学术委员会   **委员**（按姓氏笔画排序）：

主　任：厉以宁
副主任：张维迎

于鸿君　王立彦　王建国　王其文
朱善利　刘　力　邹恒甫　张国有
陆正飞　周春生　林君秀　武常岐
徐信忠　梁钧平　梁鸿飞　徐淑英
涂　平　符　丹　曹凤岐

MBA精选教材·英文影印版

MANAGEMENT INFORMATION SYSTEMS

[第9版]

管理信息系统

Raymond Mcleod, Jr.
George P. Schell 著

北京市版权局著作权合同登记图字：01-2005-5561 号

图书在版编目(CIP)数据

管理信息系统：第 9 版/麦克劳德(Mcleod, R.)等著. —影印本. —北京：北京大学出版社，2006.4

(MBA 核心课程精选教材·英文影印版)

ISBN 978-7-301-10614-3

Ⅰ. 管… Ⅱ. 麦… Ⅲ. 管理信息系统－研究生－教材－英文 Ⅳ. C931.6

中国版本图书馆 CIP 数据核字(2006)第 031254 号

Raymond Mcleod, Jr., George P. Schell
Management Information Systems, 9th edition
This book was previously published by: Pearson Education, Inc.

书　　　名：	管理信息系统(第 9 版)
著作责任者：	Raymond Mcleod, Jr.　George P. Schell　著
责 任 编 辑：	任旭华
标 准 书 号：	ISBN 978-7-301-10614-3/F·1377
出 版 发 行：	北京大学出版社
地　　　址：	北京市海淀区成府路 205 号　100871
网　　　址：	http://www.pup.cn　电子邮箱：em@pup.pku.edu.cn
电　　　话：	邮购部 62752015　发行部 62750672　编辑部 62752926　出版部 62754962
印 刷 者：	涿州市星河印刷有限公司
经 销 者：	新华书店
	850 毫米×1168 毫米　16 开本　28.75 印张　567 千字
	2006 年 4 月第 1 版　2011 年 3 月第 4 次印刷
印　　　数：	8001—11000 册
定　　　价：	45.00 元

未经许可，不得以任何方式复制或抄袭本书之部分或全部内容。

版权所有，侵权必究

举报电话：010-62752024　电子邮箱：fd@pup.pku.edu.cn

· 院长寄语 ·

　　北京大学光华管理学院秉承北大悠久的人文传统、深邃的学术思想和深厚的文化底蕴，经过多年努力，目前已经站在中国经济发展与企业管理研究的前列，以向社会提供具有国际水准的管理教育为己任，并致力于帮助国有企业、混合所有制企业和民营企业实现经营管理的现代化，以适应经济全球化趋势。

　　光华 MBA 项目旨在为那些有才华的学员提供国际水准的管理教育，为工商界培养熟悉现代管理理念、原理和技巧的高级经营管理人才，使我们的 MBA 项目成为企业发展壮大之源，为学员创造迅速成长和充分发挥优势的条件和机会。

　　为了适应现代人才需求模式和建立中国的一流商学院，同时也为了配合北大 MBA 教育工作的展开，光华管理学院与北京大学出版社联合推出本套《MBA 核心课程精选教材·英文影印版》，并向国内各兄弟院校及工商界人士推荐本套丛书。相信我们这些尝试将会得到社会的支持。而社会对我们的支持，一定会使光华 MBA 项目越办越好，越办越有特色。

北京大学光华管理学院名誉院长　厉以宁

出版者序言

自2001年12月加入世界贸易组织以来,中国进一步加强了与世界各国的政治、经济、文化各方面的交流与合作,这一切都注定中国将在未来世界经济发展中书写重要的一笔。

然而,中国经济的发展正面临着前所未有的人才考验,在许多领域都面临着人才匮乏的问题,特别是了解国际贸易规则、能够适应国际竞争需要的国际管理人才,更是中国在未来国际竞争中取胜的决定性因素。因此,制定和实施人才战略,培养大批优秀人才,是我们在新一轮国际竞争中赢得主动的关键。

工商管理硕士(MBA)1910年首创于美国哈佛大学,随后MBA教育历经百年风雨不断完善,取得了令世人瞩目的成绩。如今,美国MBA教育已经为世界企业界所熟知,得到社会的广泛承认和高度评价。MBA教育在我国虽起步较晚,但在过去十余年里,我国的MBA教育事业发展非常迅速,也取得了相当显著的成绩。

目前,国内的MBA教育市场呈现一片繁荣景象,但繁荣的背后却隐藏着种种亟待解决的问题。其中一个就是教材的问题。目前,国内市场上国外引进版教材在一定程度上还存在新旧好坏参差不齐的现象,这就需要读者在使用引进版教材时进行仔细的甄别。

北京大学出版社推出的《MBA核心课程精选教材·英文影印版》弥补了国内MBA教材市场的缺憾,给国内MBA教材市场注入了一股新鲜的血液。全套丛书基本覆盖了北京大学MBA的主修课程,包括:管理学、营销学、战略管理、管理信息系统、运作管理、人力资源管理、商务沟通、国际金融、金融管理、决策分析、货币银行学、会计学等。另外,在十几门主课的基础上又增加了几门高级选修课程,包括:国际会计学、组织行为学、投资学、商务学、财务报表解析、管理会计、管理沟通、商业伦理学、企业家精神等。

本套丛书的筛选大体上本着以下几点原则:(1)出"新"。克服以往教材知识陈旧、落后的弊端,大部分教材都与国外原版书同步出版。(2)出"好"。本套丛书收入了美国哈佛大学、斯坦福大学、麻省理工学院等著名院校所采用的教材,如《管理学》、《营销管理架构》、《管理信息系统》、《人力资源管理》、《财务会计》、《管理会计》、《面向管理的数量分析》等;本套丛书还收入了著名学术界宗师包括斯蒂芬·罗宾斯(《管理学基础》)、菲利普·科特勒(《营销管理架构》)、查尔斯·亨格瑞(《财务会计》)等人的学术巨著。(3)出"精"。大多数教材都是再版多次,经过不断的修改和完善而成的。

本套《MBA核心课程精选教材·英文影印版》集合了美国经济学界和管理学界各个学科领域专家的权威巨著,该丛书经过北京大学光华管理学院及其他著名高校知名学者的精心选编,包括了大量精深的理论指导和丰富的教学案例,真正称得上是一套优中选精的MBA教材。

致谢

本套教材是我社与国外一流专业出版公司合作出版的,是从大量外版教材中选出的最优秀的一部分。在选书的过程中我们得到了很多专家学者的支持和帮助,可以说每一本书都经过处于教学一线的专家、学者们的精心审定,北京大学出版社英文影印版教材的顺利出版离不开他们

的无私帮助,在此,我们对审读并对本套图书提出过宝贵意见的老师们表示衷心的感谢,他们是:

　　北京大学光华管理学院:符国群、李东、梁钧平、陆正飞、王建国、王其文、杨岳全、于鸿君、张国有、张圣平、张志学、朱善利

　　中央财经大学会计系:孟焰

　　本套丛书的顺利出版还得到了培生教育出版集团(Pearson Education)北京办事处的大力支持,对他们的付出我们也致以深深的谢意。

教辅材料说明

　　教材,顾名思义教学之材料,它和普通的书籍有一个很大的区别,就是必须"方便教师教学"。所以,好的教材更需有完备的教学辅助材料相匹配,且每一本教材都要有教辅材料,只有配备了齐全的辅助材料才能称其为完整的教材。《MBA核心课程精选教材·英文影印版》系北京大学出版社获全球最大的教育出版集团——美国培生教育出版集团(Pearson Education)独家授权之英文影印版本。培生教育出版集团旗下的国际知名教育图书出版公司 Prentice Hall/Addison Wesley/Longman 出版的高品质的经济管理类出版物,已成为全美乃至全球高校采用率最高的教材,享誉全球教育界、工商界。我社在选择此套教材的过程中,尽量选择了教辅材料齐全的教材,这些教辅材料包括:教学指导用书、教学提纲、测试题、解答题、课堂演示文稿等,以书、幻灯片、CD、CD-ROM 等形式出现。同时,这些材料还可通过访问培生教育出版集团的相关网址:http://www.prenhall.com、http://www.pearsoned.com、http://www.aw.com 免费下载。

　　欲获得相关教辅材料的教师烦请填写每本书后面所附的《教学支持说明》,以确保此教辅材料仅为教师获得。

出版声明

　　本套丛书是对国外原版教材的直接影印,由于各个国家政治、经济、文化背景的不同,原书中出版者和作者所持观点及结论尚需商榷。需要特别重申的是,某些书中涉及的关于台湾、香港和澳门的表述和图表与我国政府的表述和立场不尽一致,请广大读者在阅读过程中加以认真分析和鉴别。我们希望本套丛书的出版能够促进中外文化学术交流,推进国内经济与管理专业的教学,为中国经济走向世界作出一份贡献。

　　我们欢迎所有关心中国 MBA 教育的专家学者对我们的工作进行指导,欢迎每一位读者给我们提出宝贵的意见和建议。

北京大学出版社
经济与管理图书事业部
2006 年 1 月

To Carolyn
—*Ray McLeod*

To Tracy
—*George Schell*

简明目录

第一部分 核心概念 ... 1
   第一章 信息系统导论 ... 2
   第二章 竞争优势的信息系统 ... 24
   第三章 运用信息技术开展电子商务 ... 48
   第四章 系统使用者和开发者 ... 74

第二部分 信息资源 ... 99
   第五章 计算和通讯资源 ... 100
   第六章 数据库管理系统 ... 128
   第七章 系统开发 ... 156
   第八章 运用中的信息 ... 184

第三部分 管理信息和技术 ... 207
   第九章 信息安全 ... 208
   第十章 信息技术的伦理含义 ... 228
   第十一章 决策支持系统 ... 248

第四部分 项目 ... 273
   项目1 技术强化的演示 ... 274
   项目2 运用Word的Web/HTML项目 ... 282
   项目3 运用Notepad的Web/HTML项目 ... 292
   项目4 Web/HTML客户满意度表格 ... 300
   项目5 Web/HTML计算机购买表格 ... 308
   项目6 Spreadsheet基础 ... 316
   项目7 具有数据捕获功能的Spreadsheet——小型货车例子 ... 322
   项目8 具有数据捕获功能的Spreadsheet——大学计算例子 ... 332
   项目9 数据库表格和报告 ... 344
   项目10 数据库查询——Textbook数据库 ... 358
   项目11 数据库查询——Classproject数据库 ... 374
   项目12 基于查询的报告 ... 390

词汇表 ... 403
参考文献 ... 409
索引 ... 413

BRIEF CONTENTS

PART I ESSENTIAL CONCEPTS 1

Chapter 1 Introduction to Information Systems 2
Chapter 2 Information Systems for Competitive Advantage 24
Chapter 3 Using Information Technology to Engage in Electronic Commerce 48
Chapter 4 System Users and Developers 74

PART II INFORMATION RESOURCES 99

Chapter 5 Computing and Communications Resources 100
Chapter 6 Database Management Systems 128
Chapter 7 Systems Development 156
Chapter 8 Information in Action 184

PART III MANAGING INFORMATION AND TECHNOLOGY 207

Chapter 9 Information Security 208
Chapter 10 Ethical Implications of Information Technology 228
Chapter 11 Decision Support Systems 248

PART IV PROJECTS 273

Project 1 Technology Enhanced Presentations 274
Project 2 Web/HTML Project Using Microsoft Word 282
Project 3 Web/HTML Project Using Notepad 292
Project 4 Web/HTML Customer Satisfaction Form 300
Project 5 Web/HTML Computer Purchase Form 308
Project 6 Spreadsheet Basics 316
Project 7 Spreadsheets with Data Capture—Minivan Example 322
Project 8 Spreadsheets with Data Capture—College Computing Example 332
Project 9 Database Forms and Reports 344
Project 10 Database Queries—Textbook Database 358
Project 11 Database Queries—ClassProjects Database 374
Project 12 Reports Based on Queries 390
Glossary 403
References 409
Index 413

CONTENTS

Preface xxi

PART I ESSENTIAL CONCEPTS 1

Chapter 1 **Introduction to Information Systems** 2
History Of Information Systems 4
The Evolution in Computer Hardware 4
Smaller Computers 5
Moore's Law 6
Introduction to Computer Architecture 7
Introduction to Communications Architecture 8
The Evolution in Computer Applications 8
Transaction Processing Systems 9
Management Information Systems 9
Virtual Office Systems 12
Decision Support Systems 12
Enterprise Resource Planning Systems 13
Putting the Evolution in Computer Applications in Perspective 14
Information System Users 14
Managers as Information System Users 14
Where Managers Are Found 14
What Managers Do 16
The Role of Information in Management Problem Solving 16
Problem Solving and Decision Making 16
Problem-Solving Phases 17
The Future of Information Technology 18
Highlights in MIS — The World's Smallest Logic Circuit 19
SUMMARY 19 KEY TERMS 20 KEY CONCEPTS 20 QUESTIONS 20
TOPICS FOR DISCUSSION 21 PROBLEMS 21 NOTES 22
Case Problem — Freeway Ford 21

v

Chapter 2   **Information Systems for Competitive Advantage**   24

    The Firm And Its Environment   25
    The General Systems Model of the Firm   25
    The Firm in Its Environment   26
    Environmental Resource Flows   27
    Competitive Advantage   28
    Porter's Value Chains   28
    The Dimensions of Competitive Advantage   29
    Challenges from Global Competitors   31
    The Special Need for Information Processing in an MNC   31
    The Special Need for Coordination in an MNC   31
    The Advantages of Coordination   32
    Information Management   32
    The Dimensions of Information   32
    The Changing Nature of Information Management   33
    Strategic Planning for Information Resources   34
    The Chief Information Officer   35
    Strategic Planning for the Enterprise   35
    Strategic Planning for Business Areas   35
    The SPIR Approach   35
    Core Content of a Strategic Plan for Information Resources   36
    An Example Strategic Plan for Information Resources   36
    Global Business Strategies   37
    Decentralized Control Strategy   39
    Centralized Control Strategy   40
    Centralized Expertise Strategy   40
    Centralized Control and Distributed Expertise Strategy   41
    Highlights in MIS — 9/11—Not the End of Globalization   43
    SUMMARY   42   KEY TERMS   43   KEY CONCEPTS   44
    QUESTIONS   44   TOPICS FOR DISCUSSION   44
    PROBLEMS   45   NOTES   46
    Case Problem — Water Equipment Technology Company of Mexico   45

Chapter 3   **Using Information Technology to Engage in Electronic Commerce**   48

Electronic Commerce 49
Electronic Commerce Beyond the Boundary of the Firm 50
Anticipated Benefits from Electronic Commerce 51
Electronic Commerce Constraints 51
Scope of Electronic Commerce 52
The Path to Electronic Commerce 53
Business Intelligence 53
External Databases 53
Search Engines 54
Electronic Commerce Strategy and Interorganizational Systems 55
The Interorganizational System (IOS) 55
IOS Benefits 55
Electronic Data Interchange (EDI) 56
Extranet 57
Electronic Funds Transfer (EFT) 57
Proactive and Reactive Business Partners 57
Adoption Influences 57
Indirect IOS Benefits 58
A Challenge to EDI 59
Business-To-Customer Strategies For Electronic Commerce 60
Digital Products 61
Physical Products 61
Virtual versus Hybrid Sales 61
Evolution of the Internet 63
ARPANET 63
The World Wide Web 64
Cyberspace and the Information Superhighway 65
Internet Standards 66
Business Applications of the Internet 66
Marketing Research 67
Retailing Applications 67
Suggestions for Successful Internet Use 68
Future Impact of The Internet on Business 68

Highlights in MIS — Get Your Red Hot Web Domain Here 66
SUMMARY 69   KEY TERMS 70   KEY CONCEPTS 70
QUESTIONS 70   TOPICS FOR DISCUSSION 71   PROBLEMS 71
NOTES 73

Case Problem — A Buck More 71

Chapter 4 **System Users and Developers** 74
The Business Organization 75
Office Automation 76
A Shift from Clerical to Managerial Problem Solving 77
The Virtual Office 77
Telecommuting 78
Advantages of Telecommuting to Employees 78
Disadvantages of Telecommuting to Employees 78
The Decreasing Role of Telecommuting 78
Hoteling 79
Advantages of the Virtual Office 80
Disadvantages of the Virtual Office 80
The Virtual Organization 80
The Societal Impact of the Virtual Organization 81
The Information Services Organization 81
The Information Resources 81
The Information Specialists 81
The Information Services Organizational Structure 82
Innovative Organizational Structures 82
End-User Computing 86
Users As an Information Resource 88
Benefits of End-User Computing 88
Risks of End-User Computing 89
Systems Development Knowledge and Skill 89
Systems Development Knowledge 89
Systems Development Skill 90
Knowledge Management 90
KM Challenges 91
A Successful KM Development Project at Nortel Networks 92

Challenges in Developing Global Information Systems 94
Politically Imposed Constraints 94
Cultural and Communications Barriers 94
Technological Problems 94
Lack of Support from Subsidiary Managers 94
Putting The System Users And Information Specialists in Perspective 95
Highlights in MIS — Video Conferencing Alternatives 79
SUMMARY 95   KEY TERMS 96   KEY CONCEPTS 96
QUESTIONS 97   TOPICS FOR DISCUSSION 97   PROBLEMS 97
NOTES 98
Case Problem — Cyber U 98

PART II INFORMATION RESOURCES 99

Chapter 5 **Computing and Communications Resources 100**
Hardware 101
Processors 101
Memory 103
Storage 104
Input Devices 106
Output Devices 108
Multimedia 109
Personal Computing Devices 109
Tablets, Handheld, and Pocket PCs 110
Personal Digital Assistants 111
Cell Phones with Interactive Messaging 112
Software 112
System Software 112
Application Software 113
The Role of User Friendly Software 114
Communications—Public Telephone System 114
Public Connections 114
Private Lines 116
Virtual Private Network 116

Communications—Networks 118
Protocols for Computer Communication 118
Packets 120
Internet Network Addresses 120
Network Types 120
Local Area Networks 121
Metropolitan Area Networks and Wide Area Networks 122
Internet 122
Convergence of Computing and Communications 123
Highlights in MIS — Blue Gene 103
Highlights in MIS — The Impact of Wireless Networks—Convenient but Vulnerable 117
SUMMARY 124　KEY TERMS 125　KEY CONCEPTS 125
QUESTIONS 125　TOPICS FOR DISCUSSION 125
PROBLEMS 126　NOTES 127
Case Problem — Special Salmon 126

Chapter 6　**Database Management Systems 128**
Data Organization 129
The Data Hierarchy 129
The Spreadsheet As a Simple Database 130
Flat Files 130
Key Fields 131
Relating Tables 132
Database Structures 134
Hierarchical Database Structures 134
Network Database Structures 135
Relational Database Structures 135
A Relational Database Example 136
The Schedule Database 136
The Database Concept 139
Creating a Database 140
Determine the Data Needs 140
Data Modeling Techniques 141
Entity-Relationship Diagrams 141

CONTENTS ... xi

    Class Diagrams 143
    Using the Database 144
    Reports and Forms 145
    Query-by-Example 148
    Structured Query Language 148
    Advanced Database Processing 149
    Managing the Database 150
    Resources 150
    Database Personnel 150
    Database Management Systems In Perspective 152
    DBMS Advantages 152
    DBMS Disadvantages 152
    Highlights in MIS — It Can Be Healthy to Mine the Corporate Database 149
    SUMMARY 153   KEY TERMS 153   KEY CONCEPTS 154
    QUESTIONS 154   TOPICS FOR DISCUSSION 154
    PROBLEMS 154   NOTES 155
    Case Problem — Maple Tree Industries 155

Chapter 7   **Systems Development 156**
    The Systems Approach 157
    A Series of Steps 158
    Preparation Effort 158
    Definition Effort 159
    Solution Effort 161
    The Systems Development Life Cycle 162
    The Traditional SDLC 162
    Prototyping 163
    Types of Prototypes 163
    The Attraction of Prototyping 165
    Potential Pitfalls of Prototyping 165
    Rapid Application Development 165
    The Essential Ingredients of RAD 166
    Phased Development 166
    The Phased Development Stages 167
    Module Phases 168

Business Process Redesign 168
Reverse Engineering 168
Restructuring 170
Reengineering 170
Selection of the BPR Components 170
Putting The Traditional SDLC, Prototyping, RAD, Phased Development, and BPR in Perspective 170
Process Modeling 171
Data Flow Diagrams 171
Use Cases 174
Use Case Guidelines 175
When to Use Data Flow Diagrams and Use Cases 175
Project Management 175
The MIS Steering Committee 176
Project Leadership 178
The Project Management Mechanism 178
Highlights in MIS — A Quick Fix for IT at the FBI? Think Again 178
SUMMARY 180   KEY TERMS 181   KEY CONCEPTS 181
QUESTIONS 181   TOPICS FOR DISCUSSION 182
PROBLEMS 182   NOTES 183
Case Problem — A Snow Job 182

Chapter 8 **Information in Action 184**
The Transaction Processing System 185
System Overview 186
The Major Subsystems of the Distribution System 187
Systems that Fill Customer Orders 187
Systems that Order Replenishment Stock 189
Systems that Perform General Ledger Processes 189
Putting the Transaction Processing System in Perspective 190
Organizational Information Systems 190
The Marketing Information System 190
The Human Resources Information System 191
The Executive Information System 191
Customer Relationship Management 193

Data Warehousing 195
Data Warehouse Characteristics 195
The Data Warehousing System 195
How Data Is Stored in the Warehouse Data Repository 196
Information Delivery 199
OLAP 200
Data mining 201
Hypothesis Verification 201
Knowledge Discovery 203
Putting Data Warehousing in Perspective 203
Highlights in MIS — Casinos Lead the Way in Data Mining 203
SUMMARY 204   KEY TERMS 205   KEY CONCEPTS 205
QUESTIONS 205   TOPICS FOR DISCUSSION 205
PROBLEMS 206   NOTES 206
Case Problem — The Data Mine 206

PART III MANAGING INFORMATION AND TECHNOLOGY 207

Chapter 9 Information Security 208

Information Security 209
Objectives of Information Security 209
Management of Information Security 210
Information Security Management (ISM) 210
Threats 210
Internal and External Threats 211
Accidental and Deliberate 212
Risks 212
Unauthorized Disclosure and Theft 212
Unauthorized Use 212
Unauthorized Destruction and Denial of Service 213
Unauthorized Modification 213
The Most Notorious Threat—The "Virus" 213
E-Commerce Considerations 213
The American Express "Disposable" Credit Card 213

Visa's Required Security Practices 213
Risk management 214
Information security policy 215
Controls 216
Technical Controls 216
Access Controls 217
Intrusion Detection Systems 218
Firewalls 218
Cryptographic Controls 219
Physical Controls 219
Putting the Technical Controls in Perspective 219
Formal Controls 219
Informal Controls 219
Achieving The Proper Level of Controls 220
Government and Industry Assistance 220
Government Legislation 220
Industry Standards 221
Professional Certification 221
Information Systems Audit and Control Association (ISACA) 221
International Information System Security Certification Consortium (ISC) 222
SANS Institute 222
Putting Information Security Management In Perspective 222
Business Continuity Management (BCM) 222
The Emergency Plan 222
The Backup Plan 222
The Vital Records Plan 223
Putting Business Continuity Management In Perspective 223
Highlights in MIS — Recovering from 9/11 and Enron 223
SUMMARY 224   KEY TERMS 225   KEY CONCEPTS 225
QUESTIONS 225   TOPICS FOR DISCUSSION 226
PROBLEMS 226   NOTES 227
Case Problem — Confidential Reports 226

Chapter 10 **Ethical Implications of Information Technology** 228

Prescriptive Versus Descriptive Coverage 229

Morals, Ethics, and Laws 230

Morals 230

Ethics 230

Laws 230

Computer Legislation in the United States 230

Software Patents 231

Software Patent Legislation in the European Union 231

Personal Privacy Legislation in the People's Republic of China 232

Putting Morals, Ethics, and Laws in Perspective 232

Need for an Ethics Culture 232

How the Ethical Culture Is Imposed 232

Putting the Credos, Programs, and Codes in Perspective 234

Reasons for a Computer Ethic 234

Reasons for the Importance of Computer Ethics 234

Social Rights and the Computer 235

Right to Privacy 235

Right to Accuracy 235

Right to Property 236

Right to Access 236

Information Auditing 236

The Importance of Objectivity 236

Types of Auditing Activity 237

The Internal Auditor as a Member of the Development Team 238

The Internal Audit Subsystem 238

Achieving Ethics in Information Technology 239

Codes of Ethics 239

Computer Ethics Education 241

Ethics and the CIO 242

Highlights in MIS — European Union Agrees on Cookies but Not on Spam 243

SUMMARY 244   KEY TERMS 245   KEY CONCEPTS 245
QUESTIONS 245   TOPICS FOR DISCUSSION 245
PROBLEMS 246   NOTES 247

Case Problem — Need to Know 246

Chapter 11 Decision Support Systems 248
What It's All About—Decision Making 249
Problem Solving and Decision Making 249
Problem-Solving Phases 249
Problem-Solving Frameworks 250
The Systems Approach 250
The Importance of a Systems View 250
Building on the Concepts 250
Elements of a Problem-Solving Process 250
Selecting the Best Solution 251
Problems versus Symptoms 252
Problem Structure 252
Types of Decisions 252
The DSS Concept 253
A DSS Model 254
Mathematical Modeling 255
Types of Models 255
Uses of Models 256
Classes of Mathematical Models 256
Simulation 257
Simulation Technique 258
Format of Simulation Output 258
A Modeling Example 258
Model Input 258
Model Output 258
Modeling Advantages and Disadvantages 259
Mathematical Modeling Using The Electronic Spreadsheet 261
Static Modeling Capability 261
Dynamic Modeling Capability 261
Playing the "What-if" Game 262
The Spreadsheet Model Interface 263
Artificial Intelligence 263
History of AI 263
Areas of AI 263

The Appeal of Expert Systems 263
The Expert System Configuration 264
Group Decision Support Systems 265
The GDSS Concept 265
How the GDSS Contributes to Problem Solving 265
GDSS Environmental Settings 265
Putting The DSS in Perspective 266
Highlights in MIS — Fix It Before It Breaks 267
SUMMARY 267 KEY TERMS 268 KEY CONCEPTS 268
QUESTIONS 268 TOPICS FOR DISCUSSION 269
PROBLEMS 269 NOTES 271
Case Problem — Scanco 269

PART IV   PROJECTS 273

Project 1 **Technology Enhanced Presentations** 274
Presentation Basics 275
Getting Started 275
Fonts, Size, and Colors 276
Linking 277
Actions 278
Assignment 281

Project 2 **Web/HTML Project Using Microsoft Word** 282
Example 283
Making the Word Document 284
Saving the Example 290
View the Web Page 290
Advantages and Disadvantages 291
Assignment 291

Project 3 **Web/HTML Project Using Notepad** 292
Example 293
Sections of an HTML Document 294
Making the Notepad Document 294
Saving the Example 298
View the Web Page 298

	Advantages and Disadvantages 298
	Assignment 299
Project 4	**Web/HTML Customer Satisfaction Form 300**
	Example 301
	Sections of the Example Form 302
	Saving the Example 305
	View the Web Page 305
	Assignment 306
Project 5	**Web/HTML Computer Purchase Form 308**
	Example 309
	Sections of the Example Form 310
	Saving the Example 313
	View the Web Page 313
	Assignment 314
Project 6	**Spreadsheet Basics 316**
	Example 317
	Discount Datasheet 318
	Invoice Datasheet 319
	Saving The Example 321
	Assignment 321
Project 7	**Spreadsheets with Data Capture—Minivan Example 322**
	Example 323
	Options Datasheet 324
	Car Datasheet 325
	Calculating Values Based on Choices 328
	Calculating Monthly Payments 328
	Showing the Profit 328
	Saving and Editing the Example 330
	Assignment 331
Project 8	**Spreadsheets with Data Capture—College Computing Example 332**
	Example 333
	Prices Datasheet 334
	Computers Datasheet 334

	Calculating Values Based on Choices 338
	Choosing the Best Buy 339
	Saving and Editing the Example 340
	Assignment 342
Project 9	**Database Forms and Reports 344**
	Example 345
	Textbook Database 345
	Creating a Form 346
	One Table Report 351
	Report from Multiple Tables 354
	Assignment 357
Project 10	**Database Queries—Textbook Database 358**
	Example 359
	Textbook Database 360
	Creating a Query with Constraints 361
	Parameter Query 364
	Inexact Constraints 365
	Queries Requiring More Than One Table 366
	Data Field Concatenation and Calculation 369
	Assignment 373
Project 11	**Database Queries—ClassProjects Database 374**
	Example 375
	ClassProjects Database 376
	Creating a Query with Constraints 377
	Parameter Query 380
	Inexact Constraints 381
	Queries Requiring More Than One Table 381
	Data Field Concatenation and Calculation 385
	Assignment 388
Project 12	**Reports Based on Queries 390**
	Example 391
	Textbook Database 392
	Creating a Query and Report to Show Books Required for Classes 393

Creating the Query for Books 393
Creating the Report of Books Required for Classes 396
Creating a Report from a Parameter Query 398
Creating the Parameter Query 399
Creating the Report Based on the Parameter Query 400
Assignment 401

Glossary 403

References 409

Index 413

PREFACE

A textbook must be current, present concepts in an easy-to-understand format, and allow students to be active participants in learning. *Management Information Systems* has these features. The dynamic nature of the information technology and information systems field requires managers to be aware of both current and emerging technologies. Students are faced with complex subjects and need a clear, concise explanation to be able to understand and use the concepts in their careers. By engaging you with projects that enforce concepts, *Management Information Systems* creates a learning experience that will last.

The text offers a solid organization based on logical layout, thorough explanations, and a solid theoretical base.

- **Logical Layout.** You will find the text well organized with the topics flowing logically from one chapter to the next and from one section to the next. Terms are not used in a chapter without first defining them. A glossary is included. Chapters begin with learning objectives, and key terms and concepts are included at the end. Chapter questions direct you to examine key points made in the chapter. Twelve projects comprise the last section and are designed to enforce concepts from the text.
- **Thorough Explanations.** Complete coverage is provided for each topic that is introduced. Emphasis has never been on the number of topics covered but rather on the number covered well. Explanations are written so that students can understand the concept and relate it to other concepts presented in the text.
- **Solid Theoretical Base.** The text relies on current theory and practice of management information systems. References to current academic and professional journals are found throughout the text. Bibliographies for each chapter, located at the end of the text, provide a roadmap for additional, pertinent readings that can be the basis for learning beyond the scope of the chapter.

These three features—logical layout, thorough explanations, and a solid theoretical base—give you an advantage in learning about the complex and changing field of business computing.

Management Orientation with Technical Accuracy

A management orientation is the appropriate perspective for business students, but that cannot come at the expense of technical accuracy. Information technology touches almost every aspect of an organization. Understanding the trends in technology gives managers an advantage over those who simply respond to change. Information systems are built upon technologies and those systems support decisions at every level of management.

When you become a manager, you will have many opportunities to apply the material in this text. In your career, you will interact with systems analysts, network specialists, database administrators, and others who use technology to develop managerial systems. Some of you will become managers of technology-heavy areas in the organization. Regardless of where you apply your managerial expertise, this text will give you the perspective to use technology to achieve organizational goals.

New Organization

This edition has been extensively rewritten. Materials from earlier edition chapters have been reorganized into eleven chapters. The reduced number of chapters allows you to spend more time with experiential learning. Following the eleven chapters is a section of twelve projects. Presentations, Web pages, spreadsheets, and databases are included in the projects.

The text is subdivided into four parts, the last part being the projects. The first part, Chapters 1 through 4, deals with essential concepts. The history of computing technology, using technology for competitive advantage, the role of the Web and the Internet in commerce, and roles of information users in organizations are explored. You will understand how information systems and technology shape the business world after you complete this part.

Chapters 5 through 8 cover information resources. These resources are assets for the organization that are utilized to achieve organizational objectives. The days are long over for managers to think of computers as an expense—managers who do not recognize information systems and technology as a valuable asset now find themselves at a serious competitive disadvantage.

Managing information and technology is the theme for Chapters 9 through 11. The last chapter highlights information in action. Ultimately, managers make decisions and the value of the decision is built upon the information and programs supporting the decision. Because you cannot manage what you do not understand and the role of information systems and technology is so central to decision making, a course in management information systems is one of the necessities in preparing you to become a manager.

Projects

Projects are presented at different skill levels and some cover the same concepts using different examples. Your instructor can choose to assign a limited number of projects or to assign multiple projects in order to achieve a wider and deeper understanding of the topic. The projects are implemented using Microsoft Office software because it is the most popular software used for personal productivity.

Material to Encourage Discussion

All chapters contain a boxed insert entitled "Highlights in MIS" that relates the chapter material to the use of information technology in organizations. In essence, these inserts describe how firms have been either successful or unsuccessful in applying the principles of information management.

There is a brief case at the end of each chapter reflecting concepts of the chapter. These cases encourage you to consider what concepts have been presented and then apply those concepts to a situation you might find in an organization. Different people in an organization can view the same facts from different points of view and the cases will force you to consider some of those views.

You are encouraged to discuss the "Highlights in MIS" and the cases. Talk with your instructor and your classmates. Discussing your insights and viewpoints with others is a good way to attain a deeper understanding of the chapter material.

Proven Chapter Pedagogy

Each chapter begins with Learning Objectives and an Introduction, and ends with Key Terms, Key Concepts, Questions, Topics for Discussion, Problems, and Case Problems. The concepts and discussion topics focus attention on the important chapter elements. The questions and problems test knowledge and allow application of the material in a creative way.

Strong Ties to the Literature

Footnotes throughout the text, combined with the chapter bibliographies, tie the material to academic and professional literature. Many references are "classics" that have withstood the test of time. Other references shed light on applications that are just emerging. Therefore, what is given is not only a look at the field today but an appreciation for how this point was reached, and an idea of what is to come.

A Complete Supplement Package

A complete set of materials is available that will assist students and instructors in accomplishing course objectives.

INSTRUCTOR'S RESOURCE CD-ROM Available to adopting faculty, the Instructor's Resource CD-ROM contains all of the supplements in one convenient place: IM, TIF, TestGen, PPTs, and Image Library.

- **Instructor's Manual (IM) and Test Item File (TIF).** The IM, written by the text authors, includes suggestions for designing the course and presenting the material. Each chapter is supported by answers to end-of-chapter questions and problems, and suggestions concerning the discussion topics and cases. The TIF, written by Paula Ruby, consists of true-false and multiple-choice questions, plus a 10-point miniquiz for each chapter. The TIF content is provided in both Microsoft Word and in the form of TestGen on the IR CD-ROM.
- **TestGen.** This computerized package allows instructors to custom design, save, and generate classroom tests. The test program permits instructors to edit, add, or delete questions from the test banks; edit existing graphics and create new graphics; analyze test results; and organize a database of tests and student results. This new software allows for greater flexibility and ease of use. It provides many options for organizing and displaying tests, along with a search-and-sort feature.
- **PowerPoint Slides.** A set of PowerPoint slides, created by Gene Mesher and Robert Jamieson, accompanies each chapter and project, and features bulleted items that provide a lecture outline, plus key figures and tables from the text.
- **Image Library.** Text figures and tables, as permission allows, are provided in a format by which they can be imported into PowerPoint for class lectures. Each chapter is organized in its own folder for convenient use.

MyCompanion Web site www.prenhall.com/mcleod

The Prentice Hall MyCompanion Web site includes support for students and instructors. These support materials enhance the learning experience.

The student side of the Web site provides:

- **Interactive Study Guide (ISG).** Each chapter features a collection of quiz questions, including Multiple Choice, True False, and Essay, written by Pauka Ruby. Students answer the questions online and receive automatic grading and feedback. Results can be e-mailed to instructors.
- **Project Files.** The authors have provided files for Project 1-12. Students have access to files in Project examples–instructors have access to files for examples and assignments.
- **Internet Links.** Throughout the text are Web site addresses where related material can be obtained from the World Wide Web. These Web locations provide valuable information

that, when used with the text material, provides a complete, up-to-date coverage of business computing.
- **PowerPoint Slides.**
- **Glossary.**

The instructor side of the site contains:

- **Instructor's Manual (IM)**
- **Test Item File (TIF)** Available in Microsoft Word and in converted WebCT/Blackboard files.
- **Image Library**

VIDEO A video cassette covering various topics in MIS is available free to adopters. This complete set of materials provides both students and instructors with a variety of options in terms of course support.

Acknowledgments

Throughout the text the authors frequently use the term "we." The authors are not always referring to themselves but also to many people who have made valuable contributions. The people at Prentice Hall played key roles. The dedicated staff includes Executive Editor Bob Horan, VP/Publisher Natalie Anderson, Project Manager–Editorial Lori Cerreto, Production Manager John Roberts, Project Manager–Production Vanessa Nuttry, Designer Steve Frim, Senior Marketing Manager Sharon Koch, Marketing Assistant Danielle Torio, Editorial Assistant Robyn Goldenberg, and Media Project Manager Joan Waxman.

The materials in the text are based on thorough use in the classroom. The projects, the questions, the presentation of material, and so much more have been experienced by the students of the authors. We would like to thank our students for their feedback and suggestions.

Reviewers and Other Support

We also want to thank others who provided valuable support, including the following reviewers of this and past editions:

Marzie Astani, Winona State University

Michael Bartolacci, New Jersey Institute of Technology

David Bradbard, Winthrop University

Nora Braun, Augsburg College

Jack Cook, SUNY Geneseo

Robert Donnelly, Goldey-Beacom College

Charla Griffy-Brown, Pepperdine University

David T. Jones, California University of Pennsylvania

Robert M. Laurie, University of Maryland University College Asia

Donald Masselli, Northwood University

Richard Murphy, Marist College

Robert Richardson, Iona College

Randall Smith, University of Virginia

George Strouse, York College

David Whitney, San Francisco State University

Jim Wood, Arkansas Tech University

Sancy Wu, Texas A&M University

Even though we have received much help along the way, we alone are responsible for the manner in which the material is presented. Therefore, any shortcomings are our own.

—Raymond McLeod, Jr.
Austin, Texas

—George P. Schell.
Wilmington, North Carolina

ABOUT THE AUTHORS

RAYMOND MCLEOD, JR. is Adjunct Professor at the University of Texas at Austin. Findings of his research have appeared in such journals as *California Management Review*, *MIS Quarterly*, *Journal of Management Information Systems*, *Decision Sciences*, *Journal of Systems Management*, *IEEE Transactions on Engineering Management*, and *Communications of the ACM*.

In addition to coauthoring *Management Information Systems* with Dr. George Schell, Dr. McLeod is coauthor with William G. Zikmund and Faye W. Gilbert of *Customer Relationship Management: Integrating Marketing Strategy and Information Technology*, (Wiley, 2003), and co-author with Eleanor Jordan of *Systems Development: A Project Management Approach*, (Wiley, 2002). He also authored *Information Systems Concepts* (Macmillan, 1994) and *Introduction to Systems Analysis and Design: An Organizational Approach* (Dryden, 1994).

He has served on the editorial boards of the *Journal of Management Information Systems*, *Data Base*, and the *Information Resources Management Journal*, and was recently appointed to the board of the *International Journal of Information Technology Education*. He is past chair of the ACM Special Interest Group for Computer Personnel Research (SIGCPR).

GEORGE P. SCHELL is Professor of Management Information Systems at the University of North Carolina at Wilmington. He received his B.A. in Business Administration and M.A. in Management Science from the University of Florida. His Ph.D. is from Purdue University in Management Information Systems.

Professor Schell has published in the *Communications of the ACM*, *Information and Management*, *Computer Personnel*, and other scholarly journals. He has also been listed in *Who's Who in American Education*. Distance education and Web-based courses have been developed and taught by Dr. Schell. He continues to be active in consulting and professional service.

PART 1
Essential Concepts

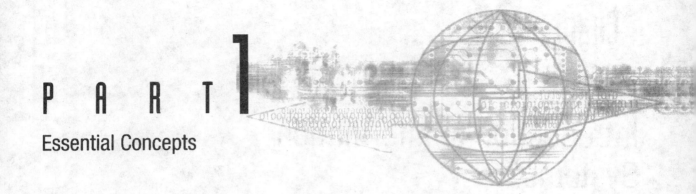

The computer has been used in business for over fifty years. During that time, dramatic changes have occurred in computer hardware and software technology and how that technology is applied to business problems. The big changes in hardware have been the trend to smaller systems and to linking computers of all sizes to form communications networks. The big change in software technology has been from customized programming to the use of prewritten software systems.

Hardware and software technologies are physical systems; they exist physically as does the firm and its physical resources such as machines, materials, and human resources. The data and information processed by the computer and stored in its storage units can be viewed as a conceptual system. The increasing use of the computer as a conceptual system to help managers manage the physical firm, not merely account for transactions, has been the big breakthrough in business computer applications.

Firms quickly realized that competitive advantage can be achieved just as effectively, or more so, with their conceptual resources as with those of a physical nature. In order to achieve this competitive advantage, the information resources must be managed. This requires development of a strategic information plan that looks into the future to identify projected computer uses and the information resources needed.

Even though these accomplishments in computer use have been substantial, the most dramatic impact of all has been achieved by the Internet and World Wide Web. This impact is seen in the increasing popularity of electronic commerce—linking businesses both to other businesses (business-to-business, or B2B), and to customers (business-to-customer, or B2C). Today's businesses have the option of utilizing either a virtual store or, one of brick and mortar, or both.

Fifty years ago, none of these innovations would have been thought possible by even the most enthusiastic of the computer visionaries. Today, they are part of the daily routine for both information specialists and users who develop part or all of their information systems.

Chapter 1

Introduction to Information Systems

Learning Objectives

After studying this chapter, you should

- Understand how computer hardware has evolved to its present level of sophistication.
- Understand the basics of computer and communications architectures.
- Know the distinction between physical and conceptual systems.
- Understand how business applications have evolved from an initial emphasis on accounting data to the current emphasis on information for problem solving.
- Understand what enterprise resource planning systems are and the reasons for their popularity.
- Know how to tailor information systems to managers based on where they are located in the organizational structure and what they do.
- Know the relationship between problem solving and decision making, and know the basic problem-solving steps.
- Know what innovations to expect in information technology.

Introduction

Computers have been used for business applications for only about fifty years. During this time, dramatic improvements have been made in both hardware and software, making it possible for the benefits of computer processing to be enjoyed by not only firms of all sizes but individuals as well.

The first widely marketed computer was the UNIVAC I, installed first at the U.S. Census Bureau in 1951 and then at General Electric (GE) in 1954. International Business Machines (IBM) quickly responded with a complete product line that led to the System/360 in the 1960s—the first computer to allow multiple users at the same time.

It didn't take long for the trend to smaller computers to gain momentum. First there were minicomputers in the 1970s, smaller than the large mainframes and popular with scientific users. Then came the microcomputers in the early 1980s aimed at not only small firms but individual users as well. IBM's personal computer, or PC, bestowed legitimacy on the small computer movement. A good measure of the improvements in hardware technology is Moore's Law, which explains the doubling of computer power every 18 months.

Computers began as machines that were as large as a room and performed only such simple tasks as adding numbers quickly. Vacuum tubes the size of small lightbulbs provided much of the circuitry. Later, transistors and chips on silicon wafers replaced those early electronics and the resulting lower costs of manufacturing led to a growing demand for computers. Computer processing speed has continually increased as the size of computer circuits decreased. Because the speed of electricity moving through the circuits is constant, making a circuit half the size will double its speed. This guiding principle of computer circuit design, miniaturization, continues to increase computer processing speed and simultaneously lower computer costs.

Communications and computers go hand-in-hand. Swiping your credit card at a store would be useless unless there were communications between the store's computer and the credit card company's computer. The difficulty is that telephone systems were designed for standards to accommodate human conversations, not the high speed and precise communications required between computers. Communications between computers has grown as computer use has grown. Communication has leapt from simple transmission down copper wires to the realm of wireless radio waves and fiber optics.

The first business applications involved processing the transactions of accounting data. The systems were conceptual systems in that they processed and maintained data that represented the physical system of the firm. In addition to being a physical system, the firm communicates with its environment and has a self-controlling capability.

With the accounting transaction processing systems in place, firms shifted their systems focus to providing information to the firm's managers for problem solving. The first information-oriented systems were called management information systems and their objective was broad support for all managers of an organizational unit. At about the same time, word processing introduced a suite of applications that eventually made the virtual office concept a reality. The next major step was the refinement of the management information system (MIS) concept to produce a class of systems called decision support systems, which were aimed at specific managers and specific problems. The first decision support systems emphasized outputs in the form of reports and results of mathematical simulations, and were subsequently refined by encompassing group problem solving, adding artificial intelligence, and incorporating on-line analytical processing. Most recently, firms have undertaken projects to integrate all of their information systems across the firm to form an enterprise resource planning system.

Users of these information systems can include managers and nonmanagers inside the firm, and also persons and organizations outside the firm. In this book, we focus on the managers. Managers are an important group of users because information is so critical to what they do. Managers exist on different organizational levels and in various business areas. Regardless of their location, they perform certain management functions and play certain managerial roles where they require information to make decisions to solve problems. Information is required as the managers search for problems to solve, develop alternative solutions, select the best solution, and review the consequences of their choice.

The future of information technology indicates a continued trend toward small size and mobility. Computer manufacturers are exploring such devices as wireless modems to be built into computer motherboards, keyboards that are simply projections of light on a flat surface, and a digital pen that remembers what it has written. The future is any place, any time, any way you want to access information technology.

HISTORY OF INFORMATION SYSTEMS

A review of the history of information systems includes a look back at the hardware and how it has been applied. In the half century since the first general-purpose digital computer was installed in a business organization, the hardware has experienced many-fold increases in speed and capacity along with dramatic reductions in size. Concurrently, the computer applications have evolved from relatively straightforward accounting processes to systems designed to support managers and other problem solvers.

THE EVOLUTION IN COMPUTER HARDWARE

Electronic computers as we know them today can be traced to a machine called the Electronic Numerical Integrator and Calculator (ENIAC), which was developed in 1946 by John W. Mauchly and J. Presper Eckert. At the time, they were working as engineers at the University of Pennsylvania. ENIAC was the predecessor of the Remington Rand UNIVAC I, which was the first widely marketed universal automatic computer.

The first UNIVAC I was installed in a government organization, the U.S. Census Bureau, in 1951. Three years later, the same type of machine was installed in the first business organization, General Electric. Figure 1.1 is a photograph of a UNIVAC. These machines performed fewer than 2,000 calculations per second—extremely slow compared to the 2 billion or more instructions per second that are common for today's smallest and least expensive microcomputers. These early computers focused on a single task requested by a single user, and were called mainframes. The term **mainframe** is still in use today, but now is used to describe the large, centrally located computers typically found in large organizations.

Although IBM was not the first computer manufacturer, it was not long before it became the industry leader. By the end of the 1950s, it had amassed a full product line and in the mid-1960s it revolutionized the computer industry by introducing the IBM System/360 line of computers. These computers were the first that could concurrently perform multiple tasks from multiple users. Although a computer processor actually performs only one task at a time, the term **multitasking** refers to the fact that more than one user appears to be working on the computer at the same time. This appearance is made possible by the fact that the computer processes pieces of each user's application, and some of the pieces may be interspersed with one or more other applications. Before the System/360, one user started, processed, and completed an entire application before another user could access any of the computer resources. Systems such as the System/360 were very expensive by today's standards and could only be afforded by large organizations.

Figure 1.1 Computer Scientists Harold Sweeney (left) and J. Presper Eckert (center) Demonstrate the UNIVAC Computer to Walter Cronkite as It Predicts the Winner of the 1952 Presidential Election

Smaller Computers

During these early years, in most firms the computer departments monopolized computer use. Users were not allowed to access the computers, which were housed in the central computing facility. The users had to communicate their information needs to **information specialists**—employees who have a full-time responsibility for developing and operating information systems. Examples of information specialists are systems analysts, programmers, database administrators, network specialists, and webmasters. As the computer became more popular, it became more difficult for the information specialists to keep up with demand, and backlogs of jobs awaiting computer processing became commonplace. Users became impatient and began wanting access to computer-based data without having to go through the information specialists. Some computer manufacturers recognized this need to make computer resources available to users and responded by manufacturing and marketing computers considerably smaller and less expensive than the mainframes.

The first small-scale systems were called minicomputers. A **minicomputer**, or **mini**, was a smaller and less powerful computer than the larger mainframe, with an ability to handle the processing of small organizations at a more affordable cost.

The mini enjoyed immediate success, especially for scientific rather than business applications. Business firms were hesitant to use them to process their data, and a main reason for this was the fact that IBM had not entered the minicomputer market.

During this time, an even smaller computer was being developed and marketed. It was called the **microcomputer**, or **micro**, because it was even smaller than the mini. Whereas the mini had been intended for small organizations, the micro was seen as a computer that could be owned and operated by an individual. Apple pioneered this market, as did the Tandy Corporation. Nonetheless, the fact that IBM had not brought out a micro dampened sales. Things changed in 1982, when IBM introduced its microcomputer, called the Personal Computer, or PC.

Figure 1.2 **A Personal Computer**
Source: *Dell Computer Corporation.*

Both the IBM product and its name were universally adopted and today the term **personal computer (PC)** is used, along with microcomputer, to describe the small, relatively inexpensive, and powerful systems used for both business and personal applications. Figure 1.2 is a photo of a modern personal computer.

Moore's Law

Processor speed has grown tremendously over the years since IBM introduced its first microcomputer. The term **Moore's Law**, named for Gordon Moore, who was one of the founders of Intel, was coined in the 1960s and stated that the storage density of integrated circuits on a silicon chip doubled about every year. By the 1970s, the rate of doubling took about 18 months but that pace has continued until today. Now, we speak of Moore's Law when we refer to the doubling of computer power every 18 months. What this means to users is that the power of a computer doubles about every 18 months for a given cost. The computer you could purchase 15 years from today would be 1,024 times as powerful, yet would cost the same as today's model. Fifteen years divided by 1 1/2 (18 months equals 1 1/2 years) yields 10, and 1,024 is 2 raised to the 10th power. In 30 years the power would be $1,024 \times 1,024$, which equals 1,048,576 times as powerful. Figure 1.3 illustrates Moore's Law in terms of Intel processors.[1]

Figure 1.3 **Increase in Processor Power as an Application of Moore's Law**

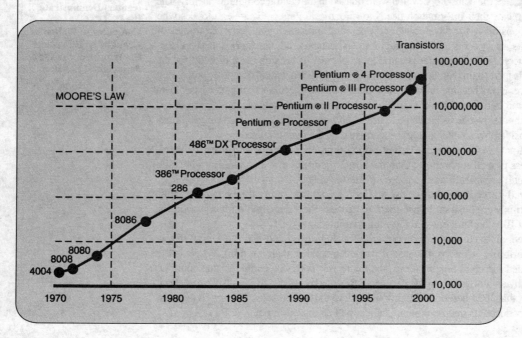

Figure 1.4 **IBM NetVista Microcomputer**

Source: IBM Corporation. Photo courtesy of International Business Machines Corporation.

INTRODUCTION TO COMPUTER ARCHITECTURE

When we think of computers, we think of the collection of the computer processor and such input and output devices as those illustrated in Figure 1.4. But the largest mainframe computer and the personal computer on your desk have a similar architecture. The computer hardware is controlled by the operating system. Application software performs tasks for the user such as word processing, calculations for spreadsheets, manipulating information via databases, and more.

At the core of a computer is its processor. The processor, controlled by an operating system such as Windows 2000, manages the input and output devices, data storage devices, and operations on the data. The central processing unit (CPU) controls all the other components. Random access memory (RAM) acts as the temporary workspace for the CPU; the greater the work area, then the more quickly the CPU can accomplish its tasks. The central processing unit and random access memory reside on the computer's motherboard, the single circuitry board that all other devices plug into. The CD-ROM, floppy drive, and hard disk (also known as the hard drive) are storage devices, but unlike the random access memory they are permanent data storage and not temporary. These devices are illustrated in Figure 1.5.

Together with a keyboard, monitor, mouse, and printer, the microcomputer can be used to support managerial decision-making.

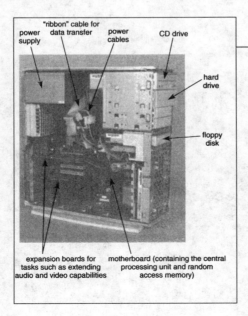

Figure 1.5 **Computer Hardware Components**

Source: James A. Folts Photography.

INTRODUCTION TO COMMUNICATIONS ARCHITECTURE

Communications between computers must deal with the fact that telephone communications between people came first. Communications standards and procedures were never meant to accommodate the extremely fast digital communications required between computers. Figure 1.6 illustrates the different paths that voice and data communications can take. Notice that the beginning and the end of the journey both connect to a modem. Any computer that will use the public telephone system must have a modem between the public telephone service and the computer. A **modem** is a hardware device that modulates the digital signals from a computer (either on or off like a light switch) into an analog signal (a continuous wave such as the sound of a voice), and vice versa.

Direct communications between computers that do not utilize the public telephone system are generally much faster. Their communications standards came later, after the standards were established for public telephone systems. Even later came wireless communications. Your computer at home may use a modem connected to your telephone running at 56,000 bits per second (56 Kbps) or to your cable television connection running at speeds as high as 2 million bits per second (2 Mbps). The most common wireless networks exchange data at 11 million bits per second (11 Mbps). Networks within a firm often run 10 to 100 Mbps.

The widespread wireless revolution cannot be stopped. The single cloud on the horizon of wireless communications is security. Although wireless networks are cheap and easy to install, most users who set them up never use any of their security features. The simplest fix to the problem is to purchase firewall hardware when the wireless network is purchased. Uncomplicated firewall hardware is inexpensive and simply plugs into the wireless access point.

THE EVOLUTION IN COMPUTER APPLICATIONS

Information systems are conceptual systems that enable management to control the operations of the physical systems of the firm.

The **physical system** of the firm consists of tangible resources—materials, personnel, machines, and money. A **conceptual system**, on the other hand, consists of the information

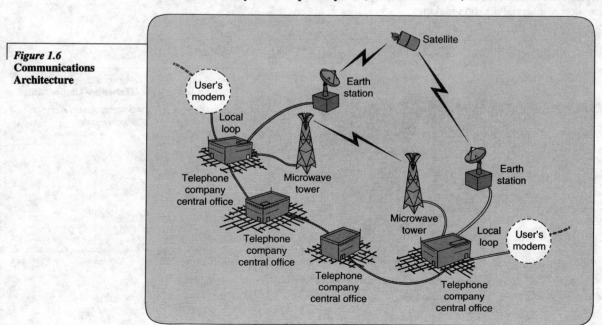

Figure 1.6 **Communications Architecture**

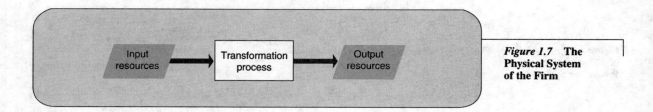

Figure 1.7 The Physical System of the Firm

resources that are used to represent the physical system. For example, an inventory storeroom containing inventory items is a physical system and the computer-based inventory master file is a conceptual system that represents the physical system. Figure 1.7 shows the physical system of the firm that transforms input resources into output resources. The input resources come from the firm's environment, a transformation occurs, and the output resources are returned to the same environment. The physical system of the firm is an **open system**, interacting with its environment by means of physical resource flows. An information system is also an open system. A closed system is one that does not communicate with its environment. A truly **closed system** would not interact with customers or managers or anyone else, and is not of interest to developers and users of information systems.

Although Figure 1.7 can represent any type of firm, it is especially easy to see how it fits a manufacturing operation where raw materials are transformed into finished products. The three other physical resources—machines, money, and human resources—flow as well.

Transaction Processing Systems

Before the computer came on the scene, the firm's conceptual systems were a combination of manual processes, key-driven bookkeeping machines, and punched card systems that processed the firm's data. **Data** consists of facts and figures that are generally unusable due to their large volume and unrefined nature. The precomputer systems processed such data as that relating to payroll, inventory, billing, and general ledger transactions. It was only natural that these same applications would be the first computer applications. After all, the applications were thoroughly understood and there was a need for better speed and accuracy that computers could provide.

The first computer-based systems were called **electronic data processing (EDP)** systems. Later the name **accounting information system (AIS)** was coined. Today, the term **transaction processing system** is common. These systems share a common bond in that all process data that reflects the activities of the firm.

Figure 1.8 is a model of a transaction processing system. The input, transformation, and output elements of the physical system of the firm are at the bottom. Data is gathered from throughout the physical system and the environment, and is entered into the database. Data processing software transforms the data into information for the firm's management and for individuals and organizations in the firm's environment.

It is important to recognize the information flow to the environment. Much, perhaps most, of the information produced by the transaction processing system is intended for use by persons or organizations outside the firm.

Management Information Systems

With the transaction processing systems up and running, both the firm's information specialists and the computer manufacturers wanted to keep the computer activity growing, so they sought new application areas. It did not take them long to realize that the informational output of the transaction processing systems left much to be desired. The systems were generally incapable of transforming the volumes of data into aggregated, sorted, organized, and processed information needed by managers.

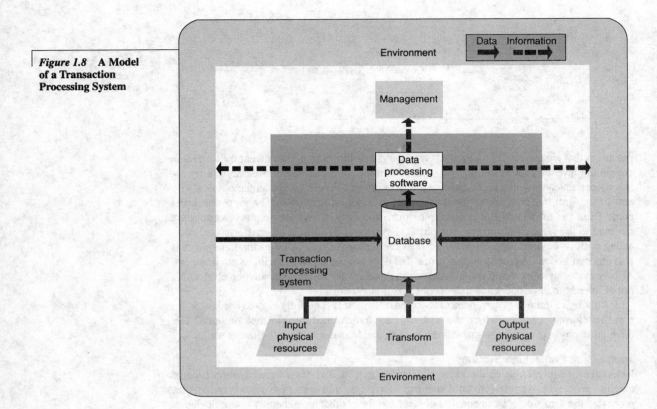

Figure 1.8 A Model of a Transaction Processing System

It looked like the development of a management information system would be easy. The firms that attempted to introduce the first management information systems learned otherwise. The big barrier turned out to be the managers, but the information specialists added to the problem as well. As a group, the managers knew nothing about how computers worked. They knew their jobs, and they had developed approaches to solving problems, but they had not given much formal thought to the role of information in their activities. As a result, it was difficult for the managers to articulate exactly what they needed from the management information system.

This situation was frustrating to the information specialists. Since they knew little about management, they did not know what questions to ask. The information specialists decided that the only solution was for them to design and implement systems to produce information that they *thought* the managers needed. This was done, but in many cases the information specialists had guessed wrong, and their systems were not used.

Over time, as managers learned about the computer, they became aware of the underlying logic of the processes that they followed in solving problems, and they were better able to describe their information needs. Information specialists, in turn, learned the basics of management and how to work with managers in designing information systems. The management information systems were redesigned so that they more closely fit managers' needs, and the systems eventually became established as a major computer application area.

We define a **management information system (MIS)** as a computer-based system that makes information available to users with similar needs. **Information** is processed data that is meaningful; it usually tells the user something that she or he did not already know. The MIS users usually compose a formal organizational entity—the firm or a subsidiary subunit. Special versions of the MIS have been tailored to the marketing unit (marketing information systems) and the executives (executive information systems) for example. The information describes the firm or one of its major systems in terms of what has happened in the past, what is happening now, and what is likely to happen in the future. The information is produced from data in the database by two types of software.

- **Report-writing software** produces both periodic and special reports. Periodic reports are coded in a programming language and are prepared according to a schedule. The special reports, often called *ad hoc* reports, are prepared in response to unanticipated information needs. Today's database management systems have features that quickly generate reports in response to requests for specific data or information.
- **Mathematical models** produce information as a result of simulations of the firm's operations. Mathematical models that describe the firm's operations can be written in any programming language. However, special modeling languages make the task easier and faster.

The output information is used by organizational problem solvers (both managers and professionals) as they make decisions to solve the firm's problems.

Our definition can be illustrated with the MIS model in Figure 1.9. The database contains the data provided by the transaction processing system. In addition, both data and information are entered from the environment. Note that some of the problem solvers can exist within the firm's environment. The environment becomes involved when the firm interacts with other organizations such as suppliers to form an **interorganizational information system (IOS)**. In that case, the MIS supplies information to the other members of the IOS as well as the firm's users.

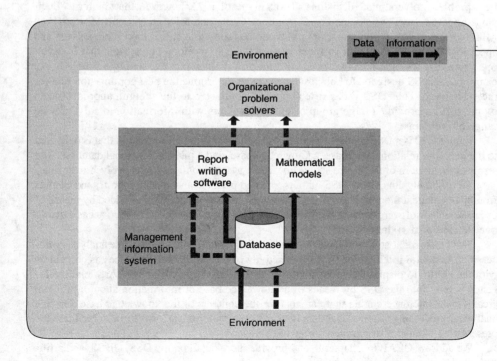

Figure 1.9 An MIS Model

Virtual Office Systems

In 1964, computer technology was applied to office tasks when IBM introduced an electric typewriter with a magnetic tape capability. The typewriter could store typed material on the magnetic tape and retrieve the material when it was needed. The application was called word processing. This was the beginning of **office automation**, the use of electronics to facilitate communication. Additional applications include electronic mail, voice mail, electronic calendaring, audio conferencing, video conferencing, computer conferencing, and facsimile transmission. Today, these applications account for a major portion of a firm's use of the computer as a communications vehicle.

These systems came from modest, clerical beginnings. But today they are generally referred to as **personal productivity systems** and they have important impacts on managers. Managers use technology to self-manage some of the clerical tasks that supported a manager in the 1960s. For example, managers keep calendars as well as an address book that contains mail addresses, e-mail addresses, and more. Phone numbers are kept in a cell phone.

Technology has not burdened managers with clerical tasks. By using technology to remove unnecessary obstructions to communications between the manager and others, technology has made managers much more efficient. The managers rapidly issue communications via e-mail and a distribution list instead of dictating a memo, having someone else type it, checking the memo for errors, and finally sending a corrected memo to others.

The ability of the office automation applications to be performed anywhere gave birth to the concept of a **virtual office**—performance of office activities free from dependence on a particular physical location. For example, managers can engage in a video conference without all gathering in the same physical location. Virtual office systems have made managers more available to customers and others within the firm.

Decision Support Systems

The MIS failures had convinced information scientists that there must be another way to help problem solvers make decisions. It was not until 1971, however, that the term "decision support system" was coined by G. Anthony Gorry and Michael S. Scott Morton, both MIT professors.[2] They felt that systems should be tailored to specific problem solvers and specific problems. A **decision support system (DSS)**, therefore, is a system that is developed to assist a single manager or small group of managers solve a single problem. An example is a DSS designed to help a sales manager determine the best commission rate for the sales force. Thus DSS was a rifle approach, contrasted to the shotgun approach taken by the MIS to provide a large group of problem solvers with information to solve a wide range of problems.

Figure 1.10 is a DSS model. There are three sources for the information that is delivered to the users—a relational database, a knowledge base, and a multidimensional database. The arrow at the bottom of the figure shows how these system configurations evolved over time.

As originally conceived, DSS outputs featured periodic and special reports, and outputs from mathematical models. Next, a group decision support capability was added by means of group-oriented software called **groupware**. The groupware enabled the DSS to act as a **group decision support system (GDSS)**.

The most recent additions have featured artificial intelligence and on-line analytical processing. **Artificial intelligence (AI)** is the activity of providing such machines as computers with the ability to display behavior similar to that of an intelligent human. Artificial intelligence is built into the DSS by means of a knowledge base of information about a problem area, and an inference engine that can analyze the contents of the knowledge base. On-line analytical processing requires that data be stored in a multidimensional form to facilitate the presentation of an almost infinite number of data views.

We address OLAP in Chapter 8, and provide more detail on the DSS, GDSS, and artificial intelligence in Chapter 11.

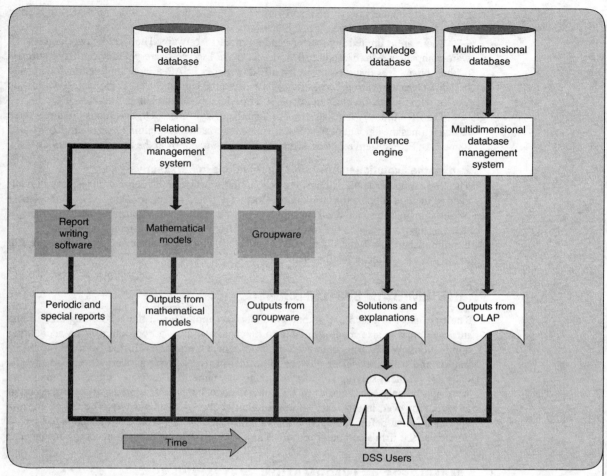

Figure 1.10 A DSS Model

Enterprise Resource Planning Systems

The transaction processing systems, MISs, and DSSs, all developed without an overall master plan. Essentially, each sprang up individually in response to a different need. During the 1990s firms began to see the value of integrating all of these systems so that they would function as a coordinated unit. Software vendors responded by developing standardized software packages aimed at meeting the needs of practically all types of organizations. The vendors named their product an **enterprise resource planning (ERP) system** and defined it as a computer-based system that enables the management of all of the firm's resources, on an organization-wide basis.

The tremendous growth in ERP software during the late 1990s can be attributed to several factors, including the Y2K problem, the difficulty in achieving enterprise-wide systems, the flurry of corporate merger activity, and a "follow the leader" competitive strategy. The Y2K (the year 2000) problem was the difficulty faced by computer programs that had stored years in a two-digit format such as storing the year 2000 as 00. When an application subtracted the year 2000 from 1998 it would actually compute 00 −98 and give a result of −98 that could cause the application to abort. The ERP software was marketed as being Y2K compliant and that capability assured firms that the information systems being replaced would not suffer errors caused by the date change from 1999 to 2000. The theory that Y2K was a driving force for implementation of ERP software was given credence when the sales growth rates of major ERP vendors slacked off in 1999.[3]

There are a limited number of vendors of ERP software. The world's two largest software companies, Microsoft and IBM, do not make ERP software yet they run large portions of their businesses using software from ERP vendors.[4] SAP, a large multinational company based in Germany with the majority of its sales in the United States, is the largest worldwide vendor with Siebel, Oracle, and PeopleSoft providing the main competition.

The ERP industry consists of more than the ERP vendors. Organizations often pay three to seven times the amount of the software price for consultants, training, and other ERP-related items.[5] An ERP system requires an enormous commitment from the using organizations.

Putting the Evolution in Computer Applications in Perspective

The first computer applications were accounting transactions. Then computer usage broadened to include support for problem solvers and decision makers in the form of management information systems, and decision support systems. With these systems in place, firms sought to bring them together in the form of an enterprise information system. The interest in ERP has diminished somewhat since 2000 but many systems are in place and many firms are still in the process of implementing them.

INFORMATION SYSTEM USERS

The first users of computer output were clerical employees in the accounting area. Some information was also made available to managers—but as a byproduct of the accounting applications. When firms embraced the MIS concept, emphasis shifted from data to information and from clerical employees to problem solvers. Systems were developed specifically for problem-solving support. Although the name MIS indicates otherwise, managers were not the only beneficiaries of MIS; nonmanagers and professional staff used the output as well. However, in this text, we will emphasize use by the managers. The reason for this approach is that before long you will be a manager, and the purpose of the text is to prepare you to use the firm's computer resources as a step toward becoming a successful manager.

MANAGERS AS INFORMATION SYSTEM USERS

Since managers are individuals, their information needs are, for all practical purposes, unique. However, some useful frameworks have been developed that make it possible to address the role of information in problem solving.

Where Managers Are Found

Managers can exist on various managerial levels and within various business areas of the firm.

MANAGEMENT LEVELS   Management theorist Robert N. Anthony coined names for the three primary management levels—top, middle, and lower.[6] Managers at the top of the organizational hierarchy, such as the president and vice-presidents, are often referred to as being on the **strategic planning level**, recognizing the impact their decisions have on the entire organization for years to come. Middle-level managers include regional managers, product directors, and division heads. Their level is tactical and has been called the **management control level** because it is their responsibility to put plans into action and to ensure that goals are met. Lower-level managers include department heads, supervisors, and project leaders—persons responsible for accomplishing the plans specified by managers on upper levels. This lowest level has been called the **operational control level**, since it is here that the operations of the firm occur.

It is important for those designing information systems to take into consideration the manager's level, because such systems can influence both the source of information and how

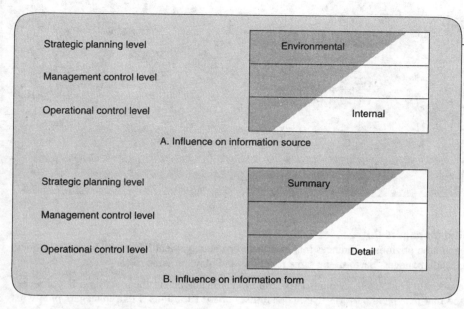

Figure 1.11
Management Level Can Influence Both the Source and Presentation Form of Information

it is presented. The upper graph of Figure 1.11 shows that managers on the strategic planning level place greater emphasis on environmental information than do managers on the lower levels, and that managers on the operational control level regard internal information as most vital. The lower graph shows that strategic-planning-level managers prefer information in a summary format, whereas operational-control-level managers prefer detail.[7]

BUSINESS AREAS   In addition to the organizational levels, managers can be found in various business areas. The three traditional areas are marketing, manufacturing, and finance. Recently, two additional areas have assumed major importance—human resources and information services. Figure 1.12 illustrates how managers can be grouped by level and business area in a manufacturing firm.

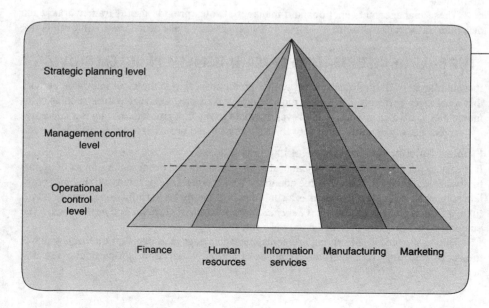

Figure 1.12
Managers Can Be Found on All Levels in All Business Areas of the Firm

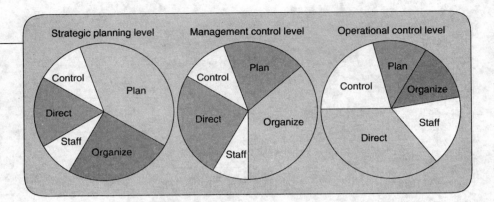

Figure 1.13 Management Level Can Influence the Relative Emphasis on the Management Functions

What Managers Do

Despite the obvious differences that exist between management levels and between business areas, all managers perform the same functions and play the same roles.

MANAGEMENT FUNCTIONS Around 1914, the French management theorist Henri Fayol recognized that managers perform five major **management functions**. First, managers *plan* what they are to do. Then, they *organize* to meet the plan. Next, they *staff* their organization with the necessary resources. With the resources in place, they *direct* them to execute the plan. Finally, they *control* the resources, keeping them on course.

All managers, regardless of their level or business area, perform these functions to some degree. Different level managers emphasize different functions. Figure 1.13 illustrates how management level can influence the emphasis on the various management functions.

MANAGERIAL ROLES Henry Mintzberg, a professor at McGill University in Montreal, decided that Fayol's functions did not tell the whole story. He developed a more detailed framework consisting of ten **managerial roles** that managers play, involving interpersonal, informational, and decisional activities. Table 1.1 lists the roles and provides brief definitions.

These management functions and managerial roles provide useful frameworks when designing information systems to support managers as they make decisions to solve problems.

THE ROLE OF INFORMATION IN MANAGEMENT PROBLEM SOLVING

It would be an oversimplification to say that problem solving is the most important activity that a manager performs. The job is more complex than that. Other activities, such as communications, are also important. However, it is safe to say that problem solving is a key activity—often spelling the difference between a successful and unsuccessful management career.

Problem Solving and Decision Making

It is easy to get the idea that a problem is always something bad because the subject of opportunity seizing receives relatively little attention. We incorporate opportunity seizing into problem solving by defining a **problem** as a condition or event that is harmful or potentially harmful to a firm in a negative way, *or is beneficial or potentially beneficial in a positive way*. The outcome of the problem-solving activity is a **solution**.

During the process of solving problems, managers engage in **decision making**, which is the act of selecting from alternative courses of action. A **decision** is a particular selected

Table 1.1
Mintzberg's Managerial Roles

INTERPERSONAL ROLES	*Figurehead* The manager performs ceremonial duties, such as giving visiting dignitaries tours of the facilities. *Leader* The manager maintains the unit by hiring and training the staff and providing motivation and encouragement. *Liaison* The manager makes contacts with persons outside the manager's own unit—peers and others in the unit's environment—for the purpose of attending to business matters.
INFORMATIONAL ROLES	*Monitor* The manager constantly looks for information bearing on the performance of the unit. The manager's sensory perceptors scan both the internal activity of the unit and its environment. *Disseminator* The manager passes valuable information along to others in the unit. *Spokesperson* The manager passes valuable information along to those outside the unit—superiors and persons in the environment.
DECISIONAL ROLES	*Entrepreneur* The manager makes rather permanent improvements to the unit, such as changing the organizational structure. *Disturbance handler* The manager reacts to unanticipated events, such as the devaluation of the dollar in a foreign country where the firm has operations. *Resource allocator* The manager controls the purse strings of the unit, determining which subsidiary units get which resources. *Negotiator* The manager resolves disputes both within the unit and between the units and its environment.

course of action. Usually, it is necessary to make multiple decisions in the process of solving a single problem.

Problem-Solving Phases

Herbert A. Simon, a Nobel prize-winning management scientist, is credited with defining four basic phases of problem solving that are universally recognized. According to Simon, problem solvers engage in:[8]

- **Intelligence Activity.** Searching the environment for conditions calling for a solution.
- **Design Activity.** Inventing, developing, and analyzing possible courses of action.
- **Choice Activity.** Selecting a particular course of action from those available.
- **Review Activity.** Assessing past choices.

In performing these activities, the problem solver must have information. Figure 1.14 illustrates this support. Information systems, developed either by users or information specialists, must provide this information.

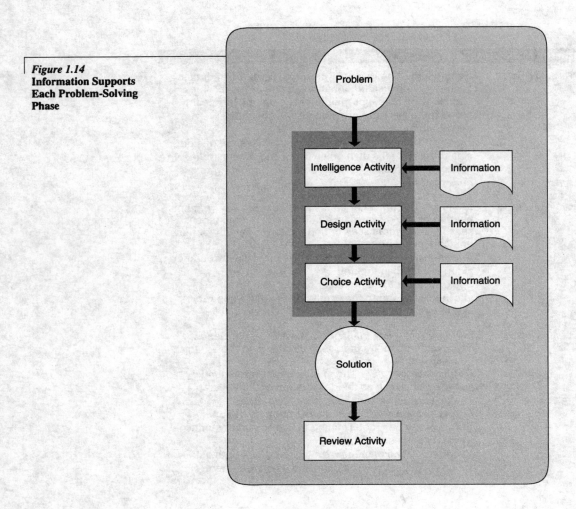

Figure 1.14
Information Supports Each Problem-Solving Phase

THE FUTURE OF INFORMATION TECHNOLOGY

The future of information technology will be driven by the reduced cost and increased power of both computers and communications. The power of computers is measured in processing speed, storage capacity, and variety of input and output. Communications power is measured by transmission speed, such as the amount of data that can be communicated in a specified amount of time. Business organizations have always shown an appetite for inexpensive assets that have the power to change their operations.

Computers and communications are converging. Intel has plans to integrate a wireless modem into the motherboard of its computers. Canesta, Inc. has developed a keyboard made only of light. It is an image of a keyboard that can be projected onto any flat surface. Logitech is close to perfecting a digital pen. The roller in the pen works much like the roller ball in a computer mouse but the pen "remembers" all the words written and images drawn. The user simply places the pen in a cradle and uploads the text and images the user made with the pen.

These advances mean that computing is going to feature low cost, small size, mobility, and connectivity to the rest of the world. To take advantage of these new possibilities, managers must learn to incorporate information systems into decision making.

Highlights in MIS

THE WORLD'S SMALLEST LOGIC CIRCUIT[9]

IBM scientists have reported a startling breakthrough in circuit design. Rather than constructing the circuit using silicon transistors, which is currently the state of the art, the scientists have used carbon monoxide molecules on a flat copper surface. The circuit makes calculations in much the same way as billiard balls roll on a billiard table. The copper atoms in the surface form tiny hollows into which the carbon monoxide molecules can settle. When three molecules settle close together, forming a "V-shape," the two outside molecules force the center one to move to the next space. When the molecules are initially positioned in the proper positions, and then nudged with an instrument in the same manner that a cue stick strikes the billiard balls, the molecules are involved in a cascade of collisions and settle in positions that represent the solution to the calculation.

The molecular circuit takes up less than a trillionth of a square inch. To give you an idea of how small this is, a silicon transistor circuit requires up to 260,000 times as much space. Although the molecular design is currently impractical because both the setting up of the molecules for the calculation and the reading of the results are very slow, the approach does offer potential for the future. It is anticipated that silicon transistor technology will reach a physical barrier in the next decade or two. Maybe by then the billiards approach will have been refined to a point where it is practical.

Summary

The first computers, called mainframes, were very large and could only be afforded by the largest firms. Innovations in hardware technology made small, powerful computers possible. IBM named its microcomputer a personal computer, or PC, and that name stuck for not only their brand but others as well. "Personal computer" was more than a catchy phrase; it described the sense of ownership that managers felt when they could access and manipulate their own data. A good measure of the rapid innovations in hardware technology is Moore's Law, which asserts that the power of a computer doubles every 18 months.

The architecture of the computer (CPU, RAM, storage, and other features) will remain similar for some time to come. But the implications of the increased power, smaller size, expanded communications, and falling costs of microcomputers cannot be ignored. They allow us to access more data, quicker, and with sophisticated analysis techniques. The constancy of computer architecture ensures that it will remain familiar, which means that managers need only understand how to increasingly use the computer power to their advantage.

Communications technology has changed dramatically; currently the big trend is to wireless technologies. The main problem with wireless communications is security. Most users never use any of the security features. The simplest solution is firewall hardware that plugs into the wireless access point.

Information systems are conceptual systems, with their data representing the physical system of the firm. Systems of both types can also be open or closed. Businesses are open systems since they interact with their environment.

The first information systems performed the firm's accounting functions and were called transaction processing systems. With those systems installed, firms turned their attention to providing information to management. First came management information systems that sought to provide support for large groups of managers, perhaps all of the managers in the firm. The introduction of the MIS was accompanied by the emergence of office-oriented applications that evolved into what is known today as the virtual office. Next came decision support systems that were designed to help one or a few managers make particular decisions. The approach was so successful that it was broadened to include group problem solving, and additions were made in the form of artificial intelligence and on-line analytical processing. An effort to integrate all of these separate systems into one overall system to manage all of the firm's operations produced what is called enterprise resource planning systems.

These information systems are used by managers, nonmanagers, professionals, and persons outside the firm. Managers can be found on management levels and in business areas. Managers make decisions to solve problems as they perform certain functions and play certain roles. The information provided to managers is most effective when it recognizes and supports the functions and roles.

Understanding the concepts of technology and their impact on decision making is crucial. With the rapid developments in technology and the continually falling prices, in 30 years you should expect to pay less than $1 for a million dollars worth of today's computer power. You will be in the job force long enough to see amazing changes in technology. The skills you learn today for spreadsheets and word processors are valuable, but the ability to adapt and utilize technology in decision making tomorrow is far more important.

KEY TERMS

multitasking
information specialist
microcomputer, micro
personal computer, PC

data
information
virtual office
personal productivity system

groupware
problem
solution
decision

KEY CONCEPTS

- Moore's law
- physical systems and conceptual systems
- transaction processing system
- management information system (MIS)

- interorganizational information system (IOS)
- decision support system (DSS)
- group decision support system (GDSS)
- artificial intelligence (AI)

- enterprise resource planning (ERP) system
- management levels
- management functions
- managerial roles
- problem-solving phases

QUESTIONS

1. What is meant by the term multitasking?
2. What is an information specialist? Give four examples.
3. What are the main functions of the central processing unit and random access memory?
4. What function does a modem provide in communications between computers?
5. What data transmission speeds can you expect for a modem? For direct computer-to-computer communications?

6. Is a computer a conceptual system or a physical system or both? Explain.
7. In what way is a computer an open system?
8. Does a transaction processing system produce information or data? Explain.
9. Where are the users of the transaction processing system located?
10. Distinguish between a periodic report and a special report.
11. What was the first office automation application?
12. How does a DSS differ from an MIS in focus?
13. Can more than a single user use a DSS? Explain.
14. What are the three primary data sources for a DSS configuration?
15. Why were firms especially attracted to enterprise resource planning systems in the late 1990s?
16. What names did Robert N. Anthony use for the three management levels?
17. Which concept explicitly recognizes the importance of information in management—management functions or managerial roles?
18. What are the four stages of problem solving, according to Herbert A. Simon?
19. If present trends continue, what will be three features of future computers?

Topics for Discussion

1. Why would a manager want to solve a "good" problem?
2. How does a manager engage in Simon's intelligence activity?

Problems

1. Assume that Moore's Law will hold true during 2000 through 2030. Prepare a table showing the increase in power for each year over the thirty-year time line.
2. Assume that you are director of recruiting for a large firm in your area that recruits graduates of your college. Describe the type of report that you would need to perform each of Fayol's management functions. You will need to describe five reports. Hint: What would you need to know to plan a recruiting campaign, what would you need to know to organize a recruiting campaign, and so on?

Case Problem: Freeway Ford

You are a management consultant working for Franklin Absolom, the majority stockholder for a group of ten automobile distributorships. He has asked you to spend several days at Freeway Ford—a dealership that is not performing up to its potential. You are not to go "looking for trouble"; instead your assignment is to find ways to help management at the dealership take advantage of opportunities.

One day while you are talking with James Kahler, the sales manager for Freeway Ford, you realize that the dealership only uses transaction processing systems—it is not utilizing the full potential of the information it has gathered for managerial decision making. For example, Freeway Ford knows the purchase date and owner of every car it sells but the dealership never contacts owners about routine maintenance. Freeway Ford knows that people who purchase a new car generally trade it in for another new car three to four years later but the dealership does not contact these previous customers.

Another opportunity comes from used car purchasing and sales. Every car has a vehicle identification number (VIN) and the dealership uses that to check for known problems with

> **Case Problem continued**
>
> a car before it makes a purchase of a used car. A data bank of car insurance claims histories and major repair histories is kept on a set of CDs that is sent to the dealership each month. At the dealership, the VIN is entered into a personal computer that accesses the CDs. However, the dealership buys twenty-five to one hundred used cars a month from other locations. Sometimes the used car buyer is at an auction and does not have access to a computer. Sometimes the buyer is at an estate sale or other private sale. Currently these sales are made "blind," without review of current VIN information because the buyer cannot get to a computer and use the CDs to check the car's history.
>
> You know that Freeway Ford collects data but the dealership is not processing the data to produce information. Also, the used car buyers' lack of access to the VIN database could be costing the dealership thousands of dollars each month. You decide that your report to Absolom and Kahler should highlight these two opportunities.
>
> **ASSIGNMENT**
> 1. In a brief summary (no more than two paragraphs) explain the difference between data and information as it applies to the data collected by Freeway Ford when it sells a car. What data should be processed into information at Freeway Ford?
> 2. How can the used car buyers access the VIN information when the buyer is not at the Freeway Ford location?
> 3. How could you expand your suggestions to the entire enterprise of ten dealerships?

NOTES

[1] "Moore's Law," Intel Technology and Manufacturing Group, obtained from the Intel Web site, 9/6/2002.
[2] G. Anthony Gorry and Michael S. Scott Morton, "A Framework for Management Information Systems," *Sloan Management Review* 13 (Fall 1971), 55–70.
[3] Richard W. Oliver, "ERP Is Dead! Long Live ERP!," *Management Review* 88 (November 1999), 12–13.
[4] Michael H. Martin, "Smart Managing," *Fortune* 137 (February 2, 1998), 149–151.
[5] August-Wilhem Scheer, and Frank Habermann, "Making ERP a Success," *Communications of the ACM* Volume 43 Issue 4 (April 2000), p. 57
[6] Robert N. Anthony, *Planning and Control Systems: A Framework for Analysis*, Harvard University Press, 1965.
[7] Figure 1.11 is a conceptual representation of a condition that is believed to exist but for which there is very little supporting evidence. Other diagrams in this text are of this type. The diagrams provide useful guidelines, but it is important to recognize that each manager has unique information needs.
[8] Herbert A. Simon, *The New Science of Management Decision*, rev. ed. (Englewood Cliffs, NJ: Prentice-Hall, 1977).
[9] Kenneth Chang, "Scientists Shrink Computing to Molecular Level," *The New York Times* October 25, 2002, p. A18.

Chapter 2

Information Systems for Competitive Advantage

Learning Objectives

After studying this chapter, you should

- Be able to use the general systems model of the firm as a template for evaluating any type of organization.
- Be able to use the eight-element environmental model as a framework for understanding the environment of a business organization.
- Recognize that competitive advantage can be achieved with conceptual as well as physical resources.
- Understand Michael E. Porter's concepts of value chains and value systems.
- Know the dimensions of competitive advantage.
- Become acquainted with the multinational corporation and recognize its special need for coordination.
- Know the basic types of information resources available to the firm.
- Know the dimensions of information that should be provided by an information system.
- Know how to manage information in the form of legacy systems, images, and knowledge.
- Know how a firm goes about strategic planning—for the firm, its business areas, and its information resources.
- Know four basic global strategies that can be practiced by multinational corporations and understand the role of information in each.

Introduction

The general systems model of the firm provides a good template for analyzing an organization. It shows the elements that should be present and how they should interact. In the same manner, the model of the eight environmental elements of a firm provides a good way to come to grips with the complexity of how the firm interacts with its environment.

During recent years, the topic of competitive advantage has received much attention. Usually it is described as being achieved by managing physical resources, but conceptual resources can also play a big role. Michael E. Porter is credited with shedding the most light on the competitive advantage concept and contributes ideas of value chains and value systems, which are compatible with taking a systems view of the firm and its environment. The firm's executives can use information to gain strategic, tactical, and operational advantages.

Firms that do business globally have special coordination needs and can meet them through the use of information. A firm's information resources include hardware, software, information specialists, users, facilities, the database, and information. Information has four desirable dimensions—relevancy, accuracy, timeliness, and completeness.

The task of information management is continually changing. Firms have been using computers since the 1950s and data formats and storage techniques have changed considerably but the data of the older, legacy systems provides valuable insights to business trends and operations. Whereas only text and numbers were stored for the legacy systems, images are becoming an important part of current information systems. Carried to its extreme, information management recognizes that the information actually represents the firm's knowledge resource. Knowledge management is required to organize, access, and leverage the firm's data and information for decision-making.

The firm's executives perform strategic planning for the entire organization, the business area, and the information resources. The chief information officer (CIO) plays a key roll in all types of strategic planning. A strategic plan for information resources identifies the objectives that the firm's information systems should meet in the coming years, and the information resources that will be necessary to meet them.

Multinational corporations face a challenge in coordinating their worldwide operations that firms with only domestic markets do not. Four strategies can be followed, given names of decentralized control, centralized control, centralized expertise, and centralized control and distributed expertise. Each of these strategies imposes unique requirements on the firm's information systems.

THE FIRM AND ITS ENVIRONMENT

In Chapter 1, we saw that a firm is a physical system that is managed through the use of a conceptual system. The physical system of the firm is an open system in that it interfaces with its environment. A firm takes resources from its environment, transforms the resources into products and services, and returns the transformed resources to its environment.

The General Systems Model of the Firm

Figure 2.1 is a diagram that shows the flow of resources from the environment, through the firm, and back to the environment. The flow of physical resources is at the bottom and the flow of conceptual resources is at the top.

THE PHYSICAL RESOURCE FLOW   The physical resources include personnel, material, machines, and money. Personnel are hired by the firm, transformed into a higher level of skill through training and experience, and eventually leave the firm. Material enters the firm in the form of raw materials and

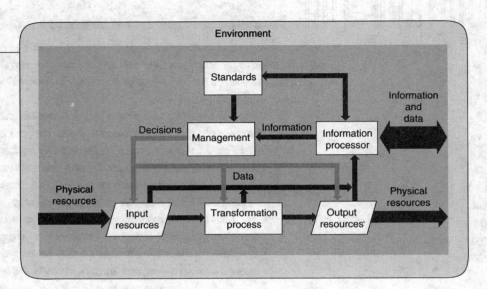

Figure 2.1 The General System Model of the Firm

is transformed into finished goods, which are sold to the firm's customers. Machines are purchased, used, and eventually scrapped or traded in on newer machines. Money enters the firm in the form of such inputs as sales receipts, shareholder investments, and loans and is transformed into such outputs as payments to suppliers, taxes to the government, and returns to stockholders. While in the firm, all of the physical resources are used to produce the firm's products and services to its customers.

THE CONCEPTUAL RESOURCE FLOW   The arrows in the upper part of the Figure 2.1 diagram show the flows of conceptual resources—data, information, and information in the form of decisions. A two-way flow of data and information that connects the firm to its environment is at the right.

THE FIRM'S CONTROL MECHANISM   The elements that enable the firm to operate as a closed-loop system are shown in the upper portion of the diagram. A **closed-loop system** is one that can control itself by means of a control mechanism and feedback loop. The control mechanism elements include (1) the standards of performance that the firm is to meet if it is to accomplish its overall objectives, (2) the management, and (3) an information processor that transforms data into information.

THE FEEDBACK LOOP   The feedback loop is composed of the conceptual resources. Data is gathered from the firm and from the environment and entered into the information processor, which transforms it into information. The information is made available to management, who makes decisions to affect necessary changes in the physical system. Management is guided in its decision making by the performance standards. The performance standards can also be utilized by the information processor in determining when the performance of the firm is not proceeding as planned.

THE USEFULNESS OF THE MODEL   The general systems model of the firm is useful to managers and systems developers alike because it shows the elements and flows that must be managed in order for the firm to function as an efficient and effective system.

The Firm in Its Environment

The general systems model of the firm makes it easy to see the importance of the environment. The firm exists for the purpose of providing products and services that meet environmental needs. Equally important, the firm could not function without the resources that the environment provides.

The environment of one firm is not exactly the same as the environment of another. A bank has a different environment than does a sporting goods store or a church, for example. However, we can identify eight major *types* of elements that exist in the environments of *all* firms.[1] These **environmental elements** are organizations and individuals that exist outside the firm and have a direct or indirect influence on the firm. These eight elements exist in a larger system called **society**. Figure 2.2 depicts the firm in its environmental context.

Suppliers, also called **vendors**, supply the materials, machines, services, people, and information that are used by the firm to produce its products and services. These products and services are marketed to the firm's **customers**, which include both current and prospective users. **Labor unions** are the organizations of both skilled and unskilled workers for certain trades and industries. The **financial community** consists of institutions that influence the money resources that are available to the firm. Examples include banks, savings and loan associations, credit unions, and other lending institutions and investment firms.

Stockholders or owners are the persons who invest money in the firm and represent the ultimate owners of the firm. **Competitors** include all of the organizations that compete with the firm in its marketplace. The **government**, on the national, state or province, and local levels, provides constraints in the form of laws and regulations and also provides assistance in the form of purchases, information, and funds. The **global community** is the geographic area where the firm performs its operations. The firm demonstrates its responsibility to the global community by respecting the natural environment, providing products and services that contribute to quality of life, and conducting its operations in an ethical manner.

Environmental Resource Flows

The firm is connected to its environmental elements by means of the resource flows. Some of the resources flow more frequently than do others. Very common flows include information flow from customers, material flow to customers, money flow to stockholders, machine flow from suppliers, and personnel flow from suppliers (schools, colleges, and employment agencies), and also the global community and labor unions. Less frequent flows include money flow from the government (such as for research), material flow to suppliers (returned merchandise), and personnel flow to competitors (employees "pirated" by other firms).

Not *all* resources flow between the firm and *all* environmental elements. For example, machines normally do not flow from the firm to stockholders, money should not flow to

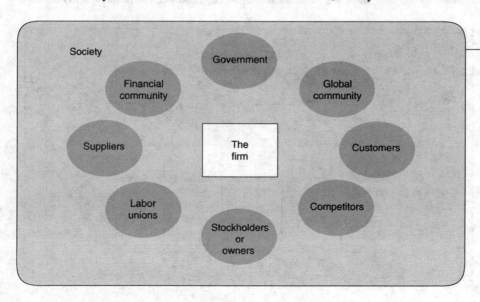

Figure 2.2 Eight Environmental Elements

competitors, and material should not flow to labor unions. The only resource that connects the firm with all of the elements is information, and the firm strives to make the connection with competitors a one-way flow—from the competitors to the firm.

COMPETITIVE ADVANTAGE

As firms go about meeting the product and service needs of their customers, firms strive to enjoy an advantage over their competitors. They achieve this advantage by accomplishing such strategies as providing products and services at a lower price, providing higher quality products and services, and meeting the special needs of certain market segments.

What is not always obvious is the fact that a firm can also achieve competitive advantage through its use of its conceptual resources. In the information systems field, **competitive advantage** refers to the use of information to gain leverage in the marketplace. An important point to recognize is that the firm's managers use both conceptual and physical resources in meeting the strategic objectives of the firm.

Porter's Value Chains

Harvard professor Michael E. Porter is the person who is most often identified with the topic of competitive advantage. His books and articles have provided guidelines and strategies for firms attempting to gain an advantage over their competitors.[2]

Porter believes that a firm achieves competitive advantage by creating a **value chain**, illustrated in Figure 2.3, that consists of primary and support activities that contribute to margin. **Margin** is the value of the firm's products and services less their costs, as perceived by the firm's customers, and margin is the objective of the chain. Firms create value by performing activities, which Porter calls **value activities**.

The primary value activities are shown on the lower layer and include *inbound logistics* that obtain raw materials and supplies from suppliers, the firm's *operations* that transform the raw materials into finished goods, *outbound logistics* that transport the goods to customers, *marketing and sales* operations that identify customer needs and obtain orders, and *service* activities that maintain good customer relationships after the sale.

The support value activities appear on the upper layer and include the *firm infrastructure*—the organizational setting that influences all of the primary activities in a general way. In addition, there are three activities that can influence the primary activities sepa-

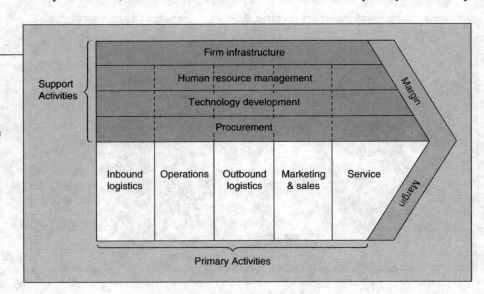

Figure 2.3 A Value Chain

Source: Represented with permission of The Free Press, a division of "Simon & Schuster, from Competitive Advantage: Creating and Sustaining Superior Performance," by Michael E. Porter, Copyright © 1985 by Michael E. Porter.

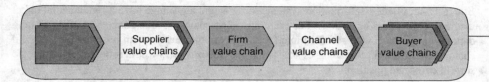

Figure 2.4 A Value System

Source: Represented with permission of The Free Press, a division of "Simon & Schuster, from Competitive Advantage: Creating and Sustaining Superior Performance," by Michael E. Porter, Copyright © 1985 by Michael E. Porter.

rately or in some combination. *Human resources management* consists of all those activities related to managing the firm's personnel, including those functions that managers perform and the roles that they play. *Technology development* includes all activities that involve technology, including the application of that technology in an effective manner. The development of information systems is an example. *Procurement* is concerned with obtaining such resources as materials and machines, which are used by the primary activities. The firm's purchasing department performs many of these procurement activities.

Each value activity, whether it be primary or support, contains three essential ingredients—purchased inputs, human resources, and technology. Also, each activity uses and creates information. For example, information specialists in the information services unit may combine purchased commercial databases, leased computing equipment, and custom-developed programs to produce decision-support information for the firm's executives.

EXPANDING THE SCOPE OF THE VALUE CHAIN   Not too long ago it might have been adequate for management to concentrate on creating the firm's value chain. Today, however, management is alert to additional advantages that can be achieved by linking the firm's value chain to those of other organizations—a linkage that creates an **interorganizational system (IOS)**. The participating firms are called **business partners** and work together as a single coordinated unit, creating a synergy that cannot be achieved by working alone. Porter had such linkages in mind when he focused on the use of information to create competitive advantage, and called the network a **value system**.

A firm can link its value chain to those of its suppliers by implementing systems that make input resources available when needed. An example is a just-in-time (JIT) agreement with a supplier to ship raw materials so that they arrive just hours before they are to be used in the production process, thus minimizing storage costs. A firm can also link its value chain with those of its distribution channel members. An example is an airline that allows travel agents to access the airline's computerized reservation system to make it easier for the agents to book passengers on the airline's flights. When the buyers of the firm's products are also organizations, their value chains can also be linked to those of the firm and its channel members. For example, a pharmaceutical manufacturer can attach retailers' price labels to its products prior to shipment, thus saving the retailers that expense. When the buyers are individual consumers, they can use their computers to log onto the firm's Web site and obtain information and make purchases. Figure 2.4 illustrates the value system containing the four links—suppliers, the firm, distribution channel, and buyers.

The value chains of firms within an industry can be very similar, but most likely the chains of each firm will be unique in some way. Since each value activity includes an informational component, managing the firm's information resources is a key step to achieving competitive advantage.

The Dimensions of Competitive Advantage

Competitive advantage can be realized in terms of achieving strategic, tactical, and operational advantages. At the highest managerial level, the strategic level, the direction of information systems can change the direction of the firm. At the tactical level, managers can specify how the strategic plans will be implemented. At the operational level, managers can use information technology in a variety of ways for data capture and information creation.

STRATEGIC ADVANTAGE   Information systems for strategic advantage have a fundamental effect in shaping the firm's operations. For example, a firm may decide to convert all of its existing data into a database with standard interfaces for possible sharing with business partners and customers. Standardized databases accessible via Web browsers would reflect such a strategic shift in corporate position.

This strategy might cause operations to be fundamentally affected in a number of ways. First, existing access may be via proprietary programs and the change would cause the firm to consider purchasing standard reporting software from an outside vendor or hire an outside firm to design and develop the new reporting systems. Also, mobility of report access is affected since the user will no longer need access to the firm's hardware resources; any connection to the Internet would allow the Web browser to access reports from virtually anywhere in the world. In a similar vein, potential suppliers and customers anywhere in the world would have potential access to the firm's raw materials and finished goods inventory levels to speed the firm's buying and selling transactions.

The element of security cannot be ignored with this example of a strategic change in information systems. Along with the greater opportunities for profits from Web access to the firm's information come greater dangers. Will a hacker pose as a vendor or customer in order to gain access to the database and damage the firm's information resource? Will a competitor access the information as part of corporate espionage? The strategic level establishes the direction and destination but there still needs to be a plan to accomplish a strategy that recognizes the importance of security.

TACTICAL ADVANTAGE   A **tactical advantage** is defined as a method of accomplishing the strategy in a better way than do competitors. In our example, customer service can be enhanced. All firms want satisfied customers because the level of satisfaction is important for repeat purchases from the customer.

Assume that a previous customer wishes to make another purchase of office supplies from your firm. The purchase of such supplies are routine and the information system notes that the customer has made purchases totaling $950 during the month and that there is a 5 percent discount of purchase costs over $1,000 during any month.

This method of accomplishing the strategy of improved customer service via the Web-based information system achieves the tactical advantage in several ways. First, the customer feels the firm's interest in the form of a 5 percent discount. Second, the information system may suggest which products the customer may wish to purchase. The firm is not only encouraging customer loyalty, it may also be increasing its profit on the sale.

Assume that the customer is purchasing cases of computer paper when the information system notes the $950 monthly amount. What if the customer routinely purchases paper but not toner cartridges? It would be safe to assume that the customer must be purchasing the toner from another supplier. This is an opportunity for the firm to offer its toner at a low price (the 5 percent discount) and possibly win future toner sales to the customer.

The discount itself is an inducement to the customer but it may also economically benefit the firm. By getting the additional $50 on this order ($1,000 minus $950) the firm saves the expense of processing a second order. Remember, the next order from this customer may reach the $1,000 level and the firm would have the expense of processing the second order and still would have to provide the discount. Providing the discount now on this order saves the firm the cost of a second order processing. Even more expenses are saved by the firm since it will make a single delivery, not two.

The strategic decision was to make the firm's information system available to customers for improved customer service. This allowed a tactical information system to be developed by the firm that not only increases customer satisfaction but improves the profitability of the firm.

OPERATIONAL ADVANTAGE   An **operational advantage** is one that deals with everyday transactions and processes. This is where the information system directly interacts with the process.

A Web site that "remembers" customers and their preferences through past transactions would reflect an operational advantage. Browsers often have **cookies**, small files of information on the user's computer, that store such information as account numbers, passwords, and other information pertinent to the user's transactions. This is a valuable convenience to the customer and directly benefits the firm. It is true that customers who use the Web to enter their purchases saves the firm from the expense of paying a clerk to enter the data, but that is a minor benefit.

User-entered data is more likely to be accurate. It is not communicated orally to someone else so it cannot be misunderstood during communication. When the information (name, address, and so on) can be retrieved from an earlier record the data has an even greater chance for likelihood of accuracy. Factor in the sense of ownership of the user-entered data. If the data is not accurate, the user does not blame the firm. For a variety of operational reasons, Web access to the firm's information systems improves customer relations.

The three levels of advantage work together. Information systems that are impacted by all three levels have the best chance to substantially increase a firm's performance.

CHALLENGES FROM GLOBAL COMPETITORS

In past years, the environmental model in Figure 2.2 would have included an element named *local community*. In order to reflect today's business realities, the term *global community* is now used. During the early years of computer use, all but the largest firms could focus on their local community in meeting needs of their customers. This narrow focus gradually gave way to the current view of the world as a marketplace. The big player in this global arena is the multinational corporation.

A **multinational corporation (MNC)** is a firm that operates across products, markets, nations, and cultures. It consists of the parent company and a group of subsidiaries. The subsidiaries are geographically dispersed, and each one may have its own unique goals, policies, and procedures.

The Special Need for Information Processing in an MNC

Although all firms have a need for information processing and coordination, these needs are especially crucial for the MNC. The MNC is an open system that seeks to minimize the uncertainty that its environment imposes. Uncertainty, in this context, is "the difference between the amount of information required to perform the task and the amount of information already possessed by the organization."[3] The MNC executives easily see that they can cope with their environmental influences by making good use of information technology.

The Special Need for Coordination in an MNC

Coordination has become a key to achieving competitive advantage in a global marketplace. Companies that are unable to gain strategic control of their worldwide operations and manage them in a globally coordinated manner will not succeed in the international economy.[4]

The bad news for the MNC executives is that the challenges of coordination are greater for the MNC than for the firm that restricts its activities to its home country. The difficulty arises from the fact that the resources used by the MNC are widely distributed. The good news is that improvements in information technology, methodology, and communications have made global coordination much easier. But even with these improvements, coordinating remains a big challenge.

The Advantages of Coordination

Many of the advantages that accrue to the MNC by virtue of having a good information processing capability are based on the ability to coordinate. These advantages include:[5]

- Flexibility in responding to competitors in different countries and markets
- The ability to respond in one country—or in a region of a country—to a change in another
- The ability to keep abreast of market needs around the world
- The ability to transfer knowledge between units in different countries
- Reduced overall costs of operation
- Increased efficiency and effectiveness in meeting customer needs
- The ability to achieve and maintain diversity in the firm's products and in how they are produced and distributed

All of these advantages are due to reductions in the time and cost of communications made possible through use of the firm's information resources.

INFORMATION MANAGEMENT

We recognized in Chapter 1 that data and information are resources—conceptual resources that represent the physical resources. A firm's information resources consist of:

- Computer hardware
- Computer software
- Information specialists
- Users
- Facilities
- The database
- Information

When a firm's managers decide to use information to achieve competitive advantage, they must manage these resources in order to achieve the desired results. The managers ensure that the necessary raw data is gathered and then processed into usable information. The managers then ensure that appropriate individuals receive the information in the proper form at the proper time so that it can be used. Finally, the managers discard information that has outlived its usefulness and replace it with information that is current and accurate. All of this activity—acquiring information, using it in the most effective way, and discarding it at the proper time—is called **information management**.

The Dimensions of Information

As the system developers (users and information specialists) define the output that the information processor is to provide, they consider four basic dimensions of information.[6] These desirable dimensions contribute to information value.

1. **Relevancy** Information has **relevancy** when it pertains to the problem at hand. The user should be able to select the data that is needed without wading through a volume of unrelated facts. In fact, only when data is relevant to the decision to be made should it be called "information."
2. **Accuracy** Ideally, all information should be accurate, but features that contribute to system accuracy add to the cost. For that reason, the user is often forced to settle for less than perfect accuracy. Applications involving money, such as payroll, billing, and accounts receivable, seek 100 percent accuracy. Other applications, such as long-range economic forecasts and statistical reports, often can be just as useful when the data is not 100 percent accurate.

3. **Timeliness** Information should be available for problem solving before crisis situations develop or opportunities are lost. The user should be able to obtain information that describes what is happening now, in addition to what happened in the past. Information that arrives after the decision is made has no value.
4. **Completeness** The user should be able to obtain information that presents a complete picture of a problem or a solution. However, systems that drown the user in a sea of information should not be designed. The term **information overload** suggests the harm that can come from too much information. The user should be able to determine the amount of detail that is needed. Information is complete when it has the correct amount of aggregation and supports all areas of the decision being made.

The users are the best persons to specify the dimensions of the information that they need. When necessary, the information specialists can help the users approach this task in a logical manner.

The Changing Nature of Information Management

For most of the computer era, information management has focused on the transaction processing systems that provide most of the data for the MISs and DSSs. That situation is changing. Many of the transaction processing systems are being made obsolete by new technology. Technology is also introducing new data-recording media, such as images, that must be managed. Finally, new views of information are regarding it as knowledge that has immense value to the firm and should be managed.

LEGACY INFORMATION SYSTEMS The task of managing and controlling information in a modern firm must recognize the limitations of past technologies. The earlier information systems and hardware that are incompatible or only partially compatible with current information technology are called **legacy systems**. Although the data captured by legacy systems produces primarily information describing what happened in the past, that information is still valuable.

Much of the legacy data can be converted to new technologies. The text and numbers that make up so much of legacy files can be imported to modern databases. Data capture may require that old data values be updated with new values. For example, obsolete product numbers are replaced with current numbers. There may be other steps necessary to merge the textual and numerical data into the current database. Firms make a decision about the amount of legacy data to capture based upon their expectations of additional profits that could be realized from the legacy data.

One problem with conversion of legacy data is that the data may not be available in digital format. Some legacy data may only exist as paper printouts. This data can still be captured as images.

IMAGE MANAGEMENT Digital photographs of printouts can be stored as computer files that can be referenced by the firm's current information systems. Special computer software exists that will translate images of textual and numerical data into a word processing file. Accuracy of the translation by these software systems depends upon several factors but generally runs between 80 percent and 95 percent. The firm must decide whether the expense of achieving 100 percent accuracy exceeds the benefits of accuracy. To achieve 100 percent accuracy involves using personnel to read and verify the translation made by the software.

The role of images has expanded with the advent of Web sites. Effective Web sites are very visual—photographs of the firm's logo, products, employees, and other images can help users navigate the Web site. Management of images becomes important as the number of images used grows. The reason is that images require a great deal of storage space compared to textual and numerical data. A consistent image format may be required so that all applications in the firm can utilize the images. Figure 2.5 lists several popular image formats.

Figure 2.5 **Common Image Management Formats**

```
COMMON IMAGE MANAGEMENT FORMATS

JPG – Joint Photographics Expert Group
        used mainly for Web images, achieves reduction of file size over most
        other formats

GIF – Graphics Interchange Format
        used mainly for Web images, uses only 256 colors, achieves some file
        size reduction, most commonly used for black and white images and for
        animated images

TIFF – Tagged Image File Format
        bit mapped images that require a large amount of storage space but can
        be rendered in most resolutions without loss of image quality

BMP – the standard bit mapped image format for Windows can require large
        amounts of storage

WMF – Windows Metafile Format
        format for graphics that are exchanged between Microsoft Windows-
        based applications (such as Word, Excel, and so on)
```

KNOWLEDGE MANAGEMENT **Knowledge management** is a broad term defined as the process of organizing a firm's information so that it can easily be captured, stored, processed, and used by decision makers. It is the management of the firm's information assets. The impetus for knowledge management is to derive more economic return to the firm from the information resources it owns.

If an organization manages its knowledge well, information will easily move from where it is captured to the decision makers who need to use it. Barriers to the movement are being unaware that pertinent data exists, inability of the decision maker to retrieve information from the system, unwillingness of different functional areas to share information, and executives who do not realize the importance of the information resource. Many tools can aid knowledge management by breaking through these barriers.

An easy-to-use database management system can greatly encourage knowledge management, and statistical software packages can provide data analysis. However, the most important tool for knowledge management is training. Managers and professionals should be trained in the recognition of information as a valuable asset to yield greater profits to the firm, and to use information systems as they make decisions. Information specialists should be trained to understand the impact of information systems to change decision making in the firm.

All of a firm's information management activities can be carried out within the scope of a strategic plan that is especially tailored to the information resources.

STRATEGIC PLANNING FOR INFORMATION RESOURCES

The first computer-using firms placed the responsibility for managing the information resources in the hands of a special unit of information professionals. This unit, which we call information services (IS), is managed by a manager who may have vice-presidential status. The accepted practice today is to establish information services as a major business area and include its top manager in the select group of executives, such as the executive committee, who make the key decisions of the firm.

The Chief Information Officer

The term *CEO*, for chief executive officer, is firmly implanted in the vocabulary of business to describe the person (president or chairperson of the board) who exerts the most influence on the direction of the firm. Terms such as *CFO*, for chief financial officer, and *COO*, for chief operating officer, have been coined as well. Similar terminology has been created for the information services manager. The term is CIO, for chief information officer. The term implies more than simply a title. It implies a recommended role that the top information services manager should play. As intended by the concept, the **chief information officer (CIO)** is the manager of information services who contributes managerial skills to solving problems relating not only to the information resources but also to other areas of the firm's operations.

The CIO can position information services as a vital element in the organizational structure of the firm by taking the following advice:[7]

- Spend time with the business and in business training. Learn the business, not just the technology.
- Build partnerships with business units and line management; don't wait to be invited.
- Focus on improving business processes.
- Explain IS costs in business terms.
- Build credibility by delivering reliable IS services.
- Be open to ideas from outside the information systems area.

From this point on in the text, we will use the term CIO when describing the top-level manager of information services.

Strategic Planning for the Enterprise

When a firm organizes its executives into an executive committee, this group invariably assumes a strategic planning responsibility for the entire firm. The committee, at a minimum, consists of the president and the vice presidents of the business areas. This committee typically schedules an annual planning session, where ideas are exchanged concerning what the firm wants to accomplish during the coming years. The output of this exercise is a strategic business plan.

With the plan in place, the executive committee monitors performance throughout the year and takes appropriate action. In some cases, the plan can be modified to reflect changing situations. Also, the committee can initiate decisions aimed at ensuring that the plan is met.

Strategic Planning for Business Areas

When a firm's executives are fully committed to strategic planning, they see a need for each business area to develop its own strategic plan. The business area plans detail how those areas will support the enterprise as it works toward its strategic objectives.

One approach to business area strategic planning would be for each area to establish its own plan independently of the others. However, that approach does not ensure that the areas will work together as synchronized subsystems. Figure 2.6 shows how all of the business areas should cooperate in their strategic planning processes. The arrows represent flows of information and influence.

During the past few years, the information services unit has probably devoted more attention to strategic planning than have most of the other business areas. The term used to describe this activity is strategic planning for information resources (SPIR).

The SPIR Approach

Strategic planning for information resources (SPIR) is the *concurrent* development of strategic plans for information services and the firm so that the firm's plan reflects the support to be provided by information services and the information services plan reflects the future

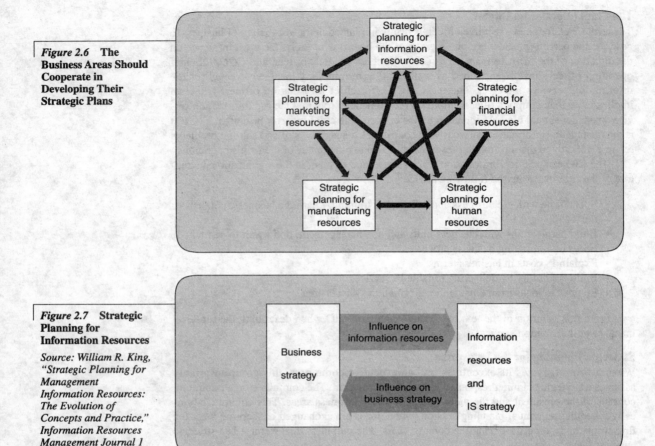

Figure 2.6 The Business Areas Should Cooperate in Developing Their Strategic Plans

Figure 2.7 Strategic Planning for Information Resources

Source: William R. King, "Strategic Planning for Management Information Resources: The Evolution of Concepts and Practice," *Information Resources Management Journal 1* (Fall 1988), 3. Used with permission.

demands for systems support. Figure 2.7 illustrates the manner in which each planning process influences the other.

Core Content of a Strategic Plan for Information Resources

Each firm will develop a strategic plan for information resources that meets its own particular needs. However, we can identify two core topics that should be included in each plan.

- The objectives to be achieved by each category of systems during the time period covered by the plan
- The information resources necessary to meet the objectives.

This content is illustrated in Figure 2.8.

An Example Strategic Plan for Information Resources

Figure 2.9 is an example of a SPIR. It is a self-contained report that includes an executive summary, spells out the goals of the firm's information services unit, defines the scope of the IT services in three organizational units, and summarizes a work plan for implementing systems that will enable the firm to meet its information services goals.

This is a fairly modest SPIR. Such plans can go into considerably more detail depending on the needs of the firm.

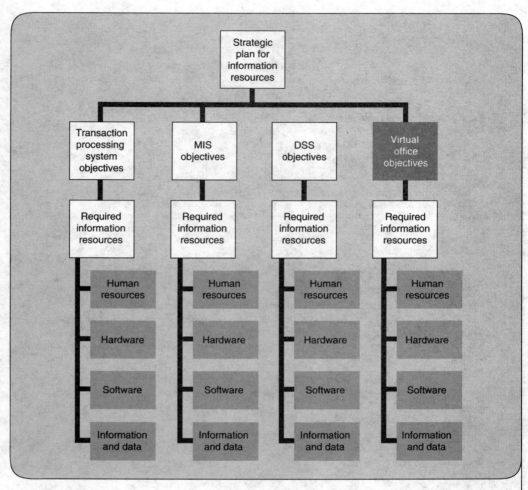

Figure 2.8 Basic Framework of a Strategic Plan for Information Resources

GLOBAL BUSINESS STRATEGIES

MNCs follow the same general strategic planning approach as do firms that confine their activities to domestic markets—following the pattern outlined above. However, MNCs have the task of tailoring their strategic plans to fit the information roles that they want their subsidiaries to play.

For some MNCs, entry into an international marketplace is a new adventure. For others, it continues a management philosophy that has influenced the firm throughout its existence. Such industry giants as Procter and Gamble, Unilever, Nestlé, Honda, and IBM have always had a global focus. IBM, for example, has always seen its potential market area as the entire world. For years its New York City headquarters was called WHQ, for World Headquarters, and one of its mottos was "World Peace Through World Trade."

MIS researchers Christopher A. Bartlett and Sumantra Ghoshal have identified four basic strategies that MNCs can follow for using information to coordinate the activities of the parent company and the subsidiaries.[8] These strategies vary in the centralization or decentralization of control, and the sharing of expertise.

A SAMPLE STRATEGIC PLAN FOR INFORMATION RESOURCES

Executive Summary

The Strategic Plan for Information Resources (SPIR) has been developed to support the Strategic Business Plan by assembling and applying the information resources that are necessary to achieve the strategic objectives. The SPIR is organized into four sections:

- Information Technology Mission Statement
- Information Technology Goals
- Scope of Information Technology Services
- Information Technology Work Plan

Information Technology Mission Statement

The mission of information technology is to provide the highest quality of information services in a supportive environment that promotes creativity, personal growth, interaction, diversity, and professional development so that the firm can leverage technology to help attain corporate objectives.

Information Technology Goals

The information technology mission will be accomplished by pursuing the following goals:

1. Build a competitive advantage in use of information technology.
2. Develop information systems that meet the needs of employees on all organizational levels and also environmental business partners.
3. Stay current on evolving information technologies so as to meet the needs of our customers.
4. Maintain operational stability and reliability in all of our information resources-people, data, facilities, hardware, and software.
5. Maintain an ongoing education and training program designed to achieve efficient and effective use of all of the information resources.

Scope of Information Technology Services

Information technology services consist of the following:

Administrative Services
- Budgeting and fiscal review
- Human resources
- Management reporting
- Stockholder relations

Engineering Services
- Strategic planning and implementation
- Capacity planning
- Network design, maintenance, troubleshooting, and administration
- Server installations
- Contingency planning and backup

Technology Services
- Technical support in the form of help desk and call management services
- User education and training
- Database management services
- Document management services
- System development and support
- World Wide Web access
- Computer graphics
- Hardware troubleshooting, upgrading, and replacement
- Antivirus and firewall services
- Systems administration and maintenance
- Systems audits

Information Technology Work Plan

Seven key projects have been identified to be completed during the next three-year period. Prior to beginning each project, a project management mechanism will be developed specifying the following:

- Required tasks
- Person(s) or organizations responsible for completion of the tasks
- Estimated amount of time required for each task

All projects will be managed using Gantt charts and network diagrams.

All projects with the exception of the knowledge-based RFP system will be accomplished with internal IT resources. The RFP system will be designed and implemented by consultants.

The projects and their estimated person months include the following. The first person listed is the project manager. Additional persons are support personnel.

Project	Project Manager(s)	Estimated Person-Months
1. Upgrade from Windows 95 to Windows XP	Carolyn Wright	0.2
2. Replace GroupWise e-mail system with an integration of Microsoft's Digital Dashboard and the corporate relationship management system.	Danny Cho Carolyn Wright	3.0
3. Implement the Outlook Telephony Interface, enabling the retrieval of e-mail from any Touch Tone telephone by callin a toll-free number.	Danny Cho Carolyn Wright	2.5
4. Conduct Java benchmark comparison of Oracle9i Application Server, IBM WebSphere, and BEA WebLogic.	Danny Cho Carolyn Wright	2.0
5. Deploy departmental-based intranet for library services and human resources information and services.	Robin Birdsong Carolyn Wright	4.0
6. Implement a Web-based human resources information system.	Robin Birdsong Carolyn Wright	18.0
7. Implement a knowledge-based system to determine personnel, production facility, and material needs in response to RFPs.	Paul Sanchez KBS Consultants	96.0

Figure 2.9 A Sample Strategic Plan for Information Resources

Decentralized Control Strategy

The **decentralized control strategy** is perhaps the oldest, pioneered by European-based firms that gave their subsidiaries much leeway in meeting the needs of the customers inside their own boundaries. It was a type of "hands-off" strategy in which the parent allowed the subsidiaries to develop their own products and practices. Figure 2.10 shows that the information flows are primarily from the subsidiaries to the parent in the form of financial reports.

Many MNCs follow a decentralized control strategy. In this setting the information systems facilitate decentralized decision making, and they consist of stand-alone databases and processes.

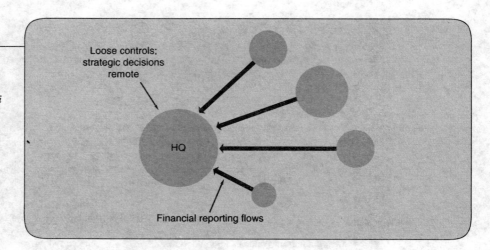

Figure 2.10
Decentralized Control Strategy

Source: Jahangir Karimi and Benn R. Konsynski, "Globalization and Information Management Strategies," Journal of Management Information Systems 7 (Spring 1991), 12. Used with permission.

Centralized Control Strategy

Whereas the decentralized control strategy leaves much of the control to the subsidiaries, the **centralized control strategy** localizes control within the parent. The firm seeks to meet the needs of its worldwide customers with standardized products. The products for all of the world markets are manufactured centrally and shipped to the subsidiaries. As Figure 2.11 shows, product and information flows between the parent and the subsidiaries travel in one direction—toward the subsidiaries.

When the MNC pursues a centralized control strategy, its information systems place the majority of the capacity at the parent location and feature centralized databases and processes.

Centralized Expertise Strategy

The **centralized expertise strategy** is a blending of the centralized control strategy and the decentralized control strategy. The centralized expertise strategy calls for a management team at the parent location that is knowledgeable and skilled at penetrating global markets. This expertise is made available to the subsidiaries. The subsidiaries use this expertise to adapt the firm's products, processes, and strategies to their own markets. Figure 2.12 shows the two-

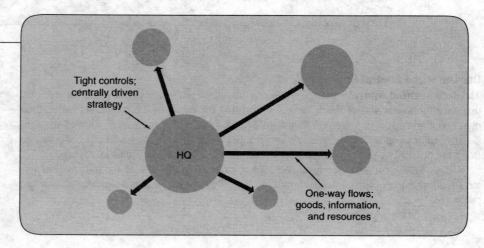

Figure 2.11
Centralized Control Strategy

Source: Jahangir Karimi and Benn R. Konsynski, "Globalization and Information Management Strategies," Journal of Management Information Systems 7 (Spring 1991), 13. Used with permission.

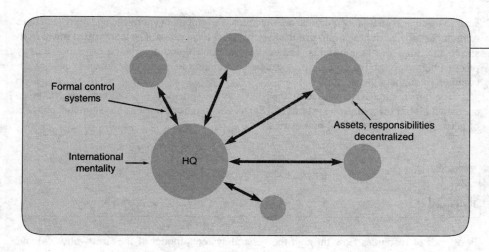

Figure 2.12
Centralized Expertise Strategy

Source: Jahangir Karimi and Benn R. Konsynski, "Globalization and Information Management Strategies," Journal of Management Information Systems 7 (Spring 1991), 14. Used with permission.

way flow of information between the parent and the subsidiaries. Expertise flows to the subsidiaries and financial information flows to the parent.

Firms that pursue this business strategy employ interorganizational systems that link databases and processes of the parent with those of the subsidiaries.

Centralized Control and Distributed Expertise Strategy

The **centralized control and distributed expertise strategy** became popular in the 1980s as firms recognized that they had to be more responsive at the subsidiary level. The parent and all of the subsidiaries work together in formulating strategies and operating policies, as well as in coordinating the logistics of getting the products to the right markets. The firm seeks to achieve global integration and efficiencies yet provide for flexibility at the local level.

Figure 2.13 recognizes the intricate control systems that are required, as well as the flows of resources from node to node as the firm functions as a coordinated system. The diagram also shows the information-processing capacity that is made available at the subsidiary level.

When a firm pursues a centralized control and distributed expertise strategy, it achieves integration in its information systems by means of standards that are applied on an international

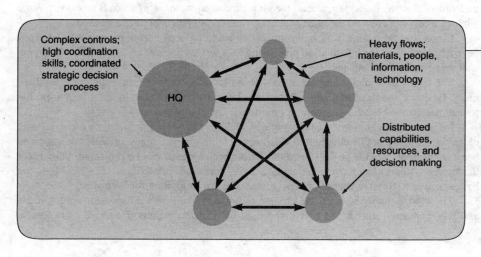

Figure 2.13
Centralized Control and Distributed Expertise Strategy

Source: Jahangir Karimi and Benn R. Konsynski, "Globalization and Information Management Strategies," Journal of Management Information Systems 7 (Spring 1991), 15. Used with permission.

scale, as well as by adopting common architectures. Development teams include representatives of multiple subsidiaries to ensure that the systems meet local needs. The teams often travel from site to site, implementing systems. The centralized control and distributed expertise strategy places a big responsibility on the firm's database specialists to ensure that database designs are common throughout the world.

The information systems used by the MNCs as they pursue these four business strategies are called **global information systems (GISs)**. A GIS can be defined as a system that consists of networks that cross national boundaries.[9]

Summary

Two types of resources flow through the general systems model of the firm—physical and conceptual. A feedback mechanism allows the flow of conceptual resources (data, information, decisions) to connect the physical system with the control mechanism. The control mechanism consists of standards, management, and an information processor.

The environment of a business organization consists of suppliers, customers, labor unions, the financial community, stockholders or owners, competitors, the government, and the global community. All of these elements are connected to the firm by flows of physical and conceptual resources.

Both physical and conceptual resources can be used to achieve a competitive advantage. Porter promoted the idea that competitive advantage could be achieved with a value chain that consists of value activities. Each chain consists of primary and support activities that are aimed at achieving margin. Each activity contains three essential ingredients—purchased inputs, human resources, and technology. The value chain concept can be expanded by linking the chains of firms that function as an interorganizational system, creating a value system.

Information systems can reflect the activities of three major managerial levels of the firm—strategic, tactical, and operational. The strategic emphasis may be to use information systems to differentiate the firm from its competition. Tactical managers on the middle level may direct the design of information systems that have common interfaces, such as browsers gaining access via the Internet, so that customers have immediate access at any time and from anywhere. On the operational level the information systems might offer complementary products as customers accesses their orders as a way to increase sales at the same time as customer satisfaction is supported. When all three levels work toward the same goal the greatest profit potential can be reached.

Firms that do business globally are called multinational corporations (MNCs). They have a special need for information processing as a way to achieve coordination, which contributes some real advantages.

The firm's information resources consist of hardware, software, information specialists, users, facilities, the database, and information. Information delivered in the proper form has four dimensions—relevancy, accuracy, timeliness, and completeness.

Information technology changes rapidly, and a consequence is that data gathered with older systems may not be compatible with current technology. Legacy systems are important because they can provide key historical data from which trends can be projected. Sometimes the legacy systems cannot provide data in a digital format. If printouts are available they can be scanned and stored as digital images. Images are also important for Web sites.

Knowledge management is the process of organizing a firm's information so that it can easily be captured, stored, processed, and used by decision makers. Database management

Highlights in MIS

9/11—Not the End of Globalization[10]

Some parties, including a professor at the London School of Economics, concluded that the terrorist acts on September 11, 2001 marked the end of globalization. The assumed basis for this belief was that nations would build walls to keep everyone else out. One year later, this had not occurred. In fact, the opposite is happening.

In building a case that 9/11 was a blow *for* globalization one can begin with the observation that the terrorists were from the parts of the world that have been the least global, open, and integrated with the rest of the world—Afghanistan, Pakistan, Yemen, and Saudi Arabia. They are a product of the part of the world that has not embraced globalization. At the opposite extreme are China and India, the two largest countries in the world that represent one-third of the world population. These countries have taken a strong globalization stance, recognizing that opening up their boundaries is a way to lift their people from poverty.

India is a case study of the benefits of globalization. In Bangalore, India's Silicon Valley, thousands of young Indians have been able to achieve social mobility not through caste, land, or heredity, but through their technical expertise. These youths work for software firms that develop software for the world's largest organizations. Not only has this been good for the "techies," but Bangalore officials believe that each technical job has generated six and a half support jobs.

What this means is that globalization is creating a generation of young people who are more interested in joining the world system than blowing it up.

---

systems and statistical software enable knowledge management but the key to successful implementation is training of managers, professionals, and information specialists.

The chief information officer (CIO) plays a key role in strategic planning for the enterprise, the business areas, and information resources. The strategic plan for information resources (SPIR) identifies the objectives that information systems are to achieve in the future and the information resources that will be required. The key to SPIR is to develop the strategic plan for the firm and for information resources at the same time.

MNCs can follow four different strategies in linking the parent company with its subsidiaries. A decentralized control strategy puts control responsibility in the hands of the subsidiaries, whereas centralized control localizes the key decision making at the parent site. A centralized expertise strategy positions the expertise at the parent but makes it available to the subsidiaries. A centralized control and decentralized expertise strategy is the most complex in terms of resource flows from node to node. The information systems used to achieve these four strategies are called global information systems.

Key Terms

closed-loop system
interorganizational system (IOS)
multinational corporation (MNC)
information management
information overload

legacy systems
knowledge management
chief information officer (CIO)
decentralized control strategy
centralized control strategy

centralized expertise strategy
centralized control and distributed expertise strategy
global information systems (GISs)

Key Concepts

- general systems model of the firm
- the eight-element environmental model
- environmental resource flows
- competitive advantage
- value chain
- value system
- dimensions of competitive advantage as management levels
- dimensions of information
- strategic planning for information resources (SPIR)

Questions

1. Why are standards provided to the information processor in the general systems model of the firm?
2. What provides the connections between the firm and its environment?
3. What are the eight environmental elements?
4. What is margin and how does it relate to competitive advantage?
5. What are Porter's primary value activities? What are his support value activities?
6. What is a value chain?
7. What is a value system?
8. How can a firm achieve strategic advantage from an information system that processes customer sales orders?
9. Explain how you would achieve a tactical advantage by tying the sales order system to the customer service system.
10. How would you design an information system to take advantage of operational opportunities?
11. What are the features that distinguish a multinational corporation (MNC)?
12. What is a source of uncertainty for an MNC?
13. How do the executives of an MNC respond to uncertainty?
14. What single word describes the key to achieving competitive advantage for an MNC?
15. List the seven types of information resources. Place an asterisk next to those that are always located in information services.
16. Name four dimensions of information that the manager should consider.
17. Comment on the following statements:
    a. Information produced by the information processor should be free of errors.
    b. An information processor should provide the manager with as much information as possible.
18. Why should an organization capture data from its legacy systems?
19. How has the increased use of Web sites by firms caused image management to increase in importance?
20. What is knowledge management?
21. Could a manager be a CIO even though he or she does not have that title? Explain your reasoning.
22. Would a degree in business administration help a CIO? Explain.
23. What are the two basic elements that should be included in a strategic plan for information resources?
24. Explain how centralized expertise can also contribute to centralized control.
25. Which of the global business strategies would require a multinational development team?

Topics for Discussion

1. The general systems model of the firm shows environmental data and information going to the information processor. Would there be any instances when the data and information would flow directly to management?
2. How has the firm's collection of data across many information system platforms over many years (resulting in legacy systems) impacted the firm's ability to make decisions?
3. Where are the information resources located that are the subject of the strategic plan for information resources?
4. Is a global information system any different from the MIS of a domestic firm?

PROBLEMS

1. Write a paragraph describing how the general systems model of the firm applies to a manufacturing firm—say a small company that manufactures window air conditioning units. Take each element in the model and resource flow and explain how it fits the manufacturer.

2. Repeat Problem 1, only use the model to explain a small law firm of three attorneys, a legal assistant, and a secretary. Each person has a desktop computer that is used for e-mail and accessing the Internet.

Case Problem: WATER EQUIPMENT TECHNOLOGY COMPANY OF MEXICO

Water Equipment Technology Company (WETCO) is a Chicago-based manufacturer of industrial wastewater treatment systems. It has subsidiary operations around the world, including Mexico. Emilio Chavez, the president of WETCO Mexico, has recently decided to implement strategic planning for information resources (SPIR). WETCO Mexico has a large computing operation but has never had a strategic information plan. Chavez sent e-mail messages to the other members of the executive committee, advising them of his intentions and asking for their ideas.

He has received replies from all three members—Benito Flores, the vice president of manufacturing and sales; Juan Alvarez, the vice president of finance; and Betty Wilson, the vice president of information systems. President Chavez reads the e-mail replies:

FROM: BENITO *I have given the subject of SPIR a great deal of thought since we discussed it in the last executive committee meeting. I would like to see manufacturing and sales develop our own strategic plan independently of the rest of the organization—including IS. We have a large amount of computing equipment that we use for our own applications and we are in the best position to know how to use it. There's no reason why another area should tell us how to use our information systems. Let Betty and Juan do the same thing—develop their own strategic plans as they see fit.*

FROM: JUAN *Thanks for the opportunity to voice my views. I think that all three vice presidents should work together in developing a single strategic plan. We have a good working relationship and cooperate on many other activities. There is no reason why a joint approach to SPIR would not work.*

FROM: BETTY *IS should prepare the strategic information resources plan for all of WETCO Mexico. Juan and Benito have enough responsibility in their own areas, so that they should not be asked to devote their valuable time to IS problems. Give IS the total strategic planning responsibility.*

After Chavez has read all three replies, he leans back in his chair and says, "Our next executive committee meeting should really be exciting."

ASSIGNMENT

1. Explain the advantages and disadvantages of each of the three approaches given by the vice presidents.
2. Which approach should WETCO Mexico take and why?
3. How should the strategic plan for information systems at WETCO Mexico relate to other WETCO subsidiaries?

Notes

[1] Richard J. Hopeman, *Systems Analysis and Operations Management* (Columbus, OH: Charles E. Merrill, 1969), 79–103.

[2] For more information on competitive advantage, see Michael E. Porter, "How Competitive Forces Shape Strategy," *Harvard Business Review* 57 (March–April 1979): 137–145, and Michael E. Porter, *Competitive Advantage* (New York: Free Press, 1985).

[3] William G. Egelhoff, "Information-Processing Theory and the Multinational Enterprise," *Journal of International Business Studies* 22 (Number 3, 1991), 343.

[4] Jahanjir Karimi and Benn R. Konsynski, "Globalization and Information Management Strategies," 7 (Spring 1991), 7.

[5] Based on Karimi and Konsynski, 9.

[6] For the classic description of information value, see Robert W. Zmud, "An Empirical Investigation of the Dimensionality of the Concept of Information," *Decision Sciences* 9 (April 1978), 187–195.

[7] Jeff Moad, "Why You Should Be Making IS Allies," *Datamation* 36 (May 1, 1990), 26*ff*.

[8] See Christopher A. Bartlett and Sumantra Ghoshal, *Managing Across Borders: The Transnational Solution* (Boston: Harvard Business School Press, 1989). The authors used the names multinational, global, international, and transnational to identify the strategies. We have changed the names to avoid the conflict of using the name *multinational* for both the corporation and the strategy.

[9] Karimi and Konsynski, "Globalization and Information Management Strategies," 18.

[10] Based on Thomas L. Friedman, "Globalization, Alive and Well," *New York Times*, September 22, 2002, page WK 13.

Chapter 3

Using Information Technology to Engage in Electronic Commerce

Learning Objectives

After studying this chapter, you should

- Recognize the importance and advantages of electronic commerce.
- Understand that within ten years electronic commerce will be blended into everyday business processes and consumers will not recognize e-commerce as a special category.
- Understand the difference between business-to-business electronic commerce and business-to-consumer electronic commerce.
- Learn examples of good business-to-business electronic commerce and business-to-consumer electronic commerce.
- Understand the role that business intelligence plays in electronic commerce.
- Know the role that interorganizational systems, the Internet, and the World Wide Web play in electronic commerce.
- Know what factors influence the adoption of interorganizational systems.
- Recognize the movement from electronic data interchange to various Web-standard data exchange practices.
- Understand why many firms choose to have both a virtual store and a physical store.

Introduction

Electronic commerce, also called e-commerce, is the use of communications networks and computers to accomplish business processes. The popular view is that e-commerce is the Internet and computers using Web browsers to buy and sell products. While this is true, it is only a small part of electronic commerce. Most electronic commerce occurs between businesses, not between a business and the consumer of the product.

Businesses have been electronically exchanging data for years in their efforts to make their operations more efficient. The communication lines they use are often leased from telephone companies (AT&T, MCI, and others) and special communications hardware is used at each end of the line to facilitate the data transfer between the businesses' computers. Standard formats for data exchange have been established so that any business that wants to electronically exchange data can do so. The business-to-business exchange of data supports electronic commerce.

Business-to-consumer electronic commerce is more recent and it seems that everyone is surfing the Web to buy books and music. Business-to-consumer sales are small compared to business-to-business sales but they still represent an opportunity for great growth and profit. A firm must understand the possibilities of electronic commerce by gathering intelligence about its customers and other environmental entities. Also, the firm must understand the role that the Internet and the World Wide Web play in providing the infrastructure required for electronic commerce to exist.

Although we see electronic commerce as a new and distinct type of commerce now, we must realize that soon it will be just another facet of everyday business transactions. The phone, invented in 1876, can give us some perspective. Like the Internet and Web, the practical applications for the phone only occurred when the phone was widely used. Businesses used phones first; they were simply too expensive to have in every household. When the phone became inexpensive it became widely popular and businesses began to devise ways that would allow customers to use phones to interact for sales and service. Businesses grow and change in order to take advantage of technology whether that technology is a phone or the World Wide Web.

ELECTRONIC COMMERCE

Some people define electronic commerce (also called e-commerce) very narrowly. Their narrow definition would only include business transactions that deal with customers and suppliers, connecting their respective computers via the Internet. Such a narrow definition implies that only transactions crossing the boundary of the firm can be classified as electronic commerce. If a transaction stays within the boundaries of the firm, these people would call it an electronic business transaction to differentiate it from electronic commerce. Trying to delineate internal versus external transactions as electronic business versus electronic commerce does not help because most people consider electronic business and electronic commerce to be synonymous.

We take the broad view of electronic commerce, that it can facilitate internal and external operations of the firm. With this view, the terms "electronic business" and "electric commerce" are truly synonyms. Many of the operations are internal—they are performed within the boundaries of the firm by the business areas of finance, human resources, information services, manufacturing, marketing, and others. Businesses have become physically dispersed with plants located across a country or even across the world. Also, business areas themselves act as the supplier or customer to other areas of the business. Under our broad definition a business transaction that uses network access, computer-based systems, and a Web browser interface qualifies as **electronic commerce**.

Electronic Commerce Beyond the Boundary of the Firm

It is useful to distinguish between the two types of electronic commerce that occur with entities beyond the firm's boundary. **Business-to-customer (B2C)** electronic commerce refers to transactions between a business and the final consumer of the product while **business-to-business (B2B)** electronic commerce refers to transactions between businesses where neither is the final consumer. For example, in the distribution chain from manufacturer to wholesaler to retail store to consumer all transactions from one entity to the next are B2B until the transactions between retail store and consumer, which is B2C.

Business-to-business transactions involve a relatively few people, generally in the information systems groups of the companies affected. The persons involved in B2B transactions are usually highly trained in the use of information systems and familiar with the business processes affected by the transactions. Since the transactions are between businesses, the number of B2B transactions may be relatively small but the dollar values are quite high. A single transaction between a manufacturer and wholesaler may involve thousands of units of a product and millions of dollars.

Business-to-consumer transactions require fundamental design differences. Customers may or may not have expertise with information technology so the site must offer instructions and help. Communications with the consumer may be over a slow phone line instead of the high-speed communication networks enjoyed by businesses, so the number of displayed images might be reduced. Payment arrangements need to be incorporated into B2C systems whereas B2B systems typically capture payment information in systems separate from the electronic commerce system. All of these differences combine to require that B2C sites have quick download times, more instructions for site navigation, shopping cart styles (that can be loaded and unloaded before actual purchase), and methods for keeping a profile of the user (address, credit card numbers, and such). Sites such as WWW.1800FLOWERS.COM and WWW.HOMEDEPOT.COM have been recognized by many Web site reviewers as well designed for B2C transactions.

Electronic commerce with external operations involve the firm's interfaces with all eight environmental elements (Table 3.1). Certain business areas may have primary responsibility for certain elements. For example, finance deals mainly with the financial community, stock-

Table 3.1

Environmental Interfaces of the Business Areas

	FINANCE	HUMAN RESOURCES	INFORMATION SERVICES	MANUFACTURING	MARKETING
FINANCIAL COMMUNITY	X				
STOCKHOLDERS AND OWNERS	X				
CUSTOMERS	X		X		X
GLOBAL COMMUNITY		X			
LABOR UNIONS		X		X	
SUPPLIERS			X	X	
COMPETITORS					X
GOVERNMENT	X	X	X	X	X

holders and owners, and the firm's customers. Human resources has a special interest in the global community and labor unions, and information services interfaces with customers, hardware, and software suppliers. Manufacturing deals with the firm's suppliers and labor unions. Marketing is primarily responsible for interfacing with the firm's customers and competitors. All of the areas interface with the government in one manner or another.

Government is increasingly participating in electronic commerce (sometimes referred to as "e-gov"). Residents of North Carolina can link to the "Click@DMV" site from the Department of Motor Vehicles Web page (WWW.DMV.DOT.STATE.NC.US) to renew their license plates. New York City (WWW.NYC.GOV) allows citizens to pay parking fines and other charges. As you think about electronic commerce, do not constrain yourself to the limited ideas of the past. A broad view is required to take advantage of the new possibilities.

Information services play a pivotal and changing role in the firm's relation to the environment. In the past, customers were not the main concern for information services but they are increasingly more important and will become a primary focus for the majority of firms in the future. All transaction interfaces from customer to supplier to government and others are being impacted by the widespread acceptance of electronic commerce.

Anticipated Benefits from Electronic Commerce

Firms engage in electronic commerce in order to achieve improvements throughout the organization. These improvements are expected to result in three main benefits:

- Improved customer service before, during, and after the sale
- Improved relationships with suppliers and the financial community
- Increased economic return on stockholder and owner investments

These benefits contribute to the firm's financial stability and enable it to better compete in a business world that is employing more and more computer technology. Note that increased profits was not listed as an anticipated benefit because profit is the result of meeting the company's goals. Profit manifests itself in the return on stockholder and owner investment.

Electronic Commerce Constraints

Just a few years ago many firms were hesitant to jump on the electronic commerce bandwagon. In a 1996 survey, 60 percent of the responding firms indicated that they had not implemented electronic commerce and had no plans to do so within the next three years.[1] Firms that had implemented systems were using them primarily for transactions with suppliers (91 percent) and customers (88 percent), and the main processes dealt with purchase orders, transfers of payment, and invoices. When asked the reasons for their caution, the firms listed three constraints in the following order:

- High costs
- Security concerns
- Immature or unavailable software

Each of these constraints is being challenged as information technology and systems become increasingly popular. The cost of computing resources inevitably comes down. As we described in Chapter 1, Moore's Law predicts the doubling of computer power every 18 months. As power doubles every 18 months, the costs of electronic commerce become lower and lower.

Security is an issue for business-to-consumer and business-to-business transactions. Firms commonly use secure telecommunications networks that are constantly monitored for unauthorized access. These networks have proven to be very secure for large firms. Consumers generally do not have access to such secure communications but companies like VeriSign (WWW.VERISIGN.COM) have added security measures that bring a high level of trust to Internet transactions. With present encryption and secure Internet Web sites there is little reason to fear an unauthorized access of a consumer's message. Consumers are much more likely to throw out sensitive information in garbage, such as credit card numbers, than to have their information compromised on the Internet.

Software for electronic commerce is moving into a new era. Instead of specialized software, firms are designing electronic commerce interfaces that take advantage of current Web browser software. The basic idea is to make a common interface suitable for both customers and electronic partners.

The constraints on electronic commerce are being disassembled because of the growing economic importance of electronic commerce. There were $10.2 billion of retail sales (i.e., B2C sales) during the second quarter of 2002.[2] Total B2C sales for 2002 topped $30 billion. As time passes, business are seeing the constraints on electronic commerce melt away in the light of its economic benefits.

Scope of Electronic Commerce

As you read this section you must understand that electronic commerce is dynamic and the scope of its influence can change in just a few months. You should visit WWW.CENSUS.GOV/EOS/ WWW/EBUSINESS614.HTM to find the most current figures.

Electronic commerce accounted for more than $1 trillion of economic activity in the United States during 2000. It is estimated that electronic commerce grows between 5 percent and 15 percent each year. That growth rate may have to slow at some point but it is likely to continue for the next several years. The amount of economic impact varies from industry to industry but about 94 percent of electronic commerce is B2B, leaving 6 percent for B2C.

Over 18 percent of sales from U.S. manufacturing plants ($777 billion) in 2000 were the result of electronic commerce. Almost 8 percent of sales from wholesalers ($213 billion) were e-commerce. The percentage of electronic commerce conducted in the retail sales sector has barely topped 1 percent. It is only because of the high dollar amount of retail sales, compared to other segments of industry, that B2C accounted for 6 percent of total U.S. electronic commerce activity in 2000.

E-commerce is particularly important to certain segments of the U.S. economy simply because it has a large percentage of sales dollars in that segment. Table 3.2 shows some examples that highlight the impact of electronic commerce in certain areas. Electronic commerce has matured to the point where it has become vital to the economy and its importance continues to grow.

Table 3.2

Percentage of Electronic Commerce Sales versus Total Sales in Selected Industry Segments for 2000

INDUSTRY SEGMENT	E-COMMERCE % OF TOTAL SALES
Apparel manufacturing	20%
Transportation equipment manufacturing	46%
Motor vehicle wholesaling	20%
Drug wholesaling	40%
Travel and reservation retail	24%

CHAPTER 3   USING INFORMATION TECHNOLOGY TO ENGAGE IN ELECTRONIC COMMERCE   •••   53

The Path to Electronic Commerce

When a firm decides that the anticipated benefits outweigh the constraints and decides to implement electronic commerce, it understands that the implementation will be a mammoth task. The strategic business plan embodies the commitment to use electronic commerce to achieve competitive advantage. The firm first gathers business intelligence so that it can understand the potential role that each of the environmental elements will play.

BUSINESS INTELLIGENCE

Engaging in electronic commerce is not a decision that should be made without first gaining knowledge about your firm and its relationships with customers, competitors, suppliers, and other external entities. There is a saying that "if you want to make chicken soup, the first thing you need is a chicken." The same logic can be applied to our subject by saying, "If you want to engage in electronic commerce with elements in the environment, the first thing you need is an understanding of the elements." This truism provides the case for business intelligence. **Business intelligence (BI)** is the activity of gathering information about the elements in the environment which interact with your firm.

External Databases

Companies do not have to gather environmental information themselves. There are a number of important commercial databases that provide information on virtually any subject. LEXIS-NEXIS (WWW.LEXIS-NEXIS.COM) provides legal, financial, and governmental information from a wide variety of sources. For a fee, the firm will provide analyses of information requested. DIALOG (WWW.DIALOG.COM) covers news, business, government, and other sources. DOWJONES.COM (at WWW.DOWJONES.COM) offers a wide variety of information concerning financial matters. Global eXchange Services (WWW.GXS.COM) sells services aimed at integrating electronic transactions for global supply chains. These are only a few of the companies that provide data and data services to firms.

Firms use these databases to gather business intelligence because it is faster and less expensive than trying to research a wide array of information sources. Reuters (WWW.REUTERS.COM) can search and analyze news media for subjects of concern to a firm much more effectively and efficiently than most firms can do for themselves. The value that these commercial databases bring to the firm is their wide knowledge of information sources.

Thomas Register Online (WWW.THOMASREGISTER.COM) is an example of a database that provides a great deal of information for free and also offers services for a fee. Thomas Register provides an index of over 170,000 U.S. and Canadian manufacturers and can be used to obtain information on products and their suppliers. All records provide the name, address, telephone number, and industry code for companies, as well as brand names, trademarks, and descriptions of the company's products. Also, many records provide such information as the number of employees and executive names and titles.

Government databases are another important source of information. The Library of Congress (WWW.LOC.GOV) offers a wide range of topics for researchers in many fields. The Census Bureau (WWW.CENSUS.GOV) contains a treasure chest of information concerning the demographics of people in the United States. Information is provided in a number of formats and can be as general as an industry or as specific as a county. Firms can tap into the Securities and Exchange Commission records (WWW.SEC.GOV) to view various required financial filings via the EDGAR databases. EDGAR is the Electronic Data Gathering, Analysis, and Retrieval system. The federal government and many state governments are under a mandate to make public information available via the Internet.

Firms are becoming more inclined to initiate their own external searches for market intelligence. External searches have been helped by the fact that more and more firms are

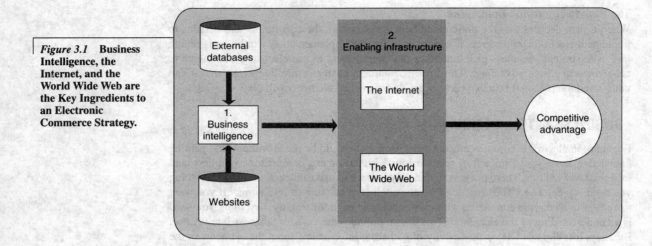

Figure 3.1 Business Intelligence, the Internet, and the World Wide Web are the Key Ingredients to an Electronic Commerce Strategy.

placing more information about themselves on the Web. Search engines are the most popular means for people to obtain information available from the Web. Figure 3.1 illustrates the use of external databases and Web searches for business intelligence.

Search Engines

A **search engine** is a special computer program that asks a user for a word or group of words to be found. The program then searches the content of Web sites on the Internet to see if the word or words exists at any Web sites. For example, you might use a search engine to find motel room availabilities (Figure 3.2). For our purposes, the specialized programs that index the sites and create directories of site categories will be considered subparts of the search engine. Customers interested in B2C electronic commerce frequently begin their transaction by using search engines to locate possible vendors. Search engines estimate the usefulness of the sites that contain the words and present the requestor with the addresses of Web sites and documents that contain the chosen words. Many users have come to view the Web site that contains the search engine computer program and organizes the results as search engines themselves. Although this is not technically true, the search engine program and the Web site that uses the engine are generally treated as the same thing.

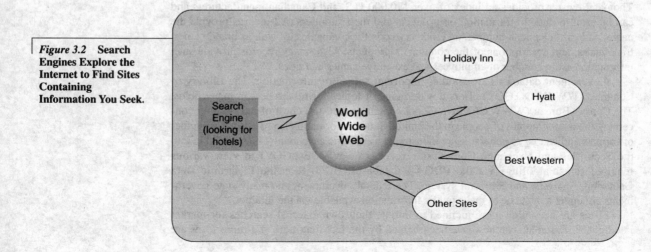

Figure 3.2 Search Engines Explore the Internet to Find Sites Containing Information You Seek.

Yahoo (WWW.YAHOO.COM), Excite (WWW.EXCITE.COM), AltaVista (WWW.ALTAVISTA.COM), HotBot (WWW.HOTBOT.COM), Google (WWW.GOOGLE.COM), and AskJeeves (WWW.ASKJEEVES.COM) are just a few of the popular search engine sites and portals available to users to search Web-accessible information. The sites are organized in a manner that makes them easy to use. Searches can be simple or use advanced features to look for complex combinations of key words. There is no charge for the use of these search engines.

The first step toward achieving electronic commerce is to gain a thorough understanding of the environment in which the commerce will be conducted. Much of this intelligence can be gathered by non-computer means—such as through surveys, observations, informal conversations, field reports, newspaper and trade paper articles, and so on. However, computer databases make it possible to scan large volumes of information quickly, easily, and thoroughly.

ELECTRONIC COMMERCE STRATEGY AND INTERORGANIZATIONAL SYSTEMS

For any problem, there are several possible solutions, and this situation applies to the problem of determining the best electronic commerce strategy. However, the strategy that is most often mentioned is one in which the elements are linked with transmissions of electronic data. The name given to this strategy is the interorganizational system (IOS). A term frequently used with IOS is EDI, which stands for electronic data interchange. The two terms are often used interchangeably, but when a distinction is drawn, EDI is considered a subset of IOS.[3] Electronic data interchange is one means for achieving an interorganizational system. Extranets, similar to Internet use but limited to selected and trusted business partners, are beginning to take the place of EDI in some organizations.

THE INTERORGANIZATIONAL SYSTEM (IOS)

We have recognized how the firm can establish electronic linkages with other firms to create an **interorganizational system (IOS)** so that all of the firms work together as a coordinated unit, achieving benefits that each could not achieve alone. The participating firms are called **trading partners** or **business partners** or a **business alliance**. In Chapter 1, we recognized that the MIS database contains data from both the transaction processing system and the firm's environment. Some of the environmental data comes from the IOS trading partners. Then, when discussing Porter's value chain in Chapter 2, we noted that when the trading partners work together as a single coordinated unit, they create a value system.

Interorganizational systems are fundamental to electronic commerce. The rapid and secure exchange of vast amounts of data is critical to support the transactions of the organizations that use information technology to compete. Without the communication networks and computer processing capabilities, organizations would be virtual islands of production with little ability to account for the services and products that create their vitality. Interorganizational systems are the highways of electronic commerce and electronic data interchange is the favorite method of traveling that highway.

IOS Benefits
The trading partners enter into an IOS venture with the expectation of realizing certain benefits—comparative efficiency and bargaining power.[4]

COMPARATIVE EFFICIENCY By joining an IOS, the trading partners can produce their goods and services with greater efficiency and, in turn, provide their goods and services at lower costs to their customers. This gives the partners in an IOS a price advantage over their competitors.

- **Internal efficiency** consists of improvements in the firm's own operations, thus enabling the firm to gather data faster, analyze it faster, and make decisions faster.

- **Interorganizational efficiency** includes improvements that are gained by working with other firms. These improvements enable the firms to offer more products and services, serve more customers, shift certain work to suppliers or customers, and gather environmental data more easily.

BARGAINING POWER   The ability of a firm to resolve disagreements with its suppliers and customers to its own advantage is called its bargaining power. The power is derived from three basic areas—by offering unique product features, by reducing search-related costs, and by increasing the switching costs.

- **Unique product features.** The electronic linkages of the IOS enable firms to offer better service to their customers in the form of easier ordering, quicker shipment, and faster response times to requests for information. This better service becomes a feature of the firm's products, making them more appealing than similar products offered by competitors.
- **Reduced search-related costs.** By belonging to an IOS, a firm can reduce the "shopping" costs that its *customers* incur in searching for a supplier, identifying alternative products, and getting the lowest price. Since the firm is a customer of its suppliers, the firm can realize the same shopping cost reductions when ordering from its *suppliers*.
- **Increased switching costs.** A firm would like to make it expensive, in cost and/or convenience, for customers to switch to a competitor. IOS achieves this benefit by providing customers with such information resources as hardware, software, and data communications channels that would have to be replaced if products were purchased from another firm.

Vendor stock replenishment. is a special type of IOS in that the customer trusts the supplier enough to allow the supplier to access its computer-based inventory system. The *supplier* can initiate the replenishment process by electronically monitoring the firm's inventory levels. This will require the firm to grant database access to the supplier. For more protection the firm may make a copy of less sensitive parts of the database and give the supplier access to only that copy instead of the firm's entire database system.

Whether the IOS firm is considering a role of sponsor or participant, each of these benefits is carefully weighed against the anticipated costs. The IOS has a strong theoretical base—the eight environmental elements connected by resource flows. For that reason, it is no surprise that the IOS has emerged as a dominant strategy for achieving competitive advantage. It is also no surprise that the data linkage is achieved electronically.

Electronic Data Interchange (EDI)

Electronic data interchange (EDI) consists of direct computer-to-computer transmissions among multiple firms of data in a machine-readable, structured format. The transmissions enable the data to be transmitted and received without rekeying.[5] There are two major standards for EDI: the American National Standards Institute standard ASC X12 is used in North America and the EDIFACT international standards are used in Europe. The communications lines, communications hardware, and support services for EDI are generally provided by telephone companies (AT&T, MCI, and others).

When the services that operate and manage the communications line (sometimes called the circuit) are provided in addition to the line itself, this is referred to as a **value-added network (VAN)**. Some argue that a VAN is simply an EDI that has been outsourced to a vendor. That view is simplistic. The vendor that provides a VAN provides expertise concerning what communications line is required, how it should be supported, opportunities and threats from the line, and a host of other valuable insights.

EDI is the dominant implementation of an interorganizational information system. More than two-thirds of electronic commerce is conducted using EDI compared to other IOS alternatives.[6] Although more costly and cumbersome than newer IOS communication systems, electronic data interchange is still the leading method.

Extranet

Extranets are another means of establishing an IOS. They allow the sharing of sensitive computer-based information with other firms using information technology commonly associated with the Internet. Firms use them in collaboration with trusted suppliers and large customers. Security and privacy are serious concerns so the extranets are generally secured behind a firewall. A firewall allows only authorized users access to the firm's information. Extranets allow for the same type of data exchange as EDI but incorporate the common protocols and communication networks of the Internet so that firms do not have to use the more costly software and communications hardware associated with EDI.

The cost of equipment to establish EDI may be thousands of dollars at each site and the secure communications lines can be hundreds of dollars each month. However, extranets use the Internet for communications and standard Web browsers for navigating to sites and exchanging data. Encryption methods that keep messages secret are easy to use. One methodology, Pretty Good Privacy®, typically known as PGP, (WWW.PGP.COM), is extremely safe, easy to use, and costs very little.

Electronic Funds Transfer (EFT)

We sometimes fail to recognize the flows of electronic data as only one piece of the puzzle. Neither the shipment of the ordered merchandise nor the firm's payment is included. The merchandise shipment cannot be accomplished electronically unless it is a digitized product such as software or a video; however, an electronic payment can be made even if the product cannot be sent electronically. When data representing money is transmitted over a computer network, it is called **EFT**, for **electronic funds transfer**. EFT is used by many firms and also by individuals who have their payroll checks deposited into their bank accounts and who pay their bills with electronic payments.

Although we do not emphasize EFT as much as EDI, EFT plays a major role in electronic commerce. The greatest advantages of EFT are that monies associated with the transfer of assets are transferred with greater speed and security compared to sending cash or checks between parties. Since the large percentage of e-commerce is B2B, electronic funds transfer is particularly important.

Proactive and Reactive Business Partners

When a firm decides to adopt IOS, it can do so in a proactive or reactive way. The IOS sponsor typically takes a *proactive* approach, stimulating interest in the IOS and encouraging participation in the network. The participants, on the other hand, typically respond in a *reactive* manner—accepting or rejecting the sponsor's offer to adopt IOS.

In Table 3.2 you read that 46 percent of transportation equipment manufacturing sales were accomplished via electronic commerce. This is a reflection of the large automobile manufacturers adopting EDI systems for acquiring supplies from vendors. The proactive approach was taken by the manufacturers and then suppliers were forced to react by either adopting the EDI system or losing the customer.

Adoption Influences

In a 1995 *Decision Sciences* article, MIS professors G. Premkumar and K. Ramamurthy studied the factors that can influence the decision to adopt an interorganizational system and identified four factors that determine whether the firm will be proactive or reactive.[7] Figure 3.3 illustrates the influences. Two are internal and two are environmental.

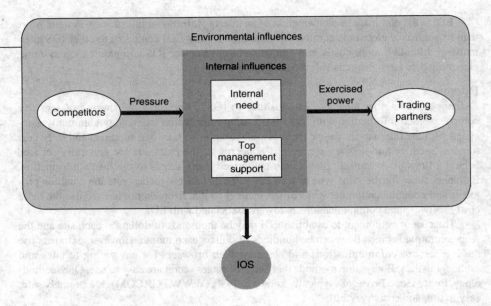

Figure 3.3 Internal and Environmental Influences on IOS Adoption

- **Competitive pressure.** When the firm is in a poor position in relation to its competitors or when industry or trade associations provide strong pressure, the firm will adopt an interorganizational system such as EDI in a *reactive* way. Later researchers[8] have suggested competitive pressure as the most frequent reason for adopting EDI.
- **Exercised power.** When a firm can exert power over other members of the IOS, it will be *proactive* in adopting IOS. Some firms are so powerful that they can demand that their trading partners either use IOS or take their business elsewhere.
- **Internal need.** When the firm sees that participation in the IOS is a way to improve its own operations, it will approach IOS in a *proactive* manner.
- **Top management support.** Regardless of whether the firm acts in a *proactive* or *reactive* manner, top management support always influences the decision. When significant benefits from IOS are intangible, top management support is critical.

Indirect IOS Benefits

Some of the benefits of interorganizational systems such as EDI and extranets are derived directly from the technology. These are the **direct benefits** of reduced date entry errors, reduced costs, and increased operational efficiency. **Indirect benefits** include the increased ability to compete, improved relationships with trading partners, and improved customer service.[9] Figure 3.4 shows this relationship between direct and indirect benefits.

- **Reduced errors.** By not having to key incoming data into the system, data entry errors can be greatly reduced. A study by EDI Group Ltd. found that the error rate can decline from 10.1 percent of the data entered without EDI to 4.4 percent with EDI.[10]
- **Reduced costs.** Cost reductions can be realized by eliminating redundant steps, eliminating paper documents, and reducing the manual labor of routing paper documents through the organization.[11] Cost reductions for all types of documents can range from $1.30 to $5.50 per document, and they can be even higher for purchase orders. The cost of preparing a purchase order in a conventional way can range from $75 to $350. With an IOS, the cost can be reduced to as low as $5. These cost savings outweigh the hardware, software, and personnel costs of EDI. The costs of extranets are very small compared to EDI and, therefore, their transaction cost reductions are even greater.

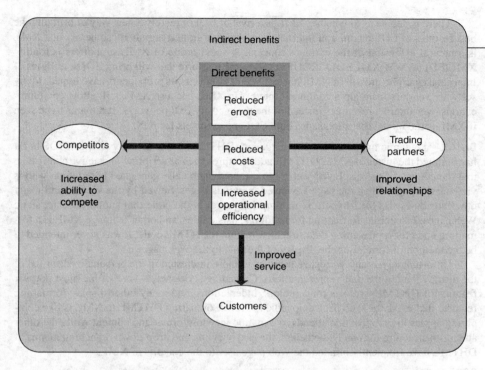

Figure 3.4 IOS Direct and Indirect Benefits

- **Increased operational efficiency.** The IOS benefits of internal and interorganizational efficiency are made possible to a large extent by EDI and extranets. By replacing paper documents in each of the flows with electronics, many opportunities for improved efficiency are possible.
- **Increased ability to compete.** The combination of reduced costs and unique product features made possible by the IOS make it exceedingly difficult for competitors to match the firm's product in terms of cost and service offerings.
- **Improved relationships with trading partners.** By entering into a formal system with trading partners, good relations come about naturally—as a byproduct of the business activity. All participants realize that they are working toward the same ends and gain mutual advantage.
- **Improved customer service.** The speed of electronic communications enables the firm to respond quickly to customer orders and requests for service. When combined with the reduced error rate and the ease with which the customer can shop for products, the result is improved customer service.

The direct benefits, often measurable in dollars, can provide a solid economic justification for using EDI. The indirect benefits, however, can well be viewed by top management as the most important reasons for approving an EDI strategy.

A Challenge to EDI

Although EDI and extranets are the most common approaches to interorganizational systems for business-to-business data transfer in the global business community, they are being challenged by extensible markup language, DHTML, and CORBA.

EXTENSIBLE MARKUP LANGUAGE (XML) XML is an extension of the hypertext markup language that is used to code Web pages. The feature of great interest is that XML can provide file formatting structure and a means for describing data within the file of the Web page. Now, even XML is being challenged by more current Web language extensions.

There is debate as to whether XML is a rival of EDI or merely a new way of bringing the best features of EDI to common Internet users. Using a similar argument, some say that XML is a natural extension of the extranet concept. A vocal group of XML supporters is touting XML/EDI (WWW.XMLEDI-GROUP.ORG) as the platform that will bring EDI to millions of Internet users. The growth of XML has not been as quick as its proponents have hoped. Many software vendors maintain a continued interest in XML because XML will allow communications over Internet resources instead of the more costly EDI networks. It remains to be seen if XML is the model that supersedes both EDI and extranets for IOS.

DHTML Dynamic hypertext markup language (DHTML) is not actually a type of IOS but it has dimmed the luster of XML. DHTML adds features such as scripting and active controls so that the content of the displayed Web page can be dynamically generated based upon who is viewing the page, when the page is viewed, previous pages viewed by the viewer, and many other attributes. HTML (hypertext markup language) is the code that supports basic, static Web pages. It specifies formatting for headings, lists, tables, and other features. XML is a formatting code for representing data structures within the HTML code. It was never intended to be the method of formatting the display of the data to the Web page.

Unfortunately, many Web page users were more interested in the personalized format of the display than in the data representations. Cascading style sheets—one of the most popular features of DHTML—allows fonts, colors, indentations, and many other display formatting features that make the Web page enjoyable to view. Comparing DHTML to XML is like comparing apples to oranges: one attends to dynamic viewing format and content while the other attends to structure format. Nonetheless, the easy viewing and drop-down branching menus of DHTML have frequently blinded the Web page user to the benefits of XML.

CORBA About the same time that DHTML grew in popularity, designers of Web pages wished for an object-oriented methodology for accessing database records. Objects are helpful because they represent logical chunks of information and methods of manipulating the information. The **Common Object Request Broker Architecture (CORBA)** grew as a standard as the software industry embraced object-oriented programming and databases. The objects are important since they can communicate among each other regardless of the programming language or operating system used.

Information pertinent to a Web page is frequently held in a database. For e-commerce applications, it is almost always held in a database. The CORBA standards specify an infrastructure that is independent of computer used, software used, operating system used, and browser used. Interoperability to access database information is the characteristic that makes this standard so appealing. CORBA combined with the ability of DHTML to display results from within powerful database management systems using a visually appealing display.

XML is still an important method for exchanging data between B2B partners. But DHTML and CORBA dominate B2C. The eventual winner for B2B data exchange is hard to predict, but DHTML and CORBA have the advantage of access and display from robust databases.

BUSINESS-TO-CUSTOMER STRATEGIES FOR ELECTRONIC COMMERCE

Business-to-business electronic commerce dwarfs the dollar value of business-to-consumer electronic commerce. Currently, only about 6 percent of electronic commerce dollars are generated by B2C. So, why is it important to understand business strategies for B2C electronic commerce?

The two reasons are that more products and services are becoming available for digital delivery and more consumers are overcoming their reluctance to purchase using the Web. Higher communications speeds for computers in homes has made delivery of digital products practical. Fear of information theft, such as credit card information, has been replaced with acceptance. B2C electronic commerce will grow significantly during the next ten years.

Digital Products
Certain products and services can be delivered to the consumer over the Internet. Entertainment has been one of the earliest products to take advantage of the Internet. Songs, albums, movies, and similar products can be bought from Web sites such as Sony (WWW.SONY.COM). Computer programs and their updates, such as virus protection software, are frequently sold using the Web so that customers get the very latest versions. Services can also be delivered via the Internet. Lending Tree (WWW.LENDINGTREE.COM) allows users to get mortgages and refinance their homes via the Internet.

One key difference between digital products and physical products purchased over the Web is that digital products can be consumed as soon as they are downloaded. Another difference is that the product itself is transferred to the purchaser's asset. For example, the music you download has to be placed into a file or onto a compact disk or to some other storage medium. The consumer pays for that medium, not the seller. You would not expect to take a blank CD into a music store when you purchase an album but you do need a blank CD if you want to play the music you purchase over the Internet on your car stereo. Purchasers of digital products incur a substantial cost of the transaction in terms of computer cost, online connection fees, storage media, and other items.

Physical Products
Physical goods cannot be consumed via the Web; instead they must be transported to the consumer. So-called "catalog" companies have faced this problem for years. Sales orders can be taken over the Web but shipment has to be arranged. The postal service provides several classes of delivery depending upon the size and weight of the item being mailed. Parcel post was frequently the least expensive mode provided by the postal service but it took the longest time for delivery.

The growth of private mail/shipping companies such as Federal Express and UPS has indirectly aided retail electronic commerce. These companies, and others, provide a number of alternative shipment methods for different prices. Urgent shipments can be delivered to the consumer within 24 hours from virtually any point in the world. Slower than standard methods can be offered that let the consumer reduce standard shipping costs. Firms engaging in electronic commerce can simply use a private mail/shipping company instead of providing the service themselves.

Most of the popular mail/shipping companies offer a service that complements a firm's B2C activity. A shipping number is assigned to each package generated by the sale. Customers can use the shipper's Web site to track the progress of the package from the firm until its delivery to the customer. If the firm were to use a vague "three to ten working days" shipment time required between purchase and delivery it could be a barrier to B2C sales. With access to the shipper's Web site the consumer has more information and control for the delivery, so online tracking can make B2C sales attractive.

Virtual versus Hybrid Sales
Virtual sales are those made by a firm that does not operate a physical storefront. There is no store in which a customer can enter and purchase the product. **Hybrid sales** occur when firms have both a physical storefront and a Web site where customers can purchase products. Both of these retail sales strategies need to inform the customer of what is available, the costs and features of products, arrange customer payments, and achieve product delivery.

A difficulty faced by firms offering virtual sales is providing necessary product information without overwhelming the customer. Browsing in a physical store can take place relatively quickly. Your eyes can view many products at a single glance. Fitting that visual experience on a computer screen is impossible; there simply is not enough room.

Figure 3.5 Home Page for Office Depot

Source: www.officedepot.com (Courtesy of Office Depot, Inc.

Another impediment is that images are large files and communicating them from the Web site to the customer's computer takes time. The problem can be lessened by restricting the number of images displayed until the customer has focused his or her search to a relatively few choices. The Web site of Office Depot (WWW.OFFICEDEPOT.COM) is a good example of this strategy. (See Figure 3.5) Its opening Web page has few images but provides a number of links to pages that search for different classes of products. If the customer wishes to purchase paper for a laser printer, it may take five successive mouse clicks to view the product but each link loads very quickly. The customer can go directly to the product, assuming the customer knows what he or she wants, by simply typing the request into a search box and letting the site search for the product. The fewer mouse clicks required to get to the product the better, but it is far more important to be fast than to reduce mouse clicks.

Product comparison in a physical store is aided by a salesperson. A Web site can provide the same information and, if well designed, much more. Once the customer has navigated to the desired product, the Web site can provide links to similar products, reviews of the product by experts and other customers, images and physical descriptions of the product, and other information. Some customers appreciate a "human touch" in the sales process but Web sites can provide far more pertinent information than most salespersons.

Payment over the Internet has suffered from bad press. There is a risk of having credit card information stolen if it is used to make a purchase over the Internet. The risk is very small, much smaller than other credit card uses. When you use your credit card to pay your restaurant bill, did the waiter copy the card number for his personal use later? You throw out old credit card statements and carbon copies in the trash; did the janitor who emptied the trash keep your credit information? You phone a florist for flowers and tell her your credit card number to pay; how do you know she will not charge more flowers to that card? These scenarios have proven to be much more conducive to credit card fraud than using the Internet. Coupled with the efforts of credit card companies and firms such as VeriSign (WWW.VERISIGN.COM) which certify secure data transfer, credit card payments over the Internet to reputable firms are probably one of the most secure means of payment.

Virtual Sales are used most frequently when the firm either cannot construct a physical storefront or finds a physical storefront to be economically unjustified. For example,

1-800-flowers (WWW.1800FLOWERS.COM) has no stores since its business model is to provide flowers across the United States and a few other countries. It would be costly to build florist shops everywhere it wishes to do business, especially when florist shops already exist in those places. Instead 1-800-flowers acts as a broker to gather and solicit orders which are in turn given to local florists to prepare and deliver.

A fee is paid to 1-800-flowers for each order. The local florist benefits since 1-800-flowers can be used by a customer (perhaps from Atlanta) who might otherwise not buy flowers because he or she would not know a florist in another town (perhaps Chicago) where the flowers are to be delivered. 1-800-flowers further increases sales by sending e-mail reminders to past customers about birthdays and other occasions when they have sent flowers. When a firm wants to avoid the cost of a store front, virtual sales are a sound way to service customers.

Hybrid Sales are sometimes known as "brick and click" operations. Most firms have a storefront because it is necessary to their business plans. Office Depot had storefronts before sales over the Internet were possible. Also, the stores act as showcases for products ranging from desks and chairs to pencils and paper. Some products, like chairs, are more likely to be sold when customers can physically interact with the product.

At the same time, Home Depot wants to offer its customers the convenience of shopping over the Web. Products such as printer paper do not require physical contact before the purchase. The customer time saved by not having to drive to the store is an added convenience for the customer. Into this situation is an added benefit to customer online shopping, free delivery when the purchase is more than a certain dollar amount. Although free delivery seems like a one-sided inducement to the customer, it actually helps Office Depot.

The B2C sales Office Depot makes lead to less inventory kept at its stores. Less inventory means less floor space at the store devoted to inventory which results in more floor space for sales. Office Depot can build smaller stores (which reduces its cost of operations) when new stores are needed. At existing stores, more floor space can be devoted to actively selling products, which in turn yields higher sales at the stores. Web sales are used to complement the traditional store sales.

EVOLUTION OF THE INTERNET

We need to understand the evolution of the Internet because of the key role it has played in providing opportunities for electronic commerce. Electronic commerce cannot occur if the participants and their computers are isolated. The Internet connects them.

Understanding the Internet's evolution will help us to forecast future opportunities. The origin of the Internet can be traced to 1969, when the U.S. government established a network called ARPANET. Efforts beginning in 1989 led to what is known today as the World Wide Web.[12]

ARPANET

The purpose of ARPANET, a product of the Advanced Research Projects Agency, was to make it possible for military personnel and civilian researchers to exchange information relating to military matters. It was the first network to demonstrate the feasibility of computer-to-computer transmission of data in the form of packets.

ARPANET still exists. In fact, along with two other networks–CSNET (Computer Science Network) and NSFNET (National Science Foundation Network)–it forms a major portion of what is today known as the Internet. **Internet** is the name given to the world's largest collection of computer networks, each of which is composed of a collection of smaller networks. Figure 3.6 illustrates this networks-of-networks concept.

When a person requests data from the Internet, the request travels from computer to computer through the network until it reaches the location where the data is stored. Likewise, the response follows a computer-to-computer path back to the person who made the request. The path taken by data in each direction may be different.

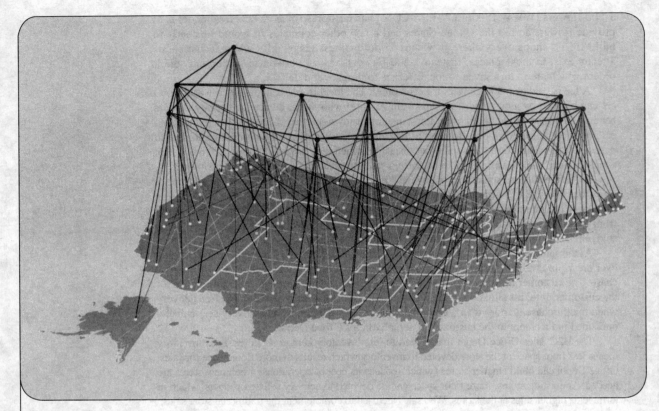

Figure 3.6 **The Internet Is a Network of Networks**

Source: Based on Parsons and Oja, "New Perspectives on Computer Technology," Course Technology, 1994, p. NP212.

During the 1970s, work on ARPANET consisted of connecting the various networks and developing the necessary internetwork software. During the early 1980s, the network became known as the Internet, and it was during this period that business firms began using it from workstations and local area networks. Although we frequently speak of the Internet and the World Wide Web as if they are the same thing, they are not.

The Internet is the communications network, similar to a system of roads for the interstate, state highways, and down to the streets in your community. The World Wide Web is the set of standards, procedures, and data formats that allow users to navigate the resources located on the Internet. Together, the Internet and World Wide Web provide the opportunity to find information all over the world.

The World Wide Web

In 1989, Tim Berners-Lee, a computer scientist working at CERN, the European Particle Physics Laboratory, came up with a better way for physicists to communicate. The idea was to use **hypertext**—documents in an electronic form that are linked together. As conceived by Berners-Lee, the physicists would be able to click on words or phrases displayed on their computer screens and retrieve the hypertext. The idea became a reality in mid-1992 in the form of the World Wide Web. Rather than handling only textual material, it is also possible to store and retrieve **hypermedia**—multimedia consisting of text, graphics, audio, and video. The **World Wide Web**, also called the **Web**, and **WWW**, is information accessible via the Internet where hypermedia documents (computer files) are stored and can be retrieved by means of a unique addressing scheme.

The Internet provides the network architecture and the Web provides the method for storing and retrieving its documents. As we've said before, the terms "Internet" and "World Wide

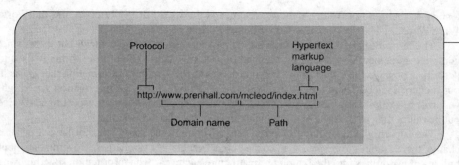

Figure 3.7 World Wide Web Terminology

Web" are frequently used as if they are the same. This is not really a problem but we should remember that the Internet itself is the global communications network that connects millions of computers. The World Wide Web is the collection of computers acting as content servers that host documents formatted to allow viewing of text, graphics, and audio as well as allowing linkages to other documents on the Web. These servers and the users that access them are connected by the Internet. Figure 3.7 defines some common WWW terms.

1. **Website.** A computer linked to the Internet that containing hypermedia that can be accessed from any other computer in the network by means of hypertext links.
2. **Hypertext Link.** A pointer consisting of text or a graphic that is used to access hypertext stored at any Website.
3. **Web Page.** A hypermedia file stored at a unique Website address.
4. **Home Page.** The first page of a Website. Other pages at the site can be reached from the home page.
5. **Browser.** Software that is designed to find and read files on the Internet that are written in hypertext markup language (HTML).
6. **URL (Universal Resource Locator).** This refers to the address of a Web page.
7. **Protocol.** A set of standards that govern the communication of data. HTTP is the protocol for hypertext, and the letters stand for HyperText Transport Protocol. Another common protocol on the Web is FTP for file transfer protocol. The protocol name is followed by a colon (:) and two slashes (//).
8. **Domain name.** The address of the Website where the Web page is stored.
9. **Path.** A certain directory/subdirectory and file at the Website. HTML (or HTM) is the suffix for the program code that designates hypertext files.

Netscape Navigator was an early browser for viewing Web content that is still used. The most popular Internet browser is Microsoft's Internet Explorer. 96 percent of global users access the Web via Internet Explorer.[13]

FTP (FILE TRANSFER PROTOCOL) This refers to software that enables you to copy files onto your computer from any Web site. In order to do this, you must know the **universal resource locator (URL)** of the Web site. Many FTP sites offer transfer of data in one direction only. Firms have used Internet sites off their premises that are devoted to providing files to users such as product information, software updates, news releases, and other information. Sensitive data is not stored at the off-premises site and large volumes of Internet traffic do not hinder the firm's operations because the firm's computer resources are physically separated from the off-premises site.

CYBERSPACE AND THE INFORMATION SUPERHIGHWAY

Two other terms are also associated with the Internet and the Web; cyberspace and the information superhighway. The term cyberspace was coined in 1984, when author William Gibson used it in his book *Neuromancer*[14] to describe a society that had become a slave to technology. Today, **cyberspace** means the world of the Internet and the World Wide Web.

The term **information superhighway** is also used in the same context, but there is not complete agreement concerning its eventual impact on society. The term is normally used to describe a positive force that gives everyone access to the wealth of information that exists in our modern society. There are dissenters, however, who fear that the information superhighway will be exploited by businesses as a way to push their wares on an unsuspecting and naive public rather than as a means of communicating worthwhile information.[15]

The superhighway analogy is very useful. Although the road does not have a per use charge, there are fees to be paid via taxes and other regulatory surcharges. Governments pour billions of tax dollars into the Internet infrastructure each year. The information superhighway user needs a computer in much the same way as a highway user needs a vehicle. There are costs to train the user just like there are costs to train new drivers. There are similar benefits and costs to superhighway users whether they travel in cars or via communications networks.

Internet Standards

A major reason why the Internet and the Web have been received with open arms by computer users around the world is because the two work together as a single system that can be used from any computer platform. A user at a Dell PC or a Sun workstation can retrieve the same Web page as can a user with an Apple PowerBook. To make this possible, everyone contributing to the Internet and Web architecture must follow the same rules.

Two organizations have assumed roles of leadership in establishing Internet and Web standards. The Internet Society was formed in 1992 to promote commercial Internet use and has delegated responsibility for Internet standards to the IETF (Internet Engineering Task Force). Web standards come from the World Wide Web Consortium (W3C).

BUSINESS APPLICATIONS OF THE INTERNET

Simply put, the Internet can be used for any business application that involves data communication, including both communication inside the firm and with the environment. Unlike proprietary networks, the Internet can be used with any computer platform without making a special effort. This is a big advantage. The Web protocol and browsers are also much easier to learn and use than the query languages that are normally used to retrieve information from

Highlights in MIS

GET YOUR RED HOT WEB DOMAIN HERE

Have you ever considered getting your own Web domain site? You can; it's easy and not very expensive. Many businesses can create a Web address for you and host your Web site. VeriSign operates a domain name site at www.netsol.com. You can enter the domain name you want to register and see if it is available or if someone else has already registered that name.

Once the fee is paid to register your domain name, you will get a choice of options about the site for your domain name. Do you want to host Web pages? Do you want an e-mail address to the domain name? What about selling products via the Website? All of these options are available for a monthly or annual fee.

Web domains are not just for large businesses; you can have your own personal Web domain. Go to www.netsol.com and see if your name is registered yet. If not, claim it and you can start your own e-commerce business right now!

databases. In addition, the Internet makes it possible to transmit a wider variety of media than many firms handle over their conventional networks.

The phenomenal growth of the number of Internet host sites has made the Internet a source of information that cannot be ignored. The Internet Software Consortium (WWW.ISC.ORG) has charted the rise in domain names from a handful in the early 1990s to over 160 million in July 2002. These new domains represent possible new customers, suppliers, and business partners.

All areas of the firm can use the Internet, but if one had to pick the area with the most untapped potential, it would be marketing. That is because so many of the Internet users are potential consumers of the firm's products and services. The Internet offers a new way to reach a market segment that can be measured in the millions. In addition, the Internet provides marketers with a way of staying current on competitors.

Marketing Research

The Golden Rule of Marketing could well be: "Know your customer." The reasoning is that if you do not know what the customer needs, you cannot meet those needs. A big segment of marketing is industrial marketing, in which one firm sells to another. In this setting, the Internet can help the industrial marketing firm know its customers and potential customers.

Two Web sites, PR Newswire (WWW.PRNEWSWIRE.COM) and MSNBC (WWW.MSNBC.COM), maintain Web pages that contain press releases and news stories providing rich information on company activities. Also, many firms have home pages that give information about their products and scope of operations.

By taking advantage of this new source of customer information, industrial marketers gain new inroads to their markets.

Retailing Applications

The Web business application with which the general public is most familiar is retailing. Most of the large retail chains have established a Web presence. JC Penney opened its Web site in 1994, allowing customers to place orders for about 350 items. Wal-Mart opened its Web site in mid-1996 and intended to target its products to a more upscale audience than the customers who normally shop its stores.

Many retailers make their home pages directly accessible through the Web. Some prefer to combine with other stores in a collection called a virtual mall in hopes that a single mall name will be easier to recognize and find than their individual store name. A virtual mall may take a traditional mall view—collections of different types of stores. CyberTown Mall (WWW.CYBERTOWN.COM/SHOPPING.HTML) and 24Hour-Mall (WWW.24HOUR-MALL.COM) are two such collections of stores.

Some retailing operations are changing in the face of Web information. Autobytel.com, Inc. (WWW.AUTOBYTEL.COM) provides customers with car selection, financing, insurance, and other services. Amazon.com (WWW.AMAZON.COM) has grown from being a seller of books to offering music, videos, electronics, and even toys and games. Many goods and services once thought to be beyond the realm of the Web are finding an electronic connection.

While all this activity is good, many retailers find that the Web does not provide sufficient market coverage to reach all their customers. CommerceNet and Nielsen Media Research released a study of North American buying via the Web based on an April 1999 survey. They found that of the 92 million North American Internet users, 55 million shop online. They defined shopping online as an actual online purchase or the research for a purchase (such as price comparisons). Twenty-eight million of the shoppers, about half, made an online purchase. While 28 million consumers is a significant number, there are over 300 million people in the United States and Canada. Electronic commerce is a needed, profitable avenue for sales but others are also needed.

SUGGESTIONS FOR SUCCESSFUL INTERNET USE

Although Web activity is relatively young, firms have identified keys that lead to successful use. The executives who make the strategic decisions in the firm should consider the following tips and assign responsibility for achieving these goals to the CIO and to information services.[16]

1. **Make sure your Website is robust.** When you commit to a Web project, be prepared to go beyond the Web pages and link your databases to the Web by means of your applications. This will enable you to integrate the Web into your computer-based information system rather than to simply use it as a way to provide and obtain information. Integration to the firm's database is important.
2. **Make sure your browser and database structure are both flexible and intuitive.** This will enable you to handle future growth and provide users with quick access.
3. **Emphasize content.** Don't get so caught up in artwork, audio, and video that you overlook the real objective of providing information. When it comes to a robust content, it is hard to beat a narrative and tabular display.
4. **Update often.** Entice business partners and browsers to keep coming back. A daily update is not too often for many firms.
5. **Look beyond customers.** Use the Internet to improve communications with all of the environmental elements—except competitors, of course.
6. **Target content to specific users' needs.** Encourage viewers to register on your site by providing names, addresses, and interests. With this understanding you can tailor your pages to their needs.
7. **Make the interface intuitive.** Do everything you can to make the Web site as fast and efficient as possible. Use graphics sparingly, since they slow down retrieval. Remember, design the interface from the perspective of the user, not the perspective of the firm.
8. **Be in the right Web location.** If your Website isn't generating as much traffic as you would like, consider linking it to such other sites as trade associations and industry and professional organizations.
9. **Create a sense of community.** Involve users in your site by providing an opportunity for them to input suggestions, complaints, and so on. Make use of such other interactive Web features as bulletin board systems and e-mail.
10. **Get help if you need it.** Web work is highly specialized. Rather than develop an internal expertise yourself, it might be better to outsource Web development and maintenance to professionals.

These suggestions make the point that taking full advantage of the Web is more than creating a home page. Considering the potential impact of the Web on a firm's business, simply putting as much planning into the Web effort as the firm usually puts into any development project might not be adequate. A good Web presence requires more than the usual amount of effort for a non-Web project.

FUTURE IMPACT OF THE INTERNET ON BUSINESS

The Internet is seen as the beginning of a **National Information Infrastructure**, or **NII** (NII.NIST.GOV).[17] Each country would have an NII, and each country would be linked in some manner that is yet to be defined.

Just how important is the NII? The U.S. House of Representatives Committee on Science adopted the Networking and Information Technology Research and Development Act (H.R. 2086) in September, 1999. It calls for almost $5 billion additional spending from 2000 through 2004 on infrastructure. That amount almost doubles the previously appropriated amount for federal information technology research over the five year period. The act addresses security and privacy issues as well as technical issues of digital communications. This substantial increase in the research for infrastructure will improve the capabilities and opportunities of e-commerce.

The NII will affect commerce in the different countries in varying ways. In such highly industrialized countries as Canada, Japan, Korea, Germany, and the United States, which make quick use of innovations in technology, the effect can be swift and dramatic.

For example, in the United States the information gathered by a firm in the normal conduct of business is typically owned by the firm. Many Web users see a notice at Websites that information gathered will not be passed on to other firms. But the U.S. firm owns the data and has the right to share it with other firms. In Europe the standard is more strict. European firms, and firms that do business in Europe, are not generally allowed to share customer information about Europeans with another firm unless they first have the written permission of the customer to allow data sharing. This difference in opinion about the privacy of customer data may have a serious impact on the ability of U.S. companies to do business in Europe.

Within a single country, the effect can vary from one industry to another. In some market segments adoption of e-commerce has been slow. But even in the U.S. retailing industry, the e-commerce strategy is not a question of "Should we do it?" or "When should we do it?" Retailers know those questions should be answered "Yes" and "Now."

Summary

When the concept of electronic commerce is defined broadly, it can include all eight environmental elements. However, firms typically implement electronic commerce with the intention of improving customer service, improving relationships with suppliers and the financial community, and increasing the return on stockholder and owner investments.

Business-to-business electronic commerce is a significant and growing force in business transactions. Some industry segments, such as transportation equipment manufacturing, have almost half of all sales accomplished via electronic commerce. Business-to-consumer electronic commerce sales comprise only about 1 percent of all retail sales. But B2C sales still represented over $30 billion of retail sales in 2002.

When the firm includes electronic commerce in its strategic business plan in order to achieve a competitive advantage, it pursues a path that begins with business intelligence. Commercial databases can provide a rich source of secondary data. Firms would be wise to take advantage of public and not-for-profit data sources. Determination of the best databases is influenced by both the business area of the firm and its environmental responsibilities.

An IOS consists of trading partners. Firms enter into an IOS to gain benefits of comparative efficiency, which exists in both an internal and an interorganizational form, and to increase their bargaining power, which is derived from unique product features, reduced search-related costs, and increased switching costs.

One way to achieve an IOS is through electronic data interchange. The most common data flows connect the firm to its suppliers. Money can also flow by means of electronic funds transfer. Firms are stimulated to adopt EDI by competitive pressure, exercised power, internal need, and top management support. Direct EDI benefits of reduced errors, reduced costs, and increased operational efficiency produce indirect benefits such as increased ability to compete, improved relationships with trading partners, and improved customer service. While EDI is the most frequent method of achieving IOS, the XML, DHTML, and CORBA methods are also important.

The data communications network that links the trading partners can be achieved with direct connectivity, one in which common carriers provide the circuits. Another option, and the one that is receiving the most attention today, is the Internet. The Internet is a global network of networks, and navigation is facilitated by the World Wide Web, the linkage of hypermedia documents. Although the Internet and Web offer great potential, there is opportunity for misuse.

Firms are using the Internet in many ways. One application is called the intranet, and it consists of transmissions within the firm. Intranets use the networks within the firm and browser software associated with the Web. Marketers can use the Internet to conduct research and gather competitive intelligence. Retailers can use the Internet to promote their products and, in some cases, deliver digital products to customers.

The ultimate in information networks would be a National Information Infrastructure (NII) that connects all countries. For highly industrialized countries, the NII might be just around the corner.

KEY TERMS

electronic commerce (e-commerce)
business-to-consumer electronic commerce (B2C)
business-to-business electronic commerce (B2B)
search engine
electronic data interchange (EDI)
interorganizational system (IOS)
extranet

extensible markup language (XML)
DHTML
CORBA
domain
virtual and hybrid sales
World Wide Web/Web page
Internet
browser

hypertext link
universal resource locator
information superhighway, cyberspace
National Information Infrastructure (NII)
Value-added networks (VAN)

KEY CONCEPTS

- business intelligence (BI)
- business-to-business and business-to-consumer transactions
- digital versus physical products
- interorganizational systems

QUESTIONS

1. How does the government, state and federal, engage in electronic commerce?
2. In terms of dollar impact, is business-to-business or business-to-consumer electronic commerce more important?
3. Why should a firm engage in business intelligence as it contemplates electronic commerce?
4. What external database provides information about U.S. and Canadian manufacturers?
5. Explain electronic data interchange.
6. What are the benefits of an interorganizational system?
7. How can XML challenge EDI? What about DHTML and CORBA?
8. What is the difference between the Internet and the World Wide Web?
9. Why should you limit the number of images on your business-to-consumer Web site?
10. What benefits does electronic commerce yield?
11. Why would a firm use an external database instead of gathering business intelligence itself?
12. How does electronic commerce benefit the internal operations of a firm?
13. How do European countries restrict the sale and distribution of information that a firm gathers about its customers?
14. Give three examples of digital products.
15. Why would a firm have both a storefront and a Web site that sell its products?
16. What is a "virtual mall"?
17. Should the design of a B2B site be from the customer's point of view or the firm's point of view? Why?
18. Should the design of a B2C site be from the customer's point of view or the firm's point of view? Why?
19. About how many people in North America make online purchases?
20. What costs do purchasers of digital products incur in their transactions?

TOPICS FOR DISCUSSION

1. What is the current percent of retail sales accomplished by business-to-consumer electronic commerce and how much can it grow?
2. Why will electronic commerce become simply one more part of everyday business practice in the near future?
3. How will the increased speed and reduced costs of Internet communications affect electronic commerce?
4. How secure is credit card payment over the Internet compared to other credit card payments such as buying a meal at a restaurant?

PROBLEMS

1. Go to the U.S. Census Bureau's Web page for e-commerce statistics at www.census.gov/eos/www/ebusiness614.htm (it is very important that all letters in the URL are in lower case). Graph the e-commerce retail sales each quarter from the first quarter of 2000 until the latest quarter shown at the Web site. Based on these figures, what do you believe will be the total e-commerce retail sales in the fourth quarter of 2010?
2. Financial information about many businesses can be found at the Web site of the Securities and Exchange Commission (www.sec.gov). If you are gathering business intelligence about a competitor, this may be a place to begin. Go to the Web site of the Securities and Exchange Commission and access EDGAR (Electronic Data Gathering, Analysis, and Retrieval) to search financial filings with the SEC. What was the last annual net income for Microsoft according to their most recently filed Form 10-K?

Case Problem

A BUCK MORE

You, Jackie Goudet, are the leader of three entrepreneurial students on your campus. You're an information systems major and working your way through school. Last year, when you were a junior, you assembled the team to form a company to buy back used books from students. The plan was simple, offer one dollar more for a used book than the campus bookstore would pay.

You found that two points of exit from the campus accounted for almost 90 percent of all traffic by cars, bikes, and pedestrians. Lucky for you there was a large parking lot at both points of exit. Students were lured to your site because it was so convenient as they left classes (or final exams) and because you offered a dollar more for used books.

It was easy to make money. First, the campus bookstore didn't mind that you bought books from students; repurchasing used texts was a headache for the bookstore. Second, your costs were low because you operated out of the back of a rental truck. You didn't have to keep a store open all year and pay employees, you simply rented two trucks and parked one in each of the parking lots where students passed as they exited campus. Third, the student government association loaned you the money to buy back texts and you repaid the loan (without interest) when you sold the texts to the used text wholesaler. Since students considered your services a great convenience and since you offered better prices to students, the student government association was happy to help.

Your book buy-back operations gave you insight into a new and possibly more profitable venture: one-stop-shopping. Students sell their old books and buy the books needed for the next semester at the same time. You're a senior this year and when you graduate you and your friends have a chance to turn a small time operation into a business that makes substantial profits.

You ask your two fellow entrepreneurs to come to a meeting where you will lay out your ideas. Allen Turning is the computer expert. He designed the Web pages and information systems that have supported the book buying operations. He is an information systems major and is experienced with databases, programming, Web-based information systems, and communications. Allen is a senior and will graduate with you.

Case Problem continued

Nina Cerro, also a senior, is an operations management major. She knows about logistics and designing systems operations. She was crucial in lining up the text wholesalers who purchased books from you and she arranged favorable shipping terms to transport the texts to the wholesalers. Since transporting texts was a major cost of the operation, her expertise was valuable. Notes of the meeting are below.

JACKIE: *Hey, guys. I've got a good idea but it's a little risky. We've done pretty good with the book setup the last three semesters. We made over $20,000 profit each semester after we paid off everybody. Not bad for some part-time work.*

ALLEN: *That's true, but there was a lot of work behind the scenes. I mean, we had to get all the programs running. The Web pages looked great but they took a long time to make them come out the way we wanted. And we got lucky that the student government let us run the pages off their Web site so we didn't have to pay somebody for hosting.*
And the cost of the laptops isn't included. I mean, well, we used our own stuff and just plugged into the truck's lighter outlet for power to run the laptops. We had a bunch of costs, they just were hidden. We just used our own computer stuff and we borrowed money and Web server space from the student government.

JACKIE: *You're right, we didn't have to pay for all the stuff we used. But the students made a lot more than $20,000; we bought back 35,000 to 40,000 books each semester. And student government didn't pay a penny, they were just using a computer that had been given to them. Before we helped them, they didn't even have their own Web page.*
So listen to my whole idea. We can form a real company and buy back books as our job. I mean, we've all gotten pretty good offers to work in companies but don't we really want to work for ourselves? Be our own bosses? We can do this, we just need to expand.
I figure that if we work enough campuses we can make a lot more money than if we work for a company. But we need to sell books, not just buy them. And we need to really capitalize on convenience. The way I see it, we need to make a Web shopping cart like you see on a lot of Web sites. Allen, remember the Web hosting sites at www.intelli-net.com and www.PrecisionWeb.net that we learned about? Either one of them could host the site for us.

ALLEN: *Yeah. We even made some shopping cart applications in one of our classes.*

NINA: *I get it, it's a kind of "shop-before-you-stop" idea. They tell us what books they are going to sell and what books they want to buy. When they drive by to sell their books, the books they want to purchase will be waiting to be picked up. Count me in!*

ASSIGNMENT

1. Assume you would buy back approximately 35,000 books at each campus each semester and sell about the same number. Your profits have been a little more than 60 cents per book (excluding the costs talked about in the case) so assume you'll also make about 60 cents when you sell a book. How many books would you need to buy and sell to make a comfortable living?
2. Visit the www.intelli-net.com and www.PrecisionWeb.net sites and determine how much it would cost to have one of them host your Web page for e-commerce. You will still have students just walk up to your truck but you expect most students will use the Web site to tell you the books they want to sell and buy.
3. This is not a virtual store and you don't have a digital product. Explain how renting trucks and using a Web page for e-commerce substantially decreases your costs of doing business and raises your profits.

NOTES

[1] Alden M. Hayashi, "Is Corporate America Ready for E-Commerce?" *Datamation* 42 (October 1996), 54–56.

[2] United States Department of Commerce News, August 22, 2002, CB-02-107.

[3] G. Premkumar, K. Ramamurthy, and Sree Nilakanta, "Implementation of Electronic Data Interchange: An Innovation Diffusion Perspective," *Journal of Management Information Systems* 11 (Fall 1994), 158.

[4] H. Russell Johnston and Michael R. Vitale, "Creating Competitive Advantage with Interorganizational Information Systems," *MIS Quarterly* 12 (June 1988), 156–158.

[5] This definition paraphrases one in G. Premkumar and K. Ramamurthy, "The Role of Interorganizational and Organizational Factors on the Decision Mode for Adoption of Interorganizational Systems," *Decision Sciences* 26 (May/June 1995), 305.

[6] United States Department of Commerce E-Stats, March 18, 2002, available at www.census.gov/, link to "E-Stats."

[7] G. Premkumar and K. Ramamurthy, "The Role of Interorganizational and Organizational Factors on the Decision Mode for Adoption of Interorganizational Systems." *Decision Sciences* 26 (May/Jun 1995), 303–336.

[8] Anitesh Barua and Byungtae Lee, "An Economic Analysis of the Introduction of an Electronic Data Interchange System," *Information Systems Research*, Vol. 8, No. 4, (December 1997), 397–422.

[9] This classification of benefits comes from Charalambos L. Iacovou, Izak Benbasat, and Albert S. Dexter, "Electronic Data Interchange and Small Organizations: Adoption and Impact of Technology," *MIS Quarterly* 19 (December 1995), 469. The authors have generalized the benefits described in the article from the narrow EDI focus to the wider interorganizational systems focus.

[10] Karen D. Schwartz, "The Electronic Antidote to Slow Business," *Enterprise Reengineering* 3 (May 1996), 18.

[11] The following costs come from Schwartz, 18–19.

[12] For more details on Internet history, see Brad Schultz, "The Evolution of ARPANET," *Datamation* 34 (August 1, 1988), 71–74; and Robert E. Kahn, "The Role of Government in the Evolution of the Internet," *Communications of the ACM* 37 (August 1994), 15–19.

[13] *ZDNet News*, April 30, 2002, zdnet.com.com/2110-1104-895496.html.

[14] William Gibson, *Neuromancer* (New York: Ace Science Fiction Books, 1984), 51.

[15] See Jeff Johnson, "The Information Superhighway: A Worst-Case Scenario," *Communications of the ACM* 39 (February 1996): 15–17.

[16] Vance McCarthy, "The Web: Open for Business," *Datamation* 41 (December 1, 1995), 32.

[17] Robert E. Kahn, "The Role of Government in the Evolution of the Internet," *Communications of the ACM* 37 (August 1994), 18.

Chapter 4

System Users and Developers

Learning Objectives

After studying this chapter, you should

- Learn that the organizational context for systems development and use is changing from a physical to a virtual structure.
- Recognize the benefits and disadvantages of the virtual office and the virtual organization.
- Know who the information specialists are and how they can be integrated into an information services organization.
- Be alerted to new directions that the information services organization might take.
- Understand what is meant by end-user computing and why it came about.
- Appreciate that users, especially those with an end-user computing capability, are a valuable information resource.
- Know the benefits and risks of end-user computing.
- Be aware of the types of knowledge and skill that are important to systems development, practiced by both end users and information specialists.
- Understand knowledge management and the challenges that must be addressed for successful implementation.
- Be aware of the special constraints that face developers of global information systems.

Introduction

The first office automation applications were designed for use chiefly by secretarial and clerical personnel but their use soon spread to managerial and professional ranks. These applications made possible a concept called the virtual office, where it is not necessary that workers be physically located at the office site. The virtual office movement, triggered by telecommuting and hoteling, became so popular that it was expanded to the concept of a virtual organization.

The firm's information specialists were initially located in an information services unit but later the specialists began to be allocated to business areas. As firms evaluated the advantages and disadvantages of centralized and decentralized information services (IS) organizations, three future structures were identified—the partner, platform, and scalable models.

As the first information systems were developed by information specialists, users were not expected (or permitted) to do more than specify their information needs. When user demand for more computer support exploded, the specialists were unable to keep up and the users sought to develop their own systems—a phenomenon called end-user computing. Today, many users do much of their own system development and some still rely one hundred percent on the information specialists. Other users are capable of doing much of their own developmental work and rely on the specialists for consulting service. A firm whose users are capable of participating in end-user computing enjoys an advantage over firms whose users do not. End-user computing can produce real benefits, but it is not without its risks.

Regardless of whether systems are developed by information specialists or users, certain knowledge and skill is required. The knowledge represents material that can be learned and the skill consists of natural capabilities, enhanced by education and experience.

Firms are recognizing the value of the knowledge possessed by their employees and are implementing knowledge management systems. When challenges are met, the firm can achieve higher levels of learning, knowledge exchange, and decision making.

Systems that span national boundaries pose unique challenges to the developers. Some challenges are politically imposed, some are technical, and some relate to the personnel.

Systems development is an evolving activity, with the organizational setting and the roles played by the users and information specialists continually changing.

THE BUSINESS ORGANIZATION

Information systems are developed and used in business organizations. In Chapter 1 we recognized that managers can be found on all levels and in all business areas of the firm. We identified the basic areas as finance, human resources, information services, manufacturing, and marketing.

Information systems have been developed to support the entire organization, the executive level, and the business areas. This framework is illustrated in Figure 4.1. The MIS is intended to meet the general information needs of managers throughout the firm; the executive information system is designed for use by the firm's strategic level managers; and the five information systems on the lower level of the figure address the unique information needs of those business areas.

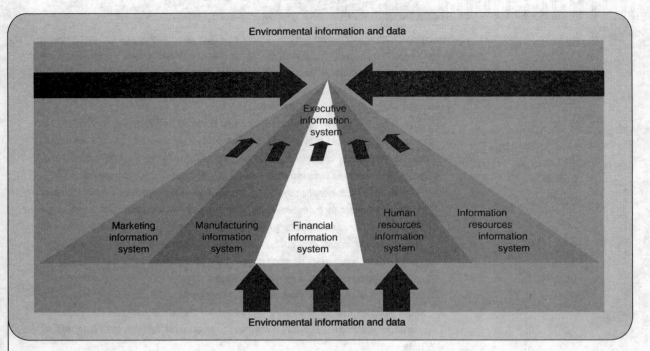

Figure 4.1
Information Systems Are Developed to Support Organizational Levels and Areas

These information systems are tailored to the **physical organization**—the way that the physical resources (human, material, machine, and money) are allocated to the various physical areas of the firm—global subsidiaries, divisions, regions, districts, branches, and so on. Innovations in information technology have made it possible for many of the firm's activities to be conducted without the constraints of physical location. Such an organization structure is called the virtual organization, and it got its start with office automation and the concept of the virtual office.

OFFICE AUTOMATION

Office automation can be traced back to the early 1960s, when IBM coined the term *word processing* to express the concept that much office activity is centered on the processing of words. Subsequently, such other technologies as electronic mail, electronic calendaring, video conferencing, and desktop publishing were applied to office work, and together they were called office automation. **Office automation (OA)** includes all of the formal and informal electronic systems primarily concerned with the communication of information to and from persons both inside and outside the firm.

Some OA systems involve the use of a computer and some do not. Figure 4.2 is an OA model that shows how the computer-based applications and the noncomputer-based applications are used by problem solvers. Some of the problem solvers reside within the firm and some are in the firm's environment. An advantage of OA is the fact that it provides a communications conduit for persons inside and outside the firm to communicate with each other. The model shows that the computer-based applications interface with a database that is populated by information gathered within the firm and from the environment.

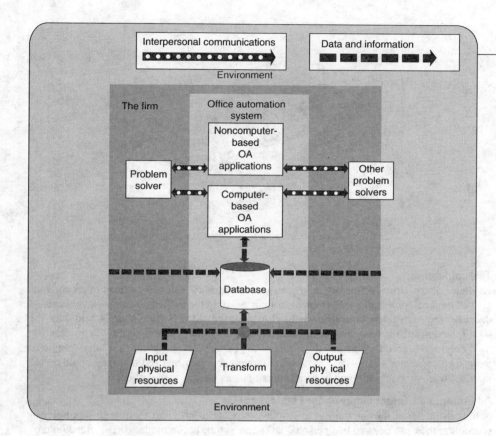

Figure 4.2 An OA Model

A Shift from Clerical to Managerial Problem Solving

The first OA applications were intended to support secretarial and clerical personnel. Word processing, electronic mail, fax, and electronic calendaring are examples. As managers and professionals became more computer literate they recognized how they could use the applications in solving their problems. They began using E-mail to communicate with other problem solvers, using electronic calendaring to schedule meetings with other problem solvers, using video conferencing to link problem solvers over a wide geographical area, and so on.

Today, managers and professionals have as much claim on OA applications as do secretarial and clerical personnel. In fact, the OA applications have been extended by such technology as hand-held computers and personal digital assistants (PDAs) to provide additional communications and computational ability. For example, the Palm i705 Handheld illustrated in Figure 4.3 provides a wireless access to E-mail and the Internet.

THE VIRTUAL OFFICE

The capability of OA to link people electronically opened up new avenues in how office work is performed. It has even made it unnecessary for office work to be performed at the office. Instead, such work can be done wherever the employee is located. This concept of a virtual office got its start with telecommuting and was refined to achieve an office facility called hoteling.

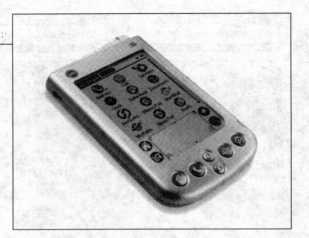

Figure 4.3 PDAs Provide a Wireless Communication Ability.

Source: Photograph of the Palm i705 Handheld printed with permission.

Telecommuting

Evidence of the virtual office began to emerge during the 1970s as low-priced microcomputers and data communications equipment made it possible for individuals to work at home. At the time, the term **teleprocessing** was used to describe data communications, and later the term **telecommuting** was introduced because it seemed like an appropriate way to describe how employees could electronically "commute" to work. Among the first telecommuters were such computer scientists as systems programmers, who realized that they could create their software products at home or on a sailboat just as well as at the office.

Advantages of Telecommuting for Employees

A big advantage of telecommuting to employees is that it provides them with flexibility in scheduling their job tasks so that personal tasks can also be accommodated. This freedom provides a flexibility that many professionals desire. Another advantage is that the firm typically pays more attention to communications needs of telecommuters than in an ordinary office environment, where much information is communicated in casual conversation and by observation.

Disadvantages of Telecommuting for Employees

The advantages are offset, however, by some real disadvantages. First, the employees can develop a sense of not belonging. When employees do not come in direct daily contact with their colleagues, they may lose the feeling of being an important part of an organization. Another disadvantage is fear of job loss or career damage. Since the employees' work is done independently of the company operation, the employees can get the idea that they are expendable. They can conclude that anybody with a computer and a modem can do their work and that they may become the victims of an "electronic layoff." Even if employees are not terminated, they can fear that not being a part of the physical organization can hurt their chances for career advancement. A third disadvantage is increased family tension. When there are tensions at home, the telecommuter is not able to escape for a few hours. Tensions can also be increased because spouses may view the job as a working arrangement that is being used to avoid family responsibilities. It is easy for the division between home and office responsibilities to become blurred.

The Decreasing Role of Telecommuting

There is an indication that there is a decreasing interest in telecommuting. A *USA Today* survey of financial and information technology (IT) firms engaged in telecommuting revealed that more than 80 percent plan to scale back, 62 percent plan a decrease, 21 percent plan a phase-out, and only 4 percent plan an increase.[1] Although telecommuting was the stimulus to the virtual office, it appears to be playing an increasingly minor role.

Highlights in MIS

VIDEO CONFERENCING ALTERNATIVES

Video conferencing is an office automation application involving the use of video equipment to link geographically dispersed conference participants. The equipment provides both sound and picture. There are three possible video conferencing configurations.

- **One-Way Video and Audio.** Video and audio signals are sent from a single transmitting site to one or more receiving sites. This is a good way for a project leader to disseminate information to team members at remote locations.
- **One-Way Video and Two-Way Audio.** People at the receiving sites can talk to people at the transmitting site, while everyone views the same video images.
- **Two-Way Video and Audio.** The video and audio communications between all sites are two-way. Although this is the most effective of the electronically aided conferencing approaches, it can be the most expensive. The first video conferencing efforts used dedicated rooms that cost in the neighborhood of $30,000 or could be rented from a common carrier or hotel chain. Although those setups are still in use, another, lower-priced option is available—desktop video conferencing.

DESKTOP VIDEO CONFERENCING With **desktop video conferencing**, video and audio equipment are attached to each workstation in the network, enabling the two-way communication of picture and sound. The networked workstations each contain a camera mounted above the screen to view the user, a microphone, add-on boards, and software. The cost of such a setup continues to come down but there are additional costs that must be considered. Desktop video conferencing typically requires a dedicated server and a high-speed channel. One alternative, NetMeeting from Microsoft, is free and easy to use over Internet connections but only two participants may connect at a time.

THE TELESUITE SOLUTION Telesuite, an Englewood, Ohio, firm, markets videoconferencing networks that utilize fiber optic broadband channels and feature high-quality video.[2] The video image is much wider than the typical 4-by-3 aspect ratio, capable of providing an image that fills a 14-foot wide wall. This wide view provides a much more natural setting and participants frequently feel that they are communicating in person.

Video conferencing has the inherent appeal of enabling managers to communicate in a way that most closely approximates the face-to-face meeting. The ability to span great geographic distances by means of video conferencing enables more managers to get involved in decision making than otherwise would be the case—another example of the virtual organization.

Hoteling

The initial narrow focus of telecommuting on certain classes of office workers who could do all of their work at home has been broadened to include all kinds of employees who come to the office only when necessary. This concept has been given the name **hoteling** and the idea is that the firm provides a central facility that can be shared by employees as the need for office space and support arises. Employees use the central facility in much the same way as they would use a hotel while on a trip. The employees make reservations for facilities with particular support resources, based on the work to be done.

In order for this vision to be achieved, the central office facility must be staffed with appropriate support personnel and must offer the needed technology. The guiding principles for achieving hoteling include:

- Design space for functional needs
- Construct offices of similar size
- Provide centralized storage space
- Decrease the number of enclosed office spaces
- Eliminate assigned offices

The benefits of hoteling are a more effective utilization of resources and space, and an improved focus on what is needed to support office personnel. The risks include perceived loss of "perks" by employees who no longer have private offices, a loss of community feeling, and a potential negative impact on corporate culture.

Advantages of the Virtual Office

Telecommuting and hoteling make possible a capability called the **virtual office**, a concept that office work can be done at virtually any geographical location as long as the work site is linked to one or more of the firm's fixed locations by some type of electronic communications capability.

The virtual office overcomes the physical constraints of the workplace with electronics and thereby makes possible several real advantages, including:

- **Reduced facility cost.** The firm does not require such a large office capacity, since some employees are working elsewhere, making possible reduced costs for office rent and expansion.
- **Reduced equipment cost.** Rather than provide a set of office equipment to everyone, the employees can share equipment in much the same way that participants in a local area network share its resources.
- **Reduced work stoppages.** When winter storms, floods, hurricanes, and the like make it impossible for employees to travel to the physical workplace, company activity can come to a screeching halt. In a virtual office setting, however, much of the work can continue.
- **Social contribution.** The virtual office makes it possible for the firm to employ persons who would not otherwise have an opportunity to work. Handicapped persons, the elderly, and parents with young children can work at home. The virtual office therefore provides the firm with an opportunity to express its social conscience.

Disadvantages of the Virtual Office

When a firm commits to a virtual office strategy, it does so with the understanding that there can be some negative impacts, such as:

- **Low morale.** A number of factors can produce low employee morale. One is the absence of positive feedback that comes from face-to-face interaction with superiors and peers.
- **Fear of security risks.** The security of data and information might be more difficult to control in a virtual office environment.

The virtual office demands cooperation by both the firm and the employees if it is to succeed. Quite possibly, the virtual office demands more dedication from employees than does the fixed office. The virtual office is not for everyone. Unless the employees can discipline themselves to do much of their work without supervision and motivation, the work will likely not get done. For employees who prefer to work alone and be their own boss, the virtual office can be the ideal setup.

THE VIRTUAL ORGANIZATION

The successes of the virtual office prompted visionaries to see how it could be expanded to apply to the entire firm—a virtual organization. In a **virtual organization**, operations throughout the firm are designed so that they that are not tied to physical locations.

The Societal Impact of the Virtual Organization

Although the virtual office and the virtual organization have been primarily identified as business strategies, the concept can eventually have a dramatic implication for society as well.[3]

The industries that are the most attracted to the concept of the virtual office and the virtual organization are those that add value in the form of information, ideas, and intelligence. The term **Three I Economy** has been coined to describe such industries. Examples are education, health care, entertainment, travel, sports, and consulting. As these industries are attracted to the virtual office in increasing numbers, the movement can affect the way that practically everyone lives and works. This effect will be most obvious in the physical appearance and function of our cities. The virtual office and the virtual organization will decrease the demand for more skyscrapers and commuters, making our cities quieter, gentler, and more appealing as places to live.

In order for this beneficial effect to take place, everyone must be able to participate. Workers on all levels will have to be attracted to jobs in the Three I Economy and must have the necessary knowledge and skills to succeed. Such a high level of competence will require a dedication on the part of our educational institutions and also governments on all levels to encourage and facilitate the change.

Today, almost every firm's activities encompass more information, ideas, and intelligence than in previous years. Because of that, universities and high schools routinely include information literacy and computer literacy in their programs. Information technology and information systems are woven into the fabric of business processes.

THE INFORMATION SERVICES ORGANIZATION

We have used the term **information services (IS)** to describe the unit of the firm that has responsibility for the majority of the information resources. Other names—MIS division or MIS department, and especially IT (information technology)—are popular.

The Information Resources

In Chapter 2, we identified the information resources as including computer hardware, computer software, information specialists, users, facilities, the database, and information. Most of these resources are located in information services and are the responsibility of the chief information officer (CIO). Information resources located in user areas are the responsibility of the user area managers.

The Information Specialists

We use the term *information specialist* to describe the employee whose full-time responsibility is to contribute to the availability of information resources in the firm. The original information specialists included the systems analyst, programmer, and operator. Subsequently, the database administrator and network specialist were added.

SYSTEMS ANALYSTS   These specialists work with the users to develop new systems and improve existing systems. Systems analysts are expert at defining problems and in preparing written documentation on how the computer will assist in solving the problems.

DATABASE ADMINISTRATORS   An information specialist who has responsibility for the database is called a **database administrator (DBA)**. The duties of the DBA fall into four major areas: planning, implementation, operation, and security. We will describe these duties in Chapter 6 when we address data resources.

WEBMASTER   The **webmaster** is responsible for the content and presentation of the firm's Web site. The webmaster must work with network specialists in order to assure that the communications network between the customer and/or business partner is always open. Web sites rely heavily on images and the webmaster will generally have some expertise in graphics manipulation or design. Often a subordinate of the webmaster will be responsible for making images available that are consistent and complementary among all of the pages at the Web site.

An important duty of the webmaster is to track people who come to the firm's Web pages. These statistics can provide important information about the Web site's effectiveness. For example, the statistics may reveal that many customers begin the purchase process but cancel their transaction after moving from one page to another. This information and the sequence of pages accessed combined with the amount of time spent on each Web page can lead to a different design of the site. Customer relations can be greatly improved by Web sites that operate all day, every day, but poor Web site design can quickly wipe out any benefits.

NETWORK SPECIALISTS **Network specialists** work with systems analysts and users in establishing the data communications networks that tie together widespread computing resources. Network specialists combine expertise from the fields of computing and telecommunications. Maintaining network requirements for Web-based applications is especially difficult since much of the communications take place beyond the boundaries of the firm.

PROGRAMMERS **Programmers** use the documentation prepared by the systems analysts to code computer programs that transform the data into information that is needed by the user. Some firms combine the functions of the systems analyst and programmer, creating a **programmer analyst** position.

OPERATORS **Operators** run the large-scale computing equipment such as mainframe computers and servers that are usually located in the firm's large computing facilities. The operators monitor the consoles, change paper forms in the printers, manage libraries of tape and disk storage, and perform other similar duties.

All of these information specialists typically are combined with representatives of the user organization to form project teams that develop the systems. The specialists are also responsible for maintaining the systems after they are implemented.

The Information Services Organizational Structure

The information specialists in information services can be organized in various ways. The first organizational units were centralized in the firm, with practically all of the information resources located in the IT unit. An organizational structure that is typical of a centralized operation is illustrated in Figure 4.4. This particular structure is tailored to the system life cycle. The firm has assigned certain systems analysts and programmers to the development of new systems and assigned other systems analysts and programmers to the maintenance of existing systems. Each of these groups is managed by a manager. The operations, database administration, and network units contribute to both development and maintenance.

During the 1970s and 1980s, some firms began decentralizing many of their information resources by allocating them to the business units and granting the units the authority to decide how the resources would be applied. The marketing unit, for example, had its own IT staff, led by a **divisional information officer (DIO)** who worked with marketing management in determining how the marketing information resources would be used.

Innovative Organizational Structures

Recognizing during the 1990s that both centralization and decentralization have their advantages, large firms sought to achieve a "centrally decentralized" organizational structure. This was accomplished by giving the corporate IS unit authority to make decisions concerning the IT infrastructure, and giving business areas authority to make decisions about the strategic use of IT in their areas. This structure faced difficulties for two reasons. First, IT is now playing a more prominent role in the firm than any time previous, and second, the rapid rate of technological change demands that a structure pay particular attention to developing information

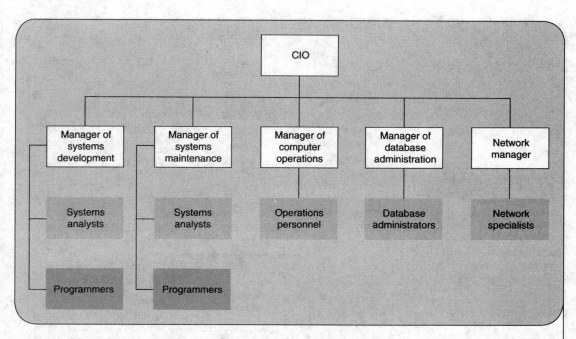

Figure 4.4 An Organizational Structure for a Firm's Centralized Information Services Unit

knowledge and skill in both system users and developers, and utilizing information resources of all types available from vendors and consultants.

In response to this need, three innovative structures have been identified. They are called the partner model, the platform model, and the scalable model.[4] Whereas the organizational structure in Figure 4.4 illustrates how the *information specialists* are grouped, the innovative structures show how the *IT functions* are grouped. Each of the innovative models incorporates three communication networks. A **visioning network** enables the CIO to work with top management in strategic planning for information resources. An **innovation network** is used by the CIO to interface with business areas so that innovative applications can be developed for those areas. A **sourcing network** is utilized to interface with vendors for the purpose of acquiring information resources.

The three models of innovative structures are explained below.

- **The Partner Model.** The basis for the partner model, illustrated in Figure 4.5, is the idea that IT works with business areas in using IT to achieve business innovation. The structure shows that the IT unit has responsibility for value innovation, strategic planning, infrastructure management, financial management, human resources management, and services provisioning. The visioning network involves the CIO with the CEO and the top management team in strategically planning how information resources are to be used. The innovation network is used by the CIO in working with the business areas and their DIOs in achieving value innovation and accomplishing solutions delivery. The sourcing network is used to interface with vendors to acquire information resources.
- **The Platform Model.** The underlying assumption of the platform model is that IT will not actively initiate business innovations but will provide the networks so that innovation can be accomplished by the business areas. Figure 4.6 shows how the same three networks are employed. The visioning network again involves the CIO in strategic information planning, but the innovation network is used by **account managers** to achieve the value innovation in the business

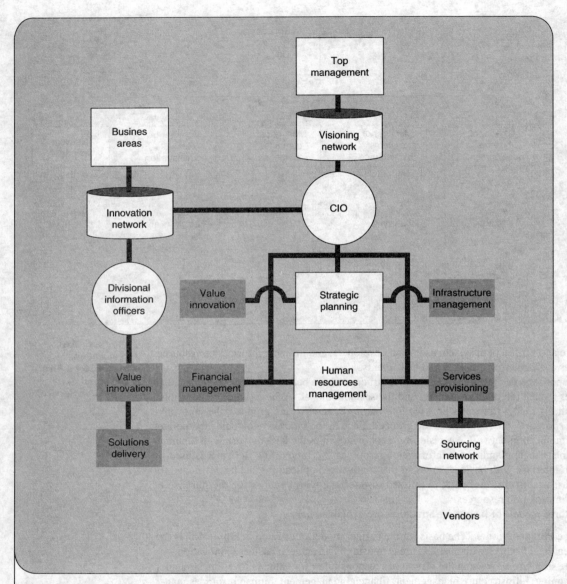

Figure 4.5 The Partner Model

Source: Adapted from Ritu Agarwal and V. Sambamurthy, "Principles and Models for Organizing the IT Function," MIS Quarterly Executive Volume 1, Number 1 (March 2002), pp. 1–16.

areas. The managers of the six other value innovation areas, especially infrastructure management, solutions delivery, and services provisioning, develop IT capabilities in their areas so that they can apply their knowledge and skill in the business areas.

- **The Scalable Model.** Some firms, especially those with cyclical operations, have a need to quickly adjust the level of their information resources to respond to market conditions. Resources must be quickly obtained when market opportunities arise and must be quickly shed when the opportunities no longer exist, keeping fixed costs to a minimum. The scalable model, illustrated in Figure 4.7, shows that two sourcing networks are utilized to interface with vendors when engaging in infra-

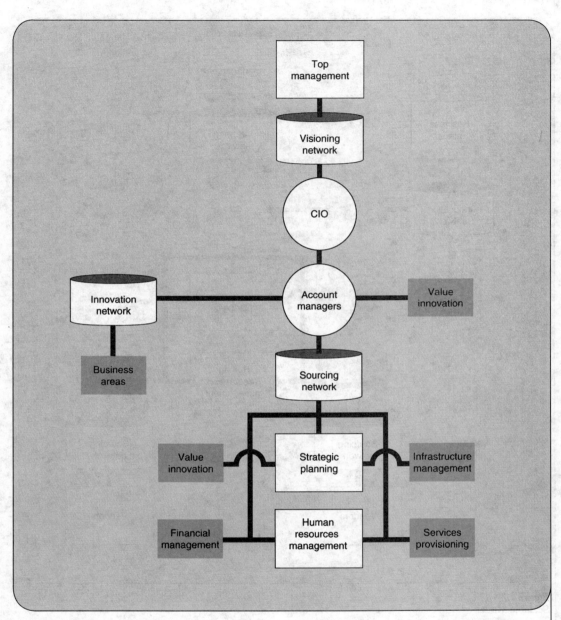

Figure 4.6 **The Platform Model**

Source: Adapted from Ritu Agarwal and V. Sambamurthy, "Principles and Models for Organizing the IT Function," MIS Quarterly Executive Volume 1, Number 1 (March 2002), pp. 1–16.

structure management and solutions delivery. In addition, the MIS steering committee has responsibility for utilizing an innovation network to achieve innovative processes in the business areas.

All three models recognize that the IT function is not a self-contained unit, housing all of the information resources and providing all of the information systems to users. It is necessary that (1) IT interface with both users and vendors, and (2) responsibilities for certain functions be allocated to such specialists as divisional information officers and account managers.

86 ••• PART 1   ESSENTIAL CONCEPTS

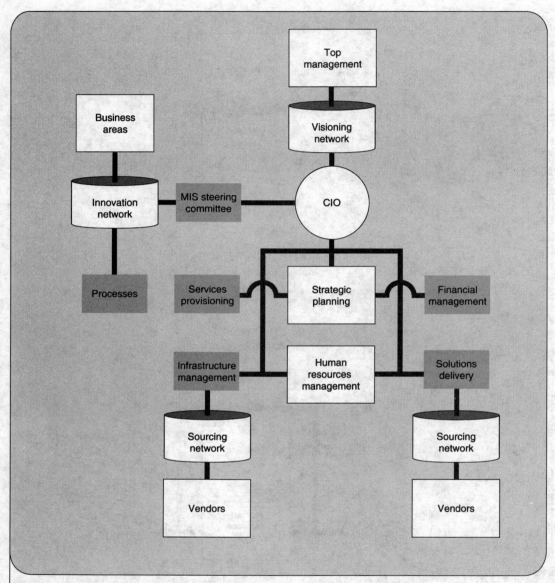

Figure 4.7 The Scalable Model

Source: Adapted from Ritu Agarwal and V. Sambamurthy, "Principles and Models for Organizing the IT Function," MIS Quarterly Executive Volume 1, Number 1 (March 2002), pp. 1–16.

All three models reflect an effort to make the IT unit a team player in the firm's use of information resources—sharing and delegating functions when it is best for the firm.

END-USER COMPUTING

The first information systems were developed with the information specialists doing all of the work for the users. This approach, illustrated in Figure 4.8 and still used for many systems development efforts today, shows how the information specialists (systems analyst, database administrator, network specialist, programmer, and operator) are intermediaries, separating the user from the computer.

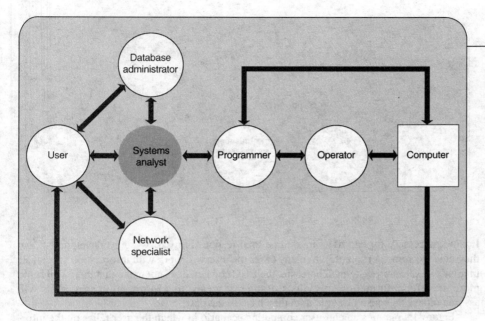

Figure 4.8 The Traditional Communication Chain (note that Webmaster could be considered a Network specialist in the traditional communication chain)

The late 1970s saw the beginning of a trend that had a big influence on computer use. The trend was a growing interest on the part of users in developing their own computer applications, an approach named end-user computing. **End user** is synonymous with user; he or she uses the end product of a computer-based system. **End-user computing (EUC)**, therefore, is the development by users of all or part of their information systems. End-user computing evolved because of four main influences:

- **The impact of computer education**. During the early 1980s, the impact of good computer education programs in public and private schools, colleges, and industrial firms became apparent. Management ranks, especially on the lower levels, began to be filled with persons having good computer skills. As the years passed these managers progressed to higher levels of management and continued their use of information systems and technology.
- **The information services backlog**. Information specialists have always had more work than they can handle. This situation became critical during the early 1980s, when users began making demands on information services for additional systems support. Information services could not respond fast enough to the users' demands, and backlogs built up with jobs waiting to go on the computer. Some users had to wait two or three years for their jobs to work their way through the backlog.
- **Low-cost hardware**. During this same period, the market became flooded with low-cost microcomputers. Users could obtain their own hardware by placing an order at the local computer store by telephone.
- **Prewritten software**. Both hardware and software firms produced software that would perform basic accounting tasks as well as provide information for decision making. This prewritten software offered enhanced support and ease of use, and it enabled firms and individual users with little computer expertise to implement computer-based systems.

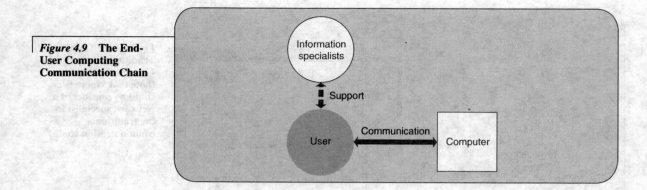

Figure 4.9 The End-User Computing Communication Chain

It is not necessary for end users to assume total responsibility for systems development, but they must do some portion of it. In many cases the user will work with information specialists in jointly developing systems. Therefore, the EUC concept does not mean that there will be no more need for information specialists. Rather, it means that information specialists will assume more of a consulting role than they have in the past.

Figure 4.9 pictures an end-user computing scenario in which the user relies on the information specialists for some degree of support.

USERS AS AN INFORMATION RESOURCE

The users of the firm's information system are important information resources who can make a real contribution to meeting strategic objectives and achieving a competitive advantage. This is especially true when the users can actively participate in systems development and practice end-user computing.

In deciding how the firm will use its information resources, top management must give considerable attention to the manner in which end-user computing will be conducted, so as to maximize the benefits and minimize the risks.

Benefits of End-User Computing

EUC can make possible two major benefits:

- **Match Capabilities and Challenges.** The shift in the workload for systems development to user areas frees up the information specialists to concentrate on organization-wide and complex systems, enabling the specialists to do a better job in these areas. The specialists also have more time to devote to maintaining existing systems—an important area of responsibility.
- **Reduce Communications Gap.** A difficulty that has plagued systems development since the first days of computing has been the communications between the user and the information specialist. The user understands the problem area better than the computing technology. The specialist, on the other hand, is expert in the technology but less knowledgeable in the problem area. When users develop their own applications, there is no communications gap because there is no need for communication. Similarly, when users develop a portion of their systems, the gap is reduced.

Both of these benefits result in the development of better systems than those produced by information specialists trying to do the majority of the work themselves.

Risks of End-User Computing

Conversely, when end users develop their own systems, they expose the firm to a number of risks:

- **Poorly Aimed Systems.** End users may apply the computer to applications that should be performed some other way, such as manually.
- **Poorly Designed and Documented Systems.** End users, although they may have high levels of technical competence, usually cannot match the professionalism of information specialists when it comes to designing systems. Also, in the rush to get systems up and running, end users tend to neglect the need to document their designs so that the systems can be maintained.
- **Inefficient Use of Information Resources.** When there is no central control over acquisition of hardware and software, the firm can end up with incompatible hardware and redundant software. Also, end users may "reinvent the wheel" by developing systems that have already been developed by information services or other end users.
- **Loss of Data Integrity.** End users may not exercise the necessary care in entering data into the firm's database. Other users use this erroneous data, assuming it to be accurate. The result is contaminated output that can cause managers to make the wrong decisions.
- **Loss of Security.** In a similar fashion, end users may not safeguard their data and software. Computer criminals can gain access to the system and harm the firm in many ways. The increasing use of networks makes security increasingly important.
- **Loss of Control.** Users develop systems to meet their own needs without conforming to a plan that ensures computer support for the firm.

Because of the potential benefits, the firm must develop a strategic plan for information resources that allows EUC to grow and flourish. As far as the risks are concerned, the same types of controls must be applied to user areas that have worked so well in information services.

SYSTEMS DEVELOPMENT KNOWLEDGE AND SKILL

The development of information systems requires certain knowledge and skill. Information specialists apply this knowledge and skill on a full-time basis. Users apply them when they engage in end-user computing to any degree.

Systems Development Knowledge

Knowledge is something that can be learned, either through formal courses of study or through such individual efforts as reading and observation. The types of knowledge that enable someone to contribute to systems development efforts include computer literacy, information literacy, business fundamentals, systems theory, the systems development process, and systems modeling.

Computer literacy is the ability to use computer resources to accomplish necessary processing. **Information literacy** consists of understanding how to use information at each step of the problem-solving process, where that information can be obtained, and how to share information with others. Although information literacy does not absolutely require computer literacy, the two go hand-in-hand to provide problem solvers with a powerful tool. **Business fundamentals** are those topics that are usually included in the undergraduate and graduate business core courses—accounting, finance, marketing, management, MIS, and operations. Most information systems are developed to support these fundamentals. **Systems theory** describes how to depict phenomena as normative systems structures. The general systems model of the firm, presented in Chapter 2, is an example. The **systems development process** consists of the steps that are taken to develop an information system. The names **system life cycle (SLC)** and **system development life cycle (SDLC)** are used to describe the process, which we describe in Chapter 7. **Systems modeling** consists of the various ways to document a system. In most cases, the

Table 4.1

Knowledge Requirements

KNOWLEDGE	GENERAL MANAGEMENT	PROFESSIONAL STAFF	CLERICAL STAFF	INFORMATION SPECIALISTS
COMPUTER LITERACY	Minor	Intermediate	Intermediate	Major
INFORMATION LITERACY	Major	Major	Intermediate	Major
BUSINESS FUNDAMENTALS	Major	Major	Minor	Intermediate
SYSTEMS THEORY	Minor	Intermediate	Minor	Major
SYSTEMS DEVELOPMENT	Intermediate	Minor	Minor	Major
SYSTEMS MODELING	Minor	Major	Minor	Major

system's data and processes are modeled using such tools as entity-relationship diagrams, data flow diagrams, and class diagrams. We describe such tools in Chapters 6 and 7.

It is possible to identify not only types of knowledge and skill that are important for information specialists and users, but also how users can be subdivided into general management and their staffs. Table 4.1 identifies whether the knowledge is of major, intermediate, or minor importance. Keep in mind that these are general observations that can vary widely, depending on the organization, the personnel, and the system being developed.

Systems Development Skill

In the same manner, we can identify the different types of development skill that are important. Although these skills can be learned, individuals usually differ in their abilities due to natural gifts, and the learning process serves to refine them. The development skills include communications, analytical ability, creativity, and leadership.

Communications skills involve the ability to transmit information to one or more other persons using verbal, written, or graphical images. **Analytical ability** involves the study and ultimate understanding of a situation for the purpose of formulating a response or solution. **Creativity** is the generation of a completely or partly new idea or solution. Creativity is especially useful in the absence of experience or knowledge gained from learning about a similar phenomenon. **Leadership** is the ability to direct others to perform tasks. For general management, this is probably the most important skill, but it is also important for information specialists as they engage in managing a system development project.

Table 4.2 shows the relative importance of these skills to general management, professional and clerical staff, and information specialists. The professional staff includes such specialists as marketing researchers and management scientists, whereas the clerical staff consists of office personnel.

Knowledge Management

We have recognized that the people in an organization represent a valuable resource. Information system users and developers are a valuable information resource. A refinement of this view that is now emerging is that the knowledge of the organization's people is a valuable

Table 4.2

Skill Requirements

SKILL	GENERAL MANAGEMENT	PROFESSIONAL STAFF	CLERICAL STAFF	INFORMATION SPECIALISTS
COMMUNICATIONS	Major	Major	Intermediate	Major
ANALYTICAL ABILITY	Intermediate	Major	Intermediate	Major
CREATIVITY	Intermediate	Major	Intermediate	Intermediate
LEADERSHIP	Major	Minor	Minor	Intermediate

resource and should be managed—**knowledge management (KM)**. The knowledge relates to the firm's processes, technology, management, and interactions with its environmental elements. Firms are embarking on projects to develop knowledge management systems for the purpose of achieving a competitive advantage. In a study of 2,073 knowledge management practitioners and managers, University of Pittsburgh researchers learned that 13 percent had developed systems, 21 percent had systems under development, and 35 percent were in the planning stage.[5]

Firms typically regard KM as another type of system to be developed by information services—in this case a system that gathers knowledge, maintains it in storage, and makes it available to users. Vendors such as KnowledgeBase.net sell knowledge management software to firms that wish the advantages of prewritten software.

KM Challenges

Since KM is so new, firms are faced with several major issues and are formulating strategies to address them. The University of Pittsburgh researchers were able to identify 20 such issues and categorized them into four logical sets—executive/strategic management; costs, benefits, risks; operational management; and standards. Table 4.3 lists the challenges that must be faced by a firm developing KM systems.

Table 4.3
Knowledge Management Challenges

EXECUTIVE/STRATEGIC MANAGEMENT	Senior management must include knowledge management in the firm's strategic plans.
	Knowledge management is an effort that requires sustained effort in an organizational climate that enhances information sharing.
	KM should be the foundation for enhancing creativity and innovation in the firm.
COST, BENEFITS, RISKS	KM costs must be evaluated in terms of measurable return to the firm in order to maintain the organization's intellectual wealth.
	Management must identify appropriate levels of investment in KM.
OPERATIONAL MANAGEMENT	Processes must be put in place for ensuring that knowledge to be incorporated in the KM system is relevant, legitimate, and current.
	KM system architecture must fit the needs of the organization.
	Attention must be given to the methodology for developing a KM system to determine whether new or existing IS methodologies should be used.
STANDARDS	Technical standards for the KM data must be established.
	A clear definition of KM must be formulated and used within the organization that fits within the existing IT infrastructure.

Source: Adapted from the work of William R. King, Peter V. Marks, Jr., and Scott McCoy, "The Most Important Issues in Knowledge Management," Communications of the ACM Volume 45 Number 9 (September 2002), pp. 93–97.

A Successful KM Development Project at Nortel Networks[6]

Nortel Networks (using knowledge management software from Excalibur Technologies) credits its pilot KM project with enabling the transformation from a technology-focused company to one that is opportunity/customer-focused. Their project involved the development of a new product development (NPD) system that enabled Nortel to (1) leverage multidisciplinary NPD knowledge assets, (2) improve NPD decision making, and (3) facilitate learning and knowledge exchange.

The old NPD system illustrated in Figure 4.10 consisted of a five-phase process. The concept development portion was ill-defined, causing the entire process to be ineffective.

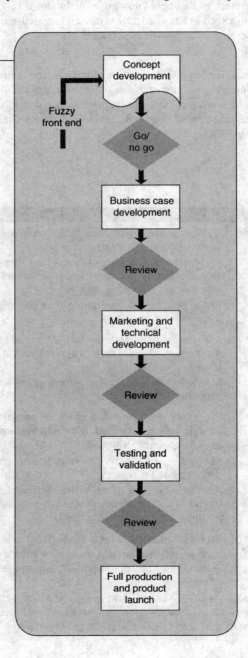

Figure 4.10 The Original Nortel Networks New Product Development System

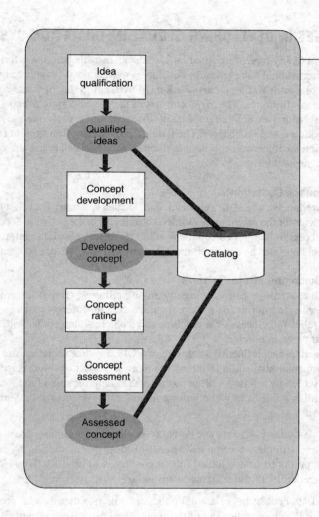

Figure 4.11 The Nortel Networks New Product Concept Development System Utilizing Knowledge Management

Management decided to redevelop the fuzzy front end, using KM. The new concept development portion shown in Figure 4.11 illustrates the four phases with rectangles. The linkages that connect the phases (the arrows) take the form of more positive why/why not decisions rather than an often hesitant go/no go attitude.

The project began in July 1995 and sufficient progress had been made by June 1996 to conduct a pilot test. The pilot involved the qualification of 112 ideas, yielding 7 product and service concepts for funding. In late 1997 and early 1998 Nortel began to implement the new NPD process, called "Time-to-Market." Two examples of successful projects have been a *Privacy Manager^{SM}* system that can ID 100% of incoming telephone calls and an *Internet Call Waiting* product that allows a user to use a single phone line to receive phone calls while connected to the Internet.

In successfully implementing KM, Nortel demonstrated its ability to address the KM challenges identified earlier. However, rather than establish a corporate knowledge officer, a new position called corporate learning officer (CLO) was created. The CLO and staff were given the task of implementing a corporate-wide KM strategy.

CHALLENGES IN DEVELOPING GLOBAL INFORMATION SYSTEMS

The development of any type of information system can be a challenging effort, but when the system spans international boundaries the developers must address several unique constraints. This is the task of a **multinational corporation** (MNC), a firm that operates across products, markets, nations, and cultures. The MNC consists of the parent company and a group of subsidiaries. The subsidiaries are geographically dispersed, and each one may have its own unique goals, policies, and procedures. The term **global information system (GIS)** has been coined to describe the information system used by an MNC. Listed below are constraints that GIS developers must address.

Politically Imposed Constraints

The national governments where the subsidiaries are located can impose a variety of restrictions that make it difficult for the parent to include the subsidiaries in the network. A common restriction is limited access to high-speed communications. Since the telephone infrastructure is frequently owned and operated by the government, not private firms, this can be an effective barrier.

Cultural and Communications Barriers

Interaction with technology can vary greatly among cultures. Global information systems need consistency in the information system interface even as different languages are used. As a result, a GIS relies more heavily on graphics and icons for interactions with users and less upon commands typed into fields.

Cultural barriers also influence the design of a GIS. In some societies, use of technology is considered a menial task while in others it is seen as a sign of importance. The issue of design may be settled by offering multiple formats that yield the same functionality. If a firm decides to establish a GIS it must be willing to adapt its systems to the varied needs of a global population.

RESTRICTIONS ON HARDWARE PURCHASES AND IMPORTS   National governments seek to protect local manufacturers and stimulate foreign investment in local manufacturing by specifying that only equipment produced or assembled in that country is to be used. This requirement can affect the interoperability of different hardware and software systems.

RESTRICTIONS ON DATA PROCESSING   National policy may dictate that data be processed within the country rather than transmitted out of the country and processed elsewhere.

RESTRICTIONS ON DATA COMMUNICATIONS   The most publicized data communications restriction is that put on transborder data flows. **Transborder data flows**, or **TDFs**, are the movements of machine-readable data across national boundaries. TDF legislation, which began in the 1970s, has been enacted by many countries as a way to protect the personal privacy of their citizens.

Technological Problems

MNCs are often plagued with problems related to the level of technology that exists in subsidiary countries. In some countries, reliable power sources are not available, resulting in frequent power outages. Telecommunications circuits often can only transmit data at slow speeds, and the transmission quality may be poor. Software can also be a problem. Because many countries do not honor software copyrights and condone blackmarket software, some software vendors refuse to do business in those countries.

Lack of Support from Subsidiary Managers

The managers of subsidiary offices often are part of the problem. Some are convinced that they can run their subsidiaries without help, and they view headquarters-imposed regulations as unnecessary. Some subsidiary managers are paid based on profitability, and they will drag their feet when they think that corporate solutions will reduce their earnings. Foreign office management can also view the GIS as a "Big Brother" type of surveillance. Middle-level managers may fear being bypassed by the new information links that funnel operational data to the parent.

With all of these potential problems, it is a minor miracle that MNCs ever attempt GISs. Although it is impossible to eliminate the problems completely, their effects can be minimized by following a well-thought-out strategy that is incorporated into the strategic plan for information resources.

PUTTING THE SYSTEM USERS AND INFORMATION SPECIALISTS IN PERSPECTIVE

The human element continues to be the most important ingredient in the development and use of information systems. The main players are the users and the information specialists. Both groups form the development team.

Early systems development was accomplished entirely by the information specialists, but over time the users have played increasingly important roles. Carried to the extreme, users can do all of the development work.

Not only has the development work changed, but the setting in which the work is performed has changed as well. No longer is the organizational setting a physical one, requiring that the work and workers be located in a particular physical location. Electronic communication networks enable firms to achieve a virtual organization, where the work can be done virtually anywhere.

Summary

The classical business organization structure consisting of such areas as finance, human resources, information services, manufacturing, and marketing is a packaging of physical resources. Office automation enabled certain office work to be performed at home—a phenomenon called telecommuting. Then it was realized that all employees did not have to do all of their work at the office; they could come to the office only when necessary. This concept, called hoteling, led to the broader concept of the virtual office, where all kinds of office work can be performed irrespective of physical location. This evolution, in turn, led to the concept of the virtual organization, where many of a firm's operations, not just office work, can be performed irrespective of physical location.

A firm's information specialists and users represent valuable information resources. The specialists include systems analysts, database administrators, and network specialists who work directly with users, and also programmers and operators who are charged with the responsibility of implementing systems to meet the users' needs. Initially, all information specialists were housed in a centralized information services unit. Over time, many of these resources were allocated to the business areas, and led by divisional information officers. Three progressive structures for capturing the organizational relationships between information services and business areas have been proposed. All three make use of networks—a visioning network that enables strategic information planning; an innovation network that ensures the achievement of innovative systems solutions in the business areas; and a sourcing network that makes maximum use of external resources. The three organizational structures are the partner model that involves: (a) IS working with business areas to achieve systems; (b) a platform model where IS provides business areas with the infrastructure so that the areas can develop their own systems; and (c) a scalable model that enables the firm to adjust the level of its information resources to fluctuating business levels.

Although users were restricted in their involvement in systems development during the early years, they gradually gained more influence, which culminated in end-user computing. End-user computing requires that a user be able to perform at least some part of the development effort for his or her system.

Users vary in their degree of computer and information literacy, and these variations, plus others, result in varying degrees of support that are provided by information specialists. When a firm's users are capable of engaging in end-user computing (EUC) they are an especially valuable information resource. EUC enables the matching of capabilities and challenges, and reduces the communications gap. Risks of EUC include poorly aimed systems, poorly designed and documented systems, inefficient use of information resources, loss of data integrity, loss of security, and loss of control.

Anyone who develops systems—user and information specialist alike—must possess certain knowledge and skill. The knowledge includes computer and information literacy, business fundamentals, systems theory, the systems development process, and systems modeling. The skills include communications, analytical ability, creativity, and leadership. The degree to which this knowledge and skill is important varies with the individual, the organization, and the system being developed.

Recognizing the value of knowledge within the organization, many firms have embarked on projects to develop knowledge management systems. This effort is so new that successful strategies have not been proven for all of the challenges that exist. The challenges have been identified and grouped into categories—executive/strategic management; costs, benefits, and risks; operational management; and standards.

Developers of global information systems face challenges that are not present in domestic systems. These challenges consist of politically imposed constraints, and restrictions on hardware purchases and imports, data processing, and data communications.

This chapter concludes the essential concepts relating to management information systems. The remainder of the book will be devoted to a discussion of the information resources and how information and technology can be managed.

KEY TERMS

office automation (OA)
computer literacy

information literacy

knowledge management (KM)

KEY CONCEPTS

- telecommuting
- hoteling
- virtual office

- virtual organization
- the partner, platform, and scalable models of IS organization

- integrating networks—visioning, innovation, sourcing end-user computing

QUESTIONS

1. In the classical business organizational structure, which physical resources are allocated to the various units?
2. Who were the original users of OA? Who were the later users?
3. What phenomenon started the movement toward the virtual office?
4. Name the five guiding principles of hoteling.
5. What are the advantages of the virtual office? What are the disadvantages?
6. Name the information resources.
7. Name the information specialists. Which ones interface directly with the user?
8. What is a visioning network used for? An innovation network? A sourcing network?
9. What are the six activities that IT has responsibility for in the partner model?
10. What is the role of the account manager in the platform model?
11. Which two IT activities have their own sourcing networks in the scalable model?
12. In order for a person to engage in end-user computing, what must he or she do?
13. What are the main benefits of EUC? What are the main risks? How can the risks be minimized?
14. What is the difference between knowledge and skills?
15. What types of knowledge does a firm seek to manage when it embarks on KM?
16. Who imposes constraints on the development of a global information system?

TOPICS FOR DISCUSSION

1. How could a manager use a PDA in a virtual organization?
2. If you were being recruited for a job as information specialist by three firms—one practicing the partner model, one the platform model, and one the scalable model—which one would you rather go to work for?
3. Which is more important for a manager—computer literacy or information literacy?
4. What courses are offered in your school to provide you with the types of systems development knowledge? Address each type separately.
5. Do you agree with the statement that "You are born with certain skills, you do not learn them"?
6. What courses are offered in your school to provide you with the types of systems development skills? Address each skill separately.
7. How could an MNC solve the problem of subsidiary managers who fail to support the firm's programs?

PROBLEMS

1. Read the Nortel article that is identified in footnote 6 and make a table to show what was done to address each of the KM challenges in Table 4.3. Your table should have two columns. The left-hand column should identify the challenge, and the right-hand column should contain a +1 or a −1 for each challenge. Enter a +1 when Nortel addressed the strategy and a −1 when there is no mention of it in the article. Tally up the points. Attach your table to an e-mail message to your instructor, explaining how well you think Nortel addressed the issues.

Case Problem

CYBER U

In this exercise you will apply the concepts of the virtual office to computer lab use on your campus. Most college campuses have computer labs for student use. These labs support course work, are located on campus, have various hours of operation, provide access to printers, provide access to help in using the computers and software, and other elements of education. However, the large majority of students today have access to computers and networks off-campus and in dorms. The question becomes, what economic advantages could be realized if your college campus applied virtual office concepts to the needs of student computing?

You may wish to make a spreadsheet for the comparison so that you can document your estimates and also make changes to gauge the economic effects of changes to your estimates. Make sure you include at least the economic factors listed below.

1. cost of student purchasing a computer and printer
2. cost of student gaining access to the Internet
3. cost of a computer lab (must be multiplied by the number of labs the college supports)
   a. computer hardware costs
   b. computer software costs
   c. cost of lab assistants
   d. cost of printers, paper, and toner cartridges
   e. cost of college support

Make one list for the costs in the current computing situation on your campus and a second list for the costs based on the campus moving to virtual computing for students. In a virtual campus computing scenario the number of computer labs and computers in those labs and hours of lab operations would be greatly reduced. Students would use their computing resources to access the software and files needed for course work. The college might then reduce the cost of fees, especially technology fees.

This exercise is simplistic but should stimulate you to consider if your college costs would actually be lowered if your college adopted more virtual office concepts.

NOTES

[1] Robert Fox, "Telecommuting Loses Appeal," *Communications of the ACM* Volume 44 Issue 9 (September 2001), pp. 9–10.
[2] Joe Sharkey, "When Having a Meeting Is Like Going to a Movie," *New York Times*, September 24, 2002, p. C6.
[3] Taken from Charles Handy, "Trust and the Virtual Organization," *Harvard Business Review*, 73 (May-June, 1995), 40–50.
[4] Material in this section is based on Ritu Agarwal and V. Sambamurthy, "Principles and Models for Organizing the IT Function," *MIS Quarterly Executive* Volume 1, Number 1 (March 2002), pp. 1–16.
[5] William R. King, Peter V. Marks, Jr., and Scott McCoy, "The Most Important Issues in Knowledge Management," *Communications of the ACM* Volume 45 Number 9 (September 2002), pp. 93–97.
[6] This section is based on Anne P. Massey, Mitzi M. Montoya-Weiss, and Tony M. O'Driscoll, "Knowledge Management in Pursuit of Performance: Insights from Nortel Networks," *MIS Quarterly* Volume 26, Number 3 (September 2002), pp. 269–289.

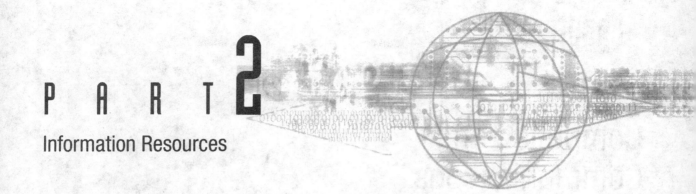

PART 2
Information Resources

Decision making is information in action. The technology of information systems supports the staff member, professional, manager, and anyone else who makes a decision in the organization. The large amount of data and short time frame for making a decision combine to require almost everyone in an organization to utilize information technology resources. Without the ability to effectively use information systems, an organization cannot compete.

Managers need to know how to use current information technology and also the trends in technology. Decision choices are influenced by the data collected and the way the data is processed. Understanding trends in information technology begins with a history and continues to a look into the next five to ten years. Planning for changes in information technology is as important as planning for growth or a changing customer base.

Technological advances in information systems provide a strategic opportunity for an organization to surpass its competitors. Understanding the data resource and the development of information systems is the foundation for achieving those opportunities. Managers must be involved in the development of information systems. Data collected by the organization will be mined and processed to support the business processes. Managerial insight into the decision-making process is crucial for designing effective information systems.

Chapter 5

Computing and Communications Resources

Learning Objectives

After studying this chapter, you should

- Know the components of computers.
- Know about personal computing devices.
- Understand the implications of the rapid advances in information and communication technologies.
- Be familiar with input and output resources.
- Recognize the differences and advantages between storage media.
- Know the advantages of prewritten software.
- Know about different networking strategies between computers.
- Understand the differences between communications over the public telephone system and networks.
- Know about network protocols.
- Distinguish between intranets, extranets, and the Internet.

Introduction

Today, the access to computer hardware and software is bound together by networks. The computer resources you use, whether printers or files, are frequently connected to your computer via a network. Your computer resources are not merely those that sit on your desk; they also include all the hardware and software and files that you can access over a network.

The speed and cost of communications and computer processors impact the use of these resources. Prices continue to drop; in fact, the power of computers doubles about every 18 months for the same prices. Conversely, in 18 months you will be able to buy a computer with today's power for half the cost. Managers tend to use inexpensive resources, so the use of computer and communications can only continue to grow.

The incentive for connecting microcomputers via networks came from the desire for higher profits. Managers who could quickly and easily share computer-based information made better, faster decisions than their competitors. Sharing music and chatting online are fine as a leisure pursuit, but they did not provide the momentum for the enormous amount of networking we see today. Businesses cannot effectively compete without being able to share their computer-based information, and that sharing requires networks.

As you study this chapter, put the change of standards, speed, and costs into perspective. Don't be lulled into a view that it is simply history to be learned for an exam. The standards for adopting new information technology are changing; firms that can look to the future and take advantage of change are the ones that survive in today's economy.

HARDWARE

Computers come in varying speeds and prices, but they all have common features that help us understand their use. The features of interest to us are the processor, memory, storage, and input and output devices (see Table 5.1). All general-purpose computers have the same types of components; larger computers have more and faster components than their microcomputer cousins.

Large computers that perform the bulk of computer operations for centralized information systems are referred to as **mainframe computers** or simply **mainframes**. Mainframes support hundreds or thousands of simultaneous users and operations. **Microcomputers** began as computers used by one person and were called **personal computers** or **PCs**. Today, microcomputers have grown in power and are connected to other computers via the Internet. However, they are still frequently called PCs because they are most often used by a single person who performs only a limited number of simultaneous tasks on the computer.

Processors

The **processor** (also called the **central processing unit** or **CPU**) is where data processing is performed. Intel, American Micro Devices (AMD), Cyrix, Motorola, and other firms manufacture the microprocessors in many popular microcomputers. A processor, such as the one shown in Figure 5.1, controls the calculations and logical comparisons of data. They also direct and control the movement of data from one location within the computer to another. Processor speed and word size combine to increase the power of computing.

Since their first introduction, computers have become less and less expensive. As firms find the costs of using information technology plummet, they use more of this inexpensive resource for decision making.

Table 5.1
Major Computer Components

Component	Description
Processor (central processing unit or CPU)	Controls calculations, controls logical comparisons of data, directs and controls movement of data from one location within the computer to another.
Memory (random access memory or primary storage)	Memory located on the computer's main circuit board called the motherboard. Data in memory is lost when the power to the computer is turned off.
Storage (disk space or secondary storage)	Memory located on a device that is not on the main circuit board. Many types of storage are removable and can be taken from one computer to another. Data in storage is not lost when the power to the computer is turned off. Common storage devices are floppy disks and CDs.
Input devices	A device that captures data by a manual or electronic method and transmits the data to storage or memory. Common input devices are keyboards, mice, and scanners.
Output device	A device that presents and/or transmits data from the computer to the user. Common output devices are computer monitors, printers, CDs, and speakers.
Input/Output devices	A device that can perform both input and output functions. Examples would be a touch-screen monitor and storage disks (such as floppies, Zip disks, and rewritable CDs).

PROCESSOR SPEED Processor speed is measured by the number of cycles that occur per second and it has grown tremendously over the years since IBM introduced its first microcomputer. Speeds were initially expressed as **megahertz (MHz)** for millions of cycles per second. Each cycle is an opportunity for an action such as comparing two characters. The Intel 8088 chip used as the processor for IBM's first microprocessor ran at 4.77 MHz (4.77 million cycles per second). The Intel Pentium 4 chip introduced in 2002 runs at 3.6 gigahertz (GHz) which is 3.6 billion cycles per second. Processor speeds are more than 750 times faster than the original PC processor introduced only 20 years ago.

WORD SIZE The first processors were called "8 bit" machines because eight bits of data made up the size of one "word." A **word** is the measure of how many bits may be moved with one cycle of the processor. A **bit** is a single value of zero or one. Eight bits make up one byte and

Figure 5.1 Intel Pentium 4 Processor

Source: Intel Corporation.

each **byte** can store a single character. For example, the string of eight bits "01000001" represents the letter "A."

Word size is important; it determines how many characters, like the "A" above, can be moved in a single cycle of the processor. The first microcomputers had a word size of eight bits but most of today's microcomputers use a 32-bit word size. So while the early microcomputers could move only a single character with a single cycle, today's microcomputers move four characters with a single cycle. Large, mainframe computers generally have word sizes of 64 and 128 bits.

POWER   The power of computers is affected by both word size and processor speed. Additionally, improvements in processor circuitry are allowing operations (such as addition, comparison of data values, and others) to be performed in fewer cycles. **Moore's Law** states that the power of a computer doubles about every 18 months. It is the combination of processor speed, word size, and circuitry improvement that achieves this remarkable growth of power.

For many people, the power growth is difficult to comprehend. Two examples will help you to understand how increased computer power has affected and will affect your life. First, the power of the first personal computer introduced by IBM was greater than the power of most mainframe computers in 1973 when Neil Armstrong was the first man to walk on the moon. Second, computer power purchased by your company for $1 million the day you start work will cost less than $1 when you retire. As the price of information technology falls we use more information technology to aid decision making, and that changes the way managers solve problems.

Memory

Data is stored in a computer in basically two ways—memory and storage. **Memory**, also called **primary storage, or random access memory (RAM)**, refers to the storage area on the computer's circuit board. Figure 5.2 depicts a circuit board. Memory is **volatile** because the contents of memory are lost when the power is turned off. This fleeting characteristic reflects that the value of bits can be changed as swiftly as processor cycles allow. Memory in a computer is extremely fast compared to accessing data on a storage device.

The amount of memory in a microcomputer can have significant impact on the user's perception of its speed. Microcomputers commonly have 128 to 256 megabytes (MB) of memory.

Highlights in MIS

BLUE GENE

Microcomputer power is not the only computing power to grow; mainframe power is also making great leaps. IBM has announced it is creating two supercomputers for the Department of Energy[1] whose combined power will be greater than the combined power of the current 500 fastest supercomputers. The computers, to be finished in 2005, are being named Blue Gene/L.

These new computer architectures are moving toward petaflops—one thousand trillion cycles per second. Machines of this speed are expected to be constructed before 2010. These amazing speeds are to be achieved by harnessing the power of an array of high speed microprocessors. The second Blue Gene/L will harness 12,000 of IBM's Power 5 microprocessor chips.

The Earth Simulator, currently the fastest computer, was developed by NEC. It functions at about 35 trillion cycles per second. With the extreme power of these supercomputers, scientists hope to model world climate conditions and similarly difficult problems.

Figure 5.2
Microcomputer Circuit Board, Also Known As a Motherboard

Source: Intel Corporation Museum. Photo courtesy of Intel Corporation.

Many microcomputers can accommodate 2 gigabytes (2 billion bytes) of memory. A table of byte, megabyte, gigabyte, terabyte, and petebyte conversions is presented in Table 5.2.

Memory can be thought of as the work space used by the processor. As an example, assume that, as you study, you are the processor. You read data from books and notes, perform mental analysis of the data, and write your conclusions on a piece of paper. You are manually performing the functions that a processor performs electronically. The memory available to the microcomputer is similar to the amount of desk space you can use when you study. If you had no room on your desk you might have to keep your books in another place—on the floor or even in another room. Every time you need to read another paragraph you would have to get up from your desk, go to where the books and notes were located, read from the books and notes only as much data as can fit into your memory, and then go back to your desk to process that data.

Having the data in an open book on your desk is much more efficient than having to get up and find the book in another room. In the same way, having the data in memory is more efficient for the processor to access and utilize. Memory has become more abundant and faster in order to keep up with the more powerful processors. Table 5.3 briefly defines several types of memory.

Storage

Storage for computers comes in the form of many different media, with each having different characteristics that make it better suited for certain tasks. Although the media types vary from large computers to small, the types have similar characteristics.

Table 5.2

Conversion from Bits to Bytes and Further

1 bit	=	a single value of 0 or 1
8 bits	=	1 byte = 1 character
2^{10} bytes	=	1,024 bytes = 1 kilobyte (1 KB)
2^{20} bytes	=	1 KB × 1 KB = 1,048,576 bytes = 1 megabyte (1 MB)
2^{30} bytes	=	1,073,741,824 bytes = 1 gigabyte (1 GB)
2^{40} bytes	=	1,099,511,627,776 bytes = 1 terabyte (1 TB)
2^{50} bytes	=	1,125,899,906,842,624 bytes = 1 petebyte (1 PB)

Table 5.3

Type	Definition
Brief Definitions of Different Memory Types	
RAM	Random access memory, the type of memory most people mean when they use the term *memory*. Computer programs and data are loaded into RAM to be executed by the computer processor.
ROM	Read-only memory cannot be changed by the user and is unaffected by turning off the power. ROM holds information used by the operating system and processor when the computer is started.
DRAM	Dynamic RAM, allows some buffering of data (temporary storage while bits are being moved about the processor) and increases the efficiency of RAM.
SDRAM	Synchronous DRAM, runs much faster than most conventional memory because it synchronizes its cycles with the processor's cycles.
SIMM	Single in-line memory module that holds a set of 9 memory chips (only 8 for Macintosh personal computers) where the 9th chip is used for error checking. Transmits 32 bits of data per cycle.
DIMM	Dual in-line memory module, transmits 64 bits per data cycle.

Storage permanently installed in the computer is referred to as "fixed." An example is the fixed hard drive of your microcomputer. Removable storage media usually take the form of a tape, a disk (also known as a diskette), a Zip disk, a CD, or some other portable medium. The computer hardware that reads from and writes to the medium is a **drive**. Media and the drives that use them have become so closely associated that the words are used synonymously by many computer users.

FIXED STORAGE   Fixed storage (sometimes called the **hard drive**) refers to storage that is permanently installed in the computer. Figure 5.3 illustrates a fixed storage disk. Microcomputers frequently come with 80 GB (80 gigabytes) for storage. Mainframes have terabytes and even petabytes of storage space—thousands of times the storage available on a microcomputer.

There is some debate as to whether the microcomputer users need such large amounts of storage space, especially when so much storage capability can be accessed via a network. But audio files, video files, and images require large amounts of storage space and these file

Figure 5.3 **Fixed Disk for Data Storage**

Source: Western Digital Corporation.

types are increasingly popular. When the price difference between a 5 GB hard drive and an 80 GB hard drive is $25, many people feel the larger amount of storage is too inexpensive to refuse.

REMOVABLE STORAGE   Removable storage can be removed from one computer and inserted in another. Table 5.4 lists popular removable disks and their storage capacities.

Three types of **high capacity media** deserve attention; Zip disks, compact disks (CDs), and digital versatile discs (DVDs). **Zip disks**, and their corresponding drives, were developed by the Iomega Corporation. They are popularly referred to as "removable" disks to differentiate them from "floppy" disks. The main advantage of Zip disks is that they store so much data that they can be effectively used as backup media for an individual's microcomputer. Zip disks hold 100 MB, 250 MB, or even 750 MB of data, depending on the model of Zip drive that is used. Users can read from and write to a Zip disk.

CDs for microcomputers originally held data that could only be read; data could not be written to them. This was a very good format for distributing software. Later, a medium called **CD-R** (for "CD-recordable") became available. It allowed users to record CDs if they had a CD writer drive and used CD-R media. The problem was that CD-R media can be recorded once and only once. You cannot rewrite to the CD-R media like you can with a floppy disk.

Then **CD-RW** for "CD rewritable" became available in 1997[2] and allowed microcomputer users with a special write-capable CD drive to write data onto the CD multiple times. The CD-RW media can take multiple recordings just like a floppy disk. Files can be read from, deleted from, and added to a CD-RW disk.

CDs hold up to 650 MB of data and data transfer speeds from the CD to the processor can reach almost five million bits per second. The large amount of data that can be quickly transferred makes CDs popular for loading software and other large programs.

DVDs hold from 5 GB to 20 GB of data and they also became available in 1997.[3] Their large storage capacity allows microcomputer users to view videos and movies on their computer. While this seems somewhat frivolous now, it may not seem so in the future. Computer users have shown an insatiable appetite for processor speed, memory, and storage space. Images require enormous amounts of storage space and are becoming increasingly important in communication. Such high-capacity DVDs hold much promise for the delivery of interactive video to microcomputer users for training and other communications purposes.

Input Devices

Computers would not be very useful without input and output devices. Business operations require enormous amounts of data input and output, and devices were developed to meet those needs. While many input and output devices are available, a relatively few have gained wide acceptance.

Human-captured data refers to input captured by a person typing on a keyboard, clicking a mouse, touching a monitor, speaking into a microphone, or a similar interaction. Figures 5.4, 5.5, and 5.6 depict human-captured input. Human-captured input is very impor-

Table 5.4

Removable Disks and Their Storage Capacities

3 ½ inch floppy disk holds 1.44 MB of data

Zip disk (developed by Iomega Corp.) may hold 100 MB, 250 MB, or 750 MB of data depending on the model of Zip drive used

CD disks hold approximately 650 MB of data

DVD disks hold from 5 to 20 GB of data

Figure 5.4 Computer Keyboard

Source: Getty Images, Inc.

Figure 5.5 Computer Mouse

Source: Microsoft Corporation. Reprinted with permission from Microsoft Corporation.

tant because it provides a direct mechanism for the user to control the computer. Much needed data is not originally in a machine-readable form and human entry of the data is necessary.

There are two constraints to human-captured data. It is slow and it generally does not achieve the very high level of accuracy of machine-captured data.

A significant machine-readable event occurred when businesses were required to place a **bar code** on every product sold.[4] The bar code appears to a person as a sequence of vertical lines, some fatter and some thinner than others. By governmental decree all items sold in the United States are required to display this code and the code encapsulates the industry,

Figure 5.6 Touch Screen Monitor

Source: Stock Boston, © Bob Daemmrich.

business, and product identity all the way down to whether it is a can or plastic bottle. Each unique product has its own unique code. Scanners can read the bar code extremely quickly and pass the data to a computer. The error rate for scanners is extremely low.

Point-of-sale terminals are a particular type of scanner used in retail stores. They interact with a computer in the store that processes the product information to determine price, change inventory levels to reflect the sale, and other actions. The computer can note when a minimal inventory level has been met and electronically order more of the product from a vendor. The real importance of point-of-sale terminals is not their technological sophistication, but their widespread use and impact on the retail sales industry.

It may seem that machine-captured data is better than human-captured data because computers capture data at less cost. This is true but it is not the compelling reason. Businesses require large amounts of accurate data for their decision-making processes. The compelling reasons for machine-captured data are the speed and accuracy of the data capture process. Lower cost is simply an added benefit.

Output Devices

Two of the most familiar output devices are the computer **screen**, sometimes called the **monitor**, and the **printer**. Although there has been much attention to the concept of a "paperless office," printed output is a fact of computing.[5]

The images on a computer screen are greatly affected by **screen resolution**. Screen resolution refers to the number of **pixels**, individual dots of light on the monitor, that are presented. Today, resolutions of 1600×1200 and greater are common. That means there are 1,600 dots on each of 1,200 lines on the screen. The high resolution of computer screens allows the practical use of enough **icons** (symbols that represent an action to be performed by the computer) so that the **graphical user interface** (GUI, pronounced "gooey") has become the dominant interface.

The monitor sizes are measured along the diagonal of the screen. Monitors with 17- and 19-inch diagonals are common with most current popular computers. The difference may not seem like much in inches but a 17-inch monitor displays over 70 percent more information than a 13-inch monitor. Flat panel monitors take up much less space on a user's desk but cost about $200 more than the price of a traditional monitor (see Figures 5.7 and 5.8).

Printers have experienced advances similar to monitors. The key characteristics of printer change are resolution for printing, the speed of printing, and color. Common printers today use either laser or ink-jet technologies. **Laser printers** are essentially copier machines, whereas **ink-jet printers** spray ink onto the surface of the paper.

Figure 5.7 **Standard Computer Monitor**

Source: *ViewSonic Corporation.*

Figure 5.8 **Flat Panel Computer Monitor**
Source: Getty Images, Inc.

The advantages of ink-jet printers are that they are mechanically small and generally lower in cost than laser printers. Ink-jet printers have a practical advantage over laser printers in that they can produce color output at a relatively low cost. Common, inexpensive ink-jet printers produce about 15 black and white pages per minute. Color printing is about half the speed of black and white printing. The resolution of printing is generally 300 to 1,200 dots per inch.

The resolution of many laser printers is also generally 1,200 dots per inch. Color laser printers have speeds of about 20 pages per minute while models that print only black and white copies may print 50 pages per minute. There are significant differences in the speed and resolution of printing among printer models. Cost is the main factor. Whereas fast, color laser printers may cost as much as $4,000, a color ink-jet printer may cost as little as $100.

Multimedia

The main evolution of input and output devices is in the direction of **multimedia**, or the use of more than a single medium at a time. For example, information in text form may be projected onto the computer screen accompanied by an image or video. Users don't just type commands; they use a pointing device such as a mouse or speak into a microphone to choose an icon that, in turn, causes the computer to operate on the screen's message. The touch of the keyboard or mouse, the spoken input, the sight of the screen images, and the sound from the speakers combine to provide a wealth of input and output possibilities.

A significant portion of today's computer users would be denied access to computer-based information systems if multimedia were not available. A number of users are illiterate, function at a low level of literacy, or are physically impaired. Children and marginally literate adults need the multimedia capabilities of computers in order to effectively use the resource. Sounds, such as voice communications for instruction and user input, and video images are important for computer interaction with these groups of computer users. Animated images moving from one step to another, possibly with a voice in the background explaining the images, can provide education to this group of users. Multimedia capabilities expand the community capable of meaningful interaction with computing resources.

PERSONAL COMPUTING DEVICES

Personal computing has long been associated with microcomputers. In fact, microcomputers were initially called personal computers. Microcomputers were not networked together when they first appeared; every microcomputer user used the resource only for his or her personal

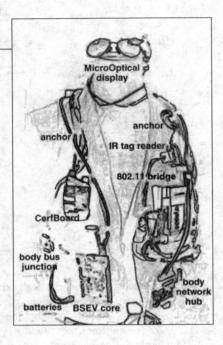

Figure 5.9 Wearable Computing Devices from the MIThril Research Project Underway at the Massachusetts Institute of Technology Media Lab

computing. Now individual users of a microcomputer can share files, printers, and other resources when connected by a network.

Today, **personal computing** is being reassociated with devices that are more personal to the user. **Handheld PCs, pocket PCs, tablet PCs, personal digital assistants**, and cell phones with **interactive messaging** capabilities are the new tools of personal computing. Even wearable computing devices like those in Figure 5.9 are beginning to appear.

Understanding more about these devices will help you see how they can change business decision making. Some features that make them especially desirable for personal computing are long battery life between recharging, wireless network access, ability to synchronize data files with other computer resources, and a small but functional display screen.

Tablets, Handheld and Pocket PCs

These **personal computing devices** (Figure 5.10) are rapidly coming together as a single product. Almost all use a version of Microsoft word processing, presentation, and spreadsheet software. Internet browser software, calendars, e-mail, and other software also come with these devices.

These devices allow users great flexibility for personal productivity. Users can work on the computer at their office desk and then transfer work to one of these personal computing devices. Battery life is not a constraint because these devices have battery lives lasting from 15 hours to several days. Once work is done, the users can upload the new and/or revised files to their desktop computers using either a device that connects the personal computing device to the computer or via a wireless network.

The key feature of these products is mobility. Each is manufactured with wireless network computing in mind. **Notebook computers** (also called **laptops**) are mobile but they are still bulky. The tablet PC[6] is the heaviest personal computing device at about 3 pounds, about half the weight of a light notebook computer. Handhelds weigh about one pound while pocket PCs weigh around eight ounces.

Figure 5.10 Examples of Personal Computing Devices: (a) Compaq Tablet PC-TC100 series; (b) iPAQ Pocket PC-h5450 Series; (c) Revo by Psion.

Source: (a) and (b) Hewlett-Packard Co; (c) Psion, PLC.

Personal Digital Assistants

Personal digital assistants, generally called **PDAs**, are devices that perform some computing but mainly personal organization tasks. Calendars, contact lists, and notes are features most people associate with their PDAs. Figure 5.11 shows some of the popular brands. The devices are pocket size and have battery lives that may last days or months without being recharged.

Figure 5.11 Examples of Popular Personal Digital Assistants: (a) Palm m500 PDA; (b) Handspring Visor Pro; (c) Blackberry Wireless Handheld Devices

Source: (a) PhotoEdit; (b) Handspring, Inc.; (c) Steve Marcus/Reuters Corbis Bettman.

Palm (WWW.PALM.COM) and Handspring (WWW.HANDSPRING.COM) are the two most popular vendors of PDAs with Palm being the most frequently sold brand. The devices include viewers for word processing, spreadsheet, and presentation files. The PDAs do not allow users to create or modify such documents, only to view the documents.

Another PDA, the BlackBerry,[7] gained its popularity by being one of the first PDAs to effectively utilize seamless communications roaming across the United States, Europe, and Asia. Research in Motion (WWW.RIM.COM) offers a number of models of the BlackBerry. Another BlackBerry feature that is popular is the small keyboard on the device. Many BlackBerry users prefer to press the keys using their stylus rather than tapping on a letter typically displayed on other PDA screens.

Cell Phones with Interactive Messaging

The distinction between cell phones and PDAs is becoming blurred. Popular cell phone manufacturers (Samsung, Nokia, Ericsson, and others) build an ability into their phones to display text messages and small images on their display screen. The phone's keypad becomes the input device, although some users find scrolling through the values on the phone's keypad to be tedious. However, the cell phone has rudimentary computing capacity and its keypad and display screen act as input and output devices.

Cell phones acting as terminals may be the next step for their computing capabilities. The cell phone connects you to a powerful computer. The only limitations of the cell phone are those restrictions relating to input and output.

SOFTWARE

There are two basic types of software—system and application. System software is required to use the computer, whereas application software processes the user's data. Application software can be obtained in a prewritten form or produced in a custom fashion for a particular user.

System Software

System software performs certain fundamental tasks that all users of a particular computer require. These are tasks that relate to the hardware and not to the applications that the firm performs. It is impossible to use a modern computer without using some of its system software. System software is usually prepared by the manufacturer of the hardware (the hardware vendor, or supplier) or by a firm that specializes in producing software (a software vendor, or supplier).

The **operating system** manages the computer's processes, functioning as an interface connecting the user, the application software, and the hardware. Examples of operating systems for microcomputers are Windows XP and Mac OS. Operating systems for smaller computers typically run on more than one manufacturer's processor, whereas the operating system for a large mainframe computer, such as IBM's OS/390, is proprietary and not shared with other computer manufacturers. UNIX is an unusual operating system in that versions run on both microcomputers and mainframes.

All computers have operating systems, but the systems vary in the number of basic functions and in how the functions are performed. The operating system of a mainframe is much more complex than that of a single-user microcomputer because the mainframe must coordinate the operations of many input and output devices, as well as handle many simultaneous users.

A **utility program**, often simply called a **utility**, is an operating system routine that enables the user to perform certain basic data processing operations that are not unique to a particular user's applications. Utilities enable users to copy files, erase files, sort the contents of files, merge two or more files together, and prepare (format) storage media for use.

Other utilities allow the computer operations manager to recover lost or corrupted files, monitor the performance of the system, and even control the flow of data between users and computers.

Application Software

When the first computers were developed, there were no programming languages. Programmers would load a series of zeros and ones into the memory of the computer to control its operations. This was extremely time-consuming, especially because many of the tasks to be performed were focused around such similar needs as finding a data record and moving its contents to memory. **Translators**, programming languages that translate the programmers' instructions into zeros and ones used by the computer, were developed to provide a more friendly way to instruct the computer. COBOL, C and C++, Java, and Visual Basic are a few examples of programming languages.

A **fourth generation language (4GL)** is one that expresses what is to be done by the computer without explicitly defining how the tasks will take place. For example, a spreadsheet software package may contain built-in capabilities to calculate the net present value of an amount of money to be paid at some future date based upon a given interest rate. In spreadsheet software such as Excel, the user simply provides the name of the built-in function that calculates net present value. Statistical packages such as SAS and SPSS allow users to accomplish sophisticated mathematical manipulations of data using computer resources without having to program the computer for those calculations. 4GL software has made the power of computing resources much more accessible to managers.

PREWRITTEN APPLICATION SOFTWARE   Some information processing tasks are so highly standardized that they function the same way from one business to the next. Software can be prewritten for these situations. Tax calculations, accounting for payroll, depreciation of fixed assets, and many other business transactions are standard. Because these and other such activities see widespread use, a great variety of prewritten application packages have been written. **Prewritten application software**, sometimes called **off-the-shelf software**, is produced by suppliers and sold to users. Users can utilize software developed by experienced programmers without either hiring the programmers or learning how to program themselves.

The users need only to install the software on their hardware, with little or no modification, in order to use it. The software generally allows the user to make small adjustments that help tailor the software to the user's needs. Prewritten software has two very important benefits:

- Prewritten software is available now. The business does not have to wait three weeks or six months for programmers to develop it.
- Prewritten software is less expensive than custom software.

All businesses know that any product development has both fixed and variable costs. Since the fixed cost of development is so high for most application software, compared to the variable costs of marketing and distributing the software, the final cost to a business for using prewritten software is modest because the development costs are spread among so many users. Prewritten application software is very attractive for smaller businesses with a limited number of employees available to write computer programs.

CUSTOM APPLICATION SOFTWARE   There are occasions when a business organization has operations that are unique. In these cases, the business might have its own programmers or a consulting group of programmers write the application software to meet its needs. Such software is called **custom application software**.

Far less custom written software is created today than in the 1960s and 1970s when computers were becoming popular in business. The cost of computing resources has fallen to the point where a very well equipped microcomputer can be purchased for less than $2,000.

However, application programmers routinely earn $60,000 to $80,000 per year.[8] Unless the firm has a unique business need, custom application software can be difficult to justify in economic terms.

The Role of User Friendly Software

Computer software that is simple and intuitive to use is frequently said to be **user friendly**. The term may elicit a negative connotation in that it implies that the application has been made very simplistic so that anyone can use it. Actually, user friendly means that the application has been carefully engineered so that the varied talents and skills of a wide range of users can be accommodated. It is far more difficult to make software "user friendly" than to make it "programmer friendly."

Business users have expertise in their business area of purchasing, manufacturing, sales, finance, or another area. Widespread use of computer-based resources is achieved when the application software is designed so that these users can apply their business expertise using the computer without special training. *Widespread use is the key.*

Computer-based resources can play a role in the tasks of most office workers from entry level clerks to the chief executive officer. A friendly interface to tap into the computer-based resources means that more data will be used to make better decisions. Here is a list of the characteristics of user friendly applications:

User Friendly Characteristics

1. Guided dialogue to direct the user concerning what data is needed, the data format, and similar issues
2. Menus, step-down lists of commands, and icons: these multiple ways to accomplish the same task provide guidance to novice users while at the same time allowing more proficient users to take shortcuts to task achievement
3. Templates and fill-out forms
4. Context sensitive help: helpful information should be provided to the specific spot where the user is having difficulty, this means the computer program must keep track of where in the application the user's specific request is originating
5. Graphical interface using standardized symbols: users should not be expected to learn new icons as each application is written, a standardization of the use of icons, their location on the interface, and their meaning must exist among a wide variety of applications

COMMUNICATIONS—PUBLIC TELEPHONE SYSTEM

The speed of data transmission between computers that takes place over public telephone systems is most often slower than when the computers are connected through their own networks. The wire making the connections is the same, yet most computer networks operate hundreds of times faster than connections routed through the public telephone system. The reason is that the protocols for the public telephone system communications were established for voice grade communication and the quality and speed of communication lines did not need to be high. A **protocol** is the specification for formatting data to be transferred between communications equipment.

Public Connections

Computers need extremely reliable connections but the humans who use the telephone system can understand communications even when the line has static or a humming noise. Protocols for the public telephone system were established to meet the minimum criteria of voice transmissions—low grade analog transmissions—and that quality for voice communications is significantly below the needs of computer data transmission. The digital signals of computers and their high speeds are beyond the original intent of telephone protocols.

Telephone modems connect most home computers to the Internet. While their speeds increased rapidly during the 1980s, the current 56 Kbps (56 thousand bits per second) is their speed limit for communication. The theoretic limit for data transmission for a standard telephone line is 64 Kbps but because of technical requirements for administering the transmission, telephone modems have a top transmission speed of 56 Kbps. See Table 5.5.

Digital protocols were introduced to the telephone system in the 1980s but did not become popular until the 1990s when the demand for computer connections from homes increased. Digital data communications, as opposed to voice communications, use packets. A **packet** is a piece of the total data to be communicated, combined with the address of the destination computer, the sending computer, and other control information. Packets will be discussed in more detail later in the chapter.

Integrated Services Digital Network (ISDN) and **Digital Subscriber Line (DSL)** protocols provide standards for transmitting data at speeds from 1.5 Mbps to 32 Mbps (32 million bits per second) over standard telephone lines.

Cable modems actually connect to the Internet via the coaxial cable that is common for receiving cable television. Cable modems generally reach a speed of 2 Mbps. However, actual speeds sometimes reach only 512 Kbps. Speed of transmission is not just dependent upon the technical capability of the cable modem but also the speed limit that the cable company wishes to enforce. The maximum transmission capacity of most cable modems is 11 Mbps but few cable companies allow that speed.

Table 5.5
Connecting to the Internet

CONNECTION	SPEED	DESCRIPTION
Telephone modem	56 Kbps	Device to connect computers over standard telephone lines.
Cable modem	2 Mbps (warning, see description)	Device that connects to the coaxial cable provided by a cable TV provider to a computer for Internet access. Speeds of these modems vary greatly with 2 Mbps being a frequently published speed advertised by the cable TV providers. However, 11 Mbps is the capability of most currently available cable modems although providers usually limit the communications speed to the customer to 2 Mbps and sometimes to 512 Kbps.
Integrated services digital network (ISDN)	128 Kbps to 1.5 Mbps	A connection using standard telephone lines as separate channels communicating at 64 Kbps each. The channels are bundled together so that the "basic" bundle of two channels results in the 128 Kbps communications rate. The most frequent bundling is 23 lines which results in a communications rate of 1.5 Mbps.
digital subscriber line (DSL)	32 Mbps	Technology similar to ISDN but more sophisticated in taking advantage of the communications speed capabilities of the telephone line. Newer versions, xDSL, can achieve speeds up to 52 Mbps

Kbps = thousands of bits per second
Mbps = millions of bits per second

The data transmission speeds described above are all for the "last mile," the link from the computer in your home to the first telephone company station or to the cable company. The data transmission capacity and speed between pieces of telephone equipment has also increased. Without its increase, improvements in "last mile" communications would be of little value.

Frame relays take advantage of the high quality communications achieved with fiber optics. Once the reliability of fiber optics was established, the need for slow protocols that tracked the sending and receiving of data from each piece of telephone equipment to the next was eliminated. **Asynchronous transfer mode (ATM)** technology offers two characteristics that improve data transmission rates. First, the size of the packet communicated is smaller than with earlier protocols for telephone systems, making it possible for packets from different users passing along the network at the same time to be more evenly intermixed. ATM's second characteristic is its speed, from 25 Mbps to 155 Mbps. In fact, ATM devices can bundle up to 16 channels together to achieve a transfer rate of almost 2.5 billion bits per second.

Private Lines

Communication requires a connection from one point to another. The possible paths across a network are numerous. Think of driving 20 people from one building to another building across town. If there are four people to a car then it would require five cars—five packets—to get the entire group across town. Each car has the address it needs to go to and each car can take a different path across the network of roads to reach the building across town. As each car (or packet) travels the network it has to stop for red lights at various points.

What if there is an arrangement to keep an open path from the first building to the building across town? What if the arrangement keeps the path, the sequence of roads, open to only the cars traveling to the other building? The path that is always open—always connected—is called a **circuit**.

A **private line** is a circuit that is always open to your communication traffic. The terms **leased line** and **dedicated line** are also used. The private line dedicated to your use is provided by the common carrier, the telephone company. Your organization pays a fixed monthly fee for the use of the line and so the more use the line receives, the smaller the per-unit data cost. Intuitively, it is as if the telephone company ran a wire directly from your firm to the destination.

Two types of private lines are popular—T-1 lines and T-3 lines. A **T-1 line**, sometimes called a **T-1** channel, has a maximum transmission speed of just over 1.5 Mbps. A **T-3 line** can transfer data at 43 Mbps. The T-1 and T-3 lines are actually collections of 64 Kbps connections between the two pieces of telephone communications equipment. Since they are collections of 64 Kbps connections, the T-1 and T-3 lines can be **multiplexed**, broken into separate lanes of communication, like dividing a highway into multiple lanes. T-1 lines are frequently used by business organizations with a high amount of data communications traffic, but T-3 lines are generally used by Internet service providers.

Virtual Private Network

Private lines are expensive, at least in comparison to Internet connections. Private lines have more security since your organization's data is the only data on the communication line, and they have more speed than secure Internet transmissions. The higher speed is due to the fact that the authentication of the message sent using the Internet is checked at multiple points as telephone equipment passes the message through multiple links of the network. What if you could achieve the security and speed of a private line by using the low cost Internet network?

Virtual private networks (VPNs)[9,10] are the answer to the question. An organization needs to use an Internet service provider that uses tunneling software. Microsoft and Cisco Systems, a major vendor of communications hardware and associated software, both support tunneling software and most major ISPs accommodate tunneling. **Tunneling software** simply establishes the set of intermediary locations of the telephone equipment that will host a given data communications transfer. Tunneling is conceptually similar to establishing a private circuit for the few milliseconds it takes to send the data.

Privacy is attained because the tunnel is not established unless the sending and receiving computers authenticate one another. Speed is attained because once the sending and receiving computers establish authenticity there is no reason for authenticity checks by each separate piece of telephone equipment as the network moves each packet of data along the communications medium. Low cost is achieved because the company is not paying for a dedicated, private communications line to each end point.

The cost savings of VPNs are particularly important when secure data transfers are required between multiple destinations. The traditional private line connects the same two end points (the same two computers) all the time. A virtual private network is established for each pair of computers and the pair may change from one transmission to another. VPNs are a secure, fast, and inexpensive connection between organizations.

Highlights in MIS

THE IMPACT OF WIRELESS NETWORKS—CONVENIENT BUT VULNERABLE

Wireless networks are popular and their popularity is growing. One area of rapid growth has been wireless networks to distribute access to a single high-speed Internet connection. Many people with cable modems and more than one computer in their home use a wireless network so that the speed of the cable modem can be utilized by all the computers in the home.

"Kits" can be purchased from electronics stores and many microcomputer vendors to set up a home wireless network very easily and for a small amount of money. This is especially attractive to many college students. Assume you have an apartment and three other roommates and all four of you have your own computer. You have a cable modem and you want to share its speed. The solution is simple; buy a wireless network access point (usually a router) and get a wireless network card for each microcomputer. Now everyone in your apartment can share the speed of the cable modem and the telephone line won't be tied up.

It sounds too good to be true. There are a few problems that you should know about. First, the "kits" sold by many electronics stores and microcomputer vendors are configured with standard settings so that they will be simple to install. This is good for the setup but not so good for you. Imagine that everyone in a neighborhood has the same garage door opener code. The same analogy applies to the standard settings to let computers with wireless network cards link to the wireless network access point.

These access points are "self detecting," which means they are continuously searching for any new wireless network card, and when one is detected it is added to the network. While you may think this is great when one roommate moves out and another moves in, what happens when someone moves into the apartment next door? The radio frequency signals pass through your apartment walls for about 100 meters. A neighbor with a wireless network card could be detected and picked up by your wireless access point. Without sharing the cost of the cable modem or the access point, the neighbor enjoys the high speed access to the Internet at your expense.

This may merely annoy you, but implications for a firm are more serious. A franchised pharmacy chain may have many stores. Each store may have a single high-speed communications line for the business transactions it must process. In order to share the high-speed communications line, the firm might use a wireless network within the store. At least, the manager thinks it is shared only within the store. Actually the wireless network spills out to the sidewalk, the parking lot, and even to adjoining buildings.

What happens if sensitive information from the network is captured by someone outside the store? What if the pharmacy records are accessed by someone outside the store? What responsibility, legal and moral, does the store have to safeguard the information? Business operations can be vulnerable to eavesdropping on wireless networks. It is the responsibility of the firm to take precautions to make wireless networks private to authorized users.

Table 5.6
Open Systems Interconnect (OSI) Reference Model

Layer	Name	Purpose
7	Application layer	Perform application-to-application communication
6	Presentation layer	Manage data representation conversions
5	Session layer	Establish and maintain communication channel
4	Transport layer	Guarantee end-to-end integrity of data transmission
3	Network layer	Route data from one network address to another
2	Data link layer	Move data from one network address to another
1	Physical layer	Put data onto and off of the network media

Communications—Networks

The International Organization for Standardization (WWW.ISO.CH) was founded in 1946 and it established the **Open Systems Interconnection (OSI)** standard architecture for network connections. OSI consists of a seven-layer model shown in Table 5.6. The levels are detailed so that the exact function for each layer of communication can be plainly defined. In current communications technology, two or more levels may be accomplished by a single piece of communications hardware.

In addition to the standard for the network architecture, a protocol is needed. As we stated earlier in the chapter, a **protocol** is a specification of the format for the data transmitted between communications devices. Once standards for communications networks have been established and protocols for data transfer are instituted the rewards of information technology can be widely shared.

Protocols for Computer Communication

Computers were not initially designed to share data with other computers, only with terminals. A **terminal** is a device that has no storage or processor; it simply provides a means for entering and displaying data for the computer. IBM recognized this communication limitation as a problem, especially since it wanted to sell multiple computers to a company. In response to the communications limitation, IBM and others began developing communications protocols.

Protocols can be proprietary, which means the data formatting specifications are owned by the company that developed them. Other protocols are "open." An **open protocol** is a format whose specifications are open to the public and allowed to be used without cost. Open protocols are favored for popular communications conduits such as the Internet.

SYSTEM NETWORK ARCHITECTURE (SNA)   IBM established System Network Architecture (SNA)[11] as a proprietary protocol in 1974 and the protocol is designed for large computers, not for microcomputers. SNA requires a main, host computer that polls other computers connected by the network in a sequence, much like taking turns. If a polled computer has data to communicate, then the data is transferred, otherwise the next computer is polled. SNA requires firms to purchase additional hardware to control communications.

TOKEN RING   IBM recognized that not all customers could or would pay the additional cost of controller hardware. The company began to develop a proprietary protocol that would not rely on a host computer to control the communications to other computers but that would treat other computers as peers. The **peer-to-peer protocol** allows each computer to

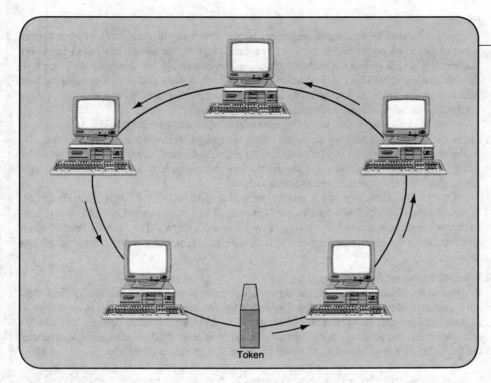

Figure 5.12 Token Ring Protocol Example

act as its own controller. IBM named its new peer-to-peer protocol **Token Ring** because a logical token is passed among the peer computers and the computer with the token is the computer that is allowed to control communications. Figure 5.12 illustrates a Token Ring network.

ETHERNET   Xerox developed a different peer-to-peer communications architecture in the early 1970s and, working in cooperation with Intel and Digital Equipment Corporation, released Ethernet. **Ethernet**[12] is an open protocol for peer-to-peer communications. The Ethernet standard is not proprietary and is presently overseen by a professional society, the Institute of Electrical and Electronics Engineers (IEEE). Unlike IBM's Token Ring, Ethernet works from a single transmission line. No token is passed that establishes which peer computer controls the communications medium. Instead, if a peer computer wishes to send data on the communications medium it simply checks to see if data is currently being transmitted. If not, the computer sends the message.

If two peer computers try to send data at the same time a **data transmission crash** occurs, with the data from each computer being mixed up with data communicated by the other computers. The data sent by each computer is lost in the crash but the data loss on the communications line does not remove the data from each computer's storage. Each peer computer that sends data will wait for a signal from the receiving computer to verify that the data arrived safely. Lacking a proper reply, as when data is lost in a data transmission crash, the sending computer merely resends the data. This strategy works well for most peer-to-peer connections since the capacity of the network is typically far greater than the amount of data likely to be passed between computers on the network.

Packets

The volume of data being communicated can become large and this is a problem when control is not enforced by a host computer. For large data transfers, the messages need to be broken into smaller pieces so that the message from one computer does not dominate the communications medium. This is accomplished with data packets. A **data packet** is a piece of the total data to be communicated, combined with the address of the destination computer, the sending computer, and other control information.

Networks may have one, ten, or even hundreds of possible routes through the communications media that connect the communicating computers. Just as there are many routes for someone to drive a car from Miami to Los Angeles, individual packets may take different routes. The packets are collected at the destination, put into proper sequence, and checked to ensure that all packets in the message have arrived.

One of the more important packet switching protocols is **TCP/IP** that stands for **Transmission Control Protocol/Internet Protocol**. The Transmission Control Protocol conducts communications over the network between two computers. The Internet Protocol handles the packet issues so that they can be routed between computers on the communications network.

Internet Network Addresses

In order to route packets through the network, each computer handling packets of data must have a unique address. When routing packets on the Internet, the **IP address** is used. The IP address is a four-part set of numbers (each from 0 to 255), separated by periods. The address parts designate the network, host, subnetwork, and computer being addressed. For example, the IP address for the University of North Carolina at Wilmington is 152.20.1.3.

Most users in a firm are linked to networks through a permanently assigned address. Users at home generally access networks using an Internet service provider (ISP). The user connects to the ISP using the public telephone system. What remains to be done is to temporarily assign an Internet address to the home user so that communications from the network reach the correct user. That address is one of many owned by the ISP and the home user simply uses the IP address only as long as he or she is connected to the Internet.

NETWORK TYPES

Although many users feel as though there is only one network, the Internet, several types of networks are the building blocks that combine together and make the Internet possible. The Internet itself is just a network of the other networks.

Understanding the different types of networks is important because each can play a different role in the firm's strategy of communications. Different network types can effectively compartmentalize communications. An analogy might be the layout of the building that houses a firm. An office suite is a collection of individual offices, perhaps in the same department. The suites connect to other suites, representing other departments. Each department suite would be its own local area; local areas would connect to other suites and eventually out of the building to other firms. The doors into a suite, a collection of suites, and the building itself each offer an opportunity to screen and possibly deny entrance. Networks need that same capability.

To be included on a network, each device—each computer, printer, or similar device—must be attached to the communications medium via a network interface card. The **network interface card (NIC)** acts as an intermediary between the data moving to and from the computer or other device and the network. The NIC is more than just a buffer between the computer and the network to allow temporary data storage. It also deciphers information from the packets to determine if the data is meant to be captured or if it should be allowed to pass down the communications line medium. Other network hardware is discussed in Table 5.7.

Table 5.7
Communications Network Hardware

NAME	DESCRIPTION
HUB	A device that receives a data packet from a computer at the end of one spoke of the star topology and copies the contents to all other devices. As vendors have tried to differentiate their products, the capabilities of hubs have increased. Some are "manageable" in that they monitor and control the flow of data among the spokes.
ROUTER	A device to connect LANs together. Routers do not simply rebroadcast data; they process control information contained in communications packets in order to determine which LAN should receive the data. Because there may be many possible paths through a network to connect two computers, the router is key to determining which path will be efficient for data transfer.
SWITCH	A device that connects LANs together. Switches perform router tasks and more. Switches filter data from a network path when that path will not contain the destination computer. As a result of filtering, switches eliminate unnecessary data traffic and make communications more efficient.

Local Area Networks

A **local area network** (LAN)[13] is a group of computers and other devices (such as printers) that are connected together by a common medium. The medium is generally copper wire but can be wireless, fiber optics, or other media. LANs typically join computers that are physically close together, such as in the same room or building. Only a limited number of computers and other devices can be connected on a single LAN.

As a general rule, a LAN will cover a total distance of less than one-half mile with the distance between any two devices being no more than 60 feet. These distances are only guidelines because the specifications imposed by the type of communications medium, the network interface card used, and the LAN software dictate actual distances. The current transmission speed of data along a LAN generally runs from 10 million bits per second to 100 million bits per second (10 Mbps to 100 Mbps) but 1,000 million bps (i.e., 1 Gigabit per second) is becoming popular. LANs use only private network media; they do not transfer data over the public telephone system.

Local area networks utilize three separate configurations (called **topologies**) for connecting the computers and other devices. Figure 5.13 illustrates those configurations. A **ring** configuration is used for IBM's Token Ring networks. The token is passed along the ring from one device to another and the device with the token gets to control communications. Ethernet networks use a **bus** (also called a **backbone**) topology. A bus is a single wire of limited length. A practical advantage of the bus over the ring is that if a single device on the ring fails, communications to the other devices are cut off. With a bus, a single device failure does not stop communications between other devices.

The third configuration is a **star** and it requires a hub. A **hub** is a device that receives a data packet from a computer at the end of one spoke of the star and copies the contents to all other devices. The star topology and hubs are important because of their simplicity and early adoption.

The importance of LANs to business professionals has less to do with the technology and more to do with communication.[14] As managers and professional staff became dependent upon personal computer resources to perform work tasks, they realized the limitations of passing computer-based information from one user to another by copying files to a disk. It was time-consuming to copy the data, walk to coworkers, and have coworkers copy the data

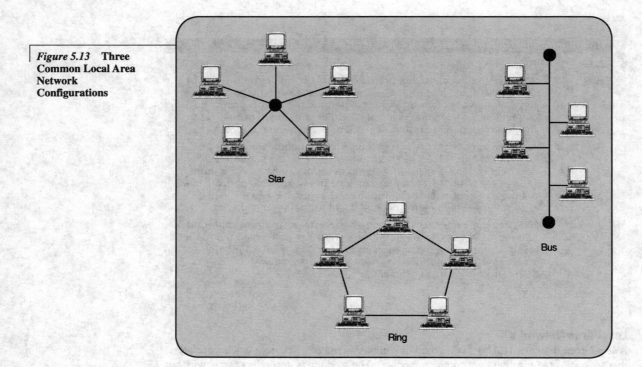

Figure 5.13 Three Common Local Area Network Configurations

onto their computers. What if the coworkers were not at their desks? As important decision-making data became computer-based, computer-to-computer communication became important.

Metropolitan Area Networks and Wide Area Networks

A **metropolitan area network (MAN)** is one that has a physical distance limit of roughly 30 miles. Distance covered is the differentiating characteristic from LANs. Conceptually, a MAN might be the network that connects all of the suites in a building (all departments) together. Linking several buildings of an organization together, such as buildings on a campus, is a common application of a MAN.

MANs typically use the topologies described for LANs. Like LANs, MANs do not use public telephone systems to transfer data. Common MANs transfer data at speeds of 100 Mbps to 1 Gigabit per second.

Wide area networks (WANs) are used to connect computers and other devices when the distance exceeds constraints of LANs and MANs. The public telephone system, the common carrier, is used for wide area networks. As Internet connections became pervasive, interest in WANs has declined. For practical purposes, WANs have been replaced by the Internet.

Internet

The Internet has had a greater impact on computer-based communications than any other development, and it has spawned such specialized applications as intranets and extranets. Simply put, an internet is just the collection of networks that can be joined together. If you have a LAN in one office suite and a LAN in a another office suite, you can join them and that will create an internet.

Using everyday transportation as an analogy, you can travel two blocks to visit a friend using the road as the medium. This is an example of an **internet**. However, with an interconnecting set of roads, rivers, train tracks, and plane routes you can travel virtually anywhere in the world. This is an example of an **Internet**. The scale of interconnection is the difference between an internet and the Internet. That is why it is common to capitalize the "I" in Internet when referring to the global set of interconnecting networks.

The Internet is public. Anyone with a computer and access to the communication medium can travel the Internet. This openness to everyone has advantages and disadvantages. If your organization is seeking new customers, then you wish to have the widest possible audience for your products. However, the person using the Internet to retrieve data from your computer resources may retrieve data that you wish to keep private.

INTRANETS   Organizations can limit access to their networks to other members of their organization by using an intranet. An **intranet** uses the same network protocols as the Internet but limits accessibility to computer resources to a select group of persons in the organization.

How is an intranet different from a LAN? Technically, a LAN has no physical connection to another network. It is important to note here that many people (incorrectly) refer to their local group of computers as their LAN even though the local network bridges to other networks. The intranet has a connection to other networks within the firm but uses software, hardware, or a combination of both to prevent communications from devices outside the firm. Firewalls (discussed in Chapter 9) are commonly used to enforce intranet security.

EXTRANETS   Some authorized users of a network may be outside the boundaries of the firm. For example, a supplier might need access to the computer-based records of inventory levels. The connection to the outside user is most likely accomplished through the Internet. When an intranet is expanded to include users beyond the firm it is called an **extranet**. Only trusted customers and business partners are afforded extranet access because this access allows possible use of information systems and computer resources not directly related to the communication. Firewalls are also used with extranets in order to prevent unauthorized users from accessing computer resources.

CONVERGENCE OF COMPUTING AND COMMUNICATIONS

Computing devices and communications devices are each incorporating features of the other into themselves. Handspring's Treo 300 is a PDA, phone, Internet browser, and e-mail retriever all-in-one. Siemens offers the SX45, another all-in-one device, but with the additional capabilities of a pocket computer. The SX45 not only allows the review of spreadsheets, documents, and other files but allows the user to create and modify files.

The limits to the possibilities relate to battery life, communication speed and security, size of display and keyboard, and the user's imagination. In the office of the future you may simply place your cell phone into a cradle on your desk. The cradle would attach to a monitor, keyboard, mouse, and any other input or output device you need. All computing would be performed by the computer processor within your phone. When you leave, your computer (inside your phone) goes with you. With cradles available for use in public areas (at a store, the library, or the gym) you can compute anywhere.

Summary

The basic architecture of computer systems includes a processor, memory, and storage. These components work together to input, manipulate, and output information. Microprocessors in microcomputers are tremendously fast, and present microprocessors are about 7,500 times faster than microprocessors in the early 1980s. The power of the computer doubles every 18 months.

Just as important as computer power, the interaction between user and the computer has become more intuitive. Input and output choices have increased to provide managers with an array of possibilities for computer interaction. These advances, in part, are facilitated by the increased power and storage capabilities of current microcomputers. Images, sounds, videos, and other input and output choices are added to the standard keyboard, mouse, computer screen, and printer. The effect is far reaching and not always obvious. If a manager can use an icon to represent a computer action then the user does not have to be able to read the same language or even be able to read at all. These multiple choices help bridge communication between users with different native languages and even to young users who have not learned to read. The new choices have made computer-assisted decision making more inclusive to a wide range of demographic groups.

Software is evolving. Features in computer applications that were expensive "extras" a few years ago are now commonly included in computer software at no cost. This reflects the increasing belief that computer assistance is part and parcel to the decision-making processes of modern managers. Managers want software that controls hardware devices, maintains data security, enables multiple users to share common resources, and can be used without special training. It is inappropriate to say software is becoming more "user friendly;" software is being better engineered to meet the needs and abilities of managers.

Computers can act as stand-alone resources but their power as business tools is increased immensely when they share data. Data communications can take place from one computer to another either directly along a network connection or through the intervening network of the public telephone system. Computer hardware is much faster at communication than telephone hardware. This means that transmission of computer data that travels across the public telephone system is slower than transmission that does not use the telephone system.

Networks started as connections from the computer to a terminal at some distance from the computer. The terminal has no processor and no storage; it simply acts to input and output data. Computer data transfer to another computer is more difficult because each computer has an operating system controlling access to its own resources. Networks are the hardware and software that act as intermediaries between computers to allow the sharing of computer resources.

Local area networks were the first to occur. They had limitations on the distance allowed between computer resources but they made a big impression on management. Workers depended upon computer-based data for decision making and when workers could easily share the computer-based data, the firm benefited. Communication requires standards because different manufacturers of computer and telephone hardware must have common, understandable representations of the data moving along communications media. Telephone systems standards were established for voice communications, and those communications can occur using low-grade, analog connections. The voice-grade medium for communication is not always reliable enough for data communications between computers so new standards were required. The International Organization for Standardization established the Open Systems Interconnection standards for data communications that we use today.

KEY TERMS

processor speed	personal digital assistant (PDA)	protocol
processor word size	system software	TCP/IP
processor power	application software	Token Ring
memory	user friendly software	Ethernet
storage	public telephone system connections	data packet
human-captured data	integrated services digital network (ISDN)	IP address
resolution		local area network (LAN)
handheld PC	digital subscriber line (DSL)	Internet
pocket PC	private line	intranet
tablet PC	virtual private network	extranet

KEY CONCEPTS

- computer power
- personal computing
- communications architectures
- network types (network topologies)
- communications and computing convergence

QUESTIONS

1. If you buy a computer today for $1,500, how many years would pass before the same amount of computer power could be purchased for $375? (Hint: Use Moore's Law.)
2. Assume your friend's computer processor runs at 500 megahertz and your computer's processor runs at 1 gigahertz. How fast is your computer processor speed compared to your friend's?
3. How does a CD-R differ from a CD-RW?
4. What are the most compelling reasons to capture data electronically instead of manually?
5. What does it mean if a monitor has a screen resolution of 1600 × 1200?
6. How is a PDA different from a personal computing device?
7. Why is custom written software more expensive than prewritten software?
8. What does the phrase "user friendly" mean?
9. Why are networks that use the public telephone system slower in transmitting data than networks that communicate directly between computers?
10. What is a virtual private network?
11. What is a peer-to-peer network?
12. Why doesn't the Ethernet protocol worry about data transmission crashes?
13. What is the difference between an intranet and the Internet?
14. What is a local area network?
15. What is a danger of connecting a wireless network access point to a cable modem?

TOPICS FOR DISCUSSION

1. How will wireless communications and cell phones change computing?
2. Make an analogy between the rapid advances of information technology according to Moore's Law and what transportation (such as cars and planes) would look like if a similarly rapid advance in technology took place.
3. How would computing change managerial decision making if your cell phone could control your computer and display the results to the cell phone's display screen?

Problems

1. A firm can achieve competitive advantage by sharing computer-based information and systems with vendors. However, such sharing has risks related to making the firm's computing resources available via the Internet. What are the risks and benefits and do the benefits outweigh the risks?
2. Communications technologies and computing technologies are converging. How are personal computing devices taking advantage of this convergence of technologies? Your answer should address computer power, software used, communications ability, and "fit" with the needs of the user. You may wish to visit Research in Motion (WWW.RIM.COM), Hewlett Packard (WWW.HP.COM), and Dell (WWW.DELL.COM) to review their products and features.

Case Problem

SPECIAL SALMON

You are the CIO of Special Salmon, one of the largest providers of fish to restaurant chains in North America. The information systems division is located in Miami with the company headquarters. Special Salmon occupies five separate office buildings in an industrial park; each building houses between 75 and 125 employees. There are also three seafood processing plants in Georgia, Texas, and Virginia.

Special Salmon has a fleet of over 200 fishing boats that fish the Atlantic and Gulf coasts of the United States. Since competition is keen, it goes without saying that you have to know where the fish are located at any given time. But you also have to know the types of fish that are processed and where they will be sold. Getting orders from your restaurant customers requires some negotiation. There are certain amounts of certain items that the restaurant requires but about half of their orders are based upon what fresh seafood is available and its price. This is a true supply-and-demand business where the demand and supply levels change daily as seafood is caught and sold. The product is perishable, so it needs to be sold quickly. At the same time, restaurants want what is fresh and that means they must buy what is available.

Special Salmon has used proprietary communications with its customers for years. Dedicated phone lines, sometimes called leased lines, were used and they provided secure communications. But the cost was high. Now you are investigating the use of extranets to communicate with your customers. Your customers will gain access to your inventory information systems via the Internet to learn what seafood items you have; the amounts in your warehouses (as well as when the seafood was caught); and the amounts of seafood due to arrive at the warehouses within the next 24, 48, and 72 hours. Prices for seafood are also provided but these are determined by amount of each type of fish purchased and the total dollar amount of the purchase, and coupled to recent purchases that lead to volume discounts.

You have already convinced the president and board of Special Salmon to switch from dedicated phone lines to an extranet. Now you need to make a plan to implement the extranet. Make the following assumptions:

- each office building and each seafood processing plant connects all of its microcomputers via a local area network
- each office building and each seafood processing plant will connect to the Internet via a digital subscriber line (DSL)

Case Problem continued

ASSIGNMENT

1. What benefits can you see from using extranets instead of dedicated phone lines?
2. What data communications speeds do you expect from the local area networks and from the DSLs? Will this speed be sufficient for your business needs?
3. How do you expect your customers, the restaurants, to react to the change to extranets?
4. What impact do you believe wireless communications to PDAs and handheld computers might have once you switch to an extranet?

Notes

[1] John Markoff, "IBM Plans a Computer that Will Set Power Record," *The New York Times*, November 19, 2002, C9.

[2] Carle Catalano, "CD-R and CD-RW," *Computerworld*, Vol. 33, Issue 6, February 8, 1999, 77.

[3] Terry Kuny, Network Notes #39, ISSN 1201-4338, Information Technology Services, National Library of Canada.

[4] Edward K. Yasaki Sr., "Bar Codes for Data Entry," *Datamation*, Vol. 21, No. 5, May 1975, 63.

[5] Jerome Nugent-Smith, "The Myth of the Paperless Office," *Modern Office*, Vol. 24, No. 9, October 1985, 8–9.

[6] John G. Spooner, "Tablet PCs Won't Come Cheap," *CNET News.com*, November 1, 2002.

[7] Michael Singer, "Nextel Connects with Walkie-Talkie Blackberry," *Internet.com*, December 4, 2003.

[8] *Informationweek*, "Salary Survey," April 29, 2002, p. 36.

[9] Joaquim Menezes, "Internet VPNs Ready to Grow," *Computer Dealer News* 15 (November 12, 1999), 43.

[10] Mike Hurwicz, "A Virtual Private Affair," *BYTE Magazine* 22 (July 1997), 79–84.

[11] Eric Krapf, "IBM-Cisco: End of an Era for Big Blue," *Business Communications Review* 29 (October 1999), 16–17.

[12] Alan Deikman, "Ethernet Maintains Its Lead with Flexibility and Compatibility," *Computer Technology Review* 10 (Fall 1990), 31–33.

[13] Sara Humphry, "The Complete Guide to NetWare LAN Analysis," *PC Week* 13 (November 4, 1996), N26–N31.

[14] Robert O'Dell, "Ethernet Joins the Factory Workforce," *Machine Design* 66 (July 11, 1994), 78–80.

Chapter 6

Database Management Systems

Learning Objectives

After studying this chapter, you should

- Understand the hierarchy of data.
- Understand database structures and how they work.
- Learn how to relate tables together in a database.
- Recognize the difference between a database and a database management system.
- Understand the database concept.
- Learn methods for determining data needs.
- Understand the basic differences between structured query language and query-by-example.
- Learn about reports and forms.
- Become familiar with entity-relationship diagrams and class diagrams.
- Learn about the important personnel who are associated with databases.
- Know the advantages and costs of database management systems.

Introduction

Database management systems organize the large volumes of data that firms use in their everyday transactions. The data organization must also allow managers to find specific data easily and quickly for decision making. Firms break the entire collection of data into a set of related tables of data. These smaller collections of related data reduce data redundancy. In turn, data consistency and accuracy are increased.

The organizational structure of the firm's data has changed over the years. Currently, most firms use databases that conform to a relational structure. Two important reasons for this are that the relational database structure is easy to use and that relationships among tables in the structure are implicit. The ease of use has emboldened many managers to become direct users of database resources.

The design of a database must be performed carefully. Information systems professionals and business users work together to create database specifications. Approaches such as process-oriented modeling and enterprise modeling allow the database design to address existing problems as well as seize opportunities through synergy among business areas. Techniques such as entity-relationship diagrams and class diagrams clarify the communications between information specialists and users so that the database design truly meets the needs of the firm.

The increased importance of databases as resources supporting decision making has required managers to learn more about database design and use. Forms and reports are the standard methods for access but queries are becoming more important. Managers who can make the best direct use of database resources make the best decisions for the firm.

In this chapter we present both examples and conceptualizations of databases. As topics are demonstrated in each we occasionally repeat a concept. Bear with us. Database concepts are so important to managers that a second telling is justified.

DATA ORGANIZATION

Computers were initially used to solve problems requiring complex and tedious numerical calculations. Those problems required little input and little output. Today, firms require huge amounts of input and output. Firms often need the computer to solve the same problem, with different inputs, many times. Calculating the bill of a customer each time a sale is made is a simple process repeated many times.

Firms need very large amounts of data stored in their computer-based information systems simply because they conduct so many business transactions. So much data exists that it would be useless for business decision making without an effective and efficient manner for organizing the data. In order to use the data and avoid chaos, the concept of "data" had to be broken down and reduced to smaller concepts. The smaller concepts of data form building blocks that can be combined to reproduce the original data in an organized, accessible form.

The Data Hierarchy

Business data has traditionally been organized into a hierarchy of data fields that combine to form records and records that combine to form files. A **data field** is the smallest unit of data; it represents the smallest amount of data that might be retrieved from a computer at a given time. An example of a data field might be a code for a course you are taking. A **record** is a collection of related data fields. Users would logically think of the data fields in a record as being related, such as a course code would be related to a course title. A **file** is a collection of related records, such as a file of all records containing course codes and title fields.

Table 6.1
The COURSE Table

CODE	DESCRIPTION
MIS105	Information Systems Literacy
MIS315	Database Management Systems
POM250	Introduction to Operations Management
MGT300	Introduction to Management
MKT300	Introduction to Marketing
MKT444	Marketing Research
STA230	Descriptive Statistics
ACG201	Financial Accounting
ACG301	Cost Accounting
FIN305	Personal Finance
ECN375	Global Markets
ECN460	Banking Regulations
INT100	Cultural Diversity
INT201	Spanish for Business
INT202	French for Business

Files can be represented as tables and Table 6.1 is an example file we can call COURSE. The records are the rows in the table. Values in the rows represent the values of the data fields—"MIS105" and "Information Systems Literacy" being the values of the course *Code* and course *Description* fields for the first record. The simple hierarchy of fields comprising records that combine into a file establishes the fundamental organization of all data used in computer-aided decision making.

A **database** is a collection of files. The **general definition of a database** is the collection of all of a firm's computer-based data. A more **restrictive definition of a database** is the collection of data under the control of database management system software. Under the restrictive definition, a firm's data controlled and administered by a database management system would be considered as the database but computer files in a manager's personal computer would be considered outside the database. In this text, we typically use the general definition of a database—the collection of all computer-based data. However, in this chapter we explore the restrictive definition—data under the control of database management system software.

The Spreadsheet As a Simple Database

The table of rows and columns can be represented in a spreadsheet. So many users are familiar with spreadsheets that they are useful to introduce database concepts.[1] The columns of the spreadsheet represent the data fields, and column headings contain data field names. Rows of the table contain the field values. Figure 6.1 illustrates an Excel spreadsheet containing the values from the COURSE table of Table 6.1. The table concept is important because the most popular database structure for business organizations, the **relational database structure**, is conceptually similar to a collection of related tables. Most terms used by information specialists working with database management systems relate to terms used to describe tables, but some additional terms and concepts are required.

Flat Files

First, we need to define a particular type of table, a flat file. A **flat file** is a table that does not have repeating columns. Look at Table 6.2. The letters of the course code that represent an academic area have been stripped off and put into a separate column. Then the courses for that academic area are shown as columns on the same row. Columns for course codes and descriptions repeat, so Table 6.2 is not a flat file.

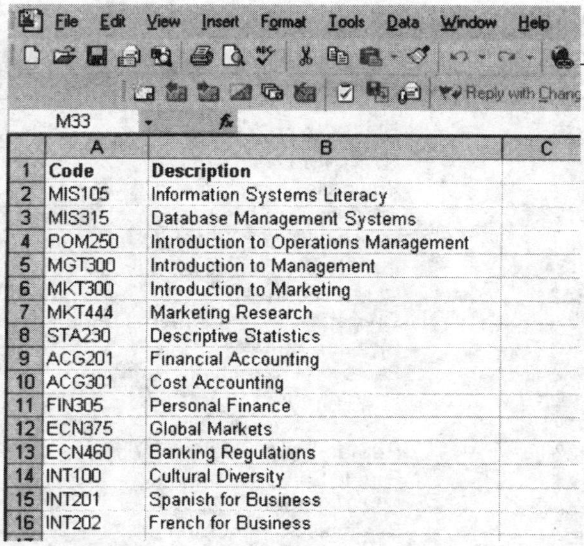

Figure 6.1
Spreadsheet Example of the COURSE Table

	A	B	C
1	Code	Description	
2	MIS105	Information Systems Literacy	
3	MIS315	Database Management Systems	
4	POM250	Introduction to Operations Management	
5	MGT300	Introduction to Management	
6	MKT300	Introduction to Marketing	
7	MKT444	Marketing Research	
8	STA230	Descriptive Statistics	
9	ACG201	Financial Accounting	
10	ACG301	Cost Accounting	
11	FIN305	Personal Finance	
12	ECN375	Global Markets	
13	ECN460	Banking Regulations	
14	INT100	Cultural Diversity	
15	INT201	Spanish for Business	
16	INT202	French for Business	

Repeating columns violate the requirements for a flat file. The reason that a table must be a flat file is because computers read data fields from a record in sequence. When the sequence is not in a constant order the computer cannot read records correctly. In the first row of Table 6.2 the computer would read five values; "MIS," "105," "Information Systems Literacy," "315," and "Database Management Systems." The computer would expect to read five values in the next record: "POM," "250," "Introduction to Operations Mgt.," "MKT," and "300." But notice that the computer has made a mistake; it confused the first two values of the third row as the fourth and fifth values on the second row. A flat file, one without repeating columns, provides the constant sequence of data fields that database management requires.

A second reason for flat files is that they allow relational database structures to be normalized. Normalization is a formal process for eliminating redundant data fields while preserving the ability of the database to add, modify, and delete records without causing errors. Normalization is beyond the scope of this text but is a primary focus of database management systems courses.

Key Fields

Table 6.3 depicts values in the BOOK table and illustrates the concept of a key. The **key** in a table is a field (or combination of fields) which contains a value that uniquely identifies each record in the table. Many times a single field serves as a key for a table. Distinguishing between two or three rows is not enough; key values must be unique for the entire table. If you

Table 6.2

The COURSE Table with Repeating Columns (Not a Flat File)				
AREA	CODE	DESCRIPTION	CODE	DESCRIPTION
MIS	105	Information Systems Literacy	315	Database Management Systems
POM	250	Introduction to Operations Mgt.		
MGT	300	Introduction to Management		
MKT	300	Introduction to Marketing	444	Marketing Research
STA	230	Descriptive Statistics		
ACG	201	Financial Accounting	301	Cost Accounting
FIN	305	Personal Finance		
ECN	375	Global Markets	460	Banking Regulations

Table 6.3
The BOOK Table

ISBN	TITLE
X-15B25	Database Examples
C-12-L	HTML for Beginners
19-63-P	Business Management
ABC-123	Product, Promotion, Placement, and Price
WJY5	Personal Sales Techniques
C-16-MN	Introduction to Accounting
43-U-523	Cost Accounting
HH-7384-GH	Operations Management Fundamentals
322-J	Risk and Returns
32K	Personal Productivity Software
5-53-921	Fundamentals of Hardware
9-7723-K	Stocks Versus Bonds
K-T-127	Human Resources for Today
7-32-881	Oracle Servers
7-32-7723	SQL Servers
A-129-X	Business Management
13-991	The Federal Reserve System
VZ-67	Business French
3-2907-X	Spanish at Work
88-PDQ	Statistics for Business

were told that the value of the *ISBN* field was "X-15B25" you would know that the *Title* field value was "Database Examples." The *ISBN* field is the key.

At first glance it may seem that the values of the *Title* field will also uniquely identify each row. However, the title "Business Management" occurs twice so the computer could not tell if the ISBN value "19-63-P" or "A-129-X" should be used. Books occasionally have the same title but an ISBN is always unique.

In some tables there may be two fields that are candidates for being the key. A **candidate key** is a field that does uniquely identify each table row but was not chosen to be the key. In the COURSE table described in Table 6.1 the *Description* field will uniquely identify each row. However, the *Code* field was chosen to be the key. Frequently, when confronted with two choices between two fields that could be the key, the field that is more compact is chosen. Field values that are longer (such as the *Description* field values versus those in *Code*) are avoided because the longer field values present a higher risk of mistyping the key field value.

Some tables require the values of two or more fields to uniquely identify each row in the table. A possible example might arise when courses have projects. Table 6.4 shows projects but note that there is no single data field value that will uniquely identify each row. Values in the *Code* field column repeat between rows. So do field values in all other columns. However, when values in the *Code* and *Number* fields are taken in combination the combined values become unique.

Relating Tables

You can easily see the relationship between the COURSE and PROJECT tables (Tables 6.1 and 6.4). The tables share a common field, *Code*, and the value of the *Code* field determines which rows in the tables are logically joined. For example, if you are curious about the projects required for the course titled "Information Systems Literacy," you must find matching values in the data field shared by both tables. The *Code* field is in both tables and allows the tables to be related together. "MIS105" is the *Code* field value when "Information System Literacy" is the *Description* field value. This relates to the *Code* field value in the PROJECT table showing that the "Information Systems Literacy" course has projects for "Home Page Development" and "Working With Windows."

Table 6.4
The PROJECT Table

Code	Number	Title	Due	Points
MIS105	1	Home Page Development	9/15/2003	25
MIS105	2	Working With Windows	11/13/2003	50
MIS316	1	Alumni Database	12/5/2003	20
MKT444	1	Finding Customers	10/31/2003	50
MKT444	2	Segmenting Customers	11/21/2003	50
MKT444	3	Customer Service	12/12/2003	40
FIN305	1	Personal Portfolio	11/14/2003	35
INT201	1	Nouns	9/17/2003	15
INT201	2	Verbs	11/21/2003	25
INT202	1	Nouns	9/17/2003	15
INT202	2	Verbs	11/21/2003	25

Sometimes tables that originally stand alone as independent may later be required to be joined. Take Table 6.5, the DEPARTMENT table. It shows the six departments offering the courses in the COURSE table. There is not a common column between the two tables. You might be able to guess which department offered each course based upon the values in the *Abbreviation* field but a computer needs an exact match, not a guess.

We will add the field *Abbreviation* to the COURSE table so that a common field between the tables can join them. Table 6.6 depicts the COURSE table with *Abbreviation* added. Now,

Table 6.5
The DEPARTMENT Table

Abbreviation	Name	Located	Phone
ISOM	Information Systems and Operations Management	Cameron Hall	910-3600
MGTMKT	Management and Marketing	Cameron Hall	910-4500
ACGFIN	Accounting and Finance	Dobo Hall	910-1800
ECN	Economics	Randall	910-0900
INT	International Business	Dobo Hall	910-0900

Table 6.6
The COURSE Table with Abbreviation Field Added

Code	Description	Abbreviation
MIS105	Information Systems Literacy	ISOM
MIS315	Database Management Systems	ISOM
POM250	Introduction to Operations Management	ISOM
MGT300	Introduction to Management	MGTMKT
MKT300	Introduction to Marketing	MGTMKT
MKT444	Marketing Research	MGTMKT
STA230	Descriptive Statistics	ISOM
ACG201	Financial Accounting	ACGFIN
ACG301	Cost Accounting	ACGFIN
FIN305	Personal Finance	ACGFIN
ECN375	Global Markets	ECN
ECN460	Banking Regulations	ECN
INT100	Cultural Diversity	INT
INT201	Spanish for Business	INT
INT202	French for Business	INT

a student having trouble in the "Introduction to Marketing" class can match the "MGTMKT" *Abbreviation* field value in the COURSE table to the "MGTMKT" *Abbreviation* field value in DEPARTMENT and know to call "910-4500" for help.

DATABASE STRUCTURES

Database structures are ways of organizing data in order to make processing that data efficient. The structure is then implemented via a database management system. Three standard structures are discussed below but there is interest in developing new structures to more efficiently process very large amounts of data.[2]

A **database management system (DBMS)** is a software application that stores the structure of the database, the data itself, relationships among data in the database, and forms and reports pertaining to the database. The data field decription is also included; field names, data types, number of decimal places, number of characters, default values, and all other field descriptions. This is why the database controlled by a database management system is called a self-describing set of related data.

Hierarchical Database Structures

The first database management system, IDS (Integrated Data Store),[3] was developed by GE in 1964. This database influenced the work of the Committee on Data Systems Languages (CODASYL). The committee had members from government, industry, and academia so that the standard developed would be open to all. CODASYL formed a Data Base Task Group and charged the group with the responsibility to develop database standards.

The IDS database management system conformed to a **hierarchical database structure**. The hierarchical structure is formed by data groups, subgroups, and further subgroups and if you were to draw the structure it would look like the branches of a tree. Like branches on a tree, to get from a record on one branch to a record on a different branch required that the database management system navigate back to a common junction for the branches. Figure 6.2 shows navigation from the DEPARTMENT table to the COURSE table.

The hierarchical structure for databases was initially popular because it worked well with the transaction processing systems that performed such tasks as inventory control, order entry, accounts receivable, and accounts payable. Accounting tasks such as these were among the first business operations to be computerized.

Figure 6.2 **The Hierarchical Structure between the DEPARTMENT and COURSE Tables**

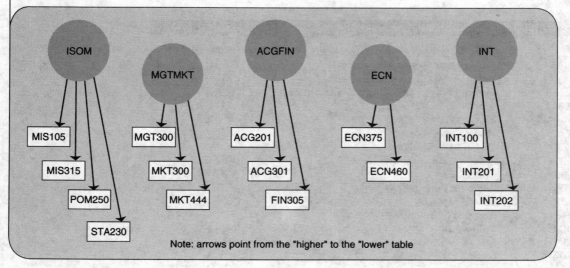

Another reason for their initial popularity was that hierarchical structures utilize computer resources efficiently, especially when the large majority of records in the database are to be used in an application. The organization wants all customers to get a bill, all vendors to be paid, and all orders to be processed. For these applications, hierarchical structures make very efficient use of database resources. In the 1960s, when the hierarchical structure was developed, computer resources were expensive.

When managers want only a few selected records from the very large number of records in the database, the hierarchical structure is not efficient. This is because each hierarchical database record has a field that points to the storage address of the next logical record in the database. Records do not have to be stored physically one after the other on a storage device. A pointer locates the "logically next" record (i.e., the subsequent record) and the database management system retrieves the "logically next" record. However, managerial decisions may require a single, specific record to address a business problem. A manager wants that specific purchase order record to address a service complaint from a particular customer, not a list of the thousands of purchase orders placed that day.

Network Database Structures

The **network database structure** was developed to allow retrieval of specific records. It allows a given record to point to any other record in the database.[4] The Data Base Task Group subcommittee of CODASYL released its specification for the network database structures in 1971.[5]

Networks solved the problem of having to backtrack all the way to a joining "branch" of the database. Conceptually, any record in the database could point to any other record in the database, intuitively like leaping to any branch on the tree. However, this wide range of possible connections was the weakness of applying network structures to practical problems. It was just too chaotic to allow every record to point to every other record. Even experienced information systems professionals found it difficult to correctly develop and use databases using network structures.

Relational Database Structures

Business organizations never widely adopted database management systems built on the network structure. However, organizations still needed a way to address managerial problems using databases and that meant the need to focus on small subgroups of data and linking from one piece of data to another without having to navigate through a large number of intermediary data records.

Another problem was that tables farther down the branches could only be related to a single higher table. Like a leaf on a tree, it is attached to only a single branch. If we wished to add a table for faculty (possibly have McLeod and Schell teach courses) the diagram would look like Figure 6.3. Conceptually, the COURSE table would have two higher tables pointing to it, FACULTY and DEPARTMENT. Such a relationship is not allowed by hierarchical database structures.

The breakthrough came from basic research conducted independently by C. J. Date[6] and E. F. Codd[7] using relational algebra. Their work is closely associated with the relational database structure that is the most commonly used today by business organizations. The database structure looks like a collection of tables similar to spreadsheet tables. Relationships between the tables are not stored as pointers or addresses; instead, the relationships between tables are implicit.

Whereas the hierarchical and network structures rely on **physical relationships** in the form of storage addresses, the relationships in relational database structures are implicit. **Implicit relationships** can be implied from the data. When a common data field (column) between two tables exists, the records (rows) from the two tables can be joined when the data field values are equal. This is how we joined the DEPARTMENT and COURSE tables together using values in the *Abbreviation* field.

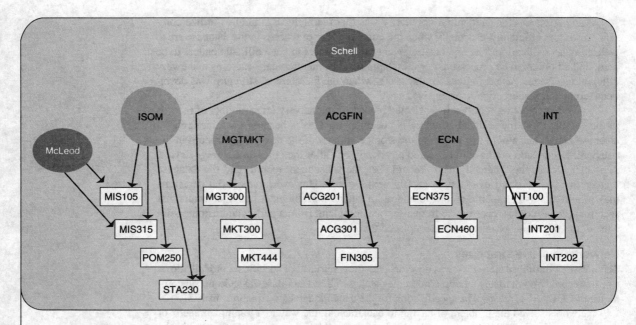

Figure 6.3 Adding a Table for FACULTY Is Beyond the Ability of Hierarchical Database Structures

The conceptualization of a database structure that consists of tables where relationships are implicitly established by matching values in common data fields is easy to use and understand. Ease of use is very important. When organizations became "flatter" (when they reorganized to have fewer layers of management), there were fewer specialists available to assemble data from computer-based systems and generate reports for managers. Today's managers and professional staff are required to directly access information from a database in order to support their decision making. The table-like structure of relational database management systems is a format that can be quickly understood by the manager and professional staff.

A RELATIONAL DATABASE EXAMPLE

An example of data fields, tables, and relationships between tables will set the stage for **database concepts** presented later in the chapter. A database named *Schedule* has been created from tables used earlier in the chapter and some others. The database is implemented in Microsoft Access 2002 (also known as Access XP). Databases break information into multiple tables because if information were stored in a single table, many data field values would be duplicated. Databases reduce **data redundancy** in tables.

Databases also increase **data consistency** and accuracy. These are critical concerns. Managers make decisions critical to the firm's operations; accordingly, they need data that is both accurate and consistent with other data in the database. Reducing the amount of redundant data is good, but data consistency and accuracy are vital.

The *Schedule* Database

The example used here is implemented on Microsoft Access database management system software but the implementation would be similar on any standard relational database structure product. DB2 and Informix from IBM, Oracle, SQL Server from Microsoft, and many others provide relational database management system software. The implementations may be slightly different but these systems all use the same structure.

The COURSE table in Access is shown in Figure 6.4. It is a list of data field values. The table itself had to be defined in Access before values were entered into the data fields. Figure 6.5 shows the definition of the *Code* field. The icon to the left of *Code* is a key, designating that

Code	Description	Abbreviation
ACG201	Financial Accounting	ACGFIN
ACG301	Cost Accounting	ACGFIN
ECN375	Global Markets	ECN
ECN460	Banking Regulations	ECN
FIN305	Personal Finance	ACGFIN
INT100	Cultural Diversity	INT
INT201	Spanish for Business	INT
INT202	French for Business	INT
MGT300	Introduction to Management	MGTMKT
MIS105	Information Systems Literacy	ISOM
MIS315	Database Management Systems	ISOM
MKT300	Introduction to Marketing	MGTMKT
MKT444	Marketing Research	MGTMKT
POM250	Introduction to Operations Management	ISOM
STA230	Descriptive Statistics	ISOM

Figure 6.4 The COURSE Table in Access

Code is the key field of the COURSE table. *Code* is a text field, in that it can be comprised of letters, digits, and/or symbols. No more than eight characters are allowed for the field.

Note that other restrictions can be placed on *Code* values. An input mask can be used to force certain characters to be entered in a particular manner. For our *Code* values, a mask of "LLL000" in an Access DBMS definition would require that the first three characters be letters and the last three characters be digits. For other types of fields, such as phone numbers or zip codes, appropriate input masks can also be established. Default values can be specified as well as rules for validating (testing) the entered value. Any user-entered value that does not meet the requirements would be rejected and not recorded into the database.

The *Code* field is the key for the table so duplicate values are not allowed. Key values must be unique. But other fields may allow duplicates if the designer chooses that option.

Figure 6.6 illustrates that *Abbreviation* field values will be looked up from a list of values in the DEPARTMENT table. Remember from Table 6.6 that the *Abbreviation* field was added

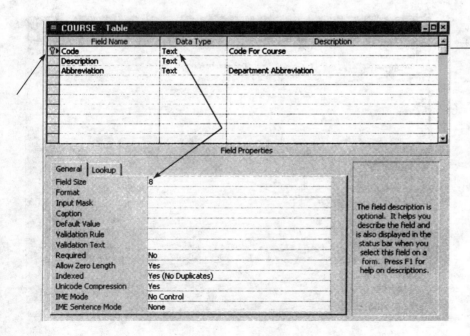

Figure 6.5 Defining the Code Field in the COURSE Table

to the COURSE table so that records from COURSE and DEPARTMENT could be logically joined. Data values from the *Abbreviation* field in the DEPARTMENT table are presented to the user in a drop-down menu when he or she tries to enter values in the *Abbreviation* field of the COURSE table. This will assure that a user entering data into the COURSE table does not make typographical errors when entering *Abbreviation* values.

The design of the fields in the COURSE table allow the user to support **data accuracy** and consistency. Consistency between the COURSE and DEPARTMENT table is enforced because data values entered into the *Abbreviation* field in the COURSE table are selected from a list of values already existing in the *Abbreviation* field of the DEPARTMENT table. An input mask can assure that Code values begin with three letters and end with three digits. Accuracy is enforced by validation rules. The definition of fields in a table are simple to use but powerful in achievement.

Redundancy is harder to conceptualize, especially after the tables have already been separated. Table 6.7 shows a single table of course and department fields before they were separated into different tables. Notice that the department name, location, and phone number is repeated. In Table 6.6, the COURSE table only has department abbreviations repeated—that repeated field allows COURSE to relate to DEPARTMENT. Redundant fields take up more storage space, slow record processing, and invite data inconsistency. Assume the International Business department changes its name to "Global Business." If only two of the three affected records in Table 6.7 were changed, the database could not be sure which department name was correct.

Moving the *Name*, *Located*, and *Phone* data fields to a separate table means that a single change to any of these fields is the one and only change required. Data inconsistency is avoided. It is necessary for the *Abbreviation* field values to be repeated in the COURSE table. That redundancy allows us to join records from the separated DEPARTMENT and COURSE tables together.

Figure 6.7 shows the *Schedule* database fields, tables, and relationships between tables. Fields within tables that represent the key are in bold font. Lines between tables delineate which fields are the common fields joining tables together in a relationship. Other features in Figure 6.7 will be discussed later in the chapter.

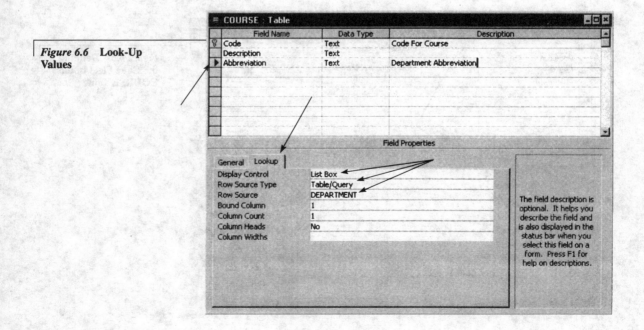

Figure 6.6 Look-Up Values

Table 6.7
Unseparated Table of Course and Department Data Fields

CODE	DESCRIPTION	ABBREVIATION	NAME	LOCATED	PHONE
MIS105	Information Systems Literacy	ISOM	Information Systems and Operations Management	Cameron Hall	910-3600
MIS315	Database Management Systems	ISOM	Information Systems and Operations Management	Cameron Hall	910-3600
POM250	Introduction to Operations Management	ISOM	Information Systems and Operations Management	Cameron Hall	910-3600
MGT300	Introduction to Management	MGTMKT	Management and Marketing	Cameron Hall	910-4500
MKT300	Introduction to Marketing	MGTMKT	Management and Marketing	Cameron Hall	910-4500
MKT444	Marketing Research	MGTMKT	Management and Marketing	Cameron Hall	910-4500
STA230	Descriptive Statistics	ISOM	Information Systems and Operations Management	Cameron Hall	910-3600
ACG201	Financial Accounting	ACGFIN	Accounting and Finance	Dobo Hall	910-1800
ACG301	Cost Accounting	ACGFIN	Accounting and Finance	Dobo Hall	910-1800
FIN305	Personal Finance	ACGFIN	Accounting and Finance	Dobo Hall	910-1800
ECN375	Global Markets	ECN	Economics	Randall	910-0900
ECN460	Banking Regulations	ECN	Economics	Randall	910-0900
INT100	Cultural Diversity	INT	International Business	Dobo Hall	910-0900
INT201	Spanish for Business	INT	International Business	Dobo Hall	910-0900
INT202	French for Business	INT	International Business	Dobo Hall	910-0900

The Database Concept

When a user thinks of records in a database, he or she intuitively feels that the sequence of records displayed in a report reflects the sequence in which the records are stored on the computer disk. A record that, to the user, appears before or after some other record may actually be stored at a completely separate part of storage. A database management system can display the data in a logically, intuitively correct sequence even though individual records of the database may be dispersed across many files and located all over the computer's storage space. For example, in Figure 6.4 the *Code* values "ACG201" and "ACG301" appear to fall one after the other but the two records may be at completely different places in storage. This logical integration of records across multiple physical locations is called the **database concept**. The physical location on the storage medium is not dependent upon the user's perception of logical location.

Two primary goals of the database concept are to minimize data redundancy and to achieve data independence. Data redundancy—discussed earlier in the chapter—wastes storage space, slows record processing, and invites data inconsistency.

Data independence is the ability to make changes in the data structure without making changes to the application programs that process the data. For example, the computer program to process purchase orders is separate from the purchase order data stored in the database. Data independence is accomplished by the placing of data specifications in tables and dictionaries that are physically separate from the programs.

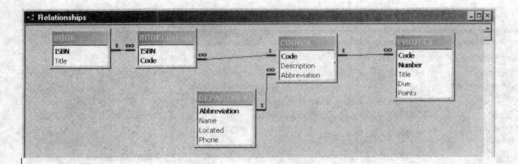

Figure 6.7 Access View of Tables, Fields, and Their Relationships

Refer back to Figure 6.5. The field size of the *Code* field could be increased from 8 to 10 characters in the table definition without affecting any application using the *Code* field. When computer programs directly access data files to retrieve data they must explicitly express the data format. That would require computer program code to be rewritten if the number of characters for *Code* were changed from 8 to 10. If there were 25 computer applications that needed access to the *Code* field, then all 25 would require modification. With data independence, no rewriting of computer code is required because the one and only change would be in the definition of that field in the database.

Data dictionary is the term that refers to the definition of data stored within the database and controlled by the database management system. Figure 6.5 depicts just one table in the *Schedule* database. The structure of the database encompassed by the data dictionary is the collection of all field definitions, table definitions, table relationships, and other issues. The data field name, type of data (such as text or number or date), valid values for the data, and other characteristics are kept within the data dictionary. Changes to data structure are made only once—in the data dictionary—and the application programs using the data are unaffected.

CREATING A DATABASE

Conceptually, the process of creating a database includes three main steps. A database example was presented earlier because it is easier to understand a conceptual model once you have seen an example. In the conceptual model you first determine the data that you need. Next, you describe the data. Then you enter the data into the database.

Determine the Data Needs

The definition of data needs is a key step to achieving a computer-based information system. There are two basic approaches—**process-oriented** and **enterprise modeling**.

A PROCESS-ORIENTED APPROACH When firms take a **process-oriented approach**, they follow the sequence of steps illustrated in the following list. First the *problem* is defined. Then the *decisions* required to solve the problem are identified, and for each decision the required *information* is described. Next, the *processing* necessary to produce the information is determined, and finally the *data* required by the processing is specified. The process-oriented approach is also called the **problem-oriented approach** and **process-oriented modeling**. To define data needs in a process-oriented approach:

1. Define the problem.
2. Identify necessary decisions.
3. Describe information needs.
4. Determine the necessary processing.
5. Specify data needs.

The reason the process-oriented approach is sometimes called the problem-oriented approach is because it begins with problems. A problem can be either good or bad, a threat to the firm or an opportunity to be exploited. Once problems are identified the data and processes dealing with problem solutions can be determined. The strength of the process-oriented approach is that it addresses problems well.

AN ENTERPRISE MODELING APPROACH   The strength of the enterprise modeling approach is that it takes advantage of a broad view of the firm's data resource.[8] All areas are considered and synergy of data resources between business areas can be leveraged. Although the process-oriented approach enables the data needs of each system to be defined in a logical manner, its weakness is the difficulty of linking the data of one business problem to that of another. Information systems cannot easily share data if they are isolated from other information systems dealing with other business problems. This weakness is overcome by determining the firm's entire data needs and then storing that data in the database. This is the underlying logic of the **enterprise modeling approach**.

When a firm is engaged in enterprise data modeling, the description of all of the firm's data is called the **enterprise data model**. This top-down process, which begins during strategic planning for information resources, is illustrated in Figure 6.8.

Data Modeling Techniques

Modeling the firm's data needs is supported by techniques that describe the data, how the data aggregates into tables, and how tables relate to each other. There are a number of techniques but we will focus on two. Entity-relationship diagrams are used to describe relationships between conceptual collections of data so that their related records can be joined together. **Class diagrams** are used to describe both the data relationships and the actions that operate on the data in the relationships. These techniques provide tools to facilitate communications between managers and information systems specialists concerning the structure of data used in an information system application.

Entity-Relationship Diagrams

Entity-relationship diagrams (ERDs),[9,10] like the name implies, deal with data in entities and the relationships between entities. When users and information specialists begin to communicate

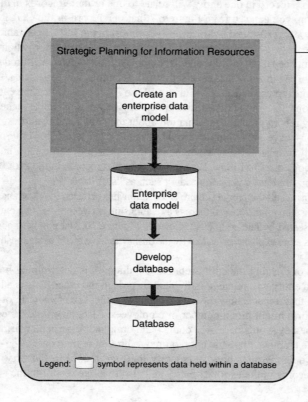

Figure 6.8 **Creating an Enterprise Data Model**

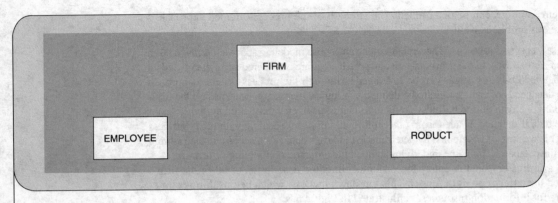

Figure 6.9 Entities

about the data needed for an information system, they speak in terms of collections of related data fields as opposed to individual data fields. These conceptual collections of related data fields are called **entities**. While it is intuitively appealing to think of entities as tables, we cannot. Tables are the result of breaking entities into smaller units that conform to the rules for database structures. An entity may turn into a table, but frequently an entity is broken into several tables. ERDs are a higher level conceptualization of data than tables.

ERDs also express which entities should conceptually be related to others. The relationships between entities are not designated by common data fields in entities because at this early stage the exact data fields for each table are not known. However, the user and information systems professional can conceptualize how records within entities might relate to records in other entities.

Entities in ERDs will have names, much like tables have names. Also, relationships link entities much like the lines joining tables via common fields between tables. ERD relationships will denote if a record in one entity will relate to one or more records in the other entity. In a similar fashion, you can see from Figure 6.7 that one record in the COURSE table may relate to many records (expressed by the infinity symbol) in the PROJECT table.

Let us assume that we need to describe the data needed for a new information system example. The system will keep track of firms and their employees as well as their products. From this brief description we can imagine that three separate data entities will exist: FIRM, EMPLOYEE, and PRODUCT. Entities are represented as boxes in an ERD so Figure 6.9 depicts the entities.

Before relationships among the entities are expressed, we must make some assumptions. First, a FIRM entity record contains information about the firm's name, address, and so forth. Second, a firm may have many employees but an employee works for only one firm. This assumption is a bit simplistic because some people work two or more jobs, but it will make the ERD explanation easier to follow. Last, we assume that records in the PRODUCT entity represent specific items and not a generic product such as "soft drink."

Because the firms sell the products there is a relationship between the FIRM and PRODUCT entities. Similarly, firms hire employees so there is a relationship between those two entities. The relationships are represented by named lines as shown in Figure 6.10. Naming is important for documentation; it serves as an explanation as to why the designers have made a relationship between the entities.

The last part of creating the entity-relationship diagram is determining how many individual records in a entity will relate to individual records in the other. This is a key step in the conceptualization that impacts how the actual database tables are created. In our example we assumed a given firm might hire a number of employees. Also, an employee could work for only one firm. The key words here are "could" and "might." A particular firm is allowed to hire more than one employee but it is not required to hire more than one.

Figure 6.11 demonstrates how we specify that one record in the FIRM entity can be related to many records in the PRODUCT entity and also that one record in the FIRM entity can

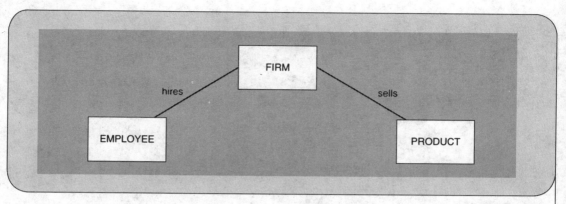

Figure 6.10 Entities and Relationships

relate to many records in the EMPLOYEE entity. The relationship "hires" has a "1" next to the FIRM entity and an "M" next to the EMPLOYEE entity. The "M" stands for "many." The relationship would be read as "one firm record may relate to many employee records and one employee record may relate to only one firm record." The relationship between the FIRM and EMPLOYEE entities is called a "one-to-many" relationship. The relationship between the FIRM and PRODUCT entities is also a one-to-many relationship.

To complete our entity-relationship discussion we need to provide a "many to many" relationship example. Suppose that another entity, PROJECT, was to be added to the application. A single project could have many employees and a single employee could be on many projects. The PROJECT entity would have a relationship to the EMPLOYEE entity. This relationship, a many-to-many relationship, is shown in Figure 6.12.

In practice, the entity-relationship diagrams are developed early in the process, before specific data fields have been identified. Later tables of data fields would be generated that lead to the creation of a database. The ERDs are a powerful means of communication and documentation between information systems professionals and information users. When ideas are clearly documented and communicated the information systems specialists are better equipped to develop a database management system structure to support decision making.

Class Diagrams

An entity-relationship diagram is a graphical representation of only the data and relationships, not actions taken on the data. A technique exists where both the data used in an application and the actions associated with the data can be graphically represented. These are called class diagrams

Figure 6.11 Entity-Relationship Diagram

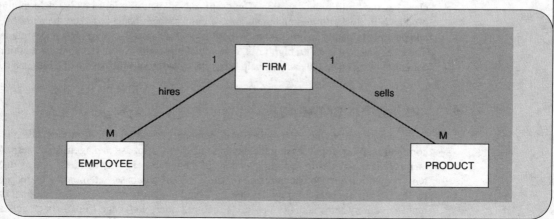

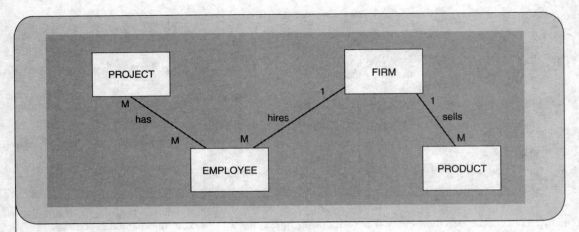

Figure 6.12 Entity-Relationship Diagram with a Many-to-Many Relationship

and they are one of several object-oriented design models. Objects are the conceptual chunks of an information system—the data, actions to be taken on the data, and relationships between objects. Objects have other characteristics that are useful in the analysis and design of information systems but here we are only interested in their impact on describing data.

Class diagrams consist of the named class, fields in the class, and actions (sometimes referred to as methods) that act upon the class. The class diagram in Figure 6.13 illustrates the entity-relationship diagram we have just completed. Notice that class diagrams begin with the class name in the top segment of the rectangle. "clsFirm" is the class name of the FIRM entity we described above. (In class diagrams it is customary, but not required, that the class name be preceded with the letters "cls.") Next, in the middle segment, the diagram explicitly states fields in the class. Unlike tables for the database structures (Figure 6.5), redundant fields between two classes are not repeated. Also notice that an asterisk represents the "many" side of a one-to-many relationship.

Looking at the relationship between the clsFirm and clsProduct classes note that the relationship is named "Sells." You would read the relationship as "one instance in the clsFirm class sells one or more instances in the clsProduct class." Also, "one instance in the clsProduct class will have only one instance in the clsFirm class." Class diagrams appear intuitively similar to entity-relationship diagrams yet the inclusion of actions that operate on the data (such as addProduct) give deeper insights into how data and applications work together.

While each class in Figure 6.13 has an add, delete, and update action, only the clsProduct class has the "sellProduct" action. The "sellProduct" action might involve determining if the product is in stock, decreasing the number of units of the product based on the number ordered, and possibly initiating an order for more product if its inventory level has fallen to a reorder point. The class diagram is still a high level, conceptual representation of data but the addition of the actions to be taken on the data can help bring clarity to the specific design of tables in a database.

USING THE DATABASE

We usually interact with a database from a personal computer. Forms, reports, and queries are common methods for accessing the database held in a database management system. A query language is the means for asking questions of the database. Many database management systems provide an easy-to-use interface for the user. The database statements actually processed by the DBMS are generated by the interface (and hidden from the user). Relational database management systems actually process structured query language (SQL) statements that are acted upon by the database.

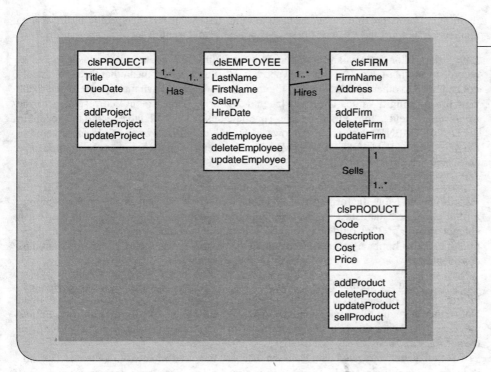

Figure 6.13 Class Diagram

Reports and Forms

The majority of users' interactions with databases are via reports and forms. Graphical user interfaces are provided by most database management software vendors that make the development of forms and reports simple. Many of the reports and forms needed by users can be created without the assistance of information systems professionals.

The greatest difference between forms and reports is in their format. **Forms** typically show one record at a time and do not provide summary data and generally do not aggregate data from many database tables. Note that forms have these abilities, but they are seldom used. Figure 6.14 shows a form for entering courses into the database. This form was developed in Access but it is representative of the major DBMS software vendors.

NAVIGATION The form user can navigate from one record to the next using the navigation bar at the bottom of the form. The "▶*" icon on the navigation bar tells the form to create a new record. A form allows both the creation of new records and the modification of existing records.

ACCURACY Forms enforce the data field definitions that were specified when the database was created. Those definitions can specify certain valid values, data ranges for numeric values, and other rules to support accuracy. They can also enforce rules beyond those in the data field

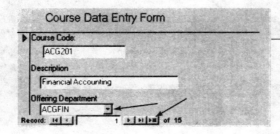

Figure 6.14 A Data Entry Form for the Course Table

definition. Forms provide an opportunity to tailor data values to the specific business area application, not just the general value rules applicable to the entire set of database users.

CONSISTENCY   Consistency is very important when field values in one table are used to join its records to another table. If a user mistyped a field value it would mean that the record could not be joined to other tables. Notice in Figure 6.14 that a drop-down menu is presented to the user for entering a value. The field labeled "Offering Department" corresponds to the *Abbreviation* field in the COURSE table. That field ties a COURSE table record to a record in the DEPARTMENT table. The drop-down menu will only display values already entered in the *Abbreviation* field of the DEPARTMENT table so entries in the form are constrained to be consistent between the two tables.

FILTERING   Databases may have enormous amounts of data. Users may wish to filter the records viewed using the form. Any field on the form could be used as a filter. For example, a filter could be established so that only junior level courses (i.e., courses with the fourth character being a "3") would be displayed. Filtering helps combat the overload of information. It can also limit a user's access to data in the database in case certain records should be confidential.

SUBFORMS   Figure 6.15 illustrates a form and subform combination. As a user enters course information, he or she may also wish to enter information about projects at the same time. Notice that there are two navigation bars, one for the form and one for the subform. Entries into the subforms are automatically associated with the form record. Subforms help to enforce the accuracy and consistency that databases require.

Reports are aggregated data from the database that are formatted in a manner that aids decision making. For example, Figure 6.16 is a report that shows each department with a list of each course taught and projects required for the course. Such aggregation seems almost trivial today but before the age of databases they could be difficult to produce. The ease of use comes at a price; users must understand how databases work to produce reports.

Look at Figure 6.17 and notice that department names (such as Economics) appear in that report that do not appear in Figure 6.16. Why were they left off? They were left off because they had no projects. For example, neither ECN375 nor ECN460 had project records in the database so the Economics department was not included in the Figure 6.16 report. Also, individual courses were left off, such as ACG201, even when the Accounting and Finance department was in the Figure 6.16 report.

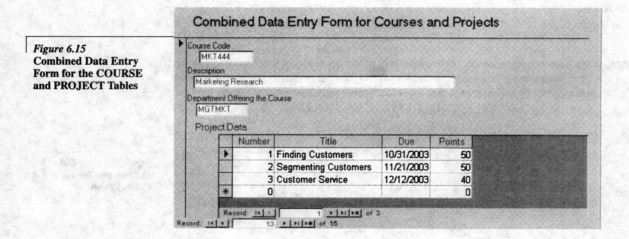

Figure 6.15
Combined Data Entry Form for the COURSE and PROJECT Tables

Courses by Department -- show projects

Department			
Accounting and Finance			
FIN305 *Personal Finance*			
	Project	Due Date	MaximumPoints
	1 Personal Portfolio	11/14/2003	35
International Business			
INT201 *Spanish for Business*			
	Project	Due Date	MaximumPoints
	1 Nouns	9/17/2003	15
	2 Verbs	11/21/2003	25
INT202 *French for Business*			
	Project	Due Date	MaximumPoints
	1 Nouns	9/17/2003	15
	2 Verbs	11/21/2003	25
Information Systems and Operations Management			
MIS10 *Information Systems Literacy*			
	Project	Due Date	MaximumPoints
	1 Home Page Development	9/15/2003	25
	2 Working With Windows	11/13/2003	50
MIS31 *Database Management Systems*			
	Project	Due Date	MaximumPoints
	1 Alumni Database	12/5/2003	20
Management and Marketing			
MKT44 *Marketing Research*			
	Project	Due Date	MaximumPoints
	1 Finding Customers	10/31/2003	50
	2 Segmenting Customers	11/21/2003	50
	3 Customer Service	12/12/2003	40

Figure 6.16 Report of Departments Showing Courses Offered and Course Projects

An assumption was made by the report generator that if details at the lowest level record do not exist then higher level records for the detail should not be displayed. Figure 6.7 illustrated that the DEPARTMENT table related down to the COURSE table which, in turn, related down to the PROJECT table. Unless there was a related entry in the PROJECT table, no COURSE record was displayed. If no record from the COURSE table was used (for example, neither economics course had a project) then a DEPARTMENT record was not displayed.

Courses by Department -- no projects

Department	
Accounting and Finance	
ACG201	Financial Accounting
ACG301	Cost Accounting
FIN305	Personal Finance
Economics	
ECN375	Global Markets
ECN460	Banking Regulations
International Business	
INT100	Cultural Diversity
INT201	Spanish for Business
INT202	French for Business
Information Systems and Operations Management	
MIS105	Information Systems Literacy
MIS315	Database Management Systems
POM250	Introduction to Operations Management
STA230	Descriptive Statistics
Management and Marketing	
MGT300	Introduction to Management
MKT300	Introduction to Marketing
MKT444	Marketing Research

Figure 6.17 Report of Departments and Courses Alone

Figure 6.18 Report of Departments and Courses Alone

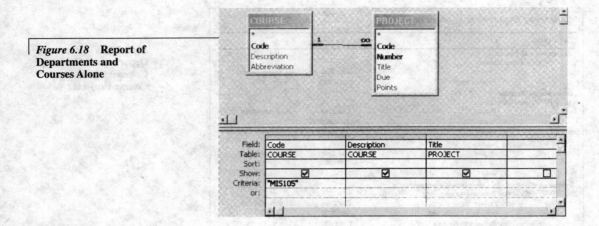

It is a simple task to require the report to display records even when no matching record at a lower table is matched. But if the user is unaware that reports created with default rules may exclude records, the user could make ill-informed decisions.

Query-by-Example
Some users wish to go beyond reports and forms to directly ask questions of the database. A **query** is a request for the database to display selected records. A query generally selects a limited number of data fields and then constrains displayed records to a set of criteria. For example, suppose you wished to see only the course code, course description, and project title of the "MIS105" course. Figure 6.18 represents how that query could be represented.

The format is called **query-by-example (QBE)** because the database management system software presents a standardized form that the user completes so that the system can generate a true query. The QBE form will display the tables involved in the query, in this case the COURSE and PROJECT tables. Next it will allow the user to choose the data fields from the tables that should be displayed. Also, criteria for limiting the search are added. In our case the column containing course code values is limited only to values of "MIS105." If projects from either the MIS105 or MIS315 courses were desired, "MIS315" would have been entered in the cell directly below the "MIS105" entry. The result of the query is the table in Figure 6.19.

The reason that query-by-example concepts are so significant is because of the importance of managers being able to directly access database values. Forms and reports may produce a volume of results that obscure what the manager is trying to find. Managers can utilize QBE to quickly find specific data to solve problems.

Structured Query Language
Structured query language (SQL) is the code that relational database management systems use to perform their database tasks. While the user may see Figure 6.18 as the QBE, the database management system sees the structured query language in Figure 6.20. DBMS software contains graphical user interfaces and "wizard" programs to walk users through queries in a user friendly manner.

SQL has become an important topic for two reasons. First, as more databases have become accessible via the Web, managers and other professionals need to know that SQL is

Figure 6.19 Results of the Query-by-Example

Code	Description	Title
MIS105	Information Systems Literacy	Home Page Development
MIS105	Information Systems Literacy	Working With Windows

> **Structured Query Language Code to Find Projects for the MIS105 Course**
>
> SELECT COURSE.Code, COURSE. Description, PROJECT.Title
> FROM COURSE, PROJECT
> WHERE COURSE.Code = PROJECT.Code
>   AND COURSE.Code = "MIS105"

Figure 6.20
Structured Query Language Code to Find Projects for the MIS105 Course

the method of choice for interacting with Web-based databases. Second, managers need to know that writing SQL statements is not difficult for most of their data needs. If managers need to hire programmers to write SQL code, they should know that the task is not one that requires overwhelming technical skill.

Advanced Database Processing

Online analytical processing (OLAP) is a feature becoming more common in database management system software.[11] Vendors are including this feature to allow data analysis similar to statistical cross-tabulation. For example, one of the fields in the PROJECTS table (Table 6.4) contains the number of points awarded for the project. If you wanted to know the sum of all points for projects in each course in each department, then online analytical processing would be beneficial.

Data mining, data marts, and data warehousing refer to the family of concepts that view the firm's data as a treasure box to be opened, examined, and conquered. They focus on methodologies to allow users quick access to aggregated data specific to their decision-making needs.

Knowledge discovery is another exciting concept. As databases grow and encompass larger and larger amounts of data, how can users recognize all of the relationships between the data? Which data fields are critical to decision making? Is there important data in the database that is not being used? Knowledge discovery attempts to answer these questions by analyzing data usage and data commonality among different tables. OLAP, data mining, data marts and warehouses, and knowledge discovery will be discussed in Chapter 8.

Highlights in MIS

IT CAN BE HEALTHY TO MINE THE CORPORATE DATABASE[12]

Everyone talks about healthy corporate profits but in the pharmaceutical industry better health does lead to healthy profits. An important part of making profits is getting the product to the market rapidly. "Any improvement in getting an innovative drug to market will have a huge payoff," says Elliot Sigal, vice president for applied genomics at Bristol-Myers Squibb.

Twelve years and $300 million to $400 million are typically what it takes to discover a drug, bring it to market, and begin making profits from the drug. For some firms, the trial and error of test tubes can be aided by the search of enormous databases. Pharmaceutical companies and biotech firms, especially those involved with the genome project to map human DNA, are sharing database information to help determine which drugs have the greatest potential. Their intent is to put more resources into those drugs likely to succeed and to reduce the flow of resources to drugs that show low potential.

Will your database wear a white lab coat?

MANAGING THE DATABASE

Database management systems perform functions that most users never see. The infrastructure is needed so that the database can be maintained and modified and also to assure its efficient operation. Just as you seldom see the electrical wiring infrastructure in your house, you'll probably have little contact with the database infrastructure.

Resources

The **performance statistics processor** component of the DBMS maintains information that identifies what data is being used, who is using it, when it is being used, and so forth. The statistics are a valuable resource used to manage the database. By analyzing the statistics, more efficient and secure processing can be achieved. This information is important to provide a profile of database use so that the structure may be altered to address possible processing efficiencies, such as breaking a large table into two separate tables. One table might be a large group of infrequently queried records and the second table might contain the few frequently queried records.

As the database management system runs it keeps a **transaction log** that notes every database action taken as well as the exact time the action was taken. This log is used in conjunction with a backup copy of the database so that when the database fails it can be quickly regenerated. All databases fail and without a transaction log and a backup the failure can be devastating to the firm.

A **backup** copy of the database is made periodically. The database itself is usually just copied to another disk or to a computer tape. The key to a backup copy is that it has a stopping point where no database activity is taking place. Each database transaction is made up of many individual subunits and the subunits of one user's transaction are intermixed with subunits from other users' transactions. Until all of the intermixed subunits are completed, a backup copy can be difficult to obtain.

Consider a busy restaurant, for example. At any given moment some customers may be waiting for an open table, some may be giving their order, others will be receiving their food, and so forth. With so many intertwined activities occurring it can be difficult to take stock of how many knives and forks are in the restaurant, how many servings of coffee are available, and many other details. Once the restaurant is closed for the evening the manager can take inventory of everything.

This analogy applies to database backups. A time is picked when database activity can be stopped or at least paused. Then, when running transactions are completed and before new transactions are begun, a backup copy is created. The backup process takes a small amount of time, with most users never noticing that it occurs.

The time of the backup is noted for the transaction log. If the database crashes, the most recent backup copy is loaded into the database and transactions from the transaction log are processed against it until a reconstructed database is established. The length of time between backups is determined by the business needs of the organization but many firms backup their database daily. Firms often keep copies of the backups for a number of years in case some extraordinary event requires their use.

Database Personnel

Several key personnel are involved with databases. The database administrator has both technical and managerial responsibilities over the database resource. Database programmers are required to create efficient data processing computer code. Some database transactions are too complex for a user to create or more sophisticated code must be written to achieve efficiency of processing so that one application does not dominate database resources.

The database end users are the other key database personnel. By virtue of the decisions made and the amount of data retrieved, end users have a major impact on database design, use, and efficiency.

DATABASE ADMINISTRATOR   Database administrators oversee all database activities. They must have managerial skills as well as high technical skills. Database administrators must understand the business operations of the firm because the decisions in those operations drive much of the database content. They must also be masters of database technology since hardware and DBMS software have a profound impact on the database speed and ease of use.

The duties of the DBA fall into four major areas: planning, implementation, operation, and security.

- **Database planning** involves working with business area managers to define the firm's data needs. The DBA should be a member of any team that is involved with a process-oriented or enterprise modeling approach to determining data needs. In addition, the DBA plays a key role in selecting the database management system software and hardware.
- **Database implementation** consists of creating the database to conform to the specifications of the selected database management system, as well as establishing and enforcing policies and procedures for database use.
- **Database operation** includes offering educational programs to database users and providing assistance when needed.
- **Database security** includes the monitoring of database activity using statistics provided by the database management system. In addition, the database management system ensures that the database remains secure. In a business environment where some vendors are allowed access to the organization's database or where the organization allows customer access to the order entry system to place their own orders, database security has become a very complex issue. It is important to remember that database security involves not only keeping unauthorized users out but also allowing authorized users easy access.

DATABASE PROGRAMMER   **Database programmers** are specialists. They often have much more experience and training than other programmers in the firm. One reason is that the database is the central repository of facts for the firm. If a programming error occurs in the database, then the consequences could be felt by a very large number of users. For this reason, firms want database programmers to be chosen from the most skilled personnel available.

Database programmers often write code to strip and/or aggregate data from the database. A single user can then download this efficiently gathered data from the firm's computer resources to their own personal computer. One benefit is that the firm's database is accessed only once and further database processing occurs only on the user's computing resource, thereby achieving a higher efficiency level for database use. Another benefit is that the user does not need to access the totality of the firm's database and since a user is more likely than a database programmer to make a mistake, the database is more secure.

END USER   End users cannot be ignored as important personnel that interact with the database. They generate reports and forms, post queries to the database, and use results from their database inquiries to make decisions that affect the firm and its customers.

Database management system software has evolved to encourage interaction by decision makers. The user does not need to know how to code structured query language statements. Query-by-example forms let the user click a few choices and run the query. The increased ease of use has caused a large increase in end-user use, which in turn can lead to increased numbers of end-user errors.

Database management systems make assumptions about what the user wants as he or she clicks through the database interface. Unless the user understands what assumptions are made, the data displayed may not be what is needed for decision making. Users need training in database systems so that the database resource can be a true asset to decision making.

DATABASE MANAGEMENT SYSTEMS IN PERSPECTIVE

The database management system makes it possible to create a database, maintain its contents, and disseminate the data to a wide audience of users without costly computer programming. Its ease of use allows managers and professional staff to access database contents with only modest training.

Every facet of information technology has its advantages and disadvantages; database management systems are no exception.

DBMS Advantages

These advantages have been stated earlier but it is important to restate them together. The DBMS enables both firms and individual users to:

- **Reduce data redundancy.** The amount of data is reduced, compared to when computer files are kept separately for each computer application. Duplicate data is limited to those fields necessary to join data from two tables. Common data among the files, in relational database management systems, is used to form implicit relationships among data.
- **Achieve data independence.** The specifications of the data are maintained in the database itself rather than in each application program. Changes may be made once, to the data structure, without requiring changes to the many application programs that access the data.
- **Retrieve data and information rapidly.** Logical relationships and structured query language enable users to retrieve data in seconds or minutes that otherwise might take hours or days to retrieve using such traditional programming languages as COBOL or Java. This is because a computer program in COBOL or Java does not need to be written to access the data. The database management system itself provides tools such as QBE and SQL to access data.
- **Improve security.** Both mainframe and microcomputer DBMSs can include multiple levels of security precautions such as passwords, user directories, and encryption. The data managed by DBMSs is more secure than most other data in the firm.

DBMS Disadvantages

A decision to use a DBMS commits a firm or user to:

- **Obtain expensive software.** Mainframe DBMSs remain expensive. The microcomputer-based DBMSs, while costing only a few hundred dollars, can represent a substantial outlay for a small organization. Fortunately, Moore's Law still holds and the cost of computer hardware and software continues to fall. This disadvantage becomes less important each year.
- **Obtain a large hardware configuration.** The ease with which the DBMS can retrieve information encourages more users to make use of the database. The increased number of users encouraged by the ease of use may lead to an increased amount of computer resources to access the database.
- **Hire and maintain a DBA staff.** The DBMS requires specialized knowledge in order to make full use of its capabilities. This specialized knowledge is best provided by the DBA and his or her staff.

A DBMS is not an absolute prerequisite to problem solving. However, information specialists and users find it to be one of the firm's greatest aids to decision making.

Summary

Computers are increasingly powerful and the cost of computing resources continues to fall. At the same time, business organizations are capturing vast amounts of data and storing the data in databases. Database management system software is crucial for organizing the data into a structure that allows rapid retrieval.

Understanding database structure begins by understanding the role the data plays in decision making. Firms can begin with the problems they face and construct required data from a process-oriented methodology. If the firm wants to take advantage of the commonality of problems across business areas, it can apply the enterprise modeling approach. Whichever method for specifying data is used, a technique must still be used to describe the required data. Entity-relationship diagrams and class diagrams are tools that allow the user and information systems specialist to effectively communicate data requirements.

Relational databases have become the dominant database structure in firms. The reasons are that they are conceptually easy to understand and relational database structures are easy to change because they use implicit relationships among data. Tables in a relational database are similar to spreadsheets; the table is the spreadsheet file, columns in the spreadsheet relate to fields, rows in the spreadsheet relate to records. Relationships are formed when the data field values of common fields are equal. Relational database management systems are relatively easy for managers to understand and use.

Data retrieval typically is via reports and forms. However, as managers need quicker direct access to data, they are writing their own database queries. This is a powerful tool for the manager but like many power tools there is a danger. If the manager is not aware of assumptions the database management system uses to process queries, reports, and forms he or she may find that the data retrieved is not the intended data.

The enormity of the data associated with modern businesses and its critical impact on business operations have combined to cause the creation of a database administrator position in most large organizations. The duties of this person include working with management to plan the structure and organization of data held by the organization. Security issues are very important, especially because the World Wide Web may allow individuals outside of the organization to access information contained in the organization's database. Less publicized but equally important is the database administrator's role of offering training to users who need to access the database to fulfill their job duties. Security requires both keeping unauthorized individuals out as well as allowing easy access for organizationally authorized individuals.

All managers need to understand basic database structures and how to retrieve data from the database. The understanding is crucial to agile decision making.

Key Terms

data field (field)
record
file
database
database management system (DBMS)
flat file
key
hierarchical database structure

relational database structure
implicit relationship
database concept
data redundancy
data consistency
data accuracy
data independence
process-oriented modeling

enterprise modeling approach
entity-relationship diagram (ERD)
class diagram
query-by-example (QBE)
structured query language (SQL)
online analytical processing (OLAP)
database administrator
database programmer

Key Concepts

- database concept
- database structures
- data modeling
- knowledge discovery

Questions

1. How do the general definition of a database and the restrictive definition of a database differ?
2. Assume you know there is a salary value of $45,000. Is the $45,000 (a) a data field value, (b) a data field name, or (c) a record?
3. You open a file (such as a spreadsheet file) and see column headings of "StudentID," "StudentName," "Semester," "Course1," "Grade1," "Course2," "Grade2," "Course3," and "Grade3." Why is this not a flat file?
4. What is a key?
5. What is a candidate key?
6. How are relationships between tables established for relational databases?
7. How does data redundancy lead to data inconsistency?
8. How are users more likely to obtain information from a database? Would they use query-by-example or structured query language?
9. Why has the relational database structure been so much more successful than the hierarchical or network structures?
10. What is data independence?
11. What is the difference between the process-oriented approach to determining data needs and the enterprise modeling approach?
12. When should a firm use a process-oriented approach to determining data needs as opposed to an enterprise modeling approach?
13. What is represented in a class diagram that is not represented in an entity-relationship diagram?
14. Who in the firm is primarily responsible for database security?
15. The cost of database management software and hardware is an often-cited disadvantage. Why are those costs becoming less significant?

Topics for Discussion

1. Why are implicit relationships among data better suited for the changing data needs of firms than explicit relationships?
2. How do techniques such as entity-relationship diagrams and class diagrams help users and information systems professionals develop information systems?
3. How can database forms improve the accuracy and consistency of the database?
4. Assume your firm has a database backup schedule and transaction logs. So far, your firm has never had to use them. What is the danger of never having tested the backup system to assure that a new database can be generated from the backup and transaction log?

Problems

1. Use a database management system software package of your choice and define the DEPARTMENT and COURSE tables shown in Tables 6.5 and 6.6. Next, enter the records from Tables 6.5 and 6.6 into your newly created database.
2. Compare the database management software features of DB2 from IBM, SQL Server from Microsoft, and Oracle (from Oracle).
3. What difficulties would your firm have in using the enterprise modeling technique if it already has an existing database management system in place?

Case Problem

MAPLE TREE INDUSTRIES

You have one of the most successful computer consulting firms in Canada that deals with helping small companies formalize their databases as they grow beyond simple computer applications for accounting and need managerial information systems. Your first consulting jobs dealt with solving quality control issues for manufacturing companies, but you have since branched out to serving other industries.

Last week you presented a database seminar in Toronto that was attended by over 25 executives in small but high-growth companies. The $2,500 tuition paid by each attending executive made the seminar a financial success, but you expect an even greater return in the form of follow-up consulting activity.

While enjoying your morning cup of coffee, you go through the stack of mail. You notice an envelope from Maple Tree Industries, and you recall that the company had a representative at the seminar. You open the envelope and read:

> Dear Sir or Madam:
>
> I greatly enjoyed the database seminar. I was surprised and excited to learn of the potential that a database management system offers. I realized that my company has many computer-based applications but no real implementation of a database. I want to change that.
>
> We are very interested in implementing a database management system and would like to consider retaining you as a consultant on the project. At present, we have no in-house database management expertise. We do use a popular software package to perform accounting transactions; order entry, accounts receivable, and such. Could you please prepare a short list of the basic steps that we should take in implementing a DBMS? The list will give us a good idea of what we must do and an indication of the support we can expect from you in project planning. I am making the same request of two other computer consultants that I know.
>
> I look forward to receiving your response.
>
> Sincerely,
> Anthony Scarmodo, President
> Maple Tree Industries

ASSIGNMENT

Assume that Maple Tree has a good information services staff and is a prospect for implementing a database management system. What steps should be made to identify data that should be incorporated into a database management system for Maple Tree? How should the users of the database and the information systems professionals communicate their ideas for the data needed in the database? Should a database administrator be identified early, while the database design is evolving, or after the database has been implemented?

NOTES

[1] David C. Hayes and James E. Hunton, "What You Better Know About Databases," *Journal of Accountancy*, Vol. 187, No. 1, January 1999, 61–63.
[2] Helen Hasan, Peter Hyland, David Dodds, and Raja Veeraraghavan, "Approaches to the Development of Multi-Dimensional Databases: Lessons from Four Case Studies," *Database for Advances in Information Systems*, Vol. 31, No. 3, Summer 2000, 10–23.
[3] Robert W. Taylor and Randall L. Frank, "CODASYL Data-Base Management Systems," *ACM Computing Surveys*, Vol. 8, No. 1, March 1976, 67.
[4] Andrew B. Whinston and Clyde W. Holsapple, "DBMS for Micros," *Datamation*, Vol. 27, No. 4, April 1981, 165–166.
[5] "CODASYL: Introduction to Feature Analysis of Generalized Data Base Management Systems," *Communications of the ACM*, Vol. 14, No. 5, May 1971, 308–318.
[6] C. J. Date, *An Introduction to Database Systems*, Addison-Wesley, Reading, MA, 1977.
[7] E. F. Codd, "A Relational Model of Data for Large Shared Databanks," *Communications of the ACM*, June 1970, 377–387.
[8] Guy Doumeingth, Yves Ducq, and Bruno Vallespir, "Production Management and Enterprise Modelling," *Computers in Industry*, Vol. 42, No. 2, 3, 245–263.
[9] Peter Chen, "The Entity-Relationship Model–Towards a Unified View of Data," *ACM Transactions on Database Systems*, Vol. 1, No. 1, March 1976, 9–36.
[10] Peter Chen, originator of the Entity-Relationship (ER) model, was awarded the Harry M. Goode Memorial Award from the IEEE Computer Society in 2002.
[11] N. Colossi, W. Malloy, and B. Reinwald, "Relational Extensions for OLAP," *IBM Systems Journal*, Vol. 41, No. 4, 714–731.
[12] Adopted from Doug Levy, "Computing Cures Database May Put Drugs on Shelves Years Faster," *USA Today* (May 17, 1998), Feature—Money Section, 1B.

Chapter 7

Systems Development

Learning Objectives

After studying this chapter, you should

- Recognize the systems approach as the basic framework for solving problems of all kinds.
- Know how to apply the systems approach in solving systems problems.
- Understand that the systems development life cycle (SDLC) is a methodology—a recommended way to develop systems.
- Be familiar with the main SDLC approaches—the traditional waterfall cycle, prototyping, rapid application development, phased development, and business process redesign.
- Know the basics of modeling processes with data flow diagrams and use cases.
- Understand how systems development projects are managed in a top-down fashion.

Introduction

Both managers and systems developers can apply the systems approach when solving problems. The approach consists of three phases of effort—preparation, definition, and solution. Within each phase is a sequence of steps. Preparation effort consists of viewing the firm as a system, recognizing the environmental system, and identifying the firm's subsystems. Definition effort involves proceeding from a system to a subsystem level and analyzing system parts in a certain sequence. Solution effort involves identifying the alternative solutions, evaluating them, and selecting the best one. The solution is then implemented and follow-up action ensures that the problem is solved.

The systems approach is applied to the problem of system development and it is called the systems development life cycle (SDLC). The traditional approach consists of five phases, taken one after the other. Prototyping is a refinement of the traditional approach that recognizes the advantage of repetitively soliciting user feedback and responding with system improvements, and continuing this cycle until the system meets user needs. Some prototypes become production systems; others serve as blueprints for systems developed using another methodology. An application of the prototyping philosophy to the development of large-scale systems is rapid application development, or RAD. In addition to incorporating prototyping, RAD also encourages the use of other approaches, such as the use of computer modeling tools and specialized teams, that are intended to speed up the development process.

An SDLC approach that is currently very popular is phased development. It is based on the idea that a project is subdivided into modules, and that analysis, design, and preliminary construction efforts are directed at each module. Then the modules are integrated in a final construction effort.

When there is a need to take a completely new approach to improving an existing system, the methodology is business process redesign. The term reengineering is also used, although that is only one aspect of the work. Other aspects can involve restructuring and reverse engineering.

Data flow diagrams, or DFDs, have been the most popular tool for modeling processes during the past twenty years or so. DFDs are a very natural way to document processes—using symbols for the processes, arrows to show how data flows link the processes, symbols for data stores, and symbols for environmental elements that interface with the system. DFDs can be prepared in a hierarchy to show varying degrees of detail. Although DFDs are good for showing the processing overview, they fail to do a good job of showing processing detail. Other tools, such as use cases, can be used at that point.

Systems development is very costly in terms of both money and time. As a result, the process should be well managed. The firm's executives provide the highest level of oversight, often with the executives participating in an MIS steering committee that oversees all of the ongoing projects. Each project is typically managed by a project leader. Such project management tools as Gantt charts, network diagrams, and reports enable the executives, managers, and developers to keep projects on track.

THE SYSTEMS APPROACH

A search for the origin of a systematic problem-solving process leads to John Dewey, a philosophy professor at Columbia University around the turn of the century. In a 1910 book he identified three series of judgments involved in adequately resolving a controversy.[1]

1. Recognize the controversy.
2. Weigh alternative claims.
3. Form a judgment.

Dewey did not use the term "systems approach," but he recognized the sequential nature of problem solving—beginning with a problem, then considering different ways to solve it, and finally selecting the solution that appears best.

Dewey's framework essentially lay dormant for many years, but during the late 1960s and early 1970s, interest in systematic problem solving came on strong. Management scientists and information specialists were searching for efficient and effective ways to solve problems and the recommended framework became known as the **systems approach**—a series of problem-solving steps that ensure the problem is first understood, alternative solutions are considered, and the selected solution works.

A Series of Steps

Although the many descriptions of the systems approach all follow the same basic pattern, the number of steps can vary. We use ten steps, grouped into three phases, as illustrated in Figure 7.1. **Preparation effort** prepares the problem solver by providing a systems orientation. **Definition effort** consists of identifying a problem to be solved and then understanding it. **Solution effort** involves identifying alternative solutions, evaluating them, selecting the one that appears best, implementing that solution, and following up to ensure that the problem is solved.

Preparation Effort

The three preparatory steps do not have to be taken in order. In addition, the steps can be taken over a long period of time—beginning now, in this course.

STEP ONE—VIEW THE FIRM AS A SYSTEM   You must be able to see your firm as a system. This can be accomplished by using the general systems model from Chapter 2 as a template. You must be able to see how your firm or organizational unit fits the model.

STEP TWO—RECOGNIZE THE ENVIRONMENTAL SYSTEM   The relationship of the firm or organization to its environment is also important. The eight environmental elements that we discussed in Chapter 2 provide an effective way of positioning the firm as a system in its environment.

STEP THREE—IDENTIFY THE FIRM'S SUBSYSTEMS   The major subsystems of the firm can take several forms. The easiest for the manager to see are the *business areas*. Each can be regarded as a separate system, as shown in Figure 7.2.

Figure 7.1 **Phases and Steps of the Systems Approach**

Phase I: Preparation effort
Step 1. View the firm as a system
Step 2. Recognize the environmental system
Step 3. Identify the firm's subsystems

Phase II: Definition effort
Step 4. Proceed from a system to subsystem level
Step 5. Analyze system parts in a certain sequence

Phase III: Solution effort
Step 6. Identify alternative solutions
Step 7. Evaluate the alternative solutions
Step 8. Select the best solution
Step 9. Implement the solution
Step 10. Follow up to ensure that the solution is effective

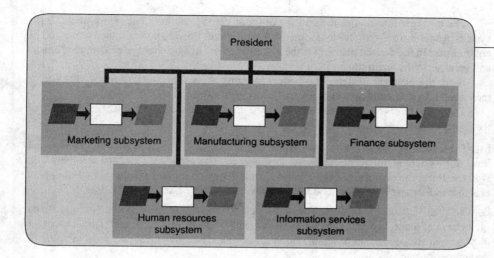

Figure 7.2 Each Business Area Is a System

The manager can also regard the *levels of management* as subsystems. The subsystems have a superior–subordinate relationship and are connected by both information and decision flows. When the manager sees the firm in this manner, the importance of information flows is clear. Without these flows, upper-level management is cut off from the lower levels.

The manager can also use *resource flows* as a basis for dividing the firm into subsystems. Finance, human resources, and information services all represent organization units dedicated to facilitate resource flows. Supply chain management is another example of managing a resource flow.

When a manager can see the firm as a system of subsystems existing within an environment, a systems orientation has been achieved. The manager has completed the preparation effort and is now ready to use the systems approach in problem solving.

Definition Effort

Definition effort is usually stimulated by a **problem trigger**—a signal that things are going better or worse than planned. The signal can originate from within the firm or its environment and initiates a problem-solving process. In most cases the trigger is a response to a symptom of a problem rather than a problem. A **symptom** is a condition that is produced by the problem and is usually more obvious than the root cause of the problem. For example, a symptom might be low sales that are reflected in a sales reporting system. Finding the root cause of the low sales might require some digging through several layers of symptoms before identifying the root cause as poor sales training.

We define a **problem** as a condition or event that is harmful or potentially harmful, or beneficial or potentially beneficial to the firm. This recognizes that managers react to things going better than expected just as well as to things going worse than expected. In the case of the better performance, the manager wants to know why it occurred so that it might be continued. In the case of the worse performance, the manager wants to bring it back up to expectations.

The manager or someone in the manager's unit usually identifies the problem or a symptom. Once the problem is identified, the manager can call on a system developer to assist in problem understanding. The definition effort consists of two steps—proceed from a system to a subsystem level, and analyze system parts in a certain sequence.

STEP FOUR—PROCEED FROM A SYSTEM TO A SUBSYSTEM LEVEL As the manager seeks to understand the problem, the analysis begins on the system for which the manager is responsible. The system can be the firm or one of its units. The analysis then proceeds down the system hierarchy, level by level.

The manager first studies the position of the system in relation to its environment. Is the system in equilibrium with its environment? Are resources flowing between the system and its environment in the desired manner? Is the system meeting its objectives of providing products and services to the environment?

Next, the manager analyzes the system in terms of its *subsystems*. Are the subsystems integrated into a smoothly functioning unit, working toward the system objectives?

The purpose of this top-down analysis is to identify the system *level* where the cause of the problem exists.

STEP FIVE—ANALYZE SYSTEM PARTS IN A CERTAIN SEQUENCE As the manager studies each system level, the system elements are analyzed in sequence. The sequence is shown in Figure 7.3, which reflects the priority of each element in the problem-solving process. For example, a problem in Element Four cannot be solved if there is a problem in Element Three.

ELEMENT ONE—EVALUATE STANDARDS The performance standards for a system are usually stated in the form of plans, budgets, and quotas. Management sets the standards and must ensure that they are realistic, understandable, measurable, and valid (i.e., they must be a good measure of system performance).

ELEMENT TWO—COMPARE SYSTEM OUTPUTS WITH STANDARDS Once managers are satisfied with the standards, they next evaluate the outputs of the system by comparing them with the standards.

If the system is meeting its standards, there is no need to continue with the systems approach to problem solving *on this particular system level*. Rather, the manager should reevaluate the standards in the light of the good current performance. Perhaps the standards should be raised. If the system is not meeting its standards, the manager must identify the cause, and the remaining system elements are possible locations.

ELEMENT THREE—EVALUATE MANAGEMENT A critical appraisal is made of the system's management and *organizational structure*. Does a management team exist in terms of both the required quantity and quality? Are there enough managers, and do they have the right skills and abilities? In a similar fashion, does the organizational structure help or hinder the problem-solving process? In some cases, the establishment of a new unit is in order.

ELEMENT FOUR—EVALUATE THE INFORMATION PROCESSOR It is possible that a good management team is present, but the team is simply not getting the information that it needs. If this is the case, the needs must be identified and an adequate information system must be designed and implemented.

ELEMENT FIVE—EVALUATE THE INPUTS AND THE INPUT RESOURCES When this level of the system analysis is reached, the conceptual system is no longer a concern, and the problem exists within the physical system. An analysis is made of both the physical resources in the input element of the system (such as the receiving dock, quality control section, and the raw materials stockroom) and the resources flowing through that element from the environment.

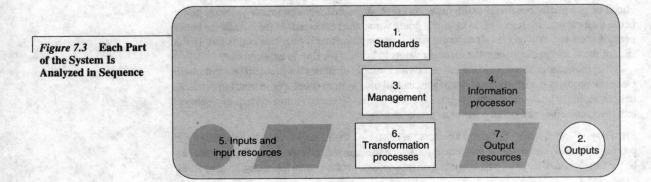

Figure 7.3 Each Part of the System Is Analyzed in Sequence

ELEMENT SIX—EVALUATE THE TRANSFORMATION PROCESSES Inefficient procedures and practices might be causing difficulties in transforming the inputs into outputs. Automation, robotics, computer-aided design and computer-aided manufacturing (CAD/CAM), and computer-integrated manufacturing (CIM) are examples of efforts to solve transformation problems.

ELEMENT SEVEN—EVALUATE THE OUTPUT RESOURCES In analyzing Element Two, we paid attention to the outputs produced by the system. Here we consider the physical resources in the output element of the system. Examples of such resources are the finished goods storeroom, shipping dock personnel and machines, and the fleet of delivery trucks.

With the definition effort completed, the location of the problem in terms of system level and element is established. Now that problem can be solved.

Solution Effort

Solution effort involves a consideration of the feasible alternatives, a selection of the best one, and its implementation.

STEP SIX—IDENTIFY ALTERNATIVE SOLUTIONS The manager identifies *different* ways to solve the *same* problem. For example, assume that the problem is a computer that cannot handle the firm's increasing volume of activity. Three alternative solutions are identified: (1) add more devices to the existing computer to increase its capacity and speed; (2) replace the existing computer with a larger computer; (3) replace the existing computer with a local area network of smaller computers.

STEP SEVEN—EVALUATE THE ALTERNATIVE SOLUTIONS All of the alternatives must be evaluated using the same **evaluation criteria**—measures of how well an alternative would solve the problem. The evaluation produces advantages and disadvantages of implementing each alternative. However, the fundamental measure is the extent to which an alternative enables the system to meet its objectives.

STEP EIGHT—SELECT THE BEST SOLUTION After evaluating the alternatives, it is next necessary to select the one that appears to be best. Henry Mintzberg, a management theorist, has identified three ways that managers go about selecting the best alternative.[2]

- **Analysis**—A systematic evaluation of options, considering their consequences on the organization's goals. An example is a presentation by the development team to the MIS steering committee, giving advantages and disadvantages of all options.
- **Judgment**—The mental process of a single manager. For example, a manufacturing manager applies experience and intuition in evaluating the layout of a new plant proposed by a mathematical model.
- **Bargaining**—Negotiations between several managers. An example is the give and take that goes on among members of the executive committee concerning which database management system to use.

The emphasis in this chapter is on analysis. However, judgment and bargaining should not be ignored. All three ways would probably be involved in the selection of the best of the three computer alternatives.

STEP NINE—IMPLEMENT THE SOLUTION The problem is not solved simply by selecting the best solution. It is necessary to implement the solution. In our example, it would be necessary to install the required computing equipment.

STEP TEN—FOLLOW UP TO ENSURE THAT THE SOLUTION IS EFFECTIVE The manager and developers should stay on top of the situation to make certain that the solution achieves the planned performance. When the solution falls short of expectations, it is necessary to retrace the problem-solving steps to determine what went wrong. Then another try is made. This process is repeated until the manager is satisfied that the problem has been solved.

THE SYSTEMS DEVELOPMENT LIFE CYCLE

The systems approach is a methodology. A **methodology** is a recommended way of doing something. The systems approach is the basic methodology for solving problems of all kinds. The **system life development cycle (SDLC)** is an application of the systems approach to the development of an information system.

THE TRADITIONAL SDLC

It didn't take the first system developers long to figure out that several stages of effort should be taken in a certain sequence if the project is to have the best chance of success. The stages are

- Planning
- Analysis
- Design
- Implementation
- Use.

The project is planned and the necessary resources to do the work are assembled. The existing system is analyzed to understand the problem and determine the functional requirements of the new system. The new system is then designed and implemented. After implementation, the system is used—ideally for a long period of time.

Because the tasks follow an orderly pattern and are performed in a top-down fashion, the traditional SDLC is often referred to as the **waterfall approach**. The flow of the activity is in one direction—leading to project completion.

Figure 7.4 illustrates how the life cycle phases can also fit into a circular pattern over time. When a system outlives its usefulness and must be replaced, a new life cycle is initiated, beginning with the planning phase.

It is easy to see how the traditional SDLC is an application of the systems approach. The problem is defined in the planning and analysis stages. Then, the alternative solutions are identified and evaluated in the design stage. Then, the best solution is implemented and used. During the use stage, feedback information is gathered to see how well the system is solving the defined problem.

Figure 7.4 The Circular Pattern of the System Life Cycle

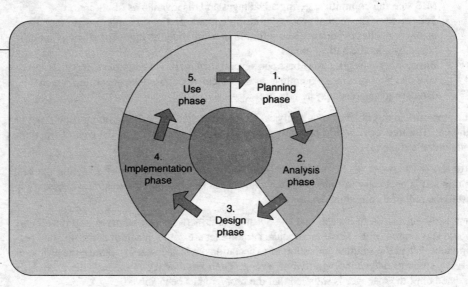

PROTOTYPING

Although it is difficult to argue with the logical unfolding of the stages of the traditional SDLC, it suffered its shortcomings. As systems grew in size and complexity, it became impossible to make a one-shot pass through the stages. Developers were always looping back and redoing things to come up with a system that satisfied the users. Also, projects tended to drag on for months and years, and almost always exceeded their budgets. In response to these limitations, systems developers decided to apply a technique that had proven effective in other pursuits, such as the design of automobiles—the use of prototypes. Applied to system development, a **prototype** is a version of a potential system that provides the developers and potential users with an idea of how the system in its completed form will function. The process of producing a prototype is called **prototyping**. The idea is to produce the prototype as quickly as possible, perhaps overnight, and obtain user feedback that will enable the prototype to be improved—again, very quickly.

Types of Prototypes[3]

A common question that people often ask when first hearing about a computer prototype is, "Does the prototype become the actual system?" The answer is, "It all depends."

There are two types of prototypes—evolutionary and requirements. An **evolutionary prototype** is continually refined until it contains all of the functionality that the users require of the new system. Then, it is put into production. So, an evolutionary prototype becomes the actual system. A **requirements prototype**, on the other hand, is developed as a way to define the functional requirements of the new system when the users are unable to articulate exactly what they want. By reviewing the requirements prototype as the features are added, the users are able to define the processing required for new system. When the requirements are defined, the requirements prototype has served its purpose and another project is initiated to develop the new system. So, a requirements prototype does not become the actual system.

DEVELOPMENT OF AN EVOLUTIONARY PROTOTYPE   Figure 7.5 shows the steps involved in developing an evolutionary prototype. There are four steps, as follows:

1. **Identify user needs.** The developer interviews the user to obtain an idea of what is required from the system.

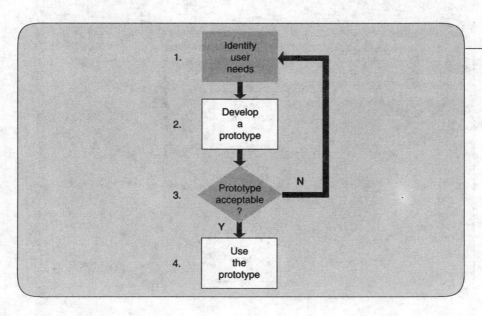

Figure 7.5
Development of an Evolutionary Prototype

2. **Develop a prototype.** The developer uses one or more prototyping tools to develop a prototype. Examples of prototyping tools are integrated application generators and prototyping toolkits. An **integrated application generator** is a prewritten software system that is capable of producing *all* of the desired features in the new system—menus, reports, screens, a database, and so on. A **prototyping toolkit** includes separate software systems, such as electronic spreadsheets or database management systems, each capable of producing a *portion* of the desired system features.
3. **Determine if the prototype is acceptable.** The developer demonstrates the prototype to the user to determine whether it is satisfactory. If so, Step 4 is taken; if not, the prototype is revised by repeating Steps 1, 2, and 3 with a better understanding of the user needs.
4. **Use the prototype.** The prototype becomes the production system.

This approach is possible only when the prototyping tools enable the prototype to contain *all* of the essential elements of the new system.

DEVELOPMENT OF A REQUIREMENTS PROTOTYPE   Figure 7.6 shows the steps involved in developing a requirements prototype. The first three are the same as those taken to develop an evolutionary prototype. The next steps are as follows:

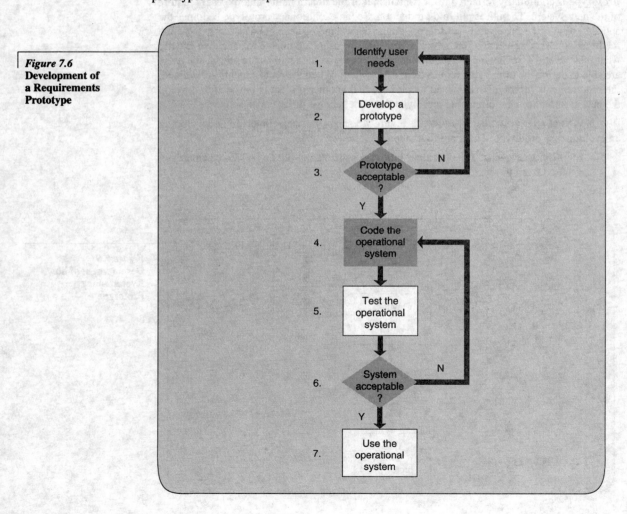

Figure 7.6
Development of a Requirements Prototype

4. **Code the new system.** The developer uses the prototype as the basis for coding the new system.
5. **Test the new system.** The developer tests the system.
6. **Determine if the new system is acceptable.** The user advises the developer whether the system is acceptable. If so, Step 7 is taken; if not, Steps 4 and 5 are repeated.
7. **Put the new system into production.**

This approach is followed when the prototype is intended only to have the *appearance* of a production system but not when it is to contain all of the essential elements.

The Attraction of Prototyping[4]
Both users and developers like prototyping for the following reasons:

- Communications between the developer and user are improved.
- The developer can do a better job of determining the user's needs.
- The user plays a more active role in system development.
- The developers and the user spend less time and effort in developing the system.
- Implementation is much easier because the user knows what to expect.

These advantages enable prototyping to cut developmental costs and increase user satisfaction with the delivered system.

Potential Pitfalls of Prototyping
Prototyping is not without its potential pitfalls. They include:

- The haste to deliver the prototype may produce shortcuts in problem definition, alternative evaluation, and documentation. The shortcuts produce a "quick and dirty" effort.
- The user may get overly excited about the prototype, thus leading to unrealistic expectations regarding the production system.
- Evolutionary prototypes might not be as efficient as systems coded in a programming language.
- The computer–human interface provided by certain prototyping tools may not reflect good design techniques.

Both the user and developers should be aware of these potential pitfalls when they elect to pursue the prototyping approach. However, on balance, prototyping has proven to be one of the most successful SDLC methodologies. It would be difficult to find a development project that did not incorporate prototyping to some degree.

RAPID APPLICATION DEVELOPMENT

A methodology that has the same objective of speedy response to user needs as does prototyping but is broader in scope is RAD. **RAD**, for **rapid application development**, is a term coined by computer consultant and author James Martin and it refers to a development life cycle intended to produce systems quickly without sacrificing quality.[5]

RAD is an integrated set of strategies, methodologies, and tools that exists within an overall framework called information engineering. **Information engineering (IE)** is the name that Martin gives to his overall approach to system development, which treats it as a firm-wide activity. The term **enterprise** is used to describe the entire firm.

Figure 7.7 illustrates the top-down nature of information engineering, involving both data (the left face of the pyramid) and activities (the right face). IE begins at the executive level, with strategic information resources planning applied to the entire enterprise. Martin uses the term **information strategy planning**. Next, each business unit within the firm is subjected to **business area analysis (BAA)** to define the activities or processes and data that are necessary for the unit to function as intended. With the BAA completed, rapid application development can proceed.

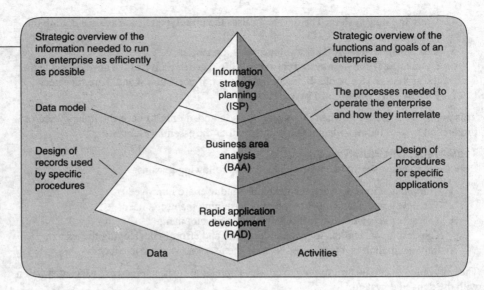

Figure 7.7 Rapid Application Development Is an Integral Part of Information Engineering

Source: James Martin, Rapid Application Development (New York: Macmillan, 1991), Figures 3.23 and 21.2 (combined). © 1991. Adapted by permission of Prentice Hall, Upper Saddle River, NJ.

The Essential Ingredients of RAD

RAD requires four essential ingredients: management, people, methodologies, and tools.

- **Management.** Management, especially top management, should be *experimenters*, who like to do things a new way, or *early adapters*, who quickly learn how to use new methodologies.
- **People.** Rather than utilize a single team to perform all of the SDLC activities, RAD recognizes the efficiencies that can be achieved through the use of specialized teams. Members of these teams are masters of the methodologies and tools that are required to perform their specialized tasks. Martin uses the term **SWAT team**, with SWAT standing for "skilled with advanced tools."
- **Methodologies.** The basic RAD methodology is the **RAD life cycle**, which consists of four phases: (1) requirements planning, (2) user design, (3) construction, and (4) cutover. Users play key roles in each phase, participating with information specialists.
- **Tools.** RAD tools consist mainly of fourth-generation languages and CASE tools that facilitate prototyping and code generation. CASE tools use the computer to prepare documentation that can be transformed into operational software and databases.

Of all the components of information engineering, RAD has probably enjoyed the greatest support. Although it might not be applied exactly as Martin envisioned, its emphasis on user involvement and speed make it very appealing. If you ask CIOs what SDLC they use, they are likely to say, "Oh, we use RAD."

PHASED DEVELOPMENT

The systems development methodology that is used by many firms today is a combination of the traditional SDLC, prototyping, and RAD—taking the best features of each. The traditional SDLC contributed the logical sequence of stages—planning or preparation, analysis, design, and implementation, followed by cutover and use. Prototyping contributed the iterative solicitation of user feedback, which makes it possible to bring a system design in line with user needs. RAD contributed the notion that user involvement goes farther than simply responding to prototypes and includes participation in development, especially the early stages. The name that we give this contemporary methodology is phased development. **Phased development** is an approach for developing information systems that consists of six stages—preliminary investigation, analysis, design, preliminary construction, final construction, and system test and installation. The analysis, design, and preliminary construction stages are taken for each system module.

The Phased Development Stages

The six phased development stages are illustrated in Figure 7.8.

PRELIMINARY INVESTIGATION   The developers, including users as well as information specialists, conduct an enterprise analysis for the purpose of learning about the organization with the systems problem; define the new system objectives, constraints, risks, and scope; evaluate both project and system feasibility; subdivide the system into major components; and obtain user feedback.

ANALYSIS   The developers analyze the users' functional requirements for each system module using a variety of information gathering techniques, and document the findings in the form of process, data, and object models.

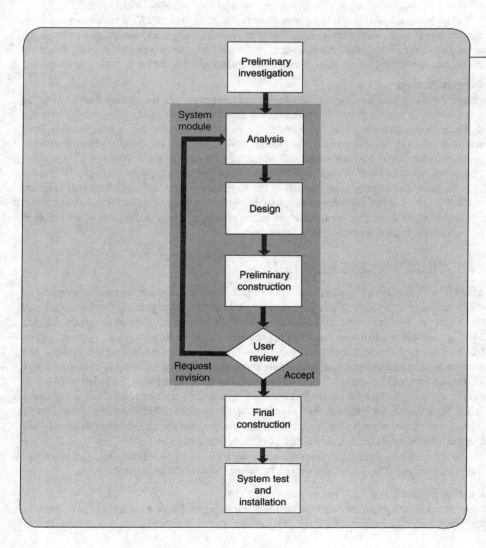

Figure 7.8 **The Stages of the Phased Development Methodology**

DESIGN   The developers design the components and interfaces with other systems for each new system module, and document the design using the various modeling techniques.

PRELIMINARY CONSTRUCTION   The developers construct and test the software and data for each system module, and obtain user feedback. For any modules that do not receive user approval, the analysis, design, and preliminary construction stages are repeated.

FINAL CONSTRUCTION   The module software is integrated to form the complete system, which is tested along with the data. In addition, any needed hardware is obtained and tested, facilities are constructed, and users are trained. The training covers the procedure that users are to follow in using the system, and often the procedure to follow in installing the system on their workstations.

SYSTEM TEST AND INSTALLATION   The developers design and perform a system test that includes not only software and data, but the other information resources as well—hardware, facilities, personnel, and procedures. The system components are installed and a user acceptance test is conducted. Acceptance by the users serves as the go-ahead to proceed to cutover. After the system has been in use for some time, perhaps a few weeks or months, a post-implementation review is conducted to ensure that the system has met the functional requirements.

This sequence of stages is not unlike those of the traditional SDLC. What distinguishes the phased development methodology is the way that analysis, design, and preliminary construction are repeated for each system module separately, rather than for the overall system. When the stages are repeated for the modules, they are called phases; hence the name phased development.

Module Phases

Figure 7.9 illustrates how the module phases are integrated into the system development. In this example, the system has been subdivided into three major modules—a report writer, a database, and a Web interface. The number of modules varies with the system, ranging from one to a dozen or so. You can see that, in the figure, the analysis, design, preliminary construction, and user review are performed separately for each module. Moreover, these three phases are repeated when necessitated by user review—reflecting the prototyping influence.

Whereas prototyping is best suited as the development methodology for small systems, and RAD is best suited for large ones, phased development can be used for the development of systems of all sizes. The key is the way that the system is subdivided into modules and each is analyzed, designed, and constructed separately.

BUSINESS PROCESS REDESIGN

Many of a typical firm's systems were put in place before computer technology became as sophisticated as it is today. These systems include both those that process the firm's data and those that perform basic functions such as drilling for oil or fabricating a manufactured part. Management often concludes that fresh approaches should be taken to these systems, taking full advantage of modern computer technology. The process of reworking the systems has been called **reengineering**. The term **business process redesign (BPR)** is also used. BPR affects the firm's IT operation in two ways. First, IT can apply BPR to the redesign of information systems that can no longer be kept alive by ordinary maintenance. Such systems are called **legacy systems**, because they are too valuable to discard but represent a drain on IS resources. Second, when a firm applies BPR to its major operations, the effort invariably has a ripple effect that results in the redesign of information systems.

IT has devised three techniques for applying BPR—reverse engineering, restructuring, and reengineering. These components can be applied separately or in combination.

Reverse Engineering

Reverse engineering had its origin in business intelligence. Firms have long kept current on their competitors' products by purchasing samples and taking them apart to see what makes

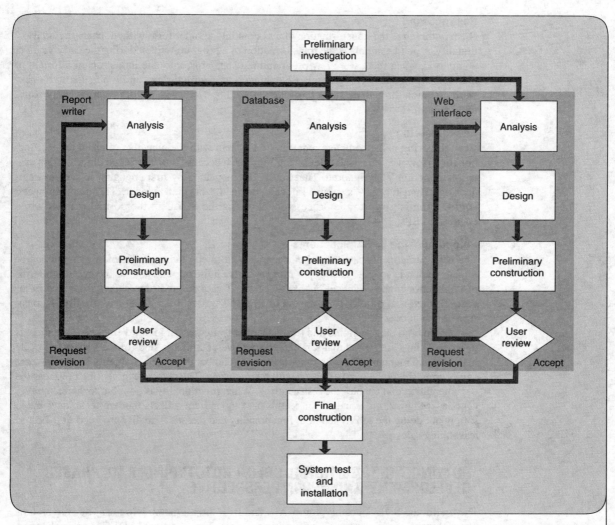

Figure 7.9 Analysis, Design, and Preliminary Construction Are Performed on Each System Module

them tick. The design specifications of the competitors' products are derived from the products themselves, reversing the normal pattern in which the design comes first.

As used in computing, **reverse engineering** is the process of analyzing an existing system to identify its elements and their interrelationships, as well as to create documentation in a higher level of abstraction than currently exists.[6]

The starting point in reverse engineering a system is the computer code, which is transformed into documentation. This documentation can, in turn, be transformed into more abstract descriptions such as data flow diagrams, use cases, and system flowcharts. The transformation can be accomplished manually or by BPR software.

Reverse engineering, therefore, follows a backward path through the system life cycle, reconstructing the system design and planning that went into the original development effort. The result is a thoroughly documented system. However, the system still does exactly what it was originally designed to do. Reverse engineering does not change the **functionality** of a system—the job that it performs. Rather, the objective is to better understand a system in order to make changes by other means, such as restructuring or reengineering.

Restructuring

Restructuring is the transformation of a system into another form without changing its functionality. A good example is the transformation of a program written during the early years of computing, when there were few programming standards, into one in a structured format of hierarchical modules. As with reverse engineering, restructuring can be pursued in a backward direction through each phase of the system life cycle. The result is a completely structured system.

Reengineering

Reengineering is the complete redesign of a system with the objective of changing its functionality. However, it is not a "clean slate" approach because the knowledge of the current system is not completely ignored. That knowledge is gained by first engaging in reverse engineering. Then the new system is developed in the normal manner. The name **forward engineering** is given to the process of following the SDLC in the normal manner while engaged in BPR.

Selection of the BPR Components

The BPR components can be applied separately or in combination, depending on the degree of change that is sought. The proper mix depends on the current state of the system in terms of its functional and technical quality. Figure 7.10 is a diagram that shows these two influences. **Functional quality** is a measure of what the system does. **Technical quality** is a measure of how it does it.

When both the functional and technical quality are poor, a forward engineering project is in order. Things are so bad that it is best to start over, taking the steps of the system life cycle in the normal manner. When the functionality is good but the technical quality is poor, reverse engineering should be pursued along with restructuring. The reverse engineering produces the documentation that enables the restructuring. When functionality is poor but technical quality is good, reengineering is called for. In this case the system reflects modern techniques but is simply not doing the job. When both functionality and technical quality are good, it is best to leave things alone.

PUTTING THE TRADITIONAL SDLC, PROTOTYPING, RAD, PHASED DEVELOPMENT, AND BPR IN PERSPECTIVE

The traditional SDLC, prototyping, RAD, and BPR are all methodologies. They are recommended ways of developing an information system. The traditional SDLC is an application of the systems approach to the problem of system development, and it contains all of the basic system approach elements, beginning with problem identification and ending with system use.

Prototyping is an abbreviated form of the systems approach that focuses on the definition and satisfaction of user needs. Prototyping can exist within the SDLC. In fact, many prototyping efforts may be required during the process of developing a single system.

RAD is an alternative approach to the design and implementation phases of the SDLC. The main contribution of RAD is the speed with which systems are put into use, achieved primarily through the use of computer-based tools and specialized project teams.

Phased development uses the traditional SDLC as a basic framework, and applies it to a project in a modular fashion, using the same tools and concept of specialized teams as does RAD.

Currently, firms are revamping many systems that were implemented with computer technology that is obsolete by today's standards. The name BPR is used for this approach of using technology to its fullest. Prototyping, RAD, and phased development can be used in a BPR project to meet users' needs in a responsive way.

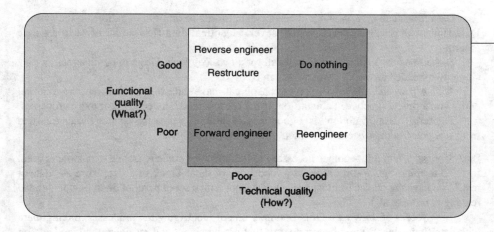

Figure 7.10 **BPR Component Selection Is Based on Both Functional and Technical Quality**

Sources: David Sharon, "The Psychology of Reengineering," IEEE Software 8 (November 1991), 74 © 1990 IEEE; and "Three R's: A White Paper on Application Re-Development," The Re-Development Investigation Team, Texaco Information Systems Enabling Center, Texaco, Inc. (January 30, 1992), 10.

PROCESS MODELING

As developers perform analysis and design, they model the system data, processes, and objects. We describe how process modeling is accomplished with data flow diagrams and use cases. Data and object oriented modeling were described in Chapter 6.

Data Flow Diagrams

A **data flow diagram (DFD)** is a graphic representation of a system that uses four symbol shapes to illustrate how data flows through interconnected processes. The symbols represent (1) environmental elements with which the system interfaces, (2) processes, (3) data flows, and (4) storage of data.

ENVIRONMENTAL ELEMENTS   Environmental elements exist outside the boundary of the system. These elements provide the system with data input and receive the system's data output. In a DFD no distinction is made between data and information. All of the flows are regarded as data.

The name **terminator** is often used to describe the environmental elements, since they mark the points where the system terminates. A terminator is represented in a DFD with a square or a rectangle, labeled with the name of the environmental element.

A terminator can be:

- A *person*, such as a manager, who receives a report from the system.
- An *organization*, such as another department within the company, or another company.
- Another *system* with which our system interfaces.

An important task in systems analysis and design is the definition of the system boundary. The terminators serve this purpose. The developer works within the boundary and establishes linkages with the system's environment in the form of data flows.

PROCESSES   A **process** is something that transforms input into output. It can be illustrated with a circle, a horizontal rectangle, or an upright rectangle with rounded corners. Each process symbol is identified with a label. The most common labeling technique is to use a *verb and an object*, but you can also use the name of a *system* or a *computer program*.

DATA FLOWS   A **data flow** consists of a group of logically related data elements (ranging from a single data element to one or more files) that travel from one point or process to another. The arrow symbol is used to illustrate the flow, and can be drawn with either a straight or curved line.

Data flows can *diverge* when the same data travels to multiple locations in the system. Data flows can also *converge* to show several identical data flows that travel to a single location.

Sometimes the system design will call for a *two-way flow*. This can be illustrated with a single two-headed arrow, or two arrows can be used.

A data flow must involve a process. You can have data flowing between an external entity and a process, between a data store and a process, and between two or more processes.

The term "data in motion" is a good way to think of a data flow, since the data moves from one point in the system to another.

DATA STORAGE When it becomes necessary to hold data for some reason, a data store is used. In DFD terminology, a **data store** is a repository of data. Think of a data store as "data at rest." You have the choice of illustrating a data store with a set of parallel lines, an open-ended rectangle, or an oval.

The process of drawing a DFD is simply one of identifying the processes, linking them with data flows, identifying the terminators that provide input and receive output, and adding data stores where needed.

The DFD in Figure 7.11 illustrates a system that a firm might use to compute commissions for its sales representatives. Here, the terminators are illustrated with rectangles, the processes with upright rectangles with rounded corners, the data flows with straight lines, and the data stores with open-ended rectangles.

A customer fills out a sales order and mails it to the company. In Process 1 the mail is opened and the sales order is removed. The data from the sales order is entered into the information system in Process 2. After the data has been entered, the sales order forms are filed away for safekeeping in the Sales Order Form file. In Process 3 the sales order data is sorted into a particular sequence. The sorted records are then used in Process 4 to prepare a sales commission report for the sales manager.

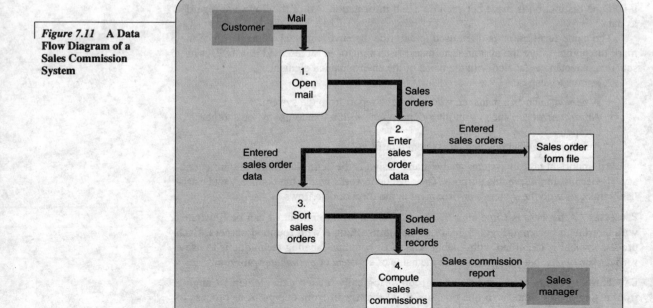

Figure 7.11 A Data Flow Diagram of a Sales Commission System

LEVELED DATA FLOW DIAGRAMS Figure 7.11 identifies the major processes of the system. It is called a **Figure 0 diagram**. We will explain how that name is derived later. It is possible to use additional DFDs to achieve documentation at both a more summarized and a more detailed level. A diagram that documents the system at a more summarized level is called a context diagram, and a diagram that provides more detail is called a Figure *n* diagram.

THE CONTEXT DIAGRAM The **context diagram** positions the system in an environmental context. The diagram consists of a single process symbol that represents the entire system. It shows the data flows leading to and from the terminators. Figure 7.12 is a context diagram of the sales commission system.

When drawing a context diagram, you:

1. Use only a single process symbol.
2. Label the process symbol to represent the entire system. You can use a verb plus object such as "Process sales commissions," or you can use the system name as in the figure.
3. Do not number the single process symbol.
4. Include all of the terminators for the system.
5. Show all of the data flows between the terminators and the system.

Although the context diagram documents a system at the highest level, it is usually easier to begin the documentation at a lower level—say, the Figure 0 level.

FIGURE *n* DIAGRAMS When it is necessary to document the system in greater detail than the Figure 0 diagram, you use one or more Figure *n* diagrams. A **Figure *n* diagram** documents a single process of a DFD in a greater amount of detail. The *n* represents the number of the process on the next higher level that is being documented. Take the sales commission system in Figure 7.11, for example. Processes 1, 2, and 3 are documented in sufficient detail; however, Process 4 represents two processes—compute the commission amounts and accumulate the totals.

Figure 7.13 shows a **Figure 4 diagram**. It explodes Process 4 of the Figure 0 diagram, making it a Figure 4 diagram. If you document Process 4.1 in still more detail, you draw another Figure *n* diagram, called a Figure 4.1 diagram. As you continue to document lower levels, you use such names as Figure 4.1.1, Figure 4.1.1.1, and so on.

Now you can understand why the DFD in Figure 7.11 is called a Figure 0 diagram. It is because the process on the next higher level, in the context diagram, is unnumbered.

Notice that the data flow into Process 4.1 in Figure 7.13 has a small circle at one end. The circle, called a **connector**, contains the number of the process that provides the data flow. A connector can also be used in the same way to show the destination process of data leaving a system. This is the way that the processes of one DFD are linked to the processes of another.

The term **leveled DFDs** is used to describe the hierarchy of diagrams, ranging from the context diagram to the lowest-level Figure *n* diagram, that are used to document a system.

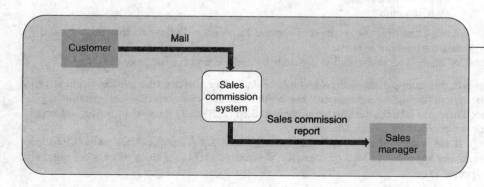

Figure 7.12 A Context Diagram of a Sales Commission System

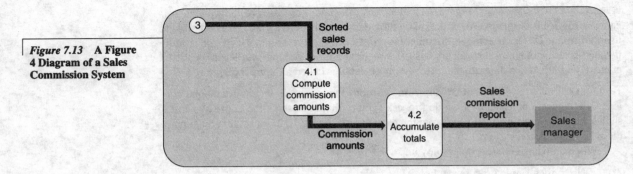

Figure 7.13 A Figure 4 Diagram of a Sales Commission System

How Much Detail to Show   There are two rules of thumb to follow when deciding how many levels of DFDs to use. One, restrict a single DFD to no more than six to eight processes. Two, use another tool to document the lowest level of detail, but use no more than a single page. If more space is required, you stopped using data flow diagramming too soon. A good process modeling tool to use for greater detail is the use case.

Use Cases

A **use case** is a narrative description in an outline form of the dialog that occurs between a primary and secondary system. In most cases, the primary system is a computer program and the secondary system is a person interacting with the computer program. The dialog usually consists of actions that are taken by the participants, such as the actions by a data entry operator and the computer system.

There are two use case formats. One is a continuous narrative with each action numbered sequentially. The other is called the **ping pong format** because it consists of two narratives and the numbering indicates how the tasks alternate between the primary and secondary systems. The ping pong format is the most popular format, and is illustrated in Figure 7.14. This example illustrates the following actions:

A data entry operator logs on with a password.

The system verifies the password or denies entry.

The data entry operator enters sales order data into the workstation. The order data includes:

- Customer number
- Item number
- Item quantity

The order entry program accesses master files to verify the accuracy of:

- Customer number
- Item number

When a number is not verified as correct, the program displays an error message and asks the operator to reenter.

When the operator wishes to conclude the order entry process, he or she logs off.

In this example, the actions involve the data entry operator (the left-hand column) and the system (the right-hand column). You begin on the left with Step 1.0—the operator logging on. Then, you take the next higher-numbered Step (2.0) where the system verifies the operator and prompts for more information.

If the system does not verify the operator, Steps 2.0-A and 2.1-A are taken. Alphabetic letters are appended to Step numbers for **alternative events**—actions that are not normally expected to occur.

Use case name:	Enter sales order data
Description:	Data entry operation for order entry system
Prerequisites:	Create customer, create item
Associations:	Main menu
Principle Actor:	Data entry operator

Data Entry Operator	System
1.0 Operator logs on with a password 1.0-A Return to main menu 1.1-A Go to 7.0-A 3.0 Operator enters customer number, item number, and item quantity 3.0-A Return to main menu 3.1-A Go to 7.0-A 6.0 Go to 3.0 6.0-A Return to main menu 6.0-A Log off	2.0 System verifies operator and prompts operator to enter additional information 2.0-A System does not verify operator and prompts to reenter 2.1-A Go to 1.0 4.0 System verifies customer number and item number 4.0-A System does not verify customer number and item number 4.1-A System displays an error message and prompts operator to reenter 4.2-A Go to 3.0 5.0 System saves order data 7.0 System logs employee off 7.0-A System displays main menu

Figure 7.14 A Use Case

If the system verifies the operator, he or she executes Step 3.0, entering the data. If the system does not verify the operator, he or she is directed to the main menu (Step 3.0-A), and Step 3.1-A specifies that Step 7.0-A next be executed with the system displaying the main menu.

In Steps 4.0 and 4.0-A through 4.2-A, the system either verifies or does not verify the entered data, and the verified data is saved in Step 5.0

After the data is saved in 5.0, Step 6.0 transfers the logic back to 3.0 where the operator can enter more data, or the operator can indicate a desire to return to the main menu (Step 6.0-A).

Use Case Guidelines
A set of guidelines for preparing a use case in the ping pong format is shown in Figure 7.15.

When to Use Data Flow Diagrams and Use Cases
Data flow diagrams and use cases are most often prepared during the preliminary investigation and analysis stages of the phased development methodology. The DFDs illustrate an overview of the processing and the use cases provide the detail. Normally, several use cases are required to support a single Figure 0 diagram. For example, the Figure 0 diagram in Figure 7.11 would be supported by two use cases—one addressing the dialog between the data entry operator in Step 2 and the sort program in Step 3, and another between the sort program and the program that computes sales commissions in Step 4.

PROJECT MANAGEMENT

The first system development projects were managed by the manager of the IT unit, assisted by the managers of systems analysis, programming, and operations. Through trial and error, the management responsibility has gradually encompassed higher management levels—the strategic level in some cases. Today, it is possible for life cycle management to span several organizational levels and to involve managers outside of IT. Figure 7.16 shows the hierarchical

> **Use Case Guidelines**
>
> 1. Begin numbering with 1.0 on the left-hand side to represent the first user action.
>   Example: 1.0 Employee logs on with a password.
> 2. The first entry in the right-hand side should be 2.0, for the first system action.
> 3. Use decimal numbers to indicate steps taken in a sequence *that are all part of a particular action*. Otherwise, use ascending whole numbers (3, 4, 5, etc.).
>   Example: 2.0 System verifies user
>   2.1 System prompts user to enter additional information
> 4. Append an alphabetical letter to a sequence number for an alternate event.
>   Example: 2.0-A System does not verify user
>   2.1-A System prompts user to reenter password
> 5. When there are mutually exclusive alternate events, use multiple alphabetical letters.
> 6. For *subsidiary* actions, use a whole number for the basic action, followed by decimal numbers for the subsidiary actions.
>   Example: 3.0 User creates report
>   3.1 User specifies starting and ending dates
>   3.2 User specifies report type
> 7. For *optional* actions, use a whole number for the basic action, followed by decimal numbers and alphabetical letters for the optional actions.
>   Example: 3.2 User specifies report type
>   3.3-A User specifies summary tabular report
>   3.4-A User specifies detailed tabular report
>   3.5-A User specifies graphical report
> 8. At the end of the process, the user should choose to repeat the process or log off.
>   Example: 10.0 User returns to the main menu
>   10.0-A User logs off
> 9. When the user logs off, the system should respond by logging the user off.
>   Example: 11.0-A System logs user off.

Figure 7.15 Use Case Guidelines

nature of project management. In this example, there are five development projects ongoing at the same time, all managed by the MIS steering committee.

When the system has strategic value or affects the entire organization, the president or the firm's executive committee of the president and vice-presidents may decide to oversee the development project. Many firms establish a special committee below the level of the executive committee that assumes responsibility for overseeing all of the systems projects. When the purpose of a committee is to provide ongoing guidance, direction, and control, it is called a steering committee.

The MIS Steering Committee

When a firm establishes a steering committee for the purpose of directing the use of the firm's computing resources, the name **MIS steering committee** is used.

Permanent members of the MIS steering committee invariably include top executives. Temporary members include lower-level managers and consultants who participate during the time that their expertise is needed.

The MIS steering committee performs three main functions:[7]

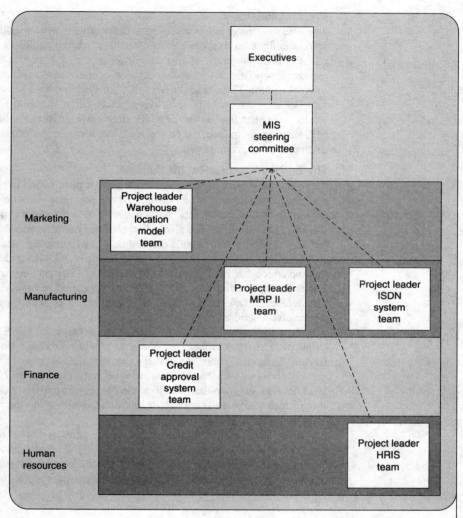

Figure 7.16
Managers of a System Life Cycle Are Arranged in a Hierarchy

- It **establishes policies** that ensure computer support for achieving the strategic objectives of the firm.
- It **provides fiscal control** by serving as the approval authority for all requests for computer-related funds.
- It **resolves conflicts** that arise concerning priorities for computer use.

In effect, the task of the MIS steering committee is to carry out both the overall strategy that is established by the executive committee and the strategic plan for information resources.

By centralizing the management of system life cycles within the steering committee, two main advantages accrue.[8] The likelihood is increased:

- that the computer will be used to support users throughout the firm.
- that computer projects will be characterized by good planning and control.

The MIS steering committee is the most visible evidence that the firm intends to make information resources available to all users who have a genuine need.

Project Leadership

The MIS steering committee seldom gets directly involved with the details of the work. That responsibility goes to project teams. A **project team** includes all of the persons who participate in the development of an information system. A team might have as many as a dozen members, consisting of some combination of users, information specialists, and perhaps an internal auditor. The auditor ensures that the system design satisfies certain requirements in terms of accuracy, controls, security, and auditability. The team activity is directed by a **team leader** or **project leader** who provides direction throughout the life of the project. Unlike the MIS steering committee, the project team is not ongoing, since it is usually disbanded when implementation is completed.

The Project Management Mechanism

The basis for project management is the project plan, which is prepared during the preliminary investigation stage when the phased development methodology is followed. When the project objectives, constraints, and scope have been defined it is possible to identify the tasks that must be performed. The plan is first sketched out in a general form but is then made more specific. A popular format for a detailed plan is a Gantt chart, which identifies the tasks, who will perform them, and when they will be performed. A **Gantt chart** is a horizontal bar chart that includes a bar for each task to be performed. The bars are arranged in a time sequence. Figure 7.17 is the first part of a Gantt chart, prepared using a Microsoft Excel spreadsheet. The number of tasks increases as the project becomes more complex. Even simple projects can involve a hundred or more tasks.

A complement to the Gantt chart is the network diagram. A **network diagram**, also called a CPM (for Critical Path Method) diagram or PERT (for Program Evaluation and Review Technique) chart, is a drawing that identifies activities, linked with arrows that show the sequence in which the activities are to be performed. Figure 7.18 is an example of a high-level network diagram that identifies the phases of a project. Microsoft Project, the project management software system from Microsoft, will prepare the network diagram automatically from the Gantt chart data.

Gantt charts and network diagrams are examples of graphic reports. Narrative reports, in the form of weekly written reports prepared by the project leader, provide another way to communicate project information to the MIS steering committee. The committee meets periodically and the project leaders supplement their written reports with oral reports that review

Highlights in MIS

A Quick Fix for IT at the FBI? Think Again.[9]

On May 7, 2001, the FBI selected DynCorp to spearhead its three-year, $400 million Trilogy IT infrastructure project. Then: September 11. All of a sudden, three years seemed way too long; there was a need for immediate action. The FBI began to put on pressure to complete the project by the end of 2002.

On July 16, 2002 the Bush administration announced the details of the National Strategy for Homeland Security. Also on that same day, the FBI informed a congressional panel that it would be impossible to speed up the Trilogy project—even with increased funding. The reason? The FBI determined that it was more important to do the project right than do it quick. Sometimes, pouring more money into a developmental project to speed things up won't work—regardless of how important the project is.

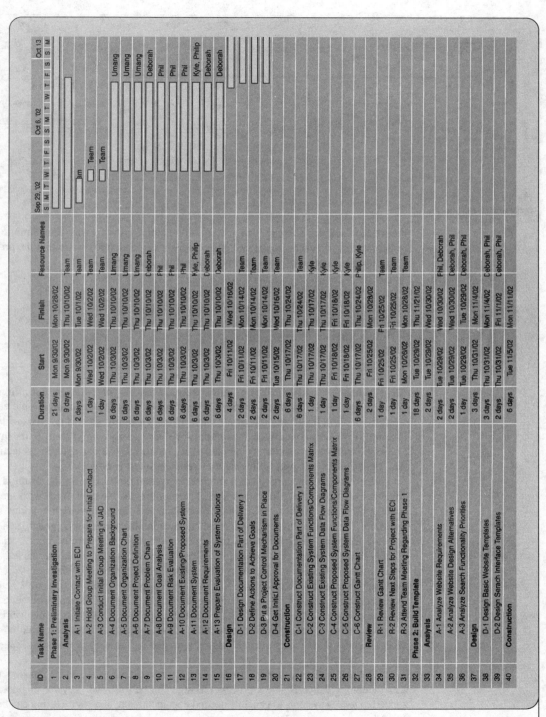

Figure 7.17 A Gantt Chart

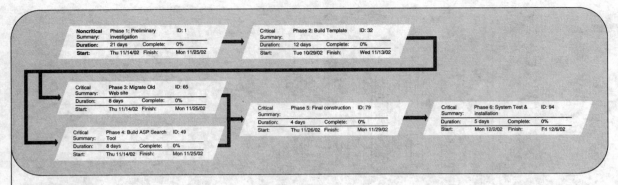

Figure 7.18 A Network Diagram

progress, identify challenges, and specify future actions. In this way, the committee is able to remain current on each project and make decisions intended to ensure that the project is successfully completed, within both time and cost budgets.

Summary

The systems approach consists of three phases of effort—preparation, definition, and solution. Preparation effort involves viewing the firm as a system, recognizing the environmental system, and identifying the firm's subsystems. Definition effort consists of two steps—proceeding from a system to subsystem level and analyzing system parts in sequence. Solution effort includes identifying alternative solutions, evaluating them, selecting the best one, implementing it, and following up to ensure that it is effective.

When the systems approach is applied to system development, the result is the system development life cycle. Numerous SDLC methodologies have evolved, with the traditional cycle, prototyping, rapid application development, and phased development drawing the most attention. The traditional SDLC approach, also called the waterfall approach, consists of five stages—planning, analysis, design, implementation, and use. In prototyping, a trial system is quickly developed and presented to the user for review. Refinements are made based on the review and this process is repeated until the prototype is approved by the user. When the prototype becomes the production system it is called an evolutionary prototype. When the prototype is used as a blueprint for another development project, it is a requirements prototype. Rapid application development (RAD) emphasizes a high level of user involvement and use of computer-based development tools. Phased development takes the best features of the other methodologies and repeats the analysis, design, and preliminary construction stages for each major module of the system being developed.

After the system has been in use and there is a need to redevelop it using modern technology, a methodology called business process redesign can be followed. Reverse engineering can be applied to legacy systems to generate needed documentation, and restructuring can be applied to provide missing system structure. Reengineering consists of reverse engineering, followed by taking the SDLC stages in the normal sequence—a process called forward engineering.

As systems are developed, the processes, data, and objects are modeled. A popular process modeling tool is data flow diagramming that uses symbols for processes and environmental elements, linked by arrows to show data flow. Data storage is illustrated with data store symbols. Leveled diagrams consist of DFDs in a hierarchy that shows varying levels of detail. The highest level DFD is the context diagram, the one on the next lower level is the Figure 0 diagram, and lower-level diagrams are called Figure *n* diagrams. DFDs are not as effective for showing details and are usually supplemented by another process modeling tool such as use cases.

As a firm goes about developing its information systems, the projects are managed by a hierarchy of managers that can include the executive committee, an MIS steering committee, and a project manger for each development team. Project management begins with a plan, specified in detail by a Gantt chart and perhaps in a summary format by a network diagram. On a periodic basis throughout the project, the project leader makes written and oral reports to the MIS steering committee, informing them of progress, problems, and plans.

KEY TERMS

methodology	restructuring	leveled DFDs
waterfall approach	forward engineering	use case
prototype	terminator	ping pong format
evolutionary prototype	data flow diagram (DFD)	MIS steering committee
requirements prototype	data store	Gantt chart
SWAT team	figure 0 diagram	network diagram
reverse engineering	context diagram	reengineering
functionality	figure *n* diagram	

KEY CONCEPTS

- systems approach
- systems development life cycle (SDLC)
- prototyping
- rapid application development (RAD)
- phased development
- business process redesign (BPR)

QUESTIONS

1. What name did Dewey use for a problem? For a decision?
2. What are the three phases of effort in applying the systems approach?
3. What is the reasoning for first evaluating a system's standards and outputs?
4. What are the three ways of selecting the best alternative, according to Mintzberg?
5. What are the five stages of the traditional system development life cycle?
6. What is the difference between an evolutionary and a requirements prototype.
7. What are the two faces of the James Martin IE pyramid?
8. What are the four essential ingredients of RAD?
9. What features does phased development take from the traditional SDLC? From prototyping? From RAD?
10. Which of the phased development stages are repeated for each system module?
11. When does a firm get involved with business process redesign?
12. When is reverse engineering performed?
13. When is restructuring performed?
14. The BPR approach that is taken depends on two kinds of quality. What are they?
15. What DFD symbols define the system boundary?
16. What is the difference between a data flow and a data store?
17. How many process symbols are on a context diagram?
18. When do DFDs become ineffective as process models?
19. What is the name of the committee that oversees a firm's system development projects and hears reports from project leaders?
20. Name two graphical reporting tools that contribute to the project management mechanism.

Topics for Discussion

1. In defining the problem, why proceed from a system to subsystem level?
2. Which of Mintzberg's three means of selecting the best solution is most susceptible to company politics?
3. How could a developer guard against the pitfalls of prototyping?
4. Would members of the MIS steering committee have to be knowledgeable in computer processing in order to do their job?

Problems

1. In describing phased development, the chapter describes the tasks that are performed in each stage. Use Figure 7.9 as a basis and prepare a Gantt chart that lists the tasks (using a verb and object) for each phase (the rectangles). Assume that you and four of your classmates will perform the work and enter the names for each task, along with estimated times for doing the work. Assume that the project must last no longer than six months. Your instructor will advise you about which software package to use.
2. For your Gantt chart in Problem 1, draw a network diagram similar to the one in Figure 7.17. Your instructor will advise you whether you can deviate from the sample format.

Case Problem

A Snow Job

You are the chief information officer of Cyan Trails Snow Products. You provide sales and rentals of ski and snowboard equipment at many ski areas. More than 200,000 people rent equipment from Cyan every year. Cyan gathers information from renters and buyers to help serve them better but also to help keep them as loyal customers. Reminders are sent each ski season about rental packages and special equipment sales offers are made to previous customers. In general, Cyan has an excellent record of using information systems to boost profits.

Your company has been profitable for 75 years because it has been able to quickly adapt to changing market conditions. This season presents a new revenue opportunity—lift ticket resale. The idea is to buy back someone's unused days of a lift pass and then sell that pass to another skier. When customers bring back their ski and snowboard rentals, it is the perfect time to buy back any lift tickets with unused days.

Some lift tickets are for a single day and some are for two, three, four, and five days. Tickets for multiple days are discounted based on the number of days of the ticket's life. Many skiers and snowboarders come to the mountains and expect to ski and snowboard the entire time. They buy a five day lift ticket because it is the best bargain. But if the skier finds that he or she cannot or does not want to ski the entire time, some of the lift days are never used. Cyan would like to buy those unused days from one skier and sell them to another.

The ski lift operators have agreed to let Cyan try this resale proposal for one season. Cyan must give the lift operators 10% of the gross sales. Annual ski passes cannot be resold since they are issued to individuals and are not part of the agreement with the lift operators. Cyan will have to design an information system that buys back lift tickets, keeps an inventory of tickets based on the number of lift days left to be used, and accounts for sales so that the lift operators can be compensated. However, the big problem is time. The ski season opens in three weeks.

Assignment

1. Why is this case well suited for rapid application development (RAD)?
2. Who would be members of your RAD team and why?
3. Briefly outline how you would implement each of the four RAD life cycle phases: requirement planning, user design, construction, and cutover.

Notes

[1] John Dewey, *How We Think* (New York: D.C. Heath & Company, 1910), 101–107.

[2] Henry Mintzberg, "Planning on the Left Side and Managing on the Right," *Harvard Business Review* 54 (July-August 1976), 55.

[3] This discussion is based on Jane M. Carey, "Prototyping Alternative Systems Development Methodology," *Information and Software Technology* 32 (March 1990), 120–121.

[4] This section and the next are from Carey, "Prototyping," 121–122.

[5] This section is based on James Martin, *Rapid Application Development* (New York: Macmillan, 1991).

[6] The definitions used in this section are based on Elliott J. Chikofsky and James H. Cross II, "Reverse Engineering and Design Recovery: A Taxonomy," *IEEE Software* 7 (January 1990), 13–17.

[7] From D. H. Drury, "An Evaluation of Data Processing Steering Committees," *MIS Quarterly* 8 (December 1984), 259.

[8] *Ibid.*, 260.

[9] "Take a Lesson from Trilogy," *Federal Computer Week*, July 29, 2002, WWW.FCW.COM.

Chapter 8

Information in Action

Learning Objectives

After studying this chapter, you should

- Recognize that the transaction processing system processes data that describes the firm's basic daily operations.
- Be familiar with the processes performed by a transaction processing system for a distribution firm.
- Recognize that organizational information systems have been developed for business areas and organizational levels.
- Understand the processes performed by a marketing information system.
- Understand the processes performed by a human resources information system.
- Know the basic architecture of an executive information system.
- Know what customer relationship management is and why it requires a large computer storage capability.
- Know how a data warehouse differs from a database.
- Know the basic architecture of a data warehouse system.
- Know how data is stored in a data warehouse.
- Know how a user navigates through a warehouse data repository.
- Know what on-line application processing is.
- Know the two basic ways to engage in data mining.

Introduction

The transaction processing system processes data that describes the firm's daily operations. This processing produces a database that is used by other systems within the firm. The transaction processing system of a firm that is in the distribution business (manufacturer, wholesaler, retailer) processes customer sales orders, orders replenishment stock, and maintains a general ledger.

Other information systems in the firm in addition to the transaction processing system are intended to support organizational units. For example, the marketing information system and human resources information system are tailored to the information needs of business areas, and the executive information system recognizes the unique information needs of users on the top organizational level.

Although the databases of the transaction processing system and the organizational systems have great value, they fall short when users want an extended history of a certain activity. This need has produced an application that is currently very popular—customer relationship management, or CRM. The data needs of CRM are so great that an innovative type of storage is used—a data warehouse. The warehouse data accumulates over time but can be quickly retrieved for use in decision making. A special type of software, called OLAP (for online application processing) has been developed to provide information to data warehouse users in a multidimensional form. An interesting feature of data warehousing is that software can provide users with patterns in the data that are unknown to the users. This type of data mining is called knowledge discovery.

In this chapter we provide examples of how information is being used in today's firms.

THE TRANSACTION PROCESSING SYSTEM

The term **transaction processing system** is used to describe the information system that gathers data describing the firm's activities, transforms the data into information, and makes the information available to users both inside and outside the firm. This was the first business application to be installed on computers when they were introduced in the 1950s. The terms **electronic data processing (EDP) system** and **accounting information system** have also been used but are not as popular today.

Figure 8.1 is a model of a transaction processing system. The model is a derivation of the general systems model of the firm that we described in Chapter 2. The input, transformation, and output elements of the physical system of the firm are at the bottom. Data is gathered from throughout the physical system and the environment, and entered into the database. Data processing software transforms the data into information for the firm's management and for individuals and organizations in the firm's environment.

The information flow to the environment is especially important. The transaction processing system is the only information system that has the responsibility to meet information needs outside of the firm. The transaction processing system has a responsibility to furnish information to each environmental element except competitors. For example, the transaction processing system provides customers with invoices and statements, provides suppliers with purchase orders, and provides stockholders and owners with data in annual reports.

A good example of a transaction processing system is one that is used by distribution firms—firms that distribute products or services to their customers. We call the system the **distribution system**. As you study this system, it will help to think of a product-oriented firm such as a manufacturer, wholesaler, or retailer. In addition, the distribution system can also be

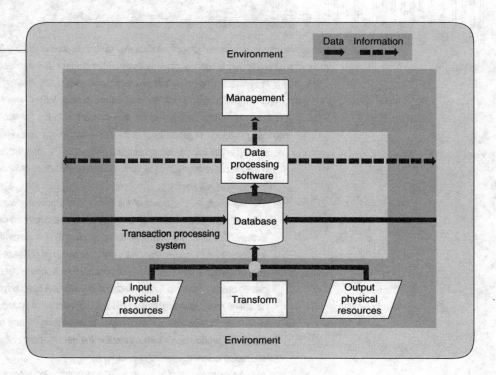

Figure 8.1 A Model of a Transaction Processing System

found in such service organizations as United Way and hospitals, and in such governmental agencies as the military and the IRS. All organizations are in the distribution business in one form or another. Also keep in mind that you probably cannot find a firm that processes its data *exactly* the same way as described here. Our model is a general one, fitting most firms in a general way.

System Overview

We will use data flow diagrams, or DFDs, to document the system. We described DFDs in Chapter 7. They document a system in a hierarchical manner, and the diagram in Figure 8.2 represents the highest level. The diagram is called a **context diagram** because it presents the system in the context of its environment.

The entire system is represented by the rectangle labeled "Distribution system" in the center. The environmental elements that interface with the system are represented by horizontal rectangles and are connected to the system by arrows called data flows.

The environmental elements of the distribution system include customers, suppliers, the materials stockroom, and management. In DFD terminology, the term *environment* applies to the *system* that is documented. For that reason, some environmental elements, such as management and the materials stockroom, exist within the firm.

The data flows that connect the firm with its customers are quite similar to the flows that connect the firm with its suppliers. That is because the firm is a customer of its supplier. The orders that the firm receives from its customers are called *sales orders*, whereas the orders that the firm places to its suppliers are called *purchase orders*. In some cases the firm will first obtain *commitments* from its suppliers before the purchase orders are prepared. Very often the firm will send *rejected sales order notices* to its customers—perhaps their credit rating is bad. Although suppliers also send rejected purchase order notices to the firm, we have omitted that flow for the sake of simplicity. Both the firm and its suppliers use *invoices* to advise customers how much money they owe, and *statements* to collect unpaid bills. Finally, both the firm and its customers must make *payments* for their purchases.

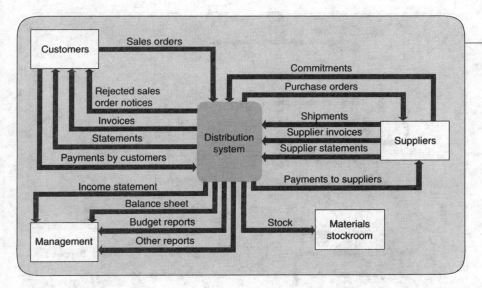

Figure 8.2 A Context Diagram of the Distribution System

The data flows from the distribution system to management consist of the standard accounting reports.

All but two of the data flows in Figure 8.2 consist of conceptual resources—data or information. The two exceptions include the one from the suppliers to the system, labeled *shipments*, and the one from the system to the materials stockroom, labeled *stock*. Data flows can reflect both conceptual and physical resources.

The Major Subsystems of the Distribution System

The context diagram is fine for defining the boundary of the system—the environmental elements and the interfaces. However, we need to learn more about the processes that are performed. We accomplish this by identifying the three major subsystems in Figure 8.3 in a *Figure 0 diagram*. Shortly you will see how that name was derived. When a series of DFDs are used in a hierarchy, they are called **leveled DFDs**.

The subsystems are identified by the numbered upright rectangles in Figure 8.3. The first subsystem is concerned with filling customer orders, the second with ordering replenishment stock from suppliers, and the third with maintaining the firm's general ledger. You will notice that all four of the environmental elements from the context diagram appear in the figure. The same is true for the data flows connecting the distribution system to those elements. This condition produces **balanced DFDs,** in that the same system connections appear on all of the systems levels where they are involved.

Systems that Fill Customer Orders

Figure 8.4 shows the four main systems that are involved in filling customer orders—order entry, inventory, billing, and accounts receivable. The **order entry system** enters customer orders into the system, the **inventory system** maintains the inventory records, the **billing system** prepares the customer invoices, and the **accounts receivable system** collects the money from the customers.

Figure 8.4 is an explosion of Process 1 in the Figure 0 diagram. For this reason, it is called a **Figure 1 diagram**. The figure number refers to the corresponding process number on the *next higher level* DFD. Now we can explain how the name *Figure 0 diagram* was derived. Since the context diagram consists of only a single, unnumbered process symbol, there is no figure number to reference and the next lower level DFD is called a **Figure 0 diagram**.

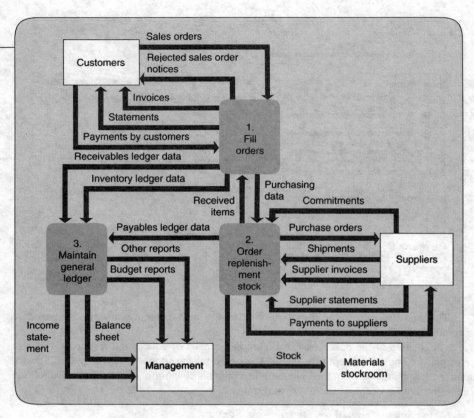

Figure 8.3 A Figure 0 Diagram of the Distribution System

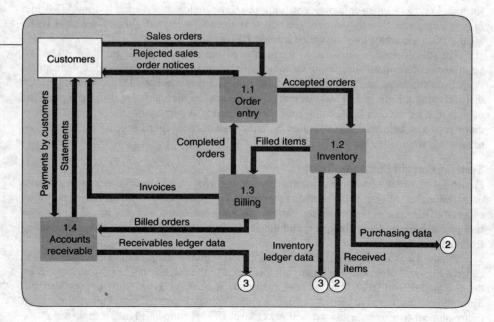

Figure 8.4 A Figure 1 Diagram of the System That Fills Customer Orders

You will notice that some of the arrows are connected to small circles with numbers in them. The circles are **connectors** that establish flows to other DFDs. The numbers identify the system numbers of the other DFDs. For example, the data flow labeled *receivables ledger data* is connected to Process 3, which is the process that maintains the general ledger.

Systems that Order Replenishment Stock

In a similar manner, we identify the subsystems that are concerned with ordering replenishment stock from suppliers. This detail is shown in Figure 8.5, and it is called a **Figure 2 diagram** since it explodes Process 2 of the Figure 0 diagram. The **purchasing system** issues purchase orders to suppliers for the needed stock, the **receiving system** receives the stock, and the **accounts payable system** makes payment.

Systems that Perform General Ledger Processes

Figure 8.6 shows the detail for the last of the three processes in the Figure 0 diagram—maintain general ledger. The **general ledger system** is the accounting system that combines data from other accounting systems for the purpose of presenting a composite financial picture of the firm's operations. The file that contains the combined accounting data is the **general ledger**.

Two subsystems are involved. The **update general ledger system** posts the records that describe the various actions and transactions to the general ledger. The **prepare management reports system** uses the contents of the general ledger to prepare the balance sheet and income statement.

Unlike previous DFDs, Figure 8.6 includes a **data store**—the DFD term for a relatively permanent storage of data such as a master file or a history file. The store is illustrated by an open-ended rectangle and labeled with the name, such as *general ledger*. We did not include stores in the higher-level DFDs because we wanted to keep those diagrams as uncluttered as possible. If we were to drop down to lower levels, we would encounter more data stores. However, we will not include that detail here.

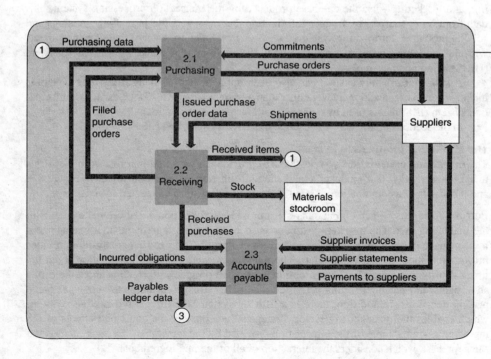

Figure 8.5 A Figure 2 Diagram of the Systems That Order Replenishment Stock

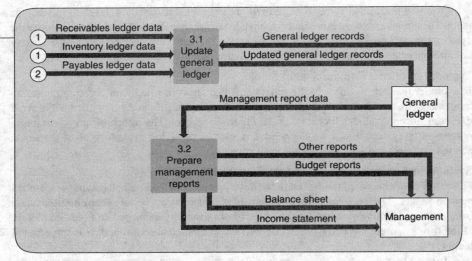

Figure 8.6 A Figure 3 Diagram of the Systems That Perform General Ledger Processes

Putting the Transaction Processing System in Perspective

It was no accident that the transaction processing system was the first application to be computerized. In addition to being the best understood application, it serves as the foundation for all other applications. The foundation exists in the form of the database, which documents everything of importance that the firm does in performing its operations and interfacing with its environment.

ORGANIZATIONAL INFORMATION SYSTEMS

The business areas of the firm—finance, human resources, information services, manufacturing, and marketing—use the database produced by the transaction processing system, plus data from other sources, to produce information that managers use in making decisions and solving problems. Information systems have been developed for each of these business areas, with the marketing information system (MKIS) and human resources information system (HRIS) being good examples.

Another information system has also been implemented in many firms; this system is intended for an organizational level rather than a business area. This is the executive information system (EIS) that is used by managers on the upper organizational levels.

In the sections below we will describe the MKIS, HRIS, and EIS.

The Marketing Information System

The **marketing information system (MKIS)** provides information that relates to the firm's marketing activities. Our model of a marketing information system is illustrated in Figure 8.7, and it consists of a combination of input and output subsystems connected by a database.

OUTPUT SUBSYSTEMS Each output subsystem provides information about critical elements in the marketing mix. The **marketing mix** consists of four main ingredients that management must manage in order to meet customers' needs at a profit. The **product subsystem** provides information about the firm's products. The **place subsystem** provides information about the firm's distribution network. The **promotion subsystem** provides information about the firm's advertising and personal selling activities. The **price subsystem** helps the manager make pricing decisions. In addition, there is a fifth subsystem, the **integrated-mix subsystem**, which enables the manager to develop strategies that consider the combined effects of the ingredients. An example of the information provided by the integrated-mix subsystem is the sales forecast, which considers the interaction of all of the mix ingredients.

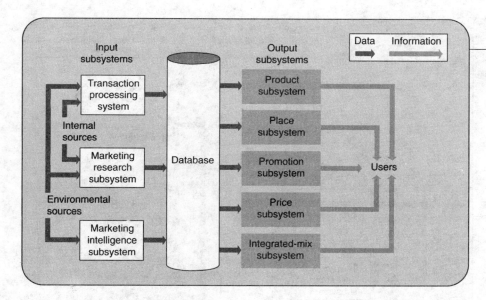

Figure 8.7 A Model of a Marketing Information System

Each of the output subsystems consists of programs in the software library. These programs enable users to obtain information in the form of periodic and special reports, the results of mathematical simulations, electronic communications, and knowledge-based systems advice. Users include managers throughout the firm who have an interest in the firm's marketing activities.

DATABASE   The data that is used by the output subsystems comes from the database. The database is populated with data provided by three input subsystems.

INPUT SUBSYSTEMS   As shown in Figure 8.7, the **transaction processing system** gathers data from both internal and environmental sources and enters the data into the database. We observed that data gathering in the discussion of the distribution system. The **marketing research subsystem** also gathers internal and environmental data by conducting special studies. The **marketing intelligence subsystem** gathers environmental data that serves to keep management informed of activities of the firm's competitors and customers and other elements that can influence marketing operations.

The Human Resources Information System

The **human resources information system (HRIS)** provides information to managers throughout the firm concerning the firm's human resources. Figure 8.8 illustrates the HRIS, using the same format as the MKIS. The transaction processing system provides input data, as does a human resources research subsystem that conducts special studies and a human resources intelligence subsystem that gathers environmental data that bears on HR issues.

The output subsystems of the HRIS each address a particular aspect of HR management—planning, recruiting, and managing the workforce; compensating the employees; providing employee benefits; and preparing the many HR reports that are required by the environment—primarily government agencies.

The Executive Information System

The **executive information system (EIS)** is a system that provides information to upper-level managers on the overall performance of the firm. The term **executive support system (ESS)** has also been used.

The firm's EIS usually consists of executive workstations that are networked to the central computer. This arrangement is shown in Figure 8.9. The workstation configuration

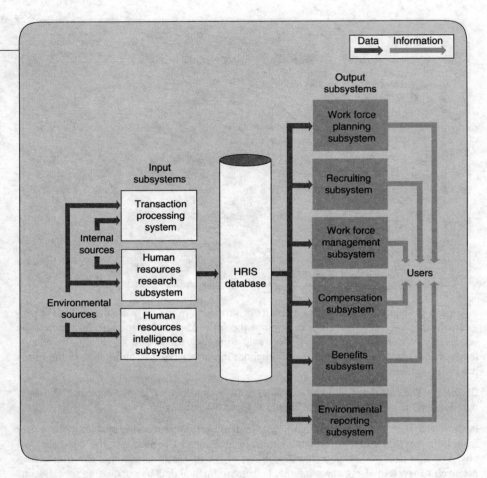

Figure 8.8 A Model of a Human Resources Information System

includes a personal computer with a secondary storage unit housing the executive database. This database contains data and information that has been preprocessed by the firm's central computer. The executive enters information requests to produce preformatted information displays or to perform a minimum amount of processing.

The EIS model also shows the composition of the central computer that relates to the EIS. Data and information can be entered into the corporate database from external sources, and current news and explanations of events can be entered by staff members using their workstations. In addition to the corporate database, the EIS includes the executives' electronic mailboxes and a software library that produces the executives' information.

Although it is generally accepted that executives prefer summary information, there are exceptions. Some executives prefer the detail. Designers of EISs build in flexibility so that the systems fit the preferences of all executives, whatever they are. One approach is to provide a **drill-down** capability. With this approach, the executive can bring up a summary display and then successively display lower levels of detail. This drilling down continues until executives are satisfied that they have obtained as much detail as is necessary.

Figure 8.10 shows a series of three screen displays that illustrate the drill-down process. In this example, an executive is reviewing profit data for the firm's product categories to see how actual performance compares to the budget, or plan. The actual and budget figures represent thousands of dollars. The display in Figure 8.10A indicates a high negative variance for radio profit when compared to the budget. The executive requests more detailed information on the

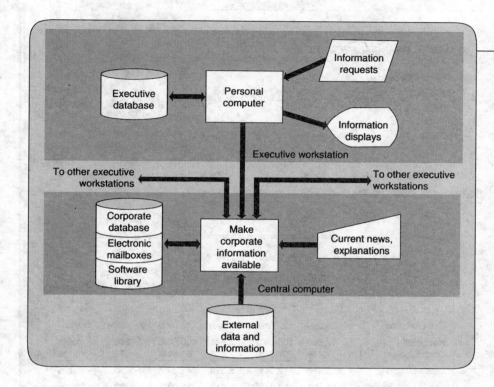

Figure 8.9 An EIS Model

radio product and receives the display in Figure 8.10B. It is now clear that research and development expenses are out of line, being 20.0 percent over budget. The executive drills down to another level and retrieves the display in Figure 8.10C, which shows the problem to be primarily with Project RA100. Now the executive knows where to concentrate problem-solving efforts.

CUSTOMER RELATIONSHIP MANAGEMENT

The databases that we included in the model of the transaction processing system (Figure 8.1), in the model of the marketing information system (Figure 8.7), and in the model of the human resources information system (Figure 8.8) are intended to support the users in performing their day-to-day activities. The other organizational information systems (finance, manufacturing, IS, and executive) all have similar databases. The data in these databases must be kept current so that users have the best basis for making decisions and solving problems. For example, if a sales manager is concerned about a particular sales region meeting its sales quota, the manager wants to see sales data that is current as of that day or perhaps even that hour or minute.

In designing these databases, there is also an effort to provide some, although limited, historical data. For example, an HR manager reviewing the overtime work for a particular employee would want to know the year-to-date overtime earnings. In this case, the total figure represents the overtime earnings from the beginning of the fiscal year to the current date.

Even though some historical data is included, very seldom will the database contain data more than a year old. There are instances, however, when users want a richer historical record in order to study behavior over time or to assemble as much information as possible to address an especially complex problem. This need for historical data has been especially strong in the marketing area, where managers want to be able to track the purchase behavior of customers over an extended period, for as many years as possible. This need has stimulated a popular marketing

AMERICAN ELECTRONICS
STANDARD FINANCIAL REPORTS

Consumer

Current Month	Actual	% Total	Budget	% Total	Variance	% Var.
Profit Before Tax						
Radio ◆	1,771	24.83%	2,084	28.71%	−313	−15.0%
Stereo	2,256	31.63%	2,193	30.21%	63	2.9%
Tape Recorder	569	7.98%	504	6.94%	65	12.9%
Television	2,537	35.57%	2,478	34.14%	59	2.4%
Total	7,133	100.00%	7,259	100.00%	−126	−1.7%

A. Summary display

AMERICAN ELECTRONICS
STANDARD FINANCIAL REPORTS

Consumer Radio

Current Month	Actual	% Total	Budget	% Total	Variance	% Var.
Net Sales	12,986	100.00%	12,741	100.00%	245	1.9%
Cost of Sales	−7,488	−57.66%	−7,213	−56.61%	−275	3.8%
Gross Margin	5,498	42.34%	5,528	43.39%	−30	−.5%
Research & Devel. ◆	1,694	13.04%	1,412	11.08%	282	20.0%
Selling & Mktg.	1,505	11.59%	1,498	11.76%	7	.5%
General & Admin.	511	3.94%	522	4.10%	−11	−2.1%
Interest Income	60	.46%	62	.49%	−2	−3.2%
Interest Expense	−77	−.59%	−74	−.58%	−3	4.1%
Before Tax Profit	1,771	13.64%	2,084	16.36%	−313	−15.0%

B. Display one level down

AMERICAN ELECTRONICS
STANDARD FINANCIAL REPORTS

Consumer Radio Research & Devel.

Current Month	Actual	% Total	Budget	% Total	Variance	% Var.
	517	30.52%	303	21.46%	214	70.6%
Project RA200 ◆	179	10.57%	176	12.46%	3	1.7%
Project RA300	115	6.79%	80	5.67%	35	43.8%
Project RA400	315	18.60%	288	20.40%	27	9.4%
Project RA500	231	13.64%	225	15.93%	6	2.7%
Project RA600	337	19.89%	340	24.08%	−3	−.9%
Total R&D Expense	1,694	100.00%	1,412	100.00%	282	20.0%

C. Display two levels down

Figure 8.10 **The Drill-Down Technique**
Source: Courtesy of Pilot Executive Software

strategy called customer relationship management. **Customer relationship management**, or **CRM**, is the management of the relationships between the firm and its customers in order for both the firm and its customers to receive maximum value from the relationship. It recognizes that cultivation of long-term customer relationships is a good marketing strategy because it usually costs less to keep an existing customer than to obtain a new one. So, efforts are made to know the customers so that their needs can be met and they will remain loyal to the firm.

When a firm seeks to practice CRM, it implements a CRM system. The **CRM system** accumulates customer data over a long term—five years, ten years, or more—and uses that data to produce information for users. The central element in a CRM system is the data warehouse.

DATA WAREHOUSING

As you can imagine, as transaction data accumulates over the years, the volume becomes enormous. Only recently has computer technology been capable of supporting a system with such large-scale data demands. All of that has changed, however, and it is now possible to build a system with almost unlimited data capacity.

Data Warehouse Characteristics

The term **data warehouse** has been coined to describe a data storage that has the following characteristics:

- The storage capacity is very large scale.
- The data is accumulated by adding new records rather than kept current by updating existing records with new information.
- The data is very easily retrievable.
- The data is used solely for decision making and is not used for the firm's daily operations.

Achieving a data warehouse sounds like a big challenge—and it is. In fact, it is so big that some experts recommend taking a more modest approach—implementing the data warehouse in a piecemeal way. When this approach is followed, the term "data mart" is used to describe the subsets. A **data mart** is a database that contains data describing only a segment of the firm's operations. For example, a firm might have a marketing data mart, a human resources data mart, and so on.

The creation and use of a data warehouse or data mart is called **data warehousing**, and is performed by a system.

The Data Warehousing System

The data warehouse is the central portion of a **data warehousing system** that enters data into the warehouse, transforms the contents into information, and makes the information available to users. Figure 8.11 is a diagram of a data warehousing system. Data is gathered from the data sources and goes through a staging area before being entered in the warehouse data repository. An information delivery system obtains data from the warehouse data repository and transforms it into information for the users.

The primary data sources are the transaction processing systems but additional data is obtained from other sources, both internal and environmental. When data is identified as having potential value in decision making, it is added to the data warehouse.

The staging area is where the data undergoes extraction, transformation, and loading, a process often abbreviated to **ETL**. The **extraction** combines the data from the various sources, and the **transformation** cleans the data, puts it into a standardized format, and prepares summaries. The data will be stored in both a detailed and summary form to provide for maximum flexibility in meeting the varying information needs of the users. The **loading** process involves the entry of the data into the warehouse data repository.

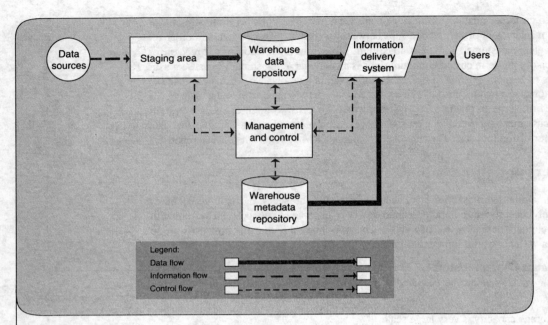

Figure 8.11 A Model of a Data Warehousing System

You will notice in Figure 8.11 that there are two repositories—one for warehouse data and one for warehouse metadata. The term **metadata** means "data about data." It is data that describes the data in the data repository. It is similar to the schema of a database, only much more detailed. In addition to describing the data, the metadata tracks the data as it flows through the data warehousing system.

The data warehousing system also includes a management and control component. This is similar to the data manager of a database management information system, controlling the movement of data through the system.

How Data Is Stored in the Warehouse Data Repository

In a database, all of the data about a particular subject is stored together in one location, usually a table. The data includes identifying data (such as customer number), descriptive data (such as customer name), and quantitative data (such as current month sales). In the warehouse data repository, two types of data are stored in separate tables. This table data is combined to produce an information package.

DIMENSION TABLES   Identifying and descriptive data are stored in **dimension tables**. The term **dimension** captures the idea that this data can provide the basis for viewing the data from various perspectives, or in various dimensions. Figure 8.12 illustrates a dimension table for the customer entity or object. The entries give you an idea of the typical makeup of the identification and descriptive data. In this example, customer number can be used to identify a customer and the remaining data elements describe various details about a customer.

With the sample dimensions in the figure, users can produce analyses by customer, by customer territory, by standard industry code (SIC), by zip code, and so on.

FACT TABLES   Separate tables are used to contain the quantitative measures of an entity, object, or activity and are called **fact tables**. A sample fact table is provided in Figure 8.13. In this example, the fact table contains data about a particular activity—commercial sales. These are all measures of that activity. Some are units, such as actual sales units and budgeted sales units. The remainder are in dollars. With these types of facts available for commercial sales, users can produce such quantitative analyses as actual sales units versus budgeted units, aver-

```
         Customer                                    Commercial Sales Facts

  Customer number                              Actual sales units
  Customer name                                Budgeted sales units
  Customer phone number                        Actual sales amount
  Customer e-mail address                      Budgeted sales amount
  Customer territory                           Sales discount amount
  Salesperson number                           Net sales amount
  Customer credit code                         Sales commission amount
  Customer standard industry code              Sales bonus amount
  Customer city                                Sales tax amount
  Customer state
  Customer zip code
```

Figure 8.12 **A Sample Dimension Table**   *Figure 8.13* **A Sample Fact Table**

age sales dollar per unit, sales commissions as a percent of actual sales, and sales bonuses as a percent of sales commissions.

Combined with the dimension table data, various analyses can be prepared such as net sales by customer territory, sales taxes by zip code, and sales commissions by credit code. Users can request information that involves *any* combination of the dimensions and facts.

INFORMATION PACKAGES   How does the data warehousing system know to associate a particular dimension table with a particular fact table? The two types of data are combined to form an information package. An **information package** identifies all of the dimensions that will be used in analyzing a particular activity. Figure 8.14 shows the format and Figure 8.15 includes some sample data.

In the Figure 8.14 example, four dimensions are linked to the facts. There can be any number of dimensions. In the Figure 8.15 example, the package includes four dimensions that can be used to analyze commercial sales by time, salesperson, customer, and product.

For each dimension, there are multiple attributes and each is arrayed in a **hierarchy** ranging from the smallest increment at the top to the largest at the bottom. For example, the smallest measure

Figure 8.14
Information Package Format

Subject: Name of Business Activity Being Measured

Dimension name	Dimension name	Dimension name	Dimension name
Dimension key	Dimension key	Dimension key	Dimension key
Dimension 1	Dimension 1	Dimension 1	Dimension 1
Dimension 2	Dimension 2	Dimension 2	Dimension 2
Dimension 3	Dimension 3	Dimension n	Dimension 3
Dimension 4	Dimension n		Dimension 4
Dimension n			Dimension n

Facts: Numeric measures of the business activity.

Subject: Commercial Sales			
Time	**Salesperson**	**Customer**	**Product**
Time key	Salesperson key	Customer key	Product key
Hour	Salesperson name	Customer name	Product name
Day	Sales branch	Customer territory	Product model
Month	Sales region	Customer credit code	Product brand
Quarter	Subsidary		Product line
Year			

Facts: Actual sales units, budgeted sales units, actual sales amount, bugeted sales amount, sales discount amount, net sales amount, sales commission amount, sales bonus amount, sales tax amount

Figure 8.15 A Sample Information Package

of time is the hour and the largest is the year. For the salesperson, the hierarchy shows how salespersons can be grouped into branches, into larger regions, and into subsidiaries of the firm.

THE STAR SCHEMA   For each dimension, there is a key that identifies the dimension and provides the link to connect the dimension tables to the fact table. Figure 8.16 shows how the keys in the four dimension tables are related to keys in the information package in the center, and Figure 8.17 provides an example using the four dimension tables—customer, time, salesperson, and product. Because of the similarity of the pattern to a star, the structure is called a **star schema**.

The warehouse data repository contains multiple star schemas, one for each type of activity to be analyzed.

Figure 8.16 Star Schema Format

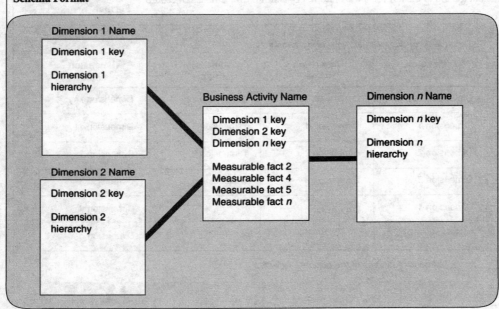

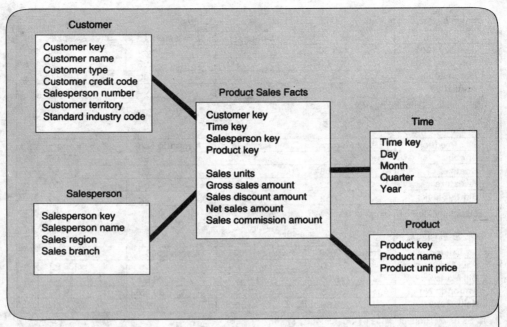

Figure 8.17 A Sample Star Schema

INFORMATION DELIVERY

We have described the staging area operations and how data is stored in the warehouse data repository. The final element in the data warehousing system is the information delivery system, which obtains data from the data repository, transforms it into information, and makes the information available to users.

The information can be made available in the form of traditional reports, responses to data warehouse queries, and outputs from mathematical models that use the warehouse data. The information can be provided in a detailed form or in various summary levels. Figure 8.18 illustrates how the user can navigate through the data repository to produce summary information (such as net sales for the midwestern sales region), detailed information (net sales for salesperson 383), and detailed data (sales units for salesperson 383).

Figure 8.18 **Navigating through the Warehouse Data Repository**

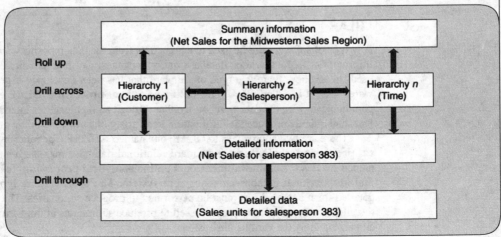

CUSTOMER: Bill Marlowe

Month	Shoes	Coats	Sweaters	Skirts/Slacks
January 2003	145.00	279.95	118.29	.00
February 2003	.00	.00	79.95	.00
March 2003	239.50	.00	.00	391.50
April 2003	49.95	.00	.00	129.95

A Sales by Customer by Product Class by Month

Month: January 2003

Product	Paul Murray	Bill Marlowe	Armondo No	Kelly Pope
Shoes	.00	145.00	89.95	234.68
Coats	234.68	279.95	.00	434.50
Sweaters	112.19	118.29	.00	.00
Skirts/Slacks	141.12	.00	217.92	.00

B Sales by Month by Product Class by Customer

Product Class: Shoes

Customer	January 2003	February 2003	March 2003	April 2003
Paul Murray	.00	.00	.00	238.92
Bill Marlowe	145.00	.00	239.50	49.95
Armondo No	89.95	122.34	89.95	119.35
Kelly Pope	234.68	.00	112.92	.00

C Sales by Product Class by Customer by Month

Figure 8.19 Drilling Across Hierarchies Produces Multiple Views.

The process of navigating down through the levels of detail is called **drill down**, the process that originated with executive information systems. The process of navigating upwards is called **roll up**, enabling the user to begin with a detail display and then summarize the details into increasingly higher summary levels. The user can also **drill across**, quickly moving from one data hierarchy to another, and can **drill through**, going from a summary level to the detailed data.

Figure 8.19 shows the results of a drill-across navigation, producing outputs in different hierarchies. The user can specify the customer hierarchy for customer Bill Marlowe and obtain the output at the top, then specify the time hierarchy for January 2003 and obtain the information in the center, and then specify the product class Shoes and obtain the output at the bottom. The information delivery software accomplishes the navigation quickly, a requirement of the data warehouse.

OLAP

Any type of software can be used to extract data from the data repository and transform it into information. Report writers, database query packages, and mathematical models can all be used. In addition, there is a type of software that has been developed especially for the data warehouse. It is called **OLAP**, for **online analytical processing**. OLAP enables the user to communicate with the data warehouse either through a graphical user interface or a Web interface, and quickly produce the information in a variety of forms, including graphics.

There are two approaches to OLAP; one named **ROLAP** (for **relational online analytical processing**) that utilizes a standard relational database management system, and one named **MOLAP** (for **multidimensional online analytical processing**) that utilizes a special multidimensional database management system. The ROLAP data typically exists in a detailed form and analyses must be performed to produce summaries. The MOLAP data, on the other hand, is typically preprocessed to produce summaries at the various levels of detail and arranged by the various dimensions.

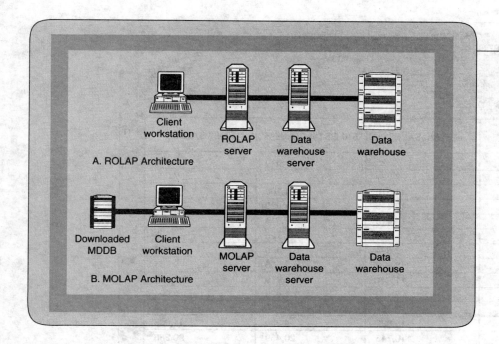

Figure 8.20 ROLAP and MOLAP Architectures

Figure 8.20 illustrates the two architectures. Both include a data warehouse server and a second server that contains the OLAP software. A major difference is that the workstation of the MOLAP user includes a downloaded multidimensional database. The data in this database has already been formatted in various dimensions so that it may be made available quickly rather than force users to go through time-consuming analyses.

ROLAP can easily produce outputs at detailed levels and perhaps at a few summary levels but must execute processes to achieve summary levels that have not been previously prepared. This means that ROLAP analysis is constrained to a limited number of dimensions. Figure 8.21 illustrates a report that is the type that ROLAP can easily prepare. This report shows sales data in three dimensions: for a particular product (DVD); in a particular region (West); and by quarter.

In addition to a faster summary ability, MOLAP can produce information in many dimensions—ten or more. Figure 8.22 illustrates a summary report in four dimensions; store type, product, age, and gender.

DATA MINING

A term that is often used in conjunction with data warehousing and the data mart is data mining. **Data mining** is the process of finding relationships in data that are unknown to the user. It is analogous to a miner panning for gold in a mountain stream. Data mining helps the user by discovering the relationships and presenting them in an understandable way so that the relationships may provide the basis for decision making.

There are two basic ways of performing data mining—hypothesis verification and knowledge discovery.

Hypothesis Verification

Assume that a bank has decided to offer mutual funds to its customers. Bank management wants to aim promotional materials at the customer segment that offers the greatest potential business. One approach is for the managers to identify the characteristics that they

ANALYSIS OF RETAIL PRICE DISCOUNTS
PRODUCT CLASS BY STORE REGION BY QUARTER
2001 THROUGH 2003
IN DOLLARS

STORE REGION: WEST

PRODUCT CLASS: DVD

QUARTER	RETAIL SALES	SALES DISCOUNTS	NET SALES
1/2001	7,525	610	6,915
2/2001	7,280	0	7,280
3/2001	11,310	1,108	10,202
4/2001	12,445	1,829	10,616
1/2002	16,418	2,314	14,104
2/2002	1,320	725	595
3/2002	6,694	890	5,804
4/2002	12,310	2,555	9,755
1/2003	11,927	3,719	8,208
2/2003	5,423	1,429	3,994
3/2003	2,764	960	1,804
4/2003	15,329	4,230	11,009
TOTAL	110,745	20,459	90,286

Figure 8.21 An Example of a Report That Could Be Produced with ROLAP

believe the members of the target market will have. Assume that the managers believe that the target market consists of young, married, two-income, and high net-worth customers. The managers believe that there is a market segment populated by people with these characteristics. This multidimensional query could be entered into the DBMS, and the appropriate records retrieved. Such an approach, which begins with the user's hypothesis of how the data is related, is called **hypothesis verification**. The shortcoming of this approach is that the retrieval process is guided entirely by the user. The selected information can be no better than the user's view of the data. This is the traditional way to query a database.

Figure 8.22 An Example of a Report that Could Be Produced with MOLAP

PRODUCT SALES BY CUSTOMER GENDER
YEAR-TO-DATE 2003
IN UNITS

STORE TYPE: DEPARTMENT

PRODUCT NUMBER: 23184

PRODUCT NAME: ROLLING CARRY-ON LUGGAGE

GENDER	AGE= 15–20	AGE= 21–30	AGE= 31–40	AGE= 41–50	AGE= OVER 50	TOTAL
FEMALE	8	23	144	124	79	378
MALE	6	17	85	63	51	222
TOTAL	14	40	229	187	130	600

Knowledge Discovery

In **knowledge discovery** the system analyzes the warehouse data repository, looking for groups with common characteristics. In the bank example, the system might identify not only the young married group but also retired married couples who rely on Social Security and pensions.

The big contribution of knowledge discovery is the fact that it gives the data warehousing system an ability to analyze data that exceeds that of the users. In order to accomplish this, the data mining software must be capable of identifying patterns in the data that are not obvious to users. Such an ability is obtained by employing such artificial intelligence methodologies as neural networks, decision trees, genetic algorithms, and memory-based reasoning.[1]

Putting Data Warehousing in Perspective

There was probably a need for data warehousing all along, but the computer technology needed to support it did not yet exist. When technology caught up to demand some dramatic accomplishments were made. Some were new innovations, such as a new way of storing data in information packages that made it possible to analyze the data in practically unlimited ways, and on-line application processing that made it possible to retrieve the data quickly. Existing methodologies and technologies were also applied, such as the concept of drilling down through layers of detail, and use of artificial intelligence to discover new relationships in data.

The ability to store practically unlimited quantities of data and retrieve it quickly opens up new doors to data processing.

Highlights in MIS

CASINOS LEAD THE WAY IN DATA MINING[2]

Although data mining is being done by firms of all kinds, the gambling industry is leading the way if the reports out of MGM Mirage, Harrah's, and Foxwoods are any indication. These resorts are able to keep track of their customers' gambling behavior and award prizes to keep them coming back. Prizes include such incentives as free hotel rooms, show tickets, and meals. The key ingredient is the loyalty card, a special barcoded card that the casino gives to its best customers. Then, when the customer engages in gambling, the card is scanned, gathering data that identifies the type of gambling, when it begins and ends, the amount of money wagered, and the amount of money won or lost. This data is stored in a data warehouse. The MGM Mirage data warehouse maintains 6 terabytes of customer information. Harrah's accumulates data on 23 million customers, 8 million of whom have the loyalty cards. The Native American-owned Foxwoods data warehouse has a smaller capacity—200 gigabytes—but this data can be matched with third-party databases that provide demographic data to learn such details as whether the customer has kids and how much he or she earns. At Foxwoods, when customers spend $100 or more a day, they receive red-carpet treatment. Harrah's knows a lot about its customers as well—whether someone likes thick steaks, oceanfront views, and Elvis slots.

All of these applications are examples of customer relationship management. The casinos believe that by knowing their customers they can offer incentives that will cause the customers to keep coming back. John Boushy, the Harrah's CIO, said, "We decided we would never be able to anticipate the questions that marketing might ask, so we keep all the data." Harrah's began populating their data warehouse in 1995 and has never deleted any data—it just keeps on accumulating.

Summary

The system that processes the firm's accounting data is called the transaction processing system. Data is gathered from the physical system of the firm and entered into a database, along with data from the environment. Data processing software transforms the data into information for management and the environment.

A distribution system consists of three main processes—fill customer orders, order replenishment stock from suppliers, and maintain the general ledger. Order processing involves an order entry system, an inventory system, a billing system, and an accounts receivable system. The stock replenishment system consists of a purchasing system, a receiving system, and an accounts payable system. The general ledger system consists of two main subsystems—update the general ledger system, and prepare management reports system.

Organizational information systems are tailored to business areas and organizational levels. Two business areas that have developed popular systems are marketing and human resources. Both types of systems consist of input subsystems that gather data and information for entry into a database, and output subsystems that transform the data into information. In both cases, the three input subsystems include the transaction processing system, a system that conducts special research projects, and a system that gathers intelligence data from the environment.

The executive information system has a different architecture, consisting of executive workstations networked to the central computer. Preformatted information displays are downloaded from the central computer and stored in an executive database.

A computer application that is currently drawing much attention is customer relationship management (CRM). It demands a supersized data storage called a data warehouse, which accumulates data rather than keeping it current, makes the data easily retrievable, and is dedicated to supporting decision making rather than supporting daily operations. Subsets of the data warehouse are called data marts.

A data warehousing system includes a staging area where ETL (extraction, transformation, and loading) are performed, a warehouse data repository where the data is stored, and an information delivery system that transforms the data into information and delivers it to users. A management and control unit controls the data flow from sources to users, and a warehouse metadata repository houses data that describes the data in the warehouse data repository and keeps track of the data as it flows through the system.

Data is stored in the warehouse data repository in dimension tables and fact tables, which are integrated in an information package. A graphical view of the information package and its dimension tables is called a star schema.

Users navigate through the warehouse data repository by performing such operations as drill down, roll up, drill across, and drill through. A special type of information delivery software has been developed especially for the data warehouse. It is called OLAP, for online analytical processing. OLAP enables data to be analyzed in multiple dimensions, a capability that is more easily performed by MOLAP (multidimensional online analytical processing) than ROLAP (relational online analytical processing) due to the fact that MOLAP provides users with downloaded multidimensional databases.

The process of looking through the data warehouse for data is called data mining and it can be performed two ways. In hypothesis verification, the user believes that certain patterns exist in the data and the system either confirms or rejects this assumption. In knowledge discovery, the user leaves it up to the system to find the patterns, which it does by using artificial intelligence logic.

In addition to the technological innovations of data warehousing, it represents a breakthrough in another way—it is a new way of thinking about data. Rather than trying to keep data current, the idea is to just accumulate it over time. The data warehouse provides users with a new approach to obtaining information for decision making.

KEY TERMS

transaction processing system
organizational information system
drill down
customer relationship management (CRM)
data warehousing
dimension tables
fact tables
information package
star schema
roll up
drill across
drill through
online analytical processing (OLAP)
relational online analytical processing (ROLAP)
multidimensional online analytical processing (MOLAP)
data mining
hypothesis verification
knowledge discovery

KEY CONCEPTS

- information systems for organizational areas and levels
- input subsystems for data entry
- output subsystems for information transformation

QUESTIONS

1. Who uses the output of the transaction processing system?
2. What are the contents of the transaction processing system database? Where do they come from?
3. What types of firms would use the distribution system?
4. What are the four environmental elements of the distribution system? Which exist inside the firm? Which outside?
5. Are the data flows in the distribution system physical or conceptual or both? Explain.
6. What are the three types of input subsystems that exist in both the marketing information system and the human resources information system?
7. Where is the data stored in an executive information system? How is it stored—in a detail or summary form or both?
8. How do EIS designers address the needs of executives who prefer both detail and summary data?
9. Why gather voluminous quantities of customer data?
10. What is the difference between a data warehouse and a database?
11. What is a data mart?
12. What do the letters ETL stand for? Where does it fit in the data warehousing system?
13. What kind of data is stored in dimension tables? Fact tables?
14. Why store detailed data in the data warehouse? Why store summary data?
15. What does an information package do?
16. What forms the connections between the fact table and the multiple dimension tables in a star schema?
17. What distinguishes drill down from drill through?
18. If a manager prefers summaries, would she or he prefer ROLAP or MOLAP? Explain.
19. If hypothesis verification is a data mining technique, which it is, how does it tell the user something that he or she did not previously know?
20. What has enabled casinos to have such successful data warehousing systems?

TOPICS FOR DISCUSSION

1. What are some areas of business other than marketing that would require data warehouses?
2. The chapter suggests that data marts can be developed for business areas. What are some other possible subsets of the data warehouse?
3. What would be an example of multidimensional analysis involving four dimensions?

PROBLEMS

1. Draw a diagram of a financial information system. Hint: use Figure 8.8 as a guideline, recognizing that the HRIS manages the flow of human resources and the financial information system handles the flow of money.

2. Assume that the manager doing the drill down in Figure 8.10 is looking for evidence of good performance related to the radio product line. What are they?

THE DATA MINE

You've been the Director of Manufacturing at Tej Electronics for five years. During that time you have repeatedly depended upon the Tej database for key decisions. A disturbing rise in the manufacturing defect rate of your signature product had your job on the line. On a hunch, you had an information analyst scour the database and an unexpected fact emerged—each defective product had the same component fail. There are 20 vendors for that component but each of the defective products used the component from the same vendor. That insight probably saved your career.

Greg Wilkins is the Director of Sales. When you mentioned your incident to him, he confided a similar episode. A multimillion dollar sale to one of the firm's most important customers was in jeopardy. After talking with the sales account representative and the customer, Greg could not understand why the sale was at risk. The customer representative began going over old database reports and noticed a peculiar pattern to the dates when the customer had cancelled past sales orders. He then went through news reports for those times and found reports about the company. When the company ran out of warehouse space, it cancelled orders.

With this information, Greg knew what to do. He arranged for the sale to go through as planned but shipment of the product was to be made on a delayed timetable set by the company. Tej made the sale by acting as the warehouse for its customer.

Tej has been relying on the company database for key decisions more and more frequently. You and Greg begin to discuss how to take their use of the database to a higher level.

Assignment

1. What can data mining do to help Tej Electronics?
2. From the examples in the case, do you think Tej will be more likely to use roll up or drill down navigation? Why?
3. How might OLAP help Tej?

NOTES

[1] For descriptions of these knowledge discovery methodologies, see William G. Zikmund; Raymond McLeod, Jr.; and Faye Gilbert, *Customer Relationship Management: Integrating Marketing Strategy and Information Technology* (New York: John Wiley & Sons, 2003).

[2] This section is based on Kim S. Nash, "Casinos Hit Jackpot with Customer Data," *Computerworld*, July 2, 2001, p. 16.

PART 3
Managing Information and Technology

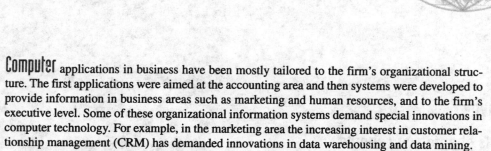

Computer applications in business have been mostly tailored to the firm's organizational structure. The first applications were aimed at the accounting area and then systems were developed to provide information in business areas such as marketing and human resources, and to the firm's executive level. Some of these organizational information systems demand special innovations in computer technology. For example, in the marketing area the increasing interest in customer relationship management (CRM) has demanded innovations in data warehousing and data mining.

Events of the past few years have imposed increased responsibilities on those who manage the firm's information resources. These events have been in the areas of security and ethics. Because the firm and its organizational units rely so completely on computer technology, it is important that the information resources be kept secure. Contingency plans that are intended to ensure the continued availability of the firm's information resources address threats and risks that were unimaginable just a few years ago. By the same token, everyone connected to the firm must ensure that information systems are used in an ethical way, protecting and respecting the rights of both persons inside and outside the firm.

As the firm's managers draft the strategic information plan they must insist on a strong security component and a basis of ethical computer use. By being vigilant to the importance of the computer to their organization, the managers put a powerful decision support tool into the hands of the firm's problem solvers.

Chapter 9

Information Security

Learning Objectives

After studying this chapter, you should

- Know that information security is concerned with securing all of the information resources, not just hardware and data.
- Know the three main objectives of information security.
- Know that management of information security consists of two areas—information security management (ISM) and business continuity management (BCM).
- See the logical relationship among threats, risks, and controls.
- Know what the main security risks are.
- Know the process for implementing an information security policy.
- Be familiar with the more popular security controls.
- Be familiar with actions of government and industry that influence information security.
- Know the types of plans that are included in contingency planning.

Introduction

Information security is intended to achieve confidentiality, availability, and integrity in the firm's information resources. The management of information security consists of both the day-to-day protection, which is called information security management (ISM), and making preparations for operating after a disaster, which is called business continuity management (BCM).

There are two approaches to developing ISM strategies. They are risk management and benchmark compliance. Paying attention to threats and risks is integral to the risk management approach. Threats can be internal or external, and accidental or deliberate. Risks are all unauthorized incidents of disclosure, use, and modification as well as theft, destruction, and denial of service. The most notorious threat is the "virus." E-commerce produces a special risk but some unique responses have come from such organizations as American Express and Visa.

There are three types of controls. Technical controls consist of restrictions on access, firewalls, cryptography, and physical controls. Formal controls are in writing and have a long-term life expectancy. Informal controls are intended to ensure that the firm's employees both understand and support the security policies.

A number of governments have established standards and passed legislation that affect information security. Industry associations have also provided standards and professional certifications.

Business continuity management consists of a set of subplans to provide for safety of employees, enable continued operation by means of backup computing facilities, and protect the firm's vital records. Firms wanting to develop a new contingency plan need not start from scratch; there are several software-based templates available, plus outlines and hints from state governments.

INFORMATION SECURITY

When government and industry first became aware of the need to secure their information resources, attention was focused almost exclusively on protecting the hardware and data and the term **systems security** was used. This narrow focus was subsequently broadened to include not only hardware and data, but also software, the computer facilities, and personnel as well. Today, the scope is even broader, to include all types of data. The term **information security** is used to describe the protection of both computer and noncomputer equipment, facilities, data, and information from misuse by unauthorized parties. This broad definition includes such equipment as copiers and fax machines, and all types of media, including paper documents.

Objectives of Information Security

Information security is intended to achieve three main objectives: confidentiality, availability, and integrity.

- **Confidentiality.** The firm seeks to protect its data and information from disclosure to unauthorized persons. Executive information systems, human resource information systems, and such transaction processing systems as payroll, accounts receivable, purchasing, and accounts payable are especially critical in this regard.
- **Availability.** The purpose of the firm's information infrastructure is to make its data and information available to those who are authorized to use it. This objective is especially important to the information-oriented systems—MIS, DSS, and organizational information systems.

- **Integrity.** All of the information systems should provide an accurate representation of the physical systems that they represent.

The firm's information systems must protect the data and information from misuse, but ensure its availability to authorized users who can have confidence in its accuracy.

Management of Information Security

Just as the scope of information security has broadened, so has the view of the management responsibility. Management is not only expected to keep the information resources secure; it is also expected to keep the firm functioning after a disaster or security breach. The activity of keeping the information resources secure is **information security management (ISM)**, and the activity of keeping the firm and its information resources functioning after a catastrophe is **business continuity management (BCM)**.

The CIO is the logical person to have responsibility for information security but the trend is to designate persons who can devote full time to the activity. The title **corporate information systems security officer (CISSO)** has been used for the person in the organization, typically a member of the information systems unit, who is responsible for the firm's information systems security. Currently, however, there is a movement to achieve a higher level of information security in the firm by designating a **corporate information assurance officer (CIAO)**, who should report to the CEO and manage an information assurance unit. As envisioned, the CIAO should possess the full range of security certifications and have a minimum of 10 years experience in managing an information security facility.[1]

In this chapter we will describe information security in its broadest form and will assume that the efforts are managed by either a corporate information systems security officer or a corporate information assurance officer. We will begin with a discussion of information security management (ISM) and then conclude with a discussion of business continuity management (BCM).

INFORMATION SECURITY MANAGEMENT (ISM)

In its most basic form, information security management consists of four steps: identifying the *threats* that can attack the firm's information resources; defining the *risks* that the threats can impose; establishing an information security policy; and implementing *controls* that address the risks. Threats impose risks, which must be controlled. The name **risk management** has been coined to describe this approach of basing the security of the firm's information resources on the risks that they face. Figure 9.1A illustrates the risk management approach.

Another option exists for formulating the firm's information security policy. It has become popular in recent years with the emergence of information security standards or benchmarks. A benchmark is a recommended level of performance. The **information security benchmark** is a recommended level of security that in normal circumstances should offer reasonable protection against unauthorized intrusion. Such standards and benchmarks are defined by governments and industry associations and reflect what those authorities believe to be the components of a good information security program. When a firm follows this approach, which we call **benchmark compliance**, it is assumed that the government and industry authorities have done a good job of considering the threats and risks and that the benchmarks offer good protection. Figure 9.1B shows the benchmark compliance approach.

THREATS

An information security **threat** is a person, organization, mechanism, or event that has potential to inflict harm on the firm's information resources. When one thinks of information security threats it is only natural to think of groups or individuals outside the firm, and to think of

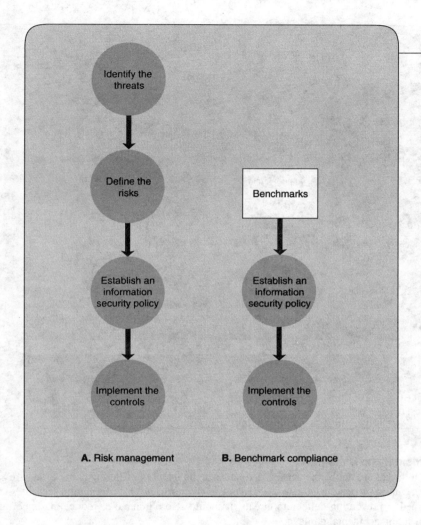

**Figure 9.1
Information Security
Management (ISM)
Strategies**

acts that are intentionally carried out. Actually, threats can be internal as well as external, and they can be accidental as well as intentional.

Figure 9.2 shows the information security objectives and how they are subjected to the four types of risks.

Internal and External Threats

Internal threats include not only the firm's employees but also temporary workers, consultants, contractors, and even the firm's business partners. A survey by the Computer Security Institute found that 49% of the respondents faced security incidents brought on by actions of legitimate users,[2] and the proportion of computer crimes committed by employees has been estimated to be as high as 81 percent.[3] Internal threats are considered to present potentially more serious damage than do external threats due to the more intimate knowledge of the system by the internal threats.

Controls that are put in place to address external threats typically go into action when an effort to breach the security is detected. Controls against internal threats are intended to predict security violations. We will describe such controls later in the chapter.

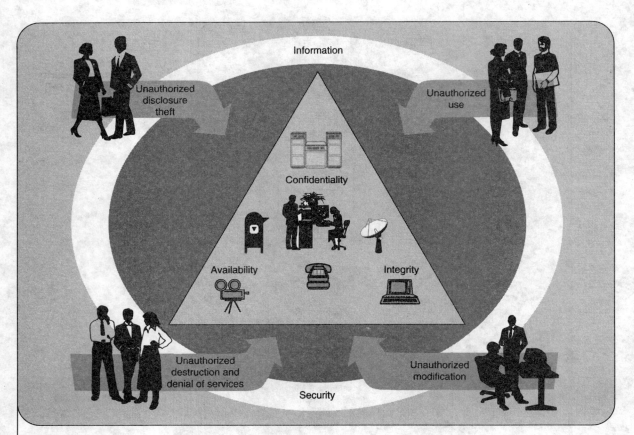

Figure 9.2
Unauthorized Acts Threaten System Security Objectives

Accidental and Deliberate
Not all threats are deliberate acts carried out with the intent of inflicting harm. Some are accidental, caused by persons both inside and outside the firm. Just as information security should be aimed at preventing deliberate threats, it should also eliminate or reduce the opportunity for inflicting accidental damage.

RISKS

We define an information security **risk** as a potential undesirable outcome of a breach of information security by an information security threat. All risks represent unauthorized acts, and there are four types: disclosure and theft, use, destruction and denial of service, and modification.

Unauthorized Disclosure and Theft
When the database and software library are made available to persons not entitled to have access, the result can be the loss of information or money. For example, industrial spies can gain valuable competitive information, and computer criminals can embezzle the firm's funds.

Unauthorized Use
Unauthorized use occurs when persons who are not ordinarily entitled to use the firm's resources are able to do so. Typical of this type of computer criminal is the hacker who views a firm's information security as a challenge to be overcome. A hacker, for example, can break

into a firm's computer network, gain access to the telephone system, and make unauthorized long-distance calls.

Unauthorized Destruction and Denial of Service
Individuals can damage or destroy the hardware or software, causing a shutdown in the firm's computer operations. It is not even necessary for computer criminals be on the premises. They can log onto the firm's computer network from a remote terminal and cause such physical destruction as damaged monitors, crashed disks, jammed printers, and disabled keyboards.

Unauthorized Modification
Changes can be made to the firm's data, information, and software. Some changes go unnoticed and cause the users of the system outputs to make the wrong decisions. An especially worrisome type of modification is that caused by malicious software, often grouped under the heading of viruses.

THE MOST NOTORIOUS THREAT—THE "VIRUS"

Everyone has heard of the computer virus. Actually a virus is only one example of a type of software that bears the name "malicious software." **Malicious software**, or **malware**, consists of complete programs or segments of code that can invade a system and perform functions not intended by the system owners. The functions can erase files or cause the system to come to a halt. There are many types of malicious software; in addition to viruses, worms and Trojan horses receive a lot of attention.

A **virus** is a computer program that can replicate itself without being observable to the user, and embed copies of itself in other programs and boot sectors. A **worm** cannot replicate itself within a system, as can the virus, but it can transmit its copies by means of E-mail. A **Trojan horse** can neither replicate nor distribute itself; the distribution is accomplished by users who distribute them as a utility and when used, they produce unwanted changes in the system's functionality.

E-COMMERCE CONSIDERATIONS

E-commerce has introduced a new security concern. It is not protection of data, information, and software, but protection from credit card fraud. According to a survey by the Gartner Group, credit card fraud is 12 times more prevalent for e-commerce retailers than for merchants who deal with their customers face-to-face.[4] In response to this problem, both American Express and Visa have implemented programs aimed specifically at e-commerce.

The American Express "Disposable" Credit Card
American Express has announced "disposable" credit card numbers—an action aimed at the 60 percent to 70 percent of consumers who fear credit card fraud arising from Internet use.[5] The disposable card works this way: When cardholders wish to purchase something online, they obtain a randomly generated number from the American Express Web site. This number, rather than the customer's credit card number, is provided to the e-commerce retailer, who submits it to American Express for repayment.

Visa's Required Security Practices
Visa has announced 10 security-related practices that they expect their retailers to follow. Retailers not following the practices face fines, loss of membership in the Visa program, or limits on Visa sales. Retailers *must*:[6]

1. Install and maintain a firewall.
2. Keep security patches up to date.
3. Encrypt stored data.

4. Encrypt transmitted data.
5. Use and update antivirus software.
6. Restrict data access to those with a need to know.
7. Assign unique IDs to persons with data access privileges.
8. Track data access with the unique ID.
9. Not use vendor-supplied password defaults.
10. Regularly test the security system.

We discuss firewalls and encryption later in the chapter.

In addition, Visa identified three general practices that retailers *should* follow in achieving information security for all activities, not only those related to e-commerce:

1. Screen employees who have access to data.
2. Not leave data (diskettes, paper, and so forth) or computers unsecured.
3. Destroy data when it is no longer needed.

RISK MANAGEMENT

Earlier, we identified risk management as one of two strategies for achieving information security. The view is that risks can be managed to apply the proper amount of controls to either remove the risks or reduce their impact. The step of defining the risks consists of four substeps:[7]

1. Identify business assets to be protected from risks.
2. Recognize the risks.
3. Determine the level of impact on the firm should the risks materialize.
4. Analyze the vulnerabilities of the firm.

A systematic approach can be taken to Substeps 3 and 4—determining the impact and analyzing the vulnerabilities.[8] Table 9.1 illustrates the options.

Impact severity can be classified as **severe impact** (put the firm out of business or severely limit its ability to function), **significant impact** (cause significant damage and cost but the firm will survive), or **minor impact** (cause breakdowns that are typical of day-to-

Table 9.1

Degree of Impact and Vulnerability Determine Controls			
	SEVERE IMPACT	SIGNIFICANT IMPACT	MINOR IMPACT
HIGH VULNERABILITY	Conduct vulnerability analysis. Must improve controls.	Conduct vulnerability analysis. Must improve controls.	Vulnerability analysis unnecessary.
MEDIUM VULNERABILITY	Conduct vulnerability analysis. Should Improve controls.	Conduct vulnerability analysis. Should Improve controls.	Vulnerability analysis unnecessary.
LOW VULNERABILITY	Conduct vulnerability analysis. Keep controls intact.	Conduct vulnerability analysis. Keep controls intact.	Vulnerability analysis unnecessary.

day operations). For both severe and significant risks, a vulnerability analysis is conducted. When the analysis indicates high vulnerability (substantial weaknesses exist in the systems) controls *must* be implemented to eliminate or reduce the vulnerability. When vulnerability is medium (some weaknesses exist), controls *should* be implemented. When vulnerability is low (the system is well constructed and is operating correctly), the existing controls should be kept intact.

At the completion of the risk analysis, the findings should be documented in a risk analysis report. Contents of this report should include information such as the following for *each risk*:[9]

1. A description of the risk
2. Source of the risk
3. Severity of the risk
4. Controls that are being applied to the risk
5. The owner(s) of the risk
6. Recommended action to address the risk
7. Recommended time frame for addressing the risk

When the firm has responded to the risk, the report should be completed by adding a final section:

8. What was done to mitigate the risk.

INFORMATION SECURITY POLICY

Regardless of whether the firm follows a risk management or a benchmark compliance strategy, a security policy should be implemented to guide the overall program. The firm can implement its security policy by following a phased approach, and Figure 9.3 illustrates the five phases.[10]

- **Phase 1—Project initiation** The team that is to develop the security policy is formed. If the corporate MIS steering committee is unable to assume responsibility for overseeing the security policy project, a special steering committee can be formed. If a special committee is formed, it will include managers in the areas where the policy will apply.
- **Phase 2—Policy Development** The project team consults with all interested and affected parties to determine the requirements of the new policy.
- **Phase 3—Consultation and Approval** The project team consults with management to inform them of findings to date and also obtain their views on policy requirements.
- **Phase 4—Awareness and Education** Training awareness and policy education programs are conducted in the organizational units. The trainees can consist of the project members, other internal representatives such as persons from IT and HR, or outside consultants.
- **Phase 5—Policy Dissemination** The security policies are disseminated throughout the organizational units where the policies apply. Ideally, the unit managers will hold meetings with employees to ensure that they understand the policies and are committed to following them.

Separate policies are developed for:

- Information systems security
- System access control
- Personnel security
- Physical and environmental security
- Telecommunications security
- Information classification

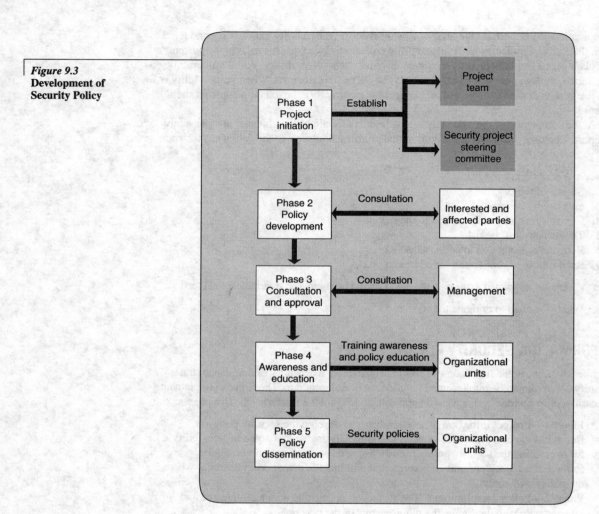

Figure 9.3
Development of Security Policy

- Business continuity planning
- Management accountability

These policies are distributed to employees, preferably in writing, and through educational and training programs. With the policies established, controls can be implemented.

CONTROLS

A **control** is a mechanism that is implemented to either protect the firm from risks or to minimize the impact of the risks on the firm should they occur. Controls fall into three categories; technical, formal, and informal.[11]

TECHNICAL CONTROLS

Technical controls are those that are built into systems by the system developers during the system development life cycle. Including an internal auditor on the project team is an excellent way to ensure that such controls are included as a part of system design. Most of the security controls are based on the hardware and software technology. The more popular ones are described below.

Access Controls

The basis for security against threats by unauthorized persons is access control. The reasoning is simple: If unauthorized persons are denied access to the information resources, then harm cannot be done.

Access control is achieved by means of a three-step process that includes user identification, user authentication, and user authorization. The incorporation of these steps into a security system is illustrated in Figure 9.4.

1. **User identification.** Users first identify themselves by providing something that they *know*, such as a password. The identification can also include the user's *location*, such as a telephone number or network entry point.
2. **User authentication.** Once initial identification has been accomplished, users verify their right to access by providing something that they *have*, such as a smart card or token, or an identification chip. User authentication can also be accomplished by providing something that they *are*, such as a signature or a voice or speech pattern.
3. **User authorization.** With the identification and authentication checks passed, a person can then be authorized to access certain levels or degrees of use. For example, one user might be authorized only to read from a file, whereas another might be authorized to make changes in the file.

Identification and authentication make use of **user profiles**, or descriptions of authorized users. Authorization makes use of **access control files** that specify the levels of access available to each user.

Once users have satisfied the three access control functions, they can use the information resources within the constraints of the access control files. An **audit log** is maintained of all access control activity, such as date and time of day and terminal identification, and it is used to prepare security reports.

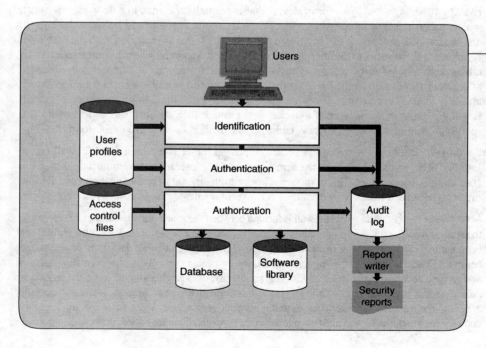

Figure 9.4 **Access Control Functions**

Source: Ken Cutler, "Hackers, Viruses, Thieves, and Other Threats to Your Information Assets," in Computer Security Seminar Course Material *(NY:ACM 1991)*

Intrusion Detection Systems

The underlying logic of intrusion detection systems is to recognize an attempt to breach the security before it has the opportunity to inflict damage. A good example is **virus protection software** that has proven to be effective against viruses transported in E-mail. The software identifies the virus-carrying messages and warns the user. The software must continually be updated to be effective against new viruses.

Another example of intrusion detection is the software aimed at identifying potential intruders before they have an opportunity to inflict harm. **Insider threat prediction tools** have been developed that consider such characteristics as the person's position in the firm, access to sensitive data, ability to alter hardware components, the types of applications used, the files owned, and the usage of certain network protocols. The output of such profilers, some of which are quantitative, can classify the internal threats in such categories as possible intentional threat, potential accidental threat, suspicious, and harmless.[12]

Firewalls

Computer resources are at risk whenever they are connected to a network. The type of network and the number of users who can travel the network to access your computer determine your level of risk.

One approach to security is to physically separate a firm's Web site from the firm's internal network that contains sensitive data and information systems. Another is to provide trading partners with passwords that enable them to enter the internal network from the Internet. A third approach is to build a protective wall, a firewall.

The **firewall** acts as a filter and barrier that restricts the flow of data to and from the firm from the Internet. The concept behind the firewall is that it establishes one safeguard for all computers on the firm's network rather than separate safeguards for each computer. Some companies producing antivirus software (such as McAfee at WWW.MCAFEE.COM and Norton at WWW.NORTON.COM) now include firewall software at no extra charge when you purchase your antivirus software.

Three types of firewalls are packet-filtering, circuit-level, and application-level.

PACKET-FILTERING FIREWALL   A type of device that is normally included in a network is a router, which directs the flow of network traffic. When the router is positioned between the Internet and the internal network, it can serve as a firewall. The router is equipped with data tables of IP addresses that reflect the filtering policy. For each transmission, the router accesses its tables and enables only certain types of messages from certain Internet locations (IP addresses) to pass through. An IP adress is a set of four numbers from 0 to 255 which uniquely identify each compuer connected to the Internet. A limitation of the router is that it is a single point of security, so if a hacker gets through then the firm can be in trouble. "IP spoofing," fooling the router's access tables, is one method hackers use to foil routers.

CIRCUIT-LEVEL FIREWALL   A step up in security over the router is a circuit-level firewall that is installed between the Internet and the firm's network but closer to the communications medium (i.e., circuit) than a router. This approach allows a high amount of authentication and filtering, much higher than a router. However, the limitation of a single point of security still applies.

APPLICATION-LEVEL FIREWALL   This firewall is located between the router and the computer performing the application. The full power of additional security checks can be performed. After the request has been authenticated as coming from an authorized network (circuit-level) and from an authorized computer (packet-filtering), the application can request further authentication information such as asking for a secondary password, confirming an identity, or even checking to see if the request is during normal business hours. While this is the most effective type of firewall, it tends to degrade access to the resource. Another issue is that a network programmer must write specific program code for each application and must change the code as applications are added, deleted, or modified.

Cryptographic Controls

Stored and transmitted data and information can be protected against unauthorized disclosure through **cryptography**, which is the use of coding by means of mathematical processes.[13] The data and information can be encrypted as it resides in storage and as it is transmitted over networks. If an unauthorized person gains access, the encryption makes the data and information meaningless and prevents misuse.

Cryptography is increasing in popularity due to e-commerce, and special protocols aimed at that application have been developed. One is SET (Secure Electronic Transactions) that performs security checks using digital signatures. The signatures are issued to the persons who can participate in an e-commerce transaction; customers, merchants, and financial institutions. Dual signatures are used rather than credit card numbers.

Considerable attention is currently being directed at encryption by governments, which fear that the coding could be used to cover up criminal or terrorist activities. Several restrictions have been placed on encryption use. Presently, there are no restrictions on importing encryption software from foreign countries but there are restrictions on export. The U.S. Department of Commerce administers U.S. policy and prohibits export to Cuba, Iran, Iraq, Libya, North Korea, the Sudan, and Syria. Organizations and countries that defend the individual's right to use encryption oppose restrictions.

With the increasing popularity of e-commerce and the continual development of encryption technology, its use is expected to increase within the bounds of government restrictions.

Physical Controls

The first precaution against unauthorized intrusions was to lock the computer room door. Subsequent refinements led to more sophisticated locks, opened by palm prints and voice prints, and to surveillance cameras and security guards. Firms can carry physical controls to the limit by locating their computer centers in remote areas far from cities and far from areas especially sensitive to such natural disasters as earthquakes, floods, and hurricanes.

Putting the Technical Controls in Perspective

You can see from this long list of technical controls (and we did not list them all), that much attention has been directed at using technology to safeguard information. The technical controls are recognized as being the best bet for security. Firms typically select from the list and implement a combination that is considered to offer the most realistic safeguard.

FORMAL CONTROLS

Formal controls include the establishment of codes of conduct, documentation of expected procedures and practices, and monitoring and preventing behavior that varies from the established guidelines. The controls are formal in that management devotes considerable time to devising them, they are documented in writing, and they are expected to be in force for the long term.

There is universal agreement that if the formal controls are to be effective, top management must participate actively in their establishment and enforcement.

INFORMAL CONTROLS

Informal controls include such activities as instilling the firm's ethical beliefs in its employees, ensuring an understanding of the firm's mission and objectives, education and training programs, and management development programs. These controls are intended to ensure that the firm's employees both understand and support the security program.

ACHIEVING THE PROPER LEVEL OF CONTROLS

All three types of controls—technical, formal, and informal—cost money. Since it is not a good business practice to spend more for a control than the expected cost of the risk that it addresses, the idea is to establish controls at the proper level. So, the control decision boils down to cost versus return, but in some industries other considerations must be addressed. In banking, for example, when engaging in risk management for ATMs, controls must keep the system secure but not at the cost of diminishing customer convenience. Also, in health care, the questions of patient health and right to privacy must be considered. The system should not be made so secure as to reduce the amount of patient information that can be made available to hospitals and physicians who are responsible for the patient's health.

GOVERNMENT AND INDUSTRY ASSISTANCE[14]

Several governments and international organizations have established standards that are intended to serve as guidelines for organizations seeking to achieve information security. Some of the standards are in the form of benchmarks, which we identified earlier as providing an alternate strategy to risk management. Some of the standard-setting entities use the term *baseline* rather than benchmark. Organizations are not required to adhere to the standards. Rather, they are intended to provide the firm with assistance in establishing a target level of security. Some examples are

- **United Kingdom's BS7799.** The UK standards establish a set of baseline controls. Both Australia and New Zealand have instituted controls based on BS 7799.
- **BSI IT Baseline Protection Manual.** The baseline approach is also followed by the German Bundesamt fur Sicherheit in der Informationstechnik (BSI). The baselines are intended to provide reasonable security when normal protection requirements are intended. The baselines can also serve as the basis for higher degrees of protection when those are desired.
- **COBIT.** COBIT, from the Information Systems Audit and Control Association & Foundation (ISACAF), focuses on the process that a firm can follow in developing standards, paying special attention to the writing and maintaining of the documentation.
- **GASSP.** Generally Accepted System Security Principles (GASSP) is a product of the U.S. National Research Council. Emphasis is on the rationale for establishing a security policy.
- **GMITS.** The Guidelines for the Management of IT Security (GMITS) is a product of the International Standards Organization (ISO) Joint Technical Committee and it provides a list of the information security policy topics that should be included in an organization's standards.
- **ISF Standard of Good Practice.** The Information Security Forum Standard of Good Practice takes a baseline approach, devoting considerable attention to the user behavior that is expected if the program is to be successful.

None of the standards offer complete coverage of the subject, but, when taken together, they form a good basis for the firm to follow in establishing its own information security policy that supports its organizational culture.

GOVERNMENT LEGISLATION

Governments in both the United States and the United Kingdom have established standards and passed legislation aimed at addressing the increasing importance of information security, especially in light of 9/11 and the pervasive nature of the Internet and the opportunities it provides for computer crime. Among these are

- **U.S. Government Computer Security Standards.** A study by the Gartner research firm predicts that through 2005, 90 percent of all computer security attacks will be aimed at weaknesses for which there is a known protection.[15] In 2002, the U.S. government responded with a program aimed at applying the known protections. The program includes a set of security standards that participating organizations should meet, plus the availability of a software program that grades users' systems and assists them in configuring their systems to meet the standards. The Department of Defense was required to implement the standards immediately and in late 2002 the White House was considering their required use throughout the federal government.
- **The U.K. Anti-Terrorism, Crime and Security Act (ATCSA) 2001.** In the United Kingdom, Parliament enacted the Anti-Terrorism, Crime and Security Act (ATCSA) 2001.[16] This act has three provisions: (1) Internet service providers (ISPs) are required to maintain for one year data about all communications events, (2) government taxing authorities are empowered to disclose information about an individual's or organization's financial affairs to the authorities that investigate crime or terrorism, and (3) the obligation of confidence is removed for public bodies that can investigate or audit other public bodies; information can be disclosed even if there is only suspicion of an impending terrorist act.
- **U.S. Government Internet Crime Legislation.** In 2002 the U.S. House of Representatives passed legislation that is similar to the U.K. act in order to address the threat of computer crime committed on the Internet.[17] ISPs are exempted from liability if they report suspicions to the government that an Internet crime might be committed. The House bill also permits the use of electronic surveillance tools for 48 hours pending authorization by courts to use such tools. Finally, the bill establishes a penalty of 10 to 20 years imprisonment for attempting to cause injury by means of the Internet, and a penalty of life imprisonment if death occurs. In late 2002, the House bill was awaiting approval by the Senate.

INDUSTRY STANDARDS

The Center for Internet Security (CIS) is a nonprofit organization dedicated to assisting computer users to make their systems more secure. The center, consisting of more than 170 member organizations, has made available standards and software similar to those of the House legislation.

CIS benchmarks have been established and are integrated in a software package that calculates a "security" score on a 10-point scale. When Virginia Tech used the software to evaluate the level of security for its network of 24,000 computers, the Sun servers scored 3.67 and the Windows 2000 servers scored 1.6. When the benchmarks were applied the Sun score was raised to 8.17 and Windows to 5.5.[18]

PROFESSIONAL CERTIFICATION

Beginning in the 1960s, the IT profession began offering certification programs. The three following examples illustrate the breadth of the subject matter.

Information Systems Audit and Control Association (ISACA)

The first certification program was Certified Information System Auditor, offered by the Information Systems Audit and Control Association (ISACA). Subsequently, ISACA developed the Certified Information Security Manager designation. In order to earn this certification, the applicant must complete an exam offered for the first time in June 2003, adhere to a code of ethics, and verify work experience in information security. Information on ISACA can be found at WWW.ISACA.ORG.

International Information System Security Certification Consortium (ISC)[19]

The Certification Information System Security Professional (CISSP) is offered by the International Information System Security Certification Consortium (ISC). The CISSP certification verifies that the holder has a general expertise in information security that encompasses such topics as access control, cryptography, security architecture, Internet security, and security management practices. Certification is based on performance on an exam of 250 multiple-choice questions. More information can be found at WWW.ISC2.ORG.

SANS Institute

SANS (SysAdmin, Audit, Network, Security) Institute offers certifications through its Global Information Assurance Certification Program that are aimed at such specialties within information security as intrusion detection, firewalls and perimeter protection, and operating system security. These certifications require the applicant to not only demonstrate the required knowledge but also to be able to apply the material in the real world. Information on SANS can be obtained from WWW.SANS.ORG.

PUTTING INFORMATION SECURITY MANAGEMENT IN PERSPECTIVE

Firms should put in place an information security management policy before putting controls in place. The policy can be based on an identification of threats and their risks or on guidelines provided by governments and industry associations. Firms implement a combination of technical, formal, and informal controls that are expected to offer the desired level of security within cost parameters and in accordance with other considerations that enable the firm and its systems to function effectively.

BUSINESS CONTINUITY MANAGEMENT (BCM)

The activity aimed at continuing to operate after an information system disruption is called **business continuity management (BCM)**. During the early years of computing, this activity was called **disaster planning**, but a more positive term, **contingency planning**, became popular. The key element in contingency planning is a **contingency plan**, which is a formal written document that spells out in detail the actions to be taken in the event that there is a disruption, or threat of disruption, in any part of the firm's computing operation.

Firms have found that, rather than relying on a single, large contingency plan, the best approach is to develop several subplans that address specific contingencies.[20] Typical subplans include the emergency plan, the backup plan, and the vital records plan.

The Emergency Plan

The **emergency plan** specifies those measures that ensure the safety of employees when disaster strikes. The measures include alarm systems, evacuation procedures, and fire suppression systems.

The Backup Plan

The firm should make arrangements for backup computing facilities in the event that the regular facilities are destroyed or damaged beyond use. These arrangements constitute the **backup plan**. Backup can be achieved by means of some combination of redundancy, diversity, and mobility.[21] Key elements might include:

- **Redundancy.** Hardware, software, and data are duplicated so that when one set is inoperable, the backup set can continue the processing.
- **Diversity.** The information resources are not all installed at the same location. Large firms typically establish separate computing centers for different areas of their operations.

- **Mobility.** Firms can enter into a **reciprocal agreement** with other users of the same type of equipment so that each firm can provide backup to the other in the event of a catastrophe. A more elaborate approach is to contract for backup service at hot or cold sites. A **hot site** is a complete computing facility that is made available by a supplier to its customers for use in the event of emergencies. A **cold site** includes only the building facilities but not the computing resources. The firm can obtain a cold site from a supplier or construct its own facilities. For either approach, the firm must provide the computing resources. The largest suppliers of hot and cold sites are IBM and SunGard.

The Vital Records Plan

A firm's **vital records** are those paper documents, microforms, and magnetic and optical storage media that are necessary for carrying on the firm's business. The **vital records plan** specifies how the vital records will be protected. In addition to safeguarding the records at the computer site, backup copies should be stored at a remote location. All types of records can be physically transported to the remote location, but computer records can be transmitted electronically.

PUTTING BUSINESS CONTINUITY MANAGEMENT IN PERSPECTIVE

Business continuity management is one area of computer use where it is easy to see major improvements. During the late 1980s, only a handful of firms had such plans and the firms seldom put them to any test. Since then, much effort has gone into contingency planning and much information and assistance is available. There are packaged plans that firms can adapt to their needs. TAMP Computer Systems markets a Disaster Recovery System (DRS) that includes a database management system, instructions, and tools that can be used in preparing a recovery plan. There are also guidelines and outlines that firms can use as starting points or benchmarks to achieve. A guideline for contingency planning prepared by the Texas Department of Information Resources can be obtained at HTTP://WW.DIR.STATE.TX.US/SECURITY/CONTINUITY/INDEX.HTM. A contingency planning outline prepared by the Kansas Department of Administration, Division of Information Systems & Communications can be obtained at WWW.DA.STATE.KS.US/DISC/BCPOUTLINE.HTM.

Highlights in MIS

RECOVERING FROM 9/11 AND ENRON

The events of September 11, 2001 were a tragedy and Enron was a scandal but they had one thing in common—they served as a wake-up call for corporate management in terms of securing information resources. The image of millions of pages of paper documents fluttering down from the World Trade towers and the news stories of the illegal shredding of documents at Enron emphasized to management the importance of its information.

September 11 introduced a new type of threat to firms. Up until that point, security precautions had been aimed at threats by rational perpetrators. Even though business continuity management usually includes backup facilities and data, the plans did not anticipate the fact that planes would not be flying for days, making it impossible to ship data to or from the backup site.

Also, little if any attention had been devoted to protecting the firm and its assets from catastrophes that far exceeded what had ever happened before. Contingency planning was usually based on the assumption that the only loss would be of such computing resources as hardware and data. No one anticipated loss of both computing resources and the entire employee force, as was the case for many firms with offices in the World Trade Center. For those firms, it quickly became clear that the loss of people was more crippling than the loss of facilities and equipment.

Faced with a new set of threats and risks, information security management is now a whole new ballgame.

Summary

The original focus of systems security on the computer and database has been broadened to include not only all types of information resources but also such noncomputer media as paper documents as well, and the activity is named information security. The three objectives of information security are confidentiality, availability, and integrity. These objectives are met by following programs of information security management (ISM) on a daily basis, and business continuity management (BCM) to remain operational after a disruption from a disaster or a security breach. Current thinking is that this security activity should be managed by a corporate information assurance officer (CIAO) who directs a separate security facility and reports directly to the CEO.

There are two approaches to ISM. Risk management involves the chain of events that includes identification of threats, definition of risks, establishment of an information security policy, and implementation of the controls. Benchmark compliance replaces the threat and risk considerations with benchmarks of good information security, which are usually made available by the government or industry associations.

Threats can be internal or external and accidental or deliberate. Much attention has been directed at both internal and external threats, with the internal controls usually taking the form of intrusion detection tools and prediction of intrusions before they occur. Risks are the unauthorized acts performed by the threats. The acts can result in disclosure, theft, unauthorized use, destruction, denial of service, and modification. The most notorious threat is the virus, which is only one example of malicious software, along with worms and Trojan horses. E-commerce produces the threat of credit card fraud, which can be minimized when participants use numbers randomly generated for transactions rather than credit cards.

When engaging in risk management, the level of impact and the degree of vulnerability can be defined in a systematic way. Severe or significant impact demands a vulnerability analysis. Controls must be implemented for severe impacts and should be implemented for significant ones.

Information security policy can be implemented by following a five-phased plan. The project includes a project team and perhaps a special steering committee. The team works with management and interested parties in developing the policy, which is then disseminated to organizational units after providing training and educational programs. Separate policies can be developed to secure the information system, personnel, telecommunications, and the physical environment.

There are three types of controls—technical, formal, and informal. Technical controls employ hardware and software. Access controls grant access only after users pass screens of user identification, authentication, and authorization. Intrusion detection systems include antivirus packages and models that can identify insider threats. Firewalls are aimed at protecting the firm's network from intrusion via the Internet. Cryptographic controls are considered to be especially effective because they do not hinge on preventing access; rather, they make data and information unusable when it is obtained. Physical controls secure the computing facility by restricting or discouraging unauthorized access. Formal controls take the form of top-down efforts such as codes of conduct, procedures, and practices. Informal controls are concerned primarily with giving employees the information that they need to carry out the controls.

Much has been accomplished in the area of security standards. Both national governments and industry associations have issued standards or provided assistance in determining what should be included in security programs. Governments have also passed legislation that requires certain standards to be followed or that enables organizations to provide information about potential terrorist or organized crime threats without fear of prosecution. Going hand-in-hand with industry support are the various security certification programs, which address such broad subjects as management practices and such narrow topics as cryptography.

Business continuity management is achieved by means of a contingency plan, which is usually divided into subplans. An emergency plan protects the employees; a backup plan enables the operation to continue even after loss of a computing capability; and the vital records plan ensures that data is not lost.

So much is available today to firms that want to improve information security. This is one area of computer activity where the correct path is well-lighted.

KEY TERMS

information security
information security management (ISM)
business continuity management (BCM)

benchmark
threat
risk
control
firewall

cryptography
contingency planning
emergency plan
backup plan
vital records plan

KEY CONCEPTS

- risk management
- benchmark compliance
- access control

QUESTIONS

1. What is included in information security that was not included in systems security?
2. What are the three objectives of information security?
3. Information security is subdivided into two separate efforts. What are they?
4. How does risk management differ from benchmark compliance?
5. What special type of risk must be addressed by e-commerce systems?
6. What type of threat is addressed by a firewall?
7. What is so great about cryptography?
8. What is the difference between formal and informal controls?
9. What distinguishes banks and health care organizations in terms of how they determine the proper security level?
10. Which countries have established security baselines?
11. What is the first government agency that is required to implement the new U.S. security standards?
12. What role can an ISP play in security against computer criminals and terrorists?
13. What types of plans are included in contingency planning?

Topics for Discussion

1. Figure 9.1A shows the security policy being established after threats and risks are defined. Shouldn't the policy be established first?
2. Why do controls aimed at internal threats emphasize intrusion detection?
3. The outline of the report to be prepared at the end of risk analysis refers to the "owner(s) of the risk." What is meant by "owning" a risk? Who would be an example of an owner?
4. Why not just rely on cryptography, and not worry about restricting access?

Problems

1. Go to WWW.SUNGARD.COM and obtain information about the business continuity services offered by SunGard. Write a paper describing your findings. Your instructor will provide the specifics in terms of format, paper length, and so on.
2. Assume that you are the newly hired corporate information systems security officer for a small Midwest manufacturing firm and you are shocked to learn that there is no virus protection software. Read the Denis Zenkin article in the bibliography and write a memo to your president, stating the case for implementing such software.

Case Problem: Confidential Reports

Your company, Fair Heights, is hired by other companies to perform background checks on executives. The executives are typically senior managers in a firm with a vice president title or higher. Most of the checks are on executives who are being considered for a job but sometimes you run background checks on current executives. The gathering of information is not the key service Fair Heights provides. Analysis of the information and the security recommendation are the services that make your company unique.

During the last 10 years of business, Fair Heights has always provided the report to their clients in person or in a written report delivered by a courier. There is a growing demand to make the recommendations accessible via the World Wide Web. The reason is that many of the firms are multinational and assembling key executives to hear Fair Height's' report can be difficult and expensive to arrange. Making the arrangements can cause delays and the companies want this vital information delivered as quickly as possible.

The move to Web-based reports is inevitable. It's your job to make a report for the planning committee that identifies and addresses key issues.

Assignment

1. You want Fair Heights reports to be confidential, available, and to have integrity. Explain how making reports Web-accessible will affect each of these.
2. List several external threats and internal threats to the security of Fair Heights reports. Make sure you address both accidental and deliberate threats to security.
3. Make a brief risk management report (about three paragraphs) that identifies several risks and classify the risk impact of each.

Notes

[1] For a detailed description of the CIAO duties, see Gerald L. Kovacich, "The Corporate Information Assurance Officer (CIAO)," *Computers & Security* Volume 20 Issue 4 (July 31, 2001), pp. 302–307.

[2] Magklaras, G. B., and Furnell, S. M., "Insider Threat Prediction Tool: Evaluating the Probability of IT Misuse," *Computers & Security* Volume 21 Issue 1 (1st Quarter 2001), pp 62–73.

[3] Dhillon Gurpreet and Steve Moores, "Computer Crimes: Theorizing About the Enemy Within," *Computers & Security* Volume 20, Issue 8 (December 1, 2001), pp. 715–723.

[4] Bill Hancock, "Visa's Ten Commandments for E-Security Online," *Computers & Security* Volume 19 Issue 6 (October 1, 2000), pp. 485–486.

[5] Bill Hancock, "American Express Creates Disposable Credit Card Numbers," *Computers & Security* Volume 19 Issue 7 (November 1, 2000), pp. 571–572.

[6] Bill Hancock, "Visa's Ten Commandments for E-Security Online."

[7] Nosworthy, Julie D., "A Practical Risk Analysis Approach: Managing BCM Risk," *Computers & Security* Volume 19 Issue 7 (November 1, 2000), pp. 596–614.

[8] Nosworthy, *op. cit.*

[9] Nosworthy, *op. cit.*

[10] Peter Ward and Clifton L. Smith, "The Development of Access Control Policies for Information Technology Systems," *Computers & Security* Volume 21 Issue 4 (August 1, 2002), pp. 356–371.

[11] Dhillon Gurpreet and Steve Moores, "Computer Crimes: Theorizing About the Enemy Within," *Computers & Security* Volume 20 Issue 8 (December 1, 2001), pp. 715–723.

[12] Magklaras and Furnell, *op. cit.*

[13] This section is based on material in Andres Torrubia; Francisco J. Mora; and Luis Marti, "Cryptography Regulations for E-commerce and Digital Rights Management," *Computers & Security* Volume 20 Issue 8 (December 1, 2001), pp. 724–738.

[14] This section is based on Karin Höne and J. H. P. Eloff, "Information Security Policy—What Do International Information Security Standards Say?" *Computers & Security* Volume 21 Issue 5 (October 1, 2002), pp. 402–407.

[15] "U.S. Government Unveils Computer Security Standards," *Information Management Journal* Volume 36 Issue 5 (September/October 2002), p. 9.

[16] Chris Pounder, "Anti-Terrorism Legislation: The Impact on the Processing of Data," *Computers & Security* Volume 21 Issue 3 (June 1, 2002), pp. 240–245.

[17] "House Votes to Increase Penalties for Cybercrime," *Information Management Journal* Volume 36 Issue 5 (September/October 2002), p. 12.

[18] Acohido, Byron, "Agency Raises the Bar on Tech Security Non-Profit Works to Plug Holes—For Free," *USA Today* February 27, 2002, p. 7B.

[19] Bill Hancock, "Truly Certified: Security Certifications Update," *Computers & Security* Volume 19 Issue 6 (October 1, 2000), pp. 479–480.

[20] The idea of separate subplans was first described in *Data Security Controls and Procedures—A Philosophy for DP Installations*, G320–5649 (White Plains, NY: IBM Corporation, 1977), 17–22.

[21] Daniel E. White, Ernst & Young, address at the ACM Computer Security Seminar, Phoenix, Arizona, October 8, 1991.

Chapter 10

Ethical Implications of Information Technology

Learning Objectives

After studying this chapter, you should

➡ Understand the distinction between morals, ethics, and laws.

➡ Be familiar with the most important computer legislation that has been passed in the United States, and know how legislation in one country can influence computer use in others as well.

➡ Know how a firm creates an ethics culture by first establishing a corporate credo, then establishing ethics programs, and lastly establishing a corporate ethics code.

➡ Know why society demands that computers be used ethically.

➡ Know the four basic rights that society has concerning the computer.

➡ Know how the firm's internal auditors can play a positive role in achieving information systems that are designed to meet ethical performance criteria.

➡ Be aware of computer industry codes of ethics, and the wide variety of educational programs that can help firms and employees use computers ethically.

➡ Know what the CIO can do to be a power center as the firm follows ethical practices.

Introduction

We are guided in our behavior by morals, ethics, and laws. Computer laws have been enacted in many countries to address such concerns as rights to data access, rights to privacy, computer crime, and software patents. Some countries are ahead of others in passing such legislation, and the laws in one country can affect computer use elsewhere in the world.

Firms have an obligation to establish an ethics culture for their employees to follow. The culture is supported by a corporate credo and ethics programs.

Computer ethics are important because society has certain perceptions, and fears, related to computer use. The features of computer use that concern society are the ability to program the computer to do practically anything, the fact that the computer can so change our daily lives, and the fact that what the computer does is invisible to viewers.

Society has four basic rights concerning the computer; rights to privacy, accuracy, property, and access.

A firm's internal auditors can contribute to the ethical use of information systems by conducting three types of audits—operational, financial, and concurrent—and engaging in internal control systems design. The financial information system includes an internal auditing subsystem as an input subsystem that enters the results of the internal audits into the database.

When a firm sets out to establish its own code of ethics and to follow ethical practices, there is much help available. Professional associations have defined ethical codes, and a wide variety of ethics courses are available from colleges, professional programs, and private educational institutions.

The CIO can play a pivotal role in the firm's practice of computer ethics. The CIO can follow a proactive program to ensure that the information systems provide the information that executives and managers need to support the firm's ethics efforts, that the executives and managers not only understand the information systems that provide financial data but contribute to their development, that such environmental elements as stockholders and owners understand that the firm uses its computers ethically, and that funds spent on IT are not wasted.

PRESCRIPTIVE VERSUS DESCRIPTIVE COVERAGE

Beginning with the first edition of this text, the approach has been to present a **prescriptive coverage** of MIS. That is, to prescribe how the MIS *ought to be* developed and used in a business firm. This appeared to be a clearly better approach for presenting the material to college students entering the business world than to provide a **descriptive coverage** that explains how things *are being* done. We never completely abandoned the descriptive approach because we have always included real-world examples, but they have, in the majority of cases, been good examples. We recall once including a description of a failed MIS project but it was included as an example of how not to develop systems. Our mission, as we have always seen it, is to provide a path that future business and information system professionals can follow—a path that will lead to a successful career and a career that makes a positive contribution to the computing profession and to business and society.

In light of recent events involving firms and executives that have not met their ethical responsibilities, the prescriptive treatment of ethics might appear to be naïve and only wishful thinking. That is not the case at all. We fully recognize that our descriptions are not always followed. However, we will continue to describe how the computer ought to be applied in an ethical manner. Our mission, as we see it, is to recognize that business persons in general and information specialists in particular have definite responsibilities in terms of performing within ethical, moral, and legal constraints, and to provide some guidelines showing how that level of integrity should be achieved.

MORALS, ETHICS, AND LAWS

As we go about our everyday lives, we are guided by many influences. As socially conscionable citizens, we want to do what is morally right, be ethical, and obey the law.

Morals

Morals are traditions of belief about right and wrong conduct.[1] Morals are a social institution with a history and a list of rules. We begin to learn the rules of moral behavior as children: "Don't pull your sister's hair." "Always say, 'Thank you.'" As we grow and mature physically and mentally, we learn the rules that our society expects us to follow. These rules of conduct are our morals.

Although societies around the world do not all subscribe to the same set of morals, there is a strong underlying commonality. "Doing what is morally right" is the bedrock of our social behavior.

Ethics

We are also guided in our actions by ethics. The word "ethics" is derived from the Greek root *ethos*, meaning *character*. **Ethics** is a suite of guiding beliefs, standards, or ideals that pervades an individual or a group or community of people.[2] All individuals are accountable to their community for their behavior. The community can exist in such forms as a neighborhood, city, state, nation, or profession.

Unlike morals, ethics can vary considerably from one community to another. We see this variability in the computer field in the form of **pirated software**—software that is illegally copied and then used or sold. In some countries the practice is more prevalent than in others. In 1994 it was estimated that 35 percent of the software in use in the United States had been pirated, and the figure jumped to 92 percent in Japan and 99 percent in Thailand.[3]

The implication of these figures is that the Japanese and Thai computer users are less ethical than those in the United States. This is not necessarily so. Some cultures, especially those of Asian countries, encourage sharing. In the words of a Chinese proverb, "He that shares is to be rewarded; he that does not, condemned."[4]

Laws

Laws are formal rules of conduct that a sovereign authority, such as a government, imposes on its subjects or citizens. For the first ten years or so of computer use in government and business, there were no computer-related laws. This was because the computer was a new innovation and the legal system had a hard time keeping up.

In 1966 the first case of computer crime made the news when a programmer for a bank put a patch in a program so that it would not flag his account as being overdrawn. He could continue writing checks even though there was no money in the account. The ruse worked until the computer went down, and manual processing revealed the unflagged, overdrawn balance. The programmer was not charged with committing a computer crime, because no laws were on the books. Rather, he was charged with making false entries in bank records.[5]

Computer Legislation in the United States

Once U.S. computer legislation began to be enacted it was focused on rights and restrictions related to data access, especially credit data and data held by the government, on privacy, computer crime, and, most recently, on software patents.

DATA ACCESS RIGHTS AND RESTRICTIONS   The Freedom of Information Act of 1966 gave citizens and organizations the right to access data held by the federal government, with a few exceptions. The 1970s brought additional laws in the form of the Fair Credit Reporting Act of 1970, which dealt with the handling of credit data, and the Right to Federal Privacy Act of 1978, which limited the federal government's ability to conduct searches of bank records. In 1988 another law aimed at restricting the federal government, the Computer Matching and Privacy Act of 1988, restricted the federal government's right to match computer files for the purpose of determining eligibility for government programs or identifying debtors.

PRIVACY   Shortly after the Freedom of Information Act went into effect, the federal government put into law the Electronic Communications Privacy Act of 1968. However, the act covered only voice communications. In 1986 it was rewritten to include digital, data, and video communications and electronic mail.[6]

COMPUTER CRIME   In 1984 the U.S. Congress put additional teeth into computer legislation by passing federal statutes that applied specifically to computer crime[7]:

- The Small Business Computer Security and Education Act established the Small Business Computer Security and Education Advisory Council. The council was assigned the responsibility to advise Congress concerning matters relating to computer crime against small businesses, and to evaluate the effectiveness of federal and state crime laws in deterring and prosecuting computer crime.
- The Counterfeit Access Device and Computer Fraud and Abuse Act made it a federal felony for someone to gain unauthorized access to information pertaining to national defense or foreign relations. The act also made it a misdemeanor to gain unauthorized access to a computer protected by the Right to Financial Privacy Act or the Fair Credit Reporting Act, and to misuse information in a computer owned by the federal government.

Software Patents

In July 1998, the U.S. Court of Appeals for the Federal Circuit affirmed that a business process could be patented. The case became known as **the State Street Decision**.[8] At issue was a software package used for managing mutual funds. Up until that time, the court's position had been that software could not be patented for two reasons: a mathematical algorithm was not patentable, and business methods could not be patented.

Apparently feeling that software patents should have some restrictions, the U.S. Congress in April 2001 introduced a bill requiring a determination of the significance of the patent and whether it is appropriate for use with computer technology. Further, after eighteen months all business-related patents would be published to provide an opportunity for holders of *prior art* to make their case.[9]

In this fashion, the U.S. federal government has gradually established a legal framework for computer use. As with ethics, however, the computer laws can vary considerably from one country to the next.

Software Patent Legislation in the European Union

In early 2002, responding to the State Street Decision that stimulated a flurry of software patent activity in the United States that affected European firms, the European Union policy body made proposals that standards for software patents be established that are much higher than those in the United States. The requirement would be that the software would have to make a "technical contribution to the state of the art."[10] If passed by the European Parliament and the Council of Ministers, the proposals would become law. However, the law would not allow software piracy to run rampant since the software would still be covered by copyright law.

Personal Privacy Legislation in the People's Republic of China[11]

Both government and citizens of the PRC are becoming aware of a need to define personal privacy. One problem is that the term "privacy" often has a negative connotation, being associated with someone who has something to hide. Chinese personal privacy activists are pressing for regulations that would protect such personal data as income level, occupation, marital status, physical attributes, and even address and phone number.

Currently, the only government action has been aimed at imposing regulations on the use of computers and the Internet. These regulations stipulate that such use cannot damage "state security," "social interest," "citizens' lawful interest," and "privacy." However, no definitions of these terms have been provided.

In making their arguments, the activists identify both the European Union and the United States as models for the type of legislation needed.

PUTTING MORALS, ETHICS, AND LAWS IN PERSPECTIVE

Computer use in business is guided by the moral and ethical values of managers, information specialists, and users, as well as by the applicable laws. The laws are the easiest to interpret because they exist in writing. Ethics, on the other hand, are not so precisely defined and are not even agreed upon by all members of a society. It is this thorny area of computer ethics that is receiving much current attention. In the remainder of the chapter, we focus on ethical use of information technology.

NEED FOR AN ETHICS CULTURE

A widely held opinion in business is that a firm reflects the personality of its leader. For example, the influence of James Cash Penney on J. C. Penney, Colonel John Patterson on National Cash Register, or Thomas J. Watson, Sr., on IBM established the personalities of those corporations. Today, the CEOs of such firms as Federal Express, Southwest Airlines, and Microsoft have such an influence on their organizations that the public tends to view the firm as the CEO.

This linkage of the CEO with the firm is the basis for the ethics culture. If the firm is to be ethical, then top-level management must be ethical in everything that it does and says. Top-level management leads by example. This behavior is the **ethics culture**.

How the Ethical Culture Is Imposed

The task of top-level management is to see to it that its concept of ethics permeates the organization, filtering down through the ranks to touch every employee. The executives achieve this implementation in a three-tiered fashion, in the form of a corporate credo, ethics programs, and tailored corporate codes.[12] Figure 10.1 shows the different tiers and their relationships.

CORPORATE CREDO   A **corporate credo** is a succinct statement of the values that the firm seeks to uphold. The purpose of the credo is to inform persons and organizations, both inside and outside the firm, of the firm's set of ethical values. Figure 10.2 shows an example of a corporate credo from Security Pacific Corporation, a Los Angeles–based bank. Security Pacific management recognized that its business was built on commitments, both internal and external.

ETHICS PROGRAMS   An **ethics program** is an effort consisting of multiple activities designed to provide employees with direction in carrying out the corporate credo. A typical activity is the orientation session that is held for new employees. During this session considerable attention is paid to the subject of ethics.

Another example of an ethics program is the ethics audit. In an **ethics audit** an internal auditor meets with a manager in a several-hour session for the purpose of learning how the manager's unit is carrying out the corporate credo. For example, an auditor might ask a sales

ETHICAL IMPLICATIONS OF INFORMATION TECHNOLOGY ••• 233

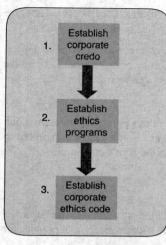

Figure 10.1 Top-Level Management Imposes the Ethics Culture in a Top-Down Manner

Figure 10.2 Example of a Corporate Credo
Source: Patrick Murphy, "Creating Ethical Corporate Structures," Sloan Management Review 30 (Winter 1989), 82. Used with permission.

Commitment to customer
The first commitment is to provide our customers with quality products and services that are innovative and technologically responsive to their current requirements, at appropriate prices. To perform these tasks with integrity requires that we maintain confidentiality and protect customer privacy, promote customer satisfaction, and serve customer needs. We strive to serve qualified customers and industries that are socially responsible according to broadly accepted community and company standards.

Commitment to employee
The second commitment is to establish an environment for our employees that promotes professional growth, encourages each person to achieve his or her highest potential, and promotes individual creativity and responsibility. Security Pacific acknowledges our responsibility to employees, including providing for open and honest communication, stated expectations, fair and timely assessment of performance, and equitable compensation that rewards employee contributions to company objectives within a framework of equal opportunity and affirmative action.

Commitment of employee to Security Pacific
The third commitment is that of the employee to Security Pacific. As employees, we strive to understand and adhere to the Corporation's policies and objectives, act in a professional manner, and give our best effort to improve Security Pacific. We recognize the trust and confidence placed in us by our customers and community and act with integrity and honesty in all situations to preserve that trust and confidence. We act responsibly to avoid conflicts of interest and other situations that are potentially harmful to the Corporation.

Commitment of employee to employee
The fourth commitment is that of employees to their fellow employees. We must be committed to promote a climate of mutual respect, integrity, and professional relationships, characterized by open and honest communication within and across all levels of the organization. Such a climate will promote attainment of the Corporation's goals and objectives, while leaving room for individual initiative within a competitive environment.

Commitment to communities
The fifth commitment is that of Security Pacific to the communities that we serve. We must constantly strive to improve the quality of life through our support of community organizations and projects, through encouraging service to the community by employees, and by promoting participation in community services. By the appropriate use of our resources, we work to support or further advance the interests of the community, particularly in times of crisis or social need. The Corporation and its employees are committed to complying fully with each community's laws and regulations.

Commitment to stockholder
The sixth commitment of Security Pacific is to its stockholders. We will strive to provide consistent growth and a superior rate of return on their investments, to maintain a position and reputation as a leading financial institution, to protect stockholder investments, and to provide full and timely information. Achievement of these goals for Security Pacific is dependent upon the successful development of the five previous sets of relationships.

manager, "Have there been any instances where we have lost business because we do not give gifts to purchasing agents?"

TAILORED CORPORATE CODES   Many firms have devised their own corporate code of ethics. Sometimes these are adaptations of codes for a particular industry or profession. Later in the chapter we will study the codes of ethics for the information systems profession.

Putting the Credos, Programs, and Codes in Perspective
The corporate credo provides the setting in which the firm's ethics programs are carried out. The ethics codes describe the specific behaviors that the firm's employees are expected to carry out in their dealings with each other and the elements in the firm's environment.

REASONS FOR A COMPUTER ETHIC

James H. Moor has defined **computer ethics** as the analysis of the nature and social impact of computer technology as well as the corresponding formulation and justification of policies for the ethical use of such technology.[13]

Computer ethics, therefore, consists of two main activities, and the person in the firm who is the logical choice for implementing the ethics programs is the CIO. The CIO must (1) be alert to the effects that the computer is having on society, and (2) formulate policies to ensure that the technology is used throughout the firm in the right way.

One point is very important and that is the fact that *the CIO does not bear this managerial responsibility for computer ethics alone*. The other executives contribute as well. This firm-wide involvement is an absolute necessity in today's world of end-user computing, in which managers in all areas are responsible for the ethical use of computers in their areas. Beyond the managers, each and every employee is responsible for his or her computer-related actions.

Reasons for the Importance of Computer Ethics
James Moor believes there are three main reasons for society's high level of interest in computer ethics. He calls these reasons logical malleability, the transformation factor, and the invisibility factor.

LOGICAL MALLEABILITY   By **logical malleability** Moor means the ability to program the computer to do practically anything you want it to do. The computer performs exactly as it is instructed by the programmer and this can be frightening. However, when the computer is used for an unethical activity it is not the computer that is the culprit. Rather, it is the person or persons behind the computer who are at fault. So, rather than fear that the computer is sometimes used in an unethical way, society should fear the persons who are directing the computer.

The Transformation Factor   This reason for concern over computer ethics is based on the fact that computers can drastically change the way we do things. We can see this transformation of duties in firms of all types. A good example is electronic mail. E-mail did not simply replace regular mail or telephone calls. It provided an entirely new means of communication. Similar transformations can be seen in how managers conduct meetings. Whereas managers once had to physically assemble in the same location, they can now meet in the form of a video conference.

THE INVISIBILITY FACTOR   The third reason for society's interest in computer ethics is that society views the computer as a black box. All of the computer's internal operations are hidden from view. Invisibility of internal operations provides the opportunity for invisible programming values, invisible complex calculations, and invisible abuse.

- **Invisible programming values** are those routines that the programmer codes into the program that may or may not produce the processing that the user desires. During the course of writing a program, the programmer must make a series of value judgments as to how the program should accomplish its purpose. This is not a malicious act on the part of the programmer but, rather, a lack of understanding. A good example of the impact that invisible programming values can have is the Three Mile Island nuclear disaster. The plant operators had been trained in handling emergencies by using a mathematical model. The model was designed to simulate single malfunctions occurring alone. What happened, however, was that multiple malfunctions occurred simultaneously. The inability of the computer to give the users what they needed was due to this invisibility factor.
- **Invisible complex calculations** take the form of programs that are so complex that users do not understand them. A manager uses such a program with no idea of how it is performing its calculations.
- **Invisible abuse** includes intentional acts that cross legal as well as ethical boundaries. All acts of computer crime fall into this category, as do such unethical acts as invasion of individuals' right to privacy and surveillance.

Society is, therefore, very concerned about the computer—how it can be programmed to do practically anything, how it is changing many of the ways that we do things, and the fact that what it does is basically invisible. Society expects business to be guided by computer ethics in order to put these concerns to rest.

Social Rights and the Computer

Society not only expects government and business to use computers in an ethical way, it also has certain computer-related rights. The most widely publicized classification of human rights in the computer area is Richard O. Mason's PAPA.[14] Mason coined the acronym **PAPA** to represent society's four basic rights in terms of information. The letters in PAPA stand for *p*rivacy, *a*ccuracy, *p*roperty, and *a*ccessibility.

Right to Privacy

Supreme Court Justice Louis Brandeis is credited with recognizing "the right to be let alone."[15] Mason feels that this right is being threatened because of two forces. One is the increasing ability of the computer to be used for surveillance, and the other is the increasing value of information in decision making. The federal government addressed a portion of this problem in the Privacy Act of 1974. However, that act only covers violations by the government.

According to Mason, decision makers place such a high value on information that they will often invade someone's privacy to get it. Marketing researchers have been known to go through people's garbage to learn what products they buy, and government officials have stationed monitors in restrooms to gather traffic statistics to be used in justifying expansion of the facilities.

These are examples of snooping that do not use the computer. The general public is aware that the computer can be used for this purpose, but it is probably not aware of the ease with which personal data can be accessed, especially using the Internet. If you know how to go about the search process and are willing to pay some fees along the way, you can obtain practically any types of personal and financial information about private citizens.

Right to Accuracy

The computer is given credit for making possible a level of accuracy that is unachievable in noncomputerized systems. The potential is certainly there, but it is not always reached. Some computer-based systems contain more errors than would be tolerated in manual systems.

Right to Property

Here we are talking about intellectual property, usually in the form of computer programs. Software vendors can guard against theft of their intellectual property by means of copyrights, patents, and license agreements. Until the 1980s, software was covered by neither copyright nor patent laws. Now, both can be used to provide some degree of protection. Patents provide especially strong protection in the countries where they are enforced because it is not necessary that a clone match the original version exactly in order for copyright protection to be obtained.

Software vendors try to plug up the loopholes in the laws by means of the license agreements that their customers accept when they use the software. Violation of the agreements can put the customers in court.

Right to Access

Prior to the introduction of computerized databases, much information was available to the general public in the form of printed documents or microform images stored in libraries. The information consisted of news stories, results of scientific research, government statistics, and so on. Today, much of this information has been converted to commercial databases, making it less accessible to the public. To have access to the information, one must possess the required computer hardware and software and pay the access fees. In light of the fact that a computer can access data from storage much more quickly and easily than any other technology, it is ironic that a right to access is a modern-day ethical issue.

INFORMATION AUDITING

As we build the case for ethical computer use, there is one group that can serve as a key building block. They are the internal auditors. Firms of all sizes rely on **external auditors** to audit the accounting records to verify their accuracy. Larger firms have their own staffs of **internal auditors**, who perform the same analyses as external auditors but have a broader range of responsibilities. Some external auditors have been doing some internal auditing and overseeing the work of the internal auditors, but after Enron, that has come to a halt. The Securities and Exchange Commission has placed restrictions on the amount of internal auditing that external auditors can perform.[16] That was one of the many downfalls of Arthur Andersen with Enron.

Figure 10.3 shows a popular way to position internal auditing in the organization. The board of directors includes an **audit committee**, which defines the responsibilities of the internal auditing department and receives many of the audit reports. The **director of internal auditing** manages the internal auditing department and usually reports to the CEO or the CFO. The **CFO**, or **chief financial officer**, is the person who manages the financial function and typically holds the title of vice-president of finance. This top-level positioning of internal auditing within the organization ensures that it is recognized as an important activity and receives the cooperation of managers on all levels.

The Importance of Objectivity

A unique ingredient that internal auditors offer is objectivity. They operate independently of the firm's business units and have no ties with any individuals or groups within the firm. Their only allegiance is to the board, the CEO, and the CFO.

In order for the auditors to retain their objectivity, they make it clear that they do not want operational responsibility for systems that they help develop. They work strictly in an advisory capacity. They make recommendations to management, and management decides whether to implement those recommendations.

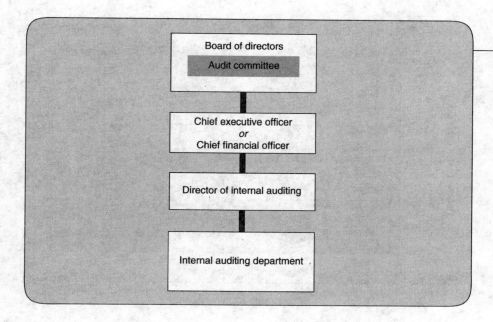

Figure 10.3 The Position of Internal Auditing in the Organization

Types of Auditing Activity

There are four basic types of internal auditing activity: financial, operational, concurrent, and internal control systems design. One internal auditor can engage in all four types.

FINANCIAL AUDITING A **financial audit** verifies the accuracy of the firm's records and is the type of activity performed by external auditors. On some assignments, the internal auditors work jointly with external auditors. On other assignments, the internal auditors do all of the auditing work themselves.

OPERATIONAL AUDITING An **operational audit** is not conducted to verify the accuracy of records but rather to validate the effectiveness of procedures. This is the type of work done by the systems analyst during the analysis phase of the system development life cycle. The systems that are studied are almost invariably conceptual rather than physical, but they do not necessarily involve the computer.

When internal auditors conduct operational audits, they look for three basic system features:

- **Adequacy of controls.** Is the system designed to prevent, detect, or correct errors?
- **Efficiency.** Are the operations of the system carried out so as to achieve the greatest productivity from the available resources?
- **Compliance with company policy.** Does the system enable the firm to meet its objectives or solve its problems in the prescribed way?

When information specialists develop systems, they should also look for these same features.

CONCURRENT AUDITING A **concurrent audit** is the same as an operational audit except that the concurrent audit is ongoing. For example, internal auditors may randomly select employees and personally hand them their paychecks rather than use the company mails. This procedure ensures that the names on the payroll represent real employees and not fictitious entries made by an unscrupulous supervisor who wants to receive some extra paychecks.

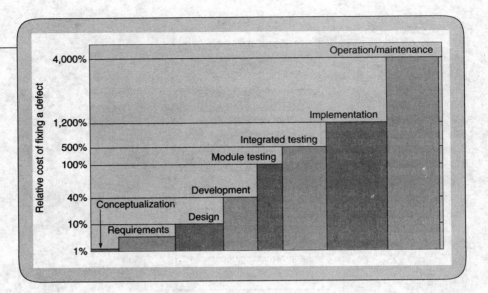

Figure 10.4 The Escalating Cost of Correcting Design Errors as the System Life Cycle Progresses

Source: Frederick Gallegos, "Audit Contributions to Systems Development," EDP Auditing 9 (Boston: Auerbach Publishers, 1991), section 72-01-70. Used with permission.

INTERNAL CONTROL SYSTEMS DESIGN   In operational and concurrent auditing, the internal auditors study existing systems. However, an auditor should not wait until a system is implemented to exert an influence on it. Internal auditors should actively participate in systems development. There are two basic reasons. First, the cost of correcting a system flaw increases dramatically as the system life cycle progresses. According to Figure 10.4, it costs 4,000 times as much to correct a design error during the operation and maintenance of a system than when the design is being conceptualized.

The second reason for involving the internal auditors in system development is that they offer expertise that can improve the quality of the system.

The Internal Auditor as a Member of the Development Team
The contributions that internal auditors can make depend on a combination of their knowledge and skills and the attitude of top management.

The Internal Audit Subsystem
In Chapter 8 we presented an architecture for information systems tailored to the business areas and illustrated the marketing information system in Figure 8.7 and the human resources information system in Figure 8.8 This architecture includes input systems that enter data into the database. In the financial information system illustrated in Figure 10.5 the internal audit subsystem is one of the input subsystems, along with the transaction processing system and a financial intelligence subsystem that gathers environmental data.

The internal audit findings enter the database, which is used by three output subsystems to produce financial information for users, who may be inside or outside the firm. The forecasting subsystem prepares long-term financial forecasts. The funds management subsystem assists managers in managing the firm's money resources, providing such abilities as performing cash flow analysis. The control subsystem enables the firm's managers to control their expenditures and consists of the operating budget and budget reports.

Including internal auditors on systems development teams is a good step toward having well-controlled information systems, and the systems are a good step toward giving management the information it needs to achieve and maintain ethical business operations.

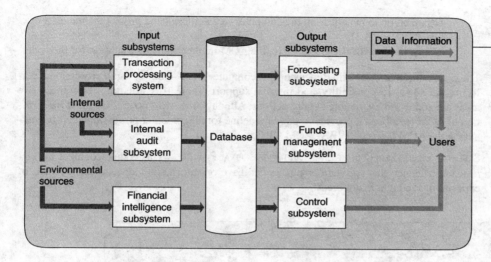

Figure 10.5 A Model of a Financial Information System

ACHIEVING ETHICS IN INFORMATION TECHNOLOGY

How is an ethics culture achieved in a firm? The firm need not attempt to do all of the work without assistance. There is assistance in the form of ethics codes and ethics educational programs that can provide the foundation for the culture. The educational programs can assist in developing a corporate credo and in putting in place ethics programs. The ethics codes can be used as is or can be tailored to the firm.

Codes of Ethics

The Association for Computing Machinery (ACM) is the oldest professional computer organization in the world, founded in 1947. ACM has developed a *Code of Ethics and Professional Conduct* that its 75,000 members are expected to follow. There is also a *Software Engineering Code of Ethics and Professional Practice* that is intended to serve as a guide for teaching and practicing software engineering, which is the use of engineering principles in software development.

CODE OF ETHICS AND PROFESSIONAL CONDUCT The current form of the ACM code of ethics was adopted in 1992 and consists of 24 "imperatives" that are statements of personal responsibility. The code is subdivided into four parts; general moral imperatives, more specific professional responsibilities, organizational leadership responsibilities, and compliance with the code. Figure 10.6 is an outline that includes the imperatives for each section. Each imperative is documented with a brief narrative.

- **General Moral Imperatives.** The first four deal with moral behavior (contributing to society; avoiding harm; being honest, trustworthy, fair), whereas the last four address issues that are currently receiving legal attention (property rights, copyrights, patents, privacy, and confidentiality).
- **More Specific Professional Responsibilities.** The first four address dimensions of professional performance. The next two (2.5 and 2.6) address moral issues of being honest in making evaluations and honoring commitments. Two (2.3 and 2.8) address legal issues, and one (2.7) is a social responsibility of contributing to public understanding of computers.
- **Organizational Leadership Imperatives.** As a leader, the ACM member has a responsibility to support only legal use of computing resources (3.3), stimulate others in the organization to meet their social responsibilities (3.1), enable others in the

organization to benefit from the computer (3.2 and 3.6), and protect the interests of users (3.4 and 3.5).
- **Compliance with the Code.** Here, the ACM member indicates support for the code.

The code addresses five main dimensions of computer work—moral, legal, professional performance, social responsibility, and internal support. Table 10.1 illustrates how these five areas are addressed by the three main sections. Although the ACM code is intended for direction of ACM members, it provides a good guideline for all computer professionals. It is available at the ACM Website, WWW.ACM.ORG.

SOFTWARE ENGINEERING CODE OF ETHICS AND PROFESSIONAL PRACTICE   This code recognizes the significant influence that software engineers can have on information systems and consists of expectations in eight major areas:

Figure 10.6 Outline of the ACM Code of Ethics and Professional Conduct

Source: Association for Computing Machinery. Printed with permission.

Outline of the ACM Code of Ethics and Professional Conduct

1. General Moral Imperatives
- 1.1 Contribute to society and human well-being.
- 1.2 Avoid harm to others.
- 1.3 Be honest and trustworthy.
- 1.4 Be fair and take action not to discriminate.
- 1.5 Honor property rights including copyrights and patents.
- 1.6 Give proper credit for intellectual property.
- 1.7 Respect the privacy of others.
- 1.8 Honor confidentiality.

2. More Specific Professional Responsibilities
- 2.1 Strive to achieve the highest quality, effectiveness, and dignity in both the process and products of professional work.
- 2.2 Acquire and maintain professional competence.
- 2.3 Know and respect existing laws pertaining to professional work.
- 2.4 Accept and provide appropriate professional review.
- 2.5 Give comprehensive and thorough evaluations of computer systems and their impacts, including analysis of possible risks.
- 2.6 Honor contracts, agreements, and assigned responsibilities.
- 2.7 Improve public understanding of computing and its consequences.
- 2.8 Access computing and communication resources only when authorized to do so.

3. Organizational Leadership Imperatives
- 3.1 Articulate social responsibilities of members of an organizational unit and encourage full acceptance of those responsibilities.
- 3.2 Manage personnel and resources to design and build information systems that enhance the quality of working life.
- 3.3 Acknowledge and support proper and authorized uses of an organization's computing and communication resources.
- 3.4 Ensure that users and those who will be affected by a system have their needs clearly articulated during the assessment and design of requirements; later the system must be validated to meet requirements.
- 3.5 Articulate and support policies that protect the dignity of users and others affected by a computing system.
- 3.6 Create opportunities for members of the organization to learn the principles and limitations of computer systems.

4. Compliance with the Code
- 4.1 Uphold and promote the principles of this code.
- 4.2 Treat violations of this code as inconsistent with membership in the ACM.

1. Public
2. Client and Employer
3. Product
4. Judgment
5. Management
6. Profession
7. Colleagues
8. Self

Five deal with responsibilities that the engineer has to constituents (Public, Client and Employer, Management, Profession, and Colleagues). Two (Product and Judgment) deal with professional performance, and one (Self) addresses self improvement. Table 10.2 shows the focus of the sections on these three main responsibilities.

Computer Ethics Education

Formal educational programs in computer ethics are available from a variety of sources—college courses, professional programs, and private educational programs.

COLLEGE COURSES   ACM is currently revising its model computing curriculum and the approved final draft includes a course to address social and professional issues. This will have a big influence on the computer science and MIS curricula of many colleges and universities.

Table 10.1

Topics Covered by the ACM Code of Ethics and Professional Conduct

	MORAL BEHAVIOR	LEGAL RESPONSIBILITY	PROFESSIONAL PERFORMANCE	SOCIAL RESPONSIBILITY	INTERNAL SUPPORT
GENERAL MORAL IMPERATIVES	X	X			
MORE SPECIFIC PROFESSIONAL RESPONSIBILITIES	X	X	X	X	
ORGANIZATIONAL LEADERSHIP IMPERATIVES		X			X

Table 10.2

Topics Covered by the ACM Software Engineering Code of Ethics and Professional Practice

	RESPONSIBILITY TO CONSTITUENTS	PROFESSIONAL PERFORMANCE	SELF-IMPROVEMENT
PUBLIC	X		
CLIENT AND EMPLOYER	X		
PRODUCT		X	
JUDGMENT		X	
MANAGEMENT	X		
PROFESSION	X		
COLLEAGUES	X		
SELF			X

Some colleges and universities have been teaching computer ethics for some time. George Mason University's introductory computer science course includes a lecture on computer ethics and law. Topics include on-line fraud, Internet privacy, and privacy versus company rights. The Johns Hopkins University offers a computer science course in computer ethics theory and practice, which addresses ethical frameworks, computers and the individual, computers and society, and ethical responsibilities for computer science professionals.

Some on-line courses are also available. The University of Phoenix offers an Ethics in Information Technology course, and the American College of Computer & Information Sciences offers a Computer Ethics course.

PROFESSIONAL PROGRAMS The American Management Association offers special programs that address subjects of current importance, such as ethics. An AMA 2002 Corporate Values Survey found that 23 percent of the respondents' firms adhered to ethical and integrity guidelines only part of the time, and 33 percent frequently issued statements that conflicted with internal realities.[17] An AMA Special Issues Forum was conducted in New York City in November, 2002 to address these issues. One of the presenters was Frank Ashen, the New York Stock Exchange Chief Ethics Officer.

PRIVATE EDUCATIONAL PROGRAMS LRM®, the Legal Knowledge Company, offers over 150 Web-based course modules that address a wide range of ethical and legal issues. Each course consists of an interactive tutorial and an on-line handbook. The courses are intended for use by firms that seek to increase the ethical awareness of their workforce.[18]

The college courses enable students to prepare to address ethical issues when they enter industry, and the professional and private programs enable managers and employees on all levels to maintain their ethical awareness and commitment as technology and social imperatives change.

ETHICS AND THE CIO[19]

At no other time in history has there been a bigger responsibility to restore integrity to American business. As of August 11, 2002, CEOs and CFOs are required to sign off on the accuracy of their financial statements. This requirement puts responsibility on the executives but also on the corporate information services unit and the information services units of the business areas to provide the executives with information that is accurate, complete, and timely.

IS only one unit in the organizational structure but it is in a key position to have the most influence on satisfying the demands of both government and society for accurate financial reporting. Moreover, as the executive with a full-time information responsibility, the CIO is the logical person to lead the efforts to meet these reporting objectives. The CIO can bring financial reporting up to expectations by following a program that includes the following:

- **Achieving a higher level of understanding of accounting principles**. The CIO has long been expected to understand the principles of business and business operations. Now, the CIO is expected to be especially knowledgeable about accounting systems. If the CIO is deficient in this area the knowledge can be gained by taking advantage of educational programs described above and by working closely with the firm's internal auditors and members of the project team that developed and maintains the firm's transaction processing systems.
- **Reviewing the information systems that accomplish financial reporting and taking remedial action**. The CIO should initiate projects to review transaction processing systems and financial information systems to ensure that they are operating at maximum effectiveness. The project leaders should submit reports of findings to the CIO, the MIS steering committee, and the executive committee. When weaknesses are identified, system development projects should be initiated to address them.

- **Educating the firm's executives on financial systems.** Formal sessions should be scheduled with the firm's executives, especially the CEO and CFO and other members of the executive committee, to review the financial systems—transaction processing, financial information, and executive information. These sessions can be conducted by information specialists who developed the systems. After an initial program aimed at bringing the executives up to the required level of understanding, the educational programs should be ongoing. One way to accomplish a continuing education is to make sure that financial managers are liberally represented on the MIS steering committee. That way, they will actively participate in all systems projects that deal with financial information.
- **Integrating alarms into information systems that alert executives to activities that require attention.** The executive information system and financial information system should be reviewed for the purpose of evaluating capabilities for alerting executives to indicators that certain activities are getting out of line. Many firms have identified critical success factors that are key to the firm meeting its objectives, and these are excellent measures for the systems to monitor on a daily basis.
- **Actively participating in the release of financial information to environmental elements.** The CIO should work with the stockholder relations department to identify the information to be included in stockholder reports and to be presented at stockholder meetings. Systems should be put in place to produce this information, and the CIO should be included on the stockholder meeting program to explain the firm's financial reporting systems and to answer questions.
- **Keeping tight control on money spent for information resources.** The CIO should be especially diligent to monitor spending on information resources. Reporting systems should involve all levels of information services management and all business units in (1) justifying expenditures on hardware and software and other information resources for inclusion in the operating budget, and (2) managing the funds once they have been approved.

By following a program such as this, the CIO can be the beacon for information integrity in the firm.

Highlights in MIS

EUROPEAN UNION AGREES ON COOKIES BUT NOT ON SPAM[20]

In the European Union, two groups set policy. They are the European Parliament and the E.U. Council of Ministers. Recently they addressed two issues affecting ethical computer use, cookies and spam. Cookies are software-based tracking devices that log actions of Web site viewers for the purpose of gaining a knowledge of the viewers' behavior. The information can be useful in such marketing strategies as customer relationship management. Spam, as we all know too well, is unwanted junk E-mail.

In addressing the two issues, the two governing groups could agree that software makers should notify Web site viewers of the presence of the cookies. However, the two could not agree on how to handle spam. The Council of Ministers wants to set it up on an "opt-in" basis where marketers and advertisers could send spam only when the viewer gives authorization. The European Parliament, on the other hand, wants to leave the spam decision to the member states.

As a result of the lack of agreement, a Conciliation Committee enters the scene to resolve the spam issue.

Summary

Morals are informal traditions of good conduct, which remain fairly constant from one society to another. Ethics are beliefs, standards, and ideals that are intended to serve as guidelines for individuals and communities. Ethics can vary from one society to another. Laws are formal rules that are enacted by governments and carry penalties for noncompliance.

U.S. computer laws have been enacted to address such subjects as data rights and restrictions, privacy, computer crime, and software patents. Court decisions, such as the State Street Decision, also contribute to the body of legislation. The European Union considered tightening the software patenting requirements of the State Street Decision. In China, attention is being given to such computer-use concerns as state security, social interest, citizens' lawful interest, and privacy. However, no definitions have been provided.

A firm imposes an ethics culture in a top-down manner, establishing a corporate credo, ethics programs, and ethics codes in that order.

Society expects computers to be used in an ethical way for three reasons: Logical malleability means that the computer can be programmed to do practically anything. The transformation factor recognizes that the computer can affect dramatic changes in our everyday lives. The invisibility factor recognizes that internal computer processing is hidden from view. The internal processing can include programming values, complex calculations, and acts of computer crime.

Richard Mason's PAPA identifies four computer rights of society; rights to privacy, accuracy, property, and access.

Large firms include a staff of internal auditors that reports to the board of directors or a high-level executive and offers the advantage of objectivity. The auditors engage in four types of activity. In operational auditing, they verify that the firm's systems have adequate controls, operate efficiently, and comply with company policy. In financial auditing, they verify the accuracy of records. In concurrent auditing, they conduct ongoing operational audits. In internal control systems design, they ensure that systems perform as intended. The financial information system includes an internal audit subsystem that enters the results of audits into the database.

The ACM has developed a code of ethics and professional conduct for its members, which can be used by anyone in the computer industry. The code consists of imperatives in three categories; general moral imperatives, more specific professional responsibilities, and organizational leadership imperatives. ACM has also developed a code for software engineering that consists of expectations in eight areas; public, client and employer, product, judgment, management, profession, colleagues, and self.

Computer ethics education can be accomplished in formal courses offered by colleges, professional programs such as the American Management Association, and private educational programs that can deliver the material using the Web.

The CIO can make a big contribution to the firm operating ethically by understanding accounting principles, ensuring that financial reporting systems are effective, educating the firm's executives on financial systems, making sure that alarms are built into financial systems to notify management when the firm is varying from its course, being an active participant in communicating information to the environment on the firm's financial systems, and keeping tight control over IT expenditures.

Key Terms

morals
ethics
laws
corporate credo
ethics program

ethics audit
logical malleability
transformation factor
invisibility factor
internal auditor

financial audit
operational audit
concurrent audit

Key Concepts

- The combination of morals, ethics, and laws as guidelines of socially expected behavior
- An ethical culture as the setting for achieving ethical behavior in an organization
- The invisibility of computer processes
- PAPA
- Ethical guidelines in the form of imperatives

Questions

1. Which is least likely to vary from one society to another—morals, ethics, or laws?
2. What is included in an ethics suite?
3. At which organization were the Freedom of Information Act, the Right to Federal Privacy Act, and the Computer Matching and Privacy Act aimed?
4. What type of organization was selected by the U.S. Congress in 1984 for protection against computer crime?
5. Has the United States taken a tight or loose view of the requirements to obtain a software patent? Explain.
6. In imposing an ethical culture, three actions are taken in order. What are they?
7. Which manager has the responsibility for computer ethics in the firm?
8. The invisibility factor consists of three components. What are they?
9. The chapter describes certain U.S. laws that address one or more of the PAPA components. Name each law and identify the component or components that it addresses.
10. Internal and external auditors frequently work together on one type of audit. What is it?
11. When an operational audit is conducted in an ongoing manner, what is it called?
12. Who is expected to conform to the ACM Code of Ethics and Professional Conduct?
13. Is the ACM Code of Ethics and Professional Conduct concerned with only ethics? Explain.
14. Who are the software engineer's constituents that are identified in the ACM Software Engineering Code of Ethics?
15. What happened on August 11, 2002 that had an effect on the firm's IT operation? Explain the effect.
16. Which information systems should have alarms built into them to notify executives when activities are not going as planned?

Topics for Discussion

1. The chapter mentions how an internal auditor conducts an ethics audit. Is there anyone else in the firm who could do that? Should they?
2. Why would a firm want to go to the trouble of devising their own corporate code of ethics when there are many standard ones available?
3. How can a firm ensure that logical malleability does not lead to ethics violations?

Problems

1. Assume that you are a world-famous computer ethics consultant and that the People's Republic of China has asked you to define the terms "state security," "social interest," "citizens' lawful interest," and "privacy" in relation to computer use. For each, provide a definition and an example.
2. The corporate credo of the Security Pacific Corporation includes responsibilities to three elements in the firm's environment; customers, communities, and stockholders. We know that the environment of the firm contains eight elements. Which of the five remaining elements should be included in a firm's corporate credo? For each one, include a statement of an ethical responsibility of the firm to that element.

Case Problem

Need to Know

A new department, Customer Analysis, has just been added to the Customer Relations Management Division of your firm and you will be the manager. Your company is a conglomerate that sells a wide variety of consumer goods including electronics, clothing, specialty foods, and much more. Data is collected from these purchases and after a period of time the spending profile of a typical customer can usually be predicted.

Your Customer Analysis department will sift through the data to predict customer demand for individual products. The prediction of customer demand will determine pricing policy. A premium price can be charged when customers *really* want the item. When demand will be low, lowering the price can stimulate sales.

You have scheduled the first department meeting for next week. Two issues about your department's mission need to be addressed: (1) manipulating product price based on customer profiles, and (2) accessing individual customer profile information. Some employees in the firm, even in your new department, have expressed concern about manipulating customer behavior based on information that the company has about their purchasing habits. The concern over access seems to be influenced by the fact that some customers might be personally known by employees who would have access to those customers' spending and purchasing habits.

For the department to operate effectively, you feel the department meeting should provide a forum for discussing these issues. You want to be open to your staff's concerns and suggestions. However, you know that as the manager you must play the leadership role in the discussion.

Assignment

1. How will you explain the use of customer profiles to affect pricing policies? Your explanation should address morals, ethics, and laws.
2. What procedures can you put in place to discourage an employee from being a "snooping neighbor" by looking up information about customers that is not needed for the job?
3. What role do you as the manager play in developing an ethics culture for your department?

NOTES

[1] Tom L. Beauchamp and Norman E. Bowie (eds.), *Ethical Theory and Business*, 2nd. ed. (Englewood Cliffs, NJ: Prentice-Hall, 1983), 1.

[2] Nilakatan Nagarajan, "What's Computer Ethics, Anyway?" *Security Audit & Control Review* 8 (Summer 1990), 24.

[3] Paul Engleman, "Raw Data: Significa, Insignifica, Stats and Facts," *Playboy* 41 (March 1994), 16.

[4] William R. Swinyard, Heikki Rinne, and Ah Keng Kau, "The Morality of Software Piracy: A Cross-Cultural Analysis," *Journal of Business Ethics* 9 (1990), 656.

[5] Donn B. Parker, "Rules of Ethics in Information Processing," *Communications of the ACM* 11 (March 1968), 200.

[6] Detmar W. Straub, Jr., and Rosann Webb Collins, "Key Information Liability Issues Facing Managers: Software Piracy, Proprietary Databases, and Individual Rights to Privacy," *MIS Quarterly* 14 (June 1990), 145.

[7] Barry Render, Richard Coffinberger, Ella P. Gardner, Stephen R. Ruth, and Linda Samuels, "Perspectives on Computer Ethics and Crime," *Business* 36 (January–March 1986), 33–35.

[8] John W. Rees, "'State Street' Decision Causes 'Boom' in Software Patent Filing," (March 1999), WWW.FINDLAW.COM/ARTICLES.

[9] Michael P. Sandonato; Ann Valdivia; and Andrew Grodin, "Software and Business-Method Patents: A Decade in Review," *Patent Journal* Volume 1 Issue 9 (June/July 2002), p. 14–19.

[10] "EU Thumbs Nose at US with Software Patent Proposals," *Computergram* (2/21/2002), p. 9.

[11] Yingxi Fu-Tomlinson, "Personal Data Protection in China," *China Business Review* Volume 29 Issue 4 (July/August 2002), p. 36–39.

[12] This section is based on Patrick E. Murphy, "Creating Ethical Corporate Structures," *Sloan Management Review* 30 (Winter 1989), 81–87.

[13] This section is based on James H. Moor, "What Is Computer Ethics?" *Metaphilosophy* 16 (October 1985), 266–275. This article was the prize-winning essay in the journal's contest concerning computer ethics.

[14] Richard O. Mason, "Four Ethical Issues of the Information Age," *MIS Quarterly* 10 (March 1986), 5–12.

[15] Richard Lacayo, "Nowhere to Hide," *Time* 138 (November 11, 1991), 34.

[16] Johnathan Weil, "Arthur Andersen's 'Double Duty' Work Raises Questions About Its Independence," *The Wall Street Journal* December 14, 2001, A4.

[17] "Building an Ethical Corporation," WWW.AMANET.ORG/EVENTS, November 3, 2002.

[18] "Creating a Legally & Ethically Aware Workforce," LRN® the Legal Knowledge Company, WWW.LRN.COM, November 3, 2002.

[19] This section is based on Eileen Colkin and Jennifer Maselli, "Priority: Integrity," *InformationWeek* Issue 899 (July 29, 2002), p. 20–21.

[20] Taken from Jason R. Boyarski; Renee M. Fishman; Kara Josephberg; Jane Linn; Jane Pollock; and Jenna Victoriano, "European Authorities Consider 'Cookies' and 'Spam,'" *Intellectual Property & Technology Law Journal* Volume 14 Issue 3 (March 2002), p. 31.

Chapter 11

Decision Support Systems

Learning Objectives

After studying this chapter, you should

- Understand the fundamentals of decision making and problem solving.
- Know how the DSS concept originated.
- Know the fundamentals of mathematical modeling.
- Know how to use an electronic spreadsheet as a mathematical model.
- Be familiar with how artificial intelligence emerged as a computer application, and its main areas.
- Know the four basic parts of an expert system.
- Know what a group decision support system (GDSS) is and the different environmental settings that can be used.

Introduction

Managers make decisions to solve problems. Problem solving is accomplished in four basic phases and makes use of such frameworks as the general systems model of the firm and the environmental model. By following the systems approach to solve problems, the manager takes a systems view.

The problem-solving process consists of basic elements—standards, information, constraints, and alternative solutions. As the process is followed, selection of the best alternative is not always accomplished by a logical analysis, and it is important to distinguish between problems and symptoms.

Problems can vary in structure, and the decisions to solve them can be programmed or nonprogrammed. The DSS concept was originally aimed at semistructured problems. The first DSS outputs consisted of reports and outputs from mathematical models. Subsequently, a group problem solving capability was added, followed by artificial intelligence and OLAP.

Mathematical models can be classified in various ways and their use is called simulation. Mathematical modeling offers several real advantages, but there are some disadvantages. The electronic spreadsheet is a good mathematical modeling vehicle. It can be used for both static and dynamic models, and can enable the manager to play the "What-if" game.

Artificial intelligence can be a component of a DSS. By adding a knowledge base and an inference engine, the DSS can suggest problem solutions to the manager.

When groupware is added to the DSS, it becomes a group decision support system (GDSS). A GDSS can exist in several different settings that are conducive to group problem solving.

WHAT IT'S ALL ABOUT—DECISION MAKING

Thus far we have devoted almost an entire book to MIS. So, it is a subject that lends itself to lengthy discussion. However, stripped of all its frills and extras, an MIS is simply "a system that provides users with information for use in making decisions to solve problems."

Although it might not have been obvious, we have used decision making and problem solving as an integrating theme throughout the text. We have distinguished between problem solving and decision making, provided a list of problem-solving steps, described two frameworks that are useful in problem solving, and presented the systems approach as the basis for problem solving of all kinds.

Problem Solving and Decision Making

In Chapter 1 we described the role of information in management problem solving, distinguishing between problem solving and decision making.

We recognized that **problem solving** consists of a response to things going good as well as things going bad by defining a **problem** as a condition or event that is harmful or potentially harmful to a firm in a negative way, or is beneficial or potentially beneficial in a positive way. We also recognized that during the process of solving problems managers engage in **decision making,** the act of selecting from alternative problem solutions. We defined a **decision** as a selected course of action, and recognized that usually it is necessary to make multiple decisions in the process of solving a single problem.

Problem-Solving Phases

In Chapter 1 we also addressed the problem-solving process by describing Herbert A. Simon's four basic phases. According to Simon, problem solvers engage in:[1]

- **Intelligence Activity.** Searching the environment for conditions calling for a solution.
- **Design Activity.** Inventing, developing, and analyzing possible courses of action.
- **Choice Activity.** Selecting a particular course of action from those available.
- **Review Activity.** Assessing past choices.

We also recognized that in performing these activities, the problem solver must have information, and we illustrated that fact with Figure 1.14.

Problem-Solving Frameworks

In Chapter 2 we presented two frameworks that are useful in problem solving, the general systems model of the firm and the eight-element environmental model. We illustrated the general systems model in Figure 2.1 and presented it as a framework of a firm as a system, identifying the important elements that should be present and the flows of data, information, and decisions that connect the elements. We illustrated the environmental model in Figure 2.2 and recommended its use in understanding the environment of the firm and the interactions between the firm and each element in the form of resource flows.

The Systems Approach

Our most elaborate treatment of problem solving came in Chapter 7 when we presented the systems approach, a series of steps grouped in three phases—preparation effort, definition effort, and solution effort. We illustrated the approach in Figure 7.1 and recommended that the general systems model be used in viewing the firm as a system and that the environmental model be used in recognizing the environmental system. We also recommended that the system elements be analyzed in a certain sequence and illustrated that sequence in Figure 7.3.

The Importance of a Systems View

In using the general systems model and the environmental model as a basis for problem solving, we are taking a **systems view**, which regards business operations as systems embedded within a larger environmental setting. This is an abstract way of thinking, but it has potential value to the manager. The systems view:

1. Prevents the manager from getting lost in the complexity of the organizational structure and details of the job.
2. Recognizes the necessity of having good objectives.
3. Emphasizes the importance of all of the parts of the organization working together.
4. Acknowledges the interconnections of the organization with its environment.
5. Places a high value on feedback information that can only be achieved by means of a closed-loop system.

If you ask managers whether they have a systems view, you may get a negative answer, or: "I don't know. I never thought much about it." However, they most likely recognize the definition and solution effort of the systems approach as things that they do, and recognize the five points above as objectives that they try to achieve.

BUILDING ON THE CONCEPTS

With this understanding of the fundamental problem-solving concepts, we can now describe how they are applied in decision support systems.

Elements of a Problem-Solving Process

Several elements must be present if a manager is to successfully engage in problem solving. These elements are pictured in Figure 11.1.

Most problems that a manager solves can be regarded as systems problems. For example, the firm as a system is not functioning as intended. Or, there is a problem with the inventory system, the sales commission system, and so on. The solution to a systems problem is one that best enables the system to meet its objectives, as reflected in the system's performance standards. These *standards* describe the **desired state**—what the system should achieve. In addition, the manager must have available *information* that describes the **current state**—what the system is now achieving. If the two states are different, some problem is the cause and must be solved.

The difference between the current state and the desired state represents the **solution criterion**, or what it will take to bring the current state to the desired state. Of course, if the current state happens to represent a *higher* level of performance than the desired state, the task is *not* to bring the current state in line. Rather, the task is to keep the current state at the higher level. If the higher-level performance can be maintained, then the desired state should be raised.

It is the manager's responsibility to identify *alternative solutions*, which always exist. This is one step of the problem-solving process where computers have been of little help. The manager typically relies on his or her own experience or obtains help from the noncomputer portion of the information processor, such as input from others both inside and outside the organization.

Once the alternatives have been identified, the information system can be used to evaluate each one. This evaluation should consider any possible *constraints*, which can be either internal or environmental. **Internal constraints** take the form of limited resources that exist within the firm. For example, the IT unit cannot develop a CRM system due to a lack of expertise in on-line analytical processing. **Environmental constraints** take the form of pressures from various environmental elements that restrict the flow of resources into and out of the firm. An example would be a raise in interest rates by the Federal Reserve Board that puts the cost of plant expansion out of reach.

When all of these elements exist and the manager understands them, a solution to the problem is possible.

Selecting the Best Solution

The selection of the best solution can be accomplished in different ways. Henry Mintzberg, a management theorist, has identified three approaches:[2]

- **Analysis**—A systematic evaluation of options, considering their consequences on the organization's goals. An example might be members of a JAD session who are deciding which approach to take in implementing an executive information system.

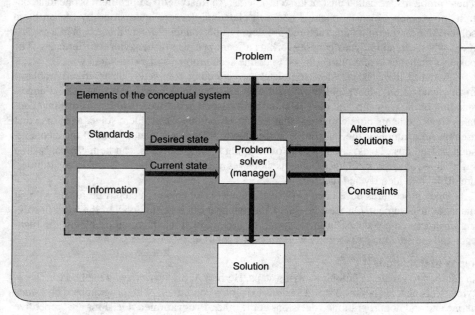

Figure 11.1 Elements of the Problem-Solving Process

- **Judgment**—The mental process of a single manager. For example, a manufacturing manager applies experience and intuition in evaluating the layout of a new plant proposed by a mathematical model.
- **Bargaining**—Negotiations between several managers. An example is the give and take that goes on among members of the executive committee concerning which functional information system to implement first. This is where the very real influence of company politics can most easily be seen.

The emphasis in this book is on analysis. However, judgment and bargaining should not be ignored. All three ways would probably be involved in the selection of alternatives to solve important problems.

Problems versus Symptoms

It is important to recognize the distinction between problems and symptoms. Otherwise, you might spend much time and money chasing the wrong problem or something that is not a problem. **Symptoms** are conditions produced by the problem. Very often the manager sees the symptoms rather than the problem. Symptoms do not tell the entire story. They are like the tip of the iceberg; the manager must look beneath the symptoms to locate the problem's real cause.

A medical doctor follows this process of sorting through symptoms to find the cause of an ailment. A manager faces the same task when confronted with a symptom such as low profits. Something is causing the low profits. The problem is the *cause* of the low profits. In fact, it is good to think of a problem as the *cause of the trouble*, or the *cause of the opportunity*.

Problem Structure

A manager may understand some problems better than others. The problem of how much replenishment stock to reorder is an example of a problem that a manager may understand very well. In fact, a mathematical model called the EOQ (economic order quantity) formula prescribes how the problem is to be solved. Such a problem is called a **structured problem** because it consists of elements and relationships between elements, all of which are understood by the problem solver.

On the other hand, there may be problems that are not understood at all by the manager. These problems are called unstructured problems. An **unstructured problem** is one that contains no elements or relationships between elements that are understood by the problem solver. An example of an unstructured problem is a personnel problem that exists in a department where the employees cannot work as a team because of behavioral differences. The business manager is often ill-equipped to define such problems in a structured way.

Actually, there are very few completely structured or completely unstructured problems in an organization. Most problems are those where the manager has a less than perfect understanding of the elements and their relationships. A **semistructured problem** is one that contains *some* elements or relationships that are understood by the problem solver and some that are not. An example is the selection of a location to build a new plant. Some of the elements, such as land cost, taxes, and the costs of shipping in raw materials, can be measured with a high degree of precision. Other elements, however, such as natural hazards and local attitudes, are difficult to identify and measure.

Once procedures have been devised, computers can solve structured problems without manager involvement. On the other hand, the manager often has to do all of the work in solving unstructured problems. In the vast middle ground of semistructured problems, the manager and the computer can jointly work toward a solution.

Types of Decisions

In addition to giving us problem-solving steps, Herbert A. Simon devised a method for classifying decisions. He believed that decisions exist on a continuum, with programmed decisions at one end and nonprogrammed decisions at the other. **Programmed decisions** are "repetitive and routine, to the extent that a definite procedure has been worked out for handling them so that they don't have to be treated *de novo* (as new) each time they occur."[3] **Nonprogrammed decisions** are "novel, unstructured, and unusually consequential. There is no cut-and-dried method for handling the problem because it hasn't arisen before, or because its precise nature and structure are elusive or complex, or because it is so important that it deserves a custom-tailored treatment."[4]

Simon explained that the two decision types are only the black and white ends of the continuum and that the world is mostly gray. However, the concept of programmed and nonprogrammed decisions is important because each calls for a different technique.

THE DSS CONCEPT

The first ten years of computer use in business consisted of only transaction processing. In the mid-1960s the MIS concept emerged in recognition of the need to provide information to managers. The MIS approach was as broad as possible, seeking to provide information to *all managers* in the firm to use in solving *all types of problems*. This proved to be an extremely ambitious undertaking and many systems failed to live up to expectations.

Two MIT professors, G. Anthony Gorry and Michael S. Scott-Morton, believed that an information system that focused on single problems faced by single managers would provide better support. They described their concept in an article titled "A Framework for Management Information Systems," published in 1971 in the *Sloan Management Review*.[5] Central to their concept was a table, called the Gorry and Scott-Morton grid. The grid, illustrated in Figure 11.2, classifies problems in terms of problem structure and management level. Gorry and Scott-Morton used names for the levels that had been coined by management theorist Robert N. Anthony. Anthony called the top level the *strategic planning level*, the middle level the *management control level*, and the lower level the *operational control level*.

The cells of the grid contain examples of problems that are typical of the corresponding management levels and problem structures. At that time, the problems above the horizontal dashed line had been well supported by computer processing. The name *structured decision system (SDS)* was used to describe the systems that were able to solve the identified problems. The problems below

Degree of problem structure		Management levels		
		Operational control	Management control	Strategic planning
	Structured	Accounts receivable	Budget analysis—engineered costs	Tanker fleet mix
		Order entry	Short-term forecasting	Warehouse and factory location
		Inventory control		
	Semistructured	Production scheduling	Variance analysis—overall budget	Mergers and acquisitions
		Cash management	Budget preparation	New product planning
	Unstructured	PERT/COST systems	Sales and production	R&D planning

Figure 11.2 The Gorry and Scott-Morton Grid

Source: G. Anthony Gorry and Michael S. Scott-Morton, "A Framework for Management Information Systems," Sloan Management Review 13 (Fall 1971); 72

Figure 11.3 **A DSS Model That Incorporates Group Decision Support, OLAP, and Artificial Intelligence**

Source: Reprinted by permission, Geraldine DeSanctis and R. Brent, Gallupe, "A Foundation for the Study of Group Decision Support Systems", Management Science, (May 1987), Copyright 1987, the Institute for Operations Research and the Management Sciences (INFORMS), 901 Elkridge Landing Road, Suite 400 Linthicum, Maryland 21090-2909 USA

the line had eluded computer processing, and Gorry and Scott-Morton used the term *decision support system (DSS)* to describe the systems that could provide the needed support.

The name DSS stuck and became used to describe a system designed to help a specific manager solve a specific problem. Emphasis was on the word *help*. The DSS was never intended to solve the problem without the help of the manager. The idea was that the manager and the computer would work together to solve the problem. The type of problem that would be solved was the semistructured problem. The computer would address the structured portion and the manager would address the unstructured portion.

Gorry and Scott-Morton achieved more than they set out to do. As evidenced by their article title, they sought to add to the MIS concept. What happened was that they identified a new type of information system.

During the period since 1971, the DSS has been the most successful type of information system, and today represents the most productive application of the computer to problem solving.

A DSS Model

Figure 11.3 is a model of a DSS. The arrow at the bottom indicates how the configuration has expanded over time. As the DSS was originally conceived, it produced periodic and special reports, and outputs from mathematical models. The special reports consisted of responses to database queries. With the DSS firmly established, an ability was added to permit problem

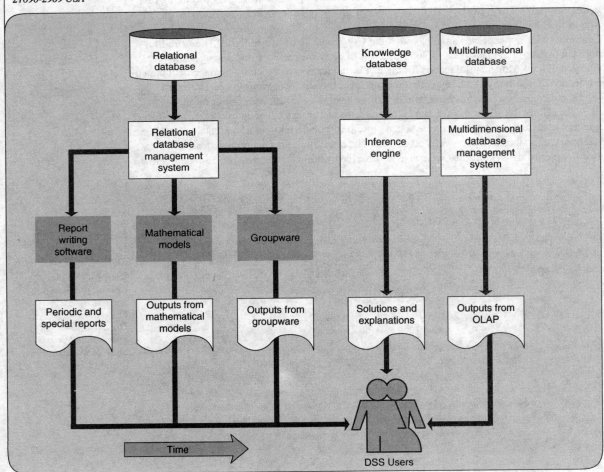

solvers to work in groups. The addition of groupware software enabled the system to function as a group decision support system (GDSS). More recently, an artificial intelligence capability has been added, along with an ability to engage in online analytical programming (OLAP).

We described OLAP in Chapter 8 when we discussed data warehousing, and will not repeat that material here. In the remainder of the chapter we will address mathematical modeling and artificial intelligence.

MATHEMATICAL MODELING

A **model** is an abstraction of something. It represents some object or activity, which is called an **entity**. Managers use models to represent problems to be solved. The objects or activities that cause problems are the entities.

Types of Models
There are four basic types of models:

1. Physical models
2. Narrative models
3. Graphic models
4. Mathematical models

PHYSICAL MODELS   A **physical model** is a three-dimensional representation of its entity. Physical models used in the business world include scale models of shopping centers and prototypes of new automobiles.

The physical model serves a purpose that cannot be fulfilled by the real thing. For example, it is much less expensive for shopping center investors and automakers to make changes in the designs of their physical models than to the real thing.

NARRATIVE MODELS   One type of model that managers use daily is the **narrative model**, which describes its entity with spoken or written words. The listener or reader can understand the entity from the narrative. All business communications are narrative models, which makes the narrative model the most popular type.

GRAPHIC MODEL   Another type of model in constant use is the graphic model. A **graphic model** represents its entity with an abstraction of lines, symbols, or shapes. The graphic model in Figure 11.4 illustrates one of the most popular concepts in business, economic order quantity. The **economic order quantity (EOQ)** is the optimum quantity of replenishment

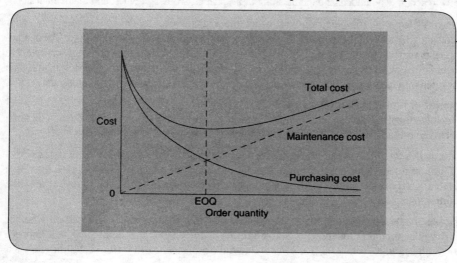

Figure 11.4 A **Graphical Model of the Economic Order Quantity Concept**

stock to order from a supplier. The EOQ balances the costs of purchasing the stock and the costs of maintaining it until it is used or sold. The line that slopes down from the left in the figure represents the unit purchasing cost, which decreases as the order quantity increases. The line that moves up from left to right represents how the maintenance cost increases in a linear fashion as the order quantity increases. Both costs are added together to yield the total cost curve. The low point on the total cost curve represents the EOQ.

Graphic models are also used in the design of information systems. Many of the tools used by systems developers are graphic in nature. Entity-relationship diagrams, object diagrams, and data flow diagrams are examples.

MATHEMATICAL MODEL Any mathematical formula or equation is a **mathematical model.** Many of the mathematical models that business managers use are no more complex than the one used to compute the EOQ:

$$EOQ = \sqrt{\frac{2PS}{M}}$$

where P is the unit purchasing cost (in dollars), S is the annual sales (in units), and M is the annual maintenance cost per unit (in dollars). The maintenance cost includes all of the costs incurred in storing the item, such as insurance, spoilage, and loss due to theft.

Some mathematical models use hundreds or even thousands of equations. For example, a financial planning model developed by the Sun Oil Company during the early years of its management information system used approximately 2,000 equations.[6] Large models of this sort tend to be cumbersome and difficult to use. The trend today is toward using smaller models.

Uses of Models

All four types of models facilitate both understanding and communication. Mathematical models have, in addition, a predictive capability.

FACILITATE UNDERSTANDING A model is typically simpler than its entity. The entity is more easily understood when its elements and their relationships are presented in a simplified way. Once a simple model is understood, it can gradually be made more complex so as to more accurately represent its entity. However, the model still only *represents* its entity and *never matches it exactly.*

FACILITATE COMMUNICATION All four types of models can communicate information quickly and accurately to people who understand the meaning of the shapes, words, graphics, and mathematics.

PREDICT THE FUTURE The precision with which the mathematical model can represent its entity endows it with a special capability that is not available with the other model types. The mathematical model can predict what might happen in the future, but it is not 100 percent accurate. No model is that good. Because assumptions usually must be made concerning much of the data that is fed into the model, the manager must use judgment and intuition in evaluating the output.

Classes of Mathematical Models

A mathematical model can be classified in terms of three dimensions; the influence of time, the degree of certainty, and the ability to achieve optimization.

STATIC OR DYNAMIC MODELS A **static model** does not include time as a variable. It deals with a situation at a particular point in time. It is like a snapshot. A model that includes time as a variable is a **dynamic model.** This model represents the behavior of the entity over time, like a motion picture.

PROBABILISTIC OR DETERMINISTIC MODELS Another way to classify models is based on whether the formulas include probabilities. A **probability** is the chance that something will happen. Probabilities range from 0.00 (for something with no chance) to 1.00 (for something that is a sure thing). A model that includes probabilities is called a **probabilistic model**. Otherwise, it is a **deterministic model**.

OPTIMIZING OR SUBOPTIMIZING MODELS   An **optimizing model** is one that selects the best solution among the alternatives. For a model to be able to do this, the problem must be very well structured. A **suboptimizing model**, often called a **satisficing model**, permits a manager to enter a set of decisions; once this step is completed the model will project an outcome. The model does not identify the decisions that will produce the best outcome but leaves that task to the manager.

Any model can be classified in terms of the three dimensions. For example, the EOQ formula is a static, deterministic, optimizing model.

Simulation

The act of using a model is called **simulation**. The simulation takes place in a particular scenario and predicts the effect of the problem solver's decision or decisions.

THE MODELING SCENARIO   The term **scenario** is used to describe the conditions that influence a simulation. For example, if you are simulating an inventory system, as shown in Figure 11.5, the scenario specifies the beginning balance and the daily sales units. The data elements that establish the scenario are called **scenario data elements**. Models can be designed so that the scenario data elements are variables, thus enabling different values to be assigned.

INVENTORY PLANNING MODEL
OCTOBER 11

SCENARIO:

BEGINNING BALANCE: 200

DAILY SALES UNITS: 20

DECISIONS:

ORDER QUANTITY: 100

REORDER POINT: 175

LEAD TIME: 3

RESULTS:

DAY	BEGINNING BALANCE	RECEIPTS	SALES	ENDING BALANCE	ORDER QUANTITY	RECEIPT DUE DAY
1	200		20	180		
2	180		20	160	100	5
3	160		20	140		
4	140		20	120		
5	120	100	20	200		
6	200		20	180		
7	180		20	160	100	10
8	160		20	140		
9	140		20	120		
10	120	100	20	200		
11	200		20	180		
12	180		20	160	100	15
13	160		20	140		
224	120	100	20	200		
225	200		20	180		

Figure 11.5   **Scenario Data and Decision Variables from a Simulation**

DECISION VARIABLES   The input values that the manager enters to gauge their impact on the entity are known as **decision variables**. In the Figure 11.5 example the decision variables include the order quantity, reorder point, and lead time (the time required for the supplier to furnish replenishment stock).

Simulation Technique
The manager usually executes an optimizing model only a single time; the model produces the best solution using the particular scenario and the decision variables. However, it is necessary to execute a suboptimizing model over and over, searching for the combination of decision variables that produces a satisfying outcome. This iterative process of trying out decision alternatives is known as playing the **what-if game**.

Each time the model is executed, only one of the decision variables should be changed, so that its influence can be seen. In this way, the problem solver systematically discovers the combination of decisions that will lead to problem solution.

Format of Simulation Output
It is a good practice to include the scenario elements and decision variables on the same screen or page as the output, as shown in Figure 11.5. With such a layout, it is always clear which inputs produced the output.

A Modeling Example
A firm's executives might use a mathematical model to make several key decisions. Perhaps the executives want to simulate the effect of:

1. the *price* of the product
2. the amount of *plant investment* that will be necessary to provide the capacity for producing the product
3. the amount to be invested in *marketing* activity, such as advertising and personal selling
4. the amount to be invested in *R & D* (research and development).

Furthermore, the executives want to be able to simulate four quarters of activity and produce two reports—an operating statement that includes such key nonmonetary values as market potential (demand) and plant capacity, and an income statement that reflects the results in monetary terms.

Model Input
Figure 11.6 shows the input screen that is used to enter the scenario data elements for the prior quarter. Some of the elements relate to the firm—its plant capacity, the number of units that were produced, the dollar value of raw materials, and so forth. The other elements relate to the influence of the firm's environment—the economic index, seasonal index, competitor price, and competitor marketing.

Figure 11.7 shows the scenario elements for the next quarter. The executives indicate how many quarters they want to simulate. Then they enter estimates for the economic and seasonal indexes, and for the competitor's price and marketing.

In the lower portion of the screen the executives enter the four decisions, with space at the right where the resulting after-tax profits will be displayed. The screen can accommodate decisions for four quarters. The screen shows default values for unsimulated quarters.

Model Output
The next quarter's activity (Quarter 1) is simulated, and the after-tax profit is displayed on the screen. The executives study the figure and decide on the set of decisions to be used in Quarter 2. These decisions are entered and the simulation is repeated. This process continues until all four quarters have been simulated. At this point the screen has the appearance shown in Figure 11.8.

The executives can obtain more detailed output in displayed or printed form. The operating statement in Figure 11.9 and the income statement in Figure 11.10 are displayed on separate screens.

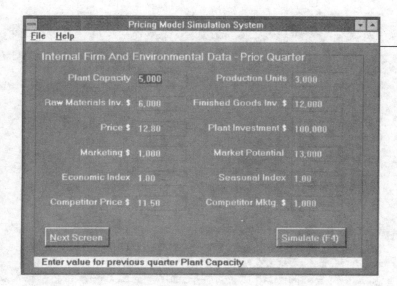

Figure 11.6 A Model Input Screen for Entering Scenario Data for the Prior Quarter

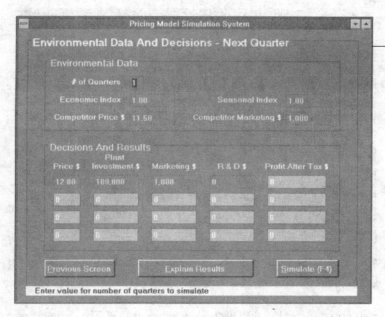

Figure 11.7 A Model Input Screen for Entering Scenario Data for the Next Quarter

Modeling Advantages and Disadvantages

A manager who uses mathematical models can expect to benefit in the following ways:

- The modeling process can be a *learning experience*. Invariably, something new is learned about the physical system with each modeling project.
- The speed of the simulation process enables the *consideration of a larger number of alternatives* by providing the ability to evaluate the impact of decisions in a short period of time. In a matter of minutes, it is possible to simulate several months, quarters, or years of company operations.
- As we have already recognized, models provide a *predictive power*—a look into the future—that no other information-producing method offers.

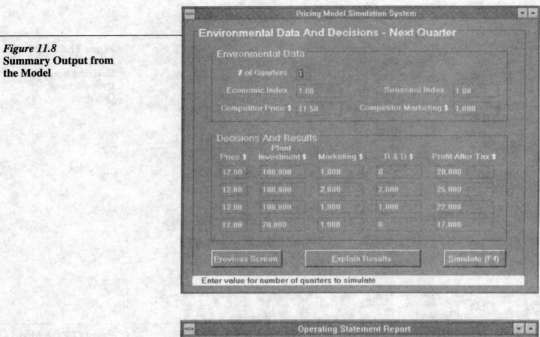

Figure 11.8
Summary Output from the Model

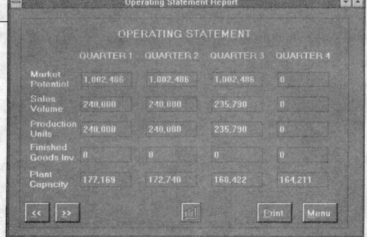

Figure 11.9 The Operating Statement Shows Nonmonetary Results of the Simulation

- Models are *less expensive* than the trial-and-error method. The modeling process is costly in terms of development time and the software and hardware required for the simulations, but the cost is not nearly as high as that of bad decisions that are implemented in the real world.

These modeling advantages can be offset to some degree by two basic disadvantages of models:

- The *difficulty of modeling a business system* will produce a model that does not capture all of the influences on the entity. For example, in the model just described, someone in the firm must estimate the values for the scenario data elements. Also, the mathematical formulas usually only approximate the behavior of the entity. This means that considerable judgment must be applied in implementing the decisions that are based on the simulation results.

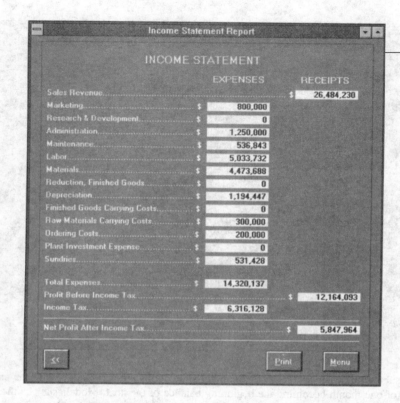

Figure 11.10 The Income Statement Shows Monetary Results of the Simulation

- A *high degree of mathematical skill* is required to personally develop more complex models. Also, such skill is necessary to properly interpret the output.

For a long time many managers believed that the disadvantages of modeling outweighed the advantages. That situation has changed, owing to a combination of more user friendly modeling tools and more computer-literate and information-literate managers.

MATHEMATICAL MODELING USING THE ELECTRONIC SPREADSHEET

The technological breakthrough that enabled problem solvers to develop their own mathematical models instead of relying completely on information specialists or management scientists was the electronic spreadsheet. Prior to the spreadsheet, mathematical models were programmed in such scientific programming languages as Fortran or APL, which were beyond the competency of all problem solvers who did not have computer backgrounds. When the spreadsheet came on the scene, it immediately became apparent that it would be a good vehicle for mathematical modeling.

Static Modeling Capability

The rows and columns of an electronic spreadsheet make it ideal for use as a static model. Figure 11.11 shows an operating budget in the form of a columnar report with columns for the budgeted expenses, actual expenses, and variance. The rows are used for the various expense items. This is a very simple model, where the only math is the subtraction of the actual from the budgeted expenses to produce the variance.

Dynamic Modeling Capability

A spreadsheet is especially well-suited for use as a dynamic model. The columns are excellent for the time periods, as illustrated in Figure 11.12. Here, the columns represent months. This is also a very simple model, with ending cash calculated by adding beginning cash and cash

Figure 11.11
Spreadsheet Rows and Columns Provide the Format for a Columnar Report.

Source: Raymond McLeod, Jr., *Decision Support Software for the IBM Personal Computer* (Chicago, Science Research Associates), 1988, p. 235.

OPERATING BUDGET

DEPARTMENT 210 – WELDING SHOP

WEEK ENDING JUNE 25

ACCOUNT	BUDGET	ACTUAL	VARIANCE
SALARIES	$9,715.00	$10,317.50	$602.50-
EQUIPMENT	$750.00	$517.50	$232.50
SUPPLIES	$1,400.00	$1,255.59	$144.41
OVERHEAD	$250.00	$250.00	$0.00
TOTAL	$12,115.00	$12,340.59	$225.59-

in, and subtracting cash out. Here, the monthly simulations are cumulative, with the ending balance of one month becoming the beginning balance of the next. Models such as the cash flow model are of special interest to financial managers or members of the financial staff, and can be much more complex.

Playing the "What-if" Game

The spreadsheet also lends itself to playing the "What-if" game, where the problem solver manipulates one or more variables to see the effect on the outcome of the simulation. For example, in the operating budget in Figure 11.11, the problem solver could make changes to the

Figure 11.12
Spreadsheet Columns Are Excellent for Time Periods in a Dynamic Model.

Source: Raymond McLeod, Jr., *Decision Support Software for the IBM Personal Computer* (Chicago, Science Research Associates), 1988, p. 234.

CASH FLOW MODEL

MONTH

	1	2	3	4	5	6
BEGINNING CASH	5000	5480	6005	6087	5975	6861
CASH IN	1800	2100	1932	1813	2987	2800
CASH OUT	1320	1575	1850	1925	2101	2495
ENDING CASH	5480	6005	6087	5875	6861	7166

actual salaries (maybe increasing them by 10 percent to simulate the effect of a pay raise), and see the effect on salary variance and overall variance. In the cash flow model in Figure 11.12, the financial manager could manipulate the cash in and cash out figures to see the effect.

The Spreadsheet Model Interface

When using a spreadsheet as a mathematical model, the user can enter data or make changes directly to the spreadsheet cells, or can use a graphical user interface. The pricing model described earlier and illustrated in Figures 11.6 through 11.10 could have been developed using a spreadsheet, and had the graphical user interface added. The interface can be prepared using such a programming language as Visual Basic, and most likely would require the work of an information specialist. A development approach would be for the user to develop the spreadsheet and then have the interface added by an information specialist.

ARTIFICIAL INTELLIGENCE

In its original form, DSS emphasized mathematical modeling and database querying. Before long, DSS developers began to recognize the need to incorporate artificial intelligence. **Artificial intelligence (AI)** is the activity of providing such machines as computers with the ability to display behavior that would be regarded as intelligent if it were observed in humans.[7] AI represents the most sophisticated computer application, seeking to duplicate some types of human reasoning.

History of AI

The seeds of AI were sown only two years after General Electric installed the first computer for business use. The year was 1956, and the term *artificial intelligence* was coined by John McCarthy as the theme of a conference held at Dartmouth College. That same year, the first AI computer program, called Logic Theorist, was announced. Logic Theorist's limited ability to reason (proving calculus theorems) encouraged researchers to develop another program called the General Problem Solver (GPS), which was intended for use in solving problems of all kinds. The task turned out to be more than the early pioneers could handle and AI research took a back seat to the less ambitious computer applications such as MIS and DSS. Over time, however, persistent research paid off and AI became established as a solid computer application area.

Areas of AI

AI is being applied in business in the form of **knowledge-based systems**, which use human knowledge to solve problems. The most popular type of knowledge-based system is the **expert system**, which is a computer program that attempts to represent the knowledge of human experts in the form of heuristics.[8] The term **heuristic** is derived from the same Greek root as the word *eureka*, which means "to discover." A heuristic is, therefore, a rule of thumb or a rule of good guessing.

Heuristics do not guarantee results as absolutely as do conventional algorithms that are incorporated into mathematical models, but they offer results that are specific enough most of the time to be useful. The heuristics allow the expert system to function in a manner consistent with a human expert, advising the user on how to solve a problem. Since the expert system functions as a consultant, the act of using it is called a **consultation**—the user consults the expert system for advice.

In addition to expert systems, AI includes work in the following areas: neural networks, perceptive systems, learning, robotics, AI hardware, and natural language processing.

The Appeal of Expert Systems

An expert system offers unique capabilities as a decision support system. First, an expert system offers the opportunity to make decisions that exceed the manager's capabilities. For example, a new investments officer for a bank can use an expert system designed by a leading financial expert and, in doing so, incorporate the expert's knowledge into his or her investment decisions. Second, the expert system can explain its line of reasoning in reaching a particular solution. Very often, the explanation of how a solution was reached is more valuable than the solution itself.

The Expert System Configuration

An expert system consists of four main parts: the user interface, the knowledge base, the inference engine, and the development engine.

THE USER INTERFACE The user interface enables the manager to enter *instructions* and *information* into the expert system and to receive information from it. The instructions specify the parameters that guide the expert system through its reasoning process. The information is in the form of values assigned to certain variables.

Expert systems are designed to recommend solutions. These solutions are supplemented by explanations. There are two types of explanations—explanations of questions that the manager asks, and explanations of the problem solution.

THE KNOWLEDGE BASE The **knowledge base** contains both facts that describe the problem area and knowledge representation techniques that describe how the facts fit together in a logical manner. The term **problem domain** is used to describe the problem area.

A popular knowledge representation technique is the use of rules. A **rule** specifies what to do in a given situation and consists of two parts: a *condition* that may or may not be true and an *action* to be taken when the condition is true. An example of a rule is:

If Economic.Index > 1.20 and Seasonal.Index > 1.30 Then Sales.Outlook = 'EXCELLENT'

All of the rules contained in an expert system are called the **rule set**. The rule set can vary from a dozen or so rules for a simple expert system to 500, 1,000, or 10,000 rules for a complex one.

THE INFERENCE ENGINE The **inference engine** is the portion of the expert system that performs reasoning by using the contents of the knowledge base in a particular sequence. During the consultation, the inference engine examines the rules of the knowledge base one at a time, and when a rule's condition is true, the specified action is taken. In expert systems terminology, the rule is *fired* when the action is taken.

The process of examining one rule after the other continues until a complete pass has been made through the entire rule set. More than one pass usually is necessary in order to assign a value to the problem solution, which is called the **goal variable**. The passes continue as long as it is possible to fire rules. When no more rules can be fired, the reasoning process ceases.

THE DEVELOPMENT ENGINE The fourth major component of the expert system is the development engine, which is used to create the expert system. There are two basic approaches: programming languages and expert system shells. An **expert system shell** is a ready-made processor that can be tailored to a specific problem domain through the addition of the appropriate knowledge base. Today, most of the interest in applying expert systems to business problems involves the use of shells.

An example of a problem domain that lends itself to an expert system shell is help desk support.[9] When a help desk expert system is used, either the user or the help desk staff member communicates directly with the system, and the system attempts to resolve the problem. One test of the degree of sophistication of artificial intelligence is whether the users can or cannot determine if they are interfacing with a human or a computer. This test is named the Turing Test, in honor of one of the great pioneers in computer science, Alan Turing. So, if the user is not aware that he or she is communicating directly with the computer, that is the sign of a good expert system.

The help desk expert systems use a variety of knowledge representation techniques. A popular approach is called **case-based reasoning (CBR)**, which uses historical data as the basis for identifying problems and recommending solutions. Some systems employ knowledge expressed in the form of a **decision tree**, a network-like structure that enables the user to progress from the root through the network of branches by answering questions relating to the problem. The path leads the user to a solution at the end of the branch.

Expert system shells have brought artificial intelligence within the reach of firms that do not have the resources necessary to develop their own systems using programming languages. In the business area, expert system shells are the most popular way for firms to implement knowledge-based systems.

GROUP DECISION SUPPORT SYSTEMS

It has always been an accepted fact that managers seldom solve problems alone. The committees, project teams, and task forces that exist in many companies are good examples of group approaches to problem solving. Recognizing this fact, system developers have adapted the DSS to group problem solving.

The GDSS Concept

A **group decision support system (GDSS)** is "a computer-based system that supports groups of people engaged in a common task (or goal) and that provides an interface to a shared environment."[10] Other terms have also been coined to describe the application of information technology to group settings. These terms include **group support system (GSS), computer-supported cooperative work (CSCW), computerized collaborative work support**, and **electronic meeting system (EMS)**.[11] The software that is used in these settings has been given the name **groupware**.

How the GDSS Contributes to Problem Solving

The underlying assumption of the GDSS is that improved communications make possible improved decisions. Improved communications are achieved by keeping the group discussion focused on the problem, resulting in less wasted time. The time gained can be devoted to a more thorough discussion of the problem, thus contributing to a better problem definition. Or the time gained can be used in identifying more alternatives than would otherwise be possible. The evaluation of more alternatives increases the likelihood of a good solution.

GDSS Environmental Settings

The GDSS contributes to problem solving by providing a setting that is conducive to communications. Figure 11.13 shows four possible GDSS settings based on the size of the group and where the members are located. In each setting, group members may meet at the same time or at different times. When members meet at the same time, it is called a **synchronous exchange**. An example is a committee meeting. When members meet at different times, it is called an **asynchronous exchange**. An example is communication by E-mail.

DECISION ROOM   A **decision room** is the setting for small groups of people meeting face-to-face. The room contributes to communication through a combination of furnishings, equipment, and layout. The equipment can include a combination of workstations, audio pick-up microphones, video cameras, and large display screens. In the center of the room is a facilitator's console. The **facilitator** is a person whose chief task is to keep the discussion on track.

Based on the arrangements that are established for each session, one group member's keyed-in messages to another member can be displayed on the large screen for the entire group to see. Other material pertinent to the discussion can also be displayed from such media as PowerPoint images, videotapes, color slides, and transparencies.

Two unique GDSS features are parallel communication and anonymity. **Parallel communication** is when all participants enter comments at the same time, and

Figure 11.13 Group Size and Location Determine DSS Environmental Settings

Source: Gerardine DeSanctis and R. Brent Gallupe, "A Foundation for the Study of Group Decision Support Systems," *Management Science 33 (May 1987)*, 598. Reprinted with permission.

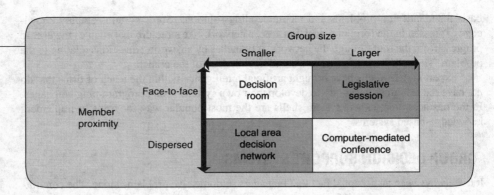

anonymity is when nobody is able to tell who entered a particular comment. Anonymity allows each participant to enter what she or he really thinks without fear of ridicule from other group members. Also, it allows each idea to be evaluated on its merits rather than on who offered it.

LOCAL AREA DECISION NETWORK   When it is impossible for small groups of people to meet face-to-face, the members can interact by means of a local area network, or LAN. A member enters comments in a workstation and views the comments of the other members on the screen.

LEGISLATIVE SESSION   When the group is too large for a decision room, a legislative session is required. The large size imposes certain constraints on the communications. Either the opportunity for equal participation by each member is removed, or less time is available. Another approach is for the facilitator to decide which material is displayed on the screen for the group to view.

COMPUTER-MEDIATED CONFERENCE   Several virtual office applications permit communication between large groups with geographically dispersed members. These are the applications that are collectively known as teleconferencing, and they include computer conferencing, audio conferencing, and video conferencing.

PUTTING THE DSS IN PERSPECTIVE

We have seen how the scope of decision support provided by the DSS has expanded greatly since Gorry and Scott-Morton first got the idea to address semistructured problems. This expansion of scope is testimony to the success that the DSS has enjoyed. The concept has worked so well that developers are continually thinking of new features to incorporate.

When artificial intelligence is added, it completely changes the character of the DSS. Someone once addressed the difference between a DSS and an expert system by explaining that when the manager uses a DSS, he or she is sitting at the workstation and is deciding how to use the information display to solve the problem. When the manager uses an expert system, the manager is sitting at the workstation but there is a consultant sitting next to the manager, giving suggestions on how to solve the problem. Artificial intelligence enables the DSS to provide a level of decision support that was not originally intended by the earliest DSS developers.

The GDSS capability is firmly established. In fact, there may be more GDSS applications today than DSS. As far as OLAP goes, it is very new to the scene and it will be interesting to follow that progress.

Highlights in MIS

Fix It before It Breaks[12]

Predictive maintenance is the name given to the activity of predicting when a machine will fail and performing maintenance on it just prior to that time to prevent the failure. This is a good idea but is not easy to accomplish. However, the SKF company in Sweden has developed a DSS with a knowledge-based capability to do just that.

SKF manufactures bearings, which are used in many types of machines, and the company has captured about 20 percent of the world market. SKF became interested in predictive maintenance as a way to generate intelligence that could be used across the entire design process. After devoting two years to the development process, the result was a decision support system named @ptitude.

@ptitude uses data from a database that contains nearly 100 years of operating data that has been gathered from hundreds of thousands of machines in use around the world. In addition, data is provided from real-time machine condition reporting. The availability of such a rich data source enables the system to relate failure data to how the parts are assembled and how they might fail in the future. Heinz Bloch, a consulting engineer, described early versions of DSS use in predictive maintenance as requiring an engineer to input all of the data that was available for a particular machine problem (say, a leaking seal). But, the engineer didn't have all the data that was necessary to answer all of the questions from the system. As a result, the system would come to some enlightening solution such as "You have a seal problem."

The robust data sources of @ptitude are expected to enable it to pinpoint when components have failed in service. This will enable SKF design engineers to focus on key elements that have the greatest impact on life-cycle costs and create designs that increase machine reliability.

In addition to making @ptitude available internally, SKF has established a Web site that offers an interactive use of @ptitude to engineers around the world on a subscription basis.

Summary

Managers make multiple decisions in the process of solving a problem, which can have a negative or positive influence on the firm. In solving the problem, the manager goes through a series of four activities: intelligence, design, choice, and review. In taking a systems view and following the systems approach, the manager can use the general systems model of the firm and the eight-element environmental model. The purpose of taking a systems view is to enable the organization to work as an efficient and effective system.

The problem-solving process consists of several key elements. Standards and information provide the desired state and the current state respectively, and the manager considers alternative solutions while adhering to the constraints. By going through this process, a solution to the problem is achieved. The selection of the best alternative can be accomplished by analysis, judgment, and bargaining.

Symptoms are only indications of a problem, which can be structured, unstructured, or semistructured, depending on the proportion of elements and relationships that are known. In solving these problems, the manager can make programmed or nonprogrammed decisions. Programmed decisions represent solutions that are known to work, whereas nonprogrammed decisions represent custom-tailored treatment.

The DSS was originally envisioned as a way to solve problems that had eluded computer processing in the early 1970s. It was intended to help the manger solve semistructured problems, with the manager addressing the structured portion and the DSS addressing the unstructured portion. The primary outputs were periodic and repetitive reports and the outputs from mathematical models. Subsequently, the DSS has been expanded to include group processing (achieving a GDSS), artificial intelligence, and OLAP.

There are four types of models; physical, narrative, graphic, and mathematical. All facilitate understanding and communication, but only the mathematical can predict the future. Mathematical models can be static or dynamic, probabilistic or deterministic. The act of using a model is called simulation, and it requires the manager to enter scenario data elements and decision variables. By trying various decisions, the manager plays the what-if game. Modeling can provide a learning experience, enable consideration of a larger number of alternatives, predict the future, and permit some problems to be solved at less cost. However, it is often difficult to model the business system and a high degree of mathematical skills are required for complex models. An electronic spreadsheet can be used for models of reasonable size.

Artificial intelligence consists of several areas but the expert system is the type that can function as a decision support system. It requires a knowledge base, which often consists of a network of rules, and an inference engine that can analyze the knowledge base and assign a value to the solution, called the goal variable. Expert systems can be developed using a programming language or an expert system shell.

Group decision support systems facilitate problem solving by providing a conducive environment, which can be achieved in the form of decision rooms, local area networks, legislative sessions, and computer-mediated conferences.

The DSS is a fitting way to conclude our discussion of MIS. The DSS was intended to improve the focus of MIS efforts and ended up being a new application of the computer to problem-solving support. Of all the efforts to apply the computer in business as an information system, the DSS has been the most successful.

KEY TERMS

desired state
current state
solution criterion
symptom
model
entity
static model
dynamic model
probabilistic model
deterministic model

optimizing model
suboptimizing model, satisficing
    model
simulation
modeling scenario
what-if game
artificial intelligence (AI)
knowledge-based system
expert system
knowledge base

problem domain
inference engine
goal variable
expert system shell
case-based reasoning
synchronous exchange
asynchronous exchange
facilitator
parallel communication
anonymity

KEY CONCEPTS

- systems view
- problem structure
- programmed and nonprogrammed decisions
- decision support system (DSS)
- group decision support system (GDSS)

QUESTIONS

1. What are Simon's four stages of problem solving?
2. Which frameworks would you use in applying the systems approach?
3. What form do both internal and environmental constraints take?
4. What are the three approaches to selecting the best alternative, according to Mintzberg?

5. What is meant by problem structure?
6. What MIS weakness did Gorry and Scott-Morton seek to overcome?
7. How did Gorry and Scott-Morton use the term *decision support system*?
8. Name the different outputs from a DSS.
9. What are the four types of models?
10. What advantages are offered by all types of models?
11. How can mathematical models be classified?
12. What two types of data are entered into a mathematical model to begin the simulation?
13. What type of data does the manager manipulate when playing the what-if game?
14. Which of the two mathematical modeling disadvantages were addressed by the electronic spreadsheet?
15. What are the spreadsheet columns used for in a dynamic model?
16. What are the four main parts of an expert system?
17. What is a goal variable?
18. Explain the difference between a synchronous and an asynchronous exchange.
19. Why is anonymity important in a GDSS setting?

Topics for Discussion

1. What would be an example of a good problem? How would the manager use the systems approach to solve it?
2. Give an example of a solution criterion and explain how it is derived.
3. Would you use programmed decisions to solve a structured problem?

Problems

1. Create an electronic spreadsheet model to prepare the operating budget in Figure 11.11. Use the same data as in the figure. Play the what-if game to see the effect of changing the actual salary to $10,500 and then to $8,500.
2. Create an electronic spreadsheet model to prepare the cash flow model in Figure 11.12. Use the same data as in the figure. Play the what-if game to see the effect of changing the cash out figure in month 1 to 2000, then 3000.
3. Create an electronic spreadsheet model to produce the inventory planning model in Figure 11.5. When the ending balance drops to or below the reorder point, the order quantity is entered as a receipt three days after the reorder point is detected (lead time of three days). Simulate 100 days.

Case Problem

SCANCO

You are sitting in your office reading yesterday's issue of The *Wall Street Journal* when the phone rings. Butch is on the phone. He says it's urgent that you come into his office—right now.

When you walk in, you are greeted by a big smile. "That budget performance system is working like a charm," he says. "All of the offices are on it, and I just got the last of the monthly reports this morning. If a little Excel is good, then some more must be great. I'm ready to talk about the next application. Sit down."

Butch begins to explain, "I have always wanted to computerize our resource planning activity. As you know, each year the marketing division projects the corporation's sales activity for the coming fiscal year. This sales forecast is used by all of the organizational units in planning their resource needs for the year. It's ironic. We prepare the forecast that everybody else uses for their planning, but we probably do the poorest job of using it ourselves. I would like for you to put it on Excel."

You respond that you think it's an excellent idea and that you would like to do it. You ask Butch to explain more about what he wants.

"The key to everything is personnel. We have to have a certain personnel mix and level in order to meet our sales objectives. All of our budgeted expenses—salaries, travel, entertainment, and so forth—are based on the number of personnel that we have."

Case Problem continued

You press Butch for some guidelines that you can use in building the Excel model. "Just what is the relationship between personnel and our objectives?" you ask.

"One sales team—a sales representative and two systems analysts—can sell one SCANCO optical scanner system per month. And, after they sell it, they can install it. We can use a figure of $325,000 for the revenue derived from one sale. A sales team should be able to sell twelve systems at $325,000, or about $4 million in annual revenue."

"3.9 million," you reply.

Butch, not breaking stride, continues. "If we want to sell $39 million, then we need ten teams working the entire year. I figure a sales rep costs about $2500 per month in salary, not counting commission, which we're not concerned with here, and a systems analyst goes for about $3300. To determine personnel needs, we start with our sales forecast, which is in numbers of systems per month. That tells us how many sales teams we need. Then, we use a cost-per-person approach in coming up with all of the budget items."

"What does our sales forecast look like for FY (fiscal year) 2003–2004?" you ask. "It's April now, and the fiscal year starts in November. That gives us seven months to get geared up."

Butch pulls out a typed forecast, which lists:

Month	Number of Systems	Month	Number of Systems
November 2003	8	May 2004	15
December 2003	9	June 2004	17
January 2004	10	July 2004	19
February 2004	10	August 2004	21
March 2004	12	September 2004	21
April 2004	13	October 2004	22

"If we're going to sell eight units in November, then we have to have eight sales teams, right?" you ask.

"Right," Butch responds. "But we can't just hire them on November 1 and expect them to start selling immediately. I estimate that a team must be on board six months before we can expect an order."

"So, we have to have eight teams on board in May if we are to meet the November target. That means we better start hiring. We have only six teams now."

"You've got it," Butch says.

"Let me see if I've got this straight," you say. "We take the number of forecast systems and convert that into a head count. Then we compute the salaries…"

Butch interrupts, "Exactly. Then we use some dollar amounts per person for the remainder of the expenses."

"Do you know what those are?" you ask.

"Not really. I think you had better come up with some," Butch says. "Why don't you do that and run all of this through Excel?"

You dig through old expense account forms and bills and develop the following average monthly expenses per person:

Telephone	$52.25	Travel	$663.70
Entertainment	$94.65	Supplies	$48.10

During an employee's first month, approximately $1,200 is spent on furniture; a desk, a chair, a wastebasket, and a file cabinet. All of these expenses vary directly with the number of personnel. The rent figure does not. Rather, it remains at a level of $9,450 per month for all of the office locations within the division. The final budget item, miscellaneous, includes everything not included in the other accounts, such as education and fringe benefits. During the past year, the miscellaneous category was about $375 per person per month.

Case Problem continued

You present these figures to Butch. "These look good. You've done a good job. On these expenses that vary with the head count, let's round them off: use $60 for telephone, $700 for travel, $70 for entertainment, $50 for supplies, and $400 for miscellaneous. Let's use $9,500 per month for rent, and a one-time expense of $1,400 per person for furniture. That should just about do it, shouldn't it?"

"Are you sure about the $70 for entertainment? They've been spending $94..."

Butch interrupts, "That's too much. I'm going to tighten up on that. The $70 is fine."

You ask, "What about salaries?"

"For the sales rep let's use $2,725 and for the analyst let's use $3,600. Now, does that do it?"

You look over your notes and keep in mind the importance of getting the specifications right the first time. "I think I need to know the system forecast for the first six months of FY 2004–2005 if I am to give you a resource projection for FY 2003–2004. You see, we must hire sales reps and analysts during the last six months of FY 2003–2004 to meet the sales forecast for the next year."

"You're right," Butch concedes. "I just happen to have those figures. Here they are."

Month	Number of Systems	Month	Number of Systems
November 2004	22	December 2004	23
January 2005	23	February 2005	24
March 2005	24	April 2005	25

Butch asks, rather impatiently, "Now, do you have everything you need?"

You reply that you believe you do, and, as final check, summarize your task. "I'll prepare a projection for the next eighteen months of these expenses for the sales division. The first six months, May through October 2003, will get us geared up to meet the FY 2003–2004 sales forecast. The last twelve months, November 2003 through October 2004, will be the budget projection that you need. Do you want all 18 months, or just the last 12?"

"Give me all 18. I'd like to be able to see what we have to do during the next six months in order to meet next year's goals. But, let me have totals for both the six-month period and the 12-month period. I want to be able to see the figures separately by fiscal year. Any more questions?"

"Only one," you reply. "What about format? What do you want the report to look like?"

"I'll leave that up to you. Just be sure and give me monthly totals on everything, and I would like to see totals for each budget item for both the six-month and 12-month periods. Let me know when you have something." With that, Butch returns to the papers on his desk.

Assignment
Prepare the spreadsheet that Butch has requested.

Notes

[1] Herbert A. Simon, *The New Science of Management Decision*, rev. ed. (Englewood Cliffs, NJ: Prentice-Hall, 1977).

[2] Henry Mintzberg, "Planning on the Left Side and Managing on the Right," *Harvard Business Review* 54 (July-August 1976), 55.

[3] Simon, *op. cit.*, 1977.

[4] Simon, *op. cit.*, 1977.

[5] G. Anthony Gorry and Michael S. Scott-Morton, "A Framework for Management Information Systems," *Sloan Management Review* 13 (Fall 1971), 55–70.

[6] George W. Gershefski, "Building a Corporate Financial Model," *Harvard Business Review* 47 (July-August 1969), 39.

[7] This definition paraphrases one found in Clyde W. Holsapple and Andrew B. Whinston, *Business Expert Systems* (Homewood, IL: Irwin, 1987), 4.

[8] The two terms are often used interchangeably. However, there is support for the view that expert systems are one example of knowledge-based systems. See Frederick Hayes-Roth and Neil Jacobstein, "The State of Knowledge-Based Systems," *Communications of the ACM* 37 (March 1994), 27.

[9] Lee Thé, "AI Automates a Help Desk," *Datamation* 42 (January 15, 1996), 54ff.

[10] Clarence Ellis, Simon Gibbs, and Gail Rein, "Groupware: Some Issues and Experiences," *Communications of the ACM* 34 (January 1991), 40.

[11] For more information on EMS, see Alan R. Dennis, Joey F. George, Len M. Jessup, Jay F. Nunamaker, Jr., and Douglas R. Vogel, "Information Technology to Support Electronic Meetings," *MIS Quarterly* 12 (December 1988), 591–624.

[12] Karen Auguston Field, "If It Ain't Broke, Fix It," *Design News* Volume 57 Issue 20 (October 21, 2002), p. 21.

PART 4
Projects

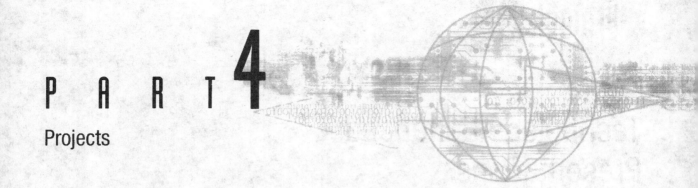

Putting what you have learned into practice is the best way to remember a lesson. There are twelve projects in this section that reinforce the lessons you learned in the chapters. Each project has specific learning objectives. You are presented with an example and then instructed to generate a similar project based upon that example.

There is one project on presentations. Four projects address hypertext markup language (HTML), three address spreadsheets, and four address databases. All projects use Microsoft software for the examples because it is the most widely used software for personal productivity. Some projects address basic concepts while others address advanced concepts and features.

These projects represent the types of applications many managers face early in their careers. Completing these projects will teach you the skills necessary to work with the types of information systems faced by new managers. Completing multiple projects on the same topic, such as databases, will give you a broader picture of the advantages and potential that these tools can render.

Project 1

Technology Enhanced Presentations

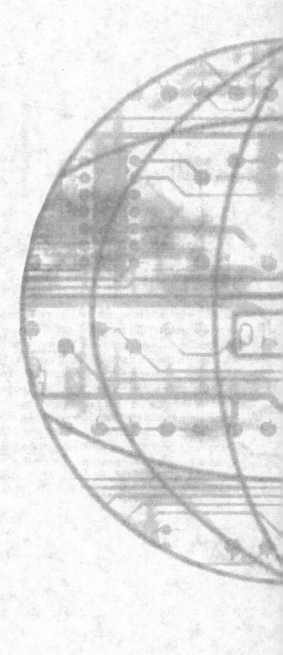

Learning Objectives

➡ Understand how presentations are organized.
➡ Learn the use of fonts, colors, headings, and footers.
➡ Learn to use slide transition and animation.
➡ Recognize the value of links from the presentation to other materials.
➡ Understand how action settings can impact the presentation.

Introduction

Using information technology to produce presentations has become the standard business practice. The main reasons are effectiveness, inexpensive technology, and linkage to other resources. Presentations make broad points but when they are enhanced with technology they can access the specific computer-based facts that led to the points in the presentation. The presentation can also provide links to electronic mail and other electronic resources so that a user can ask questions of the presenter and others in the organization.

Mastering the skill of creating technology-enhanced presentations begins with an understanding of the subject being presented and the ideas to be conveyed. The use of presentation technology serves to enhance the subject and ideas. You probably do not have a strong memory of the last glass of water you drank but you can remember a soft drink, tea or coffee, or some other drink much more clearly. While plain water is the primary component of each drink, the additional flavors can make the drink memorable. Presentations should convey the primary concepts and make them memorable.

PRESENTATION BASICS

Presentations should be organized with a clear beginning and end. Title pages are used to set the main concept to be presented and to introduce the presenters. A summary at the end of the presentation is useful for recapping and reinforcing the points within the presentation. In between, there are many techniques for bringing attention to items on an individual presentation slide. The examples that follow have been generated using Microsoft PowerPoint 2002 (also known as PowerPoint XP). Earlier versions of the software may have slightly different menus and screens.

Getting Started

Begin by opening the PowerPoint program. Select the "File" command followed by the "New" subcommand. You will be asked to choose from a variety of options but in the examples below "From Design Template" was the option chosen and the "Blends" template is used. Figure P1.1 shows that "Council of 100" was entered as the title and three names were entered into the subtitle section for the presenters. If the design choices do not appear automatically, try choosing the "Format" command followed by "Slide Design."

PowerPoint always begins presentations with a title slide. When a new slide is created after the title slide (command "Insert" followed by "New Slide") the body of the presentation is begun. There is a section for the slide title and a section for the text of the slide (see Figure P1.2). Before we begin entering the presentation we can add something to the master design of the slides to show who prepared the presentation. Choose the sequence of commands "View,"

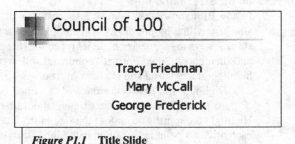

Figure P1.1 Title Slide

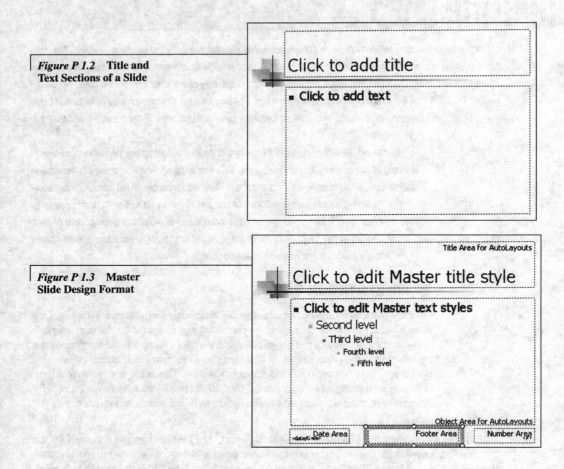

Figure P 1.2 Title and Text Sections of a Slide

Figure P 1.3 Master Slide Design Format

"Master," and "Slide Master" and then click on the "Footer Area." When the screen in Figure P1.3 appears you can type in your name so that all who see the presentation know who the author was. In the example, "Prepared By Tracy Friedman" was typed into the footer. Choosing the "View" command followed by the "Normal" subcommand returns you to a point where you can enter presentation text.

You can check the progress of the presentation at any time by clicking the "View" command followed by the "Slide Show" subcommand. Press the "Escape" key to return back to edit your PowerPoint slides.

Fonts, Size, and Colors

Figure P1.4 shows the slide we just created with "Council of 100" typed in six times—you start a new line by pressing the "enter" key each time "Council of 100" is typed. There are several ways to emphasize material typed into the presentation. You can highlight the material and then choose the "Format" command followed by the "Font" subcommand or you can highlight the material and click on an icon.

Highlight the first occurrence of "Council of 100" and click the icon to make it bold (Figure P1.5). The second occurrence should be in italics. The third should be indented. Highlight the fourth and choose the size of the letters to be 36. That refers to 36 points where each printer's point is $1/72$ of an inch high. Thirty-six points is, therefore, one half inch high.

For the fifth occurrence of "Council of 100" choose the font color to be red. The last occurrence will change the font typeface to Courier New. You may have to search the drop-

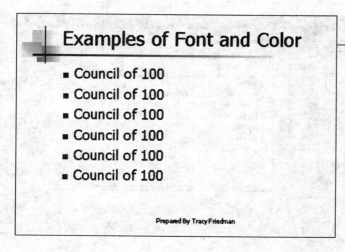

Figure P 1.4 Slide with Text Entered

Figure P 1.5 Icons

down menu choices for the Courier New typeface. Figure P 1.6 depicts the resulting slide. You can always choose the "View" and "Slide Show" commands to see the completed slides and press the "Escape" key to return to entering slide information.

Linking

Two types of linking are important: linking to E-mail and linking to a Web site. Both give the presentation user the ability to leap past the confines of the presentation itself. Linking can be from either an image or from text on the presentation.

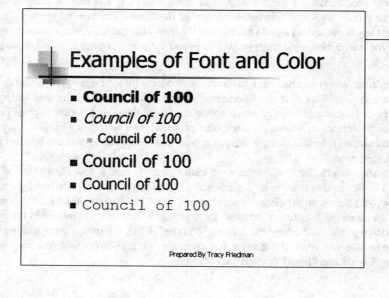

Figure P 1.6 Slide Formatted for Font, Size, and Color

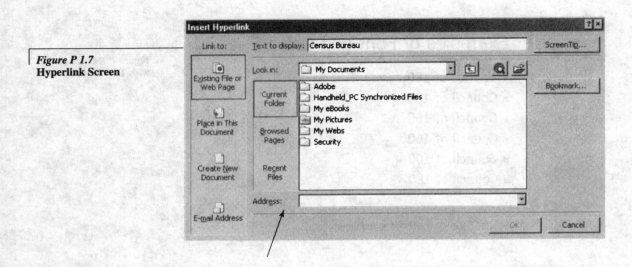

Figure P 1.7
Hyperlink Screen

Make a new slide ("Insert" followed by "New Slide" command) and give it the title of "Adding Links." Type in "Link to the Census Bureau" in the slide text. Then insert an image by choosing the "Insert" command followed by "Picture" and "Clip Art." You may be asked to search for an image based upon a search word; if so use the phrase "E-mail." If you are presented with a drop-down list of images, just choose one that is appropriate for E-mail.

Highlight the phrase "Census Bureau" and then choose the "Insert" command followed by the "Hyperlink" subcommand. Figure P 1.7 will appear. In the "Address" field type in "HTTP://WWW.CENSUS.GOV" but do not type the quotation marks. Make sure that there are no spaces. When users are viewing the presentation and click on the phrase "Census Bureau" PowerPoint will open up the Internet browser and link to the Census Bureau Web site. Closing the Internet browser will return the user to the PowerPoint presentation.

Linking to an e-mail address is a similar procedure. Your computer must have an e-mail program available but almost all computers have e-mail program software loaded. Highlight the e-mail image you inserted earlier and then choose the "Insert" command followed by the "Hyperlink" subcommand. Enter the address as "mailto:user@school.edu" where you can substitute your e-mail account information in place of the "user@school.edu" phrase. Again, do not include any blank spaces and do not include the quotation marks. When a presentation user clicks on the image the e-mail program will open and the user can enter the mail message.

Actions

Slide transition, action settings, and custom animation are three actions that can bring added life to presentations. The slide transition refers to animation caused by the change from one slide to another. Action settings cause an action outside of the slide to occur such as jumping to another presentation, starting a computer program, or causing a sound to be played. Custom animation refers to making images appear and disappear so that the illusion of animation is generated.

Animation begins by first creating the entire slide. Create a new slide that looks like Figure P 1.8. Notice that the title is "Animation" and the only slide text is "a Word document." The other two phrases on the slide are text boxes created by choosing the "Insert" command followed by choosing the "Insert Textbox" subcommand. The cursor is moved to the approximate position in the slide where the text is to be typed. Click the mouse once and begin typing in the phrase you want. Remember that there are two text boxes, not one, so you must repeat the "Insert" and "Insert Textbox" set of commands.

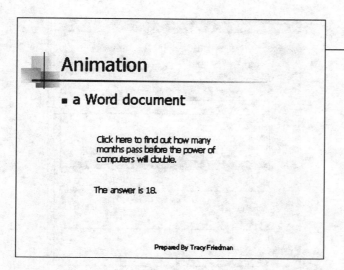

Figure P 1.8 Actions Slide

Slide transition is generally used for dramatic effect such as transitioning to the last slide. Choose the "Slide Show" and "Slide Transition" set of commands. The screen in Figure P 1.9 appears. Choose any transition you wish—such as "Blinds Horizontal"—and also choose a speed for the transition. Slower speeds create more dramatic transitions. Refrain from applying the transition effect to all slides because if all slides have a transition effect then no slide will be dramatically different from any other.

Highlight the phrase "a Word document" and choose the "Slide Show" and "Action Settings" sequence of commands. Notice in Figure P 1.10 that the resulting screen has the tab "Mouse Click" chosen. Choose "Hyperlink to:" and from the drop-down menu choose "Other File." The next PowerPoint screen will present you with a set of file choices and you can navigate to any Word file you wish and select it for action. When the user runs the PowerPoint presentation, clicking on the phrase "a Word document" will cause that document to be opened in Word. Closing the Word document returns the user to the PowerPoint presentation.

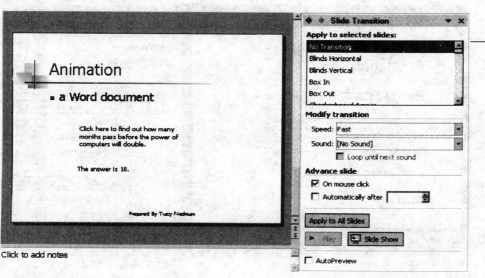

Figure P 1.9 Slide Transition

Figure P 1.10 **Action Settings**

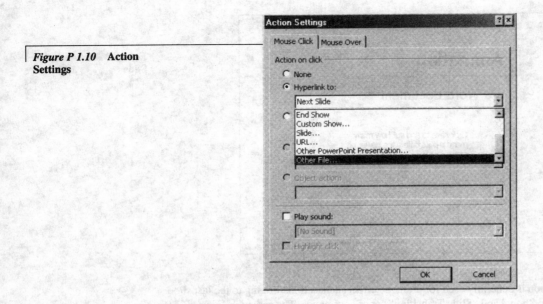

You could have chosen a spreadsheet or a database instead of a Word document and those programs would have opened in Excel and Access.

Custom animations are the most difficult animation. In our presentation the phrase "Click here to find out..." should appear three seconds after the presentation text "a Word document" appears. Then, after clicking the mouse, "The answer is 18 months" should appear.

Highlight the "Click here to find out..." phrase by clicking the mouse somewhere on the phrase and a box will appear around the phrase. Choose the "Slide Show" and "Custom Animation" commands and then choose the "Add Effect" drop-down menu. Choose "Entrance" from the drop-down menu. Figures P 1.11 and P 1.12 show you how to choose "Timing" to start with a delay of three seconds.

Figure P 1.11 **Slide Entrance Timing**

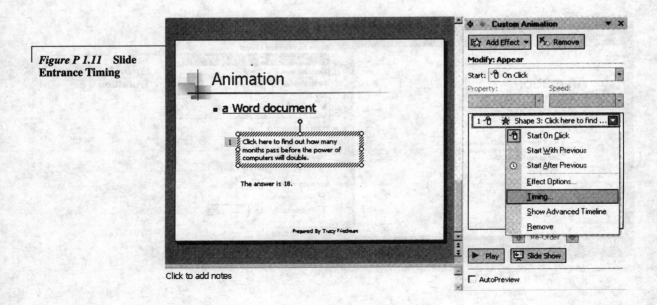

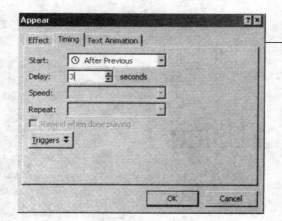

Figure P 1.12
Selecting the Start and Delay of Text Entrance

Next, click on the "The answer is 18 months" phrase to highlight it. Choose the "Slide Show" and "Custom Animation" commands again and add the effect of an entrance. From the "Entrance" command choose timing of "On Click" and a delay of zero seconds. Now when the presentation is run the question will be asked in three seconds but the answer will wait until the user clicks the mouse.

Custom animation can be used to make presentations more engaging to the audience. Sounds can be added with the animation but there is a caution. Sounds are actually computer files containing sounds and the files on one computer may not be on another. Always test your presentation on the computer that will be used to make the presentation to the audience.

ASSIGNMENT

1. Create a PowerPoint presentation that demonstrates your skills with the concepts presented here. The first slide (the title slide) should have your name as the title. In the subtitle section list your course and section along with the date. Use a design template offered by PowerPoint; do not try to create your own.
2. The second slide (the first slide of the presentation) should have its master design changed to include a footnote. The footnote should read "Project 1." If you wish, you can choose to add a date and/or slide numbers to the slide design.
3. The title of the second slide should read "Change the Master Slide Design" and the slide text should be "add a footnote." If you add a date or slide numbers then add slide text to reflect those attributes.
4. The third slide should be titled "Fonts and More." The first line of slide text should be "This line is bold," the second line should read " Courier New," the third line should read "Wingdings," and the fourth line should be "Enlarge." Indent the second and third lines. Highlight the first text line and make it bold. Highlight the second line and change its font type to Courier New. Highlight the third line and make its font type Wingdings. Highlight the fourth line and increase the font size to 48 points.
5. Create a fourth slide and enter "Links" into its title. The first line of text should be "E-mail me" and the second line should be "Link to school." Make the first text line hyperlink to your e-mail address. Make the second line link to your school's Web page.
6. Create a fifth slide and give it the title of "Actions." The slide transition to the fifth slide should be a dissolve transition with a slow speed. The first text line of the slide should be "Jump to the first slide." When the user clicks on the phrase the presentation should jump to the first slide of the presentation. Create a text box with the phrase "an apple a day" and another text box with the phrase "keeps the doctor away." The "an apple a day" phrase should appear two seconds after the slide appears. The "keeps the doctor away" phrase should appear after a mouse click and be accompanied by the sound of applause.

Project 2

Web/HTML Project Using Microsoft Word

Learning Objectives

➡ Understand the advantages and disadvantages of developing a Web page using Microsoft Word.
➡ Understand fonts, colors, and other formatting techniques.
➡ Learn how to control page lines with paragraphs, breaks, and other techniques.
➡ Learn how to create lists and tables.
➡ Learn to create links to E-mail, other parts of the same Web page, and to other Web pages.
➡ Understand how images are inserted into Web pages.

Introduction

This project uses Microsoft Word 2002 (also known as Microsoft Word XP) to make a Web page. Project 3 creates the same Web page but uses a text editor, Notepad, to generate the Web page. The two projects cover the same Web page generation in order to contrast the approaches. Your instructor may require you to complete both Project 2 and Project 3 in order to appreciate the differences between using Word and Notepad to develop a Web page.

A step-by-step example illustrates the techniques and concepts that will be needed for the project. The example is not the assignment; the assignment comes after the example. By working through the example provided, you will learn how to complete the assignment. An image of the completed example is shown in Figure P2.1.

EXAMPLE

This example creates a Word document that will be saved in an HTML format so that it can be used as a Web page. The example Web page is a product sheet for pizza so that someone browsing the Internet can see what is offered. The example contains the standard set of Web features that occur on almost all Web pages—lists, images, links, and a table.

Notice that the presentation and layout of the information is important. The company name, University Pizza, is prominently displayed at the center and top on the Web page in large, red letters. After that comes a list of locations where pizza can be purchased. The location list is indented with bullets before each location. This is a common list layout that implies no particular importance as to which location is first or last.

Now look at the list of reasons that follow "Why order from us?" That is an ordered list as opposed to the unordered list of locations. An ordered list implies the most important item is listed first. The default order is shown with numbers but Roman numerals and letters of the alphabet can also be used. Similarly, a disc (small circle) is the default bullet for an unordered list but other shapes can be used.

A table is shown after the University Pizza locations containing the prices of pizza according to the topping and size. The table has four columns and five rows. It may appear that the table has only four rows but the label "Pizza Prices" is actually in a row by itself and the label spans columns two, three, and four. "Pizza Prices" is actually a label of the other labels; "Small," "Medium," and "Large." The ability to have a label span several columns can be very useful. Tables can also have rows spanned and this is useful when rows are labeled.

The image of a chef holding a tray of pizza is just an image from clip art in Microsoft Word. You can use any image you wish but this image is one that is appropriate for a Web page that promotes pizza sales. Notice that it is centered in the Web page. Like paragraphs and words, images can be aligned to the left side of the Web page, the center, or the right side of the page.

The user has three links on the Web page. The first, "Contact Us" is a link to send e-mail. "Link to My School" is a hyperlink to your school's Web page. The last link, "Go To Top of Page," is for navigation on this Web page itself. Navigating to specific parts of the same Web page is sometimes needed for long Web pages. The technique allows users to quickly jump to the part of the page of interest and skip unwanted information. In the design of Web pages it may sometimes be better to have a single, long Web page instead of several short Web pages. This is because when users print the Web page they get all the information at once instead of having to print one short page, link to another Web page, print that short page, and so forth until all the information is printed.

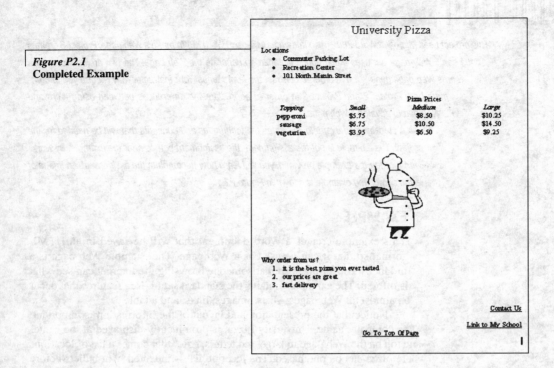

Figure P2.1
Completed Example

MAKING THE WORD DOCUMENT

Most of the basic features you want in a Web page can be created in a Microsoft Word document. Once the document is made, most users save it first as a Word document and then save it a second time as a Web page in HTML format. That process will be explained below. The instructions that follow guide you through creating a Word document that mimics Figure P2.1 Do not be alarmed if your document does not look *exactly* like Figure P2.1, but it should be close to the same format when you finish the example.

These instructions will always direct you to the commands and subcommands that achieve the desired effect. Microsoft Word has many icons that can perform the same operations with a single click of the mouse. If you move the cursor over an icon and wait a moment you will see an explanation box appear that tells what action is performed by clicking the icon. Not all computers have the same set of icons displayed, so commands and subcommands will be used in this example.

Begin by opening Word and creating a new document. Type "University Pizza" (don't type the quotation marks) and then press the "Enter" key several times to make several blank lines below "University Pizza." Use the mouse to highlight "University Pizza" and then click the "Format" command followed by the "Font" subcommand. The window shown in Figure P2.2 will appear. One of the tabs that appears is "Text Effects," but limit your actions to the "Font" tab which is shown in Figure P2.2. Although Word has a number of effects that may enliven a Word document, they can interfere with the display of a Web page and should be avoided in this project.

You want to make the phrase "University Pizza" prominent on the page so choose a "Size" that is larger (such as 18 or 20 or even 30) and choose a "Font Color" of red. You change these by using the appropriate drop-down menu choice. The particular shade of red you pick is up to you. You may notice that the "More Colors" option gives a larger choice for the shade of red to be used. Clicking the "OK" button selects these choices.

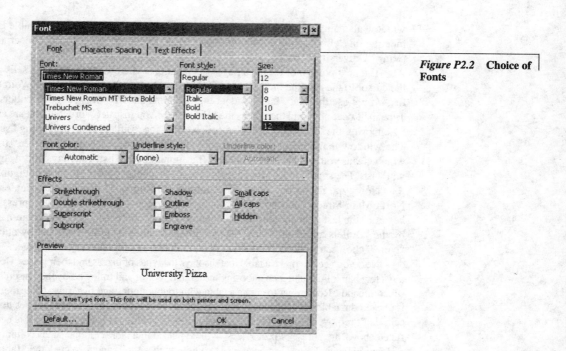

Figure P2.2 **Choice of Fonts**

After "University Pizza" has been made large and red it is time to center the phrase on the page. Use the mouse to highlight "University Pizza" (if it is not already highlighted). Click the "Format" command followed by the "Paragraph" subcommand and the window shown in Figure P2.3 will appear. You want the "Alignment" to be "Centered." Notice that this

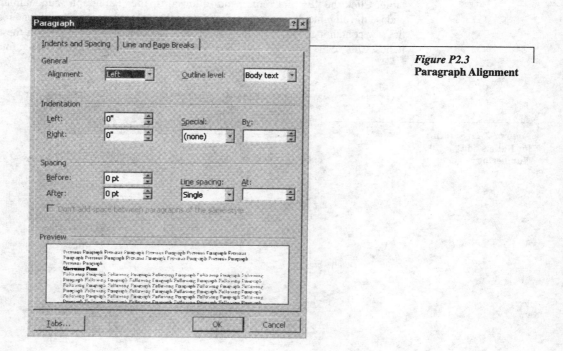

Figure P2.3 **Paragraph Alignment**

window also allows you to format paragraphs with hanging indentation, double line spacing, indentation (left and right), and other features. At this point you are only concerned with centering "University Pizza."

The next portion of the Web page lists locations where University Pizza sells pizza. Move the cursor to the last line on the page. You always want to use the features of Word to create the list; *do not* use the space bar to indent the list items and *do not* type in the bullets for the list. Type in "Locations" and then press the "Enter" key. You instruct Word that you are creating a list by choosing the "Format" command followed by the "Bullets and Numbering" subcommand. The window that appears is shown in Figure P2.4. Notice that the "Bulleted" tab is chosen which means you will have an unordered (i.e., unnumbered) list. You may choose any bullet type you wish. The small circle, also called a disc, is the choice on the example in Figure P2.1.

Now type in the list items ("Commuter Parking Lot," "Recreation Center," and "101 North Main Street") and press the "Enter" key after each item. When you press the "Enter" key after the last item another bullet appears. Simply choose the "Format" command followed by the "Bullets and Numbering" subcommand again and turn off the list by clicking on the "None" choice. You have completed a list, a feature in almost every Web page.

Next you need to make a table that displays the types of pizzas and their prices. Begin by entering a few blank lines and then choosing the "Table" command followed by the "Insert" and "Table" subcommands. Remember to create a table with four columns and five rows. Once the "OK" button is clicked the table will appear in your document. Your table will appear with lines that show each cell; don't remove the lines yet since they will help you to recognize which cell is being used. As stated above, the phrase "Pizza Prices" will be placed in a table cell that spans columns two, three, and four of the first row. Use the mouse to highlight these cells and then click the "Table" command followed by the "Merge Cells" subcommand so that columns two, three, and four are spanned.

In the merged cell type the phrase "Pizza Prices." For now, do not worry about centering the text in a cell or changing the font of the text. In the second row, first column, type "Topping." Continue by typing the pizza sizes, toppings, and prices in the appropriate cells. After you have typed the values into the cells use the mouse to highlight all the cells in the table. Click the "Format" command followed by the "Paragraph" subcommand and then choose the alignment to be centered. All the cells' values have now been centered. Highlight the row containing "Topping" through "Large" and format the font style of these phrases to italics. Choose the "Format" and "Font" sequence of commands and the italic font style.

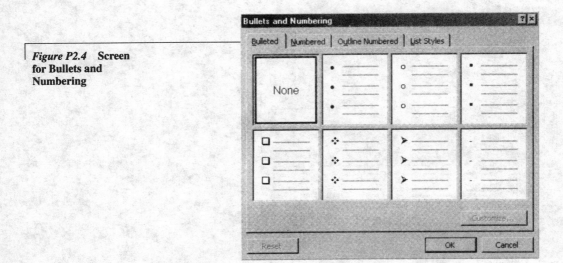

Figure P2.4 Screen for Bullets and Numbering

You may now wish to remove the lines that border each table cell. Table formatting commands let you format boundary lines of individual cells or groups of cells. For this example we choose to eliminate boundary lines for all the cells so use the mouse to highlight all table cells. With the table selected, when you click the "Format" command followed by the "Borders and Shading" subcommand the window in Figure P2.5 appears. Down the left-hand side you can see that the example eliminated the cell borders by choosing the "Setting" of "None." If you want, you can experiment with eliminating only certain cell borders by clicking on specific lines on the right-hand side of the window.

The next feature of the Web page is an image. Images inserted into a Word document from clip art must be carefully handled. Remember that after the Word document is completed you will first save it as a Word document and then you will save it a second time as a Web page in HTML format. As a Word document there is no problem since the Word software simply incorporates the image into the document itself. When saving as a Web page the process is a little more complex. Because of this we need to explain some details of saving the clip art image before you are shown how to include it in your document.

Let's assume that when you complete the document in Word you will name it PIZZA (a .doc extension will be automatically added to the name). When you save the document the second time using the "File" command followed by "Save As" you will choose the "Web Page" format type and the .htm extension will be automatically added to the file name. What you don't see is that the images in the page have been automatically saved in a subdirectory called PIZZA_files (assuming you named the document PIZZA). The images will be moved automatically from the document to the subdirectory but the subdirectory, and all the images it contains, must be submitted with the assignment document.

To insert an image into the document from clip art skip a few lines and then choose the "Insert" command and then "Picture" followed by "Clip Art" (see Figure P2.6). You could simply click on the "Search" button but you probably want to limit your search by providing a keyword such as "pizza." Simply clicking on an image will insert it into the document. To center the image in the middle of the page begin by highlighting the image. When the image "handles" appear, the dots at the corners and the edges, you know the image has been highlighted. Choose the "Format" command followed by the "Paragraph" subcommand, then choose a "Centered" alignment.

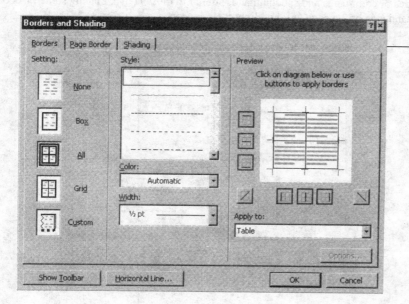

Figure P2.5 **Borders and Shading**

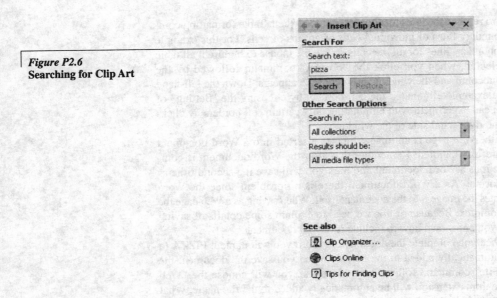

Figure P2.6
Searching for Clip Art

Back in the Word document, press the "Enter" key several times to skip a few lines and then change the paragraph alignment back to "Left" before you enter the next list. Type in "Why order from us?" and press the "Enter" key. You now want to make an ordered list—that is, a numbered list—of the reasons for ordering from University Pizza. Choose "Format" followed by "Bullets and Numbering" and then choose the "Numbered" tab. The window in Figure P2.7 appears. Several numbering schemes are available but just choose the standard 1, 2, 3 type of numbering and click the "OK" button. Enter the three choices and after pressing the "Enter" key after the third choice turn off the numbering format of the list.

The last elements on the document are links to an e-mail address, another Web page, and to another place on the Web page being constructed. Press the "Enter" key several times to leave a few blank lines and then "Format" the "Paragraph" alignment to be "Right" using the series of commands and subcommands similar to those above. Placing some links on the right-hand side of the page will highlight their existence.

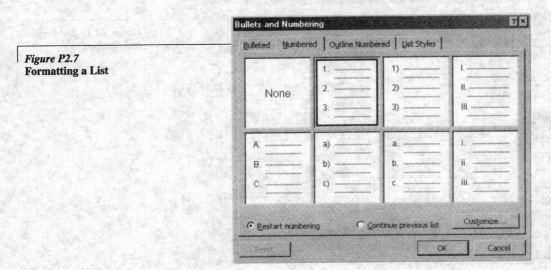

Figure P2.7
Formatting a List

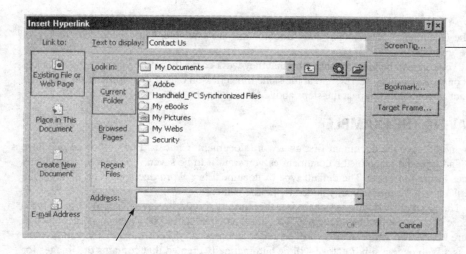

Figure P2.8 Insert an E-mail Hyperlink

Type the phrase "Contact Us," skip two lines, then type the phrase "Link to My School." Use the mouse to highlight the phrase "Contact Us" then click the "Insert" command followed by the "Hyperlink" subcommand. The window in Figure P2.8 will appear. In the box labeled "Address" enter the phrase "mailto:" followed by your e-mail address; be sure to include the @ sign and your domain name. For example, if your e-mail address is JohnDoe@aol.com then in the address box you would type "mailto:JohnDoe@aol.com" (do not type the quotation marks). There are no blank spaces in the address and you must type the colon after the phrase "mailto" or else the link will not work.

Now highlight the phrase "Link to My School" and click the "Insert" command followed by the "Hyperlink" subcommand. In the address box type in the Web address of your school, making sure to include "HTTP://" before the Web address. For example, to link to the Prentice Hall Web site you would enter "HTTP://WWW.PRENHALL.COM" (without the quotation marks) in the address box.

The last link is a navigation to a part of the same Web page. Choose to "Format" the "Paragraph" so that the alignment is "Center." Skip several lines by pressing the "Enter" key and type the phrase "Go To Top of Page." Now use the mouse to highlight "Go To Top of Page." Figure P2.9 shows the window that will appear after clicking on "Insert" and

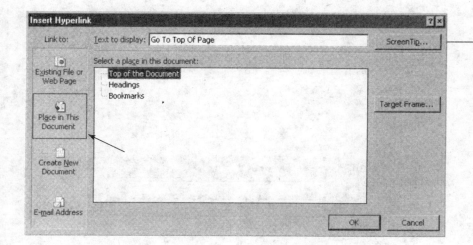

Figure P2.9 Hyperlink to a Place in the Document

"Hyperlink." Notice that the "Place in This Document" tab is selected and the choices of "Top of the Document," "Headings," and "Bookmarks" are available. Choose the "Go To Top of Page" option.

You can test the links to make sure that they work correctly before you save the file. Hold the control key down, <Ctrl>, and at the same time click on one of your links. If the link does not act as you expect, repeat the steps above for making the link.

SAVING THE EXAMPLE

You should save the document first as a Word document. Choose "File" followed by "Save As" and type the name of the document as you want it to be saved. It is best to avoid blank spaces in the file name. The default type of document is a Word document and the .doc file extension will be automatically added to the file name.

Next, save the document again but this time it should be saved as a Web page type. Choose "File" followed by "Save As." The "Save as type" should be "Web Page" as shown in Figure P2.10. The .htm extension will be added automatically. Remember, when you save the file as a Web page a subdirectory will be automatically created that contains the images for the document. If you send your assignment to your instructor via E-mail be sure to send the subdirectory of images as well as the Web page file.

VIEW THE WEB PAGE

Once the Web page has been saved, you can view it to see if it works correctly. You need to close the Word program so that the Web browser can access your Web page file. Open your Web browser and choose the "File" command followed by the "Open" subcommand. Type in the file name or "Browse" to it and click the "OK" button. Your Web page will appear in the browser.

If you need to make any corrections, close the browser and reopen Microsoft Word. Edit the document saved in Word format (not the HTML format) and save the document again in both Word format and in HTML format. Reopen the Web browser and repeat the process until you are satisfied with your Web page.

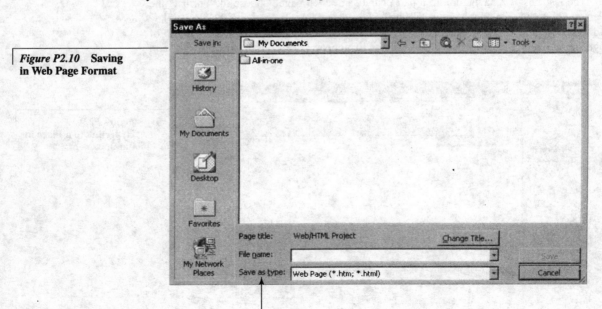

Figure P2.10 **Saving in Web Page Format**

ADVANTAGES AND DISADVANTAGES

What you see displayed on a Web page is not what the Web browser uses to create the page. While you are looking at the Web page choose the "View" command followed by the "Source" subcommand. A new window will open on your screen (probably in Notepad) that will display the code that generates the Web page. Scroll down through the code generated to create the Web page; try to find the parts where you made your lists and table.

Using Word to create a Web page is easy for many people since they are already familiar with Word. However, Word has to make many assumptions and defaults to generate the page, which results in long computer files to perform simple tasks. The great advantage of using Word to create a Web page is its ease of use. The disadvantage is the inefficient HTML code that is generated.

ASSIGNMENT

1. You are required to make a product sheet for cell phones. Your company name will be your name followed by the phrase "Cell Phone Service." For example, if your name is George Washington the company name would be "George Washington Cell Phone Service." The company name must be the first entry on the page and the words must be substantially larger than other text as well as being blue in color.
2. Next you must create an unordered (i.e., unnumbered) list of locations where the cell phones will be sold. There must be four locations; make up three locations for yourself but one location must be the room where your class meets.
3. Make a table of cell phone plans with prices like the table shown below. You may keep the border lines around the cells or you may eliminate them as you wish. Pay attention to centering of the values in the cells and the formatting of the text in cells.

		Minutes	
Price		*Day*	*Night*
$30 / month		150	450
$60 / month		500	1,000

4. Add a cell phone image from clip art. If you cannot find a cell phone image then use another image that you feel is appropriate. Center the image on the page.
5. Add an ordered list of suggested phone types such as Nokia, Ericsson, Motorola, Samsung, or others. The list should be ordered from the phone type your company feels is best to the one least preferred by your company.
6. Make three links on the page. The first link should go to your e-mail address. The second link should go to your school's Web site. The third link should go to the top of the page. All three of these links should be aligned to the right-hand side of the page.

Project 3

Web/HTML Project Using Notepad

Learning Objectives

- Understand the advantages and disadvantages of developing a Web page using the text editor Notepad.
- Understand fonts, colors, and other formatting techniques.
- Learn how to control page lines with paragraphs, breaks, and other techniques.
- Learn how to create lists and tables.
- Learn to create links to E-mail, other parts of the same Web page, and to other Web pages.
- Understand how images are inserted into Web pages.

Introduction

This project uses the text editor Notepad to create a Web page. Project 2 creates the same Web page but uses Microsoft Word 2002 (also known as Microsoft Word XP) to generate the Web page. The two projects cover the same Web page generation in order to contrast the approaches. Your instructor may require you to complete both Project 2 and Project 3 in order to appreciate the differences between using Word and Notepad to develop a Web page.

A step-by-step example illustrates the techniques and concepts that will be needed for the project. The example is not the assignment; the assignment comes after the example. By working through the example provided you will learn how to complete the assignment. An image of the completed example is shown in Figure P3.1.

EXAMPLE

This example creates a Notepad document that will be saved in a hypertext markup language (HTML) format so that it can be used as a Web page. The example Web page is a product sheet for pizza so that someone browsing the Internet can see what is offered. The example contains the standard set of Web features that occur on almost all Web pages; lists, images, links, and a table.

Notice that the presentation and layout of the information is important. The company name, University Pizza, is prominently displayed at the center and top of the Web page in large, red letters. After that comes a list of locations where pizza can be purchased. The location list is indented with bullets before each location. This is a common list layout that implies no particular importance as to which location is first or last.

Now look at the list of reasons that follow "Why order from us?" That is an ordered list as opposed to the unordered list of locations. An ordered list implies that the most important item is listed first. The default order is shown with numbers but Roman numerals and letters of the alphabet can also be used. Similarly, a disc (small circle) is the default bullet for an unordered list but other shapes can be used.

A table is shown after the locations containing the prices of pizza according to the topping and size. The table has four columns and five rows. It may appear that the table has only four rows but the label "Pizza Prices" is actually in a row by itself and the label spans columns two, three, and four. "Pizza Prices" is actually a label of the other labels, "Small," "Medium," and "Large." The ability to have a label span several columns can be very useful. Tables can also have rows spanned and this is useful when rows are labeled.

The image of a chef holding a tray of pizza is just an image found from another application. You can use any image you wish but this image is one that is appropriate for a Web page that promotes pizza sales. Notice that it is centered in the Web page. Like paragraphs and words, images can be aligned to the left side of the Web page, the center, or the right side of the page.

The user has three links on the Web page. The first, "Contact Us" is a link to send E-mail. "Link to My School" is a hyperlink to your school's Web page. The last link, "Go To Top of Page," is for navigation on this Web page itself. Navigating to specific parts of the same Web page is sometimes needed for long Web pages. The technique allows users to quickly jump to the part of the page of interest and skip unwanted information. In the design of Web pages it may sometimes be better to have a single, long Web page instead of several short Web pages. This is because when users print the Web page they get all the information at once instead of having to print one short page, link to another Web page, print that short page, and so forth until all the information is printed.

Figure P3.1
Completed Example

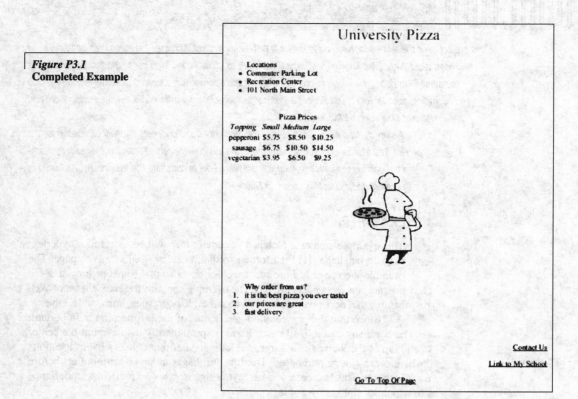

SECTIONS OF AN HTML DOCUMENT

HTML documents are comprised of two sections. The "head" section conveys information to the Web browser software and the "body" section is what the user sees displayed on the screen. Information in the head section includes the title of the Web page. The title is displayed in the top, blue line of the Web browser above the information of the Web page itself. Other information can be included in the head to denote the author of the page, keywords that will be useful for Web searches, and more. Most information in the head is never seen by the viewer of the Web page.

The body section contains the part most people think of as the Web page. Images, tables, lists, and links all occur in the body. The body lists the commands of HTML (represented as key words enclosed in angle brackets) and the actual text and images to be presented on the Web page. Commands have distinct beginnings and endings so that the Web browser software understands what commands to apply to particular Web page content.

There are many useful guides to learning HTML. An early guide that is still widely used is "A Beginner's Guide to HTML" from the National Center for Supercomputing Applications (HTTP://ARCHIVE.NCSA.UIUC.EDU/GENERAL/INTERNET/WWW/HTMLPRIMERALL.HTML). Another comprehensive set of tutorials and instructions for HTML is provided by 2K Communications (HTTP://WWW.2KWEB.NET/HTML-TUTORIAL). All of the instructions needed for this assignment are contained in this project but these two sources can aid you in the development of other Web pages.

MAKING THE NOTEPAD DOCUMENT

A short Notepad document can generate the Web page. Figure P3.2 shows the document that creates the Web page—note that the line numbers in Figure P3.2 are for your reference only, they are not typed into the Notepad document. The instructions below guide you through creating a

```
LINE01 <html>
LINE02 <head>
LINE03 <title>University Pizza</title>
LINE04 </head>
LINE05 <body>
LINE06 <a name="top_of_page">
LINE07 <p align=center>
LINE08 <font size=+3 color="red">
LINE09 University Pizza
LINE10 </font>
LINE11 </p>
LINE12 <br>
LINE13 <ul>Locations
LINE14 <li>Commuter Parking Lot</li>
LINE15 <li>Recreation Center</li>
LINE16 <li>101 North Main Street</li>
LINE17 </ul>
LINE18 <br>
LINE19 <table border=0>
LINE20 <tr>
LINE21 <td></td>
LINE22 <td colspan=3 align=center>
LINE23 Pizza Prices
LINE24 </td>
LINE25 </tr>
LINE26 <tr>
LINE27 <td align=center><i>Topping</i></td>
LINE28 <td align=center><i>Small</i></td>
LINE29 <td align=center><i>Medium</i></td>
LINE30 <td align=center><i>Large</i></td>
LINE31 </tr>
LINE32 <tr>
LINE33 <td align=center>pepperoni</td>
LINE34 <td align=center>$5.75</td>
LINE35 <td align=center>$8.50</td>
LINE36 <td align=center>$10.25</td>
LINE37 </tr>
LINE38 <tr>
LINE39 <td align=center>sausage</td>
LINE40 <td align=center>$6.75</td>
LINE41 <td align=center>$10.50</td>
LINE42 <td align=center>$14.50</td>
LINE43 </tr>
LINE44 <tr>
LINE45 <td align=center>vegetarian</td>
LINE46 <td align=center>$3.95</td>
LINE47 <td align=center>$6.50</td>
LINE48 <td align=center>$9.25</td>
LINE49 </tr>
LINE50 </table>
LINE51 <p align=center>
LINE52 <img src="pizza.gif" border=0>
LINE53 </p>
LINE54 <br>
LINE55 <ol>Why order from us?
LINE56 <li>it is the best pizza you ever tasted</li>
LINE57 <li>our prices are great</li>
LINE58 <li>fast delivery</li>
LINE59 </ol>
LINE60 <br>
LINE61 <br>
LINE62 <p align=right>
LINE63 <a href="mailto:JohnDoe@aol.com">Contact Us</a>
LINE64 <br><br>
LINE65 <a href="http://www.prenhall.com">Link to My School</a>
LINE66 <br>
LINE67 </p>
LINE68 <p align=center>
LINE69 <a href="#top_of_page">Go To Top Of Page</a>
LINE70 </body>
LINE71 </html>
```

Figure P3.2 **Notepad Document to Create the Web Page Example**

Notepad document that mimics Figure P.3.1. Do not be alarmed if your document does not look *exactly* like Figure P.3.1 but it should be close to the same format when you finish the example.

These instructions will always direct you to the commands and subcommands that achieve the desired effect. Icons exist that can perform the same operations with a single click of the mouse. If you move the cursor over an icon and wait a moment you will see an explanation box appear that tells what action is performed by clicking the icon. However, not all computers have the same set of icons displayed so commands and subcommands will be used in this example.

Begin by opening Notepad and creating a new document. To do this, click the "Start" command (bottom, left-hand side of the screen) and then choose the "Programs" subcommand. Depending upon your version of Windows, either the Notepad program will appear in a list or you may have to click the "Accessories" subcommand before the Notepad program choice is available.

Type lines 1 through 5 of Figure P3.2 into the Notepad document. **Remember, do not type in the line numbers because they are for your reference only**. Do not try to view the document using a Web browser until you have completed the entire example. HTML expects beginning and ending commands such as <html> and </html>. If you were to type only part of the example and try to view it as a Web page the browser would not find the ending commands such as </html>. The browser will try to "fix" the errors and in doing so could create a Web page very different from what you would expect. Always complete your Web page design before trying to view it using a Web browser.

These first five lines establish that the title of the Web page will be "University Pizza" and begin the body section of the HTML code. Line 6 is a place holder, a place in the Web page where the cursor can be directed. The line (<a name="top_of_page">) is an "anchor" command. We can tell this because there is a beginning angle bracket followed by the command "a" which represents an "anchor" meaning a place within the document or in some other place where the user can be directed via a hyperlink. In HTML, commands can be in upper or lower case so do not worry if, when you enter your HTML code, you use upper case letters instead of lower case letters.

The first part of our example (see Figure P3.1) is to place "University Pizza" at the top, center of the Web page in large, red letters. Line 7 instructs HTML to begin a paragraph (denoted by the command "p") that will be aligned in the center of the Web page. In line 8 the font size is increased by three steps much like choosing three items further down in a drop-down menu. Notice that the font command also changes the color of "University Pizza" to red. We must turn off these changes to the default font (line 10) and also to the default paragraph alignment (line 11) or else the font characteristics would be continued for the entire Web page.

Next we wish to make a list of locations where the pizza is sold. A blank line is left after a paragraph but in line 12 we use the command for another line break (<br>) to cause an additional blank line to be inserted into the Web page. We create an unordered list in line 13 and give it the title "Locations." Then we create three list items using the <li> command for the commuter parking lot, recreation center, and 100 North Main Street. Notice that each list item command is ended with the </li> command to turn it off and the unordered list command is turned off with the code in line 17.

After creating another blank line on the Web page (line 18) we are ready to create a table for pizza prices. The table in Figure P3.1 has five rows and four columns. The first row has the phrase "Pizza Prices" span three columns (i.e., columns two, three, and four). The text in each of the data cells of the table is centered in the cell itself. Additionally, the words "Topping," "Small," "Medium," and "Large" are in italics typeface.

Creating tables in HTML is simple but tedious. You have to specify the start and end of not only the table but of each row and each data cell in the table. Line 19 begins the table—note that the command sets the border line width of the table to be zero, which eliminates the border around the cells of the table. Some users like a thin line (such as border=1) or a thick line (such as border=10) but the example table is without border lines.

Look at line 21 in Figure P3.2. Remember that Figure P3.1 table's first row has nothing in the first table data cell. The HTML code "<td></td>" creates a table data cell but there is nothing in the cell. Line 22 commands that the next data cell of the table span 3 columns; those would be columns 2, 3, and 4. Each table data cell aligns the contents to the center of the cell by using the "align=center" phrase. The beginning and ending commands "<i>" and "</i>" cause any text between the commands to appear in italics typeface.

It is very important to remember to begin and end each table data cell, each table row, and the table itself. Forgetting one of the endings can cause the Web browser to try to correct your mistake and the result can be difficult to predict. Be very careful as you type HTML code into the Notepad document.

Images are not embedded in the HTML code but are instead referenced by an image command. In the Figure P3.1 example, the source file containing the image of the chef holding a pizza is "pizza.gif" and it is located in the same directory as the HTML file. "Img" is the abbreviation for image and "src" is the abbreviation for source. Line 52 tells HTML to use the file pizza.gif with no border around the image; that is, the border=0. Lines 51 and 53 surround the image code so that the image is located within a paragraph that is centered on the Web page.

The ordered list of "Why order from us?" is shown on lines 55 through 59. It begins with "<ol> Why order from us?" as the title of the list. An ordered list, <ol>, means that numbers will be used in sequence for the list items. You do not enter the number values, the Web browser will generate the numbers to be displayed.

The last three items in Figure P3.1 are links. The first two links are aligned to the right of the Web page. Note that the paragraph definition begins in line 62 and ends in line 67. As before, the "a" in "<a href=..." refers to the command being an anchor to a hyperlink reference. An anchor lets the user click on the Web page and hyperlink to another place on this Web page or to another page.

The first hyperlink is to "mailto:JohnDoe@aol.com." The "mailto:" segment instructs the Web browser to link to the computer's e-mail software and to insert "JohnDoe@aol.com" as the receiver of the e-mail message. For your assignment you should substitute your own e-mail address for "JohnDoe@aol.com." The phrase "Contact Us" is all that the user sees on the Web page; the anchor command itself is not seen. Do not forget to end the anchor command with "</a>" or else the rest of the Web page would link to the e-mail program.

The second hyperlink is to the Prentice Hall Web site. The phrase "Link to My School" is displayed to the user and you should use your own school Web address here. For this example, the Web address of Prentice Hall was used. Do not forget to use the whole Web address of "HTTP://WWW.PRENHALL.COM" because if you leave "HTTP://" out of the address the link will not work.

The last anchor has a hyperlink reference to a place on this Web page. Look back at line 6 in Figure P3.2. Notice that it is a named reference point within the Web page with the name being "top_of_page." Line 69 hyperlinks to that named reference point. The "#" character in the hyperlink reference "#top_of_page" tells the Web browser that the hyperlink point is within the current Web page.

The last two lines of Figure P3.2 contain "</body>" and "</html>." It is very important to end these two HTML commands so that the Web browser can interpret the Web page correctly.

SAVING THE EXAMPLE

You must save the document as an HTML file. The default type of document in Notepad is a text document and the .txt file extension will be automatically added to the file name if the file is saved in "text" mode. A Web browser will not interpret text document types. Choose "File" followed by "Save As" and Figure P3.3 will appear.

Enter a file name such as "UniversityPizza.htm" but without the quotation marks. Figure P3.4 shows that the file type chosen (i.e., "Save as type") must be "All Files" and the encoding is "ANSI." If you fail to choose "All Files" as the file type the Web page will probably not work and, even worse, the extension ".txt" will be added to the end of your file name.

VIEW THE WEB PAGE

Once the Web page has been saved you can view it to see if it works correctly. You do not need to close the Notepad program; it can remain open while you view your file with the Web browser. Open your Web browser and choose the "File" command followed by the "Open" subcommand. Type in the file name or "Browse" to it and click the "OK" button. Your Web page will appear in the browser.

If you need to make any corrections, choose the Notepad editor again. Edit the document's HTML code and save the document again. It is very important that each time you save the HTML file using Notepad that the file type is "All Files." Reopen the Web browser and choose the "View" command followed by the "Refresh" subcommand. Repeat the process until you are satisfied with your Web page.

ADVANTAGES AND DISADVANTAGES

What you see displayed on a Web page is not what the Web browser uses to create the page. Learning the HTML language is fairly easy but it is tedious and typing mistakes can have disastrous effects. Besides, the strength of managers is in their business talent and not in computer coding skills.

The disadvantage of using the text editor Notepad is the learning of HTML commands and the coding process. Though simple, it is a new language to learn and coding HTML in Notepad is time-consuming. There are two advantages to coding HTML in Notepad; the code is efficient and the manager understands more about how Web pages work.

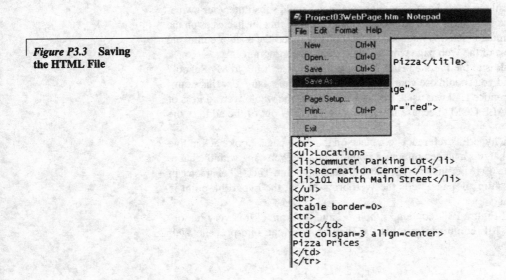

Figure P3.3 Saving the HTML File

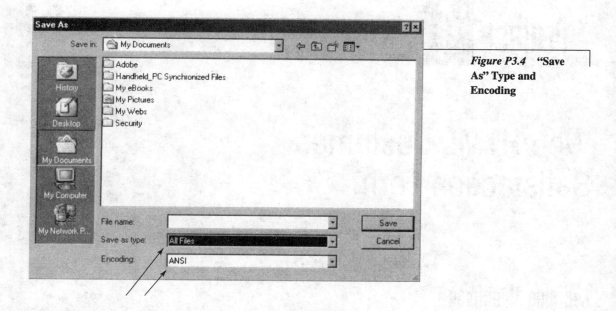

Figure P3.4 "Save As" Type and Encoding

Managers buy Web pages either as completed products from vendors or by paying wages of employees in their firm. It is important for managers to be informed consumers of the Web page development process. After having created a Web page you are in a better position to clearly express what you need in a Web page and understand if your requests should be simple or complex to the information systems specialist.

ASSIGNMENT

1. You are required to make a product sheet for cell phones. Your company name will be your name followed by the phrase "Cell Phone Service." For example, if your name is George Washington the company name would be "George Washington Cell Phone Service." The company name must be the first entry on the page and the words must be substantially larger than other text as well as being blue in color.
2. Next you must create an unordered (i.e., unnumbered) list of locations where the cell phones will be sold. There must be four locations; make up three locations for yourself but one location must be the room where your class meets.
3. Make a table of cell phone plans with prices as in the table shown. You may keep the border lines around the cells or you may eliminate them as you wish. Pay attention to centering of the values in the cells and the formatting of the text in cells.

	Minutes	
Price	Day	Night
$30 / month	150	450
$60 / month	500	1,000

4. Add a cell phone image to the Web page. If you cannot find a cell phone image then use another image that you feel is appropriate. Center the image on the page. (Note: you can capture an image from a Web page by pointing to it with the mouse, clicking the right mouse button, and then choosing the "Save Picture As" option from the menu that appears. Make sure you save the image file in the same directory as the HTML file.)
5. Add an ordered list of suggested phone types such as Nokia, Ericsson, Motorola, Samsung, or others. The list should be ordered from the phone type your company feels is best to the one least preferred by your company.
6. Make three links on the page. The first link should go to your e-mail address. The second link should go to your school's Web site. The third link should go to the top of the page. All three of these links should be aligned to the right-hand side of the page.

Project 4

Web/HTML Customer Satisfaction Form

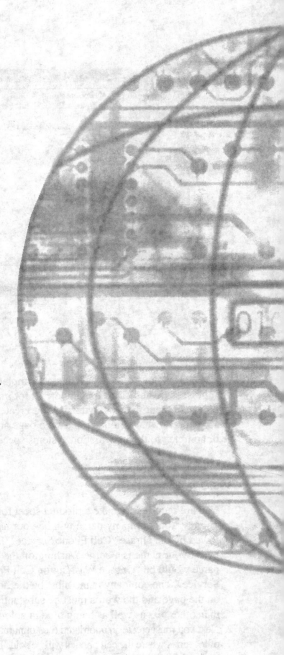

Learning Objectives

⇒ Understand how forms work to capture information from the Web-page user.

⇒ Understand the use of text boxes and text areas to acquire typed input from a user.

⇒ Learn how to create a radio button and a check box to acquire user input from a mouse click.

⇒ Learn how to create a choice of options from a drop-down menu.

Introduction

This project assumes that you have some knowledge of hypertext markup language (HTML) and the use of Notepad as a text editor. If you have completed Project 3 you have sufficient foundation knowledge to begin this project. Project 5 is a companion project; it covers the same learning objectives as this project but uses a different example. Project 4 and Project 5 both cover Web/HTML form concepts so that instructors have the option to further enforce form concepts with two projects or to assign different projects to students in different semesters.

Forms provide a mechanism for gathering information from users who visit a Web page. Without forms, information on the Web would be one-way communication to the viewer of the Web page. Organizations need to capture information from visitors to their Web site in order to make the Web site interactive. This project involves the generation of a form to support customer service operations.

This project creates the form but does not provide the Web browser with instructions for processing the form results. Information from a form is generally e-mailed back to the firm or assimilated into its database. It is not particularly difficult to generate e-mail form responses. However, many schools prohibit students from e-mailing form data or capturing it to a database because of concerns for security or excessive use of computer resources. If your school allows e-mail responses to forms you may wish to use a free service that e-mails form answers to your e-mail account. Response-O-Matic (WWW.RESPONSE-O-MATIC.COM) is a very popular service that is free and easy to use.

EXAMPLE

The example is a customer service survey about eating at Martha's Meals. The completed Web page form is shown in Figure P4.1. It represents the five most common techniques for capturing information from a Web site. The first technique is a text field (such as for the "Name" field) where the user types in one line of data. The second technique is a radio button (such as for the meal) where the possible answers are mutually exclusive. The check box (salad, pizza, or hamburger) is similar to a radio button but the user may select one or more of the choices. A drop-down menu (asking about service) uses a small amount of space on the Web page but still presents a number of mutually exclusive choices to the user. The last input technique in the example is a text area box for comments. It allows the user to enter several lines of data into a single input.

Each of these techniques has its advantages. Drop-down menus offer mutually exclusive choices just like radio buttons; however, they take up less space on the computer screen. If there are 50 or more choices (such as selecting a state for a mail address) drop-down menus obviously are superior to radio buttons. However, radio buttons have the advantage of displaying all choice options to the user at a single glance.

Text areas allow multiple lines while a text field allows only a single line. A text area could hold the entire address but firms may wish to break the address into parts using text fields. The choice of field type should be driven by how the firm wants to display the form and use the information the form gathers.

Each field containing input has at least two characteristics; a field name and a value in the field. A field could be named "Color" and its value might be either "red," "white," "blue," or some other color. The user sees information displayed on the computer screen but the computer recognizes field names and the values assigned to those fields.

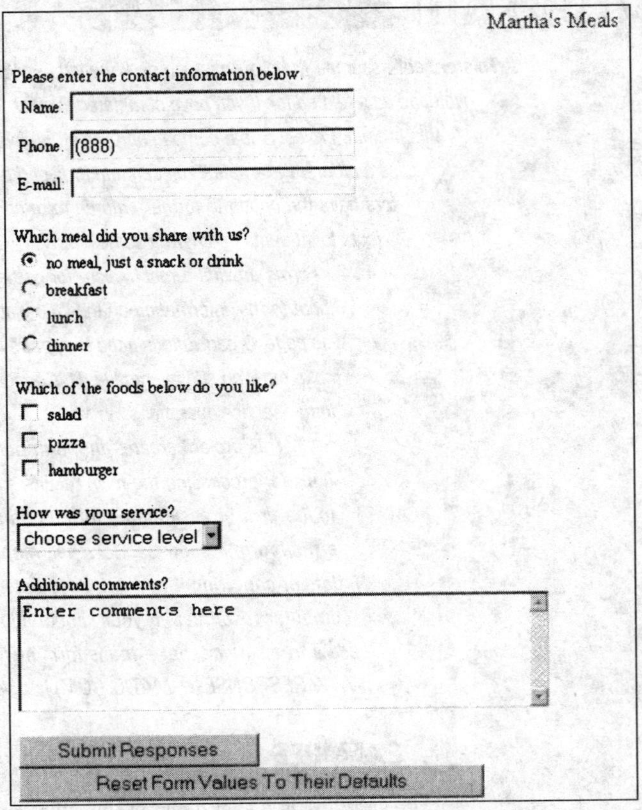

Figure P.4.1
Completed Example

SECTIONS OF THE EXAMPLE FORM

The form begins in the same manner as Project 3. A significant difference is in lines 6 and 69 of the HTML code used to generate the form (see Figure P4.2). Remember, the line numbers are in the figure as reference points only—they do not actually appear in the file of HTML code for the Web page. The set of <form> and </form> commands tells the Web browser that the Web page will engage in capturing information from the user. Without the commands to initiate and end a form the Web page cannot capture information from the user.

The first section of information to be gathered will help the firm contact the customer. From Figure P4.3 you can see that the contact information in the example is actually enclosed in a table. The dotted lines delineate the columns and rows of the table. The first column provides the labels the user sees as he or she fills out the form. Lines 17, 24, and 31 are the commands that capture input for the name, phone number, and e-mail address. Notice that the input type is "text," which instructs the Web browser that the user will type text into the input field.

From Figure P4.1 you see that the phone number field has a default area code already entered into the field. When you compare line 24 in Figure P4.2 to lines 17 and 31 you can see how this is achieved. The value field is part of the command in line 24 and "(888)" has been entered for the value. Because there is no value field as part of the input commands in lines 17 or 31, there is no value included in those fields by default. The customer name, phone, and e-mail address fields are each defined as 30 characters long.

Figure P.4.2 **HTML Code for the Example**

```
LINE01 <html>
LINE02 <head>
LINE03 <title>Customer Service</title>
LINE04 </head>
LINE05 <body>
LINE06 <form>
LINE07 <p align=center>
LINE08 <font size=+2>Martha's Meals</font>
LINE09 </p>
LINE10 Please enter the contact information below.
LINE11 <table border=0>
LINE12 <tr>
LINE13 <td align=right>
LINE14 Name:
LINE15 </td>
LINE16 <td>
LINE17 <input type="text" name="CustomerName" size=30>
LINE18 </td>
LINE19 </tr>
LINE20 <td align=right>
LINE21 Phone:
LINE22 </td>
LINE23 <td>
LINE24 <input type="text" name="CustomerPhone" size=30 value="(888)">
LINE25 </td>
LINE26 </tr>
LINE27 <td align=right>
LINE28 E-mail:
LINE29 </td>
LINE30 <td>
LINE31 <input type="text" name="E-mail" size=30>
LINE32 </td>
LINE33 </tr>
LINE34 </table>
LINE35 <br>
LINE36 Which meal did you share with us?<br>
LINE37 <input type="radio" name="Meal" value="none" checked>
LINE38 no meal, just a snack or drink<br>
LINE39 <input type="radio" name="Meal" value="B">
LINE40 breakfast<br>
LINE41 <input type="radio" name="Meal" value="L">
LINE42 lunch<br>
LINE43 <input type="radio" name="Meal" value="D">
LINE44 dinner<br>
LINE45 <br>
LINE46 Which of the foods below do you like?<br>
LINE47 <input type="checkbox" name="Salad" value="yes">
LINE48 salad<br>
LINE49 <input type="checkbox" name="Pizza" value="yes">
LINE50 pizza<br>
LINE51 <input type="checkbox" name="Burger" value="yes">
LINE52 hamburger<br>
LINE53 <br>
LINE54 How was your service?<br>
LINE55 <select name="Service">
LINE56 <option value="NoResponse">choose service level</option>
LINE57 <option value="Excellent">excellent</option>
LINE58 <option value="Average">average</option>
LINE59 <option value="Poor">poor</option>
LINE60 </select>
LINE61 <br><br>
LINE62 Additional comments?<br>
LINE63 <textarea name="Comments" rows=5 cols=45 wrap="yes">
LINE64 Enter comments here
LINE65 </textarea>
LINE66 <br><br>
LINE67 <input type="submit" value="Submit Responses"><br>
LINE68 <input type="reset" value="Reset Form Values To Their Defaults">
LINE69 </form>
LINE70 </body>
LINE71 </html>
```

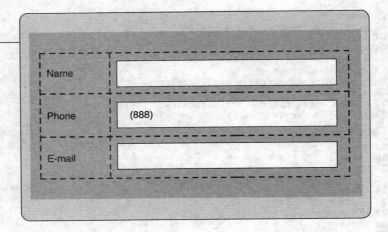

Figure P.4.3 Contact Information Fields Are Part of a Table.

The next section of the Web page asks about the meal eaten by the customer. There are four choices and the user can select one and only one choice. Radio buttons are useful when choices are mutually exclusive. Lines 37 and 38 present the choice for "no meal, just a snack or drink." Line 37 creates the radio button and line 38 creates the text that the user will see on the computer screen.

Four important features should be noticed; the field type, the field name, the field value, and the fact that this choice is checked by default. The field type of "radio" causes the Web browser to assign a circle that can be checked with a mouse click. The field name is the same value in lines 37, 39, 41, and 43. Using the same field name is what causes the choices between radio buttons to be mutually exclusive. A given field name can have only one value, the value assigned when the circle is chosen by a mouse click. A common mistake is misspelling the field name between radio button statements, which allows more than one button to be chosen.

Notice the "value" field in line 37. When the circle before the phrase "no meal, just a snack or drink" is checked the computer registers the value "none" in the "Meal" field. The Web page user sees the phrase "no meal, just a snack or drink" but the computer sees the value "none" when the circle is checked.

The word "checked" in line 37 causes the Web page to have the "no meal, just a snack or drink" choice checked by default. Only one choice for the radio button field should have "checked" in its input command. Otherwise the Web browser cannot know which of the mutually exclusive choices should be checked.

Radio buttons should be used for exclusive choices when the number of choices is limited. If many choices are presented, they can take up an excessive amount of space on the Web page. An advantage of radio buttons is that all of the available choices are presented to the users without causing them to click on the drop-down menu.

When a user should be allowed to accept more than one choice, check boxes should be used. Figure P4.1 presents check boxes for the types of food the customer likes. Lines 47 through 52 in Figure P4.2 create the check boxes in the example for salad, pizza, and hamburgers. Line 47 is representative of check box creation. Note that the field name is different in lines 47, 49, and 51 so each line creates its own field and multiple check boxes may be chosen. If the salad box is chosen with a mouse click then the "Salad" field will have the value of "yes." If the field is not chosen then the computer does not assign a value to "Salad".

Drop-down menus (also called selection boxes) present the user with a list of mutually exclusive choices where the list of choices is presented after the user clicks on the drop-down list icon. That icon is shown in Figure P4.1 just to the right of the phrase "choose service level." Lines 55 through 60 in Figure P4.2 list the commands for generating the drop-down menu of the example.

Note that there is a beginning and ending command for the selection (lines 55 and 60) and each option of the selection list has its own beginning and ending (for example, line 56). The name of the selection field is in the selection command but the value assigned to the field is generated from an option command. Generally, the first option in the list of options will be the value shown on the Web page. Note that "choose service level" is displayed in Figure P4.1 and that is the first option within the select command. However, if "<option value='Average' selected> average </option>" were substituted for line 58 the word "selected" would cause the "average" option to be the one displayed by default on the Web page.

As with other commands, what the user sees on the computer screen may not be what the computer records. If the user chooses the option of "choose service level" then the service field would contain the value "NoResponse."

The last field of the example solicits additional comments from the customer. The form assumes that the customer may need more than a single line of text to give details to the comment. A text area command is used for such comments. The name of the text area is set to "Comments" and the user is provided 5 rows with 45 characters in each row to make comments. Notice that there is a "wrap" field and its value is set to "yes." The Web browser will allow the user to type comments into the field and they will automatically wrap to the next line (like a word processor) as the comments are typed.

Line 64 lies between the beginning and ending commands of the text area. The phrase "Enter comments here" is displayed on the computer screen within the text area field. If line 64 were removed, there would be no default text in the text area field.

There are two special input types required to commit the Web browser to act upon information collected by a form: Submit and Reset. The "Submit" command is shown in line 67 of Figure P4.2. The value displayed in the button created by this command is "Submit Responses." In typical forms there would be an action specified in the form command (of line 6) and the Web browser would execute the actions specified when the "Submit" button is clicked. We have chosen not to act upon the data collected by the form and so clicking the "Submit" button merely restarts the Web page that contains the form.

The "Reset" command in line 68 presents the phrase "Reset Form Values To Their Defaults" in the button. Clicking that button on the Web page causes all choices by the user to be reset to the choices originally provided within the HTML commands. This is similar to users erasing all of their responses on a paper form.

SAVING THE EXAMPLE

You must save the document as an HTML file. The default type of document in Notepad is a text document and the .txt file extension will be automatically added to the file name if the file is saved in "text" mode. A Web browser will not interpret text document types.

Enter a file name such as "CustomerService.htm" for your project but without the quotation marks. The file type chosen (i.e., "Save as type") must be "All Files" and the encoding is "ANSI." If you fail to choose "All Files" as the file type the Web page will probably not work and, even worse, the extension ".txt" will be added to the end of your file name.

VIEW THE WEB PAGE

Once the Web page has been saved you can view it to see if it works correctly. You do not need to close the Notepad program—it can remain open while you view your file with the Web browser. Open your Web browser and choose the "File" command followed by the "Open" subcommand. Type in the file name or "Browse" to it and click the "OK" button. Your Web page will appear in the browser.

If you need to make any corrections, choose the Notepad editor again. Edit the document's HTML code and save the document again. It is very important that each time you save the HTML file using Notepad the file type is "All Files." Reopen the Web browser and choose the "View" command followed by the "Refresh" subcommand. Repeat the process until you are satisfied with your Web page.

Assignment

1. You are required to make a customer service form for the Fan See Dining restaurant. A sample of what your results should look like is shown in Figure P4.4. Notice that the name "Fan See Dining" is in a paragraph at the top of the page and is both on the right-hand side and in a font size larger than the rest of the sample.
2. Use text fields to capture the first name, last name, and phone number of the customer. Each field should be allowed a size of 30 characters of text. The default area code of "(010)" should be in the phone number field.
3. Use radio buttons to find out if the customer made reservations. The "No" choice should be checked as the default response.
4. Check boxes are used to ask the customer what was ordered. The question "What did you order?" is in a table data cell that spans two columns. The four choices are displayed in the following two rows across two columns in each row.
5. A drop-down menu is used to collect the waiter's name. The phrase "I do not know" is shown and the other choices are "Kim," "Ramon," and "Cecil."
6. A comments box should be made that is 5 rows deep and 45 characters across.
7. Create a "Submit" button and a "Reset" button similar to those in the sample of Figure P4.4.

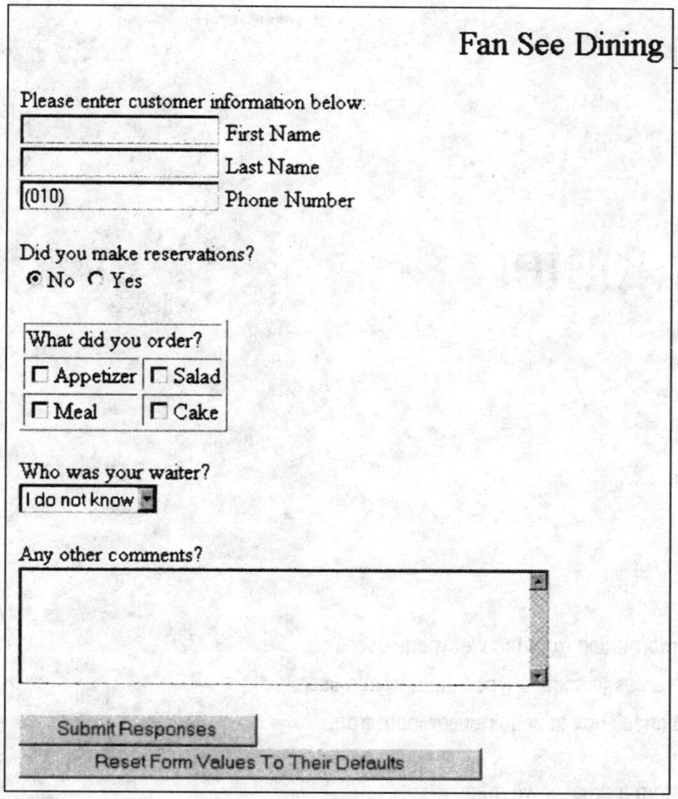

Fan See Dining

Please enter customer information below:

[_____] First Name
[_____] Last Name
[(010)_____] Phone Number

Did you make reservations?
⦿ No ◯ Yes

What did you order?
☐ Appetizer ☐ Salad
☐ Meal   ☐ Cake

Who was your waiter?
[I do not know ▼]

Any other comments?
[   ]
[   ]
[   ]

[Submit Responses]
[Reset Form Values To Their Defaults]

Figure P.4.4 **Sample Completed Assignment**

Project 5

Web/HTML Computer Purchase Form

Learning Objectives

- Understand how forms work to capture information from the Web-page user.
- Understand the use of text boxes and text areas to acquire typed input from a user.
- Learn how to create a radio button and a check box to acquire user input from a mouse click.
- Learn how to create a choice of options from a drop-down menu.

Introduction

This project assumes that you have some knowledge of hypertext markup language (HTML) and the use of Notepad as a text editor. If you have completed Project 3 you have sufficient foundation knowledge to begin this project. Project 4 is a companion project; it covers the same learning objectives as this project but uses a different example. Projects 4 and 5 both cover Web/HTML form concepts so that instructors have the option to further enforce form concepts with two projects or to assign different projects to students in different semesters.

Forms provide a mechanism for gathering information from users who visit a Web page. Without forms, information on the Web would be one-way communication to the viewer of the Web page. Organizations need to capture information from visitors to their Web site in order to make the Web site interactive. This project involves the generation of a form for a user to purchase a computer.

This project creates the form but does not provide the Web browser with instructions for processing the form results. Information from a form is generally e-mailed back to the firm or assimilated into its database. It is not particularly difficult to generate e-mail form responses. However, many schools prohibit students from e-mailing form data or capturing it to a database because of concerns for security or excessive use of computer resources. If your school allows e-mail responses to forms you may wish to use a free service that e-mails form answers to your e-mail account. Response-O-Matic (WWW.RESPONSE-O-MATIC.COM) is a very popular service which is free and easy to use.

EXAMPLE

The example creates a form to order a computer from Acme Computer Builders. The completed Web page form is shown in Figure P5.1. It represents the five most common techniques for capturing information from a Web site. The first technique is a text field (such as for the "Name" field) where the user types in one line of data. A drop-down menu (asking which computer the customer wants to buy) uses a small amount of space on the Web page but still presents a number of mutually exclusive choices to the user. The radio button technique (such as for the monitor) is used when the possible answers are mutually exclusive. The check box (larger hard drive, more memory) is similar to a radio button but the user may select one or more of the choices. The last input technique in the example is a text area box for comments. It allows the user to enter several lines of data into a single input.

Each of these techniques has its advantages. Drop-down menus offer mutually exclusive choices just like radio buttons; however, they take up less space on the computer screen. If there are 50 or more choices (such as selecting a state for a mail address) drop-down menus obviously are superior to radio buttons. However, radio buttons have the advantage of displaying all choice options to the user at a single glance.

Text areas allow multiple lines while a text field allows only a single line. A text area could hold an entire address but firms may wish to break the address into parts—city, state, and so forth—using text fields. The choice of field type should be driven by how the firm wants to display the form and use the information the form gathers.

Each field containing input has at least two characteristics; a field name and a value in the field. A field could be named "Color" and its value might be either "red," "white," "blue," or some other color. The user sees information displayed on the computer screen but the computer recognizes field names and the values assigned to those fields.

SECTIONS OF THE EXAMPLE FORM

The form begins in the same manner as Project 3. A significant difference is in lines 6 and 66 of the HTML code used to generate the form (see Figure P5.2). Remember, the line numbers are in the figure as reference points only—they do not actually appear in the file of HTML code for the Web page. The set of <form> and </form> commands tells the Web browser that the Web page will engage in capturing information from the user. Without the commands to initiate and end a form the Web page cannot capture information from the user.

The first section of information to be gathered will help the firm contact the customer. From Figure P5.3 you can see that the customer information in the example is actually enclosed in a table. The dotted lines delineate the columns and rows of the table. The second column provides the labels the users see as they fill out the form. Lines 14, 21, and 28 are the commands that capture input for the name, e-mail address, and zip code. Notice that the input type is "text," which instructs the Web browser that the user will type text into the input field.

From Figure P5.1 you see that the zip code field has a default value already entered into the field. When you compare line 28 in Figure P5.2 to lines 14 and 21 you can see how this is achieved. The value field is part of the command in line 28 and "12345" has been entered for the value. Because there is no value field as part of the input commands in lines 14 or 21, there is no value included in those fields by default. The customer name and e-mail address fields are each defined as 30 characters long while the zip code field is sized to 5 characters. That is why the table data cell for the input of the zip code is aligned to the right-hand-side of the cell.

The next section of the Web page asks about the computer to be purchased. Lines 37 through 42 show how the selection and options are defined. The name of the selection field is

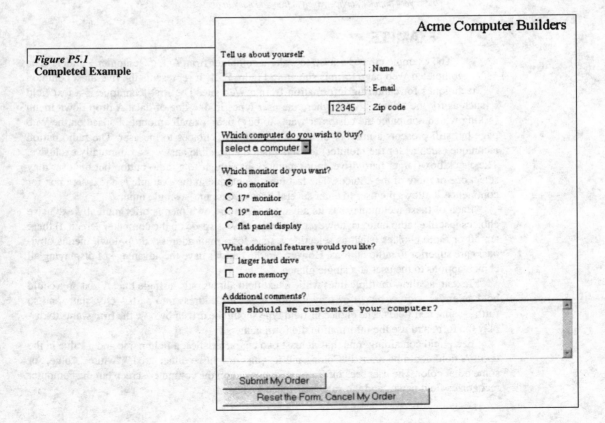

Figure P5.1
Completed Example

"Buy" and the option choices are "select a computer," "Acme 2000," "Acme 2K," and "Acme Extreme." These are the values the user sees on the Web page. The computer will store the value of "Extreme" for the "Buy" field when "Acme Extreme" is selected as the option from the drop-down menu.

Drop-down menus (also called selection boxes) present the user with a list of mutually exclusive choices where the list of choices is presented after the user clicks on the drop-down list icon. That icon is shown in Figure P5.1 just to the right of the phrase "select a computer."

Note that there is a beginning and ending command for the selection (lines 37 and 42) and each option of the selection list has its own beginning and ending (for example, line 38). The name of the selection field is in the selection command but the value assigned to the field is generated from an option command. Generally, the first option in the list of options will be the value shown on the Web page. Note that "select a computer" is displayed in Figure P5.1 and that is the first option within the select command. However, if "<option value='Extreme' selected>Acme Extreme </option>" were substituted for line 41 the word "selected" would cause the "Acme Extreme" option to be the one displayed by default on the Web page.

The next section of the form asks the user to choose a monitor. Four important features should be noticed; the field type, the field name, the field value, and the fact that the "no monitor" choice is checked by default. The field type of "radio" causes the Web browser to assign a circle that can be checked with a mouse click. The field name ("Monitor") is the same value in lines 45, 47, 49, and 51. Using the same field name is what causes the choices between radio buttons to be mutually exclusive. A given field name can have only one value, the value assigned when the circle is chosen by a mouse click. A common mistake is misspelling the field name between radio button statements, which allows more than one button to be chosen.

Notice the "value" field in line 45. When the circle before the phrase "no monitor" is checked, the computer registers the value "none" in the "Monitor" field. The Web page user sees the phrase "no monitor" but the computer sees the value "none" when the circle is checked.

The word "checked" in line 45 causes the Web page to have the "no monitor" choice checked by default. Only one choice for the radio button field should have "checked" in its input command. Otherwise the Web browser cannot know which of the mutually exclusive choices should be checked.

Radio buttons should be used for exclusive choices when the number of choices is limited. If many choices are presented, they can take up an excessive amount of space on the Web page. An advantage of radio buttons is that all of the available choices are presented to the users without causing them to click on the drop-down menu.

When a user should be allowed to accept more than one choice, check boxes should be used. Figure P5.1 presents check boxes for additional features on the computer to be purchased. Lines 55 through 58 in Figure P5.2 create the check boxes in the example for a larger hard drive and more memory. Line 55 is representative of check box creation. Note that the field name is different in lines 55 and 57 so each line creates its own field and multiple check boxes may be chosen. If a larger hard drive is chosen with a mouse click then the "HardDrive" field will have the value of "yes." If the field is not chosen then the computer does not assign a value to "HardDrive".

As with other commands, what the user sees on the computer screen may not be what the computer records. If the user chooses the option of "choose service level" then the service field would contain the value "NoResponse."

The last field of the example (lines 60 through 62) solicits additional comments from the customer. The form assumes that the customer may need more than a single line of text to give details to the comment. A text area command is used for such comments. The name of the text area is set to "Customize" and the user is provided five rows with 60 characters in each row to make comments. Notice that there is a "wrap" field and its value is set to "yes." The Web

Figure P5.2 HTML Code for the Example

```
LINE01  <html>
LINE02  <head>
LINE03  <title>Order a Computer</title>
LINE04  </head>
LINE05  <body>
LINE06  <form>
LINE07  <p align=center>
LINE08  <font size=+2>Acme Computer Builders</font>
LINE09  </p>
LINE10  Tell us about yourself.
LINE11  <table border=0>
LINE12  <tr>
LINE13  <td>
LINE14  <input type="text" name="Customer" size=30>
LINE15  </td>
LINE16  <td>
LINE17   : Name
LINE18  </td>
LINE19  </tr>
LINE20  <td>
LINE21  <input type="text" name="E-mail" size=30>
LINE22  </td>
LINE23  <td>
LINE24   : E-mail
LINE25  </td>
LINE26  </tr>
LINE27  <td align=right>
LINE28  <input type="text" name="Zip" size=5 value="12345">
LINE29  </td>
LINE30  <td>
LINE31   : Zip code
LINE32  </td>
LINE33  </tr>
LINE34  </table>
LINE35  <br>
LINE36  Which computer do you wish to buy?<br>
LINE37  <select name="Buy">
LINE38  <option value="NoResponse">select a computer</option>
LINE39  <option value="2000">Acme 2000</option>
LINE40  <option value="2K">Acme 2K</option>
LINE41  <option value="Extreme">Acme Extreme</option>
LINE42  </select>
LINE43  <br><br>
LINE44  Which monitor do you want?<br>
LINE45  <input type="radio" name="Monitor" value="none" checked>
LINE46  no monitor<br>
LINE47  <input type="radio" name="Monitor" value="17">
LINE48  17" monitor<br>
LINE49  <input type="radio" name="Monitor" value="19">
LINE50  19" monitor<br>
LINE51  <input type="radio" name="Monitor" value="flat">
LINE52  flat panel display<br>
LINE53  <br>
LINE54  What additional features would you like?<br>
LINE55  <input type="checkbox" name="HardDrive" value="yes">
LINE56  larger hard drive<br>
LINE57  <input type="checkbox" name="Memory" value="yes">
LINE58  more memory<br><br>
LINE59  Additional comments?<br>
LINE60  <textarea name="Customize" rows=5 cols=60 wrap="yes">
LINE61  How should we customize your computer?
LINE62  </textarea>
LINE63  <br><br>
LINE64  <input type="submit" value="Submit My Order"><br>
LINE65  <input type="reset" value="Reset the Form, Cancel My Order">
LINE66  </form>
LINE67  </body>
LINE68  </html>
```

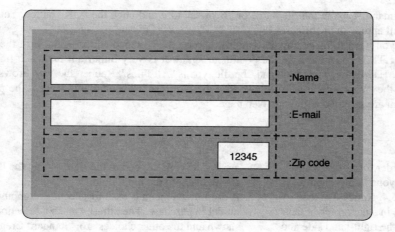

Figure P5.3
Customer Information Fields Are Part of a Table.

browser will allow the user to type comments into the field and they will automatically wrap to the next line (like a word processor) as the comments are typed.

Line 61 lies between the beginning and ending commands of the text area. The phrase "How should we customize your computer?" is displayed on the computer screen within the text area field. If line 61 were removed, there would be no default text in the text area field.

There are two special input types required to commit the Web browser to act upon information collected by a form: Submit and Reset. The "Submit" command is shown in line 64 of Figure P5.2. The value displayed in the button created by this command is "Submit My Order." In typical forms there would be an action specified in the form command (of line 6) and the Web browser would execute the actions specified when the "Submit" button is clicked. We have chosen not to act upon the data collected by the form and so clicking the "Submit" button merely restarts the Web page that contains the form.

The "Reset" command in line 65 presents the phrase "Reset the Form, Cancel My Order" in the button. Clicking that button on the Web page causes all choices by the user to be reset to the choices originally provided within the HTML commands. This is similar to users erasing all of their responses on a paper form.

SAVING THE EXAMPLE

You must save the document as an HTML file. The default type of document in Notepad is a text document and the .txt file extension will be automatically added to the file name if the file is saved in "text" mode. A Web browser will not interpret text document types.

Enter a file name such as "Acme.htm" for your project but without the quotation marks. The file type chosen (i.e., "Save as type") must be "All Files" and the encoding is "ANSI." If you fail to choose "All Files" as the file type the Web page will probably not work and, even worse, the extension ".txt" will be added to the end of your file name.

VIEW THE WEB PAGE

Once the Web page has been saved you can view it to see if it works correctly. You do not need to close the Notepad program—it can remain open while you view your file with the Web browser. Open your Web browser and choose the "File" command followed by the "Open" subcommand. Type in the file name or "Browse" to it and click the "OK" button. Your Web page will appear in the browser.

If you need to make any corrections, choose the Notepad editor again. Edit the document's HTML code and save the document again. It is very important that each time you save the HTML file using Notepad, the file type is "All Files." Reopen the Web browser and choose the "View" command followed by the "Refresh" subcommand. Repeat the process until you are satisfied with your Web page.

ASSIGNMENT

1. You are required to make an order form for Creation Computers. A sample of what your results should look like is shown in Figure P5.4. Notice that the name "Creation Computers" is in a paragraph at the top of the page and is both on the right-hand side and in a font size larger than the rest of the sample.
2. Use text fields to capture the last name, first name, and e-mail address of the customer. Each name field should be allowed a size of 20 characters of text and the e-mail address should have a field size of 30. The default e-mail domain of "@aol.com" should be in the e-mail field.
   The text fields are in a table that has two columns and three rows. "Last Name," "First Name," and "E-mail Address" are in the first column. Notice that they are in data cells aligned to the right so that the label is aligned next to the input field.
3. A drop-down menu is used to select the computer model to purchase. The phrase "make a selection" is shown and the other choices are "Standard Creation," "Deluxe Creation," and "Creation Notebook."
4. Use radio buttons to find out how the customer will pay for the purchase. Notice that the "Cash" choice should be checked as the default response.
5. Check boxes are used to ask customers how they learned about Creation Computers.
6. A comments box should be made that is five rows deep and 50 characters across.
7. Create a "Submit" button and a "Reset" button similar to those in the sample of Figure P5.4.

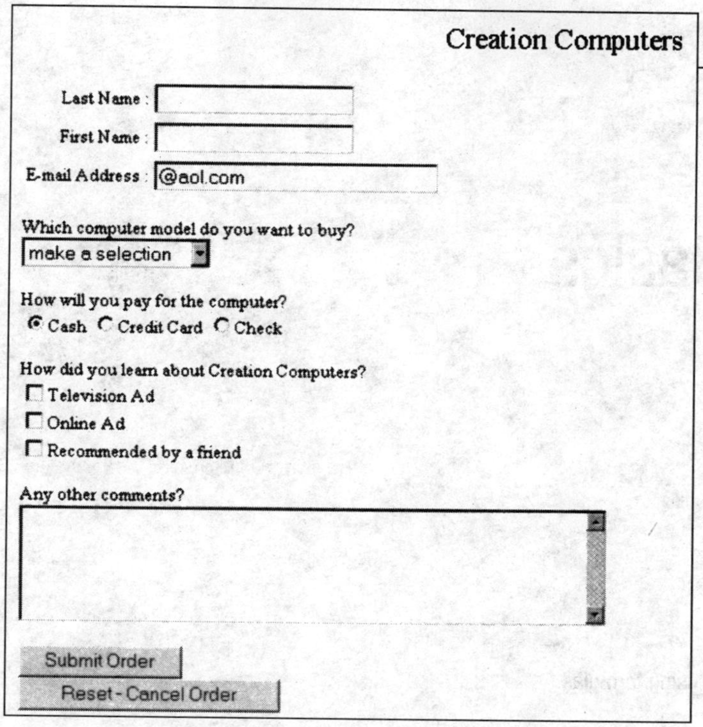

Figure P5.4 **Sample Completed Assignment**

Project 6

Spreadsheet Basics

Learning Objectives

➡ Learn to format cells of a spreadsheet.
➡ Understand how calculations are made using formulas.
➡ Learn to use multiple datasheets.
➡ Understand how to create conditional calculations using IF...THEN statements.

Introduction

This project uses Excel 2002 (also known as Excel XP) to create a basic spreadsheet. Spreadsheet appearance is important so you will need to format the values in the cells of the spreadsheet. Although there is a single spreadsheet file for the example, two datasheets are contained in the file. One sheet contains items in the invoice while the second datasheet contains information about discounting item prices. The system date (i.e., the computer's date) is captured into the invoice using an Excel built-in function.

Spreadsheets are common in business applications. They can include calculations and conditional logic that would be difficult for managers to carry out. The calculations are computed quickly and without errors. By using spreadsheets, instead of manual calculations, managers reduce the mathematical errors that can affect their decision making. As an additional benefit, the formatting of a spreadsheet can produce a visually pleasing result that can often be printed and used as documentation of the business process.

EXAMPLE

This example creates an invoice. Figure P6.1 displays the "Invoice" datasheet and Figure P6.2 displays the "Discount" datasheet. Look at the bottom of the figures and you can tell which datasheet is displayed by the tab that is highlighted.

The invoice contains four items; chair, table, lamp, and pillow. Each item has a unit price and depending upon the unit price there is a discount. The unit price, less any discount, times the number of units ordered determines the extended price.

The extended prices of all items are summed together to determine the invoice total. Additionally, the amount due from the customer is dependent upon when the customer pays the invoice. The date "1/13/03" is the date the invoice was generated. At that date, the customer simply pays the total amount. If the customer waits 30 days before paying, until 2/12/03, the amount to be paid is 101% of the total and equals $2,228.33. After 60 days from the date of purchase the amount owed is 103% of the total.

Notice that days, not months, were added to the original purchase date. That is why the subsequent dates are 2/12/03 and 3/14/03. There are not 30 days in each month.

Spreadsheet cells in the Invoice datasheet are formatted to be visually appealing. Cells in the Discount datasheet have been left in their default format. The reason is that the user will not generally view the Discount datasheet while the Invoice datasheet will be frequently viewed and possibly

	A	B	C	D	E	F	G	H
1	INVOICE							
2								
3		Item	Unit Price	Discount	Units	Extended Price		
4		chair	$52.75	10%	15	$712.125		
5		table	$105.50	15%	4	$358.700		
6		lamp	$29.00	0%	16	$464.000		
7		pillow	$11.99	0%	56	$671.440		
8						$2,206.27	Total	
9								
10						Amount Due	Date	
11						$2,206.27	1/13/03	
12						$2,228.33	2/12/03	
13						$2,272.45	3/14/03	

Figure P6.1   **Invoice Datasheet for the Example**

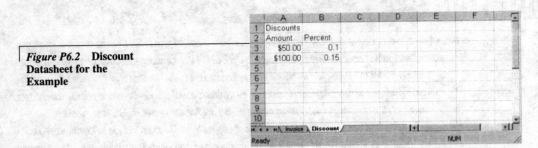

Figure P6.2 Discount Datasheet for the Example

printed as a receipt for the customer. Spreadsheets are more than simple calculating programs; they can be used to provide relatively sophisticated information systems capabilities to firms. As such, the appearance of the spreadsheet should be in a form that aids decision making.

Begin the example by opening the Excel program. Notice that there are three datasheet tabs at the bottom of the screen (see Figure P6.3) labeled "Sheet1," "Sheet2," and "Sheet3." We need only two datasheets for our example and they need to be labeled "Invoice" and "Discount." Click on the tab showing "Sheet3" and then choose the "Edit" command followed by the "Delete Sheet" command. Make sure you choose "Delete Sheet" and not the "Delete" subcommand. After deleting "Sheet3" only two datasheets will be left.

Double click on the "Sheet1" tab and you will see that the entire phrase "Sheet1" is highlighted. Press the "Delete" button to eliminate the name "Sheet1" and now type in "Invoice" for the tab label. Double click on the "Sheet2" tab, delete it, and type in "Discount." You now have the correct datasheet labels on the two sheets needed for this example.

DISCOUNT DATASHEET

The contents of the Discount datasheet (Figure P6.2) will be entered first. The purpose of this datasheet in our example is to establish two unit price amounts that establish discount percentages. In our example, if the unit price amount is greater than or equal to $100 then there is a 15% discount. A price of greater than or equal to $50 causes a 10% discount.

You must enter your values into the cells as they are shown in Figure P6.2 because formulas to calculate cell values on the "Invoice" datasheet depend upon the values of specific cells in the "Discount" datasheet. Notice that the percent values are left as .1 and .15; they have not been formatted as percentages with percent signs. The dollar amounts, $50.00 and $100.00, have been formatted. After typing the values 50 and 100 into cells A3 and A4, highlight the cells and choose the "Format" command followed by the "Cells" subcommand and the screen in Figure P6.4 appears. Choose a currency format with two decimal places to achieve the desired format for these values.

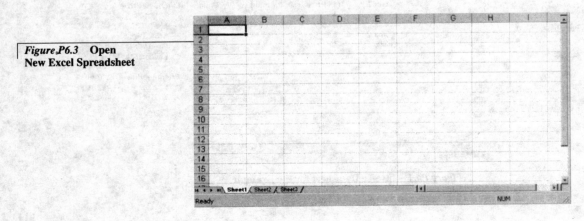

Figure P6.3 Open New Excel Spreadsheet

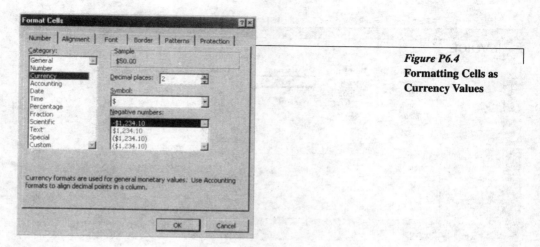

Figure P6.4
Formatting Cells as Currency Values

INVOICE DATASHEET

The "Invoice" datasheet is more complex. Begin by making the column widths wide enough to comfortably hold the values and headings of the invoice. Use the mouse to select columns A through G, then choose the "Format" command followed by the "Column" and "Width" commands. When Figure P6.5 appears choose to make the column width 13.

Now you can begin entering data without the values exceeding the size of the cells. You should begin by entering the data values into cells where no calculations are required. Your values may not appear in the same format as the "Invoice" datasheet—we will format the fields after values have been entered.

Cell A1 has the entry "Invoice." Cells B3 to B7 have the words "Item," "chair," "table," "lamp," and "pillow." The unit prices are similarly entered in cells C3 through C7. Skip the D column; those values will be calculated later. Enter the units into cells E3 through E7. Enter the words "Discount" in cell D3 and "Extended Price" in cell F3. Enter "Total," "Amount Due," and "Date" in cells G8, F10, and G10.

We wish to format the cells from A1 to G13 as centered. Highlight the entire area by clicking the mouse on cell A1 and while holding the mouse button down, drag the cursor to cell G13. Release the mouse button (the entire area will be highlighted) and choose the "Format" command followed by the "Cells" subcommand. Choose the alignment tab and Figure P6.6 appears. We wish for these values to be centered.

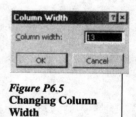

Figure P6.5
Changing Column Width

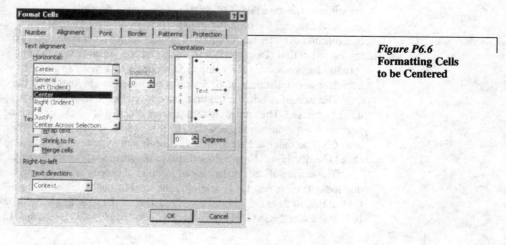

Figure P6.6
Formatting Cells to be Centered

	A	B	C	D	E	F	G
				D4		fx =IF(C4>=Discount!$A$4,Discount!$B$4,IF(C4>=Discount!$A$3,Discount!$B$3,0))	
1	INVOICE						
2							
3		Item	Unit Price	Discount	Units	Extended Price	
4		chair	$52.75	10%	15	$712.125	
5		table	$105.50	15%	4	$358.700	
6		lamp	$29.00	0%	16	$464.000	
7		pillow	$11.99	0%	56	$671.440	
8						$2,206.27	Total
9							
10						Amount Due	Date
11						$2,206.27	1/13/03
12						$2,228.33	2/12/03
13						$2,272.45	3/14/03

Figure P6.7 Formula for Calculating Discounts

The one exception for centering is the cell G8 where the word "Total" appears. The word "Total" should be aligned to the left-hand side of the cell. Using Figure P6.4 as a guide, format cells C4 through C7 as currency fields with two decimal places. Format cells D4 through D7 as percentages with zero decimal places. Cells F4 through F7 should be currency but with three decimal places. The "Total" amount (in cell F8) and the values under "Amount Due" should all be currency with only two decimal places.

The amounts of the discounts depend upon the unit price and the values in the "Discount" datasheet. This is a conditional formula which requires an "IF" statement to generate a value. Typically, an "IF" statement tells Excel that a value will be placed in the cell based on certain conditions. There will be a comparison (such as if one cell has a greater value than another) followed by the value to place in the target cell if the comparison is true followed by a value to be placed in the cell if the comparison is not true. Our "IF" statement is more complex because if the comparison is not true we wish to perform a second comparison; that is, a second "IF" statement.

Figure P6.7 illustrates the "IF" statement for cell D4. If the value in cell C4 is greater than or equal to the value in the Discount datasheet ("Discount!") cell value of $A$4 then place the value of the Discount datasheet cell $B$4 into this cell. The cell could have been denoted as simply A4 in the Discount datasheet but with the $ preceding the column and row designations we can cut and paste this formula to other cells.

If the value in C4 is not greater or equal to Discount!$A$4 then another comparison is performed. When the value in C4 is greater than or equal to Discount!$A$3 then this cell becomes the value in Discount!$B$3. If neither of the comparisons is true, the value becomes zero.

One caution: the ordering in the "IF" statements is critical when two or more are nested in a formula. An "IF" statement will stop as soon as a comparison is true. We had to take the largest value first (Discount!$A$4 equals $100). Assume that the unit price was $150. If the formula had compared the value to Discount!$A$3 first (a value of only $50) it would have been true and a discount of 10% would be placed in D4 instead of the correct value of 15%.

The extended price is the unit price times one minus the discount times the number of units purchased. The current date is placed in cell G11 as the Excel function "=NOW( )" but without the quotation marks. Cell G12 is simply cell G11 plus 30 while cell G13 is cell G11 plus 60. The dates are formatted as month-day-year only—no hours, minutes, or seconds should be displayed. Figure P6.4 displays the screen where formatting these cells occurs.

The last set of cells reflect the time value of money when paying the invoice. The amount due today (i.e., in cell G11) is simply the total of the extended prices—enter "=G8" into cell G11. After 30 days the amount owed is 101% of the total and after 60 days the amount owed is 103%. Enter "=G8*1.01" into cell G12 and "=G8*1.03" into cell G13.

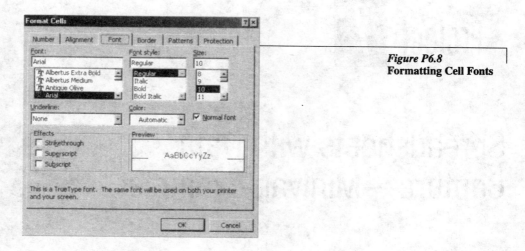

Figure P6.8
Formatting Cell Fonts

Figure P6.8 displays the screen resulting from choosing the "Format" command followed by the "Cells" command and then clicking the "Font" tab. You can make column headings bold and/or change the font size of the word "Invoice" in cell A1. Changing the fonts of cells can make the invoice example more visually appealing.

SAVING THE EXAMPLE

You should save your example as the file "ExampleP6"; Excel will automatically add the .xls extension to the file name. This way you can refer to the example as you work the assignment below.

ASSIGNMENT

1. Create a spreadsheet for orders. Figures P6.9 and P6.10 display the format of the two datasheets. Format the cells the same way (i.e., centered, currency, etc.) as they are in the figures.
2. The extended price is the price times the number of units ordered.
3. The subtotal is the sum of the extended prices.
4. The discount is obtained from the "Discount" datasheet. If the subtotal is greater than or equal to the amount in cell A4 of the "Discount" sheet then the discount amount is the value from cell B4 in the "Discount" datasheet times the subtotal. If the subtotal is greater than or equal to the amount in the "Discount" datasheet cell A3 then the discount is the percent from "Discount" datasheet cell B3 times the subtotal.
5. The total is the subtotal minus the discount amount.
6. The "Today" field should use Excel's "NOW" function.
7. The amount due after 45 days is 105% of the total. The date is 45 days past "NOW."

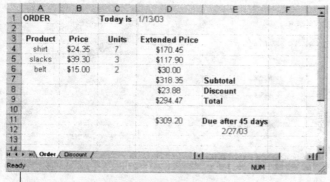

Figure P6.9 **Assignment, Order Datasheet**

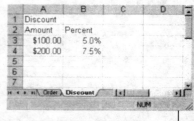

Figure P6.10 **Assignment, Discount Datasheet**

Project 7

Spreadsheets with Data Capture—Minivan Example

Learning Objectives

- Understand how calculations are made using formulas.
- Use multiple datasheets.
- Understand data capture techniques of drop-down menus, check boxes, and radio buttons.
- Learn how to use a function built into Excel.
- Learn to develop macros and to execute them with command buttons.

Introduction

This project uses Excel 2002 (also known as Excel XP) to create a spreadsheet with data capture capabilities using mouse clicks. You should have a basic understanding of spreadsheets using Excel before attempting this project. If you have completed Project 6 then you have sufficient knowledge to begin this project.

Project 8 is a companion project: it covers the same learning objectives but uses a different example. Projects 7 and 8 both cover spreadsheets with data capture concepts so that instructors have the option to further enforce those concepts with two projects or to assign different projects to students in different semesters.

Data capture in spreadsheets using a mouse click is important for two reasons: complicated or extended amounts of data can be captured easily and data entry errors are reduced. For example, book titles are frequently four words long or more. When book titles are presented to the user in a drop-down menu the user can simply click the choice and avoid typing in a long book name. Also, the choice from a list eliminates the chance that the user will incorrectly type the book title.

Data capture using mouse clicks improves the quality and speed of data capture from the user. However, these techniques require more effort in the design of the spreadsheet. The possible choices must be entered into the spreadsheet. Drop-down menus, radio buttons, and check boxes must be located on the spreadsheet. These considerations must be included in the design of the spreadsheet.

EXAMPLE

This example generates a price sheet for the Terra Traveler Minivan. The minivan has a base price and three options. The purchaser may choose a color, a type of transmission, and may choose special tires for the minivan. In the spreadsheet example a drop-down menu (also called a combo box), radio buttons, and a check box are used to capture the purchaser's choices.

As a convenience to the purchaser, the total price with options is calculated. Then the monthly payment is calculated based upon the price, interest rate, and number of months over which the minivan will be financed. The payment is calculated using a built-in Excel financial function. The last feature of the spreadsheet consists of two command buttons; one to show the amount of profit in the minivan's total price and the other to hide the amount of profit. Brief macros are written to compute and delete the profit figure and those macros are assigned to the command buttons. Figures P7.1 and Figures P7.2 display the "Car" and "Options" datasheets of the spreadsheet.

The datasheet which will supply values for data capture must be completed first. The values in the "Options" datasheet will be displayed on the "Car" datasheet. The data capture techniques, such as a drop-down menu, will not work until values are specified for the techniques.

Begin this example by opening Excel and creating a new spreadsheet. Delete a datasheet so that only two datasheets exist for the spreadsheet. Change the name of the first datasheet to "Car" and the second datasheet to "Options."

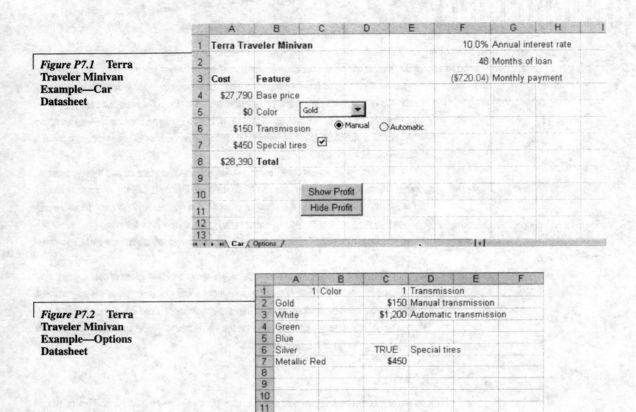

Figure P7.1 Terra Traveler Minivan Example—Car Datasheet

Figure P7.2 Terra Traveler Minivan Example—Options Datasheet

OPTIONS DATASHEET

The "Options" datasheet provides information for a drop-down menu, a set of radio buttons, and a check box. There are six color choices presented to the user and they are listed in cells A2 through A7 of the "Options" datasheet. The color choices will not incur an additional charge except for the Metallic Red color choice.

A radio button will be generated for the mutually exclusive choices of a manual transmission or an automatic transmission. Depending upon the transmission choice, the cost of the choice will change. A check box will be used to capture the purchaser's choice for special tires.

Choose the "Options" datasheet and enter the values shown in Figure P7.2. It is very important that you enter the values into the correct cells because the instructions below will assume the locations of data capture choices relate to the cells in Figure P7.2. Cells A2 through A7 present color choices. Cells C2 and C3 present the costs of transmission type choices. C7 displays the cost of choosing special tires.

Note that it is not required to have values in cells A1, C1, and C6. In general, these cells would be left blank since they are where the results of choices from the "Car" datasheet are reported. Those cells contain the results of the choices you see in Figure P7.1 so that you can see how results are reported. However, if you place a value in cell C6 make sure that it is in capital letters just like Figure P7.2.

CAR DATASHEET

The "Car" datasheet begins by placing the phrase "Terra Traveler Minivan" in cell A1. Next, format the height for rows 1 through 11 to be 18 by highlighting the rows and choosing the "Format", "Row", and "Height" commands. This will allow the data capture commands to fit easily in a row and make the spreadsheet more visually appealing. Enter "Cost" and "Feature" in cells A3 and B3. Enter the values in cells B4 through B8 as they are shown in Figure P7.1. Now enter the labels in cells G1 through G3 as shown in Figure P7.1. With these labeling values entered we are ready to define the data capture techniques.

First, the toolbar that provides form choices must be displayed. If the "Forms" toolbar is already displayed on your screen (see Figure P7.3) then you are ready to use the icons to develop data capture techniques. If the "Forms" toolbar is not already displayed, choose the "View" command followed by the "Tools" and "Forms" commands (Figure P7.4). A note of

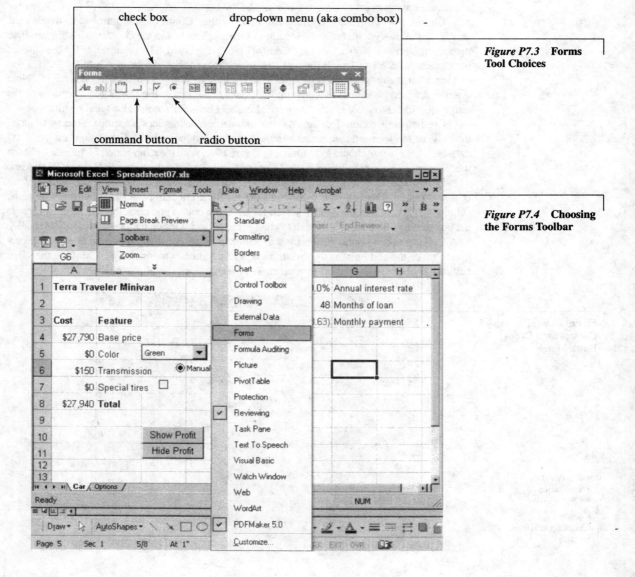

Figure P7.3 Forms Tool Choices

Figure P7.4 Choosing the Forms Toolbar

Figure P7.5 Drop-Down Menu Box with Handles

caution: the "Control Toolbox" contains icons that look similar to the "Forms" icons but it should not be chosen. Choose the "Forms" toolbar instead.

The first data capture technique will be a drop-down menu. A drop-down menu is also called a combo box. The choices to be displayed are in the "Options" datasheet in cells A2 through A7. The result of the choice should be recorded in the A1 cell. If the purchaser chooses the first choice in the list, the value 1 will be recorded. If the third choice in the list is chosen, then 3 is recorded and so forth. We need to tell Excel where to place the drop-down menu, where the choices are located, and where to record the choice.

Make sure you are in the "Car" datasheet. Click on the drop-down menu icon from the "Forms" toolbar (see Figure P7.3). Move the cursor next to the word "Color" on the datasheet. You draw the menu box by pressing the mouse button down at the top, left-hand corner of where you want the box to be and continue pressing the mouse button and releasing the button when you move the cursor to the bottom, right-hand corner of the box. The drop-down menu box appears (Figure P7.5) and you can tell it is selected to accept instructions because the handles appear at the corners and edges of the box.

Choose the "Format" command followed by the "Control" subcommand to display the screen that allows you to enter the location of menu choices and the choice result. Figure P7.6 displays the screen. Notice that the "Control" tab is displayed. The input range for the choices is "Options!$A$2:$A$7" and the cell link which records the choice is "Options!$A$1." You can see what the ranges should be from viewing the "Options" datasheet in Figure P7.2. Note that the drop-down menu is located on the "Car" datasheet so the "Options!" segment of the range tells Excel to look at the "Options" datasheet cells for menu values and results.

Creating radio buttons for manual versus automatic transmissions is a similar process. Click on the radio button icon and then create a radio button next to the word "Transmission" on the "Car" datasheet. Your button should look similar to Figure P7.7. With the radio button highlighted, choose the "Format" command followed by the "Control" command and the screen in Figure P7.8 appears.

Choose the "checked" option because you want the manual transmission to be the default option checked. The cell link value (i.e., the result of checking the radio button) should be "Options!$C$1." Close the control screen for the radio button and click the mouse cursor inside the box of the radio button. You wish to change the phrase "Option button…" to read "Manual."

Create a second radio button for the "Automatic" choice using the same method. Be certain to make the cell link for the "Automatic" radio button "Options!$C$1." Making the same cell link for both radio buttons is what makes their choice mutually exclusive.

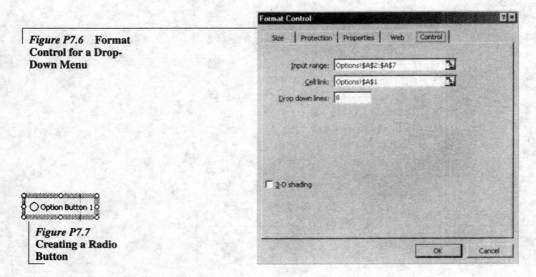

Figure P7.6 Format Control for a Drop-Down Menu

Figure P7.7 Creating a Radio Button

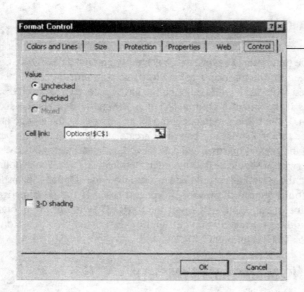

Figure P7.8 Control Screen for Radio Button

When the purchaser clicks on the "Manual" radio button a value of 1 will be placed in the cell link. Choosing the "Automatic" radio button will cause a value of 2 to be placed in the link. The order of creating the radio buttons is important: the first radio button generates a value of 1, the second generates a value of 2, and so on.

The third data capture technique is a check box. A check box in the example allows the purchaser to select special tires for the minivan. Choose the check box icon from the "Forms" toolbar and draw the check box next to the phrase "Special tires" on the "Car" datasheet. The check box appears as in Figure P7.9. Choose the "Format" command followed by the "Control" subcommand and the screen in Figure P7.10 appears. You should choose "Unchecked" so that the default for the check box is not to have special tires. The cell link is "Options!$C$6" which will record "TRUE" if the box is checked and "FALSE" if it is not checked.

Before continuing, format the cells of the datasheets as currency and percentages according to the cells in Figures P7.1 and P7.2.

Figure P7.9 Check Box Creation

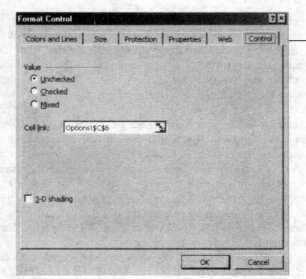

Figure P7.10 Check Box Control

CALCULATING VALUES BASED ON CHOICES

What must be done now is to associate dollar values on the "Car" datasheet based on choices captured from the purchaser. The base price is simply entered as $27,790. Cell A5 is the dollar amount charged for the minivan's color. Only one color, metallic red, incurs an additional price. Metallic red costs $250 while other colors have no cost. Create an "IF…" statement for cell A5 that tests if the value in Options!A1 is 6. "Metallic Red" is the sixth choice of the drop-down menu. If the value is 6 then charge $250; otherwise, the charge is zero.

For the price of a transmission, you must create an "IF…" statement based on the value in Options!C1. If the value is one then cell A6 on the "Car" datasheet should be set to the value in Options!C2; otherwise, it should be the amount in Options!C3. Do not code dollar figures into the "IF…" statement; those amounts should be retrieved from the "Options" datasheet.

Cell A7 should denote the price for special tires. If the special tires check box is checked, the value in cell Options!C6 will be "TRUE" (without the quotation marks) and the amount should be retrieved from cell Options!C7. This "IF…" statement would read "=IF(Options!C6=TRUE,Options!C7,0)."

CALCULATING MONTHLY PAYMENTS

The total amount in cell A8 is just the sum of cells A4 through A7. That amount is used to calculate the monthly payment. To use the built-in "PMT" financial function in Excel you must have an amount, an interest rate, and a number of payments. Purchasers normally make payments each month for a number of years. A four year loan would take 48 months of payments. Interest rates are expressed as a percentage per year.

The general expression for payments is "=PMT(interest rate, # of periods, present value)." In the example, the interest rate is contained in cell F1 while the number of periods is in F2. The present value (i.e., the amount of the loan) is the total in cell A8. We must divide the annual percentage by 12 so that the rate is expressed as the interest rate per month because the payments are made on a monthly basis. Note that dividing an annual interest rate by 12 only approximates the monthly interest rate but the approximation is sufficient for our example. The formula for a monthly payment becomes "=PMT((F1/12),F2,A8)."

SHOWING THE PROFIT

Macros in Excel can be generated either by writing programming code or by recording the sequence of keystrokes performed by the user. Keystroke recording is an effective tool that is easy to achieve. Recording a sequence of keystrokes into a macro is an important tool for completing a complex sequence of steps using a single key stroke.

At some point you may design a spreadsheet that is particularly complex. One application of the spreadsheet may require you to reformat all currency values, change row heights, add new fields, and change formulas for calculating results. Even if you are proficient at using Excel, you could make a mistake in performing one of the steps.

Even more important, you would not be able to entrust these actions to one of your subordinates who might not be proficient in Excel. In order to achieve the efficiency of processing, avoid mistakes, and enable subordinates with little training to accomplish the same results you can record the sequence of steps in a macro that can be run later with the click of a mouse.

In our example we will make two macros, one to generate and show the profit from the purchase and one to hide the profit by deleting the cell that calculates the profit. Begin by choosing the "Tools" command followed by the "Macro" and "Record New Macro" commands as shown in Figure P7.11. Name this new macro "Show."

At this point, every cursor click and key stroke will be recorded. To create a macro to show the profit, click on cell A10 in the "Car" datasheet. Every mouse click is important; it is

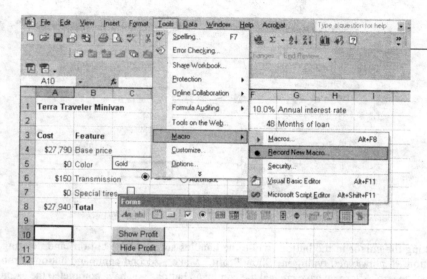

Figure P7.11 Steps to Begin Recording a Macro

important to begin this macro by choosing cell A10. Even if the cursor is already pointing to cell A10 when you begin recording the macro, click on cell A10 again.

In the cell enter the formula of "=A8*.1" to calculate the amount of profit as 10% of the total cost. Then press the "Enter" key. Now choose the "Tools" command followed by "Macro" and "Stop Recording" commands as shown in Figure P7.12.

Create another macro using the same procedure. This macro should be named "Hide." The "Hide" macro should click the cursor to cell A10 and then press the delete key. That will remove the formula that calculates the profit and therefore the profit amount becomes hidden.

Macros can be executed using a sequence of commands but that would defy the reason for creating a macro (i.e., to use a mouse click instead of commands). Refer to Figure P7.3 and choose the icon for creating a command button. Place the button in the "Car" datasheet as shown for the "Show Profit" button in Figure P7.1.

You will be asked to assign a macro to the command button you just created; choose the "Show" macro. Change the button name from "Button..." to "Show Profit." Do this by

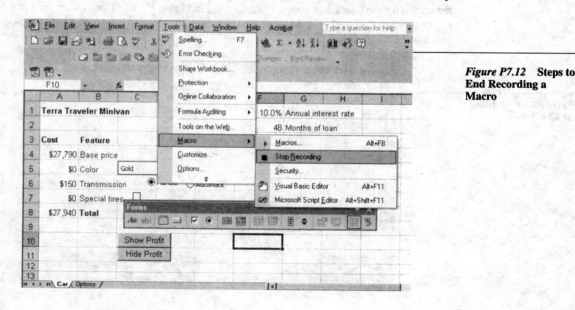

Figure P7.12 Steps to End Recording a Macro

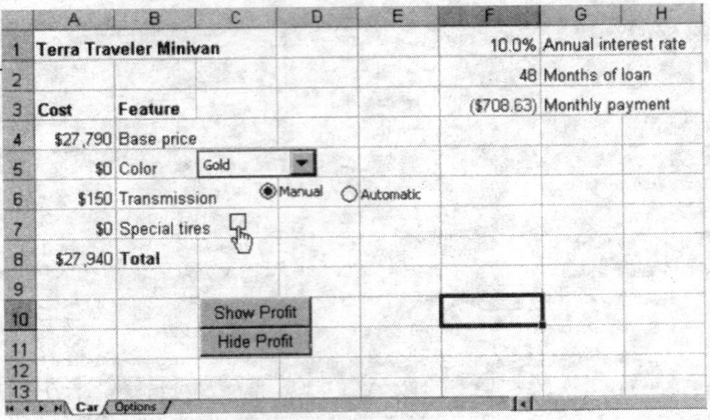

Figure P7.13
Highlighting the Check Box

clicking the cursor in the button (while the handles surround the button) and deleting the "Button..." phrase and typing in "Show Profit." Make a second command button to run the "Hide" macro. After you have created the command buttons you have completed the example.

SAVING AND EDITING THE EXAMPLE

You should save your example as the file "ExampleP7." Excel will automatically add the .xls extension to the file name. This way you can refer to the example as you work the assignment below.

Try using the spreadsheet you have just created. Make sure that the data capture techniques work correctly. Also make sure that the calculations and formatting are correct. If you have an error in a drop-down menu, check box, or radio button then you will need to edit the field. The first problem you have is the selection of the field; Excel assumes you want to enter data when you click the cursor on the field.

Assume the check box does not work correctly. Move the cursor over the check box and the cursor image changes to a fist with one finger extended (see Figure P7.13). By pressing the right mouse button (as opposed to the left mouse button which is normally pressed) you will see the menu of choices in Figure P7.14. When you choose the "Format Control" option the screen for the check box appears just as it did in Figure P7.10. Now you are able to make any changes to the check box that are necessary. Similar steps are taken to edit the drop-down menu and radio buttons.

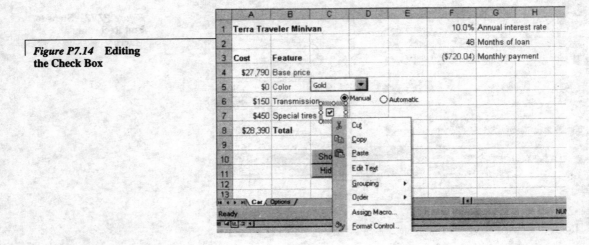

Figure P7.14 Editing the Check Box

Assignment

1. Create a spreadsheet that documents sandwich selection using datasheets similar to Figures P7.15 and P7.16.
2. Your spreadsheet should have only two datasheets and they should be labeled "Menu" and "Prices."
3. Create a drop-down menu on the "Menu" datasheet that has the choices of "Turkey," "Chicken," "Ham," "Beef," and "Vegan" as shown on the "Prices" datasheet. *Hint:* it will be easier to create data capture boxes if the row heights are set to 18.
4. The price for all drop-down menu sandwich choices is $5.95 except for the "Vegan" choice, which is $3.95.
5. Create three radio buttons for the bread type. There is no additional cost for white or wheat bread but if rye bread is chosen there should be a $.35 extra charge.
6. There are check boxes for mayonnaise, mustard, and ketchup. The additional cost of each is shown on the "Prices" datasheet. Retrieve these prices from the "Prices" datasheet.
7. Calculate the total price as the sum of the price of the sandwich, bread, and condiments. Format the prices as currency fields with two decimal places.
8. Create a macro that selects the special for the day. The special is a vegan sandwich on rye with mayonnaise, mustard, and ketchup. You should create the macro by recording key strokes as demonstrated in the example. Note that the changes you make for the special must be on the "Prices" datasheet and not the "Menu" datasheet. Macros do not record choices from form boxes.
   Hint: You should begin the macro by clicking the mouse on some cell in the "Menu" datasheet, clicking on the "Prices" datasheet, changing values on the "Prices" datasheet, and finally clicking back on a cell in the "Menu" datasheet.

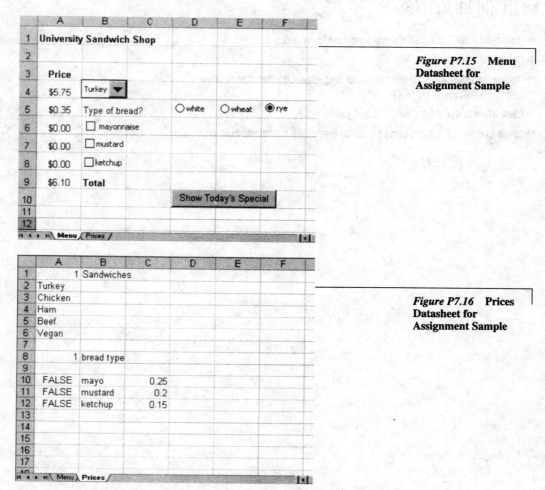

Figure P7.15 Menu Datasheet for Assignment Sample

Figure P7.16 Prices Datasheet for Assignment Sample

Project 8

Spreadsheets with Data Capture—College Computing Example

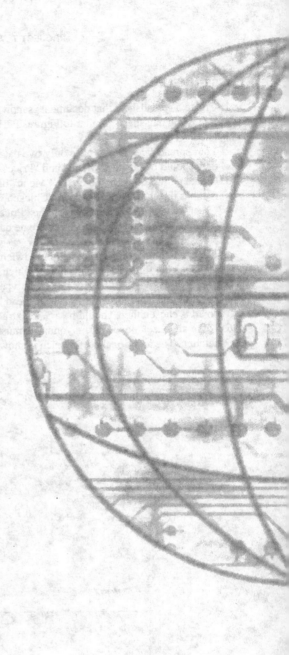

Learning Objectives

➡ Understand how calculations are made using formulas.
➡ Use multiple datasheets.
➡ Understand data capture techniques of drop-down menus, check boxes, and radio buttons.
➡ Learn how to use a function built into Excel.
➡ Learn to develop macros and to execute them with command buttons.

Introduction

This project uses Excel 2002 (also known as Excel XP) to create a spreadsheet with data capture capabilities using mouse clicks. You should have a basic understanding of spreadsheets using Excel before attempting this project. If you have completed Project 6 then you have sufficient knowledge to begin this project.

Project 7 is a companion project; it covers the same learning objectives but uses a different example. Projects 7 and 8 both cover spreadsheets with data capture concepts so that instructors have the option to further enforce those concepts with two projects or to assign different projects to students in different semesters.

Data capture in spreadsheets using a mouse click is important for two reasons: complicated or extended amounts of data can be captured easily and data entry errors are reduced. For example, book titles are frequently four words long or more. When book titles are presented to the user in a drop-down menu, the user can simply click the choice and avoid typing in a long book name. Also, the choice from a list eliminates the chance that the user will incorrectly type the book title.

Data capture using mouse clicks improves the quality and speed of data capture from the user. However, these techniques require more effort in the design of the spreadsheet. The possible choices must be entered into the spreadsheet. Drop-down menus, radio buttons, and check boxes must be located on the spreadsheet. These considerations must be included in the design of the spreadsheet.

EXAMPLE

This example generates a price sheet for purchasing a computer from College Computing. The purchaser may choose a computer model, a type of monitor, and may be able to take advantage of two discounts. In the spreadsheet example a drop-down menu (also called a combo box), radio buttons, and a check box are used to capture the purchaser's choices.

The last feature of the spreadsheet consists of a command button to automatically make selections for the "best buy." A brief macro is written to choose the options of the "best buy" and the macro is assigned to a command button. Figures P8.1 and P8.2 display the "Computers" and "Prices" datasheets of the spreadsheet.

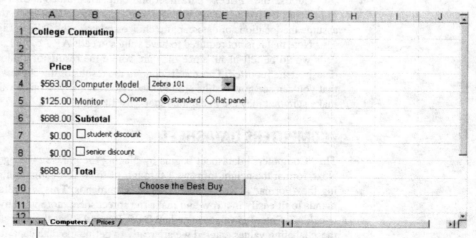

Figure P8.1 College Computing Example—Computers Datasheet

Figure P8.2 College Computing Example—Prices Datasheet

	A	B	C	D
1		1	Computer	
2	Zebra 101	563		
3	Lion 303	849		
4	Turkey 106	421		
5				
6		2	Monitor	
7	none		0	
8	standard		125	
9	flat		325	
10				
11	FALSE	student	0.05	
12	FALSE	senior	0.075	

\\ Computers \ Prices /

The datasheet that will supply values for data capture must be completed first. The values in the "Prices" datasheet will be displayed on the "Computers" datasheet. The data capture techniques, such as a drop-down menu, will not work until values are specified for the techniques.

Begin this example by opening Excel and creating a new spreadsheet. Delete a datasheet so that only two datasheets exist for the spreadsheet. Change the name of the first datasheet to "Computers" and the second datasheet to "Prices."

PRICES DATASHEET

The "Prices" datasheet provides information for a drop-down menu, a set of radio buttons, and a check box. There are three computer model choices presented to the user and they are listed in cells A2 through A4 of the "Prices" datasheet. The model choices incur specific dollar costs that are presented in cells B2 through B4 of the "Prices" datasheet.

A radio button will be generated for the mutually exclusive choices of no monitor, a standard monitor, and a flat panel monitor. Depending upon the monitor choice, the cost will change. A check box will be used to capture the information about a discount for students and for seniors.

Choose the "Prices" datasheet and enter the values shown in Figure P8.2. It is very important that you enter the values into the correct cells because the instructions below will assume the locations of data capture choices relate to the cells in Figure P8.2.

Note that it is not required to have values in cells A1, A6, A11, and A12. In general, these cells would be left blank since they are where the results of choices from the "Computers" datasheet are reported. Those cells contain the results of the choices you see in Figure P8.1 so that you can see how results are reported. However, if you place values in cells A11 and A12 make sure that they are in capital letters just like Figure P8.2.

COMPUTERS DATASHEET

The "Computers" datasheet begins by placing the phrase "College Computing" in cell A1. Next, format the height for rows 1 through 11 to be 18 by highlighting these rows and choosing the "Format", "Row", and "Height" commands. This will allow the data capture commands to fit easily in a row and make the spreadsheet more visually appealing. Enter "Price" in cell A3. Enter the values in cells B4, B5, B6, and B9 as they are shown in Figure P8.1. With these labeling values entered we are ready to define the data capture techniques.

First, the toolbar that provides form choices must be displayed. If the "Forms" toolbar is already displayed on your screen (see Figure P8.3), then you are ready to use the icons to

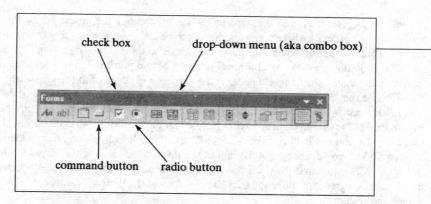

Figure P8.3 Forms Tool Choices

develop data capture techniques. If the "Forms" toolbar is not already displayed, choose the "View" command followed by the "Tools" and "Forms" commands (Figure P8.4). A note of caution: the "Control Toolbox" contains icons that look similar to the "Forms" icons but it should not be chosen. Choose the "Forms" toolbar instead.

The first data capture technique will be a drop-down menu. The drop-down menu is also called a combo box. The choices to be displayed are in the "Prices" datasheet in cells A2 through A4. The result of the choice should be recorded in the A1 cell. If the purchaser chooses the first choice in the list, the value 1 will be recorded. If the third choice in the list is chosen (Turkey 106) then 3 is recorded in cell A1 and so forth. We need to tell Excel where to place the drop-down menu, where the choices are located, and where to record the choice.

Make sure you are in the "Computers" datasheet. Click on the drop-down menu icon from the "Forms" toolbar (see Figure P8.3). Move the cursor next to the phrase "Computer

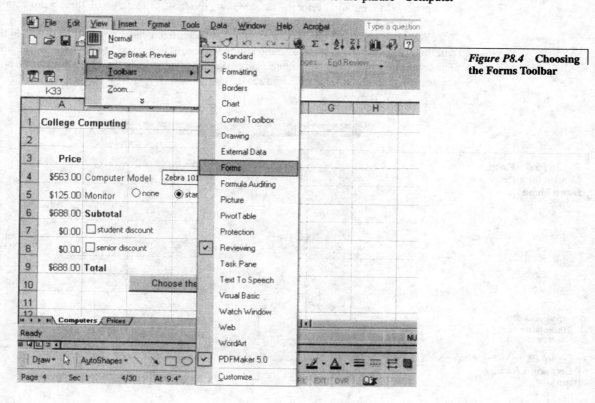

Figure P8.4 Choosing the Forms Toolbar

Figure P8.5 Drop-Down Menu Box with Handles

Model" on the datasheet. You draw the menu box by pressing the mouse button down at the top, left-hand corner of where you want the box to be and continue pressing the mouse button and releasing the button when you move the cursor to the bottom, right-hand corner of the box. The drop-down menu box appears (Figure P8.5) and you can tell it is selected to accept instructions because the handles appear at the corners and edges of the box.

Choose the "Format" command followed by the "Control" subcommand to display the screen that allows you to enter the location of menu choices and the choice result. Figure P8.6 is the format control screen. Notice that the "Control" tab is displayed. The input range for the choices is "Prices!$A$2:$A$4" and the cell link which records the choice is "Prices!$A$1." You can see what the ranges should be from viewing the "Options" datasheet in Figure P8.2. Note that the drop-down menu is located on the "Computers" datasheet so the "Prices!" segment of the range tells Excel to look at the "Prices" datasheet cells for menu values and results.

Creating radio buttons for monitor choices is a similar process. Click on the radio button icon (Figure P8.3) and then create a radio button next to the word "Monitor" on the "Computers" datasheet. Your button should look similar to Figure P8.7. With the radio button highlighted, choose the "Format" command followed by the "Control" command and the screen in Figure P8.8 appears.

Choose the "checked" option because you want no monitor (i.e., "none") to be the default option checked. The cell link value (i.e., the result of checking the radio button) should be "Prices!$A$6." Close the control screen for the radio button and click the mouse cursor inside the box of the radio button. You wish to change the phrase "Option button..." to read "none."

Create a second radio button for the "standard" choice using the same method and a third radio button for the "flat panel" choice. Be certain to make the cell link for the "standard" and "flat panel" radio buttons "Prices!$A$6." Making the same cell link for all three radio buttons is what makes their choice mutually exclusive.

When the purchaser clicks on the "none" radio button a value of 1 will be placed in the cell link. Choosing the "standard" radio button will cause a value of 2 to be placed in the link. The order of creating the radio buttons is important: the first radio button generates a value of 1, the second generates a value of 2, and so on.

Figure P8.6 Format Control for a Drop-Down Menu

Figure P8.7 Creating a Radio Button

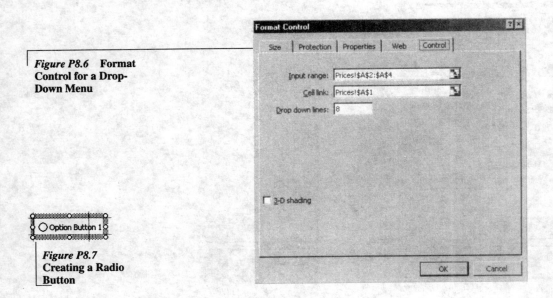

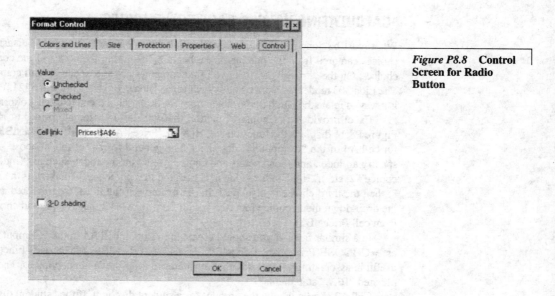

Figure P8.8 Control Screen for Radio Button

The third data capture technique is a check box. This technique will be used to capture data about two types of discounts. One check box in the example allows the purchaser to select a student discount and the other selects a senior discount. Choose the check box icon from the "Forms" toolbar and draw the check box across cells B7 and C7 as shown on the "Computers" datasheet. The check box appears as in Figure P8.9. Choose the "Format" command followed by the "Control" subcommand and the screen in Figure P8.10 appears. You should choose "Unchecked" so that the default for the check box is not to have a student discount. The cell link is "Prices!$A$11" which will record "TRUE" if the box is checked and "FALSE" if it is not checked.

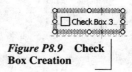

Figure P8.9 Check Box Creation

Add a check box for a senior discount in a similar manner. Then format the cells of the datasheets according to the cells in Figures P8.1 and P8.2.

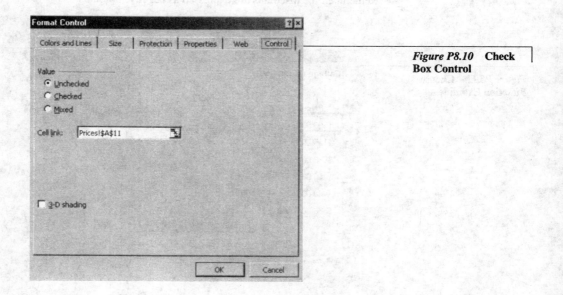

Figure P8.10 Check Box Control

CALCULATING VALUES BASED ON CHOICES

What must be done now is to associate dollar values on the "Computers" datasheet based on choices captured from the purchaser. We begin by capturing the prices of the computer model choices. On the "Prices" datasheet you find computer prices associated with computer models. The Lion 303 model has a price of $849 while the Turkey 106 has a price of $421. What is needed is a way to relate the purchaser's choice from the drop-down menu to the list of prices.

Excel provides a "Choose" function that will let us associate prices to menu choices. Figure P8.11 displays the function "=CHOOSE(Prices!A1,Prices!B2,Prices!B3,Prices!B4)" for cell A4 of the "Computers" datasheet. The general format of the "Choose" function is to specify an index and then specify the choices based on the index such as "(index, choice #1, choice #2, etc.)." If the index value is 1, then the first choice is displayed. If the index value is 3, then the third choice is displayed. In our example if the index (represented as the result of the drop-down menu choice reported in cell Prices!A1) is 2 then the second choice (the value from cell Prices!B3) is reported.

In a similar fashion you should create the value in cell A5 in the "Computers" datasheet as "=CHOOSE(Prices!A6, Prices!B7, Prices!B8, Prices!B9)." "Choose" functions are very useful in associating prices and other attributes to drop-down menu choices. They avoid complicated "IF..." statements.

Cell A7 should denote the amount for a student discount. If the "student discount" check box is checked, the value in cell Prices!A11 will be "TRUE" (without the quotation marks) and the amount of the discount should be retrieved from cell Prices!C11. The calculation for cell A7 in the "Computers" datasheet (Figure P8.12) should read "=IF(Prices!A11=TRUE, (-Prices!C11*A6), 0)." This statement says that if the student discount is checked (i.e., the value in cell Prices!A11 is "TRUE") then enter the discount amount here. The amount is a negative number showing the product of the discount amount from Prices!C11 times the subtotal amount from cell A6 on the "Computers" datasheet. If the check box is not checked, the value is zero.

You must make a similar formula for the senior discount. The values of the discount must be retrieved from the "Prices" datasheet and not coded into the "IF..." statements. The actual dollar amount of the discounts depends upon the dollar amount of the subtotal.

The subtotal is the sum of cells A4 and A5 while the total is the sum of cells A6, A7, and A8. Remember, the discounts are expressed as negative amounts.

Figure P8.11 Choose Function Example

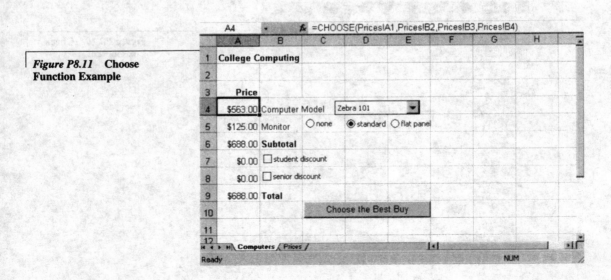

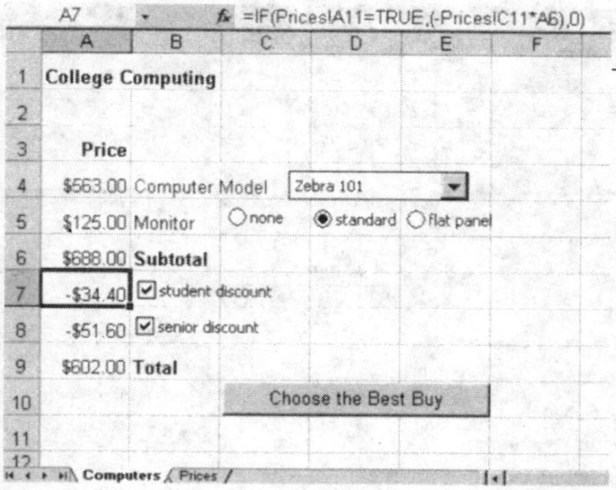

Figure P8.12
Computing the Student Discount

CHOOSING THE BEST BUY

Macros in Excel can be generated either by writing programming code or by recording the sequence of keystrokes performed by the user. Keystroke recording is an effective tool that is easy to achieve. Recording a sequence of keystrokes into a macro is an important tool for completing a complex sequence of steps using a single keystroke.

At some point you may design a spreadsheet that is particularly complex. One application of the spreadsheet may require you to reformat all currency values, change row heights, add new fields, and change formulas for calculating results. Even if you are proficient at using Excel, you could make a mistake in performing one of the steps.

Even more important, you would not be able to entrust these actions to one of your subordinates who might not be proficient in Excel. In order to achieve the efficiency of processing, avoid mistakes, and enable subordinates with little training to accomplish the same results, you can record the sequence of steps in a macro that can be run later with the click of a mouse.

The "best buy" for our example will be the choice of a Zebra 101 computer model and a standard monitor. The best buy is not affected by discounts so you ignore those check boxes. Choices are made by specifying values in the "Prices" datasheet. Mouse clicks for form choices are not recorded by the macro.

To make a macro that chooses the "best buy" for the purchaser begin by choosing the "Tools" command followed by the "Macro" and "Record New Macro" commands as shown in Figure P8.13. Name this new macro "Best."

At this point, every cursor click and key stroke will be recorded. To create a macro to choose the best buy, click on cell A10 in the "Computers" datasheet. If you are not in the "Computers" datasheet when you begin the macro, navigate to the "Computers" datasheet. Every mouse click is important: It is important to begin this macro by choosing a cell in the "Computers" datasheet. Even if the cursor is already pointing to cell A10 in the "Computers" datasheet when you begin recording the macro, click on cell A10 again.

Navigate to the "Prices" datasheet and enter the value "1" (without quotation marks) in cell A1. That selects the first menu choice, Zebra 101, for the computer model. Next enter the value "2" in cell A6. That relates to the second radio button created, the button for a standard monitor.

Even if the values "1" and "2" are already in cells A1 and A6, enter the values again. The macro must record that you are entering values, not just moving the cursor around on the datasheet.

Figure P8.13 Steps to Begin Recording a Macro

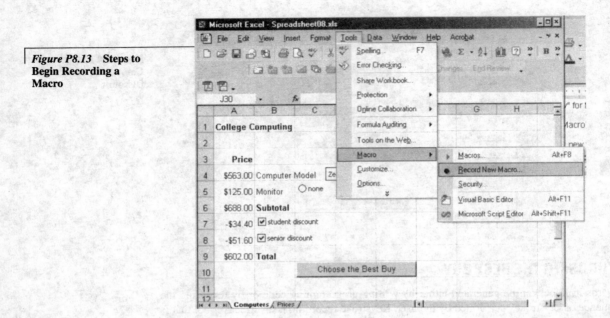

Navigate back to the "Computers" datasheet. Click the cursor on cell A10 so that at the end of the macro execution you are taken to the "Computers" datasheet to the same cell where the macro begins. Now choose the "Tools" command followed by "Macro" and "Stop Recording" commands as shown in Figure P8.14.

Macros can be executed using a sequence of commands but that would defy the reason for creating a macro: that is, to use a mouse click instead of commands. Refer to Figure P8.3 and choose the icon for creating a command button. Place the button in the "Computers" datasheet as shown for the "Choose the Best Buy" button in Figure P8.1.

You will be asked to assign a macro to the command button you just created; choose the "Best" macro. Change the button name from "Button…" to "Choose the Best Buy." Do this by clicking the cursor in the button (while the handles surround the button) and deleting the "Button…" phrase and typing in "Choose the Best Buy." After you have created the command button you have completed the example.

SAVING AND EDITING THE EXAMPLE

You should save your example as the file "ExampleP8." Excel will automatically add the .xls extension to the file name. This way you can refer to the example as you work the assignment below.

Try using the spreadsheet you have just created. Make sure that the data capture techniques work correctly. Also make sure that the calculations and formatting are correct. If you have an error in a drop-down menu, check box, or radio button, then you will need to edit the field. The first problem you have is the selection of the field; Excel assumes you want to enter data when you click the cursor on the field.

Assume the drop-down does not work correctly. Move the cursor over the drop-down menu and the cursor image changes to a fist with one finger extended (see Figure P8.15). By pressing the right mouse button (as opposed to the left mouse button which is normally pressed), you will see the menu of choices in Figure P8.16. When you choose "Format Control" option the screen for the drop-down menu appears just as it did in Figure P8.6. Now you are able to make any changes to the drop-down menu that are necessary. Similar steps are taken to edit the check boxes and radio buttons.

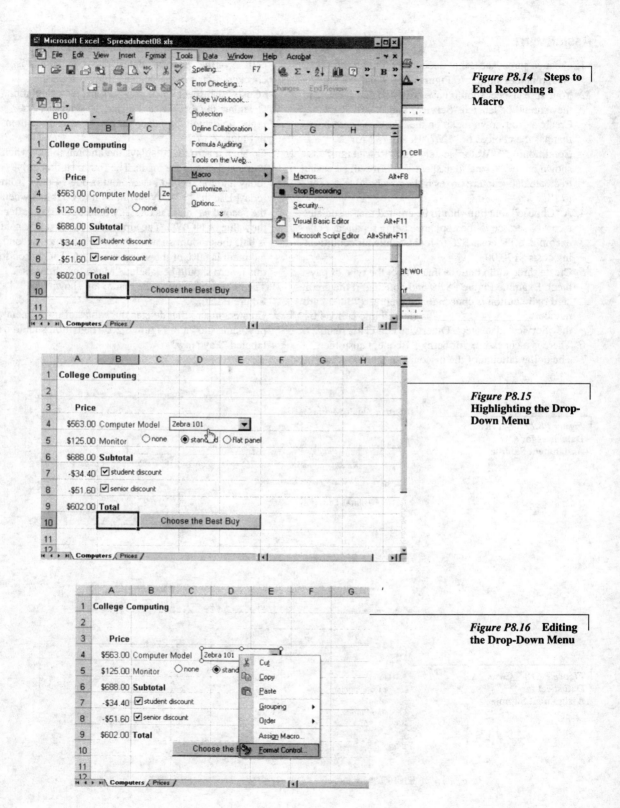

Figure P8.14 Steps to End Recording a Macro

Figure P8.15 Highlighting the Drop-Down Menu

Figure P8.16 Editing the Drop-Down Menu

Assignment

1. Create a spreadsheet that documents routine service on appliances similar to Figures P8.17 and P8.18.
2. Your spreadsheet should have only two datasheets and they should be labeled "Service" and "Costs."
3. Create a drop-down menu on the "Service" datasheet that has the choices of "TV," "Heating," "Air Conditioning," "Water Heater," and "Refrigerator" as shown on the "Costs" datasheet. *Hint:* it will be easier to create data capture boxes if the row heights are set to 18.
4. A "Choose" function should be created that associates a cost of service to the appliance being repaired. For example, a TV costs $25 to repair while air conditioning costs $170.00.
5. Create three radio buttons that reflect the type of payment. Examine Figure P8.19 and note that if the credit card radio button is chosen that the phrase "Enter card number _____" is entered into cell G4 of the "Service" datasheet. Otherwise cell G4 is blank.
6. There is a check box for being a frequent customer. The dollar amount of the discount should be shown in cell A5 of the "Service" datasheet when the box is checked. Retrieve the percent amount from the "Costs" datasheet when you perform the calculation.
7. Calculate the total price. Format the prices as currency fields with two decimal places as you see them in Figure 8.17.
8. Create a macro that displays the amount to pay when two installments are made. The first installment is today and the second installment is due 14 days from today. Use the "=NOW()" function to establish when the second payment is due; it would be 14 days after the value of NOW(). The amount of the first payment is half the amount shown in cell A6 while the second payment is 60% of the value in cell A6. The button for this macro should be labeled "Make Installments." The results of running the macro are shown in Figure P8.20.
9. Create a macro that deletes the values of installment payments shown in Figure 8.20. The button should be labeled "Pay Now."

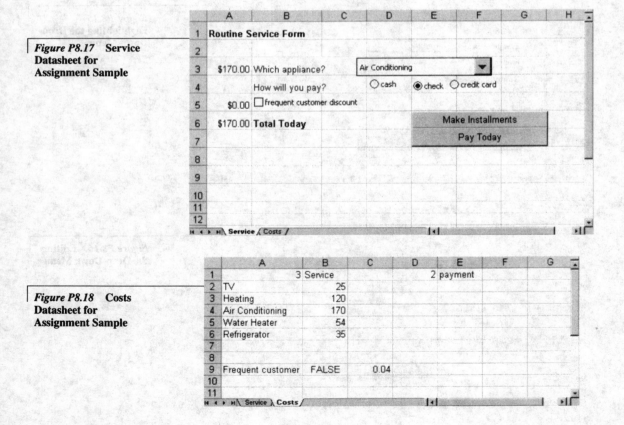

Figure P8.17 Service Datasheet for Assignment Sample

Figure P8.18 Costs Datasheet for Assignment Sample

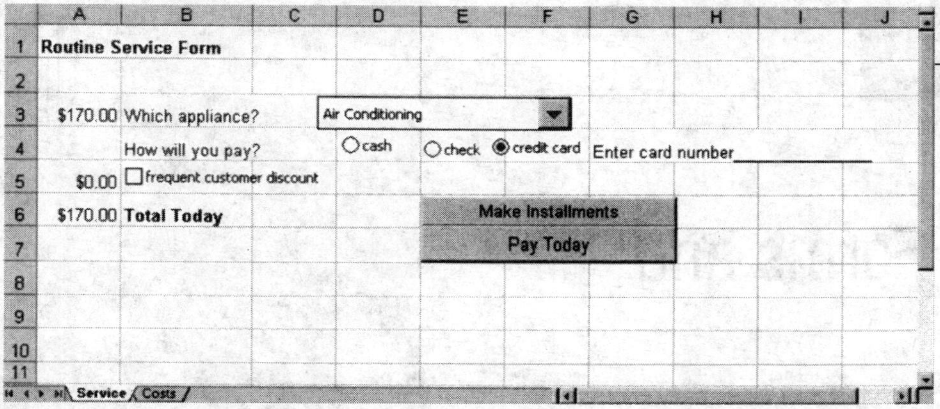

PROJECT 8 SPREADSHEETS WITH DATA CAPTURE—COLLEGE COMPUTING EXAMPLE ••• **343**

Figure P8.19
Showing an Entry for Credit Card Number

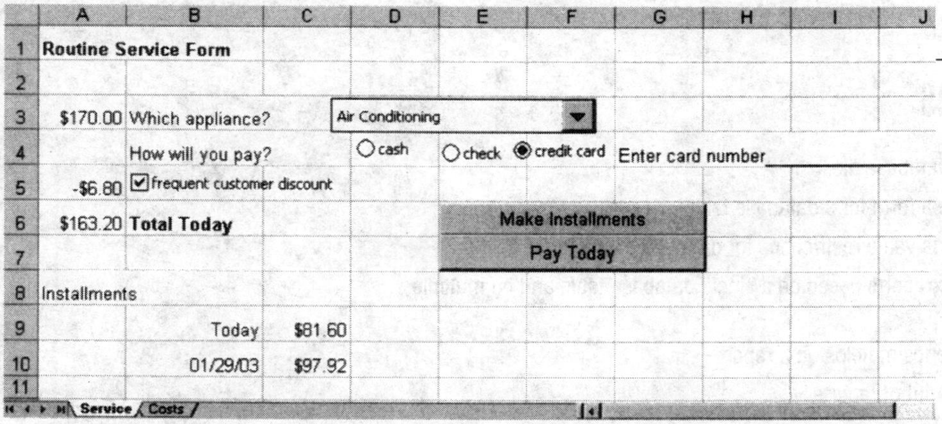

Figure P8.20 **Results of Clicking the "Make Installments" Macro**

Project 9

Database Forms and Reports

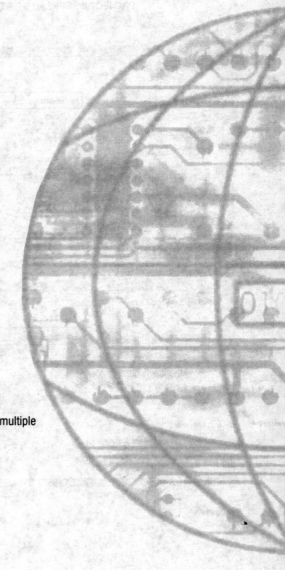

Learning Objectives

- Learn to use an existing database file.
- Understand how to create a form for a database table.
- Learn how to generate data value restrictions for data fields on a form.
- Understand how to create reports based on a single database table and on multiple database tables.
- Learn to calculate summaries of fields on a report.
- Learn how to alter the format of reports.

Introduction

This project uses Access 2002 (also known as Access XP) to create a form and several reports for an existing database. The initial database can be downloaded from the Prentice Hall Web site for the text at WWW.PRENHALL.COM/MCLEOD—"mcleod" must be in lower-case letters. The database for this project concerns classes and the books used in those classes. The database also contains records of students who have copies of books to sell.

An Access database is a single file. Although there may be many tables in a database, they are all contained in the single database file along with any forms, reports, or other components of the database. You should create a copy of the data file with your database on a regular basis. You can save the copy to a diskette, a Zip disk, or some other medium of your choice.

If you use a floppy disk or Zip disk to store your database, always wait until you have completely exited Access and writing to the database has stopped before you remove the disk from the drive. Database management software works closely with the computer's operating system and sometimes the writing of information back to the database file occurs when you exit the database. Removing the disk early could result in losing your entire database.

Within Access you are able to use the "Edit" command to cut and paste objects. Those objects are tables, reports, and similar components of the database. You cannot copy the database itself from within Access. To copy the entire database, such as for a backup copy, you must copy the entire database file using Windows Explorer or clicking on the "My Computer" icon.

One last caution about using database software is that the database file size can grow quickly. Users like features such as the "Undo" command that can easily reverse mistakes. Such features come at a price—they require much disk space in the database file to guide the reversal of actions taken. To keep your database file at a reasonable size you should compact it on a regular basis, such as every time you exit Access.

From within Access, the "Tools," "Database Utilities," and "Compact and Repair Database" sequence of commands will compact your database to remove all of the deletions and missteps that you may have performed while using the database. You can change the Access settings to automatically compact the database each time you exit Access. "Tools," followed by "Options," "General," and "Compact on Close" will have Access automatically compact the database. However, many universities limit the ability of students to change computer settings so you may have to explicitly compact your database each time you use Access.

EXAMPLE

This example will generate a form for data entry into the STUDENT table. It will also create a report of class enrollments and a list of books used in classes along with their prices. These exercises illustrate the common applications for which many people use a database. This project uses the Textbook database which will be provided by your instructor or downloaded from the Prentice Hall Web site.

Textbook Database

The Textbook database consists of four tables that relate to each other by common values. The tables and their data fields are shown in Figure P9.1. The STUDENT table contains four fields; FirstName, LastName, BookNumb, and CopiesToSell. The key fields of the tables are shown in bold font. It takes the combination of values from the FirstName, LastName, and BookNumb fields to make a key (i.e., a unique value) for the STUDENT table. The ClassNumb field is the only field needed to be the key of the CLASS table.

The fields from different tables can be combined when a common value exists between the two tables. For example, the field BookNumb is in both the STUDENT table and the BOOK table. If the value of BookNumb is 409 in the BOOK table and in the STUDENT table, then the name of the student from the STUDENT table can be associated with the book title of the BOOK record. From Figure P9.2 you can see Amy Abner and Brian Janski both have book number 409 to sell. Book number 409 (see Figure P9.3) has a title of "Management Information Systems" and was authored by McLeod and Schell.

For the projects and assignments in this text you will only have to use an existing database; you will not be required to create a database or tables within a database. Any changes to the format or values in fields will be accomplished through the use of forms and reports in this project.

Begin this project by opening the Access program and then opening the Textbook database. Figure P9.4 will appear. Notice from Figure P9.4 that the "Tables" tab is chosen.

Creating a Form

Entering data into a table can be aided by the use of a form. Table forms not only allow for data entry but they display one record from a table at a time. Since a database table can contain very many records, displaying one record at a time can make it easier for a user to view records. In our example we will create a form for the STUDENT table.

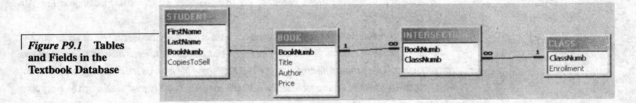

Figure P9.1 Tables and Fields in the Textbook Database

Figure P9.2 Values in the STUDENT Table

FirstName	LastName	BookNumb	CopiesToSell
Amy	Abner	409	1
Bell	Ringer	32	1
Bette	Chancer	32	10
Betty	Donner	12	1
Betty	Donner	371	1
Bill	Eschew	16	3
Bill	Eschew	31	2
Bill	Eschew	32	2
Bill	Eschew	191	2
Bill	Eschew	200	1
Bill	Leer	191	1
Bill	Leer	371	5
Brian	Janski	409	1
Charles	Darling	121	1
Charles	Darling	371	1
Chris	Lee	12	1
Cindy	Rellash	12	2
Cindy	Rellash	24	1
Cindy	Rellash	191	5
Claire	Moore	27	6

Record: 38 of 60

BookNumb	Title	Author	Price
12	Finance for Me	Poe and Tattem	$78.75
16	Stock Crisis	Plankton	$35.90
24	Counting Pennies	Durgee	$108.10
31	Costing Products	Gough and Howe	$123.45
32	The Growing Economy	Birch	$72.00
101	Personnel Files	Hiram	$78.24
121	Employee Termination	Fletcher	$72.10
191	Selling Yourself	Tattem and Green	$83.00
206	Market Research	Shi	$95.62
231	Data Mining	Thurston and Gradston	$101.50
276	Cash Management	Packard	$29.75
371	Counting By The Numbers	Bongberd	$61.00
409	Management Information Systems	McLeod and Schell	$60.50

Figure P9.3 Values in the BOOK Table

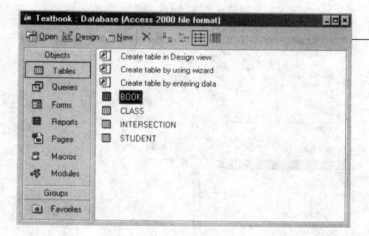

Figure P9.4 Textbook Database Screen

In addition to simple data viewing and data entry, forms can be used to test the values entered and reject values that are in error. In the Textbook database, book numbers should have values less than 1,000 and that rule will be placed in the form design. Data rules in the definition of the data field itself are automatically enforced within a form. During the definition of the STUDENT table, the data field CopiesToSell was constrained to be 10 or less so any form generated will enforce that rule.

Click on the "Forms" tab and the "Create form by using wizard" option as shown in Figure P9.5. A "wizard" is a procedure Access uses to walk you through the development of an object (such as a form) in a step-by-step method. Wizards can generate many of the forms and reports you need. Sometimes you may need to modify the form or report generated but that will be discussed later.

Double-click on the "Create form by using wizard" option. When the screen in Figure P9.6 appears, you must use the drop-down menu to choose the STUDENT table. When Figure P9.7 appears, highlight each field (such as FirstName) and then move it to the "Selected Fields" area by clicking the ">" button. Now click on the "Next" button.

You want a "Columnar" choice of form layout in the next screen followed by a "Standard" choice of style in the following screen. Moving from one screen to the next is achieved by clicking the "Next" button. When the screen in Figure P9.8 appears, change the title to be "Student Data Entry Form." Now click the "Finish" button. Figure P9.9 appears with the completed form. Spend a moment clicking on the buttons that move through the

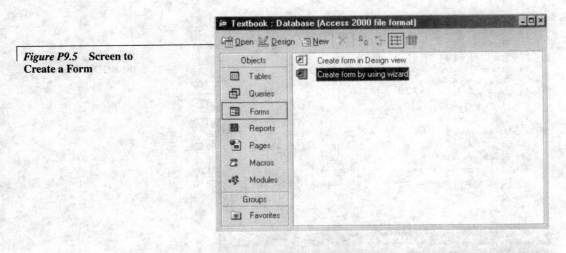

Figure P9.5 Screen to Create a Form

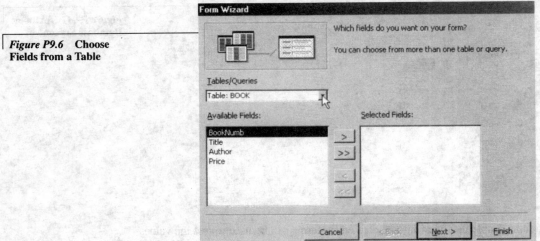

Figure P9.6 Choose Fields from a Table

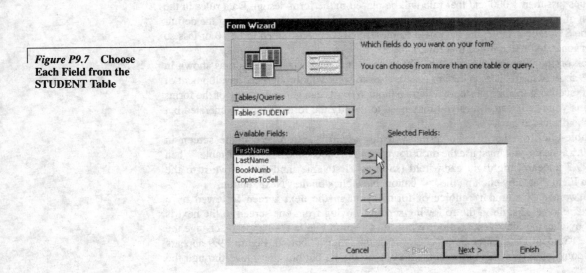

Figure P9.7 Choose Each Field from the STUDENT Table

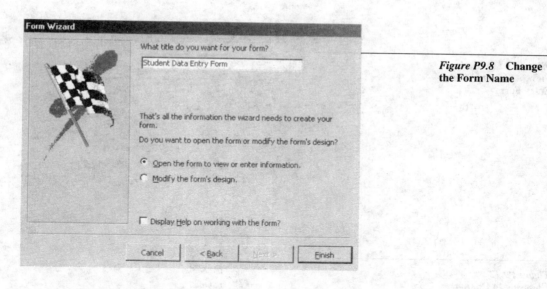

Figure P9.8 Change the Form Name

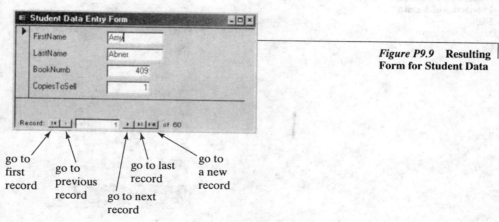

Figure P9.9 Resulting Form for Student Data

records. If you click on the navigation button that moves to a new record all the fields are blank and Access expects you to enter new data.

Enter a new record. The first name should be "Aaron" (do not include the quotation marks around any of these data entries). The last name should be "Ackerman," the number of the book is "409," and the copies to sell should be "11". When you try to move to the next record Figure P9.10 appears. Remember that the data field definition for the CopiesToSell field was set to 10 or less. Access enforces this rule as values are entered into the form. Records with more than 10 copies to sell will not be added to the STUDENT table. You must change the number of books to sell to be 10 before you can continue.

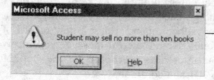

Figure P9.10 The Number of Copies to be Sold Must Be 10 or Less

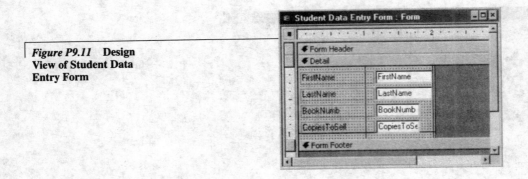

Figure P9.11 Design View of Student Data Entry Form

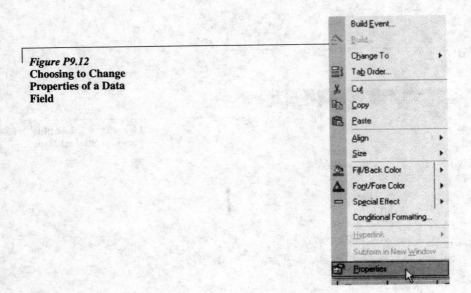

Figure P9.12 Choosing to Change Properties of a Data Field

Choose the "View" command followed by the "Design View" subcommand and Figure P9.11 appears. You may have to expand the image by dragging one of its corners in order to see the entire design of the form. Click on the BookNumb field with the right mouse button. Make sure the data field is chosen and not the field label; the data field has a white background. Choose the "Properties" option as shown in Figure P9.12.

When Figure P9.13 appears, enter the validation rule and validation text as they appear on the screen. The "All" tab is selected so that all properties are displayed. Note that the value "1000" does not have a comma for the validation rule but in the validation text shows "1,000." Do not enter quotation marks in properties of data fields. Close the screen in Figure P9.13 and go back to data entry by choosing the "View" command followed by the "Form View" subcommand. Enter a new record of "Aaron," "Ackerman," "1010," and "1" for the fields. Note the error message you receive after entering "1010" is the validation text you entered as a property of the BookNumb field. Change the BookNumb field value to 101 and continue.

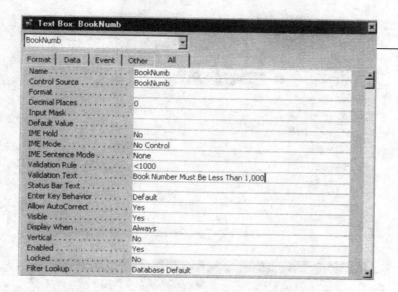

Figure P9.13
Changing the Rule for Book Number Values

One Table Report

A report on class enrollments can be made from the table CLASS. The completed report should look like Figure P9.14. The class and the number of students enrolled is all that needs to be displayed.

Create a report by choosing the "Report" tab and the "Create report by using wizard" option shown in Figure P9.15. Choose the CLASS table from the drop-down menu and both the ClassNumb and Enrollment fields as shown in Figure P9.16 by using the ">" button. Click the "Next" button to move to the next screen.

You do not want any additional grouping, so simply choose the "Next" button when that screen appears. You do wish to sort the report by ClassNumb records so choose ClassNumb from the drop-down menu in the screen shown in Figure P9.17. For the next two report wizard screens you want a tabular layout and a corporate style.

Make the report title "Report of Class Enrollments" and click the "Finish" button. What you see should be similar to the report shown in Figure P9.14. A small change should be made for the label of the class; it should be changed from the default field name "ClassNumb" to simply "Class."

Report of Class Enrollments

Class	Enrollment
ACG205	117
ACG206	102
ECN401	49
FIN201	25
FIN301	15
MGT305	68
MIS330	152
MIS370	24
MIS401	78
MKT305	55
MKT405	2

Figure P9.14 **Report of Class Enrollments**

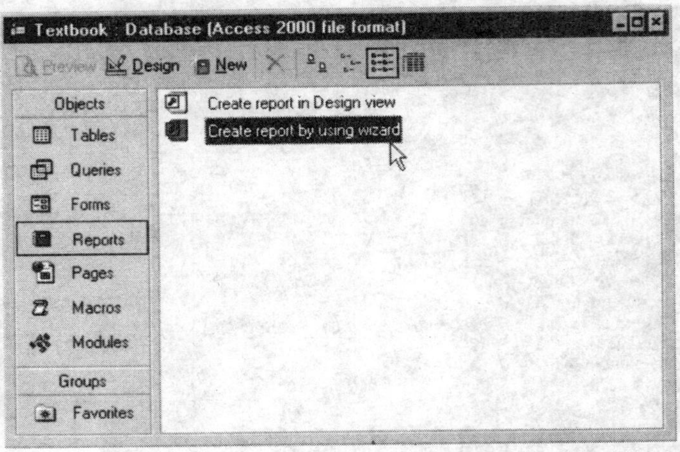

Figure P9.15 **Steps to Begin Creating a New Report**

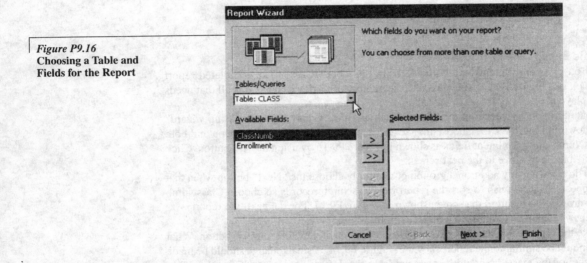

Figure P9.16 **Choosing a Table and Fields for the Report**

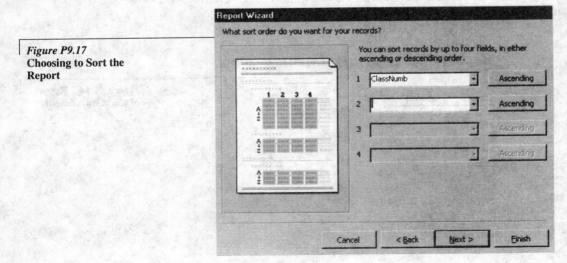

Figure P9.17 **Choosing to Sort the Report**

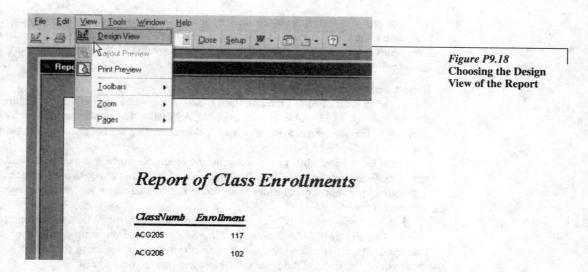

Figure P9.18
Choosing the Design View of the Report

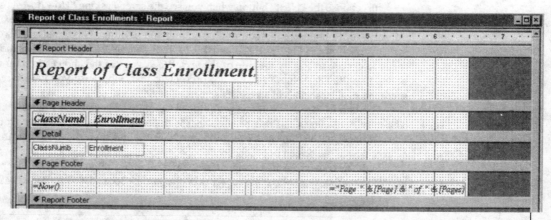

Figure P9.19 **Design View of Report of Class Enrollments**

Choose the "View" command followed by the "Design View" command as shown in Figure P9.18 and Figure P9.19 will appear. Several parts of the report design require your attention. First, look at the ruler space and see that the report width is 6.5 inches. That relates to a standard sheet of paper which is 8.5 inches wide less the 2 inches of margins for the report. If you accidentally extend the width of the report then you will see one page of report followed by what appears to be a blank page. The page is not blank; Access is merely trying to display the part of the report beyond the 6.5 inch range.

There is a header and a footer for the report. That means a section of the report is reserved at the beginning and end. Items in the report header will be written only once, at the beginning of the report. Items in the report footer will be written only once, at the end of the report. As you can see, this report has nothing in the report footer. There are also headers and footers for pages; this information appears at the top and bottom of each page of the report. The page footer shows the date (i.e., the Now() function) and the page of the report. The detail section displays every record retrieved from the database for the report.

Click on the "ClassNumb" label in the page header and the field is selected; the handles appear at the field's edges and corners. Click once again inside the field and the cursor changes so that you can edit the text of the label. The label should be changed to read "Class" instead of "ClassNumb."

You can save the report by closing the screen and following the choices given. You can also choose the "File" command followed by the "Save" command and then close the screen. The name of the saved report will be the name you provided to the wizard— "Report of Class Enrollments."

Report from Multiple Tables

Part of the "Report of Books Used in Each Class" is shown in Figure P9.20. It requires information from the BOOK table as well as the CLASS table. The books used for each class are shown with the book price; at the end of each class record the sum of prices for the books used in the class is displayed.

To achieve the ability to make a sum, the report has to be grouped on a field. In this report the field ClassNumb is used for grouping and the prices of books used in each member of the group are summed. A header and a footer can be created for any data field upon which a group is formed.

Create a new report by using the same process as above. When you are presented a screen (like Figure P9.16) choose the CLASS table from the drop-down menu and the ClassNumb field. Then go back to the drop-down menu and choose the BOOK table and choose the Title field and the Price field. Now move to the next screen.

Just choose the "Next" button when you see the screen asking "How do you want to view your data?" The default displayed is the way you wish to view the data. At the next screen you do not want to choose any additional grouping so click the "Next" button. Two important screens are shown in Figures P9.21 and P9.22. In Figure P9.21 you should use the drop-down menu to choose to sort by the title of the text. When you see the choices in drop-down menu notice that the ClassNumb field is not presented; that is because you have already chosen grouping by ClassNumb in an earlier screen.

The button labeled "Summary Options" should be clicked and Figure P9.22 appears. The only field choice is Price because that is the only numeric field being grouped by the ClassNumb field values. Choose the "Sum" option and then the "OK" button. You will be returned to the screen in Figure P9.21.

In the next two screens presented by the wizard you want to choose the "stepped" layout and "corporate" style. Make the report title "Report of Books Used in Each Class" and then

Figure P9.20 Part of the Report of Books Used in Each Class

Report of Books Used in Each Class

Class	Book	Price	
ACG205			
	Costing Products	$123.45	
		$123.45	Sum
ACG206			
	Counting By The Numbers	$61.00	
		$61.00	Sum
ECN401			
	The Growing Economy	$72.00	
		$72.00	Sum
FIN201			
	Finance for Me	$78.75	
	Stock Crisis	$35.90	
		$114.65	Sum
FIN301			
	Cash Management	$29.75	
	The Growing Economy	$72.00	

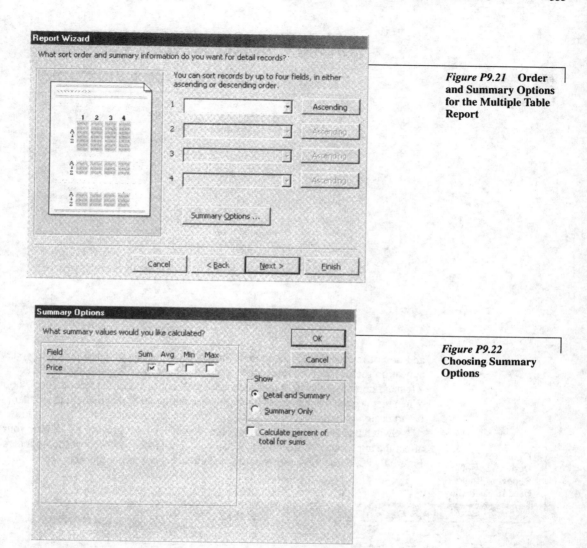

Figure P9.21 Order and Summary Options for the Multiple Table Report

Figure P9.22 Choosing Summary Options

choose the "Finish" button. The report you see in Figure P9.23 must now be modified to produce the report as shown in Figure P9.20.

Begin by changing to the design view—the "View" command followed by the "Design View" subcommand. When the screen in Figure P9.24 appears you can make the modifications. Change the "ClassNumb" label in the page header to be "Class." Do not change the ClassNumb field in the ClassNumb header. Click the mouse once on the field "='Summary for' & …" in the ClassNumb footer. Once it is highlighted with handles, press the "Delete" key to remove the field.

Notice that the Price field is summed in the ClassNumb footer. That means that for each ClassNumb value in the report, the sum of the prices of books used in the class will be reported in the ClassNumb footer. There is also a sum of prices for the entire report shown in the report footer of the design view. The report sum is labeled as the "Grand Total" while the sum for a given ClassNumb is labeled simply as "Sum."

You need to drag the "Sum" label to the right-hand side of the "=Sum([Price])" field in the ClassNumb footer so that you report looks like Figure P9.20. Click on the "Sum" label

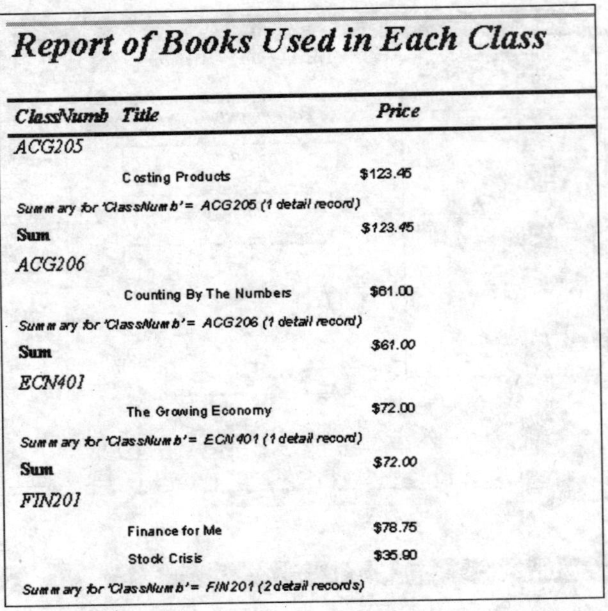
Report of Books Used in Each Class
ClassNumb Title Price
ACG205
Costing Products $123.45
Summary for 'ClassNumb' = ACG205 (1 detail record)
Sum $123.45
ACG206
Counting By The Numbers $61.00
Summary for 'ClassNumb' = ACG206 (1 detail record)
Sum $61.00
ECN401
The Growing Economy $72.00
Summary for 'ClassNumb' = ECN401 (1 detail record)
Sum $72.00
FIN201
Finance for Me $78.75
Stock Crisis $35.90
Summary for 'ClassNumb' = FIN201 (2 detail records)

Figure P9.23 **Initial Report of Books Used in Each Class**

and do not release the mouse button. Simply drag the "Sum" label to where you wish it to appear on the report. Any selected field can also be moved by moving the cursor to the top, left-hand corner of the field and the cursor will change to a fist with a finger pointing up. When that occurs, you can press the left mouse button and drag the field to another part of the report design screen.

Switch back and forth from the design view to the print preview to see how your changes affect the appearance of the report. When you are finished your report should look similar to Figure P9.20. Close the report window and choose to save your changes.

Figure P9.24 **Design View of Report of Books Used in Each Class**

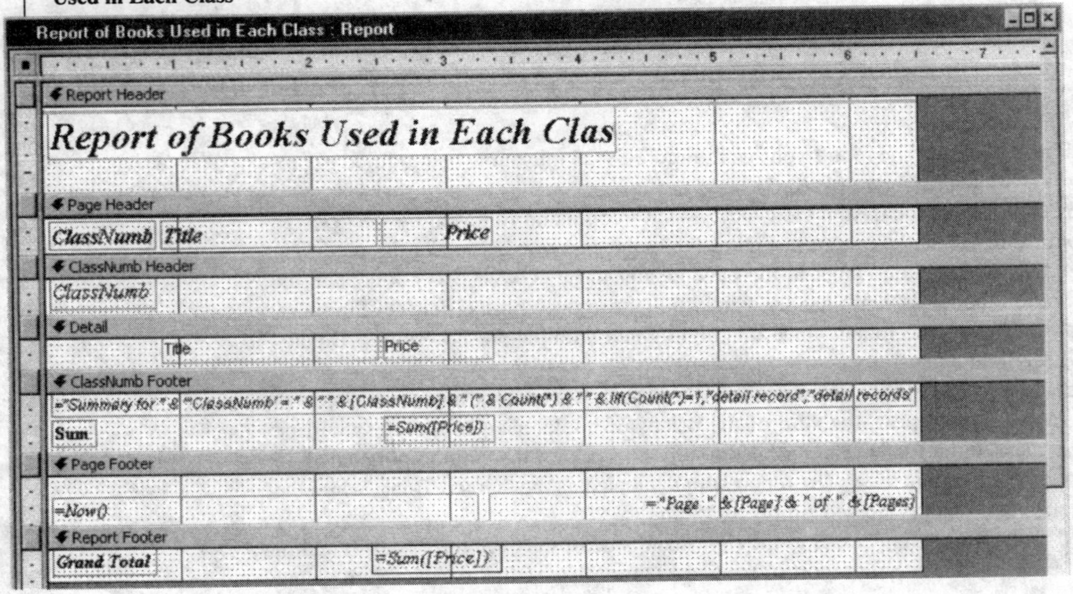
Report of Books Used in Each Class : Report
Report Header
Report of Books Used in Each Clas
Page Header
ClassNumb Title Price
ClassNumb Header
ClassNumb
Detail
Title Price
ClassNumb Footer
="Summary for " & "'ClassNumb' = " & " " & [ClassNumb] & " (" & Count(*) & " " & IIf(Count(*)=1,"detail record","detail records")
Sum =Sum([Price])
Page Footer
=Now() ="Page " & [Page] & " of " & [Pages]
Report Footer
Grand Total =Sum([Price])

Assignment

1. Make a form for the CLASS table. Place both the ClassNumb and Enrollment fields in the form. For the Enrollment field on the form, create a validation rule that the value must be less than or equal to 200. When the validation rule is violated a message should appear stating "Enrollment Must Be Less Than Or Equal To 200."
2. Make a report of books used in each class. The finished report should look similar to Figure P9.25. Note any changes in labels from the default field names. Move the labels "Sum" and "Grand Total" to be on the right-hand side of the totals. Make sure your fields are wide enough to show the entire field value; that is, do not let the book titles get truncated by fields that are too narrow. Make sure your report design does not go past 6.5 inches wide, which would cause blank pages to appear.

Report of Classes Using Each Book

Book Title	Class	Enrollment	
Finance for Me			
	FIN201	25	
		25	Sum
Stock Crisis			
	FIN201	25	
		25	Sum
Costing Products			
	ACG205	117	
	MKT305	55	
		172	Sum
The Growing Economy			
	ECN401	49	
	FIN301	15	
		64	Sum
Personnel Files			
	MGT305	68	
	MKT305	55	
		123	Sum

Figure P9.25 Partial Listing of Report of Classes Using Each Book

Project 10

Database Queries—Textbook Database

Learning Objectives

- Learn to create queries using one or multiple tables.
- Understand how to limit query results with single and multiple constraints.
- Understand how a query can request constraint values from the query user.
- Learn to use queries that look for partial values in fields.
- Learn to make computations within queries on both numeric and text fields.

Introduction

This project uses Access 2002 (also known as Access XP) to create queries for an existing database. The initial database can be downloaded from the Prentice Hall Web site for the text at WWW.PRENHALL.COM/mcleod—"mcleod" must be in lower case letters. The database for this project, Textbook, concerns classes and the books used in those classes. The database also contains records of students who have copies of books to sell.

Project 11 is a companion project; it covers the same learning objectives but uses a different database example. Projects 10 and 11 both cover query concepts so that instructors have the option to further enforce those concepts with two projects or to assign different projects to students in different semesters.

An Access database is a single file. Although there may be many tables in a database, they are all contained in the single database file along with any queries, reports, or other components of the database. You should create a copy of the data file with your database on a regular basis. You can save the copy to a diskette, a Zip disk, or some other medium of your choice.

If you use a floppy disk or Zip disk to store your database, always wait until you have completely exited Access and writing to the database has stopped before you remove the disk from the drive. Database management software works closely with the computer's operating system and sometimes the writing of information back to the database file occurs when you exit the database. Removing the disk early could result in losing your entire database.

Within Access you are able to use the "Edit" command to cut and paste objects. Those objects are tables, queries, and similar components of the database. You cannot copy the database itself from within Access. To copy the entire database, such as for a backup copy, you must copy the database file using Windows Explorer or clicking on the "My Computer" icon.

One last caution about using database software is that the database file size can grow quickly. Users like features such as the "Undo" command that can easily reverse mistakes. Such features come at a price: They require much disk space in the database file to guide the reversal of actions taken. To keep your database file at a reasonable size you should compact it on a regular basis, such as every time you exit Access.

From within Access, the "Tools," "Database Utilities," and "Compact and Repair Database" sequence of commands will compact your database to remove all of the deletions and missteps that you may have performed while using the database. You can change the Access settings to automatically compact the database each time you exit Access. "Tools," followed by "Options," "General," and "Compact on Close" will have Access automatically compact the database. However, many universities limit the ability of students to change computer settings so you may have to explicitly compact your database each time you use Access.

EXAMPLE

This example will generate a number of queries from the Textbook database. The Textbook database will be provided by your instructor or downloaded from the Prentice Hall Web site. Managers typically use queries to look for specific records, and so the query is constrained to records that have certain values for fields. Other queries compute new values from the values of other fields in the query.

It is important for decision makers to be able to generate their own queries. First, the decision maker who can create a query gains immediate access to the power of a database. Second, the decision maker may not know exactly which records in the database are needed until a query is generated, its results are seen, and more queries are created in an iterative process until the results desired are ultimately generated. The third reason is that an intuitive understanding of the database cannot occur unless the decision maker gains a hands-on understanding of the data values and relationships in the database.

Information is the essential tool of a decision maker. The understanding of the database gained by writing queries trains a decision maker to use that tool better.

Textbook Database

The Textbook database consists of four tables that relate to each other by common values. The tables and their data fields are shown in Figure P10.1. The STUDENT table contains four fields; FirstName, LastName, BookNumb, and CopiesToSell. The key fields of the tables are shown in bold font. It takes the combination of values from the FirstName, LastName, and BookNumb fields to make a key (i.e., a unique value) for the STUDENT table. The ClassNumb field is the only field needed to be the key of the CLASS table.

The fields from different tables can be combined when a common value exists between the two tables. For example, the field BookNumb is in both the STUDENT table and the BOOK table. If the value of BookNumb is 409 in the BOOK table and in the STUDENT table then the name of the student from the STUDENT table can be associated with the book title of the BOOK record. From Figure P10.2 you can see Amy Abner and Brian Janski both have book number 409 to sell. Book number 409 (see Figure P10.3) has a title of "Management Information Systems" and was authored by McLeod and Schell.

For the projects and assignments in this text you will only have to use an existing database, you will not be required to create a database or tables within a database.

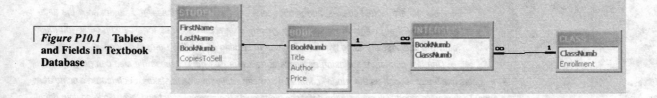

Figure P10.1 Tables and Fields in Textbook Database

Figure P10.2 Fields and Values in the STUDENT Table

FirstName	LastName	BookNumb	CopiesToSell
Amy	Abner	409	1
Bell	Ringer	32	1
Bette	Chancer	32	10
Betty	Donner	12	1
Betty	Donner	371	1
Bill	Eschew	16	3
Bill	Eschew	31	2
Bill	Eschew	32	2
Bill	Eschew	191	2
Bill	Eschew	200	1
Bill	Leer	191	1
Bill	Leer	371	5
Brian	Janski	409	1
Charles	Darling	121	1
Charles	Darling	371	1
Chris	Lee	12	1
Cindy	Rellash	12	2
Cindy	Rellash	24	1
Cindy	Rellash	191	5
Claire	Moore	27	6

BookNumb	Title	Author	Price
12	Finance for Me	Poe and Tattem	$78.75
16	Stock Crisis	Plankton	$35.90
24	Counting Pennies	Durgee	$108.10
31	Costing Products	Gough and Howe	$123.45
32	The Growing Economy	Birch	$72.00
101	Personnel Files	Hiram	$78.24
121	Employee Termination	Fletcher	$72.10
191	Selling Yourself	Tattem and Green	$83.00
206	Market Research	Shi	$95.62
231	Data Mining	Thurston and Gradston	$101.50
276	Cash Management	Packard	$29.75
371	Counting By The Numbers	Bongberd	$61.00
409	Management Information Systems	McLeod and Schell	$60.50

Figure P10.3 Fields and Values in the BOOK Table

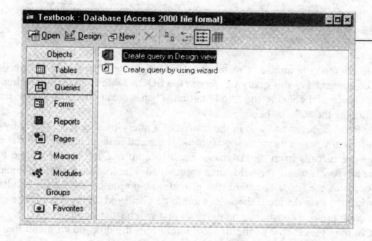

Figure P10.4 Textbook Database Screen

Begin this project by opening the Access program and then opening the Textbook database. Notice from Figure P10.4 that the "Queries" tab is chosen.

Creating a Query with Constraints

Records in the BOOK table are shown in Figure P10.5. If a query were constructed without constraints, all of the records in the table would be displayed in the query result. It is more productive to restrict the records displayed to those which fit some decision making criteria. Let's look at books with a price greater than $100.

BookNumb	Title	Author	Price
12	Finance for Me	Poe and Tattem	$78.75
16	Stock Crisis	Plankton	$35.90
24	Counting Pennies	Durgee	$108.10
31	Costing Products	Gough and Howe	$123.45
32	The Growing Economy	Birch	$72.00
101	Personnel Files	Hiram	$78.24
121	Employee Termination	Fletcher	$72.10
191	Selling Yourself	Tattem and Green	$83.00
206	Market Research	Shi	$95.62
231	Data Mining	Thurston and Gradston	$101.50
276	Cash Management	Packard	$29.75
371	Counting By The Numbers	Bongberd	$61.00
409	Management Information Systems	McLeod and Schell	$60.50

Figure P10.5 Fields and Values in the BOOK Table

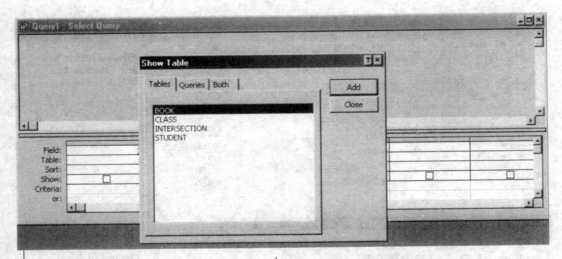

Figure P10.6 Choosing a Table for a Query

Double-click on the phrase "Create query in Design view" shown in Figure P10.4 and Figure P10.6 appears. For this query we choose the BOOK table from the list by highlighting the BOOK choice and clicking the "Add" button. Then we can close the screen that shows tables by clicking the "Close" button.

Figure P10.7 appears and it is in the format of a query-by-example. Query-by-example (QBE) is a format where a user can specify what is desired without having to write computer code to retrieve records from the database. Each column in QBE can be a field to be displayed. The top row is where the field name is provided. The second row tells the name of the table that contains the field. The third row provides an option of sorting the results and the fourth row lets the user decide if the values are to be displayed on the report. The remaining rows are used to provide constraints on the rows that will be displayed.

Click in the "Field" row of the first column. From the drop-down menu that appears, choose the Title field. Click on the "Field" row of the second column and choose the Price field. An alternative way to select fields is to click the mouse on the name of the field in the BOOK table box and drag the field name into place.

Now choose the "View" command followed by the "Datasheet View" subcommand. A table of the results is presented with all records from the BOOK table being presented but

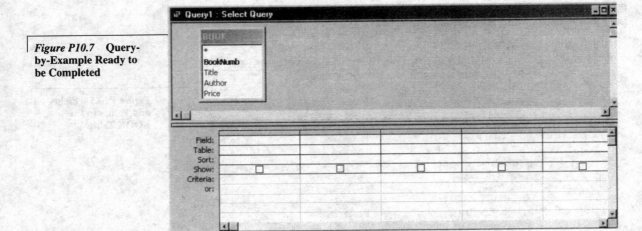

Figure P10.7 Query-by-Example Ready to be Completed

only the two fields Title and Price are displayed. Notice that the records are not sorted in a meaningful way. Choose the "View" command followed by the "Design View" subcommand so that we can change the query design.

Click on the "Sort" row of the Title column and from the drop-down menu choose "Ascending" for the sorting method. Now when the results are shown they will be sorted by the book title. In the "Criteria" row for Price, enter the constraint ">100" as shown in Figure P10.8. Notice that there is no dollar sign in the constraint and you would not put a comma in values of $1,000 or more. The constraint is just the digits, not the formatting.

View the datasheet again ("View" command followed by "Datasheet View") and Figure P10.9 appears. Notice that only the three books with a price greater than $100 are displayed. To generate a report of books whose price is greater than or equal to $50 but less than or equal to $75 use the constraint in Figure P10.10.

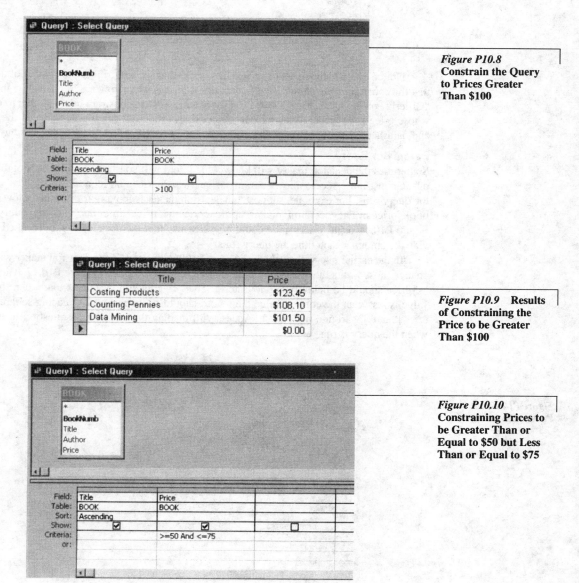

Figure P10.8 Constrain the Query to Prices Greater Than $100

Figure P10.9 Results of Constraining the Price to be Greater Than $100

Figure P10.10 Constraining Prices to be Greater Than or Equal to $50 but Less Than or Equal to $75

Figure P10.11
Constraining Prices to be Less Than $75 or Greater Than $100

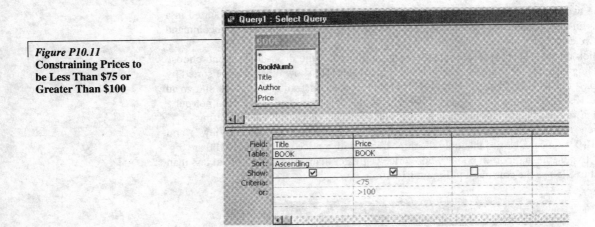

Notice that when one set of constraints or another set will trigger the display of a record that the constraints are shown on different lines. That is why the word "or" is below the word "Criteria" on the QBE. Figure P10.11 demonstrates how to constrain query results to records whose price is either less than $75 or greater than $100. You can toggle between the design and datasheet views to see how the queries are constructed and the results they display.

Parameter Query

Sometimes the decision maker will know which field will constrain a query but not the value of the constraint. Access allows parameter queries, queries that let a user provide a value as the query runs. For example, suppose the decision maker is looking for unusually low or high book prices. The decision maker could code the price amounts into the query as in Figure P10.11 or the query code could be written so that the decision maker is asked to provide the amounts each time the query runs.

In the earlier query, the values of $75 or $100 were used. If the decision maker wished to change those limits the query would have to be rewritten. Look at Figure P10.12. The phrase "<[price should be below]" is one criteria. The "<" sign simply means that when the price value is less than the entered value the record should be displayed. By placing square brackets, "["and"]," around the phrase, Access will display the phrase as a question to the user when the query is run.

Figure P10.12 A **Parameter Query**

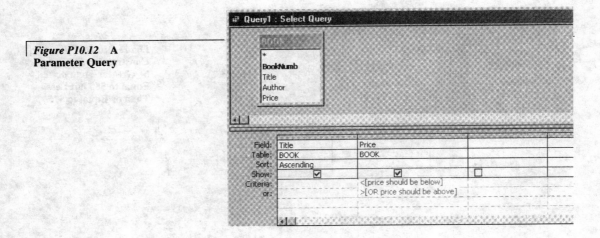

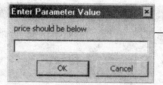

Figure P10.13 The Query Will Ask for a Parameter Value

Figure P10.13 shows the screen displayed by the first query criteria. It is important to note that the parameter query requires square brackets, not parentheses, around the phrase to be asked of the user. Save the query by using the "File" command followed by the "Save" subcommand. When asked, name the query "Book Prices" but do not include the quotation marks.

Inexact Constraints

Constraints on fields containing text can be difficult to create because what constitutes a match might be ambiguous. For example, what if you are looking for an author named "Tattem?" You can see from the values of the Author field in Figure P10.3 that Tattem is a coauthor of two books. If the constraint is entered as Figure P10.14, Access will not find the record.

The "Tattem" phrase looks for an exact match for the entire field value in the database records. Since "Tattem" is not an exact match of an entire Author field, no records are displayed by the query. Access uses two characters as wildcards in the matching of text fields.

The asterisk, "*," is a wildcard that matches any value or string of values, even a null value. A null value is the special case where there is no value at all. A question mark, "?," is a wildcard match for a single character. Table P10.1 shows how wildcards match with certain phrases. Figure P10.15 shows a query with a wildcard match looking for the word "and" so that books with more than one author are displayed.

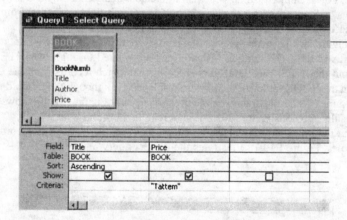

Figure P10.14 Incorrect Constraint to Find the "Tattem" Record

Table P10.1

Examples of Wildcard Matching		
WILDCARD PHRASE	MATCHES	DOES NOT MATCH
Like "*Tattem"	Poe and Tattem	Tattem and Green
Like "Tattem*"	Tattem and Green	Poe and Tattem
Like "*Tattem*"	Poe and Tattem	
	Tattem and Green	
Like "?i*"	Birch	Shi
	Hiram	

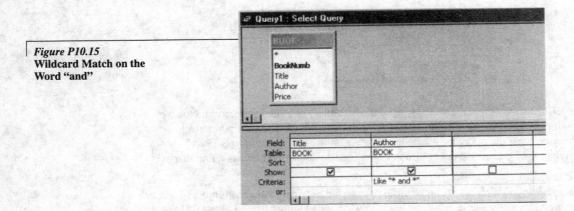

Figure P10.15
Wildcard Match on the Word "and"

Note that since a word, such as "and," is surrounded by spaces the constraint uses "* and *" and not "*and*." The constraint "*and*" would display a record if the sole author was "Mandy." Also, Access will find a match even if the letter case does not match. "AAA" in the database record would match the constraint of "aaa." Some database management software requires the case to match as well as the letters.

Queries Requiring More Than One Table

Queries that require data fields from more than one table require that the tables supplying field values as well as tables used to navigate between those tables be included in the query-by-example. For example, assume you wish to create a query that displays the class number and the titles of books used for the class. The ClassNumb field is needed from the CLASS table and the Title field is needed from the BOOK table.

From Figure P10.1 you can see that the records in the CLASS table do not relate directly to the records in the BOOK table. Instead, they are related through the INTERSECTION table. Without the INTERSECTION table records that match records from the CLASS table to records in the BOOK table, all records are displayed even though they should not be joined together. Figure P10.16 illustrates the incorrect query and Figure P10.17 shows some of the incorrect results. Obviously, ACG205 does not require all of those texts.

Without the links between tables the query does not restrict itself to records that match between tables. Figure P10.18 illustrates the correct query and Figure P10.19 displays the query results.

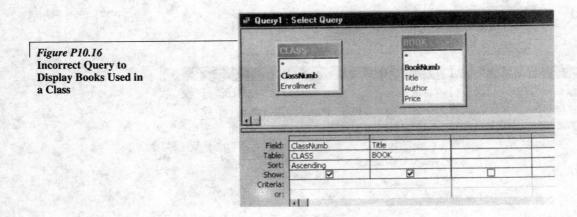

Figure P10.16
Incorrect Query to Display Books Used in a Class

ClassNumb	Title
ACG205	The Growing Economy
ACG205	Personnel Files
ACG205	Counting By The Numbers
ACG205	Counting Pennies
ACG205	Stock Crisis
ACG205	Cash Management
ACG205	Management Information Systems
ACG205	Market Research
ACG205	Data Mining
ACG205	Selling Yourself
ACG205	Employee Termination
ACG205	Finance for Me
ACG205	Costing Products

Record: 143 of 143

Figure P10.17 Some Results from the Incorrect Query to Display Books Used in a Class

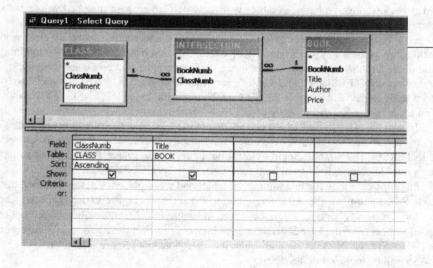

Figure P10.18 Correct Query to Display Books Used in Classes

ClassNumb	Title
ACG205	Costing Products
ACG206	Counting By The Numbers
ECN401	The Growing Economy
FIN201	Stock Crisis
FIN201	Finance for Me
FIN301	Cash Management
FIN301	The Growing Economy
MGT305	Employee Termination
MGT305	Personnel Files
MIS330	Management Information Systems
MIS401	Data Mining
MKT305	Selling Yourself
MKT305	Personnel Files
MKT305	Costing Products
MKT405	Market Research

Figure P10.19 Query Results Showing Books Used in Classes

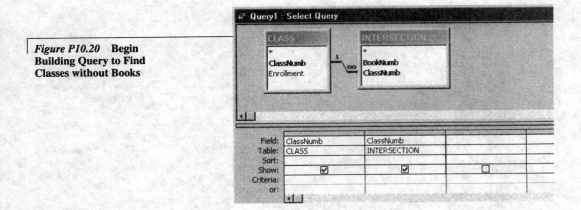

Figure P10.20 Begin Building Query to Find Classes without Books

There is a note of caution when using multiple tables in a query. When there is no matching value between the tables, the records with no match are not displayed in the query results. That is because linkage between tables is usually performed with matched values between tables. To display unmatched records we must modify the linkage between the tables.

Let's assume that you need to know which classes do not require a text. By looking at the relationships among tables in Figure P10.1 we can see that if a class (i.e., a ClassNumb field value in the CLASS table) does not require a book then there will be no corresponding class number in the INTERSECTION table. In query-by-example terms, there will be a ClassNumb record value in the CLASS table but the ClassNumb value in the INTERSECTION table will be null.

To write a query to find which classes do not use a book we must edit the property joining the CLASS and INTERSECTION tables and place a constraint on the ClassNumb field in the INTERSECTION table. Begin by creating a query as in Figure P10.20. Notice that it is taking the ClassNumb field from both the CLASS and INTERSECTION tables.

Place the cursor on the line joining the tables and try to place it halfway between the two tables. When you press the right mouse button the screen in Figure P10.21 appears. Choose the "Join Properties" option. From the screen in Figure P10.22, choose the second option so that all records from the CLASS table will be included. Even if there is no matching record in the INTERSECTION table, such as when the class does not require a text, the record from CLASS will be included in the report.

You can see from running the query (Figure P10.23) that the class "MIS370" does not require a text. To display only the classes that do not require texts we constrain the ClassNumb value in the INTERSECTION table to be null. That query is shown in Figure P10.24. The phrase "Is Null" is a special constraint in Access.

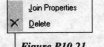

Figure P10.21 Choices after Selecting the Line Joining Tables

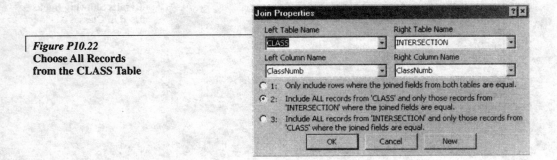

Figure P10.22 Choose All Records from the CLASS Table

CLASS.ClassNumb	INTERSECTION.ClassNumb
ACG205	ACG205
ACG206	ACG206
ECN401	ECN401
FIN201	FIN201
FIN201	FIN201
FIN301	FIN301
FIN301	FIN301
MGT305	MGT305
MGT305	MGT305
MIS330	MIS330
MIS370	
MIS401	MIS401
MKT305	MKT305
MKT305	MKT305
MKT305	MKT305
MKT405	MKT405

Figure P10.23 Query Results after Modifying the Join Properties

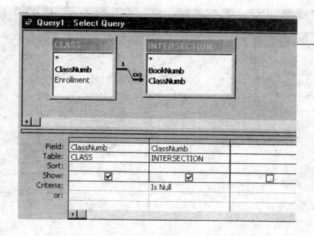

Figure P10.24 Using the "Is Null" Constraint

Data Field Concatenation and Calculation

Data fields with text values can be concatenated—the characters can be added together with other characters and other text fields. Numeric fields are subject to mathematical operations. These operations can take place within a query so that values in the database do not need to be changed.

For example, the STUDENT table has separate fields for the FirstName and LastName of students. Figure P10.25 demonstrates how the fields can be shown separately and together in a last name, first name format. For example, the name "Michael Jordan" would become "Jordan, Michael." "Name:[LastName] & ', '& [FirstName]" shows that the field names from the Access database are surrounded by square brackets. Notice that there is a comma and a blank space between "Jordan" and "Michael." Also notice in Figure P10.25 that the phrase "Name:" appears before the concatenation of the FirstName and LastName fields. This is so Access can give this new field a label for its column in the display.

Since some students sell more than one text, student names may repeat in the query results. The duplicate names can be removed by grouping same value records together. Choose the "View" command followed by the "Totals" subcommand and another row, "Total," is inserted in the query design as shown in Figure P10.26. By running the new query you can see that duplicate names are removed from the results.

With the "Total" row in the query we have a new set of query options that can be used for decision making. We may wish to know how many books a student has to sell. There are two

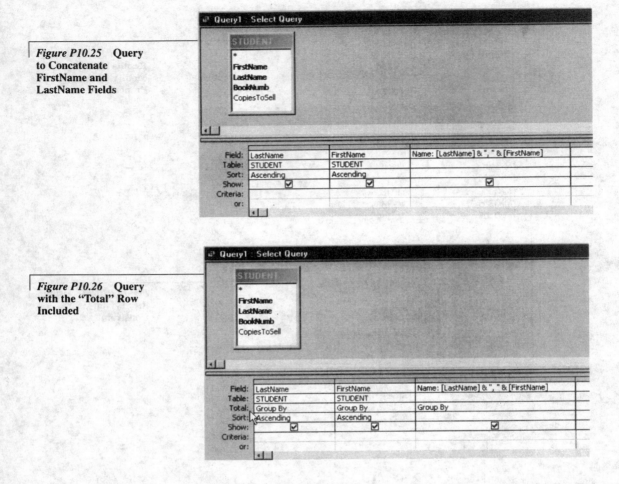

Figure P10.25 Query to Concatenate FirstName and LastName Fields

Figure P10.26 Query with the "Total" Row Included

ways at looking at the number; first as the count of different texts the student has to sell and second as the sum of the copies to sell. When the "Total" row is added to the query design the default value for a column is "Group By" but by clicking on the drop-down menu many other choices are possible.

One option, "Count" tells Access to record the number of times a record is encountered. Another option, "Sum," calculates the mathematical total of the values in the field. For a sum or count to be computed they have to apply to a field or fields that are grouped together. In our example we have been grouping student records together by the combination of their last and first names.

Figure P10.27 shows a query that will calculate both the count of the number of BookNumb field values for a given student as well as the sum of the number of copies the student has to sell. Figure P10.28 is a partial listing of the query results.

Numeric fields can be subjected to mathematical computations. Assume the decision maker wants to know the extended price of each book a student has to sell. To calculate that value, for every book number of each student you would multiply the value in the CopiesToSell field of the STUDENT table by the Price field value in the BOOK table.

Figure P10.29 illustrates a new field named "Extended" which is calculated as the product of CopiesToSell times Price values. Figure P10.30 displays some of the query results. In this example no summation was needed so the "Totals" row was removed. Choosing the

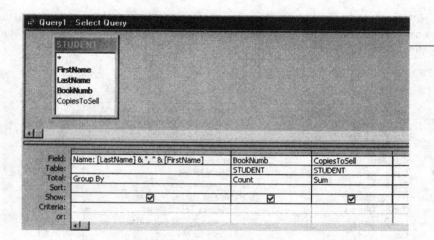

Figure P10.27 Query Design With Count and Sum Features

Name	CountOfBookNumb	SumOfCopiesToSell
Abner, Amy	1	1
Ackerman, Aaron	1	10
Chancer, Bette	1	10
Cole, Lee	1	1
Cole, Nick	2	4
Costa, Maria	2	3
Darling, Charles	2	2
Donner, Betty	2	2
Eschew, Bill	5	10
Fazool, Leon	1	1
Fender, Keri	4	4
Fryz, Julianne	2	2
Hinkle, Herman	2	3
Hogue, James	2	2
Hogue, Patty	2	3

Figure P10.28 Some Query Results Showing Count and Sum Functions

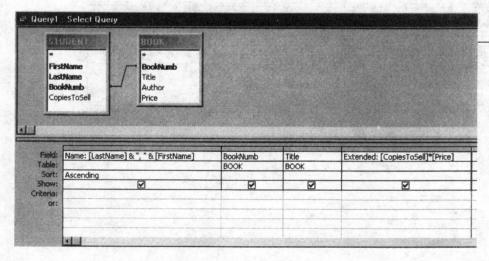

Figure P10.29 Query to Calculate Extended Prices

"View" command followed by the "Totals" subcommand toggles the "Total" row in and out of the query design. If the sum of extended prices across all books being sold by a given student is desired, construct a query such as Figure P10.31.

Figure P10.30 **Some Results from the Query to Calculate Extended Prices**

Name	BookNumb	Title	Extended
Abner, Amy	409	Management Information Systems	$60.50
Ackerman, Aaron	409	Management Information Systems	$605.00
Chancer, Bette	32	The Growing Economy	$720.00
Cole, Lee	16	Stock Crisis	$35.90
Cole, Nick	409	Management Information Systems	$60.50
Costa, Maria	12	Finance for Me	$78.75
Costa, Maria	32	The Growing Economy	$144.00
Darling, Charles	371	Counting By The Numbers	$61.00
Darling, Charles	121	Employee Termination	$72.10
Donner, Betty	371	Counting By The Numbers	$61.00
Donner, Betty	12	Finance for Me	$78.75
Eschew, Bill	191	Selling Yourself	$166.00
Eschew, Bill	32	The Growing Economy	$144.00
Eschew, Bill	31	Costing Products	$246.90
Eschew, Bill	16	Stock Crisis	$107.70
Fazool, Leon	121	Employee Termination	$72.10

Figure P10.31 **Query to Calculate the Sum of Extended Prices**

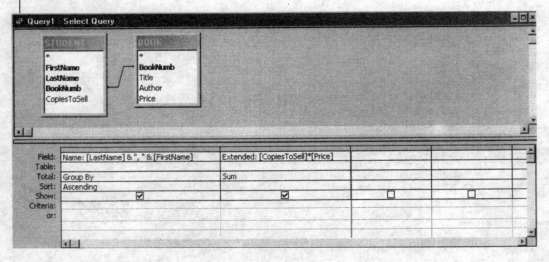

ASSIGNMENT

1. Create a query using the CLASS table that shows the class number and enrollment where the enrollment is less than 25 students. Sort the results by the class number field.
2. Create a query that shows the class number (sorted) of classes that have either less than 25 students or more than 100 students. Show only the ClassNumb field, not the field or fields you use to constrain the results.
3. Create a query that shows the class number (sorted) of classes that have an enrollment of greater than 25 and less than 100 students. Show only the ClassNumb field in the query results.
4. Create a query that displays all of the MIS classes. These classes will begin the ClassNumb field with "MIS" and you should use an inexact constraint match.
5. Create a query that finds all senior level classes in the CLASS table based upon values in the ClassNumb field. A senior level class will always have the fourth character of the ClassNumb field be the value "4."
6. Make a parameter query that asks the user to provide a ClassNumb value and limit the query results to the ClassNumb and Enrollment field values for that class.
7. What books are not being sold by any student? Show the book title (sorted) and book number.
8. For each class, count the number of books used in the class. Show the class number (sorted) and the count of the books. For this query you need two tables.
9. Count the number of copies of all books that each student has to sell. The student name should be in first name, last name format such that one field (called "Name") is created as the first name, a blank space, and the last name. Sort by the "Name" field you create.
10. Which book has the highest price? Show the book to price, title, and author.

Project 11

Database Queries—ClassProjects Database

Learning Objectives

- Learn to create queries using one or multiple tables.
- Understand how to limit query results with single and multiple constraints.
- Understand how a query can request constraint values from the query user.
- Learn to use queries that look for partial values in fields.
- Learn to make computations within queries on both numeric and text fields.

Introduction

This project uses Access 2002 (also known as Access XP) to create queries for an existing database. The initial database can be downloaded from the Prentice Hall Web site for the text at WWW.PRENHALL.COM/MCLEOD—"mcleod" must be in lower-case letters. The database for this project, ClassProjects, concerns classes and the projects used in those classes.

Project 10 is a companion project; it covers the same learning objectives but uses a different database example. Projects 10 and 11 both cover query concepts so that instructors have the option to further enforce those concepts with two projects or to assign different projects to students in different semesters.

An Access database is a single file. Although there may be many tables in a database, they are all contained in the single database file along with any queries, reports, or other components of the database. You should create a copy of the data file with your database on a regular basis. You can save the copy to a diskette, a Zip disk, or some other medium of your choice.

If you use a floppy disk or Zip disk to store your database, always wait until you have completely exited Access and writing to the database has stopped before you remove the disk from the drive. Database management software works closely with the computer's operating system and sometimes the writing of information back to the database file occurs when you exit the database. Removing the disk early could result in losing your entire database.

Within Access you are able to use the "Edit" command to cut and paste objects. Those objects are tables, queries, and similar components of the database. You cannot copy the database itself from within Access. To copy the entire database, such as for a backup copy, you must copy the database file using Windows Explorer or clicking on the "My Computer" icon.

One last caution about using database software is that the database file size can grow quickly. Users like features such as the "Undo" command that can easily reverse mistakes. Such features come at a price—they require much disk space in the database file to guide the reversal of actions taken. To keep your database file at a reasonable size you should compact it on a regular basis, such as every time you exit Access.

From within Access, the "Tools," "Database Utilities," and "Compact and Repair Database" sequence of commands will compact your database to remove all of the deletions and missteps that you may have performed while using the database. You can change the Access settings to automatically compact the database each time you exit Access. "Tools," followed by "Options," "General," and "Compact on Close" will have Access automatically compact the database. However, many universities limit the ability of students to change computer settings so you may have to explicitly compact your database each time you use Access.

EXAMPLE

This example will generate a number of queries from the ClassProjects database. The ClassProjects database will be provided by your instructor or downloaded from the Prentice Hall Web site. Managers typically use queries to look for specific records and so the query is constrained to records that have certain values for fields. Other queries compute new values from the values of other fields in the query.

It is important for decision makers to be able to generate their own queries. First, the decision maker who can create a query gains immediate access to the power of a database. Second, the decision maker may not know exactly which records in the database are needed until a query is generated, its results are seen, and more queries are created in an iterative process until the results desired are ultimately generated. The third reason is that an intuitive understanding of the database cannot occur unless the decision maker gains a hands-on understanding of the data values and relationships in the database.

Information is the essential tool of a decision maker. The understanding of the database gained by writing queries trains a decision maker to use that tool better.

ClassProjects Database

The ClassProjects database consists of three tables that relate to each other by common values. The tables and their data fields are shown in Figure P11.1. The COURSE table contains three fields; Code, Description, and Abbreviation. The key fields of the tables are shown in bold font. It takes the combination of values from the Code and Number fields to make a key (i.e., a unique value) for the PROJECT table. The Abbreviation field is the only field needed to be the key of the DEPARTMENT table.

The fields from different tables can be combined when a common value exists between the two tables. For example, the field Abbreviation is in both the DEPARTMENT table and the COURSE table. If the value of Abbreviation is "INT" in the DEPARTMENT table and in the COURSE table then the name of the department from the DEPARTMENT table can be associated with the description of the course in the COURSE record. From Figure P11.2 you can see the courses "Cultural Diversity," "Spanish for Business," and "French for Business" each has the value "INT" for the Abbreviation field. Finding the "INT" value in the Abbreviation field of the DEPARTMENT table (see Figure P11.3) lets us know that the three courses are in the International Business department.

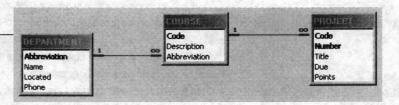

Figure P11.1 Tables and Fields in the ClassProjects Database

Figure P11.2 Fields and Values in the COURSE Table

Code	Description	Abbreviation
ACG201	Financial Accounting	ACGFIN
ACG301	Cost Accounting	ACGFIN
ECN375	Global Markets	ECN
ECN460	Banking Regulations	ECN
FIN305	Personal Finance	ACGFIN
INT100	Cultural Diversity	INT
INT201	Spanish for Business	INT
INT202	French for Business	INT
MGT300	Introduction to Management	MGTMKT
MIS105	Information Systems Literacy	ISOM
MIS315	Database Management Systems	ISOM
MKT300	Introduction to Marketing	MGTMKT
MKT444	Marketing Research	MGTMKT
POM250	Introduction to Operations Management	ISOM
STA230	Descriptive Statistics	ISOM

Figure P11.3 Fields and Values in the DEPARTMENT Table

Abbreviation	Name	Located	Phone
ACGFIN	Accounting and Finance	Dobo Hall	910-1800
ECN	Economics	Randall	910-0900
INT	International Business	Dobo Hall	910-0900
ISOM	Information Systems and Operations Management	Cameron Hall	910-3600
MGTMKT	Management and Marketing	Cameron Hall	910-4500

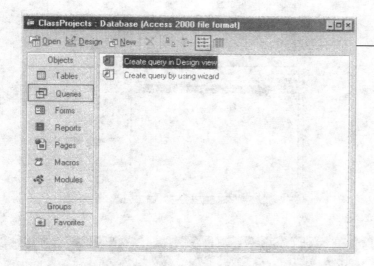

Figure P11.4
ClassProjects Database Screen

For the projects and assignments in this text you will only have to use an existing database; you will not be required to create a database or tables within a database.

Begin this project by opening the Access program and then opening the ClassProjects database. Notice from Figure P11.4 that the "Queries" tab is chosen.

Creating a Query with Constraints

Records in the PROJECT table are shown in Figure P11.5. If a query were constructed without constraints, all of the records in the table would be displayed in the query result. It is more productive to restrict the records displayed to those which fit some decision making criteria. Let's look at projects that earn more than 35 points.

Double-click on the phrase "Create query in Design view" shown in Figure P11.4 and Figure P11.6 appears. For this query we choose the PROJECT table from the list by highlighting the PROJECT choice and clicking the "Add" button. Then we can close the screen that shows tables by clicking the "Close" button.

Figure P11.7 appears and it is in the format of a query-by-example. Query-by-example (QBE) is a format where a user can specify what is desired without having to write computer code to retrieve records from the database. Each column in QBE can be a field to be displayed. The top row is where the field name is provided. The second row tells the name of the table that contains the field. The third row provides an option of sorting the results and the fourth row lets the user decide if the values are to be displayed on the report. The remaining rows are used to provide constraints on the rows that will be displayed.

Code	Number	Title	Due	Points
FIN305	1	Personal Portfolio	11/14/2003	35
INT201	1	Nouns	9/17/2003	15
INT201	2	Verbs	11/21/2003	25
INT202	1	Nouns	9/17/2003	15
INT202	2	Verbs	11/21/2003	25
MIS105	1	Home Page Development	9/15/2003	25
MIS105	2	Working With Windows	11/13/2003	50
MIS315	1	Alumni Database	12/5/2003	20
MKT444	1	Finding Customers	10/31/2003	50
MKT444	2	Segmenting Customers	11/21/2003	50
MKT444	3	Customer Service	12/12/2003	40

Figure P11.5 **Fields and Values in the PROJECT Table**

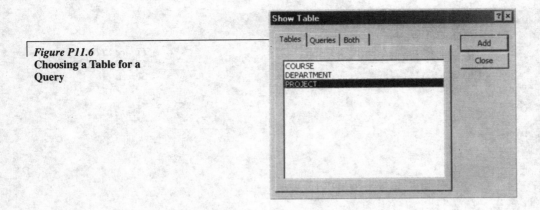

Figure P11.6
Choosing a Table for a Query

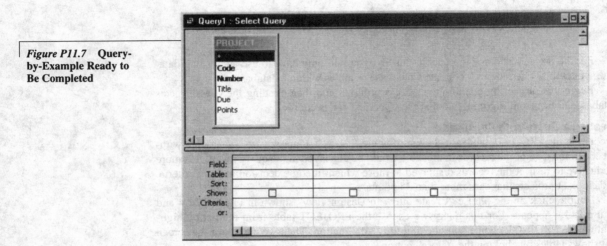

Figure P11.7 **Query-by-Example Ready to Be Completed**

Click in the field row of the first column. From the drop-down menu that appears, choose the Code field. Click on the field row of the second column and choose the Number field. Click on the field row of the third column and choose the Points field from the drop-down menu. An alternative way to select fields is to click the mouse on the name of the field in the PROJECT table box and drag the field name into place.

Now choose the "View" command followed by the "Datasheet View" subcommand. A table of the results with all records from the BOOK table is presented but only the three fields Code, Number, and Points are displayed. The records are sorted by values in the Code and Number fields because those two fields comprise the key of the PROJECT table. It is better to explicitly control sorting of the query than to rely on the default sorting from Access. Choose the "View" command followed by the "Design View" subcommand so that we can change the query design.

Click on the "Sort" row of the Code column and from the drop-down menu choose "Ascending" for the sorting method. Also choose the ascending sorting method for the Number field. In the "Criteria" row for Points, enter the constraint ">35" as shown in Figure P11.8.

View the datasheet again ("View" command followed by "Datasheet View") and Figure P11.9 appears. Notice that only projects with more than 35 points are displayed. Since the "FIN305," project "1" earns 35 points and the constraint called for more than 35

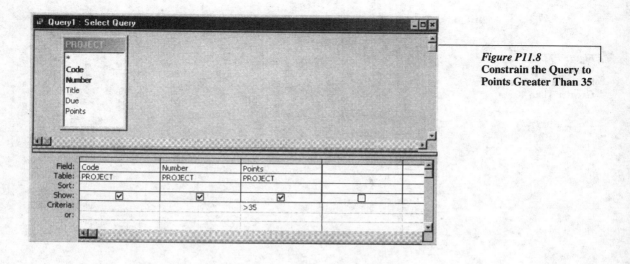

Figure P11.8 Constrain the Query to Points Greater Than 35

Figure P11.9 Results of Constraining the Points Greater Than 35

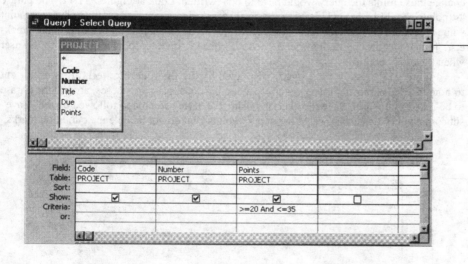

Figure P11.10 Constraining Points to Be Greater Than or Equal to 20 But Less Than or Equal to 35

points, that project does not appear in the results. To generate a report of projects whose points are greater than or equal to 20 but less than or equal to 35 use the constraint in Figure P11.10.

Notice that when one set of constraints or another set will trigger the display of a record that the constraints are shown on different lines. That is why the word "or" is below the word "Criteria" on the QBE. Figure P11.11 demonstrates how to constrain query results to records whose points are either less than 20 or greater than 40. You can toggle between the design and datasheet views to see how the queries are constructed and the results they display.

Figure P11.11
Constraining Points to be Less Than 20 or Greater Than 40

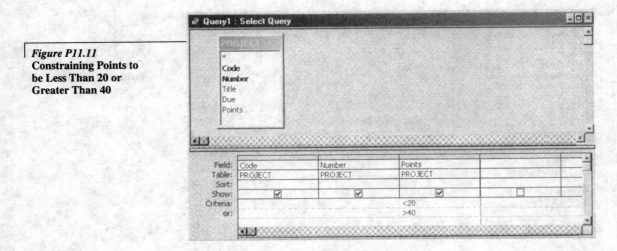

Parameter Query

Sometimes the decision maker will know which field will constrain a query but not the value of the constraint. Access allows parameter queries, queries that let a user provide a value as the query runs. For example, suppose the decision maker is looking for unusually low or high points for projects. The decision maker could code the point amounts into the query as in Figure P11.11 or the query code could be written so that the decision maker is asked to provide the amounts each time the query runs.

In the earlier query, the values of 20 or 40 were used. If the decision maker wished to change those limits the query would have to be rewritten. Look at Figure P11.12. The phrase "<[points should be below]" is one criteria. The "<" sign simply means that when the point value is less than the entered value, the record should be displayed. By placing square brackets, "[" and "]," around the phrase, Access will display the phrase as a question to the user when the query is run.

Figure P11.13 shows the screen displayed by the first query criteria. It is important to note that the parameter query requires square brackets, not parentheses, around the phrase to be asked of the user. Save the query by using the "File" command followed by the "Save" subcommand. When asked, name the query "Points" but do not include the quotation marks.

Figure P11.12 **A Parameter Query**

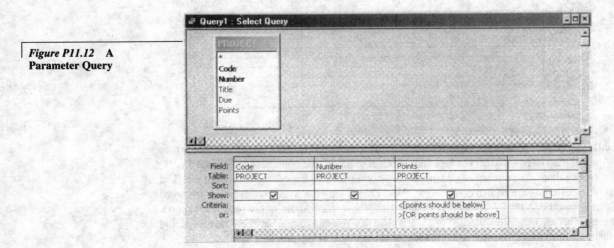

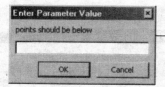

Figure P11.13 The Query Will Ask for a Parameter Value

Inexact Constraints
Constraints on fields containing text can be difficult to create because what constitutes a match might be ambiguous. For example, what if you are looking for a course named "Management?" You can see from the values of the Description field in Figure P11.2 that the word "Management" is part of three course descriptions. If the constraint is entered as Figure P11.14 Access will not find the record.

The "Management" phrase looks for an exact match for the entire field value in the database records. Since "Management" is not an exact match of an entire Description field, no records are displayed by the query. Access uses two characters as wildcards in the matching of text fields.

The asterisk, "*," is a wildcard that matches any value or string of values, even a null value. A null value is the special case where there is no value at all. A question mark, "?," is a wildcard match for a single character. Table P11.1 shows how wildcards match with certain phrases. Figure P11.15 shows a query with a wildcard match looking for the word "for."

Note that since a word, such as "for," is surrounded by spaces the constraint uses "* for *" and not "*for*." The constraint "*for*" would display the record "Information Systems Literacy." Also, Access will find a match even if the letter case does not match. "AAA" in the database record would match the constraint of "aaa." Some database management software requires the case to match as well as the letters.

Queries Requiring More Than One Table
Queries that require data fields from more than one table require that the tables supplying field values as well as tables used to navigate between those tables be included in the query-by-example. For example, assume you wish to create a query that displays the department name associated with each project title. The Name field is needed from the DEPARTMENT table and the Title field is needed from the PROJECT table.

From Figure P11.1 you can see that the records in the DEPARTMENT table do not relate directly to the records in the PROJECT table. Instead, they are related through the COURSE table. Without DEPARTMENT records matching records in the COURSE table and then those COURSE records matching records in the PROJECT table, all records are

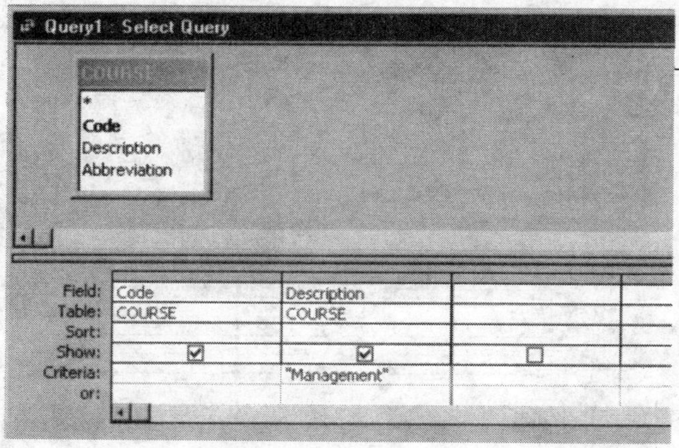

Figure P11.14 Incorrect Constraint to Find a "Management" Record

Table 11.1

Examples of Wildcard Matching

WILDCARD PHRASE	MATCHES	DOES NOT MATCH
Like "*Management"	Introduction to Management	Database Management Systems
	Introduction to Operations Management	
Like "Management*"		Introduction to Management
		Introduction to Operations Management
		Database Management Systems
Like "*Management*"	Introduction to Management	
	Introduction to Operations Management	
	Database Management Systems	
Like "?i*"	FIN305	INT100
	MIS105	INT201
	MIS315	INT202

displayed in the query results even though they should not be joined together. Figure P11.16 illustrates the incorrect query and Figure P11.17 shows some of the incorrect results. Obviously, the Personal Portfolio project is not used in all of the departments.

Without the links between tables the query does not restrict itself to records that match between tables. Figure P11.18 illustrates the correct query and Figure P11.19 displays the query results. Note that since the INT201 and INT202 courses use the same project titles ("Nouns" and "Verbs"), these titles are shown twice on the report.

There is a note of caution when using multiple tables in a query. When there is no matching value between the tables, the records with no match are not displayed in the query results. That is because linkage between tables is usually performed with matched values between tables. To display unmatched records we must modify the linkage between the tables.

Let's assume that you need to know which courses do not require a project. By looking at the relationships among tables in Figure P11.1 we can see that if a course (i.e., a Code field

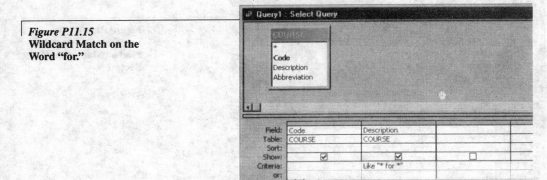

Figure P11.15
Wildcard Match on the Word "for."

value in the COURSE table) does not require a project then there will be no corresponding course code in the PROJECT table. In query-by-example terms, there will be a Code record value in the COURSE table but the Code value in the PROJECT table will be null.

To write a query to find which courses do not require a project we must edit the property joining the COURSE and INTERSECTION tables and place a constraint on the Code field in

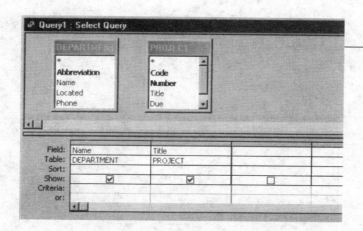

Figure P11.16 Incorrect Query to Display Department Names with Project Titles

Name	Title
Accounting and Finance	Personal Portfolio
Economics	Personal Portfolio
International Business	Personal Portfolio
Information Systems and Operations Management	Personal Portfolio
Management and Marketing	Personal Portfolio
Accounting and Finance	Nouns
Economics	Nouns
International Business	Nouns
Information Systems and Operations Management	Nouns
Management and Marketing	Nouns
Accounting and Finance	Verbs
Economics	Verbs
International Business	Verbs

Figure P11.17 Some Results from the Incorrect Query to Display Department Names with Project Titles

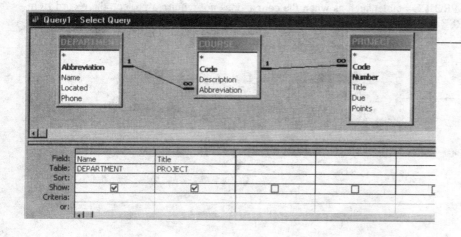

Figure P11.18 Correct Query to Display Departments for Projects

Figure P11.19 Query Results Showing Departments and Project Titles

Name	Title
Accounting and Finance	Personal Portfolio
International Business	Nouns
International Business	Verbs
International Business	Nouns
International Business	Verbs
Information Systems and Operations Management	Home Page Development
Information Systems and Operations Management	Working With Windows
Information Systems and Operations Management	Alumni Database
Management and Marketing	Finding Customers
Management and Marketing	Segmenting Customers
Management and Marketing	Customer Service

Figure P11.20 Begin Building Query to Find Courses without Projects

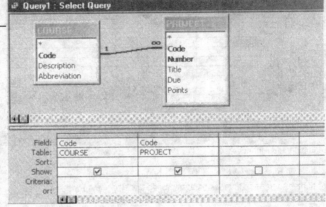

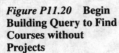

Figure P11.21 Choices after Selecting the Line Joining Tables

the PROJECT table. Begin by creating a query as in Figure P11.20. Notice that it is taking the Code field from both the COURSE and PROJECT tables.

Place the cursor on the line joining the tables and try to place it halfway between the two tables. When you press the right mouse button the screen in Figure P11.21 appears. Choose the "Join Properties" option. From the screen in Figure P11.22, choose the second option so that all records from the COURSE table will be included. Even if there is no matching record in the PROJECT table, such as when the course does not require a project, the record from COURSE will be included in the report.

Figure P11.22 Choose All Records from the COURSE Table

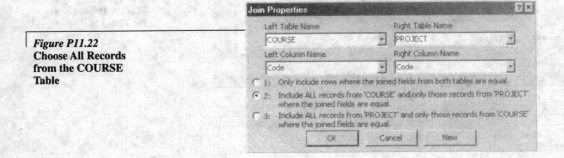

PROJECT 11 DATABASE QUERIES—CLASSPROJECTS DATABASE ••• 385

COURSE.Code	PROJECT.Code
ACG201	
ACG301	
ECN375	
ECN460	
FIN305	FIN305
INT100	
INT201	INT201
INT201	INT201
INT202	INT202
INT202	INT202
MGT300	
MIS105	MIS105
MIS105	MIS105
MIS315	MIS315
MKT300	
MKT444	MKT444
MKT444	MKT444
MKT444	MKT444
POM250	
STA230	

Figure P11.23 **Query Results after Modifying the Join Properties**

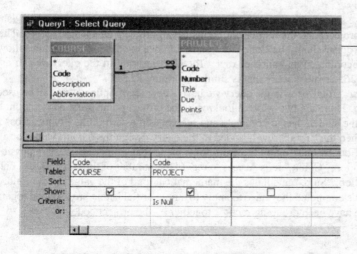

Figure P11.24 **Using the "Is Null" Constraint**

You can see from running the query (Figure P11.23) that the course "ACG201" and others do not require a project. To display only the courses that do not require projects we constrain the Code field value in the PROJECT table to be null. That query is shown in Figure P11.24. The phrase "Is Null" is a special constraint in Access.

Data Field Concatenation and Calculation

Data fields with text values can be concatenated; the characters can be added together with other characters and other text fields. Numeric fields are subject to mathematical operations. These operations can take place within a query so that values in the database do not need to be changed.

For example, the PROJECT table has separate fields for the Code and Number fields. Figure P11.25 demonstrates how the fields can be shown separately and together in a single, concatenated field label. For example, the second project for MIS105 would be "MIS105-2." "Label:[Code] & "-" & [Number]" shows that the field names from the Access database are surrounded by square brackets. Notice that a dash has been inserted between "MIS105" and "2."

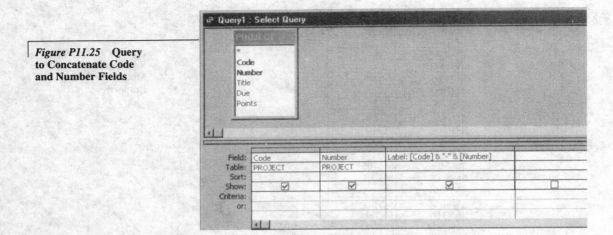

Figure P11.25 Query to Concatenate Code and Number Fields

Also notice in Figure P11.25 that the phrase "Label:" appears before the concatenation of the Code and Number fields. This is so Access can give this new field a description for its column in the display.

Because some courses have more than one project, a decision maker may wish to see the number of projects and the number of points for all projects on a single record. The only two fields in the query should be Code and Points. Choose the "View" command followed by the "Totals" subcommand and another row, "Total," is inserted in the query design as shown in Figure P11.26. Create a query that is similar to Figure P11.26.

With the "Total" row in the query we have a new set of options that can be used for decision making. There are two ways at looking at the project points; first as the count of number of projects the student has to complete and second as the sum of the points across the course projects. When the "Total" row is added to the query design the default value for a column is "Group By" but by clicking on the drop-down menu many other choices are possible.

One option, "Count," tells Access to record the number of times a record is encountered. Another option, "Sum," calculates the mathematical total of the values in the field. For a sum or count to be computed they have to apply to a field or fields that are grouped together. In our example we have been grouping records together by the project code.

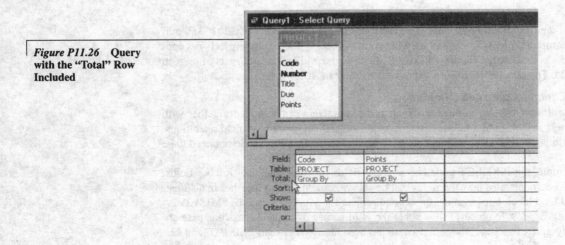

Figure P11.26 Query with the "Total" Row Included

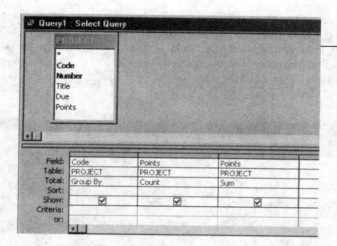

Figure P11.27 **Query Design With Count and Sum Features**

Query1 : Select Query

Code	CountOfPoints	SumOfPoints
FIN305	1	35
INT201	2	40
INT202	2	40
MIS105	2	75
MIS315	1	20
MKT444	3	140

Figure P11.28 **Query Results of Count and Sum Functions**

Figure P11.27 shows a query that will calculate both the count of the number of projects for a given course as well as the sum of the project points for that course. Notice that the Points field is in the query twice, once with the "Count" option and once with the "Sum" option. Figure P11.28 is a listing of the query results.

Numeric fields and date fields can be subjected to mathematical computations. Assume the decision maker wants to know the number of points needed for an "A" grade for each project. An "A" would be calculated as 90% of possible points. Figure P11.29 shows the query that would generate such a report. (Notice that the "Total" row has been removed from the query since no summing or counting is required for the query.)

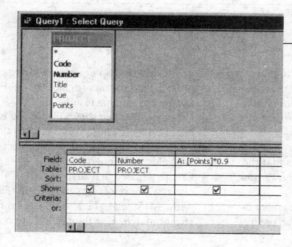

Figure P11.29 **Query to Calculate Project Points Needed for an "A" Grade**

Assume the instructor decides that projects could be turned in one week late with a deduction of 5 points from the maximum grade. The query calculations are shown in Figure P11.30. The calculated field "Late" adds 7 days to the original due date while 5 points are subtracted from the original number of points assigned to the project. The results of the query are shown in Figure P11.31.

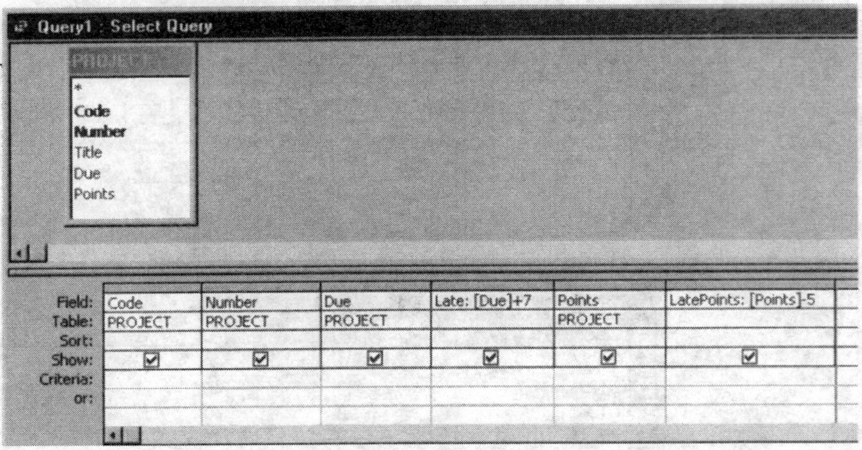

Figure P11.30 Query to Calculate Late Due Dates and Reduced Points

Figure P11.31 Results of Query to Calculate Late Due Dates and Reduced Points

Code	Number	Due	Late	Points	LatePoints
FIN305	1	11/14/2003	11/21/2003	35	30
INT201	1	9/17/2003	9/24/2003	15	10
INT201	2	11/21/2003	11/28/2003	25	20
INT202	1	9/17/2003	9/24/2003	15	10
INT202	2	11/21/2003	11/28/2003	25	20
MIS105	1	9/15/2003	9/22/2003	25	20
MIS105	2	11/13/2003	11/20/2003	50	45
MIS315	1	12/5/2003	12/12/2003	20	15
MKT444	1	10/31/2003	11/7/2003	50	45
MKT444	2	11/21/2003	11/28/2003	50	45
MKT444	3	12/12/2003	12/19/2003	40	35
	0			0	

Assignment

1. Create a query using the PROJECT table that shows the code and number of projects that are worth more than 40 points. Project codes should be the combination of the Code and Number fields such that code and number values "FIN305" and "1" become "FIN305, Project 1." Sort the results by the number of points that the project is worth. Hint: Figure P11.25 shows how concatenate fields.
2. Create a query that shows the project code and number of projects whose points are greater than or equal to 30 and less than or equal to 40. Show only the project code and number, not the field or fields you use to constrain the results.
3. Create a query that shows the project code and number of projects whose points are less than 30 or greater than 40. Show only the project code and number fields in the query results.
4. Create a query that displays all of the MIS classes. These classes will begin the Code field with "MIS" and you should use an inexact constraint match. Use the table that contains all the

course codes for this query. Sort in descending order.
5. Create a query that finds all senior level classes in the COURSE table based upon values in the Code field. A senior level class will always have the fourth character of the Code field be the value "4."
6. Make a parameter query that asks the user to provide a Code value in the COURSE table and limit the query results to the Description field value for that course.
7. What courses from the International Business department (the Abbreviation field value of "INT") do not have any projects? Only display the course code for courses that have no projects.
8. For each department, count the number of courses offered by the department. Show the department name and count of courses. For this query you need two tables.
9. Sum the number of project points for each department (not for each individual course). The department name and the summed value of points should be displayed. Sort in descending order by the number of points.
10. Which project is due first from the PROJECT table? Show the code, number, and title.

Project 12

Reports Based on Queries

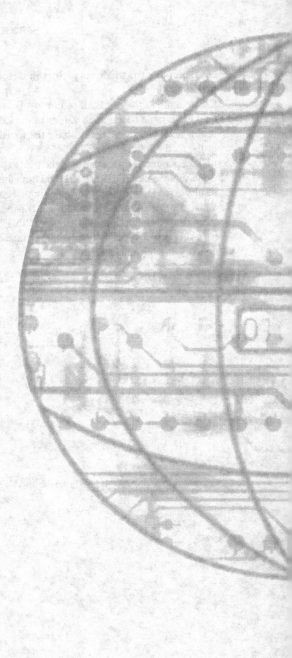

Learning Objectives

- Learn to create a report based on query results.
- Learn to pass query parameters to reports.
- Understand how built-in Access functions can change report content.
- Understand how to generate field values based upon query values.
- Learn to make calculations within reports.

Introduction

This project uses Access 2002 (also known as Access XP) to create queries for an existing database. The initial database can be downloaded from the Prentice Hall Web site for the text at WWW.PRENHALL.COM/MCLEOD – "mcleod" must be in lower case letters. The database for this project, Textbook, concerns classes and the books used in those classes. The database also contains records of students who have copies of books to sell.

Project 12 contains some advanced database concepts for queries and reports. If you have completed Project 9 and either Project 10 or 11 then you should be prepared for this project. Managers often need to build reports based upon the results of queries. The reports may need calculated fields to display meaningful labels on codes from the database. Fields in the report may need to be moved and reformatted to create visually appealing reports. Decision makers need to understand how to generate reports from queries so that data can be filtered to a relevant set of facts for decision making.

An Access database is a single file. Although there may be many tables in a database, they are all contained in the single database file along with any queries, reports, or other components of the database. You should create a copy of the data file with your database on a regular basis. You can save the copy to a diskette, a Zip disk, or some other medium of your choice.

If you use a floppy disk or Zip disk to store your database, always wait until you have completely exited Access and writing to the database has stopped before you remove the disk from the drive. Database management software works closely with the computer's operating system and sometimes the writing of information back to the database file occurs when you exit the database. Removing the disk early could result in losing your entire database.

Within Access you are able to use the "Edit" command to cut and paste objects. Those objects are tables, queries, reports, and similar components of the database. You cannot copy the database itself from within Access. To copy the entire database, such as for a backup copy, you must copy the database file using Windows Explorer or clicking on the "My Computer" icon.

One last caution about using database software is that the database file size can grow quickly. Users like features such as the "Undo" command that can easily reverse mistakes. Such features come at a price: They require much disk space in the database file to guide the reversal of actions taken. To keep your database file at a reasonable size you should compact it on a regular basis, such as every time you exit Access.

From within Access, the "Tools," "Database Utilities," and "Compact and Repair Database" sequence of commands will compact your database to remove all of the deletions and missteps that you may have performed while using the database. You can change the Access settings to automatically compact the database each time you exit Access. "Tools," followed by "Options," "General," and "Compact on Close" will have Access automatically compact the database. However, many universities limit the ability of students to change computer settings so you may have to explicitly compact your database each time you use Access.

EXAMPLE

This example will generate queries and reports from data in the Textbook database. The Textbook database will be provided by your instructor or downloaded from the Prentice Hall Web site. Managers typically use queries to look for specific records and so the query is constrained to records that have certain values for fields. Reports based on query results must usually be modified from the default report settings in order to create visually appealing reports.

Information is the essential tool of a decision maker. The understanding of the database gained by writing queries trains a decision maker to use that tool better. Creating reports based upon query results is valuable so that the decision maker can produce documents for his or her subordinates.

Textbook Database

The Textbook database consists of four tables that relate to each other by common values. The tables and their data fields are shown in Figure P12.1. The STUDENT table contains four fields; FirstName, LastName, BookNumb, and CopiesToSell. The key fields of the tables are shown in bold font. It takes the combination of values from the FirstName, LastName, and BookNumb fields to make a key (i.e., a unique value) for the STUDENT table. The ClassNumb field is the only field needed to be the key of the CLASS table.

The fields from different tables can be combined when a common value exists between the two tables. For example, the field BookNumb is in both the STUDENT table and the BOOK table. If the value of BookNumb is 409 in the BOOK table and in the STUDENT table then the name of the student from the STUDENT table can be associated with the book title of the BOOK record. From Figure P12.2 you can see Amy Abner and Brian Janski both have book number 409 to sell. Book number 409 (see Figure P12.3) has a title of "Management Information Systems" and was authored by McLeod and Schell.

For the projects and assignments in this text you will only have to use an existing database; you will not be required to create a database or tables within a database.

Begin this project by opening the Access program and then opening the Textbook database. Notice from Figure P12.4 that the "Queries" tab is chosen.

Figure P12.1 Tables and Fields in the Textbook Database

Figure P12.2 Fields and Values in the STUDENT Table

FirstName	LastName	BookNumb	CopiesToSell
Amy	Abner	409	1
Bell	Ringer	32	1
Bette	Chancer	32	10
Betty	Donner	12	1
Betty	Donner	371	1
Bill	Eschew	16	3
Bill	Eschew	31	2
Bill	Eschew	32	2
Bill	Eschew	191	2
Bill	Eschew	200	1
Bill	Leer	191	1
Bill	Leer	371	5
Brian	Janski	409	1
Charles	Darling	121	1
Charles	Darling	371	1
Chris	Lee	12	1
Cindy	Rellash	12	2
Cindy	Rellash	24	1
Cindy	Rellash	191	5
Claire	Moore	27	6

Record: 38 of 60

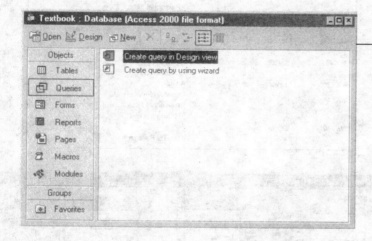

BookNumb	Title	Author	Price
12	Finance for Me	Poe and Tattem	$78.75
16	Stock Crisis	Plankton	$35.90
24	Counting Pennies	Durgee	$108.10
31	Costing Products	Gough and How	$123.45
32	The Growing Economy	Birch	$72.00
101	Personnel Files	Hiram	$78.24
121	Employee Termination	Fletcher	$72.10
191	Selling Yourself	Tattem and Gre	$83.00
206	Market Research	Shi	$95.62
231	Data Mining	Thurston and Gr	$101.50
276	Cash Management	Packard	$29.75
371	Counting By The Numbers	Bongberd	$61.00
409	Management Information Systems	McLeod and Scl	$60.50

Figure P12.3 Fields and Values in the BOOK Table

Figure P12.4 Textbook Database Screen

CREATING A QUERY AND REPORT TO SHOW BOOKS REQUIRED FOR CLASSES

A decision maker may need to see books required for each class. A standard report will generate this information as long as each class requires a book. But classes that do not require a book would not be shown on a standard report. A query must be made that will include all classes whether or not they require a book. As an additional piece of information, the course level for a class (i.e., "Freshman," "Sophomore," "Junior," and "Senior") should be shown. Figure P12.5 displays the final report.

The course level is determined from the class number. If the fourth character is a "4" then the class is a "senior" class. Values of "3," "2," and "1," relate to "Junior," "Sophomore," and "Freshman" classes. These labels for course levels can be calculated in the report itself using a series of embedded "IF..." statements but they will be easier to create in the report if the fourth character of the class number is extracted using a query.

Creating the Query for Books

Reporting unmatched class records (class records without corresponding book records) is achieved by editing the relationships between tables in a query design. Figure P12.1 is the map that allows us to determine which tables and fields are needed for the query. The CLASS table will be needed for the ClassNumb field values and the BOOK table will be needed for the Titles field. The INTERSECTION table is needed to relate class numbers to book titles.

Books Required for Classes

Class	Course Level	Title
ACG205	Sophomore	Costing Products
ACG206	Sophomore	Counting By The Numbers
ECN401	Senior	The Growing Economy
FIN201	Sophomore	Finance for Me Stock Crisis
FIN301	Junior	Cash Management The Growing Economy
MG7305	Junior	Employee Termination Personnel Files
MIS330	Junior	Management Information Systems
MIS370	Junior	
MIS401	Senior	Data Mining
MK7305	Junior	Costing Products Personnel Files Selling Yourself
MK7405	Senior	Market Research

Figure P12.5 **Report of Books Required for Classes**

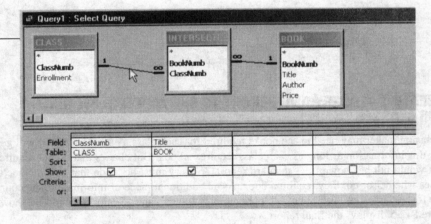

Figure P12.6 **Initial Query to Support Finding Books for Classes**

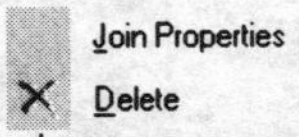

Figure P12.7 **Choose the "Join Properties" Option**

Begin by building the query shown in Figure P12.6. When you run the query you should notice that the "MIS370" class is not listed. That class does not require a text book. In order to have the query show all class numbers, whether or not they require a book, relationships joining the tables in the query must be modified.

Move the cursor to the line connecting the BOOK table to the INTERSECTION table as shown in Figure P12.6. Click the right mouse button and the screen in Figure P12.7 appears. Choose the "Join Properties" option. When Figure P12.8 appears, choose to include all records from the CLASS table. Also edit the relationship line joining the INTERSECTION and BOOK tables so that all records from the INTERSECTION table are included in the query. Your resulting table should look like Figure P12.9. When you run the edited query you see the "MIS370" ClassNumb value appear in the results.

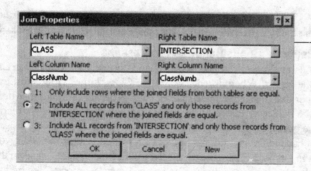

Figure P12.8 Choose to Include All Records from the CLASS Table

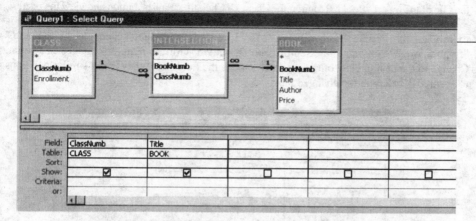

Figure P12.9 Query with Relationships Edited to Show All Records

Another column should be added to the query in order to determine the fourth character in the ClassNumb field. This could be done in the report itself but the calculation would be more complex. In the query we can simply make a new field called "Level" that contains nothing but the fourth character from ClassNumb. The entry is " Level: Mid$([CLASS.ClassNumb],4,1)" and it is placed in the third column as shown in Figure P12.10.

"Mid$" is a function in Access to take values from within a text field. It begins by naming the targeted text field, then tells where the desired string begins, and finishes with the number of characters to take out of the field. In our example Access goes to the ClassNumb

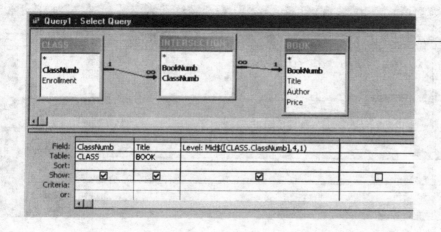

Figure P12.10 Query with Function to Determine Course Level

field in the CLASS table, finds the 4th character, and takes and returns that one character from the field. Run the query to see the results. Exit and save the query as "Books for Classes."

Creating the Report of Books Required for Classes

Create a report using Access' "report wizard" and choose the "Books for Classes" query as the source for the report. When asked, choose the ClassNumb, Title, and Level fields for the report. Remember that the field named "Level" was generated using the "Mid$" function. It is important that the field was named in the query; that name is how Access recognizes the value generated by the query.

You do not have to do any grouping other than what is default but when you advance to the screen shown in Figure P12.11, choose to sort the results based on the values in the Title field. The report layout and style can be your choice but "Stepped" and "Corporate" are frequently used. Make the title of the report "Books Required for Classes." Click the "Finish" button and view the results.

The report is similar to Figure P12.5 but requires some changes. The greatest change is to replace the course level values (1, 2, 3, and 4) with labels such as "Freshman," "Sophomore," "Junior," and "Senior." We can begin with the simpler changes in format. Change to the design view of the report and move the fields until they are in similar positions to Figure P12.12 with the changed labels.

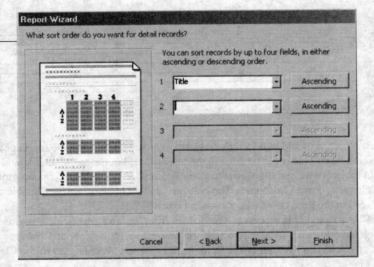

Figure P12.11 Sort Report Records by Title

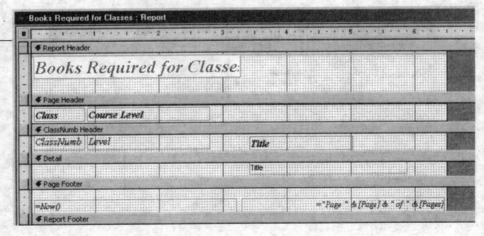

Figure P12.12 Design View of Books for Classes with Some Modifications

Notice that the label is now "Class" and not "ClassNumb" and that the label "Level" is now "Course Level." Also notice that the label "Title" has been dragged into the ClassNumb header.

Highlight the Level field, in the ClassNumb header, and delete the field. In its place we will create a new field to choose a "Freshman," "Sophomore," "Junior," or "Senior" value. If the Toolbox is not already visible on the design, choose the "View" command followed by the "Toolbox" subcommand to make the toolbox appear. Click the textbox icon ("ab|") and place a box in the design where you just deleted the Level field. You want to have some room so begin the box about two inches from the left-hand side. Remember that there is a ruler at the top of the design so you can tell where you are on the design screen. Your screen will look similar to Figure P12.13.

Click on the label field "Text..." and delete it. Click on the "Unbound" field and then click the right mouse button so you can choose "Properties." Figure P12.14 shows the control source formula for choosing the course level. "=Choose([Level], "Freshman," "Sophomore," "Junior," "Senior")" begins by calling the Access function "Choose." The function has an index and a set of values. The index is a number (in our case 1, 2, 3, or 4) and based on the index value, the value displayed in the report is either the first, second, third, or fourth value in the set of values. If the value of the Level field for a record is three, the value displayed would be "Junior," which is the third value in the list of values provided. When you display the report in print preview form you see the course level values are shown as "Freshman," "Sophomore," "Junior," or "Senior."

Formatting fields is the last step for the "Books Required for Classes" report. Return to the design view of the report and select the course level field you just created. The font name should be "Arial" and the font size should be "8" as shown in Figure P12.15. Make the font size "8" and font name "Arial" for the ClassNumb field in the ClassNumb header, the "Title" label in the ClassNumb header, and the Title field in the Detail section of the report design. The last formatting task is to select the "Title" label in the ClassNumb header and change the "Font Underline" property to be "Yes." When you run the report it should now look like Figure P12.5.

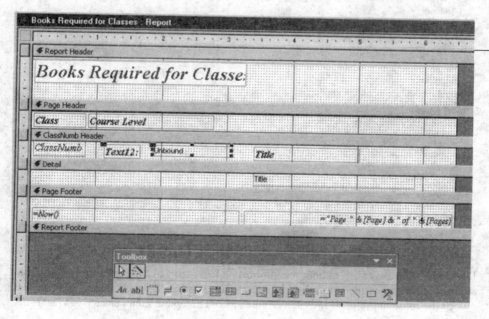

Figure P12.13 Design with Inserted Text Box

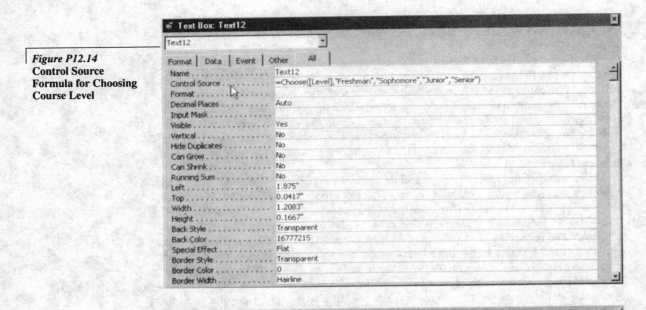

Figure P12.14
Control Source Formula for Choosing Course Level

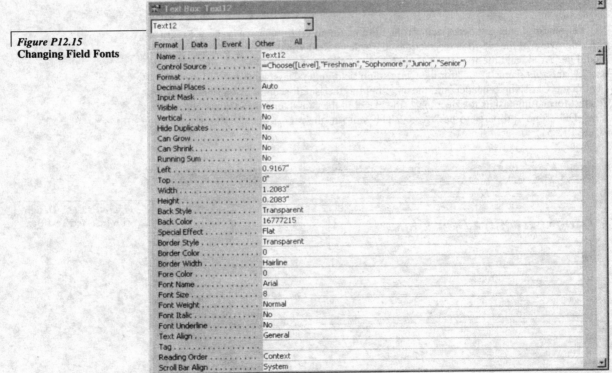

Figure P12.15
Changing Field Fonts

CREATING A REPORT FROM A PARAMETER QUERY

Decision makers may wish to limit the information in a report by basing the report on a constrained query. When the constraint is constant the report can be generated with a title that reflects the constraint value. However, it is more difficult to capture values entered in a parameter

Students Selling Books With a Price of at Least $78.75

Name	Title	Price
Costa, Maria		
	Finance for Me	$78.75
Donner, Betty		
	Finance for Me	$78.75
Eschew, Bill		
	Costing Products	$123.45
	Selling Yourself	$83.00
Fender, Keri		
	Finance for Me	$78.75
	Market Research	$95.62
	Selling Yourself	$83.00
Hinkle, Herman		
	Finance for Me	$78.75
Hogue, James		
	Counting Pennies	$108.10
Hogue, Patty		
	Counting Pennies	$108.10
Lee, Chris		
	Finance for Me	$78.75

Figure P12.16 **Partial Report of Students Selling Books**

query to be displayed in a report. Yet the parameter value is a significant piece of information that should be displayed so that the reader of the report knows how the results were constrained.

The report generated here is based upon a minimum book price which is supplied by the user at the time the report is generated. Figure P12.16 shows part of the report. The report is based upon a parameter query that passes both the parameter value and the resulting records to the report.

Creating the Parameter Query

Begin by creating a parameter query as shown in Figure P12.17. When the query is run the results are displayed but the value of the parameter is not reported. Without reporting the parameter value, the report will lack critical information.

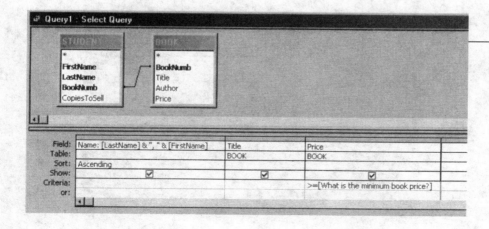

Figure P12.17 **Beginning Parameter Query**

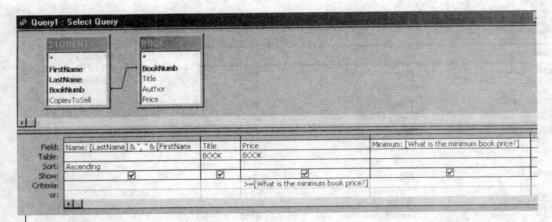

Figure P12.18
Parameter Query with Added Field to Capture Constraint Value

Another column must be added to the parameter query, see Figure P12.18. The field is given the name "Minimum" so that the field and its value can be passed to the report generator. When you run the query, notice that the value of Minimum is a constant; it is always the value you supplied to the query. A note of caution; the parameter "[What is the minimum book price?]" and the value added in the field row must be spelled exactly the same. Otherwise Access believes two parameters are in the query. Exit the query building process and name the query "Ask Minimum Price."

Creating the Report Based on the Parameter Query

Begin creating a new report using the report wizard feature of Access. The source for the report should be the "Ask Minimum Price" query you just created. Choose all the fields (Name, Title, Price, and Minimum) for the report. Group the report based on the Name field. When Figure P12.19 appears, choose to sort on Title field values.

The stepped layout and corporate style should be chosen. Name the report "Students Selling Books" and click the "Finish" button. The report created will need to be changed before it resembles the finished report shown in Figure P12.16. Begin the changes by changing to the report design view. Delete the report title (in the report header), the Minimum field,

Figure P12.19 Sort Based on Title Values

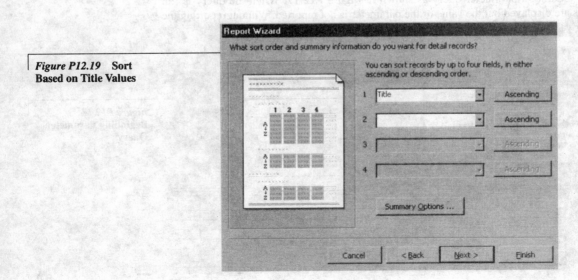

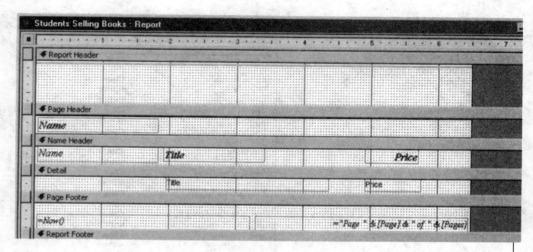

Figure P12.20
Intermediate Design of Report Based on Parameter Query

and the "Minimum" label. Then move titles and fields until they are arranged in the same manner as Figure P12.20.

The last step is to make the report title. Make sure the Toolbox is displayed in the design and choose the "Text Box" icon ("ab|"). Create a field in the "Report Header" section. Delete the "Text" box and click on the "Unbound" box with the right mouse button so that you can choose the Properties field. Enter the formula shown in Figure P12.21 into the control source of the unbound field. The formula concatenates the string "Students Selling Books With a Price of at Least $" with the field Minimum.

One reason the parameter value is placed in the title is that it needs to be shown only once since the value is a constant. Another reason is the parameter value entered should be displayed in a prominent part of the report. While you are in the properties, change the font size and font type of the report title to look like Figure P12.16.

Figure P12.21
Control Source Formula

ASSIGNMENT

1. Create a report of classes using each book. Use Figure P12.22 to guide your report creation. Note that the book title "Counting Pennies" is not used in any class.
2. Create a report similar to Figure P12.23. That report is based upon a parameter query that asks the user to supply the class number for the report. One note of caution: Some courses will not have any students who sell books for that course. In those cases, there will be no records in the report.
3. Create a report similar to Figure P12.24. That report is based upon a parameter query that asks the user to provide a minimum enrollment size. The parameter value (55 for this example) should be displayed in the report title.

Figure P12.22
Sample Report of Classes Using Each Book

Classes Using Each Book

Title	
Cash Management	**Class**
	FIN301
Costing Products	**Class**
	ACG205
	MKT305
Counting By The Numbers	**Class**
	ACG206
Counting Pennies	**Class**
Data Mining	**Class**
	MIS401
Employee Termination	**Class**
	MGT305
Finance for Me	**Class**
	FIN201
Management Information Systems	**Class**
	MIS330
Market Research	**Class**
	MKT405
Personnel Files	**Class**
	MGT305
	MKT305
Selling Yourself	**Class**
	MKT305
Stock Crisis	**Class**
	FIN201
The Growing Economy	**Class**
	ECN401
	FIN301

Figure P12.23
Sample Report of Students Selling Books

Students Selling Books for MKT305

Title	
Costing Products	Name
	Eschew, Bill
Personnel Files	Name
	Hinkle, Herman
	Jihn, San
	Vashing, Ed
Selling Yourself	Name
	Eschew, Bill
	Fender, Keri
	Leer, Bill
	Rellash, Cindy

Figure P12.24
Sample Report of Classes with Minimum Enrollments

Classes With Enrollment Greater Than or Equal to 55

Class	Enrollment
ACG205	117
ACG206	102
MGT305	68
MIS330	152
MIS401	78
MKT305	55

GLOSSARY

Chapter 1

multitasking when more than one user appears to be working on the computer at the same time. Caused by the computer's ability to break tasks into subtasks and intersperse the work of subtasks among more than one task.

information specialist a person who has a full-time responsibility for developing and operating information systems.

microcomputer (micro) a small, relatively inexpensive, and powerful system, given the name because it was even smaller than the minicomputer when it was announced.

personal computer (PC) a small, relatively inexpensive, and powerful system used for both business and personal applications.

data facts and figures that are generally unusable due to their large volume and unrefined nature.

information processed data that is meaningful, usually telling users something that they did not already know.

virtual office the performance of office activities free from dependence on a particular physical location.

personal productivity system an example of such electronic systems as electronic spreadsheets, electronic mail, voice mail, electronic calendaring, audio conferencing, video conferencing, computer conferencing, and facsimile transmission that increase the productivity of problem solvers.

groupware group-oriented software that aids group decision making.

problem a condition or event that is harmful or potentially harmful to a firm in a negative way, or is beneficial or potentially beneficial in a positive way.

solution the outcome of a problem-solving activity.

decision a particular selected course of action.

Chapter 2

closed-loop system a system that can control itself by means of a control mechanism and feedback loop.

interorganizational system (IOS) electronic linkages among firms so that all of the firms work together as a coordinated unit, achieving benefits that each could not achieve alone.

multinational corporation (MNC) a firm that operates across products, markets, nations, and cultures.

information management the process of acquiring information, using it in the most effective way, and discarding it at the proper time.

information overload the harm that can come from too much information.

legacy system an earlier information system that is incompatible or only partially compatible with current information technology.

knowledge management a broad term that describes the process of organizing a firm's information so that it can easily be captured, stored, processed, and used by decision makers.

chief information officer (CIO) the senior manager of information services who contributes managerial skills to solving problems relating not only to the information resources but also to other areas of the firm's operations.

decentralized control strategy a type of "hands-off" global strategy in which the parent allows the subsidiaries to develop their own products and practices.

centralized control strategy a global strategy that concentrates control within the parent.

centralized expertise strategy a blending of the centralized control and the decentralized control global strategies, calling for a management team at the parent location that is knowledgeable and skilled at penetrating global markets.

centralized control and distributed expertise strategy a global strategy where the parent and all of the subsidiaries work together in formulating strategies and operating policies, as well as in coordinating the logistics of getting the products to the right markets.

global information systems (GIS) an information system used by a multinational corporation.

Chapter 3

electronic commerce (e-commerce) a business transaction that uses network access, computer-based systems, and a Web browser interface.

business-to-customer (B2C) electronic commerce referring to transactions between a business and the final consumer of the product.

business-to-business (B2B) electronic commerce referring to transactions between businesses where neither is the final consumer.

business intelligence (BI) is the activity of gathering information about the elements in the environment that interact with your firm.

search engine is a special computer program that asks a user for a word or group of words to be found; typically searches Web sites on the Internet.

interorganizational system (IOS) electronic linkages among firms so that all of the firms work together as a coordinated unit, achieving benefits that each could not achieve alone.

electronic data interchange (EDI) consists of direct computer-to-computer transmissions among multiple firms of data in a machine-readable, structured format.

value-added network (VAN) when the services that operate and manage the communications line (sometimes called the circuit) are provided in addition to the communications line itself.

extranets allow the sharing of sensitive computer-based information with a few trusted firms using information technology commonly associated with the Internet.

electronic funds transfer (EFT) when data representing money is transmitted over a computer network.

extensible markup language (XML) an extension of the hypertext markup language that provides file formatting structure and a means for describing data within the file of the Web page.

virtual sales sales made by a firm that does not operate a physical storefront.

hybrid sales sometimes called "brick and click," sales from firms that have both a physical storefront and a Web site where customers can purchase products.

hypertext documents in an electronic form that are linked together—usually with Web browser software.

Chapter 4

office automation (OA) all of the formal and informal electronic systems primarily concerned with the communication of information to and from persons both inside and outside the firm.

computer literacy the ability to use computer resources to accomplish necessary processing.

information literacy understanding how to use information at each step of the problem-solving process, where that information can be obtained, and how to share information with others.

knowledge management (KM) the view that the knowledge of the organization's people is a valuable resource and should be managed.

Chapter 5

mainframe computer a large computer which performs the bulk of computer operations for centralized information systems.

processor (central processing unit or CPU) where data processing is performed.

Moore's Law states that the power of a computer doubles about every 18 months.

Memory (random access memory or RAM) the storage area on the computer's circuit board.

human-captured data input captured by a person typing on a keyboard, clicking a mouse, touching a monitor, speaking into a microphone, or a similar interaction.

screen resolution the number of pixels, individual dots of light on the monitor or dots of ink on a printed page.

personal computing computing associated with devices that are more personal to the user such as handheld PCs, pocket PCs, tablet PCs, personal digital assistants, and cell phones with interactive messaging.

personal digital assistant (PDA) a device capable of performing some computing but mainly devoted to personal organization tasks.

system software software performing certain fundamental tasks that relate to the hardware and not to the applications.

fourth generation language (4GL) is one that expresses what is to be done by the computer without explicitly defining how the tasks will take place.

user friendly computer software that is simple and intuitive to use.

protocol specification for formatting data to be transferred between communications equipment.

packet a piece of the total data to be communicated, combined with the address of the destination computer, the sending computer, and other control information.

cable modem a modem connection to the Internet via the coaxial cable that is common for receiving cable television.

private line a circuit that is always open to only your communication traffic.

Token Ring peer-to-peer communication protocol allowing each computer to act as its own controller when it controls the "token" (proprietary to IBM).

Ethernet an open protocol for peer-to-peer communications.

data transmission crash two peer computers try to send data at the same time, causing the data from each computer to be mixed up with data communicated by the other computers.

IP address a four-part set of numbers (each ranging from 0 to 255), separated by periods designating the network, host, subnetwork, and computer being addressed.

local area network (LAN) group of computers and other devices (such as printers) that are connected together by a common medium—will not use the public telephone system.

Internet the collection of networks worldwide that can be joined together.

intranet uses the same network protocols as the Internet but limits accessibility to computer resources to a select group of persons in the organization.

Chapter 6

data field the smallest unit of data representing the smallest amount of data that might be retrieved from a computer at a given time.

record is a collection of related data fields.

file is a collection of related records.

database, general definition the collection of all of a firm's computer-based data.

database, restrictive definition the collection of data under the control of database management system software.

database management system (DBMS) a software application that stores the structure of the database, the data itself, relationships among data in the database, and forms and reports pertaining to the database.

flat file a table that does not have repeating columns.

key a field (or combination of fields) which contains a value that uniquely identifies each record in the table.

hierarchical structure data groups, subgroups, and further subgroups.

relational structure joining tables by implicit relationships.

implicit relationships implied from the data values being the same in fields common between tables.

database concept logical integration of records across multiple physical locations.

data independence the ability to make changes in the data structure without making changes to the application programs that process the data.

entity-relationship diagram (ERD) graphical documentation of entities—logical chunks of data—and the relationships between entities.

class diagram graphical documentation of an object class, showing fields in the class and actions (sometimes referred to as methods) that act upon the class.

consistency data values in two fields which logically should have the same value do in fact have the same value.

redundancy repeating data fields and values in a table or group of tables.

structured query language (SQL) the code that relational database management systems use to perform their database tasks.

transaction log a list of every database action taken as well as the exact time the action was taken.

Chapter 7

methodology a recommended way of doing something.

waterfall approach a name given to the traditional system development life cycle.

prototype a version of a potential system that provides the developers and potential users with an idea of how the system in its completed form will function.

evolutionary prototype a prototype that is continually refined until it contains all of the functionality that the users require of the new system.

requirements prototype a prototype that is developed as a way to define the functional requirements of the new system when the users are unable to articulate exactly what they want.

SWAT team a development team with specialized skills, with SWAT standing for "skilled with advanced tools."

reverse engineering the process of following the system development life cycle in a backward sequence to identify a system's elements and their interrelationships, as well as to create documentation in a higher level of abstraction than currently exists.

functionality the job that a system performs.

restructuring the transformation of a system into another form without changing its functionality.

forward engineering the process of following the system development life cycle in the normal manner while engaged in business process reengineering.

terminator an environmental element that interfaces with a system, given the name because it marks the point where the system terminates.

data flow a group of logically related data elements (ranging from a single data element to one or more files) that travel from one process to another or between a process and a data store or terminator.

process an action taken on data.

data flow diagram (DFD) a graphic representation of a system that uses symbols to depict processes, data flows, data stores, and environmental elements.

context diagram a data flow diagram that positions the system in an environmental context.

figure 0 diagram a data flow diagram that identifies the major processes of the system.

figure *n* diagram a data flow diagram that documents a single process of a DFD in a greater amount of detail than the Figure 0 diagram, with the letter *n* representing the number of the process on the next higher level that is being documented.

leveled DFDs a hierarchy of data flow diagrams, ranging from the context diagram to the lowest-level diagram, that are used to document a system.

use case a narrative description in an outline form of the dialog that occurs between a primary and secondary system.

ping pong format a use case diagram consisting of two narratives, where the numbering indicates how the tasks alternate between the primary and secondary systems.

MIS steering committee a committee that directs the use of the firm's computing resources.

Gantt chart a horizontal bar chart that includes a time-phased bar for each task to be performed.

network diagram a drawing that identifies activities, linked to show the sequence in which the activities are to be performed; also called a CPM (for Critical Path Method) diagram or PERT (for Program Evaluation and Review Technique) chart.

Chapter 8

transaction processing system an information system that gathers data describing the firm's activities, transforms the data into information, and makes the information available to users both inside and outside the firm.

organizational information system an information system tailored to one of the business areas of the firm—such as finance, human resources, information services, manufacturing, and marketing—that produces information that managers use in making decisions and solving problems.

drill down a way to obtain information whereby the problem solver can bring up a summary display and then successively display lower levels of detail.

customer relationship management (CRM) the management of the relationships between the firm and its customers in order for both the firm and its customers to receive maximum value from the relationship.

data warehouse, warehousing a data storage where the storage capacity is very large-scale; the data is accumulated by adding new records rather than kept current by updating existing records with new information; the data is very easily retrievable; and the data is used solely for decision making and is not used with the firm's daily operations.

dimension table a stored table that contains identifying and descriptive data that can be used for viewing the data from various perspectives, or in various dimensions.

fact tables stored tables that are used to contain the quantitative measures of an entity, object, or activity.

information package a combination of dimension and fact tables that identifies all of the dimensions that can be used in analyzing a particular activity.

star schema a connection of dimension tables to the fact table that has the appearance of a star.

roll up the process of navigating upwards, enabling the user to begin with a detail display and then summarize the details into increasingly higher summary levels.

drill across quickly moving from one data hierarchy to another.

drill through going from a summary level to the detailed data.

online analytical processing (OLAP) the method that enables the user to communicate with the data warehouse either through a graphical user interface or a Web interface, and quickly produce the information in a variety of forms, including graphics.

relational online analytical processing (ROLAP) a type of OLAP that utilizes a standard relational database management system.

multidimensional online analytical processing (MOLAP) a type of OLAP that utilizes a special multidimensional database management system.

data mining the process of finding relationships in data that are unknown to the user.

hypothesis verification an approach to data mining that begins with the user's hypothesis of how the data is related.

knowledge discovery a data mining approach whereby the system analyzes the warehouse data repository, looking for groups with common characteristics.

Chapter 9

information security the protection of both computer and non-computer equipment, facilities, data, and information from misuse by unauthorized parties.

information security management (ISM) the activity of keeping the information resources secure.

business continuity management (BCM) the activity of keeping the firm and its information resources functioning after a catastrophe.

benchmark a recommended level of information security that in normal circumstances should offer reasonable protection against unauthorized intrusion.

threat a person, organization, mechanism, or event that has potential to inflict harm on the firm's information resources.

risk a potential undesirable outcome of a breach of information security by an information security threat.

control a mechanism that is implemented to either protect the firm from risks or to minimize the impact of the risks on the firm should they occur.

firewall a filter that restricts the flow of data between points on a network—usally the firm's internal network and the Internet.

cryptography the coding of stored or transmitted data by means of mathematical processes as a security precaution.

contingency planning the activity aimed at being able to continue to operate after an information system disruption, called disaster planning during the early years of computing.

emergency plan those measures that ensure the safety of employees when disaster strikes.

backup plan arrangements for backup computing facilities in the event that the regular facilities are destroyed or damaged beyond use.

vital records plan the plan that specifies how paper documents, microforms, and magnetic and optical storage media that are necessary for carrying on the firm's business will be secured.

Chapter 10

morals traditions of belief about right and wrong conduct.

ethics a suite of guiding beliefs, standards, or ideals that pervades an individual or a group or community of people.

laws formal rules of conduct that a sovereign authority, such as a government, imposes on its subjects or citizens.

corporate credo a succinct statement of the values that the firm seeks to uphold.

ethics program an effort consisting of multiple activities designed to provide employees with direction in carrying out the corporate credo.

ethics audit a meeting between an internal auditor and a manager for the purpose of learning how the manager's unit is carrying out the corporate credo.

logical malleability the ability to program the computer to do practically anything you want it to do.

transformation factor the fact that computers can drastically change the way we do things.

invisibility factor a view of the computer as a black box, where processing is unobservable.

internal auditor a person who performs the same analyses as an external auditor but who has a broader range of responsibilities and is an employee of the firm.

financial audit an audit that verifies the accuracy of the firm's records and is the type of activity performed by external auditors.

operational audit an audit that is not conducted to verify the accuracy of records but rather to validate the effectiveness of procedures.

concurrent audit an ongoing operational audit.

Chapter 11

desired state what the system should achieve.

current state what the system is achieving.

solution criterion what it will take to bring the current state to the desired state.

symptom a condition produced by the problem.

model an abstraction of something.

entity the object or activity that is represented by a model.

static model a model that does not include time as a variable.

dynamic model a model that includes time as a variable.

probabilistic model a model that includes probabilities.

deterministic model a model that does not include probabilities.

optimizing model a model that selects the best solution among the alternatives.

suboptimizing model a model that permits a manager to enter a set of decisions; once this step is completed the model will project an outcome.

simulation the act of using a model.

modeling scenario the conditions that influence a simulation.

what-if game the iterative process of trying out decision alternatives, using a mathematical model.

artificial intelligence (AI) the activity of providing such machines as computers with the ability to display behavior that would be regarded as intelligent if it were observed in humans.

knowledge-based system a system that uses human knowledge to solve problems.

expert system a computer program that attempts to represent the knowledge of human experts in the form of heuristics.

knowledge base the portion of an expert system that contains facts that describe the problem area and knowledge representation techniques that describe how the facts fit together in a logical manner.

problem domain the problem area addressed by an expert system.

inference engine the portion of an expert system that performs reasoning by using the contents of the knowledge base in a particular sequence.

goal variable the solution of a problem to be solved by an expert system.

expert system shell a ready-made processor that can be tailored to a specific problem domain through the addition of the appropriate knowledge base.

case-based reasoning the logic applied by an expert system that uses historical data as the basis for identifying problems and recommending solutions.

synchronous exchange the interaction among group problem solvers who meet at the same time.

asynchronous exchange the interaction among group problem solvers who do not meet at the same time.

facilitator a person whose chief task is to keep a group discussion on track.

parallel communication when all participants of a group problem solving session enter comments at the same time.

anonymity when members of a group problem solving session are unable to tell who entered a particular comment.

REFERENCES

Chapter 1

Ackoff, Russell L. "Management Misinformation Systems." *Management Science* 14 (December 1967): B147–B156.

Alter, Steven L. "How Effective Managers Use Information Systems." *Harvard Business Review* 54 (November–December 1976): 97–104.

Aron, Joel D. "Information Systems in Perspective." *Computing Surveys* 1 (December 1969): 213–236.

Bingi, Prasad; Sharma, Maneesh K.; and Godla, Jayanth. "Critical Issues Affecting an ERP Implementation." *Information Systems Management* 16 (Summer 1999): 7–14.

Cameron, Preston D. and Meyer, Stuart L. "Rapid ERP Implementation—A Contradiction?" *Strategic Finance* 80 (December 1998): 58–60.

Dash, Julekha. "Oracle Outsourcing ERP Applications." *Computerworld* 33 (October 11, 1999): 20.

Dearden, John. "MIS Is a Mirage." *Harvard Business Review* 50 (January–February 1972): 90–99.

Gill, T. Grandon. "Early Expert Systems: Where Are They Now?" *Management Information Systems Quarterly* 19 (Spring 1995): 51–76.

Piturro, Marlene. "How Midsize Companies Are Buying ERP." *Journal of Accountancy* (September 1999): 41–48.

Scott, Judy, and Vessey, Iris, "Managing Risks in Enterprise Systems Implementations: What Determines If a System Implementation Will Be Successful," *Communications of the ACM* Volume 45 Issue 4 (April 2002), pp. 74–81.

Smith, Mark. "Realizing the Benefits from Investment in ERP." *Management Accounting* 77 (November 1999): 34.

Chapter 2

Byrd, Terry Anthony; Sambamurthy, V.; and Zmud, Robert W. "An Examination of IT Planning in a Large, Diversified Public Organization." *Decision Sciences* 26 (January–February 1995): 49–72.

Cale, Edward G., Jr., and Kanter, Jerry. "Aligning Information Systems and Business Strategy: A Case Study." *Journal of Information Technology Management* 9 (Number 1, 1998): 1–12.

Hagland, Mark, "Going for the Goals: IT for Competitive Advantage," *Health Management Technology* Volume 19 Issue 2 (February 1998), pp. 24–ff.

Henderson, John C., and Treacy, Michael E. "Managing End-User Computing for Competitive Advantage." *Sloan Management Review* 27 (Winter 1986): 3–14.

Jarvenpaa, Sirkka L., and Ives, Blake. "Organizing for Global Competition: The Fit of Information Technology." *Decision Sciences* 24 (May/June 1993): 547–580.

Karimi, Jahangir; Gupta, Yash P.; and Somers, Toni M. "Impact of Competitive Strategy and Information Technology Maturity on Firms' Strategic Response to Globalization." *Journal of Management Information Systems* 12 (Spring 1996): 55–88.

Karimi, Jahangir; Gupta, Yash P.; and Somers, Toni M. "The Congruence between a Firm's Competitive Strategy and Information Technology Leader's Rank and Role." *Journal of Management Information Systems* 13 (Summer 1996): 63–88.

King, William R., and Sethi, Vikram. "An Empirical Assessment of the Organization of Transnational Information Systems." *Journal of Management Information Systems* 15 (Spring 1999): 7–28.

Lederer, Albert L., and Sethi, Vijay. "Critical Dimensions of Strategic Information Systems Planning." *Decision Sciences* 22 (Winter 1991): 104–119.

Lederer, Albert L., and Sethi, Vijay. "Key Prescriptions for Strategic Information Systems Planning." *Journal of Management Information Systems* 13 (Summer 1996): 35–62.

Prahalad, C. K., and Krishnan, M. S. "The Dynamic Synchronization of Strategy and Information Technology," *MIT Sloan Management Review* Volume 43 Issue 4 (Summer 2002), pp. 24–33.

Teo, Thompson S. H., and Ang, James S. K., "How Useful Are Strategic Plans for Information Systems?" *Behaviour & Information Technology* Volume 19 Issue 4 (June 2000), pp. 275–282.

Tillquist, John, "Institutional Bridging: How Conceptions of IT-Enabled Change Shape the Planning Process," *Journal of Management Information Systems* Volume 17 Issue 2 (Fall 2000), pp. 115–152.

Chapter 3

Barney, Jay B., "Strategies for Electronic Commerce and the Internet," *Academy of Management Review*, Vol. 27, No. 4, October 2002, pp. 628–630.

Berghel, Hal, "The Client's Side of the World Wide Web," *Communications of the ACM* 39 (January 1996): 30–40.

Chan, Stephen; Dillon, Tharam; and Siu, Andrew, "Applying a Mediator Architecture Employing XML to Retailing Inventory Control," *The Journal of Systems Software*, Vol. 60, No. 3, February 15, 2002, pp. 239–248.

Coltman, Tim; Devinney, Timothy M.; and Latukefu, Alopi S., "Keeping e-Business in Perspective," *Communications of the ACM*, Vol. 45, No. 8, August 2002, pp. 69–73.

Hart, Paul J. and Saunders, Carol S., "Emerging Electronic Partnerships: Antecedents and Dimensions of EDI Use from the Supplier's Perspective," *Journal of Management Information Systems* 14 (Spring 1998): 87–111.

Kujubu, Laura, "Web Procurement Picks Up Speed," *InfoWorld* 21, September 13, 1999: 8.

Purao, Sandeep; Jain, Hemant K., and Nazareth, Derek L., "ODE: A Tool for Distributing Object-Oriented Applications", *Information & Management*, Vol. 39, No. 8, September 2002, pp. 689–703.

Sliwa, Carol, "XML Poses No Big Threat to EDI—Yet," *Computerworld* 33 (April 26, 1999): 69.

Yoo, Sang Gong and Kim, Yeongho, "Web-based Knowledge Management for Sharing Product Data in Virtual Enterprises," *International Journal of Production Economics*, Vol. 75, No. 1–2, January 10, 2002, pp. 173–183.

Zuckerman, Amy, "EDI: Not Dead Yet," *Purchasing* 127, (September 16, 1999): 26–28.

Chapter 4

Agarwal, Ritu, and Thomas W. Ferratt. "Enduring Practices for Managing IT Professionals: Assessing Existing Business Practices to Determine Staff Recruitment and Retention Capabilities," *Communications of the ACM* Volume 45, Issue 9 (September 2002), pp. 73–79.

Bergeron, François; Rivard, Suzanne; and Raymond, Louis. "Assessment of End-User Computing from an Organizational Perspective," *Information Resources Management Journal* 6 (Winter 1993): 14–25.

Chan, Yolande E. "Why Haven't We Mastered Alignment? The Importance of the Informal Organization Structure," *MIS Quarterly Executive* Volume 1, Number 2 (June 2002), pp 97–112.

Edberg, Dana T., and Bowman, Brent J. "User-Developed Applications: An Empirical Study of Application Quality and Developer Productivity," *Journal of Management Information Systems* 13 (Summer 1996): 167–185.

Hazelhurst, Scott. "Developing IT Skills Internationally: Who's Developing Whom?" *Communications of the ACM* Volume 44 Number 7 (July 2001), pp. 27–28.

Klein, Gary; Jiang, James J.; and Tesch, Debbie B. "Wanted: Project Teams with a Blend of IS Professional Orientations; Desired Qualities Include a Strong Technical Orientation, End-User Empathy, and Organizational Awareness," *Communications of the ACM* Volume 45 Issue 6, pp. 81–87.

Kock, Ned. "Benefits for Virtual Organizations from Distributed Groups," *Communications of the ACM* Volume 43 Issue 11 (November 2000), pp. 107–112.

Moore, Jo Ellen. "One Road to Turnover: An Examination of Work Exhaustion in Technology Professionals," *MIS Quarterly* Volume 24 Issue 1 (March 2000), pp. 141–166.

Schambach, Thomas, and Blanton, J. Ellis. "The Professional Development Challenge for IT Professionals," *Communications of the ACM* Volume 45 Issue 4 (April 2002), pp. 83–87.

Wade, Michael R., and Michael Parent. "Relationships Between Job Skills and Performance: A Study of Webmasters," *Journal of Management Information Systems* Volume 18 Number 3 (January 2002), pp. 71–96.

Chapter 5

Baker, Sunny, "Getting the Most from Your Intranet and Extranet Strategies," *The Journal of Business Strategy*, Vol. 21, No. 4, July/August 2000, 40–43.

Bergenti, Federico. "A Collaborative Platform for Fixed and Mobile Networks," *Communications of the ACM*, Vol. 45, No. 11, November 2002, 39–44.

Ewalt, David M. "Handheld's New Role Includes Global Outreach," *InformationWeek*, Vol. 905, September 9, 2002, 76–78.

Fotedar, Shivi; Gerla, Mario; Crocetti, Paola; and Frata, Luigi. "ATM Virtual Private Networks," *Communications of the ACM*, Vol. 38, No. 2, February 1995, 101–109.

Glatzer, Hal. "Is There a Killer-app for DVD-Writers?" *Computer Technology Review* 19, September 1999, 48–49.

Grover, Varun and Goslar, Martin. ""Telecommunications Technologies: Patterns of Usage," *DATABASE*, Vol. 24, No. 1, Winter 1993, 16–22.

Joseph, Celia and Muralidhar, Kurudi. "Integrated Network Management in an Enterprise Environment," *IEEE Network Magazine*, Vol. 4, July 1990, 7–13.

Kay, Alan S. "The Business Case for Multimedia," *Datamation*, 41, June 15, 1995, 55.

McGuire, David and Krebs, Brian. "Attack on Internet Called Largest Ever," washingtonpost.com, October 22, 2002.

Mier, Edwin E. "Making VPNs Work," *Business Communications Review*, Vol. 29, November 1999, 41–49.

Salamone, Salvatore. "VPN Secures Access to Policies—Insurer's Upgraded Network Eases Installation, Firewall Woes," *InternetWeek*, 792, December 6, 1999, 17.

Schmerken, Ivey. "WiFi Hits the Street," *Wall Street & Technology*, June 2002, 45–46.

Thompson, Arthur. *Understanding Local Area Networks: A Practical Approach*, Prentice Hall, Upper Saddle River, New Jersey, 2000.

Chapter 6

Aiken, Peter. "Requirements-driven Data Engineering." *Information & Management* 35 (March 8, 1999): 155–168.

Hadjiefthymiades, Stathes. "Stateful Relational Database Gateways for the World Wide Web." *The Journal of Systems and Software* 48 (November 1999): 177–187.

Hammond, Chad. "Wired for OLAP Lets Your Users Hit the Road." *InfoWorld* 21 (August 23, 1999): 63–64.

Gwynne, Peter. "Digging for Data." *IBM Research* (Number 2, 1996): 14–19.

Hamilton, Dennis. "Give Your Database Administrators More Leverage." *Datamation* 40 (December 1, 1994): 51–53.

Hatten, Kenneth J. "Managing the Process-Centered Enterprise." *Long Range Planning* 32 (June 1999); 293–310.

Jackson, M. "Thirty Years (and More) of Databases." *Information and Software Technology*, Vol. 41, No. 14, November 15, 1999, 969–978.

Leitheiser, Robert L., and March, Salvatore T. "The Influence of Database Structure Representation on Database System Learning and Use." *Journal of Management Information Systems* 12 (Spring 1996): 187–213.

Navathe, Shamkrant B. "Evolution of Data Modeling for Databases." *Communications of the ACM* 35 (September 1992): 112–123.

Scheer, August-Wilhelm, and Hars, Alexander. "Extending Data Modeling to Cover the Whole Enterprise." *Communications of the ACM* 35 (September 1992): 166–172.

Shoval, Peretz and Kabeli, Judith. "FOOM: Functional and Object-Oriented Analysis & Design of Information Systems: An Integration Methodology." *Journal of Database Management*, Vol. 12, No. 1, January–March 2001, 15–26.

Verton, Dan. "Hacking Syndicates Threaten Banking." *Computerworld*, Vol. 36, No. 45, November 4, 2002, 14.

Weippl, Edgar; Klug, Ludwig; and Essmayr, Wolfgang. "A New Approach to Secure Federated Information Bases Using Agent Technology," *Journal of Database Management*, Vol. 14, No. 1, January–March 2003, 48–68.

Chapter 7

Ackoff, Russell L. "Towards a System of Systems Concepts." *Management Science* 17 (July 1971): 661–671.

Broadbent, Marianne, and Weill, Peter. "The Implications of Information Technology for Business Process Redesign," *MIS Quarterly* Volume 23 Issue 2 (June 1999), 159–182.

Churchman, C. West. *The Systems Approach*. New York: Delacorte Press, 1968.

Eliot, Lance B. "Project Management: IS Needs It." *Decision Line* 27 (March 1996): 12–13.

Gavurin, Stuart L. "Where Does Prototyping Fit in IS Development?" *Journal of Systems Management* 42 (February 1991): 13–17.

Gupta, Yash P., and Raghunathan, T. S. "Impact of Information Systems (IS) Steering Committees on IS Planning." *Decision Sciences* 20 (Fall 1989): 777–793.

Hammer, Michael. "Reengineering Work: Don't Automate, Obliterate." *Harvard Business Review* 68 (July–August 1990); 104–112.

Hume, Stan; DeVane, Tom; and Slater, Jill Smith. "Transforming an Organization Through Prototyping: A Case Study," *Information Systems Management* Volume 16 Issue 4 (Fall 1999), 49–59.

Klein, Gary, and Beck, Philip O. "A Decision Aid for Selecting Among Information System Alternatives." *MIS Quarterly* 11 (June 1987): 177–185.

Nolan, Richard L. "Managing Information Systems by Committee." *Harvard Business Review* 60 (July–August 1982): 72–79.

Stoddard, Donna B., and Jarvenpaa, Sirkka L. "Business Process Redesign: Tactics for Managing Radical Change." *Journal of Management Information Systems* 12 (Summer 1995): 81–107.

Tilles, Seymour. "The Manager's Job: A Systems Approach." *Harvard Business Review* 41 (January–February 1963), 73–81.

Chapter 8

Hildebrand, Carol. "What Elephant? Storage Is Already As Big As an Elephant and Getting Bigger." *CIO Magazine*, Volume 15 Number 15 (May 15, 2002), 101ff.

Codd, E. F. "Providing On-Line Analytical Processing to User Analysts." White paper, E. F. Codd and Associates, 1993.

Cox, Donald F., and Good, Robert E. "How to Build a Marketing Information System." *Harvard Business Review* 45 (May/June 1967): 145–154.

"IBM DB2 OLAP Miner: An Opportunity-Discovery Feature of DB2 OLAP Server." *IBM Business Intelligence Solutions*, November 2001.

Leff, Avraham, and Carlton, Pu. "A Classification of Transaction Processing Systems." *Computer* 24 (June 1991): 63–75.

McLeod, Raymond Jr., and DeSanctis, Gerardine. "Resource Flow Model of the Human Resource Information System." *Journal of Information Technology Management* 6 (Number 3, 1995): 1–15.

"Microsoft Corp. SQL Server 2000 Analysis Services." *Datapro Application Development Software Report 3054*, November 2000.

Rainer, R. Kelly, Jr., and Watson, Hugh J. "The Keys to Executive Information System Success." *Journal of Management Information Systems* 12 (Fall 1995): 83–98

Tweney, Dylan. "Cleaning Up Dirty Data." *Business*, August 30, 2001, Internet display.

Vandenbosch, Betty, and Higgins, Christopher A. "Executive Support Systems and Learning: A Model and Empirical Test." *Journal of Management Information Systems* 12 (Fall 1995): 99–130.

Wasserman, Todd; Khermouch, Gerry; and Green, Jeff. "Mining Everyone's Business." *Brandweek*, February 28, 2000, 34.

Chapter 9

Chien, Hung-Yu; Jan Jinn-Ke; and Tseng Yuh-Min. "An Efficient and Practical Solution to Remote Authentication: Smart Card." *Computers & Security* Volume 21 Issue 4 (August 1, 2002), pp. 372–375.

Finne, Thomas. "Information Systems Risk Management: Key Concepts and Business Processes." *Computers & Security* Volume 19, Issue 3 (2000), pp. 234–242.

Frantzen, Mike; Kerschbaum, Florian; Schultz, E. Eugene; and Fahmy, Sonia. "A Framework for Understanding Vulnerabilities in Firewalls Using a Dataflow Model of Firewall Internals." *Computers & Security* Volume 20 Issue 3 (May 1, 2001), pp. 263–270.

"House Votes to Increase Penalties for Cybercrime." *Information Management Journal* Volume 36 Issue 5 (September/October 2002), p. 12.

Reid, Randall C., and Floyd, Stephen A. "Extending the Risk Analysis Model to Include Market-Insurance," *Computers & Society* Volume 20 Issue 4 (July 31, 2001), pp. 331–339.

Schultz, E. Eugene. "A Framework for Understanding and Predicting Insider Attacks," *Computers & Security* Volume 21 Issue 6 (October 1, 2002), pp. 526–531.

Zenkin, Denis. "Guidelines for Protecting the Corporation Against Viruses," *Computers & Security* Volume 20 Issue 8 (December 1, 2001), pp. 671–675.

Chapter 10

De Jager, Peter. "Ethics: Good, Evil, and Moral Duty." *Information Management Journal* Volume 36 Issue 5, (September/October 2002), pp. 82–85.

Ota, Alan K. "Internet Privacy Issue Beginning to Click." *CQ Weekly* Volume 58 Issue 13 (March 25 2000), 637–640.

Ross, Paul F. "Whatever Became of Integrity: What Responsibilities Do Those in the Computing Profession Have for the Moral Integrity of What They Do? (On Site)." *Communications of the ACM* Volume 45, Issue 9 (September 2002), p. 27.

"Scramble for Web Services Patents in US and UK." *Computergram* (12/3/2001), p. 2.

Tillman, Rob. "Internet Privacy Legislation Emerges." *Information Management Journal* Volume 36 Issue 5 (September/October 2002), pp. 14–18.

Chapter 11

"An Interactive Decision Support System for the Design of Rapid Public Transit Networks." *INFOR*, Volume 40 Issue 2 (May 2002), pp. 111–118.

Beckers, Astrid M., and Bsat, Mohammad Z. "A DSS Classification Model for Research in Human Resource Information Systems." *Information Systems Management* Volume 19 Issue 3 (Summer 2002), pp. 41–50.

Berardinis, Lawrence A. "Untangling the Mystery of Neural Networks." *Technology Edge* (February 1993): 22–24.

Benaroch, Michel, and Tanniru, Mohan. "Conceptualizing Structurable Tasks in the Development of Knowledge-Based Systems." *Decision Sciences* 27 (Summer 1996): 415–449.

Chabrow, Eric. "Financial Execs ID Tech Barriers." *InformationWeek* Issue 902 (8/19/2002), p. 18.

Church, Kenneth W., and Rau, Lisa F. "Commercial Applications of Natural Language Processing." *Communications of the ACM* 38 (November 1995): 71–79.

Clawson, Victoria K., and Bostrom, Robert P. "The Facilitation Role in Group Decision Support Systems Environments." In Mohan Tanniru (ed.), *Proceedings of the 1993 ACM SIGCPR Conference*. New York: Association for Computing Machinery, 1993, pp. 323–335.

Dennis, Alan R.; Pootheri, Sridar K.; and Natarajan, Vijaya L. "Lessons from the Early Adopters of Web Groupware." *Journal of Management Information Systems* 14 (Spring 1998); 65–86.

Dennis, Alan R.; Hayes, Glenda S.; and Daniels, Jr., Robert M. "Business Process Modeling with Group Support Systems." *Journal of Management Information Systems* 15 (Spring 1999): 115–142.

Fazlollahi, Bijan, and Vahidov, Rustam. "A Method for Generation of Alternatives by Decision Support Systems," *Journal of Management Information Systems* Volume 18, Number 2 (October 1, 2001), 229–250.

Hall, Mark. "Decision-Support Systems." *Computerworld* Volume 36 Issue 27 (July 2002), p. 31.

Huber, George P. "Issues in the Design of Group Decision Support Systems." *MIS Quarterly* 8 (September 1984): 195–204.

Kim, Choong Nyong, and McLeod, Jr., Raymond. "Expert, Linear Models, and Nonlinear Models of Expert Decision Making in Bankruptcy Prediction." *Journal of Management Information Systems* 16 (Summer 1999): 189–206.

Nunamaker, J. F.; Dennis, Alan R.; Valacich, Joseph S.; Vogel, Douglas R.; and George, Joey F. "Electronic Meeting Systems to Support Group Work." *Communications of the ACM* 34 (July 1991): 40–61.

Rumelhart, David E.; Widrow, Bernard; and Lehr, Michael A. "The Basic Ideas in Neural Networks." *Communications of the ACM* 37 (March 1994): 87–92.

Shim, Sung J. "Characteristics and Adoption of Generic Financial Expert Systems: A Case Study of Failure." *Journal of Information Technology Management* 9 (Number 3, 1998): 43–55.

Sprague, Ralph H., Jr. "A Framework for the Development of Decision Support Systems." *MIS Quarterly* 4 (December 1980): 1–26.

Tata, Cyrus. "Judicial Decision Support Systems as Tools to Transform Justice?" *Information & Communications Technology Law* Volume 11 Issue 1 (March 2002), pp 5–13

Yoon, Youngohc, and Guimaraes, Tor. "Developing Knowledge-Based Systems: An Object-Oriented Organizational Approach." *Information Resources Management Journal* 5 (Summer 1992): 15–32.

Zeleznikow, John. "Using Web-based Legal Decision Support Systems to Improve Access to Justice." *Information & Communications Technology Law* Volume 11 Issue 1 (March 2002), pp. 15–33.

INDEX

A

Access controls for security, 217
Access rights, 236
Accidental threats to security, 212
Accounting information system (AIS), 9, 185
Account managers, 83
Accounts payable system, 189
Accounts receivable system, 187
Accuracy of data, 138
Accuracy of information, 32
Accuracy rights, 235
Advanced Research Projects Agency, 63
Advantage, competitive, 28–31
Alternative events in use cases, 174
Alternative solutions, 251
Amazon.com, 67
American College of Computer & Information Sciences, 242
American Express, 213
American Management Association, 242
American Micro Devices (AMD), 101
American National Standards Institute, 56
Analysis in solution effort, 161, 251
Analytical ability, 90
Andersen, Arthur, 236
Anonymity, 266, 408
Anthony, Robert N., 14, 253
Anti-terrorism, Crime and Security Act (ATCSA), 221
Antivirus software, 218
Apple Computer, 5
Application-level firewall, 218
Application software, 113–114
ARPANET, 63–64
Artificial intelligence (AI), 12, 263–265, 266, 408
Ashen, Frank, 242
Association for Computing Machinery (ACM), 239
Asynchronous exchange, 265, 408
Asynchronous transfer mode (ATM), 116
Audio conferencing, 79, 266
Audit committee, 236
Auditing, 236–238
Audit log, 217
Autobytel.com, Inc., 67
Availability of information, 209

B

Backbone topology, 121

Backup copy of database, 150
Backup plan, 222–223, 407
Balanced data flow diagram, 187
Bar code, 107–108
Bargaining in solution effort, 161, 252
Bargaining power, 56
Bartlett, Christopher A., 37
Baseline, *See* Benchmark
Battery life of PC, 110
Benchmark, information security, 210, 220, 221, 407
Benchmark compliance, 210
Berners-Lee, Tim, 64
Billing system, 187
Bit, 102–103
BlackBerry PDA, 112
Blue Gene supercomputers, 103
Brandeis, Louis, 235
Brick and click operations, 63
Bristol-Myers Squibb, 149
Browser, 65
BS 7799, 220
BSI IT Baseline Protection Manual, 220
Business alliance, 55
Business applications of the Internet, 66–67
Business area analysis (BAA), 165
Business areas, 15, 158–159
Business continuity management (BCM), 210, 222–223, 407
Business fundamentals, 89
Business intelligence (BI), 53–55, 404
Business organization, 75–76
Business partners, 29, 55, 57–58
Business process redesign (BPR), 168–170
Business-to-business (B2B) e-commerce, 50, 404
Business-to-customer (B2C) e-commerce, 50, 60–63, 404
Business transactions, *See* Electronic commerce
Bus topology, 121
Byte, 102–104

C

Cable modems, 115, 404
Candidate key, 132
Canesta, Inc., 18
Cascading style sheets, 60
Case-based reasoning (CBR), 264–265, 408
Case problems
 communications, 126–127
 confidential reports, 226

customer profiles, 246
database management system, 155
data mining, 206
electronic commerce, 71–72
processing data info information, 21–22
rapid application development, 182
sales forecast spreadsheet, 269–271
strategic planning for information resources, 45
virtual computing on campus, 98
CASE tools, 166
Catalog companies, 61
CDs, 106
Cell phones with interactive messaging, 112
Census Bureau, 52, 53
Center for Internet Security (CIS), 221
Centralized control and distributed expertise strategy, 41–42, 403
Centralized control strategy, 40, 403
Centralized expertise strategy, 40–41, 403
Central processing unit (CPU), 7, 101–103,404
Certification, professional, 221–222
Chief financial officer (CFO), 236
Chief information officer (CIO), 35, 403
 and ethics responsibility, 234, 242–243
Chinese personal privacy, 232
Circuit, private line, 116
Circuit board, 19,103
Circuit-level firewall, 218
Cisco Systems tunneling software, 116
Class diagram, 143–144, 405
Clerical tasks and automation, 12, 77
Closed-loop system, 26, 403
Closed system, 9
COBIT, 220
Codd, E.'F., 135
Code for product identity, 107–108
Codes of ethics, 232–234, 239–241
Cold site, 223
College ethics education, 241–242
CommerceNet, 67
Commercial databases, 53, 236
Committee on Data Systems Languages (CODASL), 134, 135
Common Object Request Broker Architecture (CORBA) standards, 60
Communications
 architecture, 8
 and computing, 123
 networks, 83

413

INDEX

Communications *(cont.)*
  network types, 120–123
  public telephone system, 114–120
  skills, 90
Compact disks, 106
Comparative efficiency, 55–56
Competitive advantage, 28–31
  See also Information systems for competitive advantage
Competitors, 27–28, 31–32
Completeness of information, 33
Computer crime, 231
  See also Ethics
Computerized collaborative work support, 265
Computer literacy, 89, 404
Computer Matching and Privacy Act, 231
Computer network, 63–65
Computer power, 6, 103
Computers, 100–114
  and communications, 123
  hardware, 101–109
    architecture, 7, 19
    evolution of, 4–6
    input devices, 106–108
    memory, 103–104
    multimedia, 109
    output devices, 108–109
    processors, 101–103
    storage, 104–106
  personal computing devices, 109–112
  software (*See* Software)
Computer screen, 108
Computer Security Standards, 221
Computer-supported cooperative work (CSCW), 265
Conceptual resources represented as data flows, 26, 187
Conceptual systems of a firm, 8–9
Concurrent audit, 237, 407
Confidentiality of information, 209
Connector, 173, 189
Consistency of data, 136–138, 405
Consultation with expert system, 263
Context diagram, 173, 186, 406
Contingency planning, 222, 407
Controls for security, 216–220, 407
Cookies, 31, 243
Coordination in MNCs, 31–32
Copyright protection, 236
CORBA standards, 60
Corporate code of ethics, 234
Corporate credo, 232–233, 407
Corporate information assurance officer (CIAO), 210
Corporate information systems security officer (CISSO), 210
Cost
  of computing resources, 6, 51
  of correcting design errors, 238
  hard drive comparison, 106
  of models, 260
  of prewritten application software, 113
  of printers, 109
Cost reductions of IOS, 58
Counterfeit Access Device and Computer Fraud and Abuse Act, 231
Creativity, 90
Credit card fraud, 62, 213–214
Crime, computer, 231
Critical path method (CPM) diagram, 178
Crytographic controls for security, 219, 407
CSNET (Computer Science Network), 63
Cultural barriers to global information systems, 94
Current state, 251, 407
Custom application software, 113
Customer order systems, 187–189
Customer relationship management (CRM), 193–195, 406
Customers, 27
Customer service, 59
Cyberspace, 65–66
  See also Internet; World Wide Web
CyberTown Mall, 67
Cycles per second, 102–103
Cyrix, 101

D

Data, 9, 403
  computer word size, 102–103
  human-captured *vs.* machine-captured, 106–108, 404
Data access rights and restrictions, 231, 236
Data accuracy, 138
Database
  commercial, 53, 236
  creation of, 140–144
  defined, 130, 405
  in global business strategies, 39–42
  managing it, 150–151
  programmers, 151
  structures, 134–136
  usage, 144–149
Database administrator (DBA), 81, 151
Database concept, 139–140, 405
Database management systems (DBMS), 128–155
  advantages and disadvantages, 152
  creating a database, 140–144
  database structures, 134–136
  data organization, 129–134
  defined, 134, 405
  example of relational database, 136–140
  managing a database, 150–151
  using a database, 144–149
Data consistency, 136–138, 405
Data dictionary, 140
Data elements, scenario, 257–258
Data entry, 58, 191
Data field, 129, 405
Data flow, 171, 406
Data flow diagram (DFD), 171–174, 175, 186–187, 406
Data independence, 139–140, 152, 405
Data integrity, 89
Data mart, 195
Data mining, 201–203, 406
Data organization, 129–134
  data hierarchy, 129–130
  flat files, 130–131
  key fields, 131–132
  relating tables, 132–134
  spreadsheet, 130
Data packets, 120
Data redundancy, 136, 138, 152, 405
Data store, 172, 189
Data transmission crash, 119, 405
Data transmission speeds, 115–116, 121
  See also Communications
Data warehousing, 195–203, 406
Date, C. J., 135
DB2, 136
Decentralized control strategy, 39, 403
Decision, 16–17, 252–253, 403
Decision making, 16–17, 249
Decision room, 265
Decision support system (DSS), 12, 248–271
  artificial intelligence, 263–265
  building on concepts, 250–253
  decision making, 249–250
  DSS concept, 253–255
  group decision support systems, 265–266
  mathematical modeling, 255–263
  spreadsheet use, 261–263
Decision tree, 265
Decision variables, 258
Dedicated line, 116
Definition effort in systems approach, 159–161
Degree of certainty on models, 256–257
Deliberate threats to security, 212
Denial of service, 213
Department of Defense, 221
Desired state, 250, 407
Desktop video conferencing, 79, 266
Destruction, 213
Deterministic model, 257, 407
Development engine in expert system, 264
Dewey, John, 157–158
Dialog database, 53
Digital Equipment Corporation communications protocols, 119
Digital products, 61
Digital subscriber line (DSL), 115
Dimension tables, 196, 406
Direct communications, 8
Director of internal auditing, 236
Disaster planning, 222
Disaster Recovery System (DRS), 223
Disclosure, 212

INDEX

Disposable credit card, 213
Distribution system, 185–186
Divisional information officer (DIO), 82
Documentation
   in database creation, 142–143
   by end users, 89
   of security controls, 219
Domain names, 65, 66
Dow Jones, 53
Drill across, 200, 406
Drill down, 192, 200, 406
Drill through, 200, 406
Drop-down menu, 146
DVDs, 106
Dynamic hypertext markup language (DHTML), 60
Dynamic model, 256, 407
Dynamic modeling capability of spreadsheet, 261–262
DynCorp, 178

E

Earth Simulator, 103
Eckert, J. Presper, 4, 5f
E-commerce, *see* Electronic commerce
Economic order quantity (EOQ), 255–256
Economics of electronic commerce, 52
EDGAR databases, 53
EDIFACT international standards, 56
Education
   on computer ethics, 241–242
   of computer skills, 87
   on financial systems, 243
Efficiency, 55–56, 59
Eight-element environmental model, 27, 50–51, 250
Electronic business, 49
Electronic commerce, 48–73, 403
   B2C strategies, 60–63
   benefits, 51
   business intelligence, 53–55
   constraints, 51–52
   described, 49–53
   information superhighway, 65–66
   Internet applications, 66–67
   Internet evolution, 63–65
   Internet future impact on business, 68–69
   Internet usage, 67–68
   interorganizational system (IOS), 55–60
   security considerations, 213–214
Electronic Communications Privacy Act, 231
Electronic data interchange (EDI), 55, 56–57, 404
Electronic data processing (EDP) systems, 9, 185
Electronic funds transfer (EFT), 57, 404
Electronic meeting system (EMS), 265
Electronic spreadsheet as mathematical model, 261–263

Embezzlement, 212
Emergency plan, 222, 407
Employees in virtual office, 12, 77–80
Encryption, 213–214, 219
End user, 87, 151
End-user computing (EUC), 86–89
ENIAC computer, 4
Enron, 223, 236
Enterprise, term for firm, 165
Enterprise data model, 141
Enterprise modeling approach, 141
Enterprise resource planning (ERP) system, 13–14
Entities, data fields, 142
Entity, mathematical model, 255, 407
Entity-relationship diagram (ERD), 141–143, 405
Environment, data flow diagram definition, 186
Environmental constraints, 251
Environmental elements, 27, 50–51, 250
Environmental model of the firm, 250
Environmental resource flows, 27–28
Environment and firms, 25–28
Ethernet networks, 119, 121, 405
Ethics, 228–247
   and CIO, 234, 242–243
   codes of ethics, 239–242
   computer ethics reasons, 234–236
   defined, 230, 407
   education, 241–242
   information auditing, 236–238
   morals, ethics, and laws, 230–232
   need for ethics culture, 232–234
   prescriptive *vs.* descriptive coverage, 229–230
Ethics audit, 232–234, 407
Ethics program, 232–234, 407
European Union software patents, 231
Evaluation criteria, 161
Evolutionary prototype, 163–164, 405
Executive committee, 35
Executive information system (EIS), 191–193
Executive support system (ESS), 191
Expert systems, 263–265, 408
Expert system shell, 264–265, 408
Extensible markup language (XML), 59–60, 404
External auditors, 236–237
External threats to security, 211
Extraction, transformation, and loading (ETL), 195
Extraction in data warehouse, 195
Extranets, 57, 123, 404

F

Facilitator, 265, 408
Fact tables, 196, 406
Fair Credit Reporting Act, 231
Fayol, Henri, 16

FBI Trilogy project, 178
Federal Express, 61, 232
Feedback loop, 26
Fiber optics, 116
Figure 0 diagram, 173, 187, 406
Figure 1 diagram, 187
Figure 2 diagram, 189
Figure 4 diagram, 173
Figure n diagram, 173, 406
File, 129–130, 405
File transfer protocol (FTP), 65
Filtering data, 146
Financial audit, 237, 407
Financial community, 27
Financial systems, 242–243
Finding Web sites, *See* Search engines
Firewall, 407
   in extranets, 57, 123
   hardware, 8
   required security practice, 213–214
   technical control for security, 218
   See also Security
Firms
   and electronic commerce, 50
   evaluation for systems approach, 158–159
   and their environment, 25–28
Fixed storage, 105–106
Flat files, 130–131, 405
Flat panel monitor, 108
1-800-flowers, 50, 63
Formal controls for security, 219–220
Forms for databases, 145–146
Forward engineering, 170, 405
Fourth-generation languages (4GL), 113, 166, 404
Frame relay, 116
Freedom of Information Act, 231
FTP (file transfer protocol), 65
Functionality of a system, 169, 405
Functional quality, 170
Funding for infrastructure, 68
Funds transfer, 57
Future
   of information technology, 18–20
   of Internet and business, 68–69

G

Gantt chart, 178–179, 406
Gartner research firm, 221
General Electric, 4, 134, 263
General ledger system, 189
Generally Accepted System Security Principles (GASSP), 220
General Problem Solver (GPS), 263
General systems model of the firm, 25–26, 250
George Mason University, 242
German security standards, 220
Ghoshal, Sumantra, 37
Gibson, William, 65

Gigahertz (GHz), 102
Global business strategies, 37, 39–42
Global communications network, *See* Internet
Global community, 27, 31
Global competition, 31–32
Global eXchange Services, 53
Global information systems (GIS), 42, 94–95, 403
Goal variable, 264, 408
Gorry, G. Anthony, 12, 253–254
Gorry-Scott Morton grid, 253
Government, 27
 databases, 53
 and electronic commerce, 51
 legislation and security standards, 220–221
 role in global information systems, 94
Graphical user interface (GUI), 108
Graphic model, 255–256
Group decision support system (GDSS), 12, 265–266
Group support system (GSS), 265
Groupware, 12, 265, 403
Guidelines for Management of IT Security (GMITS), 220

H

Hackers, 212–213
Handheld PC, 110
Handspring PDA, 112, 123
Hard drive, 105–106
Hardware
 communications network, 121
 computers (*See* Computers)
Heuristic, 263
Hierarchical database structure, 134–135, 405
High capacity media, 106
Highlights in MIS
 Blue Gene supercomputers, 103
 circuit design, 19
 data mining by casinos, 203
 European Union on cookies and spam, 243
 FBI Trilogy project, 178
 globalization, 43
 pharmaceutical companies, 149
 predictive maintenance, 267
 recovering from 9/11 and Enron, 223
 video conferencing, 79
 Web domain, 66
 wireless networks, 117
Historical data needs, 193
Honda, 37
Hoteling, 79–80
Hot site, 223
24Hour-Mall, 67
Hub device, 121
Human-captured data, 106–108, 404

Human resources information system (HRIS), 191
Hybrid sales, 61, 63, 404
Hypermedia, 64
Hypertext link, 64
Hypertext markup language, 59–60, 404
Hypothesis verification, 201–202, 406

I

IBM
 Blue Gene supercomputers, 103
 circuit design, 19
 communications protocols, 118–119
 database software, 136
 ethics culture, 232
 hot and cold sites, 223
 LANs, 121
 Personal Computer, 5
 System/360, 4
 World Headquarters, 37
Icons, 108, 114
Image management, 33
Impact severity of risks, 214–215
Imperatives, ethical guidelines, 239–241
Implicit relationships in databases, 135, 405
Independence of data, 139–140, 152, 405
Industrial marketing, 67
Industry security standards, 220–221
Inference engine in expert system, 264, 408
Informal controls for security, 219–220
Information, 10, 16–17, 403
Information auditing, 236–238
Information delivery system, 199–200
Information engineering (IE), 165
Information in action, 184–206
 customer relationship management, 193–195
 data mining, 201–203
 data warehousing, 195–203
 information delivery, 199–200
 OLAP, 200–201
 organizational information systems, 190–193
 transaction processing system, 185–190
Information literacy, 89, 404
Information management, 32–34, 403
Information officer, *See* Chief information officer (CIO); Divisional information officer (DIO)
Information overload, 33, 403
Information package, 197, 406
Information security, 209–210, 407
 See also Security
Information security management (ISM), 210, 407
Information services organization, 81–86
Information specialists, 5, 10, 81–82, 403
Information strategy planning (ISP), 165
Information superhighway, 65–66
 See also Internet
Information systems, 2–22

communications architecture, 8
computer applications evolution, 8–14
computer architecture, 7
computer hardware evolution, 4–6
future of technology, 18
management problem solving, 16–17
managers as MIS users, 14–16
Information Systems Audit and Control Association (ISACA), 221
Information systems for competitive advantage, 24–46
 competitive advantage, 28–31
 the firm and its environment, 25–28
 global business strategies, 37–42
 global competition, 31–32
 information management, 32–34
 strategic planning, 34–36
Information systems for organizational areas, 190–193, 406
Informix, 136
Infrastructure development, 65, 68–69
 See also Internet
Ink-jet printers, 108–109
Innovation communications networks, 83
Innovative organizational structures, 82–86
Input device, 106–108
Inputs to mathematical model, 258
Input subsystems
 for data entry, 191
 for internal audit, 238
Insider threat prediction tools, 218
Institute of Electrical and Electronics Engineers (IEEE), 119
Integrated application generator, 164
Integrated Data Store (IDS), 134
Integrated-mix subsystem, 190
Integrated services digital network (ISDN), 115
Integrity, *See* Ethics
Integrity of information, 89, 210
Intel
 communications protocols, 119
 future plans, 18
 processors, 6, 101, 102
Intellectual property rights, 236
Interactive messaging, 112
Internal auditors, 236–238, 407
Internal audit subsystem, 238
Internal contraints, 251
Internal control systems design, 238
Internal efficiency, 55
Internal support, 239
Internal threats to security, 211
International economy, *see* Global competition
International Information System Security Certification Consortium (ISC), 222
International Organization for Standardization (ISO), 118, 220
Internet, 405

business applications, 66–67
crime legislation, 221
evolution of, 63–65
host sites growth, 66
network address, 120
network types, 122–123
successful use of, 67–68
Internet Engineering Task Force (IETF), 66
Internet service providers (ISPs), 120, 221
Internet Society, 66
Internet Software Consortium, 66
Interorganizational efficiency, 56
Interorganizational information system (IOS), 11
Interorganizational system (IOS), 29, 55–60, 403, 404
    benefits, 55–56, 58–59
    business partners, 57–58
    challenges, 59–60
    electronic data exchange, 56–57
    electronic funds transfer, 57
    Extranet, 57
Intranet, 123, 405
Intrusion detection system, 218
Inventory system, 187
Invisibility factor, 234–235, 407
Iomega Corporation, 106
IP address, 120, 405
IP spoofing, 218
ISF Standard of Good Practice, 220

J

J.C. Penney, 67, 232
Johns Hopkins University, 242
Judgment in solution effort, 161, 252

K

Key fields, 131–132, 405
Knowledge-based system, 263, 408
Knowledge base in expert system, 264, 408
KnowledgeBase.net, 91
Knowledge discovery, 149, 203, 406
Knowledge management (KM), 34, 90–93, 403, 404
Knowledge of systems development, 89–91

L

Labor unions, 27–28
Laptop, 110
Laser printer, 108–109
Last mile communications, 116
Laws, 230, 407
    See also Legislation
Leadership, 90
Leased line, 116
Legacy system, 33, 168, 403
Legal responsibility, 239
Legislation
    computer, 230–231
    computer security, 220–221

Internet, 68
Legislative session, 266
Lending Tree, 61
Leveled data flow diagram, 173, 187, 406
LexisNexis, 53
Library of Congress, 53
License agreement, 236
Loading in data warehouse, 195
Local area decision network, 266
Local area networks (LANs), 121–122, 405
Logical malleability, 234, 407
Logic Theorist, 263
Logitech, 18
LRM®, Legal Knowledge Company, 242

M

Machine-captured data, 107–108
Mainframe computer, 4, 101, 112, 404
Malicious software, 213
Malware, 213
Management control level, 14–15, 253
Management functions, 16
Management information systems, 9–11, 253
    See also Information systems; Information systems for competitive advantage
Management levels, 14–15, 159
Managerial roles, 16–17
Managers
    and information management, 32
    and problem solving, 158–161
    role in MIS development, 10
    support for global information systems, 94–95
    use of automation, 77
    as users of information systems, 14–16
Many-to-many relationship, 143
Margin, 28
Marketing information system (MKIS), 190–191
Marketing intelligence subsystem, 191
Marketing mix, 190
Marketing research, 66–67
Marketing research subsystem, 191
Martin, James, 165
Mason, Richard O., 235
Mathematical encryption, 219
Mathematical models, 11, 255–261
    advantages and disadvantages, 259–261
    classes, 256–257
    electronic spreadsheet, 261–263
    example, 258
    simulation, 257–258
    types of, 255–256
    uses, 256
Mauchly, John W., 4
McAfee, 218
McCarthy, John, 263
Meeting room, 265
Megahertz (MHz), 102

Memory, 103–104, 404
Metadata, 196
Methodology, 162, 405
Metropolitan area networks (MANs), 122
Microcomputer, 5, 403
Microsoft
    Access, 136
    ethics culture, 232
    Internet Explorer, 65
    Project, 178
    SQL Server, 136
    tunneling software, 116
Military network, 63
Minicomputer, 5
Mining of data, 201–203, 406
Mintzberg, Henry, 16, 161, 251
MIS, *See* Management information systems
MIS steering committee, 176–177, 215, 406
Model, 255, 407
Models, mathematical, *See* Mathematical models
Modems, 8, 115
Modification, unauthorized, 213
Module phases of phased development, 168
Molecular circuit design, 19
Money, theft of, 212
Money transfers, 57
Monitor, computer, 108
Moor, James H., 234
Moore, Gordon, 6
Moore's Law, 6, 51, 103, 404
Moral behavior, 239–240
Morals, 230, 407
Motherboard, 7
Motorola, 101
MSNBC, 67
Multidimensional online analytical processing (MOLAP), 200, 406
Multimedia, 109
Multinational corporation (MNC), 31–32, 37, 39–42, 94–95, 403
Multiplexed line, 116
Multitasking, 4, 403

N

Narrative model, 255
National Cash Register, 232
National Information Infrastructure (NII), 68
National Science Foundation Network (NSFNET), 63
Nestlé, 37
Netscape Navigator, 65
Network database structure, 135
Network diagram, 178, 406
Networking and Information Technology Research and Development Act, 68
Network interface card, 117, 120
Networks, computer, 63–65
Network specialist, 82
Network topology, 120–123
New product development (NPD), 92–93

News media, 53
Nielsen Media Research, 67
Nonprogrammed decision, 253
Normalization, 131
Nortel Networks, 92–93
Norton, 218
Notebook computer, 110

O

Object-oriented database, 60, 144
Office automation (OA), 12, 76–77, 404
Office Depot Web site, 50, 62, 63
Off-the-shelf software, 113
One-to-many relationship, 143
Online analytical processing (OLAP), 149, 200–201, 406
Open protocol, 118
Open system, 9, 25
Open Systems Interconnection (OSI), 118
Operating system, 7, 112
Operational advantage, 31
Operational audit, 237, 407
Operational control level, 14–15, 253
Operational efficiency, 59
Operators, 82
Optimizing model, 257, 258, 407
Oracle, 14, 136
Order entry system, 187
Organizational information system, 190–193, 406
Organizational structure, 82–86, 160
Output devices, 108–109
Outputs from mathematical model, 258
Output subsystem
    for information transformation, 190–191
    for internal audit, 238
Owners, 27

P

Packet-filtering firewall, 218
Packets, 115, 120, 404
Palm PDA, 112
Paper cost savings, 58
Parallel communication, 265, 408
Parent companies in global business strategies, 37, 39–42
Partner model of innovative structures, 83
Patents for software, 231, 236
Peer-to-peer protocol, 118–119
PeopleSoft, 14
People's Republic of China, personal privacy, 232
Performance standards, 26, 160, 250
Performance statistics processor, 150
Personal computer (PC), 403
    devices, 109–112
    history, 5–6, 19
Personal computing, 404
Personal digital assistant (PDA), 77, 111–112, 404

Personal privacy legislation in China, 232
Personal productivity systems, 12, 403
Petaflops, 103
Phased development, 166–168, 170
Photograph management, 33
Physical controls for security, 219
Physical model, 255
Physical organization of firms, 76
Physical products, 61
Physical relationships in databases, 135
Physical resources, 25–26, 187
Physical systems of a firm, 8–9
Ping pong format, 174, 406
Pirated software, 230
Pixels, 108
Place subsystem, 190
Platform model of innovative structure, 83–84
Pocket PCs, 110
Point-of-sale terminal, 108
Policy for information security, 215–216
Porter, Michael E., 28–29
Porter's value chains, 28–29
Postal service, 61
Power of computers, 6, 103
Prediction using mathematical models, 256
Predictive maintenance, 267
Premkumar, G., 57
Preparation effort in systems approach, 158–159
Pretty Good Privacy, 57
Prewritten application software, 113
Price subsystem, 190
Primary storage, 103
Printers, 108–109
Printouts of legacy data, 33
Privacy
    of customer data, 68
    of extranets, 57
    legislation, 231–232
    rights, 235
Privacy, accuracy, property, and accessibility (PAPA), 235
Privacy Act, 235
Private educational programs on ethics, 242
Private mail, 61
Private telephone lines, 116, 404
PR Newswire, 67
Proactive business partners, 57–58
Probabilistic model, 257, 407
Probability, 256–257
Problem, 159, 403
Problem domain, 264, 408
Problem-oriented approach, 140
Problem solving, 16–17, 157–161, 249–253
    See also Decision support systems (DSS)
Problem structure, 252–253
Problem trigger, 159
Process, 171
Process modeling, 171–175

Process-oriented approach, 140
Process-oriented modeling, 140
Processors, 7, 101–103, 404
Processor speed, 6, 102–103
Procter and Gamble, 37
Product features, 56
Product identity barcode, 107–108
Products for B2C electronic commerce, 61
Product subsystem, 190
Professional certification, 221–222
Professional performance, 239
Professional programs on ethics education, 242
Program evaluation and review technique (PERT) chart, 178
Programmed decision, 252–253
Programmers, 82, 151
Project leader, 178
Project management, 175–180
Project team, 178
Promotion subsystem, 190
Property rights, 236
Protocol, 114, 404
Protocols for computer communications, 118–119
Prototype, 163, 405
Prototyping, 162–165, 170
Prototyping toolkit, 164
Public telephone system, See Telephone system
Purchase orders cost reductions, 58
Purchasing system, 189

Q

Query, 148
Query-by-example, 148
Query language, 144

R

Ramamurthy, K., 57
Random access memory (RAM), 7, 103, 404
Rapid application development (RAD), 165–166, 170
Reactive business partners, 57–58
Receiving system, 189
Reciprocal agreement for backup plan, 223
Record, 129–130, 405
Redundancy of data, 136, 138, 152, 405
Reengineering, 168, 170
Relating tables, 132–134
Relational database, 130, 135–140, 405
Relational online analytical processing (ROLAP), 200, 406
Relevancy of information, 32
Remington Rand UNIVAC I computer, 4
Removable storage, 106
Replenishment order systems, 189
Reports
    for databases, 146–148
    weekly written, 178

Report-writing software, 11
Requirements prototype, 163–165, 405
Research in Motion, 112
Research marketing, 66–67
Resolution of screens and printers, 108, 109, 404
Resource flows in problem solving, 159
Resources
    for information services organization, 81
    in problem solving, 160–161
    users as information resource, 88–89
Restructuring, 170, 405
Retailing application, 67
Reuters, 53
Reverse engineering, 168–169, 405
Rights in terms of information, 235–236
Right to Federal Privacy Act, 231
Ring topology, 121
Risk controls, 216–219
Risk management, 210, 214–215
Risks, 212–213, 407
Roll up, 200, 406
Router as firewall, 218
Rule in expert system, 264
Rule set, 264

S

Sales
    in electronic commerce, 52
    forecast, 190
    virtual *vs.* hybrid, 61–63
SANS Institute, 222
SAP, multinational company, 14
Satisficing model, 257, 258
Scalable model of innovative structures, 84–85
Scanner, 108
Scenario, 257, 407
Scenario data elements, 257–258
Scott-Morton, Michael S., 12, 253–254
Screen resolution, 108, 404
Search engine, 54–55, 404
Search-related costs, 56
Secure electronic transactions (SET), 219
Securities and Exchange Commission, 53, 236
Security, 208–227
    business continuity management (BCM), 222–223
    controls, 216–220
    of database, 151, 152
    of electronic commerce, 51–52, 213–214
    by end users, 89
    of extranets, 57
    government assistance, 220–221
    industry assistance, 220, 221
    information security, 209–210
    information security management (ISM), 210
    of intranet, 123
    legislation, 220–221
    policy, 215–216
    professional certification, 221–222
    risk management, 214–215
    risks, 212–213
    and strategic advantage, 30
    telephone lines, 116–117
    threats, 210–212
    virus, 213
    of wireless communications, 8
    See also Firewall
Security Pacific Corporation, 232
Semistructured problem, 252
Server, 65
Shipping services, 61
Siebel, 14
Siemens, 123
Silicon transistors, 3, 19
Simon, Herbert A., 17, 249, 251
Simulation, 257–258, 407
SKF company in Sweden, 267
Skills in systems development, 90
Small Business Computer Security and Education Act, 231
Social responsibility, 239
Social rights, 235–236
Society
    environmental elements, 27
    impact of virtual organization, 81
Software
    antivirus, 218
    applications evolution, 8–14
    basic types, 112–114
    for electronic commerce, 51–52
    for intrusion detection, 218
    malicious, 213
    patents, 231, 236
    pirated, 230
Software vendors and theft, 236
Solution, 16–17, 403
Solution criterion, 251, 407
Solution effort in systems approach, 161
Sourcing communications networks, 83
Southwest Airlines, 232
Spam, 243
Spreadsheet, 130, 261–263
SQL Server, 136
Standards
    ANSI ASC X12, 56
    communications networks, 118
    EDIFACT international, 56
    information security, 220–221
    Internet, 66
Star schema, 198, 406
Star topology, 121
State Street Decision, 231
Static model, 256, 407
Static modeling capability of spreadsheet, 261
Statistical packages, 113
Stockholders, 27, 243
Stock replenishment, 56
Storage for computers, 104–106
Strategic planning for information resources (SPIR), 34–39
Strategic planning level, 14–15, 253
Structured decision system (SDS), 253
Structured problem, 252
Structured query language (SQL), 144, 148–149, 405
Subforms in database, 146
Suboptimizing model, 257, 258, 407
Subsidiaries in global business strategies, 37, 39–42
Subsystems analyzed for problem solving, 159, 160
SunGard, 223
Sun Oil Company, 256
Supercomputer, 103
Superhighway, information, 65–66
Suppliers, 27, 56
SWAT team, 166, 405
Sweeney, Harold, 5f
Switching costs, 56
SX45, 123
Symptom, 159, 252, 407
Synchronous exchange, 265, 408
System Network Architecture (SNA), 118
Systems analyst, 81, 237
Systems approach, 157–161, 250
Systems development, 156–183
    business process redesign, 168–170
    knowledge and skill, 89–93
    phased development, 166–168, 170
    process modeling, 171–175
    project management, 175–180
    prototyping, 163–165, 170
    rapid application development (RAD), 165–166, 170
    systems approach, 157–161
    systems development life cycle (SDLC), 162, 170
Systems development life cycle (SDLC), 82
    internal auditing, 237, 238
    technical controls for security, 216–219
    traditional, 162, 170
Systems life cycle (SLC), 89
Systems modeling, 89
System software, 112–113, 404
Systems theory, 89
Systems view, 250
System users and developers, 74–98
    business organization, 75–76
    end-user computing, 86–88
    global information systems, 94–95
    information services organization, 81–86
    office automation, 76–77
    systems development, 89–93
    users as information source, 88–89
    virtual office, 77–80
    virtual organization, 80–81

T

T-1 and T-3 lines, 116
Tables in database, 130
Tablet PC, 110
Tactical advantage, 30
TAMP Computer Systems, 223
Tandy Corporation, 5
Team leader, 178
Technical controls for security, 216–220
Technical quality, 170
Telecommuting, 78
Teleconferencing, 79, 266
Telephone system, 8, 114–120
   communications networks, 118
   Internet network addresses, 120
   packets, 120
   private lines, 116
   protocols for computer communications, 118–119
   public connections, 114–116
   virtual private network, 116–117
Teleprocessing, 78
Telesuite, 79
Terminal, 108, 118
Terminator, 171, 406
Theft, 62, 212–214
Thomas Register Online database, 53
Threats to security, 210–212, 407
Three I economy, 81
Three Mile Island nuclear disaster, 235
Time influence on models, 256
Timeliness of information, 33
Token Ring, 118–119, 121, 405
Tracking package shipments, 61
Trading partners, 55
Training in knowledge management, 34
Transaction log, 150, 405
Transaction processing systems, 9, 185–190, 406
Transborder data flow (TDFs), 94
Transformation factor, 234, 407
Transformation in data warehouse, 195
Transformation processes, 161
Transistor, 3, 19
Translator programming languages, 113
Transmission Control Protocol/Internet Protocol (TCP/IP), 120
Trial and error method, 260
Trojan horse, 213
Tunneling software, 116–117
Turing, Alan, 264
Turing Test, 264

U

Unauthorized breach of security, 212–213
Unauthorized use, 212–213
Uncertainty, 31
Unilever, 37
United Kingdom security standards, 220, 221
United States legislation, *See* Legislation
UNIVAC I computer, 4
Universal resource locator (URL), 65
University ethics education, 241–242
University of Phoenix, 242
UNIX operating system, 112
Unstructured problem, 252
UPS, 61
URL, 65
Use, unauthorized, 212–213
Use cases, 174–175, 406
User, *See* End user; System users and developers
User friendly software, 114, 404
User identification, 217
User interface in expert system, 264
User profile, 217
Users of information systems, 14–16
Utility program, 112–113

V

Vacuum tube, 3
Value activities, 28
Value-added network (VAN), 56, 404
Value chains, 28–29
Value system, 29
Vendors, 14, 27, 236
Vendor stock replenishment, 56
VeriSign, 51, 62, 66
Video conferencing, 79, 266
Virginia Tech, 221
Virtual office, 12, 77–80, 403
Virtual organization, 80–81

Virtual private networks (VPNs), 116–117
Virtual sales, 61–63, 404
Virus, 213
Virus protection software, 218
Visa, 213–214
Visioning communications networks, 83
Vital records plan, 223, 407
Vulnerability of firm, 214–215

W

Wal-Mart, 67
Waterfall approach, 162, 405
Web, *See* World Wide Web
Web-based education on ethics, 242
Webmaster, 81
Web site design
   markup languages, 59–60
   statistics for webmaster, 82
Web sites
   sales, 61–62
   successful use of, 67–68
What-if game, 258, 262–263, 408
Wide area networks (WANs), 122
Wireless communications, 8
Wireless networks, 117
Word processing origins, 12, 76
Word size, 102–103
World Trade Center, 223
World Wide Web, 64–65
See also Internet
World Wide Web Consortium (W3C), 66
Worm, 213
Written reports, 178

X

Xerox communications protocols, 119
XML, *See* Extensible markup language (XML)

Y

Y2K problem, 13–14

Z

Zip disk, 106

影印版教材可供书目

经济与金融经典入门教材 · 英文影印版

	书号	英文书名	中文书名	版次	编著者	定价
1	08961	Public Finance: A Contemporary Application of Theory to Policy	财政学：理论在政策中的当代应用	第8版	David N. Hyman/著	59.00元
2	08132	Fundamentals of Investments: Valuation and Management	投资学基础：估值与管理	第3版	Charles J. Corrado 等/著	58.00元
3	08126	Microeconomics for Today	今日微观经济学	第3版	Irvin Tucker/著	45.00元
4	08125	Macroeconomics for Today	今日宏观经济学	第3版	Irvin Tucker/著	48.00元

管理学经典入门教材 · 英文影印版

	书号	英文书名	中文书名	版次	编著者	定价
5	08129	Management: Skills and Application	管理学：技能与应用	第11版	Leslie W. Rue 等/著	45.00元
6	08128	Information Technology and Management	信息技术与管理	第2版	Ronald L. Thompson 等/著	45.00元
7	08665	Marketing: An Introduction	营销学导论	第1版	Rosalind Masterson 等/著	45.00元
8	09061	Communicating at Work: Principles and Practices for Business and the Professions	商务沟通：原则与实践	第8版	Ronald B. Adler 等/著	54.00元

经济学精选教材 · 英文影印版

	书号	英文书名	中文书名	版次	编著者	定价
9	12633	World Trade and Payments: An Introduction	国际贸易与国际收支	第10版	Richard E. Caves, Jeffrey A. Frankel 等/著	68.00元
10	08130	Economics: Principles and Policy	经济学：原理与政策	第9版	William J. Baumol 等/著	79.00元
11	08127	Microeconomic Theory: Basic Principles and Extensions	微观经济理论：基本原理与扩展	第9版	Walter Nicholson/著	59.00元
12	09693	Macroeconomics: Theories and Policies	宏观经济学：理论与政策	第8版	Richard T. Froyen/著	48.00元
13	14529	Econometrics: A Modern Introduction	计量经济学：现代方法(上)	第1版	Michael P. Murray/著	54.00元
14	14530	Econometrics: A Modern Introduction	计量经济学：现代方法(下)	第1版	Michael P. Murray/著	41.00元

管理学精选教材 · 英文影印版

	书号	英文书名	中文书名	版次	编著者	定价
15	12091	Operations Management: Goods, Services and Value Chains	运营管理：产品、服务和价值链	第2版	David A. Collier 等/著	86.00元
16	18239	Management Fundamentals: Concepts, Applications, Skill Development	管理学基础：概念、应用与技能提高	第4版	Robert N. Lussier/著	68.00元
17	06380	E-Commerce Management: Text and Cases	电子商务管理：课文和案例	第1版	Sandeep Krishnamurthy/著	47.00元

金融学精选教材 · 英文影印版

	书号	英文书名	中文书名	版次	编著者	定价
18	12306	Fundamentals of Futures and Options Markets	期货与期权市场导论	第5版	John C. Hull/著	55.00元
19	12040	Financial Theory and Corporate Policy	金融理论与公司决策	第4版	Thomas E. Copeland 等/著	79.00元
20	09657	Bond Markets: Analysis and Strategies	债券市场：分析和策略	第5版	Frank J. Fabozzi/著	62.00元
21	09984	Money, Banking and Financial Markets	货币、银行与金融市场	第1版	Stephen G. Cecchetti/著	65.00元

22	09767	Takeovers, Restructuring and Corporate Governance	接管、重组与公司治理	第4版	J. Fred Weston 等/著	69.00元
23	13206	Management of Banking	银行管理	第6版	S. Scott MacDonald 等/著	66.00元
24	10933	International Corporate Finance	国际财务管理	第8版	Jeff Madura/著	69.00元
25	13204	Financial Markets and Institutions	金融市场和金融机构	第7版	Jeff Madura/著	78.00元
26	05966	International Finance	国际金融	第2版	Ephraim Clark/著	66.00元
27	05965	Principles of Finance	金融学原理(含CD-ROM)	第2版	Scott Besley 等/著	82.00元
28	10916	Risk Management and Insurance	风险管理和保险	第12版	James S. Trieschmann 等/著	65.00元
29	05963	Fixed Income Markets and Their Derivatives	固定收入证券市场及其衍生产品	第2版	Suresh M. Sundaresan/著	72.00元

会计学精选教材 · 英文影印版

	书号	英文书名	中文书名	版次	编著者	定价
30	17348	Advanced Accounting	高级会计学	第10版	Paul M. Fischer 等/著	79.00元
31	14752	Advanced Accounting	高级会计学	第9版	Joe Ben Hoyle 等/著	56.00元
32	17344	Management Decisions and Financial Accounting Reports	中级会计:管理决策与财务会计报告	第2版	Stephen P. Baginski 等/著	56.00元
33	13200	Financial Accounting: Concepts & Applications	财务会计:概念与应用	第10版	W. Steve Albrecht 等/著	75.00元
34	13201	Management Accounting: Concepts & Applications	管理会计:概念与应用	第10版	W. Steve Albrecht 等/著	55.00元
35	13202	Financial Accounting: A Reporting and Analysis Perspective	财务会计:报告与分析	第7版	Earl K. Stice 等/著	85.00元
36	12309	Financial Statement Analysis and Security Valuation	财务报表分析与证券价值评估	第3版	Stephen H. Penman/著	69.00元
37	12310	Accounting for Decision Making and Control	决策与控制会计	第5版	Jerold L. Zimmerman/著	69.00元
38	05416	International Accounting	国际会计学	第4版	Frederick D. S. Choi 等/著	50.00元
39	14536	Managerial Accounting	管理会计	第8版	Don R. Hansen 等/著	79.00元

营销学精选教材 · 英文影印版

	书号	英文书名	中文书名	版次	编著者	定价
40	13205	Services Marketing: Concepts, Strategies, & Cases	服务营销精要:概念、战略与案例	第3版	K. Douglas Hoffman 等/著	63.00元
41	13203	Basic Marketing Research	营销调研基础	第6版	Gilbert A. Churchill, Jr. 等/著	66.00元
42	12305	Selling Today: Creating Customer Value	销售学:创造顾客价值	第10版	Gerald L. Manning, Barry L. Reece/著	52.00元
43	11213	Analysis for Marketing Planning	营销策划分析	第6版	Donald R. Lehmann 等/著	32.00元
44	09654	Market-based Management: Strategies for Growing Customer Value and Profitability	营销管理:提升顾客价值和利润增长的战略	第4版	Roger J. Best/著	48.00元
45	09655	Customer Equity Management	顾客资产管理	第1版	Roland T. Rust 等/著	55.00元
46	09662	Business Market Management: Undertstanding, Creating and Delivering Value	组织市场管理:理解、创造和传递价值	第2版	James C. Anderson 等/著	45.00元
47	10013	Marketing Strategy: A Decision Focused Approach	营销战略:以决策为导向的方法	第5版	Orville C. Walker, Jr. 等/著	38.00元
48	05971	Marketing	市场营销学(含CD-ROM)	第6版	Charles W. Lamb Jr. 等/著	80.00元
49	10983	Principles of Marketing	市场营销学	第12版	Louis E. Boone 等/著	66.00元
50	11108	Advertising, Promotion, & Supplemental Aspects of Integrated Marketing Communication	整合营销传播:广告、促销与拓展	第7版	Terence A. Shimp/著	62.00元

| 51 | 11251 | Sales Management: Analysis and Decision Making | 销售管理：分析与决策 | 第6版 | Thomas N. Ingram 等/著 | 42.00元 |
| 52 | 11212 | Marketing Research: Methodological Foundations | 营销调研:方法论基础 | 第9版 | Gilbert A. Churchill, Jr. 等/著 | 68.00元 |

人力资源管理精选教材 · 英文影印版

书号		英文书名	中文书名	版次	编著者	定价
53	08536	Human Relations in Organizations: Applications and Skill Building	组织中的人际关系：技能与应用	第6版	Robert N. Lussier/著	58.00元
54	08131	Managerial Communication: Strategies and Applications	管理沟通：策略与应用	第3版	Geraldine E. Hynes/著	38.00元
55	07408	Human Resource Management	人力资源管理	第10版	Robert L. Mathis 等/著	60.00元
56	07407	Organizational Behavior	组织行为学	第10版	Don Hellriegel 等/著	48.00元

国际商务精选教材 · 英文影印版

书号		英文书名	中文书名	版次	编著者	定价
57	14176	International Business	国际商务	第4版	John J. Wild 等/著	49.00元
58	12886	International Marketing	国际营销	第8版	Michael R. Czinkota 等/著	65.00元
59	06522	Fundamentals of International Business	国际商务基础	第1版	Michael R. Czinkota 等/著	45.00元
60	11674	International Economics: A Policy Approach	国际经济学：一种政策方法	第10版	Mordechai E. Kreinin/著	38.00元
61	06521	International Accounting: A User Perspective	国际会计：使用者视角	第2版	Shahrokh M. Saudagaran/著	26.00元

MBA精选教材 · 英文影印版

书号		英文书名	中文书名	版次	编著者	定价
62	12838	Quantitative Analysis for Management	面向管理的数量分析	第9版	Barry Render 等/著	65.00元
63	12675	The Economics of Money, Banking, and Financial Markets	货币、银行和金融市场经济学	第7版	Frederic S. Mishkin/著	75.00元
64	11221	Analysis for Financial Management	财务管理分析	第8版	Robert C. Higgins/著	42.00元
65	12302	A Framework for Marketing Management	营销管理架构	第3版	Philip Kotler/著	42.00元
66	14216	Excellence in Business Communication	卓越的商务沟通	第7版	John V. Thill 等/著	73.00元
67	12304	Understanding Financial Statements	财务报表解析	第8版	Lyn M. Fraser 等/著	34.00元
68	10620	Principles of Operations Management	运作管理原理	第6版	Jay Heizer 等/著	72.00元
69	05429	Introduction to Financial Accounting and Cisco Report Package	财务会计	第8版	Charles T. Horngren 等/著	75.00元
70	16407	Introduction to Management Accounting	管理会计	第14版	Charles T. Horngren 等/著	79.00元
71	11451	Management Communication: A Case-Analysis Approach	管理沟通：案例分析法	第2版	James S. O'Rourke/著	39.00元
72	10614	Management Information Systems	管理信息系统	第9版	Raymond McLeod 等/著	45.00元
73	10615	Fundamentals of Management	管理学基础:核心概念与应用	第4版	Stephen P. Robbins 等/著	49.00元
74	10874	Understanding and Managing Organizational Behavior	组织行为学	第4版	Jennifer M. George 等/著	65.00元
75	15177	Essentials of Entrepreneurship and Small Business Management	小企业管理与企业家精神精要	第5版	Thomas W. Zimmerer 等/著	68.00元
76	11224	Business	商务学	第7版	Ricky W. Griffin 等/著	68.00元
77	11452	Strategy and the Business Landscape: Core Concepts	战略管理	第2版	Pankaj Ghemawat/著	18.00元
78	13817	Managing Human Resources	人力资源管理	第5版	Luis R. Gomez-Mejia 等/著	60.00元
79	09663	Financial Statement Analysis	财务报表分析	第8版	John J. Wild 等/著	56.00元

经济学前沿影印丛书

	书号	英文书名	中文书名	版次	编著者	定价
80	09218	Analysis of Panel Data	面板数据分析	第2版	Cheng Hsiao/著	48.00元
81	09236	Economics, Value and Organization	经济学、价值和组织	第1版	Avner Ben-Ner 等/著	59.00元
82	09217	A Companion to Theoretical Econometrics	理论计量经济学精粹	第1版	Badi H. Baltagi/著	79.00元
83	09680	Financial Derivatives: Pricing, Applications, and Mathematics	金融衍生工具:定价、应用与数学	第1版	Jamil Baz 等/著	45.00元

翻译版教材可供书目

重点推荐

	书号	英文书名	中文书名	版次	编著者	定价
1	14749	A Monetary History of The United States, 1867—1960	美国货币史(1867—1960)	第1版	米尔顿·弗里德曼(Milton Friedman)等/著	78.00元
2	18236	American Economic History	美国经济史	第7版	Jonathan Hughes 等/著	89.00元
3	06693	The World Economy: A Millennial Perspective	世界经济千年史	第1版	安格斯·麦迪森(Angus Maddison)/著	58.00元
4	14751	The World Economy: Historical Statistics	世界经济千年统计	第1版	安格斯·麦迪森(Angus Maddison)/著	45.00元
5	10004	Fundamental Methods of Mathematical Economics	数理经济学的基本方法	第4版	蒋中一(Alpha C. Chiang)等/著	52.00元
6	08088	Fundamentals of Economics	经济学基础	第5版	曼昆(N. Gregory Mankiw)/著	65.00元
7	15089	Principles of Economics	经济学原理(微观经济学分册)	第5版	曼昆(N. Gregory Mankiw)/著	54.00元
8	15090	Principles of Economics	经济学原理(宏观经济学分册)	第5版	曼昆(N. Gregory Mankiw)/著	42.00元
9	15088	Study Guide for Principles of Economics	曼昆《经济学原理》学习指南	第5版	大卫·R.哈克斯(David R. Hakes)/著	48.00元

经济与金融经典入门教材译丛

	书号	英文书名	中文书名	版次	编著者	定价
10	11274	Fundamentals of Investments: Valuation and Management	投资学基础:估值与管理	第3版	Charles J. Corrado 等/著	76.00元
11	09320	Public Finance: A Contemporary Application of Theory to Policy	财政学:理论在政策中的当代应用	第8版	David N. Hyman/著	78.00元
12	09847	Microeconomics for Today	今日微观经济学	第3版	Irvin Tucker/著	58.00元
13	09750	Macroeconomics for Today	今日宏观经济学	第3版	Irvin Tucker/著	66.00元

管理学经典入门教材译丛

	书号	英文书名	中文书名	版次	编著者	定价
14	10006	Marketing: An Introduction	营销学导论	第1版	Rosalind Masterson 等/著	58.00元
15	10003	Information Technology and Management	信息技术与管理	第2版	Ronald L. Thompson 等/著	68.00元
16	11152	Management: Skills and Application	管理学:技能与应用	第11版	Leslie W. Rue 等/著	55.00元

经济学精选教材译丛

	书号	英文书名	中文书名	版次	编著者	定价
17	15917	Microeconomics	微观经济学	第1版	B. Douglas Bernheim 等/著	89.00元
18	13812	Macroeconomics: Theories and Policies	宏观经济学:理论与政策	第8版	Richard T. Froyen/著	49.00元
19	13815	World Trade and Payments: An Introduction	国际贸易与国际收支	第10版	Richard E. Caves 等/著	69.00元
20	13814	Macroeconomics	宏观经济学	第2版	Roger E. A. Farmer/著	46.00元

21	12289	Microeconomic Theory: Basic Principles and Extensions	微观经济理论：基本原理与扩展	第9版	Walter Nicholson/著	75.00元
22	11222	Economics: Principles and Policy	经济学：原理与政策(上、下册)	第9版	William J. Baumol 等/著	96.00元
23	10992	The History of Economic Thought	经济思想史	第7版	Stanley L. Brue 等/著	59.00元
24	13800	Urban Economics	城市经济学	第6版	Arthur O'Sullivan/著	49.00元

管理学精选教材译丛

	书号	英文书名	中文书名	版次	编著者	定价
25	14519	Operations Management: Goods, Services and Value Chains	运营管理：产品、服务和价值链	第2版	David A. Collier 等/著	79.00元
26	11210	Strategic Management of E-business	电子商务战略管理	第2版	Stephen Chen/著	39.00元
27	10005	Management Fundamentals: Concepts, Applications, Skill Development	管理学基础：概念、应用与技能提高	第4版	Robert N. Lussier/著	82.00元
28	16772	Applied Multivariate Statistical Analysis	应用多元统计分析	第2版	Wolfgang Härdel 等/著	65.00元

会计学精选教材译丛

	书号	英文书名	中文书名	版次	编著者	定价
29	14531	Fundamentals of Financial Accounting	财务会计学原理	第2版	Fred Phillips 等/著	82.00元
30	14532	Managerial Accounting	管理会计	第8版	Don R. Hansen 等/著	99.00元

金融学精选教材译丛

	书号	英文书名	中文书名	版次	编著者	定价
31	16298	International Corporate Finance	国际财务管理	第9版	Jeff Madura/著	82.00元
32	13806	Principles of Finance	金融学原理	第3版	Scott Besley 等/著	69.00元
33	12317	Management of Banking	银行管理	第6版	S. Scott MacDonald 等/著	78.00元
34	12316	Multinational Business Finance	跨国金融与财务	第11版	David K. Eiteman 等/著	78.00元
35	10007	Capital Budgeting and Long-Term Financing Decisions	资本预算与长期融资决策	第3版	Neil Seitz 等/著	79.00元
36	10609	Money, Banking, and Financial Markets	货币、银行与金融市场	第1版	Stephen G. Cecchetti/著	75.00元
37	11463	Bond Markets, Analysis and Strategies	债券市场：分析和策略	第5版	Frank J. Fabozzi/著	76.00元
38	10624	Fundamentals of Futures and Options Markets	期货与期权市场导论	第5版	John C. Hull/著	62.00元
39	09768	Takeovers, Restructuring and Corporate Governance	接管、重组与公司治理	第4版	J. Fred Weston 等/著	79.00元

营销学精选教材译丛

	书号	英文书名	中文书名	版次	编著者	定价
40	13808	Basic Marketing Research	营销调研基础	第6版	Gilbert A. Churchill, Jr. 等/著	82.00元
41	12301	Principles of Marketing	市场营销学	第12版	Dave L. Kurtz 等/著	65.00元
42	15716	Selling Today: Creating Customer Value	销售学：创造顾客价值	第10版	Gerald L. Manning/著	62.00元
43	13795	Analysis for Marketing Planning	营销策划分析	第6版	Donald R. Lehmann/著	35.00元
44	13811	Services Marketing: Concepts, Strategies, & Cases	服务营销精要：概念、战略与案例	第2版	K. Douglas Hoffman 等/著	68.00元
45	12312	Customer Equity Management	顾客资产管理	第1版	Roland T. Rust 等/著	65.00元
46	16316	Marketing Research: Methodological Foundations	营销调研：方法论基础	第9版	Gilbert A. Churchill, Jr. 等/著	62.00元
47	11229	Market-based Management: Strategies for Growing Customer Value and Profitability	营销管理：提升顾客价值和利润增长的战略	第4版	Roger J. Best/著	58.00元
48	10010	Marketing Strategy: A Decision-Focused Approach	营销战略：以决策为导向的方法	第5版	Orville C. Walker, Jr. 等/著	49.00元

| 49 | 11226 | Business Market Management: Understanding, Creating and Delivering Value | 组织市场管理：理解、创造和传递价值 | 第2版 | James C. Anderson 等/著 | 52.00元 |

人力资源管理精选教材译丛

	书号	英文书名	中文书名	版次	编著者	定价
50	16619	Human Relations in Organizations: Applications and Skill Building	组织中的人际关系：技能与应用	第6版	Robert N. Lussier/著	75.00元
51	10276	Human Resource Management	人力资源管理	第10版	Robert L. Mathis/著	68.00元
52	15982	Fundamentals of Organizational Behavior	组织行为学	第11版	Don Hellriegel 等/著	56.00元
53	09274	Managerial Communication: Strategies and Applications	管理沟通：策略与应用	第3版	Geraldine E. Hynes/著	45.00元
54	10275	Supervision: Key Link to Productivity	员工监管：提高生产力的有效途径	第8版	Leslie W. Rue 等/著	59.00元

国际商务精选教材译丛

	书号	英文书名	中文书名	版次	编著者	定价
55	16334	International Economics: A Policy Approach	国际经济学：政策视角	第10版	Mordechai E. Kreinin/著	45.00元
56	14525	International Business	国际商务	第4版	John J. Wild 等/著	62.00元
56	10001	Fundamentals of International Business	国际商务基础	第1版	Michael R. Czinkota 等/著	58.00元

全美最新工商管理权威教材译丛

	书号	英文书名	中文书名	版次	编著者	定价
57	16318	Essentials of Managerial Finance	财务管理精要	第14版	John V. Thill 等/著	88.00元
55	16319	Understanding and Managing Organizational Behavior	组织行为学	第5版	Jennifer M. George 等/著	75.00元
59	13810	Crafting and Executing Strategy: Concepts and Cases	战略管理：概念与案例	第14版	Arthur A. Thompson 等/著	48.00元
60	14518	Management Communication: A Case-Analysis Approach	管理沟通：案例分析法	第3版	James S. O'Rourke/著	44.00元
61	16549	Quantitative Analysis for Management	面向管理的数量分析	第9版	Barry Render 等/著	85.00元
62	13790	Case Problems in Finance	财务案例	第12版	W. Carl Kester 等/著	88.00元
63	13807	Analysis for Financial Management	财务管理分析	第8版	Robert C. Higgins/著	42.00元
64	14515	Understanding Financial Statements	财务报表解析	第8版	Lyn M. Fraser 等/著	34.00元
65	13809	Strategy and the Business Landscape	战略管理	第2版	Pankaj Ghemawat/著	25.00元
66	16171	Principles of Operations Management	运作管理原理	第6版	Jay Heizer 等/著	86.00元
67	13500	Managerial Economics	管理经济学	第3版	方博亮、武常岐、孟昭莉/著	80.00元
68	16011	Managerial Economics: A Problem Solving Appreach	管理经济学：一种问题解决方式	第1版	Luke M. Froeb 等/著	35.00元
69	11609	Management: The New Competitive Landscape	管理学：新竞争格局	第6版	Thomas S. Bateman 等/著	76.00元
70	09690	Product Management	产品管理	第4版	Donald R. Lehmann 等/著	58.00元
71	12885	Entrepreneurial Small Business	小企业创业管理	第1版	Jerome A. Katz 等/著	86.00元
72	16780	Introduction to Management Accounting	管理会计	第14版	Charles T. Horngren 等/著	99.00元

经济与管理经典教材译丛

	书号	英文书名	中文书名	版次	编著者	定价
73	06415	Business Economics	企业经济学	第2版	Maria Moschandreas/著	47.00元
74	08651	International Finance	国际金融	第2版	Ephraim Clark/著	68.00元
75	07048	Fundamentals of Investment Appraisal	投资评估基础	第1版	Steve Lumby 等/著	28.00元
76	07047	Electronic Commerce and the Revolution in Financial Markets	金融市场中的电子商务与革新	第1版	Ming Fan 等/著	36.00元

77	06455	Management Accounting	管理会计	第3版	Robert S. Kaplan 等/著	52.00元
78	08621	Advertising, Promotion, & Supplemental Aspects of Integrated Marketing Communications	整合营销传播：广告、促销与拓展	第6版	Terence A. Shimp/著	58.00元
79	08101	International Accounting: A User Perspective	国际会计：使用者视角	第2版	Shahrokh M. Saudagaran/著	32.00元
80	08323	E-Commerce Management: Text and Cases	电子商务管理：课文和案例	第1版	Sandeep Krishnamurthy/著	45.00元

增长与发展经济学译丛

书号	英文书名	中文书名	版次	编著者	定价
81	05742	Introduction to Economic Growth	经济增长导论	第1版	Charles I. Jones/著	28.00元
82	05744	Development Microeconomics	发展微观经济学	第1版	Pranab Bardhan 等/著	35.00元
83	05743	Development Economics	发展经济学	第1版	Debraj Rag/著	79.00元
84	06905	Endogenous Growth Theory	内生增长理论	第1版	Philippe Aghion 等/著	75.00元

国际经典教材中国版系列

书号	英文书名	中文书名	版次	编著者	定价
85	14516	Investments: Analysis and Behavior	投资学：分析与行为	第1版	Mark Hirschey, John Nofsinger,林海/著	58.00元
86	11227	International Financial Management	国际金融管理	第1版	Michael B. Connolly,杨胜刚/著	38.00元

北京培生信息中心
中国北京海淀区中关村大街甲 59 号
人大文化大厦 1006 室
邮政编码:100872
电话:(8610)57355175
传真:(8610)58257961

北京大学出版社
经济与管理图书事业部
北京市海淀区成府路 205 号 100871
联系人:徐 冰 张 燕
电话: 010-62767312 / 62767348
传真: 010-62556201

尊敬的老师:

您好!

  为了确保您及时有效地申请教辅资源,请您务必完整填写如下教辅申请表,加盖学院的公章后传真给我们,我们将会为您开通属于您个人的唯一帐号以供您下载与教材配套的教师资源。

请填写所需教辅的开课信息:

采用教材				☐中文版 ☐英文版 ☐双语版
作 者		出版社		
版 次		ISBN		
课程时间	始于 年 月 日	学生人数		
	止于 年 月 日	学生年级	☐专科 ☐研究生	☐本科 1/2 年级 ☐本科 3/4 年级

请填写您的个人信息:

学 校			
院系/专业			
姓 名		职 称	☐助教 ☐讲师 ☐副教授 ☐教授
通信地址/邮编			
手 机		电 话	
传 真			
official email (eg:XXX@crup.edu.cn)		email (eg:XXX@163.com)	
是否愿意接受我们定期的新书讯息通知:	☐是 ☐否		

系 / 院主任:_____(签字)

(系 / 院办公室章)

____年____月____日

Please send this form to: em@pup.pku.edu.cn 或 Service.CN@pearson.com
Website: www.pearsonhighered.com/educator